NATION
OF NATIONS

VOLUME II: SINCE 1865

Here is not merely a nation but a teeming nation of nations.
—WALT WHITMAN

NATION
OF NATIONS

A NARRATIVE
HISTORY
OF THE AMERICAN REPUBLIC

VOLUME II: SINCE 1865

THIRD EDITION

JAMES WEST DAVIDSON

WILLIAM E. GIENAPP
Harvard University

CHRISTINE LEIGH HEYRMAN
University of Delaware

MARK H. LYTLE
Bard College

MICHAEL B. STOFF
University of Texas, Austin

Boston, Massachusetts   Burr Ridge, Illinois
Dubuque, Iowa   Madison, Wisconsin
New York, New York   San Francisco, California
St. Louis, Missouri

McGraw-Hill

A Division of The McGraw·Hill Companies

NATION OF NATIONS
A Narrative History of the American Republic
Volume II: Since 1865

Photo Credits appear on pages P.1 et seq., and on this page by reference.

This book is printed on acid-free paper.

2 3 4 5 6 7 8 9 0 VNH VNH 9 0 9 8

ISBN 0-07-015799-5

This book was set in Caledonia by York Graphic Services, Inc.
The editors were Lyn Uhl and Linda Richmond;
the production supervisor was Richard A. Ausburn;
the design manager was Joseph A. Piliero.
The cover was designed by Joan Greenfield.
The photo editor was Deborah Bull/Photosearch.
Von Hoffmann Press, Inc., was printer and binder.

Reproduced on the cover:
E. Dankworth, Scoville's Restaurant & Pavillion.
From the collection of Kert Lundell.

PERMISSIONS ACKNOWLEDGMENTS

1030, 1154: Taken from Frank Levy, Dollars and Dreams: The Changing American
Income Distribution. © 1987 Russell Sage Foundation. Used with permission of the Russell
Sage Foundation; **1104:** Excerpt from Nikki Giovanni, "The True Import of Present
Dialogue: Black vs. Negro" from Black Feeling, Black Talk, Black Judgment, William
Morrow & Co., © 1968, 1970 by Nikki Giovanni; **1155:** From "I Am Changing My Name
to Chrysler," by Tom Paxton. © Copyright 1980 Pax Music. Used by permission.

Library of Congress Has Cataloged the One Volume Edition as Follows

Nation of nations: a narrative history of the American republic /
    James West Davidson . . . [et al.].—3rd ed.
        p.   cm.
    Includes bibliographical references and index.
    ISBN 0-07-015794-4 (acid-free paper)
    1. United States—History.   I. Davidson, James West.
E178.1.N346   1997
973—dc21   97-1197

http://www.mhhe.com

ABOUT THE AUTHORS

JAMES WEST DAVIDSON received his Ph.D. from Yale University. A historian who has pursued a full-time writing career, he is the author of numerous books, among them *After the Fact: The Art of Historical Detection* (with Mark H. Lytle), *The Logic of Millennial Thought: Eighteenth-Century New England,* and *Great Heart: The History of a Labrador Adventure* (with John Rugge).

WILLIAM E. GIENAPP has a Ph.D. from the University of California, Berkeley. He taught at the University of Wyoming before going to Harvard University, where he is Professor of History. In 1988 he received the Avery O. Craven Award for his book *The Origins of the Republican Party, 1852–1856.* His essay on "The Antebellum Era" appeared in the *Encyclopedia of Social History* (1992), and he is a coauthor of *Why the Civil War Came* (1996).

CHRISTINE LEIGH HEYRMAN is Associate Professor of History at the University of Delaware. She received a Ph.D. in American Studies from Yale University and is the author of *Commerce and Culture: The Maritime Communities of Colonial Massachusetts, 1690–1750.* Most recently she has written *Southern Cross: The Beginnings of the Bible Belt,* a book about popular religious culture in the Old Southwest.

MARK H. LYTLE, who was awarded a Ph.D. from Yale University, is Professor of History and Environmental Studies and Chair of the American Studies Program at Bard College. He is also Director of the Master of Arts in Teaching Program at Bard. His publications include *The Origins of the Iranian-American Alliance, 1941–1953, After the Fact: The Art of Historical Detection* (with James West Davidson), and most recently, "An Environmental Approach to American Diplomatic History," in *Diplomatic History.* He is at work on *The Uncivil War: America in the Vietnam Era.*

MICHAEL B. STOFF is Associate Professor of History at the University of Texas at Austin. The recipient of a Ph.D. from Yale University, he wrote *Oil, War, and American Security: The Search for a National Policy on Foreign Oil, 1941–1947* and co-edited *Manhattan Project: A Documentary Introduction to the Atomic Age.* He has been honored many times for his teaching, most recently with the Friar's Centennial Teaching Excellence Award.

CONTENTS

CHAPTER 22   The Progressive Era   758

LIST OF MAPS AND CHARTS

PREFACE
TO THE THIRD EDITION

The third edition of *Nation of Nations* holds firm to its original premise: that students will be drawn more readily to the study of history if they are presented with an engaging narrative of past events rather than with a mere encyclopedic compendium. Inevitably the creation of such a narrative has entailed difficult choices. The undergrowth of facts, dates, and qualifying clauses must be pruned and shaped so that what remains appears in bolder relief. Fortunately the job was made easier because the authors recently prepared a concise version of *Nation of Nations.* That task suggested to us ways we could profitably sharpen the full edition without losing either our narrative thread or the more detailed context provided by a full-length survey. Consequently, this edition is shorter than the second and, we believe, all the better for it.

Paradoxically, several changes have been inspired by the very success of our narrative approach. Some professors have written suggesting that just because the tale flows so smoothly, students may be seduced into thinking that the writing of history is without controversy—that the past must have occurred just as we have sketched it and that any questions of interpretation must be minor matters. To combat this misimpression every chapter now incorporates a discussion labelled "Counterpoint," which explores contrasting ways historians have interpreted one of the chapter's central topics. These discussions are deliberately not separated out as boxed features; instead, they are integrated into the narrative so that students come to understand such debates as an inevitable (and productive) part of writing history. In addition, we have added six longer essays focusing on the process of doing history. Entitled "After the Fact: Historians Reconstruct the Past," the essays introduce students to the methods used by historians to analyze a variety of sources, ranging from typescript drafts of presidential memoirs or handwritten notations in church records to military casualty estimates, public monuments, and even climate data derived from the analysis of tree rings.

Other changes in the new edition reflect history's inevitable expansion, both chronologically and thematically. Late nineteenth-century topics originally covered in Chapters 21 and 22 ("The Failure of Traditional Politics" and "The New Empire") have been incorporated into a single chapter, "The Political System Under Strain." The text's final chapter, "A Nation Still Divisible," brings the narrative up through the Republican resurgence of 1994 and the reelection of President Clinton. Many other changes both large and small have been made throughout. Coverage of environmental history has been expanded, and there is an increased emphasis on the new western history, particularly in Chapter 20. New maps and charts have been added, including some never before seen in a survey text. Finally, in addition to the full bibliographies appearing at the back of the book, each chapter has an expanded annotated bibliography, called "Additional Reading," as well as specific bibliographical references within the "After the Fact" features.

Despite these changes, the text's basic structure remains. Each of the book's six parts begins with an essay setting American events in a global context. We believe it is important to show that the United States did not develop in a geographic or cultural vacuum and that the broad forces shaping it also influenced other nations. Each global essay features a timeline comparing political and social events in the United States with developments elsewhere. Marginal headings throughout the entire text help students focus on key terms and concepts, while each chapter concludes with a succinct summary and a timeline of significant events. Complementing the core narrative are our "Daily Lives" essays, focusing on one of five themes that give insight into the lives of ordinary Americans: clothing and fashion; time and travel; food, drink, and drugs; public space/private space; and popular entertainment.

We are grateful to the many reviewers who were generous enough to offer comments and suggestions at various stages in our development of this manuscript. Our thanks go to Thomas Altherr, Metropolitan State College of Denver; Carol Berkin, Baruch College and the Graduate Center of the City University of New York; Winifred E. A. Bernhard, University of Massachusetts, Amherst; Roger W. Biles, Oklahoma State University; Carol Brown, Houston Community College; Victor Chen, Chabot College; Vincent A. Clark, Johnson County Community College; Mario S. DePillis, University of Massachusetts, Amherst; Leonard Dinnerstein, University of Arizona; Mark Dollinger, Pasadena City College; Alan Downs, Georgia Southern University; Lynn Dumenil, Claremont McKenna College; Robert Elam, Modesto Junior College; Robert G. Fricke, West Valley College; Richard Frucht, Northwest Missouri State University; John Gauger, Lehigh Carbon Community College; James L. Gormly, Washington and Jefferson College; Robert Greenblatt, Mass Bay Community College; Peter Iverson, Arizona State University; Priscilla Jackson-Evans, Longview Community College: George Juergens, Indiana University; Burton I. Kaufman, Virginia Polytechnic Institute and State University; John L. Larson, Purdue University; Mark H. Leff, University of Illinois, Urbana–Champaign; John Little, St. Augustine's College; Norman Love, El Paso Community College; John McCardell, Middlebury College; C. K. McFarland, Arkansas State University; Gerald W. McFarland, University of Massachusetts, Amherst; William E. Mahan, Sacramento City College; John Maner, TriCounty Technical College; Sonya Michel, University of Illinois, Urbana–Champaign; William Howard Moore, University of Wyoming; Christopher Morris, University of Texas, Austin; Betty Owens, Greenville Technical College; Robert Pierce, Foothill College; Charles Pilant, Cumberland College; Leo P. Ribuffo, George Washington University; Randolph Roth, Ohio State University; Dennis C. Rousey, Arkansas State University; Tom Ryan, Broward Community College; Susan Rugh, St. Cloud State University; James C. Schneider, University of Texas, San Antonio; Ronald Schultz, University of Wyoming; Rebecca Shoemaker, Indiana State University; Lewright B. Sikes, Middle Tennessee State University; Nina Silber, Boston University; Gregory Holmes Singleton, Northeastern Illinois University; David Sloan, University of Arkansas, Fayetteville; Daniel B. Smith, University of Kentucky; Donna J. Spindel, Marshall University; Thomas E. Terrill, University of South Carolina; Emory M. Thomas, University of Georgia; Richard H. Thompson, Indiana University—Purdue University, Indianapolis; Stephen G. Weisner, Springfield Technical Community College; Frank J. Wetta, Galveston College; William Bruce Wheeler, University of Tennessee, Knoxville; Gerald Wilson, Duke University; Phillip B. Winkler, Dyersburg State College; and

William Young, Johnson County Community College. In addition, many friends and colleagues contributed their advice and constructive criticism in ways both small and large. These included Michael Bellesiles, Lawrence A. Cardoso, Dinah Chenven, James E. Crisp, R. David Edmunds, George Forgie, Erica Gienapp, Drew McCoy, James McPherson, Stephen E. Maizlish, Jim Sidbury, Harold Silesky, David J. Weber, and Virginia Joyner.

The division of labor for this book was determined by our respective fields of scholarship: Christine Heyrman, the colonial era, in which Europeans, Africans, and Indians participated in the making of both a new America and a new republic; William Gienapp, the 90 years in which the young nation first flourished, then foundered on the issues of section and slavery; Michael Stoff, the post-Civil War era, in which industrialization and urbanization brought the nation more centrally into an international system constantly disrupted by depression and war; and Mark Lytle, the modern era, in which Americans finally faced the reality that even the boldest dreams of national greatness are bounded by the finite nature of power and resources both natural and human. Finally, because the need to specialize inevitably imposes limits on any project as broad as this one, our fifth author, James Davidson, served as a general editor and writer, with the intent of fitting individual parts to the whole, as well as providing a measure of continuity, style, and overarching purpose. In producing this collaborative effort, all of us have shared the conviction that the best history speaks to a larger audience.

JAMES WEST DAVIDSON
WILLIAM E. GIENAPP
CHRISTINE LEIGH HEYRMAN
MARK H. LYTLE
MICHAEL B. STOFF

INTRODUCTION

History is both a discipline of rigor, bound by rules and scholarly methods, and something more: the unique, compelling, even strange way in which we humans define ourselves. We are all the sum of the tales of thousands of people, great and small, whose actions have etched their lines on us. History supplies our very identity—a sense of the social groups to which we belong, whether family, ethnic group, race, class, or gender. It reveals to us the foundations of our deepest religious beliefs and traces the roots of our economic and political systems. It explores how we celebrate and grieve, sing the songs we sing, weather the illnesses to which time and chance subject us. It commands our attention for all these good reasons and for no good reason at all, other than a fascination with the way the myriad tales play out. Strange that we should come to care about a host of men and women so many centuries gone, some with names eminent and familiar, others unknown but for a chance scrap of information left behind in an obscure letter.

Yet we do care. We care about Sir Humphrey Gilbert, "devoured and swallowed up of the Sea" one black Atlantic night in 1583; about George Washington at Kips Bay, red with fury as he takes a riding crop to his retreating soldiers. We care about Octave Johnson, a slave fleeing through Louisiana swamps trying to decide whether to stand and fight the approaching hounds or take his chances with the bayou alligators; about Clara Barton, her nurse's skirts so heavy with blood from the wounded she must wring them out before tending to the next soldier. We are drawn to the fate of Chinese laborers, chipping away at the Sierras' looming granite; a Georgian named Tom Watson seeking to forge a colorblind political alliance; and desperate immigrant mothers, kerosene in hand, storming Brooklyn butcher shops that had again raised prices. We follow, with a mix of awe and amusement, the fortunes of the quirky Henry Ford ("Everybody wants to be somewhere he ain't"), turning out identical automobiles, insisting his factory workers wear identical expressions ("Fordization of the Face"). We trace the career of young Thurgood Marshall, crisscrossing the South in his own "little old beat-up '29 Ford," typing legal briefs in the back seat, trying to get black teachers to sue for equal pay, hoping to get his people somewhere they weren't. The list could go on and on, spilling out as it did in Walt Whitman's *Leaves of Grass:* "A southerner soon as a northerner, a planter nonchalant and hospitable,/A Yankee bound my own way . . . a Hoosier, a Badger, a Buckeye, a Louisianian or Georgian. . . ." Whitman embraced and celebrated them all, inseparable strands of what made him an American and what made him human:

> In all people I see myself, none more and not one a barleycorn less,
> And the good or bad I say of myself I say of them.

To encompass so expansive an America Whitman turned to poetry; historians have traditionally chosen *narrative* as their means of giving life to the past. That mode of explanation permits them to interweave the strands of economic, political, and social history in a coherent chronological framework. By choosing narrative, they affirm the multicausal nature of historical explanation—the insistence that events be portrayed in context. By choosing narrative, they are also acknowledging that, while long-term economic and social trends shape societies in significant ways, events often take on a logic (or an illogic) of their own, jostling one another, being deflected by unpredictable personal decisions, sudden deaths, natural catastrophes, and chance. There are literary reasons, too, for preferring a narrative approach, since it supplies a dramatic force usually missing from more structural analyses of the past.

In some ways, surveys like this one are the natural antithesis of narrative history. They strive, by definition, to be comprehensive: to furnish a broad, orderly exposition of their chosen field. Yet to cover so much ground in so limited a space necessarily deprives readers of the context of more detailed accounts. Then, too, the resurgence of social history—with its concern for class and race, patterns of rural and urban life, the spread of market and industrial economies—lends itself to more analytic, less chronological treatments. The challenge facing historians is to incorporate these areas of research without losing the story's narrative drive or the chronological flow that orients readers to the more familiar events of our past.

With the cold war of the past half-century at an end, there has been increased attention to the worldwide breakdown of so many nonmarket economies and, by inference, to the greater success of the market societies of the United States and other capitalist nations. As our own narrative makes clear, American society and politics have indeed come together centrally in the marketplace. What Americans produce, how and where they produce it, and the desire to buy cheap and sell dear have been defining elements in every era. That market orientation has created unparalleled abundance and reinforced striking inequalities, not the least a society in which, for two centuries, human beings themselves were bought and sold. It has made Americans powerfully provincial in protecting local interests and internationally adventurous in seeking to expand wealth and opportunity.

It goes without saying that Americans have not always produced wisely or well. The insistent drive toward material plenty has levied a heavy tax on the global environment. Too often quantity has substituted for quality, whether we talk of cars, education, or culture. When markets flourish, the nation abounds with confidence that any problem, no matter how intractable, can be solved. When markets fail, however, the fault lines of our political and social systems become all too evident.

In the end, then, it is impossible to separate the marketplace of boom and bust and the world of ordinary Americans from the corridors of political maneuvering or the ceremonial pomp of an inauguration. To treat political and social history as distinct spheres is counterproductive. The primary question of this narrative—how the fledgling, often tumultuous confederation of "these United States" managed to transform itself into an enduring republic—is not only political but necessarily social. In order to survive, a republic must resolve conflicts between citizens of different geographic regions and economic classes, of diverse racial and ethnic origins, of competing religions and ideologies. The resolution of these conflicts has produced tragic consequences, perhaps as often as noble ones. But tragic or noble, the destiny of these states cannot be understood without comprehending both the social and the political dimensions of the story.

20°E 40°E 60°E 80°E 100°E 120°E 140°E 160°E

CTIC OCEAN

RUSSIAN FEDERATION

NORWAY SWEDEN FINLAND
DENMARK RUSS.
GER. POLAND BELARUS
UKRAINE
ITALY 10 18
13 14 15 ROMANIA
BULGARIA
16 TURKEY 19
GREECE 20
MALTA 22 SYRIA
TUNISIA CRETE CYPRUS 23 21
IRAQ IRAN

KAZAKHSTAN

UZBEKISTAN KYRGYZSTAN
TURKMENISTAN TAJIKISTAN
AFGHAN.
PAKISTAN

MONGOLIA

CHINA

N. KOREA
S. KOREA JAPAN

PACIFIC

LIBYA EGYPT
JORDAN KUWAIT
BAHRAIN QATAR
SAUDI
ARABIA U.A.E.

NIGER
CHAD SUDAN ERITREA
BENIN DJIBOUTI
NIGERIA
CENTRAL
AFRICAN
CAMEROON REPUBLIC ETHIOPIA
ANGOLA CONGO UGANDA
GABON ZAIRE KENYA
CAPE RWANDA
BURUNDI
TANZANIA
MALAWI
ANGOLA ZAMBIA
NAMIBIA ZIMBABWE
BOTSWANA
SOUTH SWAZILAND
AFRICA LESOTHO

YEMEN
OMAN
SOMALIA

SEYCHELLES
COMOROS

MADAGASCAR

MAURITIUS

NEPAL BHUTAN
BANGLADESH

INDIA
MYANMAR
(BURMA)

SRI
LANKA
MALDIVES

INDIAN

OCEAN

TAIWAN
HONG KONG (U.K.)
MACAU (Port.)

24
25 VIETNAM
26

LAOS
THAILAND
CAMBODIA

PHILIPPINES

BRUNEI
MALAYSIA
SINGAPORE

INDONESIA

GUAM (U.S.)
NORTHERN
MARIANAS (U.S.)

OCEAN

MARSHALL
ISLANDS

FEDERATED STATES
OF MICRONESIA
NAURU

KIRIBATI

PAPUA
NEW
GUINEA

SOLOMON
ISLANDS

VANUATU

NEW
CALEDONIA
(FR.)

FIJI

AUSTRALIA

NEW
ZEALAND

ANTARCTICA

1. NETHERLANDS
2. BELGIUM
3. LUXEMBOURG
4. ESTONIA
5. LATVIA
6. LITHUANIA
7. CZECH REPUBLIC
8. SLOVAKIA
9. SWITZERLAND
10. AUSTRIA
11. HUNGARY
12. SLOVENIA
13. CROATIA
14. BOSNIA AND HERCEGOVINA
15. YUGOSLAVIA
16. MACEDONIA
17. ALBANIA

18. MOLDOVA
19. GEORGIA
20. ARMENIA
21. AZERBAIJAN
22. LEBANON
23. ISRAEL
24. LAOS
25. THAILAND
26. CAMBODIA
27. PUERTO RICO (U.S.)
28. ST. KITTS AND NEVIS
29. ANTIGUA AND BARBUDA
30. DOMINICA
31. ST. LUCIA
32. ST. VINCENT AND THE GRENADINES
33. BARBADOS
34. TRINIDAD AND TOBAGO

Vancouver I.

L. Winnipeg

Puget Sound

L. Winnipegosis

Seattle

Olympia ★ WASHINGTON

CASCADE MTS.

Great Falls

Missouri R.

Portland

Columbia R.

Salem

Helena

MONTANA

NORTH DAKOTA

Bismarck ★

Fargo

OREGON

IDAHO

ROCKY

Boise ★

WYOMING

SOUTH DAKOTA

Pierre ★

Sioux Falls

Sacramento R.

Snake R.

BLACK HILLS

Cheyenne ★

NEBRASKA

Sacramento ★

SIERRA NEVADA

Carson City ★

Great Salt L.

Salt Lake City ★

MOUNTAINS

Omaha

San Francisco

NEVADA

UTAH

Denver ★

Lincoln

San Joaquin R.

CALIFORNIA

Las Vegas

COLORADO

Colorado R.

KANSAS

Topeka ★

Arkansas R.

Wichita

Los Angeles

ARIZONA

Santa Fe ★

Oklahoma City ★

San Diego

Phoenix ★

Albuquerque

NEW MEXICO

OKLAHOMA

PACIFIC OCEAN

Red R.

Dallas

TEXAS

MEXICO

Rio Grande

Austin ★

San Antonio

HAWAII

Kauai

Niihau

Oahu ★

Molokai

Honolulu

Lanai

Maui

Kaho'olawe

Hawaii

SOVIET UNION

ARCTIC OCEAN

BROOKS RANGE

Bering Strait

0   75   150 Miles

0   75   150 Kilometers

PACIFIC OCEAN

Yukon R.

ALASKA

BERING SEA

ALASKA RANGE

Anchorage

CANADA

Aleutian Islands

0   200   400 Miles

0   200   400 Kilometers

Juneau ★

17

Reconstructing the Union

Joseph Davis had had enough. Well on in years and financially ruined by the war, he decided to quit farming. In November 1866, he sold his Mississippi plantations Hurricane and Brierfield to Benjamin Montgomery and his sons. The sale of southern plantations was common enough after the war, but this transaction was bound to attract attention, since Joseph Davis was the elder brother of Jefferson Davis. Indeed, before the war the Confederate president had operated Brierfield as his own plantation, although his brother retained legal title to it. In truth, the sale was so unusual that the parties involved agreed to keep it secret, since the Montgomerys were black, and Mississippi law prohibited African Americans from owning land.

Though a slave, Montgomery had been the business manager of the two Davis plantations before the war. He had also operated a store on Hurricane Plantation for white as well as black customers with his own line of credit in New Orleans. In 1863 Montgomery fled to the North, but when the war was over, he returned to Davis Bend, where the federal government was leasing plots of the land on confiscated plantations, including Hurricane and Brierfield, to black farmers. Montgomery quickly emerged as the leader of the African American community at the Bend.

Then, in 1866, President Andrew Johnson pardoned Joseph Davis and restored his lands. By then Davis was over 80 years old and lacked the will and stamina to re-build, yet unlike many ex-slaveholders, he still felt bound by obligations to his former slaves. Convinced that with proper encouragement African Americans could succeed economically in freedom, he sold his land secretly to Benjamin Montgomery. Only when the law prohibiting African Americans from owning land was overturned in 1867 did Davis publicly confirm the sale to his former slave.

For his part, Montgomery undertook to create a model society at Davis Bend based on mutual cooperation. He rented land to black farmers, hired others to work his own fields, sold supplies on credit, and ginned and marketed the crops. To the growing African American community, he preached the gospel of hard work, self-re-liance, and education.

Various difficulties dogged these black farmers, including the destruction caused by the war, several disastrous floods, insects, droughts, and declining cotton prices. Yet before long, cotton production exceeded that of the prewar years, and in 1870 the black families at Davis Bend produced 2500 bales. The Montgomerys eventually ac-

A Visit from the Old Mistress, *by Winslow Homer, captures the conflicting, often awkward, emotions felt by both races after the war.*

quired another plantation and owned 5500 acres, which made them reputedly the third largest planters in the state. They won national and international awards for the quality of their cotton. Their success demonstrated what African Americans, given a fair chance, might accomplish.

The experiences of Benjamin Montgomery during the years after 1865 were not those of most black southerners, who did not own land or have a powerful white benefactor. Yet Montgomery's dream of economic independence was shared by all African Americans. As one black veteran noted, "Every colored man will be a slave, and feel himself a slave until he can raise him own bale of cotton and put him own mark upon it and say dis is mine!" Blacks could not gain effective freedom simply through a proclamation of emancipation. They needed economic power, including their own land that no one could unfairly take away.

For nearly two centuries the laws had prevented slaves from possessing such economic power. If those conditions were to be overturned, black Americans needed political power too. Thus the Republic would have to be reconstructed to give African Americans political power that they had been previously denied.

War, in its blunt way, had roughed out the contours of a solution, but only in broad terms. Clearly, African Americans would no longer be enslaved. The North, with its industrial might, would be the driving force in the nation's economy and retain the dominant political voice. But beyond that, the outlines of a reconstructed Republic remained vague. Would African Americans receive effective power? How would the North and the South readjust their economic and political relations? These questions lay at the heart of the problem of Reconstruction.

PRESIDENTIAL RECONSTRUCTION

Throughout the war Abraham Lincoln had considered Reconstruction his responsibility. Elected with less than 40 percent of the popular vote in 1860, he was acutely aware that once the states of the Confederacy were restored to the Union, the Republicans would be weakened unless they ceased to be a sectional party. By a generous peace, Lincoln hoped to attract former Whigs in the South, who supported many of the Republicans' economic policies, and build up a southern wing of the party.

Lincoln's 10 Percent Plan

Lincoln outlined his program in a Proclamation of Amnesty and Reconstruction issued in December 1863. When a minimum of 10 percent of the qualified voters from 1860 took a loyalty oath to the Union, they could organize a state government. The new state constitution had to be republican in form, abolish slavery, and provide for black education, but Lincoln did not insist that high-ranking Confederate leaders be barred from public life. Once these requirements had been met, the president would recognize the new civilian state government.

Disavowing any thought of trying prominent Confederate leaders, Lincoln indicated that he would be generous in granting pardons and did not rule out compensation for slave property. Moreover, while he privately suggested permitting some black men to vote in the disloyal states, "as for instance, the very intelligent and especially those who have fought gallantly in our ranks," he did not demand social or political equality for black Americans, and he recognized pro-Union governments in Louisiana, Arkansas, and Tennessee that allowed only white men to vote.

Radical Republicans   The Radical Republicans found Lincoln's approach much too lenient. Strongly antislavery, Radical members of Congress had led the struggle to make emancipation a war aim. Now they were in the forefront in advocating rights for the freedpeople. They were also disturbed that Lincoln had not enlisted Congress in devising Reconstruction policy. Lincoln argued that the executive branch should bear the responsibility for restoring proper relations with the former Confederate states. The Radicals, on the other hand, believed that it was the duty of Congress to set the terms under which states would regain their rights in the Union. Though the Radicals often disagreed on other matters, they were united in a determination to readmit southern states only after slavery had been ended, black rights protected, and the power of the planter class destroyed.

Under the direction of Senator Benjamin Wade of Ohio and Representative Henry Winter Davis of Maryland, Congress formulated a much stricter plan of Reconstruction. It proposed that Confederate states would be ruled temporarily by a military governor, required half the white adult males to take an oath of allegiance before drafting a new state constitution, and restricted political power to the hard-core Unionists in each state. When the Wade–Davis bill passed on the final day of the 1864 congressional session, Lincoln exercised his right of a pocket veto.* Still, his own program could not succeed without the assistance of Congress, which refused to seat Unionist representatives who had been elected from Louisiana or Arkansas. As the war drew to a close, Lincoln appeared ready to make concessions to the Radicals. He suggested that he might favor different—and conceivably more rigorous—Reconstruction plans for different states. At his final cabinet meeting, he approved placing the defeated South temporarily under military rule. But only a few days later Booth's bullet found its mark, and Lincoln's final approach to Reconstruction would never be known.

Wade–Davis bill

The Mood of the South

Northerners worried about the attitude of ex-Confederates at war's end. In the wake of defeat, the immediate reaction among white southerners was one of shock, despair, and hopelessness. Some former Confederates, of course, were openly antagonistic. A North Carolina innkeeper remarked bitterly that Yankees had stolen his slaves, burned his house, and killed all his sons, leaving him only one privilege: "To hate 'em. I git up at half-past four in the morning, and sit up till twelve at night, to hate 'em." Most Confederate soldiers were less defiant, having had their fill of war. Even among hostile civilians the feeling was widespread that the South must accept northern terms. A South Carolina paper admitted that "the conqueror has the right to make the terms, and we must submit."

This psychological moment was critical. To prevent a resurgence of resistance, the president needed to lay out in unmistakable terms what white southerners had to do to regain their old status in the Union. Any confusion in policy, or wavering on the peace terms, could only increase the likelihood of resistance. Perhaps even a clear and firm policy would not have been enough. But with Lincoln's death, the executive power came to rest in far less capable hands.

Johnson's Program of Reconstruction

Andrew Johnson, the new president, had been born in North Carolina and eventually moved to Tennessee, where he worked as a tailor. Barely able to read and write when he married, he rose to political power by portraying himself as the champion of the people against the wealthy planter class. "Some day I will show the stuck-up aristocrats who is running the country," he vowed as he began his political career. He had not opposed slavery before the war—in fact, he hoped to disperse slave ownership more widely in southern society. Although he accepted emancipation as one consequence of the war, Johnson remained a confirmed racist. "Damn the negroes," he said during the war, "I am fighting these traitorous aristocrats, their masters."

Johnson's character and values

*If a president does not sign a bill after Congress has adjourned, it has the same effect as a veto.

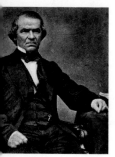

Andrew Johnson's contentious personality masked a deep-seated insecurity.

Because Johnson disliked the planter class so strongly, Republican Radicals in Congress expected him to uphold their views on Reconstruction. In fact, the new president did speak of trying Confederate leaders and breaking up planters' estates. Unlike most Republicans, however, Johnson strongly supported states' rights and opposed government aid to business. Given such differences, conflict between the president and the majority in Congress was inevitable, but Johnson's personality and political shortcomings made the situation worse. Scarred by his humble origins, he remained throughout his life an outsider. When challenged or criticized, he became tactless and inflexible, alienating even those who sought to work with him.

Johnson's program

At first, Johnson seemed to be following Lincoln's policy of quickly restoring the southern states to their rightful place in the Union. He prescribed a loyalty oath ordinary white southerners would have to take to have their property, except for slaves, restored and to regain their civil and political rights. Like Lincoln, Johnson excluded high Confederate officials from this group, but he added those with property worth over $20,000, which included his old foes in the planter class. These groups had to apply to the president for individual pardons.

Loyal state governments could be formed after a provisional governor, appointed by the president, called a convention to draft a new state constitution. Voters and delegates had to qualify under the 1860 state election laws and take the new loyalty oath. Once elections were held to choose a governor, legislature, and members of Congress, Johnson announced he would recognize the new state government, revoke martial law, and withdraw Union troops. Again, the plan was similar to Lincoln's, though more lenient. Unlike Lincoln's formula, Johnson spoke only informally of requiring southern states to repeal their ordinances of secession, repudiate the Confederate debt, and ratify the proposed Thirteenth Amendment abolishing slavery.

The Failure of Johnson's Program

Southern defiance

The southern delegates who met to construct new governments soon demonstrated that they were in no frame of mind to follow Johnson's recommendations. Several states merely repealed instead of repudiating their ordinances of secession, rejected the Thirteenth Amendment, or refused to repudiate the Confederate debt.

Nor did any of the new governments allow African Americans any political rights or make any effective provisions for black education. In addition, each state passed a series of laws, often modeled on its old slave code, that applied only to African Americans. These "black codes" did grant African Americans some rights that had not been enjoyed by slaves. They legalized marriages from slavery and allowed black southerners to hold and sell property and to sue and be sued in state courts. Yet their primary purpose was to keep African Americans as propertyless agricultural laborers with inferior legal rights. The new freedpeople could not serve on juries, testify against whites, or work as they pleased. South Carolina forbade blacks from engaging in anything other than agricultural labor without a special license; Mississippi prohibited them from buying or renting farmland. Most states ominously provided that black people who were vagrants could be arrested and hired out to landowners. Many

Black codes

SELLING A FREEDMAN TO PAY HIS FINE, AT MONTICELLO, FLORIDA.—FROM A SKETCH BY JAS. E. TAYLOR.—SEE PAGE 275.

The black codes enacted under presidential Reconstruction provided for fines for unemployed blacks. If they were unable to pay the fine, their services could be sold to the highest bidder. Here a Florida freedman watches as white landlords bid for his labor at an auction. Critics charged that this system constituted quasi-slavery.

northerners were incensed by the restrictive black codes, which violated their conception of freedom.

Elections in the South

Southern voters under Johnson's plan also defiantly elected prominent Confederate military and political leaders to office, headed by Alexander Stephens, the vice president of the Confederacy, who was elected senator from Georgia. At this point, Johnson could have called for new elections or admitted that a different program of Reconstruction was needed. Instead he caved in. For all his harsh rhetoric, he shrank from the prospect of social upheaval, and he found it enormously gratifying when upper-class planters praised his conduct and requested pardons. As the lines of ex-Confederates waiting to see him lengthened, he began issuing special pardons almost as fast as they could be printed. In the next two years he pardoned some 13,500 former rebels.

In private, Johnson warned southerners against a reckless course. Publicly he put on a bold face, announcing that Reconstruction had been successfully completed. But many members of Congress were deeply alarmed, and the stage was set for a serious confrontation.

Johnson's Break with Congress

The new Congress was by no means of one mind. A small number of Democrats and a few conservative Republicans backed the president's program of immediate and unconditional restoration. At the other end of the spectrum, a larger group of Radical Republicans, led by Thaddeus Stevens, Charles Sumner, Benjamin Wade, and others, was bent on remaking southern society in the image of the North. Reconstruction must "revolutionize Southern institutions, habits, and manners," thundered Representative Stevens, ". . . or all our blood and treasure have been spent in vain."

As a minority, the Radicals could accomplish nothing without the aid of the moderate Republicans, the largest bloc in Congress. Led by William Pitt Fessenden and Lyman Trumbull, the moderates hoped to avoid a clash with the president, and they had no desire to foster social revolution or promote racial equality in the South. But they wanted to keep Confederate leaders from reassuming power, and they were convinced that the former slaves needed federal protection. Otherwise, Trumbull declared, the freedman would "be tyrannized over, abused, and virtually reenslaved."

Issue of black rights

The central issue dividing Johnson and the Radicals was the place of African Americans in American society. Johnson accused his opponents of seeking "to Africanize the southern half of our country," while the Radicals championed civil and political rights for African Americans. Convinced that southern white Unionists were too small a nucleus to build a party around, Radicals believed that the only way to maintain loyal governments and develop a Republican party in the South was to give black men the ballot. Moderates agreed that the new southern governments were too harsh toward African Americans, but they feared that too great an emphasis on black civil rights would alienate northern voters.

In December 1865, when southern representatives to Congress appeared in Washington, a majority in Congress voted to exclude them. Congress also appointed a joint committee, chaired by Senator Fessenden, to look into Reconstruction.

Johnson's vetoes

The growing split with the president became clearer when Congress passed a bill extending the life of the Freedmen's Bureau. Created in March 1865, the Bureau provided emergency food, clothing, and medical care to war refugees (including white southerners) and took charge of settling freedpeople on abandoned lands. The new bill gave the Bureau the added responsibilities of supervising special courts to resolve disputes involving freedpeople and establishing schools for black southerners. Although this bill passed with virtually unanimous Republican support, Johnson nevertheless vetoed it, and Congress failed to override his veto.

Johnson also vetoed a civil rights bill designed to overturn the more flagrant provisions of the black codes. The law made African Americans citizens of the United States and granted them the right to own property, make contracts, and have access to courts as parties and witnesses. For most Republicans Johnson's action was the last straw, and in April 1866 Congress overrode his veto, the first major legislation in American history to be enacted over a presidential veto. Congress then approved a slightly revised Freedmen's Bureau bill in July and promptly overrode the president's veto. Johnson's refusal to compromise drove the moderates into the arms of the Radicals.

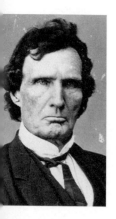

Thaddeus Stevens, Radical leader in the House

The Fourteenth Amendment

To prevent unrepentant Confederates from taking over the reconstructed state governments and denying African Americans basic freedoms, the Joint Committee on Reconstruction proposed an amendment to the Constitution, which passed both houses of Congress with the necessary two-thirds vote in June 1866. The amendment, coupled with the Freedmen's Bureau and civil rights bills, represented the moderates' terms for Reconstruction.

Provisions of the amendment

The Fourteenth Amendment put a number of matters beyond the control of the president. The amendment guaranteed repayment of the national war debt and prohibited repayment of the Confederate debt. To counteract the president's wholesale pardons, it disqualified prominent Confederates from holding office and provided that only Congress by a two-thirds vote could remove this penalty. Because moderates, fearful of the reaction of white northerners, balked at giving the vote to African Americans, the amendment merely gave Congress the right to reduce the representation of any state that did not have impartial male suffrage. The practical effect of this provision, which Radicals labeled a "swindle," was to allow northern states to restrict suffrage to whites if they wished, since unlike southern states they had few African Americans and thus would not be penalized.

The amendment's most important provision, Section 1, defined an American citizen as anyone born in the United States or naturalized, thereby automatically making African Americans citizens. Section 1 also prohibited states from abridging "the privileges or immunities" of citizens, depriving "any person of life, liberty, or property, without due process of law," or denying "any person . . . equal protection of the laws." The framers of the amendment probably intended to prohibit laws that applied to one race only, such as the black codes, or that made certain acts felonies when committed by black but not white people, or that decreed different penalties for the same crime when committed by white and black lawbreakers. The framers probably did not intend to prevent African Americans from being excluded from juries or forbid segregation (the legal separation of the races) in schools and public places.

Nevertheless, Johnson denounced the proposed amendment and urged southern states not to ratify it. Ironically, of the seceded states only the president's own state ratified the amendment, and Congress readmitted Tennessee with no further restrictions. The telegram sent to Congress by a longtime foe of Johnson announcing Tennessee's approval ended, "Give my respects to the dead dog in the White House." The amendment was ratified in 1868.

The Elections of 1866

When Congress blocked his policies, Johnson undertook a speaking tour of the East and Midwest in the fall of 1866 to drum up popular support. But the president found it difficult to convince northern audiences that white southerners were fully repentant. News that summer of major race riots in Memphis and New Orleans heightened northern concern. Forty-six African Americans died when white mobs invaded the black section of Memphis, burning homes, churches, and schoolhouses. About the same number were killed in New Orleans when whites attacked both black and white delegates to a convention supporting black suffrage. "The negroes now know, to their sorrow, that it is best not to arouse the fury of the white man," boasted one Memphis

Antiblack riots

newspaper. When the president encountered hostile audiences during his northern campaign, he only made matters worse by trading insults and ranting that the Radicals were traitors. Even supporters found his performance humiliating.

Not to be outdone, the Radicals vilified Johnson as a traitor aiming to turn the country over to rebels and Copperheads. Resorting to the tactic of "waving the bloody shirt," they appealed to voters by reviving bitter memories of the war. In a classic example of such rhetoric, Governor Oliver Morton of Indiana proclaimed that "every bounty jumper, every deserter, every sneak who ran away from the draft" was a Democrat; everyone "who murdered Union prisoners," every "New York rioter in 1863 who burned up little children in colored asylums called himself a Democrat. In short, the Democratic party may be described as a common sewer. . . ."

Repudiation of Johnson

Voters soundly repudiated Johnson, as the Republicans won more than a two-thirds majority in both houses of Congress, every northern gubernatorial contest, and control of every northern legislature. The Radicals had reached the height of their power, propelled by genuine alarm among northerners that Johnson's policies would lose the fruits of the Union's victory. Johnson was a president virtually without a party.

CONGRESSIONAL RECONSTRUCTION

With a clear mandate in hand, congressional Republicans passed their own program of Reconstruction, beginning with the first Reconstruction Act in March 1867. Like all later pieces of Reconstruction legislation, it was repassed over Johnson's veto.

Placing the 10 unreconstructed states under military commanders, the act provided that in enrolling voters, officials were to include black adult males but not former Confederates who were barred from holding office under the Fourteenth Amendment. Delegates to the state conventions would frame constitutions that provided for black suffrage and disqualified prominent ex-Confederates from office. The first state legislatures to meet under the new constitution were required to ratify the Fourteenth Amendment. Once these steps were completed and Congress approved the new state constitution, a state could send representatives to Congress.

Resistance of southern whites

White southerners found these requirements so obnoxious that officials took no steps to register voters. Congress then enacted a second Reconstruction Act, also in March, ordering the local military commanders to put the machinery of Reconstruction into motion. Johnson's efforts to limit the power of military commanders produced a third act, passed in July, that upheld their superiority in all matters. When elections were held to ratify the new state constitutions, white southerners boycotted them in large numbers. Undaunted, Congress passed the fourth Reconstruction Act (March 1868), which required ratification of the constitution by only a majority of those voting rather than those who were registered.

By June 1868 Congress had readmitted the representatives of seven states. Texas, Virginia, and Mississippi did not complete the process until 1869. Georgia finally followed in 1874.

The Land Issue

Blacks' desire for land

While the political process of Reconstruction proceeded, Congress confronted the question of whether land should be given to former slaves to foster economic inde-

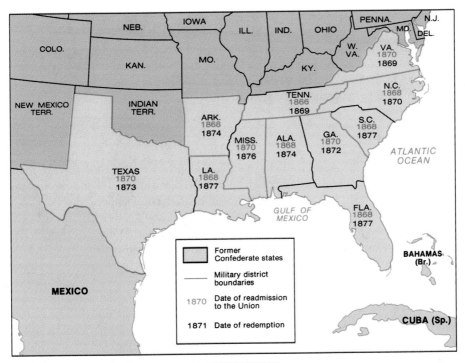

THE SOUTHERN STATES DURING RECONSTRUCTION

pendence. At a meeting with Secretary of War Edwin Stanton near the end of the war, African American leaders declared, "The way we can best take care of ourselves is to have land, and till it by our own labor." During the war, the Second Confiscation Act of 1862 had authorized the government to seize and sell the property, including land, of supporters of the rebellion. In June 1866, however, President Johnson ruled that confiscation laws applied only to wartime.

Congress debated land confiscation off and on from December 1865 until early 1867. Thaddeus Stevens, a leading Radical in the House, advocated confiscating 394 million acres of land from about 70,000 of what he termed the "chief rebels" in the South, who comprised less than 5 percent of the South's white families. He proposed to give 40 acres to every adult male freedman and then sell the remaining land, which would amount to nine-tenths of the total, to pay off the public debt, compensate loyal southerners for losses they suffered during the war, and fund Union veterans' pensions. Land, he insisted, would be far more valuable to African Americans than the right to vote.

But in the end Congress rejected all proposals. Even some Radicals were opposed. Given Americans' strong belief in self-reliance, little sympathy existed for the idea that government should support any group. In addition, land redistribution represented an attack on property rights, another cherished American value. "A division of rich men's lands amongst the landless," argued the *Nation,* a Radical journal, "would give a shock to our whole social and political system from which it would hardly recover without the loss of liberty." By 1867 land reform was dead.

Failure of land redistribution

Few freedpeople acquired land after the war, a development that severely limited African Americans' economic independence and left them vulnerable to white coercion. It is doubtful, however, that this decision was the basic cause of the failure of Reconstruction. In the face of white hostility and institutionalized racism, African Americans probably would have been no more successful in protecting their property than they were in maintaining the right to vote.

Impeachment

Throughout 1867 Congress routinely overrode Johnson's vetoes. Still, the president had other ways of undercutting congressional Reconstruction. He interpreted the new laws as narrowly as possible and removed military commanders who vigorously enforced them. Congress responded by restricting Johnson's power to issue orders to

Tenure of Office Act

military commanders in the South. It also passed the Tenure of Office Act, which forbade Johnson from removing any member of the cabinet without the Senate's consent. The intention of this law was to prevent him from firing Secretary of War Edwin Stanton, the only Radical in the cabinet.

When Johnson tried to dismiss Stanton in February 1868, the determined secretary of war barricaded himself in his office (where he remained night and day for about two months). Angrily, the House of Representatives approved articles of impeachment. The articles focused on the violation of the Tenure of Office Act, but the charge with the most substance was that Johnson had conspired to systematically obstruct Reconstruction legislation. In the trial before the Senate, his lawyers argued that a president could be impeached only for an indictable crime, which Johnson clearly had not committed. The Radicals countered that impeachment applied to political offenses and not merely criminal acts.

Johnson acquitted

In May 1868 the Senate voted 36 to 19 to convict, one vote short of the two-thirds majority needed. The seven Republicans who joined the Democrats in voting for acquittal were uneasy about using impeachment as a political weapon. Their vote against conviction established the precedent that a president could be removed from office only for indictable offenses, which greatly lessened the effectiveness of the threat of impeachment.

Facsimile of a ticket of admission to the impeachment trial of President Andrew Johnson

COUNTERPOINT

Should Johnson have been removed from office?

For the first half of the twentieth century, most historians viewed Reconstruction as an undertaking that was tragically flawed at best or vindictive and misconceived at worst. Beginning in the 1960s historians increasingly found much to praise in the experiment of Reconstruction and much to condemn in Andrew Johnson's leadership. (It is no coincidence that the reevaluation gained momentum just as the civil rights movement was forcing Americans to rethink attitudes about segregation, racism, and equality.)

Controversy persists, however, over the narrower issue of whether congressional Republicans were wise to pursue impeachment. Some historians point out that when the Constitution was first drafted, James Madison argued that impeachment should apply to political misdeeds as well as crimes. Johnson, after all, had never been elected president in his own right. In 1866 the voters in congressional elections had rejected his clumsy attempts to gain support. Furthermore, as president he had taken an oath to uphold the laws of the nation. Yet time after time Johnson interpreted those laws as narrowly as possible, refusing to enforce them in the manner that Congress clearly intended. When Congress voted to not convict the president, these historians argue, it lessened the threat of impeachment ever being used. Yet that was one of the legislative branch's most important weapons to control an abuse of power by a president.

Other historians, while not sympathetic to Johnson's policies, believe that his acquittal was fortunate. The Constitution states only that the president could be removed for "Treason, Bribery, or other high Crimes and Misdemeanors." Johnson's lawyers ably argued that whatever his "misdeeds" in the eyes of Congress, he had not committed "high Crimes." Historians who sympathize with that view argue that a conviction would have upset the constitutional doctrine of separation of powers. Removing Johnson from office would have seriously weakened the presidency, placed too much power in the hands of Congress, and provided a dangerous precedent for the future. The best course, they conclude, was the one Congress actually followed: to let Johnson finish his term as an ineffective president.

RECONSTRUCTION IN THE SOUTH

The refusal of Congress to convict Johnson sent a clear signal: the power of the Radicals in Congress was waning. Increasingly the success or failure of Reconstruction hinged on developments not in Congress but in the southern states themselves. Power there rested with the new Republican parties, representing a coalition of black and white southerners and transplanted northerners.

Black Officeholding

Almost from the beginning of Reconstruction, African Americans had lobbied for the right to vote. After they received the franchise, black men constituted as much as 80 percent of the Republican voters in the South. They steadfastly opposed the Democratic party with its appeal to white supremacy. As one Tennessee Republican explained, "The blacks know that many conservatives [Democrats] hope to reduce

Hiram Revels, a minister and educator, became the first African American to serve in the United States Senate, representing Mississippi. Later he served as president of Alcorn University.

them again to some form of peonage. Under the impulse of this fear they will roll up their whole strength and will go entirely for the Republican candidate whoever he may be."

Throughout Reconstruction, African Americans never held office in proportion to their voting strength. No African American was ever elected governor, and only in South Carolina, where more than 60 percent of the population was black, did they control even one house of the legislature. During Reconstruction between 15 and 20 percent of the state officers and 6 percent of members of Congress (2 senators and 15 representatives) were black. Only in South Carolina did black officeholders approach their proportion of the population.

Background of black political leaders

Those who held office generally came from the top levels of African American society. Among state and federal officeholders, perhaps four-fifths were literate, and over a quarter had been free before the war, both marks of distinction in the black community. Their occupations also set them apart: two-fifths were professionals (mostly clergy), and of the third who were farmers, nearly all owned land. Among black members of Congress, all but three had a secondary school education, and four had gone to college. In their political and social values, African American leaders were more conservative than the rural black population, and they showed little interest in land reform.

White Republicans in the South

Black citizens were a majority of the voters only in South Carolina, Mississippi, and Louisiana. Thus in most of the South the Republican party had to secure white votes to stay in power. Opponents scornfully labeled white southerners who allied with the Republican party scalawags, yet an estimated quarter of white southerners at one time voted Republican. Although the party appealed to some wealthy planters, they were outnumbered by Unionists from the upland counties and hill areas who were largely yeoman farmers. Such voters were attracted by Republican promises to rebuild the South, restore prosperity, create public schools, and open isolated areas to the market with railroads.

The other group of white Republicans in the South were known as carpetbaggers. Originally from the North, they allegedly had arrived with all their worldly possessions stuffed in a carpetbag, ready to loot and plunder the defeated South. Some did, certainly, but northerners moved south for a variety of reasons. Those in political office were especially well educated. Though carpetbaggers made up only a small percentage of Republican voters, they controlled almost a third of the offices. More than half of all southern Republican governors and nearly half of Republican members of Congress were originally northerners.

Divisions among southern Republicans

The Republican party in the South had difficulty agreeing on a program or maintaining unity. Scalawags were especially susceptible to the race issue and social pressure. "Even my own kinspeople have turned the cold shoulder to me because I hold office under a Republican administration," testified a Mississippi white Republican. As black southerners pressed for greater recognition and a greater share of the offices, white southerners increasingly defected to the Democrats. Carpetbaggers, by contrast, were less sensitive to race, although most felt that their black allies needed guidance and should be content with minor offices. The friction between scalawags and carpetbaggers, which grew out of their rivalry for party honors, was particularly intense.

The New State Governments

The new southern state constitutions enacted several significant reforms. They put in place fairer systems of legislative representation, allowed voters to elect many officials who before had been appointed, and abolished property requirements for officeholding. In South Carolina, for the first time, voters were allowed to vote for the president, governor, and other state officers.° The Radical state governments also assumed some responsibility for social welfare and established the first statewide systems of public schools in the South. Although the Fourteenth Amendment prevented high Confederate officials from holding office, only Alabama and Arkansas temporarily forbade some ex-Confederates from voting.

Reconstruction state constitutions

All the new constitutions proclaimed the principle of equality and granted black adult males the right to vote. On social relations they were much more cautious. No state outlawed segregation, and South Carolina and Louisiana were the only states that required integration in public schools (a mandate that was almost universally ignored). Sensitive to status, mulattoes pushed for prohibition of social discrimination, but white Republicans refused to adopt such a radical policy.

Race and social equality

Economic Issues and Corruption

The war left the southern economy in ruins, and problems of economic reconstruction were as difficult as those of politics. The new Republican governments encour-

---

°Previously, presidential electors as well as the governor had been chosen by the South Carolina legislature.

From the beginning of Reconstruction, African Americans demanded the right to vote as free citizens. The Fifteenth Amendment, ratified in 1870, secured that right for black males. In New York, black citizens paraded in support of Ulysses Grant for president. Parades played a central role in campaigning: Here, there are the usual banners, flags, costumes, and a band. Blacks in both the North and the South voted solidly for the Republican party as the party of Lincoln and emancipation, although while violence in the South increasingly reduced black turnout.

aged industrial development by providing subsidies, loans, and even temporary exemptions from taxes. These governments also largely rebuilt the southern railroad system, often offering lavish aid to railroad corporations. These investments in the South's industrial base helped: in the two decades after 1860, the region doubled its manufacturing establishments. Yet the harsh reality was that the South steadily slipped further behind the booming industrial economy of the North. Between 1854 and 1879, 7000 miles of railroad track were laid in the South, but in the same period 45,000 miles were constructed in the rest of the nation.

Corruption   The expansion of government services offered temptations for corruption. In many southern states, officials regularly received bribes and kickbacks for their award of railroad charters, franchises, and other contracts. By 1872 the debts of the 11 states of the Confederacy had increased by $132 million, largely because of railroad grants and new social services such as schools. The tax rate grew as expenditures went up, so that by the 1870s it was four times the rate of 1860.

Corruption, however, was not only a southern problem: the decline in morality affected the entire nation. During these years in New York City alone, the Democratic Tweed Ring stole more money than all the Radical Republican governments in the South combined. Moreover, corruption in the South was hardly limited to Republicans. Many Democrats and white business leaders participated in these corrupt practices both before and after the Radical governments were in power. Louisiana Governor Henry Warmoth, a carpetbagger, told a congressional committee that the legislature was as good as the people it represented. "Everybody is demoralizing down here. Corruption is the fashion."

Corruption in Radical governments undeniably existed, but southern whites exaggerated its extent for partisan purposes. Conservatives just as bitterly opposed honest Radical regimes as they did notoriously corrupt ones. In the eyes of most white southerners, the real crime of the Radical governments was that they allowed black citizens to hold some offices and tried to protect the civil rights of African Americans.

Race was the conservatives' greatest weapon. And it would prove the most effective means to undermine Republican power in the South.

BLACK ASPIRATIONS

Emancipation came to slaves in different ways and at different times. For some it arrived during the war when Union soldiers entered an area; for others it came some time after the Confederacy's collapse, when Union troops or officials announced that they were free. Whatever the timing, freedom meant a host of precious blessings to people who had been in bondage all their lives.

Experiencing Freedom

The first impulse was to think of freedom as a contrast to slavery. Emancipation immediately released slaves from the most oppressive aspects of bondage—the whippings, the breakup of families, the sexual exploitation. Freedom also meant movement, the right to travel without a pass or white permission. Above all, freedom meant that African Americans' labor would be for their own benefit. One Arkansas freedman, who earned his first dollar working on a railroad, recalled that when he was paid, "I felt like the richest man in the world."

Changing employment

Freedom included finding a new place to work. Changing jobs was one concrete way to break the psychological ties of slavery. Even planters with reputations for kindness sometimes found that most of their former hands had departed. The cook who left a South Carolina family, even though they offered her higher wages than her new job, explained, "I must go. If I stays here I'll never know I'm free."

Importance of names

Symbolically, freedom meant having a full name, and African Americans now adopted last names. More than a few took the last name of some prominent individual; more common was to take the name of the first master in the family's oral history as far back as it could be recalled. Most, on the other hand, retained their first name, especially if the name had been given to them by their parents (as most often had been the case among slaves). It had been their form of identity in bondage, and for those separated from their family it was the only link with their parents. Whatever name they took, it was important to black Americans that they made the decision themselves without white interference.

The Black Family

Upholding the family

African Americans also sought to strengthen the family in freedom. Since slave marriages had not been recognized as legal, thousands of former slaves insisted on being married again by proper authorities, even though this was not required by law. Those who had been forcibly separated in slavery and later remarried confronted the dilemma of which spouse to take. Laura Spicer, whose husband had been sold away in slavery, received a series of wrenching letters from him after the war. He had thought her dead, had remarried, and had a new family. "You know it never was our wishes to be separated from each other, and it never was our fault. I had rather anything to had happened to me most than ever have been parted from you and the chil-

PUBLIC SPACE/PRIVATE SPACE

The Black Sharecropper's Cabin

On the plantations of the Old South, slaves had lived in cabins along a central path in the shadow of the white master's "big house." These quarters were the center of their community, where marriages and other festivals were celebrated and family life went on. But with the coming of emancipation, freedpeople looked to leave the old quarters, which stood as a symbol of bondage and of close white supervision. African Americans either built new housing or dismantled their old cabins and hauled them to the plots of land they rented as tenants or sharecroppers. This enabled them to live on the land they farmed, just as white farmers and tenants did.

In selecting a cabin site, freedpeople tried to locate within a convenient distance of their fields but close to the woods as well, since cutting wood was a year-round task for boys. To improve drainage, cabins were often built on a knoll or had a floor raised above the ground. A nearby stream, spring, or well provided not only water but a place to cool butter and other perishable dairy products.

Like slave cabins, most sharecroppers' dwellings were one story high, about 16 feet square, and usually built of logs chinked with mud. The few windows had shutters to protect against the weather; glass was rare. Though the inside walls normally lacked plaster or sheeting, they were given a coat of whitewash annually to brighten the dark interior. To provide a bit of cheer, women often covered the walls with pictures from seed catalogues and magazines. The floor, packed dirt that was as smooth and hard as concrete, was covered with braided rugs made from scraps of cloth and worn-out clothing.

The main room served as kitchen and dining room, parlor, bathing area, and the parents' bedroom. To one side might be a homemade drop-leaf table (essential because of cramped space), which served as a kitchen work counter and a dining table. The other side of the room had a few plain beds, their slats or rope bottoms supporting corn shuck or straw mattresses. (Featherbeds were considered a remarkable luxury.) The social center of the room was the fireplace, the only source of heat and the main source of light after dark. Pots and pans were hung on the wall near the fireplace, and the mother and daughters did the cooking stooped over an open fire. Clothing was hung on pegs in the wall.

The cabin's chimney was made of small logs notched together and covered with several layers of clay to protect it from the heat. It often narrowed toward the top, and sometimes its height was extended by empty flour barrels, for a taller chimney drew better. That kept smoke from blowing back down into the house and kept sparks away from the roof. After the evening meal the family gathered around the fireplace, the children to play with homemade dolls and toys, the mother to sew, and the father perhaps to play the fiddle. At bedtime a trapdoor in the ceiling offered access up a

dren," he wrote. "As I am, I do not know which I love best, you or Anna." Declining to return, he closed, "Laura, truly, I have got another wife, and I am very sorry. . . ."

As in white families, black husbands deemed themselves the head of the family and acted legally for their wives. They often insisted that their wives would not work in the fields as they had in slavery, a decision that had major economic repercussions

Daily Lives

Chimneys on share-croppers' cabins were often tilted deliber-ately so that they could be pushed away from the house quickly if they caught fire.

ladder to the loft beneath the gabled roof, where older children slept, usually on pallets on the floor, as had been the case in slavery.

In the summer cooking was done outdoors over an open fire. Women generally preferred to cook under a tree, which offered some protection from rain as well as relief from the sun and the high humidity. Sharecropper families rarely had separate cooking rooms attached to or next to the cabin. Separate kitchens, which were a sign of prosperity, were more common among black landowners and white tenant farmers.

Gradually, as black sharecroppers scraped together some savings, they improved their homes. By the end of the century, frame dwellings were more common, and many older log cabins had been covered with wood siding. The newer homes were generally larger, with wood floors, and often had attached rooms such as a porch or kitchen. In addition, windows had glass panes, roofs were covered with shingles instead of planking, and stone and brick chimneys were less unusual. Ceramic dishes were more frequently seen, and wood-burning stoves made cooking easier for women and provided a more efficient source of heat.

Without question, the cabins of black sharecroppers provided more space than the slave quarters had, and certainly more freedom and privacy. Still, they lacked many of the comforts that most white Americans took for granted. Such housing reflected the continuing status of black sharecroppers as poverty-stricken laborers in a caste system based on race.

for agricultural labor. "The [black] women say they never mean to do any more outdoor work," one planter reported, "that white men support their wives and they mean that their husbands shall support them." In negotiating contracts, a father also demanded the right to control his children and their labor. All these changes were designed to insulate the black family from white control.

The Schoolhouse and the Church

*Black
education*

In freedom, the schoolhouse and the black church became essential institutions in the black community. Next to ownership of land, African Americans saw education as the best hope for advancement. At first, northern churches and missionaries, working with the Freedmen's Bureau, set up black schools in the South. Tuition represented 10 percent or more of a laborer's monthly wages. Yet these schools were full. Many parents sent their children by day and attended classes themselves at night. Eventually, the freedmen's schools were replaced by the new public school systems, which by 1876 enrolled 40 percent of African American children.

Black adults had good reasons for seeking literacy. They wanted to be able to read the Bible, to defend their newly gained civil and political rights, and to protect themselves from being cheated. One elderly Louisiana freedman explained that giving children an education was better than giving them a fortune, "because if you left them even $500, some man having more education than they had would come along and cheat them out of it all." Both races saw that education would undermine the old servility that slavery had fostered.

*Teachers in
black schools*

Teachers in the Freedmen's Bureau schools were primarily northern middle-class white women sent south by northern missionary societies. "I feel that it is a precious privilege," Esther Douglass wrote, "to be allowed to do something for these poor people." Many saw themselves as peacetime soldiers, struggling to make emancipation a reality. Indeed, on more than one occasion, hostile white southerners destroyed black schools and threatened and even murdered white teachers. Teachers in urban schools often lived together in comfortable housing, which provided a social network, created a sense of sisterhood, and helped sustain morale. In rural areas, however, teachers often had to live alone or with black families because of white hostility. Then there were the everyday challenges: low pay, dilapidated buildings, lack of sufficient books, classes of 100 or more children, and irregular attendance. Meanwhile, the Freedmen's Bureau undertook to quickly train black teachers, and by 1869 a majority of the approximately 3000 teachers in freedmen's schools were black.

*Independent
black
churches*

Before the war, most slaves had attended white churches or services supervised by whites. Once free, African Americans quickly established their own congregations led by black preachers. In the first year of freedom, the Methodist Church South lost fully half of its black members. By 1870 the Negro Baptist Church had increased its membership threefold compared to 1850, and the African Methodist Episcopal Church expanded at an even greater rate.

Black churches were so important because they were the only major organizations in the African American community controlled by blacks. A white missionary reported that "the Ebony preacher who promises perfect independence from White control and direction carried the colored heart at once." Black ministers were respected leaders, and many of the black men elected to office during Reconstruction were preachers. As it had in slavery, religion offered African Americans a place of refuge in a hostile white world and provided them with hope, comfort, and a means of self-identification.

New Working Conditions

As a largely propertyless class, blacks in the postwar South had no choice but to work for white landowners. Except for paying wages, whites wanted to retain the old system of labor, including close supervision, gang labor, and physical punishment. Determined to remove all emblems of servitude, African Americans refused to work under these conditions, and they demanded time off to devote to their own interests. Convinced that working at one's own pace was part of freedom, they simply would not work as long or as hard as they had in slavery. Because of shorter hours and the withdrawal of children and women from the fields, work output declined by an estimated 35 percent in freedom. Blacks also refused to live in the old slave quarters located near the master's house. Instead, they erected cabins on distant parts of the plantation. Wages at first were $5 or $6 a month plus provisions and a cabin; by 1867, they had risen to an average of $10 a month.

These changes eventually led to the rise of sharecropping. Under this arrangement African American families farmed separate plots of land and then at the end of the year divided the crop, normally on an equal basis, with the white landowner. Sharecropping had higher status and offered greater personal freedom than being a wage laborer. "I am not working for wages," one black farmer declared in defending

Sharecropping

A GEORGIA PLANTATION AFTER THE WAR

After emancipation, sharecropping became the dominant form of agricultural labor in the South. Black families no longer lived in the old slave quarters but dispersed to separate plots of land that they farmed themselves. At the end of the year each sharecropper turned over part of the crop to the white landowner.

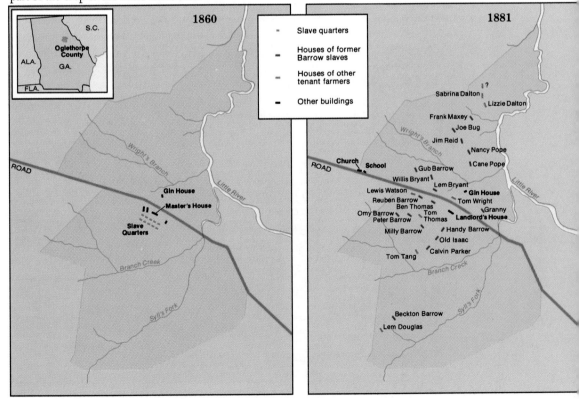

his right to leave the plantation at will, "but am part owner of the crop and as [such,] I have all the rights that you or any other man has. . . ." Although black per capita agricultural income increased 40 percent in freedom, sharecropping was a harshly exploitative system in which black families often sank into perpetual debt.

The Freedmen's Bureau

The task of supervising the transition from slavery to freedom on southern plantations fell to the Freedmen's Bureau, a unique experiment in social policy supported by the federal government. Assigned the task of protecting freedpeople's economic rights, approximately 550 local agents supervised and regulated working conditions in southern agriculture after the war. The racial attitudes of Bureau agents varied widely, as did their commitment and competence. Then, too, they had to depend on the army to enforce their decisions.

Bureau's mixed record   Most agents encouraged or required written contracts between white planters and black laborers, specifying not only wages but also the conditions of employment. Although agents sometimes intervened to protect freedpeople from unfair treatment, they also provided important help to planters. They insisted that black laborers not desert at harvest time; they arrested those who violated their contracts or refused to

After living for years in a society where teaching slaves to read and write was usually illegal, freedpeople viewed literacy as a key to securing their newfound freedom. Blacks were not merely "*anxious* to learn," a school official in Virginia reported, they were "*crazy* to learn."

sign new ones at the beginning of the year; and they preached the gospel of work and the need to be orderly and respectful. Given such attitudes, freedpeople increasingly complained that Bureau agents were mere tools of the planter class. "They are, in fact, the planters' guards, and nothing else," claimed the New Orleans *Tribune*, a black newspaper. One observer reported, "Doing justice seems to mean seeing that the blacks don't break contracts and compelling them to submit cheerfully."

The primary means of enforcing working conditions were the Freedmen's Courts, which Congress created in 1866 in order to avoid the discrimination African Americans received in state courts. These new courts functioned as military tribunals, and often the agent was the entire court. The sympathy black laborers received varied from state to state. In 1867 one agent summarized the Bureau's experience with the labor contract system: "It has succeeded in making the freedman work and in rendering labor secure and stable—but it has failed to secure to the Freedman his just dues or compensation."

In 1869, with the Bureau's work scarcely under way, Congress decided to shut it down, and by 1872 it had gone out of business. Despite its mixed record, it was the most effective agency in protecting blacks' civil and political rights. Its disbanding signaled the beginning of the northern retreat from Reconstruction. *End of the Bureau*

Planters and a New Way of Life

Planters and other white southerners faced emancipation with dread. "All the traditions and habits of both races had been suddenly overthrown," a Tennessee planter recalled, "and neither knew just what to do, or how to accommodate themselves to the new situation."

The old ideal of a paternalistic planter, which required a facade of black subservience and affection, gave way to an emphasis on strictly economic relationships. Mary Jones, a Georgia slaveholder before the war who did more for her workers than the law required, lost all patience when two workers accused her of trickery and hauled her before a Freedmen's Bureau agent, with whom she won her case. Upon returning home, she announced to the assembled freedpeople that "I have considered them friends and treated them as such but now they were only laborers under contract, and only the law would rule between us." Only with time did planters develop new norms and standards to judge black behavior. What in 1865 had seemed insolence was viewed by the 1870s as the normal attitude of freedom. *Planters' new values*

Slavery had been a complex institution that welded black and white southerners together in intimate relationships. After the war, however, planters increasingly embraced the ideology of segregation. Since emancipation significantly reduced the social distance between the races, white southerners sought psychological separation and kept dealings with African Americans to a minimum. By the time Reconstruction ended, white planters had developed a new way of life based on the institutions of sharecropping and segregation and undergirded by a militant white supremacy.

While most planters kept their land, they did not regain the economic prosperity of the prewar years. Rice plantations, which were not suitable to tenant farming, largely disappeared after the war. In addition, southern cotton growers faced increased competition from new areas such as India, Egypt, and Brazil. Cotton prices began a long decline, and southern per capita income suffered as a result. By 1880 the value of southern farms had slid 33 percent below the level of 1860.

THE ABANDONMENT OF RECONSTRUCTION

On Christmas Day, 1875, a white acquaintance approached Charles Caldwell on the streets of Clinton, Mississippi, and invited him into Chilton's store to have a drink to celebrate the holiday. A former slave, Caldwell was a state senator and the leader of the Republican party in Hinds County, Mississippi. But the black leader's fearlessness made him a marked man. Only two months earlier, he had been forced to flee the county to escape an armed white mob angry about a Republican barbecue he and his fellow Republicans had organized. For four days the mob hunted down and killed nearly 40 Republican leaders for presuming to hold a political meeting. Despite that hostility, Caldwell had returned to vote in the November state election. Even more boldly, he had led a black militia company through the streets to help quell the disturbances. Now, as Caldwell and his "friend" raised their glasses in a holiday toast, a gunshot exploded through the window. Caldwell collapsed, mortally wounded from a bullet to the back of his head. He was taken outside, where his assassins riddled his body with bullets. He died in the street.

Charles Caldwell shared the fate of more than a few black Republican leaders in the South during Reconstruction. Southern whites used violence, terror, and political assassination to challenge the federal government's commitment to sustaining Reconstruction. If northerners had boldly countered such terrorism, Reconstruction might have ended differently. But in the years following President Johnson's impeachment trial in 1868, the influence of Radical Republicans steadily waned. The Republican party was being drained of the crusading idealism that had stamped its early years.

The Election of Grant

Immensely popular after the war, Ulysees S. Grant was the natural choice of Republicans to run for president in 1868. Although Grant was elected, Republicans were shocked that despite his great military stature, his popular margin was only 300,000 votes. Since an estimated 450,000 black Republican votes had been cast in the South, that meant that a majority of whites casting ballots had voted Democratic. The 1868 election helped convince Republican leaders that an amendment securing black suffrage throughout the nation was necessary.

Fifteenth Amendment

In February 1869 Congress sent the Fifteenth Amendment to the states for ratification. It forbade any state from denying the right to vote on grounds of race, color, or previous condition of servitude. Some Radicals had hoped to forbid literacy or property requirements to protect blacks further. Others wanted a simple declaration that all adult male citizens had the right to vote. But the moderates in the party were aware that many northerners were increasingly worried about the number of immigrants who were again entering the country and wanted to be able to restrict their voting. As a result, the final amendment left loopholes that eventually allowed southern states to disfranchise African Americans. The amendment was ratified in March 1870, aided by the votes of the four southern states that had not completed the

Lucy Stone, a major figure in the women's rights movement.

process of Reconstruction and thus were also required to endorse this amendment before being readmitted to Congress.

Proponents of women's suffrage were gravely disappointed when Congress refused to prohibit voting discrimination on the basis of sex as well as race. The Women's Loyal League, led by Elizabeth Cady Stanton and Susan B. Anthony, had pressed for first the Fourteenth and then the Fifteenth Amendment to recognize women's public role. But even most Radicals, contending that black rights had to be assured first, were unwilling to back women's suffrage. The Fifteenth Amendment ruptured the feminist movement. While disappointed that women were not included in its provisions, Lucy Stone and the American Woman Suffrage Association urged ratification. Anthony and Stanton, on the other hand, broke with their former allies among the Radicals, denounced the amendment, and organized the National Woman Suffrage Association to work for passage of a new amendment giving women the ballot. The division hampered the women's rights movement for decades to come.

Women's suffrage rejected

The Grant Administration

Ulysses Grant was ill at ease with the political process. His simple, quiet manner, while superb for commanding armies, did not serve him as well in public life, and his well-known resolution withered when he was uncertain of his goal. Also, he lacked the moral commitment to make Reconstruction succeed.

Grant swings from a trapeze while supporting a number of associates accused of corruption. Among those holding on are Secretary of the Navy George M. Robeson (top center), who was accused of accepting bribes in the awarding of navy contracts; Secretary of War William W. Belknap (top right), who was forced to resign for selling Indian post traderships; and the president's private secretary, Orville Babcock (bottom right), who was implicated in the Whiskey Ring scandal. While not personally involved in the scandals during his administration, Grant was reluctant to dismiss supporters accused of wrongdoing from office.

Corruption under Grant

A series of scandals wracked Grant's presidency. Although Grant did not profit personally, he remained loyal to his friends and displayed little zeal to root out wrongdoing. His relatives were implicated in a scheme to corner the gold market, while his private secretary escaped conviction for stealing federal whiskey revenues only because Grant interceded on his behalf. His secretary of war resigned to avoid impeachment. James W. Grimes, one of the party's founders, denounced the Republican party under Grant as "the most corrupt and debauched political party that has ever existed."

Nor was Congress immune from the lowered tone of public life. In such a climate ruthless state machines, led by men who favored the status quo, came to dominate the party. Office and power became ends in themselves, and party leaders worked in close cooperation with northern industrial interests. The few Radicals still active in public life increasingly repudiated Grant and the Republican governments in the South. Congress in 1872 passed an amnesty act, removing the restrictions of the Fourteenth Amendment on officeholding, except for about 200 to 300 ex-Confederate leaders.

Liberal Republican movement

As corruption in both the North and the South worsened, reformers became more interested in cleaning up government than in protecting blacks' rights. These liberal Republicans opposed the continued presence of the army in the South, denounced the corruption of southern governments as well as the national government, and advocated free trade and civil service reform. In 1872 they broke with the Republican party and nominated for president Horace Greeley, the editor of the New York *Tribune*. A one-time Radical, Greeley had become disillusioned with Reconstruction and urged a restoration of home rule in the South as well as adoption of civil service reform. Democrats decided to back the Liberal Republican ticket. The Republicans renominated Grant, who, despite the defection of a number of prominent Radicals, won an easy victory with 56 percent of the popular vote.

Growing Northern Disillusionment

Civil Rights Act of 1875

During Grant's second term, Congress passed the Civil Rights Act of 1875, the last major piece of Reconstruction legislation. This law prohibited racial discrimination in all public accommodations, transportation, places of amusement, and juries. At the same time, Congress rejected a ban on segregation in public schools, which was almost universally practiced in the North as well as the South. While some railroads, streetcars, and public accommodations in both sections were desegregated after the bill passed, the federal government made little attempt to enforce the law, and it was ignored throughout most of the South. In 1883 the Supreme Court struck down its provisions except the one relating to juries.

Waning northern concern

Despite passage of the Civil Rights Act, many northerners were growing disillusioned with Reconstruction. They were repelled by the corruption of the southern governments, they were tired of the violence and disorder in the South, and they had little faith in black Americans. William Dodge, a wealthy New York capitalist and an influential Republican, wrote in 1875 that the South could never develop its resources "till confidence in her state governments can be restored, and this will never be done by federal bayonets." It had been a mistake, he went on, to make black southerners feel "that the United States government was their special friend, rather than those . . . among whom they must live and for whom they must work. We have tried this long enough," he concluded. "Now let the South alone."

As the agony of the war became more distant, the Panic of 1873 diverted public attention from Reconstruction to economic issues. In the severe depression that followed over the next four years, some 3 million people found themselves out of work. Congress became caught up in the question of whether printing greenbacks would help the economy prosper. Battered by the panic and the corruption issue, the Republicans lost a shocking 77 seats in Congress in the 1874 elections, and along with them control of the House of Representatives for the first time since 1861. "The truth is our people are tired out with the worn out cry of 'Southern outrages'!!" one Republican concluded. "Hard times and heavy taxes make them wish the 'ever lasting nigger' were in hell or Africa." Republicans spoke more and more about cutting loose the unpopular southern governments.

Depression and Democratic resurgence

The Triumph of White Supremacy

As northern commitment to Reconstruction waned, southern Democrats set out to overthrow the remaining Radical governments. Already white Republicans in the South felt heavy pressure to desert their party. In Mississippi one party member jus-

Two Ku Klux Klan members pose in full regalia. Violence played a major role in overthrowing the Radical governments in the South. One South Carolina paper openly praised Klan attacks on blacks and the Republican Union Leagues:

> Born of the night, and
>   vanish by day;
> Leaguers and niggers,
>   get out of the way!

tified his decision to leave on the grounds that otherwise he would have "to live a life of social oblivion" and his children had no future.

Racism

To poor white southerners who lacked social standing, the Democratic appeal to racial solidarity offered great comfort. As one explained, "I may be poor and my manners may be crude, but . . . because I am a white man, I have a right to be treated with respect by Negroes. . . . That I am poor is not as important as that I am a white man; and no Negro is ever going to forget that he is not a white man." The large landowners and other wealthy groups that led southern Democrats objected less to black southerners voting. These well-to-do leaders did not face social and economic competition from African Americans, and in any case, they were confident that if outside influences were removed, they could control the black vote.

Democrats also resorted to economic pressure to undermine Republican power. In heavily black counties, white observers at the polls took down the names of black residents who cast Republican ballots and published them in local newspapers. Planters were urged to discharge black tenants who persisted in voting Republican. But terror and violence provided the most effective means to overthrow the Radical regimes. A number of paramilitary organizations broke up Republican meetings, terrorized white and black Republicans, assassinated Republican leaders, and prevented black citizens from voting. The most famous was the Ku Klux Klan, founded in 1866 in Tennessee. It and similar groups functioned as unofficial arms of the Democratic party.

Terror and violence

Congress finally moved to break the power of the Klan with the Force Act of 1870 and the Ku Klux Klan Act of 1871. These laws made it a felony to interfere with the right to vote; they also authorized use of the army and suspension of the writ of habeas corpus. The Grant administration eventually suspended the writ of habeas corpus in nine South Carolina counties and arrested hundreds of suspected Klan members throughout the South. Although these actions weakened the Klan, terrorist organizations continued to operate underground.

Mississippi Plan

Then in 1875 Democrats inaugurated what became known as the Mississippi Plan, the decision to use as much violence as necessary to carry the state election. Several local papers trumpeted, "Carry the election peaceably if we can, forcibly if we must." When Republican Governor Adelbert Ames requested federal troops to stop the violence, Grant's advisers warned that sending troops to Mississippi would cost the party the Ohio election. In the end the administration told Ames to depend on his own forces. Bolstered by terrorism, the Democrats swept the election in Mississippi. Violence and intimidation prevented as many as 60,000 black and white Republicans from voting, converting the normal Republican majority into a Democratic majority of 30,000. Mississippi had been "redeemed."

The Disputed Election of 1876

With Republicans on the defensive across the nation, the 1876 presidential election was crucial to the final overthrow of Reconstruction. The Republicans nominated Ohio Governor Rutherford B. Hayes to oppose Samuel Tilden of New York. Once again, violence prevented an estimated quarter of a million Republican votes from being cast in the South. Tilden had a clear majority of 250,000 in the popular vote, but the outcome in the Electoral College was in doubt because both parties claimed South Carolina, Florida, and Louisiana, the only reconstructed states still in Republican

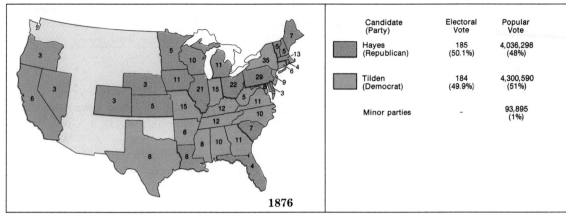

Candidate (Party)	Electoral Vote	Popular Vote
Hayes (Republican)	185 (50.1%)	4,036,298 (48%)
Tilden (Democrat)	184 (49.9%)	4,300,590 (51%)
Minor parties	–	93,895 (1%)

1876

ELECTION OF 1876

hands. Hayes needed all three states to be elected, for even without them, Tilden had amassed 184 electoral votes, one short of a majority. Republican canvassing boards in power disqualified enough Democratic votes to give each state to Hayes.

To arbitrate the disputed returns, Congress established a 15-member electoral commission: 5 members each from the Senate, the House, and the Supreme Court. By a straight party vote of 8–7, the commission awarded the disputed electoral votes—and the presidency—to Hayes.

When angry Democrats threatened a filibuster to prevent the electoral votes from being counted, key Republicans met with southern Democrats on February 26 at the Wormley Hotel in Washington. There, they reached an informal understanding, later known as the Compromise of 1877. Hayes's supporters agreed to withdraw federal troops from the South and not oppose the new Democratic state governments. For their part, southern Democrats dropped their opposition to Hayes's election and pledged to respect African American rights.

Compromise of 1877

Without federal support, the Republican governments in South Carolina and Louisiana promptly collapsed, and Democrats took control of the remaining states of the Confederacy. By 1877, the entire South was in the hands of the Redeemers, as they called themselves. Reconstruction and Republican rule had come to an end.

Redeemers take control

Racism and the Failure of Reconstruction

Reconstruction failed for a multitude of reasons. The reforming impulse that had created the Republican party in the 1850s had been battered and worn down by the war. The new materialism of industrial America inspired in many a jaded cynicism about the corruption of the age and a desire to forget uncomfortable issues. In the South, African American voters and leaders inevitably lacked a certain amount of education and experience; elsewhere, Republicans were divided over policies and options.

Yet beyond these obstacles, the sad fact remains that the ideals of Reconstruction were most clearly defeated by a deep-seated racism that permeated American life. Racism was why the white South so unrelentingly resisted Reconstruction. Racism was why most white northerners had little interest in black rights except as a means to pre-

Benjamin Montgomery, together with his sons, purchased Jefferson Davis's plantation along the Mississippi River after the war. A former slave, Montgomery pursued the dream of black economic independence by renting land to black farmers at Davis Bend.

serve the Union or to safeguard the Republic. Racism was why northerners were willing to write off Reconstruction and with it the welfare of African Americans. While Congress might pass a constitutional amendment abolishing slavery, it could not overturn at a stroke the social habits of two centuries.

Certainly the political equations of power, in the long term, had been changed. The North had fought fiercely during the war to preserve the Union. In doing so, it had secured the power to dominate the economic and political destiny of the nation. With the overthrow of Reconstruction, the white South had won back some of the power it had lost in 1865. But even with white supremacy triumphant, African Americans did not return to the social position they had occupied before the war. They were no longer slaves, and black southerners who walked dusty roads in search of family members, sent their children to school, or worshiped in churches they controlled knew what a momentous change this was. Even under the exploitative sharecropping system, black income rose significantly in freedom. Then, too, the principles of "equal protection" and "due process of law" had been written into the Constitution. These guarantees would be available for later generations to use in championing once again the Radicals' goal of racial equality.

End of the Davis Bend experiment

But this was a struggle left to future reformers. For the time being, the clear trend was away from change or hope—especially for former slaves like Benjamin Montgomery and his sons, the owners of the old Davis plantations in Mississippi. In the 1870s bad crops, lower cotton prices, and falling land values undermined the Montgomerys' financial position, and in 1875 Jefferson Davis sued to have the sale of Brierfield invalidated.

A lower court ruled against Davis, since he had never received legal title to the plantation. Davis appealed to the state supreme court, which, following the overthrow of Mississippi's Radical government, had a white conservative majority. In a politically motivated decision, the court awarded Brierfield to Davis in 1878, and the Montgomerys lost Hurricane as well. The final outcome was not without bitter irony. In applying for restoration of his property after the war, Joseph Davis had convinced skeptical federal officials that he—and not his younger brother—held legal title to Brierfield. Had they decided instead that the plantation belonged to Jefferson Davis, it would have been confiscated.

But the waning days of Reconstruction were times filled with such ironies: of governments "redeemed" by violence, of Fourteenth Amendment rights designed to protect black people being used by conservative courts to protect giant corporations, of reformers taking up other causes. Disowned by its northern supporters and unmourned by public opinion, Reconstruction was over.

CHAPTER SUMMARY

Even before the Civil War ended, Abraham Lincoln began to develop a program of Reconstruction. His 10 percent plan sought to quickly restore the Confederate states to the Union. Lincoln's assassination, however, elevated Andrew Johnson, a war Democrat from Tennessee, to the presidency. Johnson moved in the summer of 1865 to put Lincoln's program into operation, but in the process he changed its terms and lessened its requirements. When Congress assembled in December 1865, it repudiated Johnson's state governments and eventually enacted its own program of Reconstruction, which included the principle of black suffrage. Of particular importance were the Fourteenth and Fifteenth amendments and the Freedmen's Bureau, a unique experiment in social welfare in nineteenth-century America. Congress rejected land reform, however, and the effort to remove Johnson from office through impeachment failed. The Radical regimes that took power in the South compiled a mixed record on matters such as racial equality, education, economic issues, and corruption.

Reconstruction had a major impact on the aspirations and experiences of African Americans. In their actions after the war, former slaves demonstrated their understanding of the meaning of freedom in its many dimensions and revealed the importance that they attached to the family and black-controlled churches and their widespread desire for land and education. Although the failure of land reform left blacks a propertyless laboring class, they refused to toil under the old system on southern plantations. Black resistance eventually led to the adoption of sharecropping as the primary means of organizing black labor in the South. The Freedmen's Bureau played a critical role in the creation of these new working arrangements and also in the beginnings of black education in the South.

During the presidency of Ulysses S. Grant, northern public opinion became increasingly disillusioned with Reconstruction and affairs in the South. The use of violence to defeat the Republican party, the adoption of economic coercion against black voters, and the power of the ideology of white supremacy further undermined Reconstruction in the South. With the outcome of the 1876 presidential election in doubt, national Republican leaders agreed to jettison Reconstruction and abandon the cause of southern blacks in exchange for Hayes's election as president, and the last remaining Republican regimes in the South collapsed. Racism played a key role in the eventual failure of Reconstruction.

ADDITIONAL READING

Historians' views of Reconstruction have dramatically changed in recent decades. Modern studies offer a more sympathetic assessment of Reconstruction and the experience of African Americans. Indicative of this trend is Eric Foner, *Reconstruction* (1988), the fullest modern treatment. Foner devotes considerable attention to black southerners' experiences. The book is also available in an abridged edition.

Eric L. McKitrick, *Andrew Johnson and Reconstruction* (1966), while very critical of Johnson and his policies, argues that impeachment was unjustified. A different conclusion is reached by Michael Les Benedict in *The Impeachment and Trial of Andrew Johnson* (1973), which is the most thorough treatment of Congress's effort to remove Johnson from office. Political affairs in the South during Reconstruction are examined in Dan T. Carter, *When the War Was Over* (1985) and Thomas Holt, *Black Over White* (1977), an imaginative study of black political leadership in South Carolina. Leon Litwack, *Been in the Storm So Long* (1979) and Willie Lee Rose,

Rehearsal for Reconstruction (1964) sensitively analyze former slaves' transition to freedom, while James L. Roark, *Masters without Slaves* (1977) discusses former slaveholders' adjustment to the end of slavery. An excellent study of changing labor relations in southern agriculture is Julie Saville, *The Work of Reconstruction* (1995). George R. Bentley, *A History of the Freedmen's Bureau* (1955) is a sympathetic treatment of that unique institution; Donald Nieman, *To Set the Law in Motion: The Freedmen's Bureau and the Legal Rights of Blacks, 1865–1868* (1979) is more critical. Different perspectives on the overthrow of Reconstruction appear in William Gillette, *Retreat from Reconstruction, 1869–1879* (1980), which focuses on national politics and the federal government, and Michael Perman, *The Road to Redemption* (1984), which looks at developments in the South. For a fuller list of readings, see the Bibliography.

SIGNIFICANT EVENTS

1863	Lincoln outlines Reconstruction program
1864	Lincoln vetoes Wade–Davis bill; Louisiana, Arkansas, and Tennessee establish governments under Lincoln's plan
1865	Freedmen's Bureau established; Johnson becomes president; presidential Reconstruction completed; Congress excludes representatives of Johnson's governments; Thirteenth Amendment ratified; Joint Committee on Reconstruction established
1865–1866	Black codes enacted
1866	Civil rights bill passed over Johnson's veto; Memphis and New Orleans riots; Fourteenth Amendment passes Congress; Freedmen's Bureau extended; Ku Klux Klan organized; Tennessee readmitted to Congress; Republicans win decisive victory in congressional elections
1867	Congressional Reconstruction enacted; Tenure of Office Act
1867–1868	Constitutional conventions in the South; blacks vote in southern elections
1868	Johnson impeached but acquitted; Fourteenth Amendment ratified; Grant elected president
1869	Fifteenth Amendment passes Congress
1870	Last southern states readmitted to Congress; Fifteenth Amendment ratified; Force Act passed
1871	Ku Klux Klan Act
1872	General Amnesty Act; Freedmen's Bureau closes down; Liberal Republican revolt
1873–1877	Panic and depression
1874	Democrats win control of the House
1875	Civil Rights Act; Mississippi Plan
1876	Disputed Hayes–Tilden election
1877	Compromise of 1877; Hayes declared winner of electoral vote; last Republican governments in South fall

PART FOUR

THE UNITED STATES IN AN INDUSTRIAL AGE

GLOBAL ESSAY The Statue of Liberty has now stood watch over New York harbor for more than a hundred years. Looking back today, most Americans view the tired, huddled masses who passed beneath Liberty's torch as part of the continuing stream of immigrants stretching back to the English Pilgrims, the French fur traders of Canada, and the Spanish friars of Old California. But the tide of immigration that swelled during the mid-nineteenth century was strikingly different from the great majority of those who traveled to America in an earlier age. Innovations in transportation, communications, and industry created an international network that for the first time made possible voluntary migration on a massive scale.

Before 1820 most new arrivals in North and South America did not come voluntarily. Nearly 8 million Africans were brought to the Americas during those years, virtually all as slaves. That number was four to five times the number of Europeans who came during the same period. In contrast, between 1820 and 1920 nearly 30 million free immigrants arrived from Europe.

Nor was this new flood directed only toward America. At least as many Europeans settled in other regions of Europe or the world. From eastern Europe millions followed the Trans-Siberian Railway (completed in 1905) into Asiatic Russia. The Canadian prairie provinces of Manitoba and Saskatchewan competed for homesteaders with Montana and the Dakotas. And as cowboys began driving American steers to railheads for shipment east, gauchos in western Argentina were rounding up cattle to be shipped to Buenos Aires. Before 1900 two out of three emigrating Italians booked passage not for the United States but for Brazil or Argentina.

This broad movement could not have taken place without a global network of communication, markets, and transportation. By midcentury, urbanization and industrialization were well under way in both America and Europe. The British, who led in revolutionizing industry, also discovered its harsh side effects. Without efficient transportation, British urban workers were forced to live within walking distance of factories. The resulting overcrowding and filth were almost stupefying. Families jammed into dark, dingy row houses built with few windows. In the streets and alleys

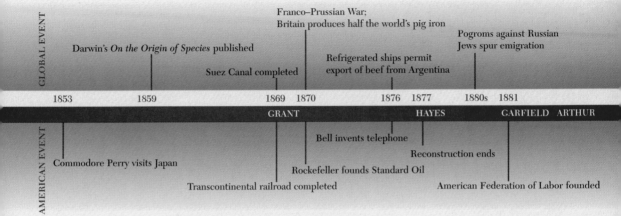

GLOBAL EVENT

Franco–Prussian War;
Britain produces half the world's pig iron

Pogroms against Russian
Jews spur emigration

Darwin's *On the Origin of Species* published

Refrigerated ships permit
export of beef from Argentina

Suez Canal completed

| 1853 | 1859 | 1869 | 1870 | 1876 | 1877 | 1880s | 1881 |

GRANT   HAYES   GARFIELD ARTHUR

AMERICAN EVENT

Bell invents telephone

Reconstruction ends

Commodore Perry visits Japan

Rockefeller founds Standard Oil

Transcontinental railroad completed

American Federation of Labor founded

beyond, open sewers flowed with garbage. In London one construction engineer reported that the overflow from privies had collected to the depth of three feet in the cellars of nearby houses.

Spurred by a deadly cholera epidemic in 1848, social reformer Edwin Chadwick led a campaign to install a system of cheap iron pipes and tile drains to provide running water and sewers throughout major cities. In addition, French and German research during the 1860s and 1870s established the germ theory of disease, confirming the need for better sanitation.

Other urban planners admired the radical renovation of Paris begun in the 1850s by Baron Georges Haussmann. Haussmann's workers tore down the city's medieval fortress walls, widened major streets into boulevards, and set aside land for pleasant green parks. American cities had no ancient walls and fewer narrow roads, and Americans were often more willing to rebuild and enlarge. Their innovations led Europeans to adopt horse-drawn streetcars and, later, electric trolleys. With an intracity transportation network in place, the old "walking cities" were able to add suburbs, partially easing the crush of earlier industrial crowding.

As hubs of the new industrial networks, cities needed efficient links to raw materials, as well as markets for their finished products. Much of the late nineteenth century can be seen as a scramble of Western nations for those natural resources and markets. Miners combed the hills of California for gold in 1849, as they did two years later in Victoria, Australia. In South Africa, the rush was for diamonds discovered

595

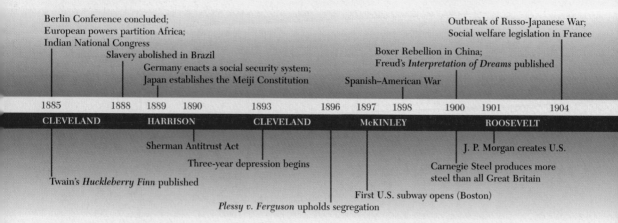

Berlin Conference concluded;
European powers partition Africa;
Indian National Congress

Slavery abolished in Brazil

Germany enacts a social security system;
Japan establishes the Meiji Constitution

Boxer Rebellion in China;
Freud's *Interpretation of Dreams* published

Spanish–American War

Outbreak of Russo-Japanese War;
Social welfare legislation in France

| 1885 | 1888 | 1889 | 1890 | 1893 | 1896 | 1897 | 1898 | 1900 | 1901 | 1904 |

CLEVELAND   HARRISON   CLEVELAND   McKINLEY   ROOSEVELT

Sherman Antitrust Act

Three-year depression begins

Twain's *Huckleberry Finn* published

Plessy v. Ferguson upholds segregation

First U.S. subway opens (Boston)

Carnegie Steel produces more
steel than all Great Britain

J. P. Morgan creates U.S.

along the Vaal and Orange rivers and gold near present-day Johannesburg. In Canada, Argentina, Australia, and New Zealand, farmers and cattle ranchers moved steadily toward larger commercial operations. All these enterprises extracted value from previously untapped natural resources.

The end result of the scramble was the age of imperialism, as the European powers sought to dominate newly acquired colonies in Africa and Asia. The United States joined the rush somewhat late, in part because it was still extracting raw materials from its own "colonial" regions, the booming West and the defeated South.

European imperialists sometimes justified their rule over nonwhite races in Darwinian fashion, as the survival of the fittest. "The path of progress is strewn with

the wreck . . . of inferior races," one English professor proclaimed in 1900. British poet Rudyard Kipling even suggested that Europeans were making a noble sacrifice on behalf of their subject peoples. "Take up the White Man's Burden," he exhorted them. "Send forth the best ye breed— / Go bind your sons to exile / To serve your captives' need."

But the burdens were far greater for the coolie laborers of Kipling's India, who died by the thousands clearing jungles for tea plantations. Imperialism's costs were also harsh for black miners laboring in South Africa and for Chinese workers in Australia and the United States who found themselves excluded and segregated after both gold rushes. A similar racialism—the widely accepted practice of categorizing and ranking

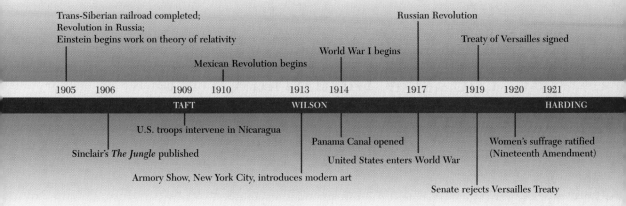

Trans-Siberian railroad completed;
Revolution in Russia;
Einstein begins work on theory of relativity

Russian Revolution

Treaty of Versailles signed

World War I begins

Mexican Revolution begins

| 1905 | 1906 | 1909 | 1910 | 1913 | 1914 | 1917 | 1919 | 1920 | 1921 |

TAFT   WILSON   HARDING

U.S. troops intervene in Nicaragua

Panama Canal opened

Women's suffrage ratified
(Nineteenth Amendment)

Sinclair's *The Jungle* published

United States enters World War

Armory Show, New York City, introduces modern art

Senate rejects Versailles Treaty

people according to race—thwarted southern black sharecroppers in the United States and made it easier for successive waves of prospectors, cowhands, and sodbusters to drive American Indians off their lands.

The racial undercurrent of both European imperialism and American expansion was something most white Americans of the era ignored. But farmers in both the South and the West did lash out at industrial "robber barons" and railroad "monopolists." These business leaders seemed to epitomize the abuses of the new industrial order. As we shall see, the underlying causes of the era's social strain could not be so conveniently placed at the door of a few greedy villains. Industrialization created a whole new order of complex, interlocking systems that fostered an increasingly stratified society.

The social strains arising out of such wrenching changes forced political systems to adjust as well. In the United States both Populist and Progressive reformers called on the government to play a more active part in managing the excesses of the new industrial order. In Europe, both radical reformers like Karl Marx and more moderate socialists pushed for change. As strikes became more common and labor unions more powerful, industrializing nations passed social legislation that included the first social security systems and health insurance. In the end, however, the political system was unable to manage the new global order of commerce and imperialism. With the coming of World War I, it was shaken to its roots.

18

The New Industrial Order

It was so dark, Robert Ferguson could not see his own feet. Inching along the railroad tracks, he suddenly pitched forward and felt his breath taken away as the ground vanished beneath him. To his dismay, he found himself wedged between two railroad ties, his legs dangling in the air. Scrambling back to solid ground, he retreated along the tracks to the railroad car, where he sat meekly until dawn.

Ferguson, a Scot visiting America in 1866, had been in Memphis, Tennessee, only two days earlier, ready to take the "Great Southern Mail Route" east some 850 miles to Washington. Things had gone badly from the start. About 50 miles outside of town, a broken river bridge forced him to take a ferry and spend 10 miles bumping along in a mule-drawn truck before learning that the rail line did not resume for another 40 miles. Disheartened, he decided to return to Memphis to try again.

The train to Memphis arrived six hours late, dawdled its way home, and then, barely three miles from the city, derailed in the middle of the night. When a few passengers decided to hike the remaining distance into town, Ferguson tagged along. It was then that he had fallen between the tracks and retreated to the railcar. At dawn he discovered to his horror that the tracks led onto a flimsy, high river bridge. Ferguson had trouble managing the trestle even in daylight.

Before he finally reached Washington, Robert Ferguson faced six more days of difficult travel. One line would end, and passengers and freight would be forced onto another because rail gauges—the width of the track—differed from line to line. Or a bridge would be out, or there would be no bridge at all. Trains had no meals "on board" or any sleeping cars. "It was certainly what the Americans would call 'hard travelling,'" Ferguson huffed; "—they do not make use of the word 'rough,' because roughness may be expected as a natural condition in a new country."

Cross-country travel proved so rough that it inspired even an American to fantasy. In 1859, the *Southern Literary Messenger* carried the first of several installments describing Miss Jane Delaware Peyton's trip to Washington, D.C. from Rasselas, Oregon, 170 years in the future—in 2029. Posh trains whisked her from one end of the country to the other in only 8 days at speeds of 60 miles an hour. While this "immense velocity" presented no physical problems, Miss Peyton had to guard against "Tourbilliere," an all-too-common mental disorder of the twenty-first century. After 10 or more hours on a speeding train, quick-witted passengers found perception accelerated but memory lapsing. "The mind loses an idea almost as soon as it has

Giant egg-shaped Bessemer converters remove carbon from molten iron ore to make steel at Andrew Carnegie's steelworks in Pittsburgh. Factory temperatures soared to over 100 degrees, and Carnegie ran his mills 24 hours a day, every day a year except for July 4th.

been formed," Miss Peyton reported. The only cure was to stop and let the mind catch up to its changing surroundings. So every few days Miss Peyton and her fellow travelers disembarked from their train to sit quietly at a depot until their symptoms subsided. Such persons were said to be "waiting for their brains."

By the 1880s, some of our writer's fantasies had actually come true, as T. S. Hudson discovered in 1882 when he launched a self-proclaimed "Scamper Through America." Hudson, another British tourist, did not cross the continent in quite 8 days, but it took him just 60 days to go from England to San Francisco and back. And he booked his rail ticket from a single agent in Boston. Such centralization would have been unthinkable in 1859, when a transcontinental railroad was still a decade from completion.

Hudson's trains had Pullman Palace cars with luxury sleeping quarters. A full breakfast of coffee, iced milk, eggs, "game in their season," and fresh fruits cost him 75 cents. Newly installed air brakes made trains safer and their stops smoother. Bridges appeared where none had been before, including a "magnificent" span over the Mississippi at St. Louis. Hudson marveled at its three arches of "five hundred feet each, approached by viaducts, and, on the western shore, also by a tunnel." He also found himself in the midst of a communications revolution. Traveling across the plains, he was struck by the number of telephone poles along the route.

An industrial transformation   What made America in the 1880s so different from just a few decades earlier was not the speed and comfort of travel or the wonders of the new technology. The true marvel was the emerging industrial order that underlay those technologies and made them possible. Because this order was essentially in place by the beginning of the twentieth century, we tend to take its existence for granted. Yet its growth in scale and complexity was at first slow and required innovations in many different areas of society in order to achieve its effects. The process of industrialization began in the United States at least three decades before the Civil War, with small factories producing light consumer goods like clothing, shoes, and furniture. Despite these early national markets, much of the economy remained local. Only after the 1850s did the industrial economy develop a set of interlocking systems that allowed larger factories, using more and bigger machines, to produce goods with greater efficiency and market them on a national and international scale.

The transformation, remarkable as it was, brought pain along with progress. The demand for natural resources led to virgin forests being cut down and open-pit mines spewing hazardous runoffs. Factories along the rivers of the Northeast were left murky with industrial wastes. In 1882, the year Hudson scampered by rail across America, an average of 675 people were killed on the job every week. Like most people, workers scrambled—sometimes literally—to adjust. Few Americans anywhere had time to "wait for their brains" to catch up to the dizzying pace of change.

THE DEVELOPMENT OF INDUSTRIAL SYSTEMS

The new industrial order can best be understood as a web of complex industrial systems woven together in the second half of the nineteenth century. Look, for example, at the industrial systems required to build the bridge across the Mississippi that

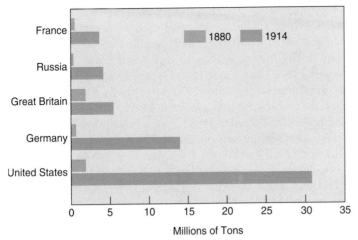

STEEL PRODUCTION, 1880 AND 1914
While steel production jumped in western industrial nations from 1880 to 1914, it skyrocketed in the United States because of rich resources, cheap labor, and aggressive management.

T. S. Hudson so admired. When James B. Eads constructed his soaring arches in 1874, he needed steel, most likely made from iron ore mined in northern Michigan. Giant steam shovels scooped up the ore and loaded whole freight cars in a few strokes. A transportation system—railroads, boats, and other carriers—probably moved the ore to Pittsburgh, where the factory system furnished the labor and machinery to finish the steel. The capital to create such factories came itself from a system of finance that linked investment banks and stock markets to entrepreneurs in need of money. Only with such a national network of industrial systems could the Eads bridge be built and a new age of industry arise.

Natural Resources and Industrial Technology

The earliest European settlers had marveled at the "merchantable commodities" of America, from the glittering silver mines of the Spanish empire to the continent's hardwood forests. One thing setting the new industrial economy apart from that older America was the scale and efficiency of using such natural resources. New technologies made it possible to exploit them in ways undreamed of only decades earlier.

Iron, for example, had been forged into steel swords as far back as the Middle Ages. In the 1850s, inventors in England and America discovered a cheaper way—called the Bessemer process after its British inventor—to convert large quantities of iron into steel. By the late 1870s, the price of steel had dropped by more than half. Steel was lighter than iron, could support 20 times as much weight, and lasted 20 years instead of 3. Steel tracks soon carried most rail traffic; steel girders replaced the old cast iron frames; steel cables supported new suspension bridges.

Bessemer process

Petroleum industry

Industrial technology made some natural resources more valuable. New distilling methods transformed a thick, smelly liquid called petroleum into kerosene for lighting lamps, oil for lubricating machinery, and paraffin for making candles. Beginning in 1859, new drilling techniques began to tap vast pools of petroleum below the surface. About the same time, Frenchman Etienne Lenoir constructed the first practical internal combustion engine. After 1900, new vehicles like the gasoline-powered carriage turned the oil business into a major industry.

Environmental costs

The environmental price of industrial technology soon became evident. Loggers cut down the trees of the Pacific Northwest so quickly that they threatened to destroy whole forests. Coal mining scarred the hills of Pennsylvania and West Virginia. In California, water cannons blasted away hillsides in search of gold. The rocks and gravel washed into rivers and raised their beds, threatening farms and cities with floods. Levies downstream reached the height of rooftops, and in some towns the Sacramento River flowed above street level.

The environmental degradation of industrial cities was astonishing. By the turn of the century the Homestead steel mill was belching enough waste to turn the trees of nearby Pittsburgh a sooty gray and to leave the Monongahela River, in the words of an English visitor, "a turbid yellowy stream." To remove the refuse from the Chicago River after decades of dumping by local meatpackers, city engineers actually reversed the river's flow, so it emptied into the Illinois River rather than Lake Michigan. But solving one environmental problem only produced another. "What right does Chicago have to pour its filth down into what was before a sweet and clean river, pollute its waters, . . . and bring sickness and death to the citizens?" fumed one downstate resident.

Some industrialists tried to limit the pollution created by technology. Chicago meatpackers stretched their imaginations to use every conceivable part of the animals that came to their plants. Straight-length bones went into cutlery, hoofs and feet into glue and oil, fat into oleomargarine. Even blood was dried and sold as powder. "There was a time," recalled the meatpacker Philip Armour at the turn of the century, "when many parts of cattle were wasted, and the health of the city was injured by refuse. Now . . . nothing is wasted." And, he might have added, even "refuse" was made to turn a profit.

Systematic Invention

Industrial technology rested on invention. For sheer inventiveness, the 40 years following the Civil War have rarely been matched in American history. Between 1790 and 1860, 36,000 patents had been registered with the government. Over the next three decades, the U.S. Patent Office granted more than half a million. The process of invention became systematized as small-scale inventors were replaced by orderly "invention factories"—forerunners of expensive research labs.

Thomas Edison, unkempt and wrinkled, in his research lab

No one did more to bring system, order, and profitability to invention than *Edison's* Thomas Alva Edison. In 1868, at the age of 21, Edison went to work for a New York *contributions* brokerage house and promptly improved the design of the company's stock tickers. Granted a $40,000 bonus (worth perhaps $400,000 in current dollars), he set himself up as an independent inventor. For the next five years, Edison patented a new invention almost every five months. His innovations included an electric voting machine, the memograph, and a device capable of sending four messages over a single telegraph wire at once.

Edison was determined to bring system and order to the process of invention. Only then could breakthroughs come in a steady and profitable stream. He moved 15 of his workers to Menlo Park, New Jersey, where in 1876 he created an "invention factory." Like a manufacturer, Edison subdivided the work among gifted inventors, engineers, toolmakers, and others.

This orderly bureaucracy soon evolved into the Edison Electric Light Company. Its ambitious owner aimed at more than perfecting his new electric light bulb. Edison *The spread of* wanted to create a unified electrical power system—central stations to generate elec- *an electrical* tric current, wired to users, all powering millions of small bulbs in homes and busi- *power system* nesses. To launch his enterprise, Edison won the backing of several large banking houses by lighting up the Wall Street district in 1882. It was like "writing by daylight," recorded one reporter. Soon Edison power plants sprang up in major cities across the country.

Correcting a critical mistake Edison had made, George Westinghouse relied on high-voltage alternating current, since Edison's low-voltage direct current could travel only a mile or two. He installed transformers to reduce voltage back to low levels for household use. Despite initial worries about safety (for years "to Westinghouse" meant to electrocute), the improvements worked. By 1898 there were nearly 3000 power stations in America, lighting some 2 million bulbs.

Electricity was more flexible than earlier sources of energy. Factories no longer had to be built near rivers and falls to make use of water power. Before the end of the century, electricity was running automatic looms, trolley cars, subways, and factory machinery. Electricity not only revolutionized industry; it also worked in the homes of ordinary citizens. The electric motor, developed commercially by Westinghouse and Nikola Tesla in 1886, powered everything from sewing machines to Edison's "gramophone," later known as the record player.

George Eastman revolutionized photography by making the consumer a part of his inventive system. In 1888 Eastman marketed the "Kodak" camera. The small black box weighed just over two pounds and contained a strip of celluloid film that replaced hundreds of pounds of photography equipment. After 100 snaps of the shutter, the owner simply sent the camera back to the store or factory and waited for the developed photos, along with a reloaded camera, to return by mail. "You press the button—we do the rest" was Eastman Kodak's apt slogan.

What united these innovations was the notion of rationalizing inventions—of making a systematic process out of them. By 1913, Westinghouse Electric, General *The research* Electric, U.S. Rubber Company, and other firms had set up research laboratories. *laboratory* And by the middle of the century research laboratories had spread beyond business to the federal government, to universities, to trade associations, and to labor unions.

Transportation and Communication

The problem of scale

Abundant resources and new inventions remained worthless to industry until they could be moved to processing plants, factories, and offices. With more than 3.5 million square miles of land in the United States, distance alone was daunting. Where 100 miles of railroad track would do for shipping goods in Germany and England, 1000 miles was necessary in America. Railroads in Europe, moreover, were usually built along existing roads and horse tracks. In America routes often broke new ground, a more costly process that also opened areas to development.

An efficient transportation network tied the United States into an emerging international system. By the 1870s railroads crisscrossed the country, and steam-powered ships (introduced before the Civil War) were pushing barges down rivers and carrying passengers and freight across the oceans. Ever-larger ships with more powerful engines cut the time of transatlantic travel in half, to about 10 days. Between 1870 and 1900, the value of American exports tripled. Eventually the rail and water transportation systems fused. By 1900 railroad companies owned nearly all of the country's domestic steamship lines.

Telegraph

A thriving industrial nation also required effective communication. In the early 1840s, it took newspapers as many as 10 days to reach Indiana from New York and 3 months to arrive by ship in San Francisco. In 1844 Samuel Morse succeeded in sending the first message over an electrical wire between cities. By 1861 the Western Union Company had strung 76,000 miles of telegraph lines across the country. If a bank collapsed in Chicago, bankers in Dallas knew of it that day. Railroads could keep traffic unsnarled through the dots and dashes of Morse's code. So useful to railroads was the telegraph that they allowed poles and wires to be set along their rights of way in exchange for free telegraphic service. By the turn of the century a million miles of telegraph wire handled some 63 million messages a year, not to mention those flashing across underwater cables to China, Japan, Africa, and South America.

Telephone

A second innovation in communication, the telephone, vastly improved on the telegraph. Alexander Graham Bell, a Scottish immigrant, was teaching the deaf when he began experimenting with ways to transmit speech electrically. In 1876, he transmitted his famous first words to a young assistant: "Mr. Watson, come here! I want you." No longer did messages require a telegraph office, the unwieldy Morse code, and couriers to deliver them.

President Rutherford B. Hayes installed the first telephone in the White House in 1878, when the instrument was still a curiosity. The same year, the city of New Haven, Connecticut, opened the first telephone exchange in America. By 1895 there were 310,000 of Bell's machines in America. Five years later there were 1.5 million. The telephone patent proved to be the most valuable ever granted. In the scramble for profits, the Bell Telephone Company fought off challenges from competitors and suits from rivals who claimed that their contributions were worth a share of the rights.

Along with other innovations in communication (see "Daily Lives"), telephones modernized offices and eased business transactions. In 1915, when the American Telephone and Telegraph Company opened the first transcontinental line, a business executive in New York could speak personally to an associate in San Francisco. The telephone became part of a social revolution. Like the railroad and the telegraph, it compressed distances and homogenized the country. In time, remote farms and isolated villages would be connected to distant neighbors and vital hospitals and fire departments.

Finance Capital

As industry grew, so did the demand for investment capital—the money spent on land, buildings, and machinery. The scale of industry required more funds than ever. Between 1870 and 1900, the number of workers in an average iron and steel firm grew from 100 to 400, and the capital invested jumped to nearly $1 million, about seven times what it had been in 1870.

The need for capital was great especially because so many new industrial systems were being put into place at once. In the old days, a steamboat could be set afloat for the price of the boat itself. A railroad, on the other hand, had enormous start-up costs. Miles of track had to be laid, workers hired, engines and cars bought, depots constructed. Industrial processes involving so many expensive systems could not take shape until someone raised the necessary funds.

Where did the money come from? For the first three-quarters of the nineteenth century, investment capital came mostly from the savings of firms. In the last half of the century "capital deepening"—a process essential for industrialization—took place. Simply put, as national wealth increased, people began to save and invest more of their money. This meant that more funds could be loaned to companies seeking to start up or expand. *Sources of capital*

Savings and investment grew more attractive with the development of a complex network of financial institutions. Commercial and savings banks, investment houses, and insurance companies gave savers new opportunities to channel money to industry. The New York Stock Exchange, in existence since 1792, linked eager investors with money-hungry firms. By the end of the nineteenth century the stock market had established itself as the basic means of making capital available to industry.

The Corporation

For those business leaders with the skill to knit the industrial pieces together, large profits awaited. This was the era of the "robber barons," those notorious entrepreneurs who bulled their way to success at the expense of competitors and employees. To be sure, sheer ruthlessness went a long way in the fortune-building game. "Law? Who cares about law!" railroad magnate Cornelius Vanderbilt once boasted. "Hain't I got the power?"

But to survive in the long term, business leaders could not depend on ruthlessness alone. Imagination was also necessary. The growing scale of enterprise and need for capital led them to adapt an old device, the corporation, to new needs. Corporations had existed since colonial times, when governments granted charters of incorporation to organizations that ran public facilities such as turnpikes, canals, and banks. After the Civil War the modern corporation came into use for raising money and protecting business holdings.

The corporation had several advantages over more traditional forms of ownership: the single owner and the partnership. A corporation could raise large sums quickly by selling "stock certificates," or shares in its business. It could also outlive its *Advantages of the corporation*

TIME AND TRAVEL

The Rise of Information Systems

In 1877, a year after its invention, advertisements were already touting Alexander Graham Bell's "speaking telegraph": "Conversation can easily be carried on after slight practice and occasional repetition of a word or sentence. . . . [A]fter a few trials the ear becomes accustomed to the peculiar sound."

It was not so for everyone. Some people had great difficulty understanding the strange sounds. Others reported terrifying "stage fright" that left them speechless. Still others had no idea how to greet callers. Bell answered with a chipper "Ahoy!" Operators at the first public telephone exchange used the old-fashioned "What is wanted?" But it was Thomas Edison's melodious "Hello" (derived from "Halloo," the traditional call to bring hounds to the chase) that won out by 1880.

At first Bell's electrical toys could be rented only in pairs by individuals who wanted to connect two places. In 1877 the advantages of such direct communication led to the first intercity hookup, between New York and Boston. Before the turn of the century, the Bell-organized American Telephone and Telegraph Company had combined more than 100 local telephone companies to furnish business and government with long-distance service. When rates dropped after 1900, telephones found their way into ordinary American homes.

Systems of finance and communications intersected at Wall Street, New York, where the nation's most important investment banks and markets were located. The Great Blizzard of 1888 buried the district with snow and also shadowed in white the crisscrossing "blizzard" of wires needed for the communications networks.

The telephone revolutionized communications, cutting time and obliterating distances. It also liberated social relations by freeing people from the nineteenth-century

owners (or stockholders) because it required no legal reorganization if one of the owners died. It limited liability since owners were no longer personally responsible for corporate debts. And it separated owners from day-to-day management of the convention of addressing only those to whom they had been properly introduced. And it acted as a great social leveler. Almost overnight, telephone operators (called "hello girls") began connecting people of different locales and classes, who might never have spoken to each other at all, let alone as peers.

The telephone and other innovations were the basis of the information system required of any thriving industrial nation. Information was a precious commodity, as essential to industrialization as capital or labor. The increased specialization at all stages of production required information about markets, prices, and supply sources—and required it quickly.

During the first half of the nineteenth century, information had traveled mostly through the mails. In 1844 Samuel F. B. Morse sent the first inter-city message across electrical wires, thereby achieving instantaneous communication. But the telegraph had drawbacks. Instantaneous communication was hardly direct. Messages had to be taken to a telegraph office, where trained clerks could translate them into Morse code, an unwieldy system of dots and dashes. Only then could they be transmitted by electrical impulse. When they arrived at the receiving station, messages were recast into understandable language, then carried by hand to their precise destination. This was a far cry from the telephone, which was both instantaneous and direct.

Another device that helped businesses was the typewriter. C. Latham Sholes, a Milwaukee printer and editor, had been tinkering with an automatic numbering machine when a friend suggested he develop a mechanical letter-writing device. In 1868 he patented the "Type-Writer." In the 1870s the Remington Arms Company began mass-producing them. By the early twentieth century the typewriter had taken its modern shape—a keyboard with upper- and lower-case letters and a carriage that allowed typists to see the output.

At first typewriters were used mainly by writers, editors, ministers, and others from the world of letters. (Legend has it that Mark Twain's *The Adventures of Tom Sawyer* was the first book manuscript to be typed.) Early critics charged that "machine-made" letters were too impersonal. When farmers complained about receiving them, Sears, Roebuck hired secretaries to write their business letters by hand. Nevertheless, machine writing soon became standard business practice.

The need for speed and efficiency in the office led to other breakthroughs. Carbon paper, designed for making a typewritten copy along with the original, was patented in 1872. In 1890 Alfred Dick invented the mimeograph to reproduce many copies of a single document cheaply, a communications boon not only to businesses but also to churches, reform organizations, and political groups. Communications, like the rest of the new industrial order, were steadily becoming more orderly and efficient, permitting the rapid distribution of information to those who desired it.

company. Professional managers could now operate complex businesses. So clear were these advantages that before the turn of the century, corporations were making two-thirds of all manufactured products in the United States.

A Pool of Labor

Last, but hardly least important for the new industrial order, was a pool of labor. In the United States the demand for workers was so great that the native-born could not fill it. In 1860 it took about 4.3 million workers to run all the factories, mills, and shops in the United States. By 1900 there were approximately 20 million workers in industrial and associated enterprises.

European sources

Europe was one recruiting ground. Mechanization, poverty, and oppression pushed many laborers from farms into cities and finally off the continent entirely. To pull them across the Atlantic, industrialists advertised in newspapers, distributed pamphlets, and sent agents to Europe. The Contract Labor Law allowed employers to recruit laborers abroad, pay their passage, and deduct the cost from their wages. The repeal of the law in 1885 did little to dampen their efforts. In the 1880s incoming iron workers from Sweden demonstrated how successful the recruiters had been. Often the only three words of English the newcomers knew were "Charlie—Deere—Moline" (Charlie was the president of the John Deere Plow Company in Moline, Illinois).

More than 8 million immigrants arrived in the United States between 1870 and 1890, another 14 million by 1914. As mechanized agriculture and religious persecution took hold in eastern and southern Europe, those regions replaced northern and western Europe as the chief sources of immigration. Most new arrivals settled in industrial cities in hopes of returning home with fatter purses. Often unskilled, many of them peasants, they found jobs in factories and mines or on construction and road gangs. They were willing to work harder for less than those they replaced. "Immigrants work for almost nothing," complained a native-born laborer, "and seem to be able to live on wind."

Migration chains

To get those jobs, immigrants relied on well-defined migration chains of friends and family. A brother might find work with other Slavs in the mines of Pennsylvania; or the daughter of Greek parents, in a New England textile mill filled with relatives. Labor contractors also served as a funnel to industry. Tough and savvy immigrants themselves, they met newcomers at the docks and train stations with contracts to work in local factories, mines, and other industries. For their trouble they took a fee or a slice of the new workers' wages. Among Italians they were known as *padrones;* among Mexicans, as *enganchistas.* By the end of the nineteenth century such contractors controlled two-thirds of the labor in New York.

Domestic sources

A massive migration of rural Americans—some 11 million between 1865 and 1920—provided a home-grown source of labor. Driven from the farm by machines and bad times or just following dreams of a new life, they moved first to small, then to larger cities. Most lacked the skills for high-paying work. But they spoke English, and many could read and write. In iron and steel cities as well as in coal-mining towns, the better industrial jobs and supervisory positions often went to them. Others found work in retail stores or offices and slowly entered the new urban middle class of white-collar workers.

Most African Americans continued to work the fields of the South. About 300,000 moved to northern cities between 1870 and 1910, perhaps more to southern

Chicago laborer

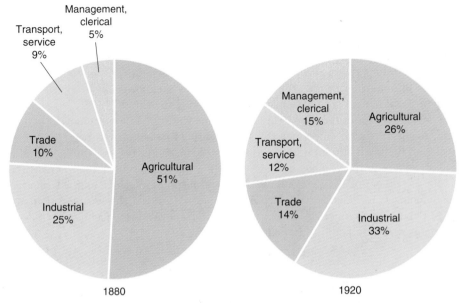

OCCUPATIONAL DISTRIBUTION, 1880 AND 1920
Between 1880 and 1920, management and industrial work—employing white- and blue-collar workers—grew at the expense of farm work.

cities. Like the new immigrants, they were trying to escape discrimination and follow opportunity. And they too relied on family migration chains, often bringing the members of their families one by one. But unlike many immigrants, few blacks returned home to the Old South, where they met increasingly with intimidation and violence.

Black migrants to cities, North or South, failed to evade discrimination but did find employment. They usually worked in low-paying jobs as day laborers and janitors or laundresses and domestic servants. By 1890 only 7 percent of all black men worked in industry. Yet to serve growing black neighborhoods, black-owned businesses thrived by catering to a black clientele, especially in southern cities.

Mexicans, too, came in search of jobs, mainly in agriculture but also in industry. Again family networks played a critical role. One man was responsible for bringing some 27 families to California. "Come! come! come over," a Mexican recalled being told by friends. "It is good here." Mexicans helped to build the transcontinental railroad and worked the crops from Texas to California. After the turn of the century, a smaller number turned farther north for jobs in the tanneries, meatpacking plants, foundries, and rail yards of Chicago, St. Louis, and other centers of industry. Soon Mexican neighborhoods, or barrios, sprang up in cities across the Midwest.

RAILROADS: AMERICA'S FIRST BIG BUSINESS

The system was a mess: any good railroad man knew as much. Along the tracks that spanned the country, each town—each rail station—set its clocks separately by the

Railroad time

sun. In 1882, the year T. S. Hudson scampered across America, New York and Boston were 11 minutes and 45 seconds apart. Stations often had several clocks showing the time on different rail lines, along with one displaying "local mean time." In 1883, without consulting anyone, the railroad companies organized time by dividing the country into four zones, each an hour apart. One Chicago newspaper compared the feat to Joshua's making the sun stand still. Cities and towns soon adjusted, but Congress did not get around to making the division official until 1918.

At the center of the new industrial systems were the railroads, moving people and freight, spreading communications, reinventing time, ultimately tying the nation together. Railroads also stimulated economic growth, simply because the sheer building of them required so many resources—coal, wood, glass, rubber, brass, and by the 1880s 75 percent of all U.S. steel. By lowering transportation costs, railroads allowed manufacturers to reduce prices, attract more buyers, and increase business. Perhaps most important, as America's first big business they devised new techniques of management, soon adopted by other companies.

A Managerial Revolution

To the men who ran them, railroads provided a challenge in organization and finance. In the 1850s, one of the largest industrial enterprises in America, the Pepperell textile mills of Maine, employed about 800 workers. By the early 1880s the Pennsylvania Railroad had nearly 50,000 people on its payroll. From setting schedules and rates to determining costs and profits, everything required a level of coordination unknown in earlier businesses.

Pioneering trunk lines

The so-called trunk lines pioneered in devising new systems of management. Scores of early companies had serviced local networks of cities and communities, often with less than 50 miles of track. During the 1850s trunk lines emerged east of the Mississippi to connect the shorter branches, or "feeder" lines. By the outbreak of the Civil War, with four great trunk lines under a single management, railroads linked the eastern seaboard with the Great Lakes and western rivers. After the war, trunk lines grew in the South and West.

The new managers

The operations of large lines spawned a new managerial elite, beneath owners but with wide authority over operations. Cautious by nature, they preferred to negotiate and administer rather than compete. Daniel McCallum, superintendent of the New York and Erie in the 1850s, laid the foundation for this system by drawing up the first table of organization for an American company. A tree trunk with roots represented the president and board of directors; five branches constituted the main operating divisions; leaves stood for the local agents, train crews, and others. Information moved up and down the trunk so that managers could get daily reports to and from the separate parts.

By the turn of the century, these managerial techniques had spread to other industries. Local superintendents were responsible for daily activities. Central offices served as corporate nerve centers, housing divisions for purchases, production, transportation, sales, and accounting. A new class of middle managers ran them and imposed new order on business operations. Executives, managers, and workers were being taught to operate in increasingly precise and coordinated ways.

An 1886 office furniture catalog underlines the need for efficiency that was a hallmark of the rising middle-level office manager. Filing cabinets and one of Edison's mimeograph machines are near at hand. Workers dress in a more dignified style reserved for professionals, while framed pictures on the wall lend a homey air.

Competition and Consolidation

While managers made operations more systematic, the struggle among railroad companies to dominate the industry was anything but precise and rational. In the 1870s and 1880s the pain of railroad progress began to tell.

By their nature, railroads were saddled with enormous fixed costs—expensive equipment, huge payrolls, high debts. These remained constant regardless of the volume of traffic. To generate added revenue, railroads constructed more lines in hopes of increasing their traffic. Soon the railroads had overbuilt. With so much extra capacity, railroad owners schemed to win new accounts. They gave free passes to favored shippers, promised them free sidings at their plants, offered free land to lure businesses to their territory.

Railroad problems

The most savage and costly competition came over the rates charged for shipping goods. Managers lowered rates for freight that was shipped in bulk, on long hauls, or on return routes (since the cars were empty anyway). They used "rebates"— secret discounts to preferred customers—to drop prices below the posted rates of competitors (and then recouped the losses by overcharging small shippers like farmers). When the economy plunged or a weak line sought to improve its position, rate wars broke out. By 1880, 65 lines had declared bankruptcy.

Rebates

One way to prevent the ravages of competition was to buy up competing lines. It was often expensive and could lead to even fiercer war. From 1866 to 1868

Cornelius Vanderbilt of the New York Central waged a futile battle to gain control of the Erie Railroad. It was headed by a trio of railroad sharks: the corporate buccaneer Daniel Drew, the flamboyant speculator James Fisk, Jr., and the unscrupulous Jay Gould. Vanderbilt fought the trio in the courts, where each side bought its own judges. He fought them in the legislature, where both sides bribed legislators (for $15,000 apiece, some said). He fought them on the streets with gangs of hired toughs and on the seas, where Fisk himself served as admiral of a Hudson River fleet armed with riflemen.

The "Erie Wars" ended in a standoff. The Erie paid Vanderbilt a huge ransom to end his offensive. Gould and Drew retained control of the company, until they turned against each other. By 1877, the Erie was bankrupt, mismanaged, and drowned in a sea of "watered stock." (Such stock, issued in excess of the company's assets, derived its name from the rancher's trick of having cattle drink water before weighing in for sale.) Gould emerged unscathed from the fight. When he died of tuberculosis at the age of 56 in 1892, his estate totaled $74 million.

Pooling   During the 1870s railroad managers created regional federations to pool traffic, set prices, and divide profits among members. Pooling—informal agreements among competing companies to act together—was designed to remove the competition that led to rate wars. Without the force of law, however, pools failed. Members broke ranks by cutting prices in hopes of quick gain. In the end, rate wars died down only when weaker lines failed or stronger ones bought up competitors.

In the East purchases, leases, and mergers helped to reduce competition. In the West new construction produced self-contained systems like the Atchison, Topeka and Santa Fe. By 1890 it stretched from Chicago to the Pacific coast and operated more than 9000 miles of track. But in the depression of 1893, it too went bankrupt, the victim of overexpansion. Railroad executives learned a lesson: although they had gained control through consolidation, they had also grown too big. By the mid-1890s, a third of the mileage of American railroads was tied up in foreclosure or bankruptcy.

The Challenge of Finance

Earlier in the nineteenth century, many railroads relied on state governments for financial help. Backers also looked to counties, cities, and towns for bonds and other forms of aid. People living near the ends of rail lines, who stood to gain from construction, were persuaded to take railroad stock in exchange for land or labor. In the 1850s and 1860s western promoters went to Washington for federal assistance. Congress loaned $65 million to six western railroads and granted some 131 million acres of land.

New ways of   Federal aid helped to build only part of the nation's railroads. Most of the money
raising money   came from private investors. The New York Stock Exchange expanded rapidly as railroad corporations began to trade their stocks there. Large investment banks developed financial networks to track down money at home and abroad. By 1898 a third of the assets of American life insurance companies had gone into railroads, while Europeans owned nearly a third of all American railroad securities.

Because investment bankers played such large roles in funding railroads, they found themselves advising companies about their business affairs. If a company fell

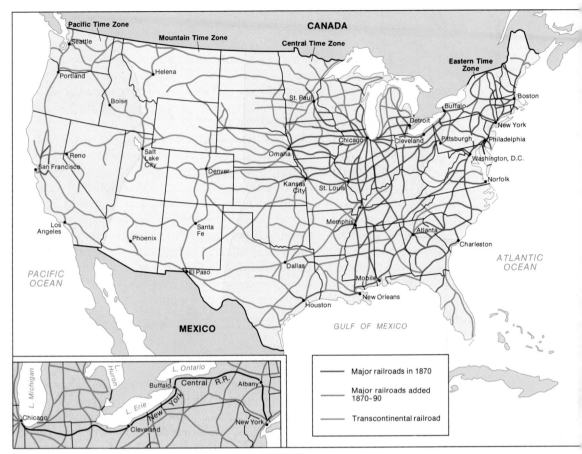

RAILROADS, 1870–1890
By 1890, the railroad network stretched from one end of the country to the other, with more
miles of track than all of Europe combined. New York and Chicago, linked by the New York
Central trunk line, became the new commercial axis.

into bankruptcy, bankers sometimes served as the "receivers" who oversaw the property until financial health returned. By absorbing smaller lines into larger ones, eliminating rebates, and stabilizing rates, the bankers helped to reduce competition and impose order and centralization. In the process, they often came to control the companies they counseled.

By 1900, the new industrial systems had transformed American railroads. Some 200,000 miles of track were in operation, 80 percent of it owned by only six groups of railroads. Time zones allowed for coordinated schedules; standardized track permitted easy cross-country freighting. Soon passengers were traveling 16 billion miles a year. To that traffic could be added farm goods, raw materials, and factory-finished products. Everything moved with a new regularity that allowed businesses to plan and prosper.

THE GROWTH OF BIG BUSINESS

In 1865, 26-year-old John D. Rockefeller sat in the office of his Cleveland oil refinery, about to conclude the biggest deal of his life. Yet his blank face betrayed not the slightest emotion. Rockefeller's business was flourishing, but not his partnership with Maurice Clark. The two had fallen out over how quickly to expand. Rockefeller was eager to grow fast; the cautious Clark was not. They dissolved their partnership and agreed to bid for the company. Bidding opened at $500, rocketed to $72,500, and abruptly stopped. "The business is yours," said Clark, and the men shook hands. Only then did a thin smile creep across Rockefeller's angular face.

Twenty years later, Rockefeller's Standard Oil Company controlled 90 percent of the nation's refining capacity and an empire that stretched well beyond Cleveland. Day and night, trains sped Standard executives to New York, Philadelphia, and other eastern cities. The railroads were a fitting form of transportation for Rockefeller's company; in many ways they were the key to his oil empire. They pioneered the business systems upon which Rockefeller was building. And they carried his oil products for discounted rates, giving him the edge to squeeze out rivals. Like other American firms, Standard Oil was improving on the practices of the railroads to do bigger and bigger business.

Growth in Consumer Goods

How to control the ravages of competition? In Michigan in the 1860s, salt producers found themselves fighting for their existence. The presence of too many salt makers had begun an endless round of price-cutting that was driving them all out of business. Seeing salvation in combination, they drew together in the nation's first pool. In 1869 they formed the Michigan Salt Association. They voluntarily agreed to divide production, assign markets, and set prices—at double the previous rate.

Horizontal growth

Salt processing and other industries that specialized in consumer goods had low start-up costs, so they were often plagued by competition. Horizontal combination—joining loosely together with rivals—had saved Michigan salt producers. The railroads were among the first big businesses to employ pools. By the 1880s there was a whiskey pool, a cordage pool, and countless others. Such informal arrangements ultimately proved unenforceable and therefore unsatisfactory. (After 1890 they were also considered illegal restraints on trade.) But other forms of horizontal growth, such as formal mergers, spread in the wake of an economic panic in the 1890s.

Vertical integration

Some makers of consumer products worried less about direct competition and concentrated on boosting efficiency and sales. They adopted a vertical-growth strategy that integrated several different activities under one company. Gustavus Swift, a New England butcher, saw the advantages of such integration when he arrived in Chicago in the mid-1870s. Aware of the demand for fresh beef in the East, he acquired new refrigerated railcars to ship meat from western slaughterhouses and a network of ice-cooled warehouses in eastern cities to store it. By 1885 he had created the first national meatpacking enterprise, Swift and Company.

Swift moved upward, closer to consumers, by putting together a fleet of wagons to distribute his beef to retailers. He moved down toward raw materials, extending and coordinating the purchase of cattle at the Chicago stockyards. By the 1890s Swift and

Company was a fully integrated, vertically organized corporation operating on a nationwide scale. Soon Swift, Armour and Company, and three other giants—together called the "Big Five"—controlled 90 percent of the beef shipped across state lines.

Vertical growth generally brought producers of consumer goods closer to the marketplace. For them profit came from high-volume sales. The Singer Sewing Machine Company and the McCormick Harvester Company created their own retail sales arms. Manufacturers began furnishing ordinary consumers with technical information, credit, and repair services in an effort to expand sales. Advertising expenditures grew, to some $90 million by 1900, to identify markets, shape buying habits, and drum up business. Armies of traveling salesmen scoured towns and cities in search of consumers.

Carnegie Integrates Steel

Industrialization encouraged vertical integration in heavy industry but more often downward, toward reliable sources of raw materials. These firms made heavy machinery and materials for big users like railroads and factory builders. Their markets were easily identified and changed little. For them, profits lay in securing limited raw materials and in holding down costs.

Andrew Carnegie led the way in steel. More than any of his contemporaries, Carnegie personified the American dream of success. A Scottish immigrant, he worked his way up from bobbin boy in a textile factory to expert telegrapher to superintendent of the western division of the Pennsylvania Railroad at the age of 24. A string of wise investments paid off handsomely. He owned a share of the first sleeping car, the first iron railroad bridge, a locomotive factory, and finally an iron factory that became the nucleus of his steel empire.

In 1872, on a trip to England, Carnegie chanced to see the new Bessemer process for making steel. Awestruck by its fiery display, he rushed home to build the biggest steel mill in the world. The J. Walter Thomson Mills (shrewdly named in honor of the president of the Pennsylvania Railroad) opened in 1875, in the midst of a severe depression. Over the next 25 years, Carnegie added mills at Homestead and elsewhere in Pennsylvania and moved from railroad building to city building. He supplied steel for the Brooklyn Bridge, New York City's elevated railway, and the Washington Monument.

Carnegie succeeded, in part, by taking advantage of the boom-and-bust business cycle. He jumped in during hard times, building and buying when equipment and businesses were cheap. But he also found skilled managers who employed the administrative techniques of the railroads. And Carnegie knew how to compete. He scrapped machinery, workers, even a new mill to keep costs down and undersell competitors.

Keys to Carnegie's success

The final key to Carnegie's success was expansion. His empire spread horizontally by purchasing rival steel mills and constructing new ones. It spread vertically, buying up sources of supply, transportation, and eventually sales. Controlling such an integrated system, Carnegie could ensure a steady flow of materials from mine to mill and market, as well as a steady stream of profits. In 1900 his company turned out more steel than Great Britain and netted him $40 million.

Integration of the kind Carnegie employed expressed the logic of the new industrial age. More and more, the industrial activities of society were being linked together in one giant, interconnected process.

Rockefeller and the Great Standard Oil Trust

John D. Rockefeller accomplished in oil what Carnegie achieved in steel. And he went further, developing an innovative business structure—the trust—that promised greater control than even Carnegie's integrated system. At first Rockefeller grew horizontally by buying out or joining other oil refiners. To cut costs, he expanded vertically, with oil pipelines, warehouses, and barrel factories. By 1870, when he and five partners formed the Standard Oil Company of Ohio, his high-caliber, low-cost products could compete with any other. The very name of the company was chosen to bespeak quality.

Rockefeller's methods of expansion

Since the oil refining business was a jungle of competitive firms, Rockefeller proceeded to twist arms. He bribed rivals, spied on them, created phony companies, and slashed prices. His decisive edge came from the railroads. Desperate for business, they granted Standard Oil not only rebates on shipping rates but also "drawbacks," a fee railroaders paid Standard for any product shipped by a rival oil company. Within a decade Standard dominated American refining with a vertically integrated empire that stretched from drilling to selling.

Throughout the 1870s Rockefeller kept his empire stitched together through informal pools and other business combinations. But they were weak and afforded him too little control. He could try to expand further, except that corporations were restricted by state law. In Rockefeller's home state of Ohio, for example, corporations could not own plants in other states or own stock in out-of-state companies.

The trust

In 1879 Samuel C. T. Dodd, chief counsel of Standard Oil, came up with a solution, the "trust." Under the trust, the stockholders of a corporation surrendered their shares "in trust" to a central board of directors with the power to control all property. In exchange, stockholders received certificates of trust that paid hefty dividends. Since it did not literally own other companies, the trust violated no state law. In 1882 the Standard Oil Company of Ohio formed the country's first great trust. It brought Rockefeller what he sought so fiercely—centralized management of the oil industry. Other businesses soon created trusts of their own—in meatpacking, wiremaking, farm machinery, and elsewhere. Just as quickly, trusts became notorious for crushing rivals and fixing prices.

The Mergers of J. Pierpont Morgan

The trust was only a stepping-stone to an even more effective means of avoiding competition, managing people, and controlling business: the corporate merger. The idea of two corporations merging—combining several corporations under one giant—remained impossible until 1889, when New Jersey began to permit corporations to own other corporations.

The holding company

In 1890, the need to find a substitute for the trust grew urgent. Congress outlawed trusts under the Sherman Antitrust Act. The Sherman Act specifically banned business from "restraining trade" by setting prices, dividing markets, or engaging in other unfair practices. The ever-inventive Samuel Dodd came up with a new idea, the "holding company," a corporation of corporations that had the power to hold shares of other companies. Many industries converted their trusts into holding companies, including Standard Oil, which moved to New Jersey in 1899.

Two years later came the biggest corporate merger of the era. It was the creation of a financial wizard named J. Pierpont Morgan. After the Civil War Morgan had become head of the powerful investment house that bore his father's name. Born rich, he made the House of Morgan richer still by buying, holding, and merging companies. For the next 50 years Morgan had a hand in reorganizing almost every important industry in America: railroads, coal, steel, steamships, electricity. His orderly mind detested chaotic competition, especially when it threatened profits. "I like a little competition," he said, "but I like combination more." Between 1892 and 1902 he was instrumental in creating such corporate giants as General Electric, American Telephone and Telegraph, and International Harvester.

Morgan's greatest triumph was in steel, where for years Carnegie had refused to combine with rivals. In January 1901, with the threat of a colossal steel war looming, Morgan convinced Carnegie to put a price tag on his company. When a messenger brought back the scrawled reply—more than $400 million—Morgan merely nodded and said, "I accept this price." Within three months he had bought Carnegie's eight largest competitors and announced the formation of the United States Steel Corporation.

A mammoth holding company, U.S. Steel embraced every aspect of steelmaking from ore beds to finishing plants. It gobbled up more than 200 manufacturing and transportation companies, 1000 miles of railways, and the whole Mesabi iron range of Minnesota. It was the largest industrial combine in the world and America's first billion-dollar corporation. Capitalized at $1.4 billion, its value exceeded the national debt. All the same, U.S. Steel was a bloated giant with far too many costs ever to realize Morgan's dream of high profits.

What Morgan helped to create in steel was rapidly coming to pass in other industries. A wave of mergers swept through American business after the depression of 1893. As the economy plunged, cutthroat competition bled businesses until they were eager to sell out. Giants sprouted almost overnight. By 1904, in each of 50 industries one firm came to account for 60 percent or more of the total output.

The merger movement

Corporate Defenders

As Andrew Carnegie's empire grew, his conscience turned troubled. Preaching a "gospel of wealth," he urged the rich to act as stewards for the poor, "doing for them better than they would or could do for themselves." He devoted his time to philanthropy by creating foundations and endowing libraries and universities with some $350 million in contributions.

The gospel of wealth

Defenders of the new corporate order were less troubled than Carnegie about the rough-and-tumble world of big business. They justified the system by stressing the opportunity created for individuals by economic growth. Through frugality, acquisitiveness, and discipline—the sources of cherished American individualism—anyone could rise like Andrew Carnegie.

When most ordinary citizens failed to follow in Carnegie's footsteps, defenders of the corporate order blamed the individual. Laziness, ignorance, and moral depravity were the true sources of failure, they said. British philosopher Herbert Spencer added the weight of science by applying Charles Darwin's theories of evolution where naturalist Darwin had never intended—to the social order. Spencer maintained that in society, as in biology, only the "fittest" survived. The competitive social jungle doomed the unfit to poverty and rewarded the most fit with property and privilege. (As much as Spencer praised the competitive jungle, he preferred the quiet

Social Darwinism

The cartoon satirizes Andrew Carnegie as a little boy playing at building libraries. Before he died in 1919, Carnegie gave away $350 million of his $400 million fortune. He built not just libraries but also museums and colleges, as well as public-spirited institutions, including the Carnegie Endowment for Peace. "The wealthy person who dies without giving away money," Carnegie wrote, "dies disgraced."

life. When the great philosopher toured Pittsburgh, he was appalled by the sooty pollution and the booming noise of the steel mills. "Six months' residence here would justify suicide," he told Carnegie.)

Spencer's American apostle, William Graham Sumner, argued that competition was natural and had to proceed without any interference, including government regulation. Millionaires were simply the "product of natural selection." Such "social Darwinism" found strong support among turn-of-the-century business leaders. The philosophy of ruthless competition certified their success even as they worked to destroy that competition through consolidation.

Corporate Critics

Andrew Carnegie invoked the gospel to wealth to justify his millions, but a group of radical critics looked on his libraries and foundations as desperate attempts to buy peace of mind. For all the contemporary celebrations of wealth and big business, they saw the new industrial order as exploitative, divisive, and immoral. It was built on the backs of ordinary "toilers," separated by caste from those few who profited from their labor. Day by day, the toilers were being transformed into "wage slaves"—chained and bound to their meager industrial wages as much as antebellum slaves had been to the plantations of the Old South. These moral critics of capitalism called for a more humane industrial America based on cooperation and communal values. Some went so far as to draw up blueprints for a new cooperative community, but the aim was always the same: to escape the inequalities and tensions of the new industrial order by redistributing its abundance and reapportioning its power.

New York's wealthy called their elaborate summer homes "cottages," but they were mansions by any standard. The Breakers, designed by Richard Morris Hunt for Cornelius Vanderbilt II, looks like an Italian palace with his grand music room among its 70 rooms. Now open to the public, the mansion cost $5 million to build.

Henry George, a journalist and self-taught economist, began his critique with a simple question. How could poverty exist when industrial progress had created such wealth? George pointed to greedy landowners who bought property when it was cheap and then held it until the forces of society—labor, technology, and speculation on nearby sites—had increased its value. They reaped most of the rewards, despite the hard work of others. In his best-selling book *Progress and Poverty* (1879), George proposed a single tax on these "unearned" profits to end monopoly landholding. With all other taxes abolished, income would be slowly redistributed. "Single-tax" clubs sprang up throughout the country, and George nearly won the race for mayor of New York in 1886.

Henry George's single tax

The journalist Edward Bellamy tapped the same popular resentment against the inequalities of industrial capitalism in his novel *Looking Backward*. Published in 1888, it sold over 500,000 copies in the United States and was translated into more than a dozen languages. One of many utopian novels published at the end of the nineteenth century, it described a future in which all were guaranteed a life of material security but were expected to contribute to the public good. Julian West, a fictional Bostonian, falls asleep in 1887 and awakens Rip Van Winkle-like in the year 2000. The competitive, class-ridden society of the nineteenth century is gone. Instead there is an orderly utopia managed by a benevolent government trust. Want has been banished. Competition, exploitation, and class divisions have disappeared. In their place is a society governed by "fraternal cooperation," shared abundance, and "nationalism," which puts the interests of the community above those of the individual. By 1892, Bellamy's philosophy had spawned over 160 clubs in 27 states with followers demanding redistribution of wealth, civil service reform, and nationalization of railroads and utilities.

Socialist
Labor party

Less popular but equally hostile to capitalism was the Socialist Labor party, formed in 1877. Under Daniel De Leon, a West Indian immigrant, it stressed class conflict and called for a revolution to give workers control over production. De Leon refused to compromise his radical beliefs, and the socialists ended up attracting more intellectuals than workers. Some immigrants found its class consciousness appealing, but most rejected its radicalism and rigidity. A few party members, bent on gaining greater support, revolted and in 1901 founded the more successful Socialist Party of America. Workers were beginning to organize their own responses to industrialism.

The Costs of Doing Business

The heated debates between the critics and defenders of industrial capitalism made clear that the changes in American society were two-edged. Big businesses certainly helped to rationalize production, increase national wealth, and tie the country together. Yet they also concentrated power, corrupted politics, and made the gap between rich and poor more apparent than ever. In 1890, the richest 9 percent of Americans held nearly three-quarters of all wealth in the United States. But by 1900, one American in eight (nearly 10 million people) lived below the poverty line.

In truth, the concentration of wealth differed little from the 1850s. What had changed was the rise of a visible class of millionaires who flaunted their new wealth. The fabulously well-to-do Vanderbilts had not one but two mansions on New York's

BOOM AND BUST BUSINESS CYCLE, 1865–1900
Between 1865 and 1900, industrialization produced great economic growth but also wild swings of prosperity and depression. During booms, productivity soared, and near-full employment existed. But the rising number of industrial workers meant high unemployment during deep busts.

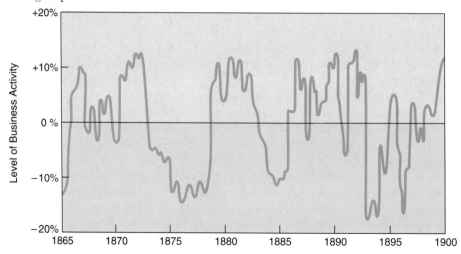

Fifth Avenue, along with five other homes and several country estates. Such tycoons lived like royalty, and much of the country either envied or hated them for it.

More to the point, the practices of big business subjected the economy to enormous disruptions. The banking system could not always keep pace with the demand for capital, and businesses failed to distribute enough profits to sustain the purchasing power of workers. The supply of goods regularly outstripped the demand for them, and then the wrenching cycle of boom and bust set in. The first of the great busts came in 1873. In September, several prominent brokerage houses declared bankruptcy. Financial panic escalated into a major depression as the economy contracted after years of expansion. Before recovery took hold 6 years later, over 10,000 businesses had failed, nearly 1 worker in 10 had been thrown out of work, and those who kept their jobs found their pay cut, often below the poverty line. Altogether three severe depressions—1873–1879, 1882–1885, and 1893–1897—rocked the economy in the last third of the nineteenth century. With hard times came fierce competition as managers searched frantically to cut costs, and the industrial barons earned their reputations for ruthlessness.

The boom- and-bust cycle

COUNTERPOINT

Attacks and celebrations have continued to characterize portraits of entrepreneurs such as Carnegie and Rockefeller. Some historians, following the lead of nineteenth-century critics, have depicted them as unscrupulous hypocrites who extolled the virtues of competition while ruthlessly crushing it. A lust for profits alone drove them, and they cared little for the needs of society, according to this portrait. The leaders of big business resembled nothing so much as medieval barons who had oppressed their serfs and robbed them of the fruits of their labors. Using corporations, trusts, and other devices, these nineteenth-century "robber barons" similarly exploited their workers and concentrated wealth and power in the hands of a relatively small elite. Such centralization, these historians argue, threatened the fundamentals of democracy.

American business leaders: robber barons or captains of industry?

Standing in sharp contrast to the image of business leaders as robber barons is the notion of them as "industrial statesmen." Some business historians, interested in examining the growth of industry, concede that the Rockefellers and Carnegies employed methods of doubtful morality. But in their eyes business leaders were not greedy robber barons. Instead they are depicted as captains of industry whose creativity and ambition helped to promote an economy of mass-produced abundance. Still other business historians have shown little interest in questions of morality or the tension between democracy and economic concentration. They emphasize less the people than the processes by which new strategies, structures, and forms of doing business increased efficiency and productivity.

THE WORKERS' WORLD

At seven in the morning, Sadie Frowne sat at her sewing machine in a Brooklyn garment factory. The factory was crowded and dark, filled with immigrant women like Sadie sitting straight-backed and ready. It was nothing at all like the small, open village in Russia where her people had started. The boss, a man she barely knew, dropped a pile of unfinished skirts next to her. She pushed one under the needle and began to rock her foot quickly on the pedal that powered her machine. Sometimes Sadie pushed the skirts too hastily, and the needle pierced her finger. There was pain and usually a moment's confusion; perhaps those at nearby machines stopped to help, but then it was back to stitching. To stop, even to slow down, was ordinarily unthinkable. "The machines go like mad all day because the faster you work the more money you get," Sadie explained of the world of industrial work in 1902.

The cramped sweatshops, the vast steel mills, the dank tunnels of the coal fields—all demanded workers and required them to work in new ways. Farmers or peasants who had once timed themselves by the movement of the sun now lived by the clock and labored in the twilight of gaslit factories. Instead of being self-employed, they had to deal with supervisors and were paid by the piece or hour. Not the seasons but the relentless cycle of machines set their pace. Increasingly, workers bore the brunt of depressions, faced periodic unemployment, and toiled under dangerous conditions as they struggled to bring the new industrial processes under their control.

Industrial Work

In 1881, the Pittsburgh Bessemer Steel Company opened its new mill in Homestead, Pennsylvania. Nearly 400 men and boys went to work in its 60 acres of sheds. They kept the mill going around the clock by working in two shifts: 12 hours a day the first week, 12 hours a night the next, except for the weekly "swing shift," when the Saturday night crew took Sunday off, and the Sunday swing worked a full 24 hours. In the furnace room, some men fainted from the heat, while the vibration and screeching of machinery deafened others. There were no breaks, even for lunch. "Home is just the place where I eat and sleep," said a steelworker. "I live in the mills."

Carnegie Furnaces, Braddock, Pennsylvania

Few industrial workers labored under conditions quite so harsh, but the Homestead mill reflected the common characteristics of industrial work: the use of machines for mass production; the division of labor into intricately organized, menial tasks; and the dictatorship of the clock. At the turn of the century, two-thirds of all industrial work came from large-scale mills.

Pattern of industrial work

Under such conditions labor paid dearly for industrial progress. By 1900, most of those earning wages in industry worked 6 days a week, 10 hours a day. They held jobs that required more machines and fewer skills. Repetition of small chores replaced fine craftwork. In the 1880s, for example, almost all the 40 different steps that had gone into making a pair of shoes by hand could be performed by a novice or "green hand" with a few days of instruction at a simple machine.

With machines also came danger. Tending furnaces in a steel mill or plucking tobacco from cigarette-rolling machines was tedious. If a worker became bored or tired, disaster could strike. Each year from 1880 to 1900 industrial mishaps killed an average of 35,000 wage earners and injured more than 500,000. Workers and their families could expect no payment from employers or the government for death or injury. The idea of workers' compensation was unknown.

Industrial workers rarely saw an owner. The foreman or supervisor exercised complete authority over the unskilled in his section, hiring and firing them and even setting their wages. Skilled workers had greater freedom, yet they too felt the pinch of technology and organization. By the 1880s, carpenters were finding that machine-made doors were replacing the ones they once constructed at the site. Painters no longer mixed their own paints. "I regard my people," reflected one manager, "as I regard my machinery. So long as they can do my work for what I choose to pay them, I keep getting out of them all I can."

Taylorism   Higher productivity and profits were the aims, and for Frederick W. Taylor, efficiency was the way to achieve them. During the 1870s and 1880s, Taylor undertook careful time-and-motion studies of workers' movements in the steel industry. He set up standard procedures and offered pay incentives for beating his production quotas. On one occasion, he designed 15 ore shovels, each for a separate task. One hundred forty men were soon doing the work of 600. By the early twentieth century "Taylorism" was a full-blown philosophy, complete with its own professional society. "Management engineers" prescribed routines from which workers could not vary.

For all the high ideals of Taylorism, ordinary laborers refused to perform as cogs in a vast industrial machine. In a variety of ways, they worked to maintain control. Many European immigrants continued to observe the numerous saints' days and other religious holidays of their homelands, regardless of factory rules. When the pressure of six-day weeks became too stifling, workers took an unauthorized "blue Monday" off. Or they slowed down to reduce the grueling pace. Or they simply walked off the job. Come spring and warm weather, factories reported turnover rates of 100 percent or more.

Worker   For some, seizing control of work was more than a matter of survival or self-re-
citizens   spect. Many workers regarded themselves as citizens of a democratic republic. They expected to earn a "competence"—enough money to support and educate their families and enough time to stay abreast of current affairs. Few but highly skilled workers could realize such democratic dreams. More and more, labor was being managed as another part of an integrated system of industry.

Children, Women, and African Americans

In the mines of Pennsylvania, nimble-fingered eight- and nine-year-olds snatched bits of slate from amid the chunks of coal. In Illinois glass factories, quick-footed "dog boys" dashed with trays of red-hot bottles to the cooling ovens. By 1900, the industrial labor force included some 1.7 million children, more than double the number 30 years earlier. Parents often had no choice. As one union leader observed, "Absolute necessity compels the father . . . to take the child into the mine to assist him in winning bread for the family." On average, children worked 60 hours a week and carried home paychecks a third the size of those of adult males.

Women had always labored on family farms, but by 1870 one out of every four nonagricultural workers was female. In general they earned one-half of what men did. Nearly all were single and young, anywhere from their mid-teens to their mid-twenties. Most lived in boardinghouses or at home with their parents. Usually they contributed their wages to the family kitty. Once married, they took on a life of full-time housework and child rearing.

Only 5 percent of married women held jobs outside the home in 1900. Married black women (in need of income because of the low wages paid to their husbands) were four times more likely than married whites to work away from home. Industrialization inevitably pushed women into new jobs. Mainly they worked in industries considered extensions of housework: food processing, textiles and clothing, cigar making, and domestic service.

Injured boy from the mills

New methods of management and marketing opened positions for white-collar women as "typewriters," "telephone girls," bookkeepers, and secretaries. On rare occasions women entered the professions, though law and medical schools still regarded them as unwelcome invaders. Such discrimination drove ambitious, educated women into nursing, teaching, and library work. Their growing presence soon "feminized" these professions, pushing men upward into managerial slots or out of these professions entirely.

Feminization of work

Even more than women, African Americans faced discrimination in the workplace. They were paid less than whites and given menial jobs. Their greatest opportunities in industry often came as strikebreakers to replace white workers. Once a strike ended, however, black workers were replaced themselves and hated by the white regulars whom they had replaced. The service trades furnished the largest single source of jobs. Waiting on whites in restaurants or on railroads lay within the boundaries set by the prevailing color line. Craftworkers and a sprinkling of black professionals could usually be found in cities. After the turn of the century, black-owned businesses thrived in the growing black neighborhoods of the North and South.

The American Dream of Success

Whatever their separate experiences, working-class Americans did improve their overall lot. Though the gap between the very rich and the poor widened, most wage earners made some gains. Between 1860 and 1890 real daily wages—pay in terms of buying power—climbed some 50 percent as prices gradually fell. And after 1890, the number of hours on the job began a slow decline.

Rising real wages

Yet most unskilled and semiskilled workers in factories continued to receive low pay. In 1890, an unskilled laborer could expect about $1.50 for a 10-hour day; a

Clerks' jobs, traditionally held by men, came to be filled by women as growing industrial networks created more managerial jobs for men. In this typical office, male managers literally oversee female clerks.

skilled one, perhaps twice that amount. It took about $600 to make ends meet, but most manufacturing workers made under $500 a year. Native-born white Americans tended to earn more than immigrants, those who spoke English more than those who did not, men more than women, and all others more than African Americans, Latinos, and Asians.

Social mobility

Few workers repeated the rags-to-riches rise of Andrew Carnegie. But some did rise despite periodic unemployment and ruthless wage cuts. About one-quarter of the manual laborers in one study entered the lower middle class in their own lifetimes. More often such unskilled workers climbed in financial status within their own class. And most workers, seeing some improvement, believed in the American dream of success, even if they did not fully share in it.

THE SYSTEMS OF LABOR

Putting in more hours to save a few pennies, walking out in exhaustion or disgust, slowing down on the job—these were the ways individual workers coped with industrial America. Sporadic and unorganized, such actions stood little chance of bringing the new industrial order under the control of labor. For ordinary workers to begin to shape industrialization they had to combine, just as businesses did. They needed to combine horizontally—organizing not just locally but on a national scale. And they needed to integrate vertically by coordinating action across a wide range of jobs and skills, as Andrew Carnegie coordinated the production of steel.

For workers, unions were their systematic response to industrialization. The most radical unions echoed the moral critics of capitalism by pointing to the oppressiveness of the new industrial order and worked to overturn it. Others embraced the new order but wanted to improve the position of workers within it. Yet whatever their views, unionists believed that power had swung out of balance and only an organized response could correct things.

Early Unions

In the United States unions began forming before the Civil War. Skilled craftworkers—carpenters, iron molders, cigar makers—joined together to protect themselves against the growing power of management. Railroad "brotherhoods" also furnished insurance for those hurt or killed on the accident-plagued lines. Largely local and exclusively male, these early craft unions remained weak and unconnected to each other as well as to the growing mass of unskilled workers.

National Labor Union

After the Civil War, a group of craft unions, brotherhoods, and reformers united skilled and unskilled workers in a nationwide organization. The National Labor Union (NLU) hailed the virtues of a simpler America, when workers controlled their workday, earned a decent living, and had time to be good citizens. NLU leaders attacked the wage system as unfair and enslaving and urged workers to manage their own factories. By the early 1870s, NLU ranks swelled to more than 600,000.

The NLU pressed energetically for the eight-hour workday, the most popular labor demand of the era. Workers saw it as a way not merely of limiting their time on the job but of limiting the power of employers over their lives. "Eight hours for work; eight hours for rest; eight hours for what we will!" proclaimed a banner at one labor rally. Despite the popularity of the issue, the NLU wilted during the depression of 1873.

The Knights of Labor

More successful was a national union born in secrecy. In 1869 Uriah Stephens and nine Philadelphia garment cutters founded the Noble and Holy Order of the Knights of Labor. They draped themselves in ritual and regalia to deepen their sense of solidarity and met in secret to evade hostile owners. The Knights remained small and fraternal for a decade. Their strongly Protestant tone repelled Catholics, who made up almost half the workforce in many industries.

In 1879 the Knights elected Terence V. Powderly as their Grand Master Workman. Handsome, dynamic, Irish, and Catholic, Powderly threw off the Knights' secrecy, dropped their rituals, and opened their ranks. He called for "one big union" to embrace the "toiling millions"—skilled and unskilled, men and women, natives and immigrants, all religions, all races. By 1886, membership had leaped to over 700,000, including nearly 30,000 African Americans and 3000 women.

Terence Powderly

Like the NLU, the radical Knights of Labor looked to abolish the wage system. In its place they wanted to construct a cooperative economy of worker-owned mines, factories, and railroads. The Knights set up more than 140 cooperative workshops, where workers shared decisions and profits, and sponsored some 200 political candidates. To tame the new industrial order, they supported the eight-hour workday and the regulation of trusts. Underlying this program was a moral vision of society. If only people renounced greed, laziness, and dishonesty, Powderly argued, corruption and class division would disappear. Democracy would flourish. To reform citizens, the Knights promoted the prohibition of child and convict labor and the abolition of liquor.

It was one thing to proclaim a national union, quite another to coordinate the activities of so many members. Powderly soon found locals resorting to strikes and violence, actions he condemned. In the mid-1880s, such stoppages wrung concessions from the western railroads, but the organization soon became associated with unsuccessful strikes and violent extremists. Even the gains against the railroads were wiped out when the Texas and Pacific Railroad broke a strike by local Knights. By 1890 the Knights of Labor, symbol of organized labor's resistance to industrial capitalism, teetered near extinction.

The American Federation of Labor

The Knights' position as the premier union in the nation was taken by the rival American Federation of Labor (AFL). The AFL reflected the practicality of its leader, Samuel Gompers. Born in a London tenement, the son of a Jewish cigar maker, Gompers had immigrated in 1863 with his family to New York's Lower East Side. Unlike the visionary Powderly, Gompers preached accommodation, not resistance. He urged his followers to accept capitalism and the wage system. What he wanted was "pure and simple unionism"—higher wages, fewer hours, improved safety, more benefits.

Samuel Gompers

Gompers chose to organize highly skilled craftworkers because they were difficult to replace. He bargained with employers and used strikes and boycotts only as last resorts. With the Cigar Makers' Union as his base, Gompers helped create the first national federation of craft unions in 1881. In 1886, it was reorganized as the American Federation of Labor. Twenty-five labor groups joined, representing some 150,000 workers.

Here was labor's answer to the corporation and the trust: a consolidated organization for controlling resources (workers) and competition (for jobs). Gompers fought off radicals and allied himself with whatever candidate supported labor. Stressing gradual, concrete gains, he made the AFL the most powerful union in the country. By 1901 it had more than a million members, almost a third of all skilled workers in America.

Gompers was less interested in vertical integration: combining skilled and unskilled workers. For most of his career, he preserved the privileges of craftsmen and accepted their prejudices against women, African Americans, and immigrants. Only two locals—the Cigar Makers' Union and the Typographers' Union—enrolled women. Most affiliates restricted black membership through high entrance fees and other discriminatory practices.

Failure of organized labor

Despite the success of the AFL, the laboring classes did not organize themselves as systematically as the barons of industrial America. At the turn of the century, union membership included less than 10 percent of industrial workers. Separated by language and nationality, divided by race and gender, workers resisted unionization during the nineteenth century. In fact, a strong strain of individualism often made them regard any collective action as un-American.

The Limits of Industrial Systems

It was the vagaries of the marketplace and stubbornness of owners that in the end broke the labor movement and set the limits of industrial systems for workers. As managers increased their control over the workplace, workers often found themselves at the mercy of the new industrial order. Even in boom times, one in three workers was out of a job at least three or four months a year. The word "unemployment" dates from the late nineteenth century.

Spontaneous protests

When a worker's pay dropped and frustration mounted, when a mother worked all night and fell asleep during the day while caring for her children, when food prices suddenly jumped—anger might boil over into protest. "A mob of 1,000 people, with women in the lead, marched through the Jewish quarter of Williamsburg last evening and wrecked half a dozen butcher shops," reported the *New York Times* in 1902. In the late nineteenth century a wave of labor activism swept the nation. More often than mobs, it was strikes and boycotts that challenged the authority of employers and gave evidence of working-class identity and discontent.

Most strikes broke out spontaneously, organized by informal leaders in a factory. "Malvina Fourtune and her brother Henry Fourtune it was them who started the strike," declared a company informer in Chicopee, Massachusetts. "They go from house to house and tells the people to keep up the strike." Thousands of rallies and organized strikes were staged as well, often on behalf of the 8-hour workday, in good times and bad, by union and nonunion workers alike.

Great Railroad Strike

In 1877, in the midst of a deep depression, the country's first nationwide strike opened an era of confrontation between labor and management. When the Baltimore and Ohio Railroad cut wages by 20 percent, a crew in Martinsburg, West Virginia, seized the local depot and blocked the line. Local militiamen refused to clear the

In this painting by Robert Koehler, entitled *The Strike* (1886), labor confronts management in a strike that may soon turn bloody. One worker reaches for a stone as an anxious mother and her children look on. Barely visible on the desolate horizon is a smoke-enshrouded factory.

tracks. The strikers, after all, were their friends and neighbors. President Rutherford Hayes sent federal troops to enforce a court order ending the strike, but instead two-thirds of the nation's tracks were shut down in sympathy. The novel tactic suggested a growing sense of solidarity among workers. Almost overnight, the country ground to a halt.

When owners brought in strikebreakers, striking workers torched rail yards, smashed engines and cars, and tore up track. In St. Louis a workers' government ran the city for 2 days. Local police, state militia, and federal troops finally quashed the strike after 12 bloody days. Sympathy strikes in factories and coal mines lasted through the summer. In its wake, the "Great Railroad Strike" of 1877 left 100 people dead and more than $10 million worth of railroad property in rubble. It signaled the rising power and unity of labor and sparked fears, as one newspaper warned, that "this may be the beginning of a great civil war in this country, between labor and captial."

Tension between labor and capital exploded in the "Great Upheaval"—a series of strikes, boycotts, and rallies in 1886. One of the most violent episodes occurred at Haymarket Square in Chicago. A group of anarchists was protesting the recent killing of workers by police at the McCormick Harvester Company. As rain drenched the small crowd, police ordered everyone out of the square. Suddenly a bomb exploded. One officer was killed; 6 others were mortally wounded. When police opened fire, the crowd fired back. Nearly 70 policemen were injured, and at least 4 civilians died.

Haymarket Square riot

Conservatives charged that radicals were responsible for the "Haymarket Massacre." Ordinary citizens who had supported labor grew fearful of what a newspaper editorial called its "Samson-like power." Though the bomb thrower was never identified, the courts found eight anarchists guilty of conspiracy to murder. Seven were sentenced to death. Cities enlarged their police forces, and states built more National Guard armories on the borders of working-class neighborhoods.

Management Strikes Again

The strikes, rallies, and boycotts of 1886 were followed by a second surge of labor activism in 1892. In the remote silver mines of Coeur d'Alene, Idaho, at the Carnegie steel mill in Homestead, Pennsylvania, in the coal mines near Tracy City, Tennessee, strikes flared, only to be crushed by management. Often state and federal troops joined company guards and private detectives from the Pinkerton agency to fight workers.

Pullman strike

The broadest confrontation between labor and management took place two years later. A terrible depression had shaken the economy for almost a year when George Pullman, owner of the Palace Car factory and inventor of the plush railroad car, laid off workers, cut wages (but kept rents high on company-owned housing), and refused to discuss grievances. In 1894 workers struck and managed to convince the new American Railway Union (ARU) to support them by boycotting all trains that used Pullman cars. Quickly the strike spread to 27 states and territories.

Anxious railroad owners appealed to President Grover Cleveland for federal help. On the slim pretext that the strike obstructed mail delivery (strikers had actually been willing to handle mail trains without Pullman cars), Cleveland secured a court order halting the strike. He then called several thousand special deputies into Chicago to enforce it. In the rioting that followed, 12 people died and scores were arrested. But the strike was put down.

Government troops were often called in to help management quell strikes. In the Pullman Strike of 1894, U.S. Regulars "give the butt" to angry laborers in this drawing by Frederick Remington.

"GIVING THE BUTT"—THE WAY THE "REGULAR" INFANTRY TACKLES A MOB.

In all labor disputes the central issue was the power to shape the new industrial systems. Employers always enjoyed the advantage. They hired and fired workers, set the terms of employment, and ruled the workplace. They fought unions with "yellow dog" contracts that forced workers to refuse to join. Blacklists circulated the names of labor agitators. Lockouts kept protesting workers from plants, and company spies infiltrated their organizations. With a growing pool of labor, employers could replace strikers and break strikes. As the railroad mogul and financier Jay Gould once remarked, "I can hire one half the working class to kill the other half." *Management weapons*

Management could also count on local, state, and federal authorities for troops to break strikes. In addition, businesses used a powerful new legal weapon, the injunction. These court orders prohibited certain actions, including strikes, by barring workers from interfering with their employer's business. It was just such an order that had brought federal deputies into the Pullman strike and put Eugene Debs, head of the American Railway Union, behind bars. The Indiana-born Debs, a former locomotive fireman and early labor organizer, received a six-month jail sentence for violating the court injunction. When the Supreme Court upheld the sentence in *In re Debs* (1895), it legalized the use of the federal injunction against strikers. The broken strike, Debs said bitterly, was "an exhibition of the debauching power of money." After his release, he abandoned the Democratic party to become the foremost Socialist leader in America. Meanwhile, despite the protests of workers like Debs, employers had become masters of the mightiest industrial economy on earth.

In a matter of only 30 or 40 years, the new industrial order transformed the landscape of America. Whether rich or poor, worker, entrepreneur, or industrial baron, Americans were being drawn closer by the new industrial systems. Ore scooped from Mesabi might end up in a steel girder on James Eads's Mississippi bridge, in a steel needle for Sadie Frowne's sewing machine in Brooklyn, or in a McCormick reaper slicing across the Nebraska plains. When a textile worker in Massachusetts struck, a family in Alabama might well pay more for clothes. A man in Cleveland now set his watch to agree with the time of a man in New York, regardless of the position of the sun.

Such changes might seem effortless to someone like T. S. Hudson, scampering across the rails of America in 1882. But as the nineteenth century drew to a close, material progress went hand in hand with social pain and upheaval.

CHAPTER SUMMARY

In the last third of the nineteenth century a new industrial order reshaped America. New industrial systems—of resource development, technology, invention, transportation, communication, finance, corporate management, and labor—boosted economic growth and industrial productivity. Businesses grew big, expanding vertically and horizontally in an effort to curb costs and competition. New business consolidations, such as trusts and holding companies, gave managers unparalleled control.

The costs were high. The power of business to exploit workers and befoul the environment grew. The number of those in control shrank. The gulf between rich and poor seemed to widen, and the economy endured a vicious cycle of boom and bust. Workers found themselves reduced to cogs in the new industrial system, with less independence and satisfaction from their jobs. They struggled to maintain their dignity and regain control, whether through slowdowns, absenteeism, quitting, unionizing, or striking. All too frequently, violence erupted as managers and workers fought to control the new industrial order.

Yet the overall gains for the economy were undeniable. On average, real wages rose for laborers, and Samuel Gompers agreed that "the social conditions of the working people have improved very materially within the past 35 years." At the end of the Civil War the United States had been fourth in the world in industrial production. By the mid-1890s the value of American manufactured goods nearly totaled those of France, Britain, and Germany combined, and by 1900 America ranked first among all industrial nations. With deeply mixed feelings, Americans tried to adjust.

SIGNIFICANT EVENTS

1859	First oil well drilled near Titusville, Pennsylvania
1866	National Labor Union founded
1869	Knights of Labor created
1870	John D. Rockefeller incorporates Standard Oil Company of Ohio
1873	Carnegie Steel Company founded; Panic of 1873
1874	Massachusetts enacts first 10-hour workday law for women
1876	Alexander Graham Bell invents telephone
1877	Railroad wage cuts lead to violent strikes; Thomas Edison invents phonograph
1879	Edison develops incandescent light bulb; Henry George's *Progress and Poverty* published
1882	Rockefeller's Standard Oil Company becomes nation's first trust; Thomas Edison's electric company begins lighting New York City
1883	Railroads establish standard time zones
1886	American Federation of Labor organized; Haymarket Square bombing
1892	Homestead Steel strike
1893	Panic of 1893
1894	Pullman strike
1901	U.S. Steel Corporation becomes nation's first billion-dollar company

ADDITIONAL READING

For a useful introduction to the period, see Edward C. Kirland, *Industry Comes of Age: Business, Labor, and Public Policy, 1860–1897* (1967). Mechanization and its impact are the focus of Siegfried Giedion's classic *Mechanization Takes Command* (1948). The best overview of American labor is American Social History Project, *Who Built America? Working People and the Nation's Economy, Politics, Culture, & Society*, Volume Two: *From the Gilded Age to the Present* (1992). Herbert Gutman's

Work, Culture and Society in Industrializing America: Essays in American Working-Class History (1976) explores the development of working-class communities in the nineteenth century, especially the role of ethnicity in creating a working-class culture. David Montgomery offers a broad look at the impact of industrialization on American labor in *The Fall of the House of Labor: The Workplace, the State, and American Labor Activism, 1865–1925* (1987), while Leon Fink's *Workingmen's Democracy: The Knights of Labor and American Politics* (1983) examines early efforts of the Knights of Labor to challenge corporate capitalism by organizing workers and socializing them into a labor culture. Alice Kessler-Harris, *Out to Work: A History of Wage-Earning Women in the United States* (1982) surveys female wage earners and their effect on American culture, family life, and values.

No book did more to set the idea of big businessmen as ruthless "robber barons" than Matthew Josephson's *The Robber Barons: The Great American Capitalists, 1861–1901* (1934). An early revision of this bleak image can be found in Allan Nevins's biography of John D. Rockefeller, *A Study in Power: John D. Rockefeller, Industrialist and Philanthropist*, 2 vols. (1953). Business historian Alfred D. Chandler, Jr.'s *Strategy and Structure: Chapters in the History of American Industrial Enterprise* (1962) and *The Visible Hand: The Managerial Revolution in American Business* (1977) are seminal accounts of business organization and management that stress the adaptations of business structures and the emergence of a new class of managers. For a comparative view of the rise of big business in the United States, Great Britain, and Germany, see his *Scale and Scope* (1988). For a fuller list of readings, see the Bibliography.

19

The Rise of an Urban Order

raziano's bootblack stand was jammed with people milling about, looking for help. Above the crowd, enthroned like an Irish king, sat George Washington Plunkitt, ward boss of Manhattan's Fifteenth Assembly District. Doing what he could to help, Plunkitt asked little in return, only votes on election day.

Plunkitt understood the close relationship between help and votes. "There's got to be in every ward," another boss explained, "somebody that any bloke can come to—no matter what he's done—and get help. *Help, you understand; none of your law and justice, but help.*" The reverse was also true: to maintain power, bosses like Plunkitt had to be able to count on the political support of those they helped. For years Plunkitt had been a leader of Tammany Hall, the Democratic party organization that ruled New York City politics from 1850 to 1930. Like other political machines in cities across America, the Hall maintained its power by helping and, if necessary, by knocking heads.

A boss at work

Much of Plunkitt's daily routine was taken up with helping. One typical day began when a bartender roused him at two in the morning to get a friend out of jail. Plunkitt succeeded but didn't return to bed until after three. Howling fire sirens woke him at six. Before dawn he was assisting burned-out tenants with food, clothing, and shelter. By eleven he was home, where four out-of-work men were waiting for help. Within hours each had a job. A quick bite of lunch and it was off again, this time to a pair of funerals. Plunkitt brought flowers for the bereaved and offered condolences, all in full view of the assembled. From there he rushed to attend a "Hebrew confirmation." Early evening found him at district headquarters, helping his election captains plot ways of "turning out the vote."

From there, Plunkitt dashed off to a church fair. Then it was back to the party clubhouse. He helped some local teams by buying tickets for their next game. Before leaving, he pledged to two dozen pushcart peddlers that he would try to stop the police from harassing them. He arrived at a wedding reception at half past ten (already having helped the bride and groom with "a handsome wedding present"). Finally, at midnight, he crawled into bed, after a day of helping all he could.

Such relentless effort helped Plunkitt as well. Born poor to Irish immigrants in a Manhattan shantytown called "Nanny Goat Hill," he died a millionaire in 1924 at the age of 82. His pluck and practicality would have made him the envy of any industrialist. Like the Carnegies and Rockefellers, fierce ambition fueled his rise from

Realist painters like George Bellows, who were scorned by critics as the "Ashcan School,"
captured the grittiness and vibrancy of teeming urban life. Cliff Dwellers *makes dramatic use*
of light and dark, relying on line, mass, and color to achieve its naturalism.

butcher boy to political boss. City politics was his way out of the slums in a world that
favored the rich, the educated, and the well-established.

In the late nineteenth century the needs of rapidly growing cities gave political
bosses like George Washington Plunkitt their chance. "I seen my opportunities and I
took 'em," Plunkitt used to say. Every city contract and bond issue, every tax assessment, every charter for a new business offered Plunkitt and his cronies an opportunity to line their pockets. Money made from inside knowledge of city projects was
known as "boodle" or honest graft. ("Black" graft came from vice and extortion.) How   *Boodle*
much boodle bosses collected depended on how well their organization managed to
elect sympathetic officials. That explained why Plunkitt spent so much time helping
his constituents.

Plunkitt's New York was the first great city in history to be ruled by men of the
people in an organized and continuing way. Bosses and their henchmen came from

the streets and saloons, the slums and tenements, the firehouses and funeral homes. Many of their families had only recently arrived in America. While the Irish of Tammany Hall ran New York, Germans governed St. Louis, Scandinavians Minneapolis, and Jews San Francisco.

In an earlier age political leadership had been drawn from the ranks of the wealthy and native-born. America had been an agrarian republic where personal relationships were grounded in small communities. By the late nineteenth century, the country was in the midst of an urban explosion. Cities of unparalleled size and diversity were transforming American life. They lured people from all over the globe, created tensions between natives and newcomers, reshaped the social order. For Plunkitt, as for so many Americans, a new urban age was dawning. The golden door of opportunity opened onto the city.

A NEW URBAN AGE

The modern city was the product of industrialization. Cities contained the great investment banks, the smoky mills and dingy sweatshops, the spreading railroad yards, the grimy tenements and sparkling mansions, the new department stores and skyscrapers. People came from places as near as the countryside and as far as Italy, Russia, and Armenia. By the end of the nineteenth century America had entered a new urban age, with tens of millions of "urbanites," an urban landscape, and a growing urban culture.

The Urban Explosion

During the 50 years after the Civil War, the population of the United States quadrupled—from 23 million to 92 million. Yet the number of people living in American cities increased nearly sevenfold. In 1860, only one American in six lived in a city with a population of 8000 or more; in 1900, one in three did. By 1910 nearly half the nation lived in cities large and small.

Cities grew in every region of the country, some faster than others. In the Northeast and upper Midwest early industrialization created more cities than in the West and the South, although those regions contained big cities as well. Atlanta, Nashville, and later Dallas and Houston boomed under the influence of railroads. Los Angeles had barely 6000 people in 1870. By 1900 it trailed only San Francisco among large cities on the Pacific coast, with a population of 100,000.

Large urban centers dominated whole regions and tied the country together in a complex urban network. New York, the nation's banker, printer, and chief marketplace, ruled the East. Smaller cities operated within narrower spheres of influence and often specialized. Milwaukee was famous for its beer, Tulsa for oil, and Hershey, Pennsylvania, for chocolate.

Cities' relations to regions around them   Cities even shaped the natural environment hundreds of miles beyond their limits. Chicago became not only the gateway to the West but a powerful agent of ecological change. As its lines of commerce and industry radiated outward, the city transformed the ecosystems of the West. Wheat to feed Chicago's millions replaced sheltering prairie grasses. Great stands of white pine in Wisconsin vanished, only to reappear in the furniture and frames of Chicago houses or as fence rails shipped to prairie farms. Yet for all its power, even Chicago had to contend with the limits imposed by nature. Built on low prairie flats, Chicago suffered from poor drainage and chronic flooding. Citizens were forced literally to raise the city with pilings and landfills 7 to 12 feet above the prairie.

The Great Global Migration

Between 1820 and 1920, some 60 million people left farms and villages for cities across the globe. Mushrooming population gave them a powerful push. In Europe the end of the Napoleonic Wars in 1815 launched a cycle of baby booms that continued at 20-year intervals for the rest of the century. Improved diet and sanitation, aided by Louis Pasteur's discovery that bacteria cause infection and disease, reduced deaths. Meanwhile machinery cut the need for farm workers. In 1896 one man in a wheat field could do what had taken 18 men just 60 years earlier.

Surplus farm workers formed a ragtag army of migrants both in America and in Europe. The prospect of factory work for better pay and fewer hours especially lured the young to cities. In America, young farm women spearheaded the migration. Mechanization and the rise of commercial agriculture made them less valuable in the fields, while mass-produced goods from mail-order houses made them less useful at home.

IMMIGRATION AND POPULATION, 1860–1920
Between 1860 and 1920, immigration increased dramatically as the sources of immigrants shifted from northern Europe to southeastern Europe. Despite fears to the contrary, the proportion of newcomers as a percentage of population increases did not show nearly the same jump.

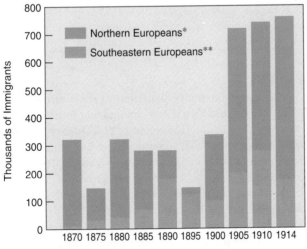

*Includes immigrants from Great Britain, Ireland, Germany, and the Scandinavian countries.

**Includes immigrants from Poland, Russia, Italy, and other Baltic and East European countries.

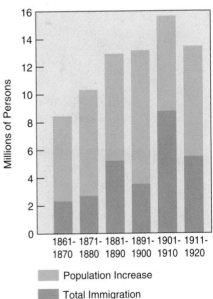

THE GREAT FEAR OF THE PERIOD
THAT UNCLE SAM MAY BE SWALLOWED BY FOREIGNERS.

By the 1890s, European immigrants were arriving at the new receiving center on Ellis Island in New York harbor (left). Asian immigrants came through Angel Island in San Francisco Bay (right). On both coasts, physical examinations, like the eye inspections shown, became part of standard screening practices as immigration policies stiffened. The rapid rise in immigration ignited nativist fears that immigrants were taking over the country. In the 1870s cartoon, immigrants literally gobble up Uncle Sam.

The "new" immigration

Earlier in the century, European immigrants had come to the United States from northern and western Europe. In the 1880s, "new" immigrants from southern and eastern Europe began to arrive. Some, like Russian and Polish Jews, were fleeing religious and political persecution. Others left to evade famine or diseases such as cholera, which swept across southern Italy in 1887. But most came for the same reasons as migrants from the countryside—a job, more money, a fresh start.

Ambitious, hardy, and resourceful, immigrants found themselves tested every step of the way to America. They left behind the comfort of family, friends, and old ways. The price of one-way passage by steamship—about $50 in 1904—was far too expensive for most to bring relatives, at least at first. And the trip was dangerous even before immigrants stepped on board a ship. They traveled for weeks, stealing across heavily guarded borders, just to reach a port like Le Havre in France. At dockside, shipping lines vaccinated, disinfected, and examined them to ensure against their being returned at company expense.

It took from one to two weeks to cross the Atlantic aboard steam-powered ships. Immigrants spent most of the time below decks in cramped, filthy compartments called "steerage." One passenger described the journey as "a kind of hell that cleanses a man of his sins before coming to the land of Columbus." Most arrived at New York's Castle Garden or the newer facility on nearby Ellis Island, opened in 1892. Immigrants who crossed the Pacific were processed at Angel Island in San Francisco Bay. Sometimes they were held in the facility for weeks. As one Chinese newcomer gazed out on San Francisco Bay, he scribbled a poem on the gray walls:

> Why do I have to languish in this jail?
> It is because my country is weak and my family poor.
> My parents wait in vain for news;
> My wife and child, wrapped in their quilt, sigh with loneliness.

Immigrants had to pass another medical examination at these facilities, have their names recorded by customs officials, and pay an entry tax. At any point, they could be detained or shipped home.

Immigrants arrived in staggering numbers—over 6 million between 1877 and 1890, some 30 million by 1920. By 1900 they made up nearly 15 percent of the population. Most were young, between the ages of 15 and 40. Few spoke English or had skills or much education. Unlike earlier arrivals, who were mostly Protestant, these new immigrants worshiped in Catholic, Greek, or Russian Orthodox churches and Jewish synagogues. Almost two-thirds were men. A large number came to make money for buying land or starting businesses back home. Some changed their minds and sent for relatives, but those returning were common enough to be labeled "birds of passage." *Immigrant profile*

Jews were an exception. Russian Jews escaped from Europe by the tens of thousands after the assassination of Czar Alexander II in 1881 rekindled anti-Semitic "pogroms," or riots. Between 1880 and 1914, a third of eastern Europe's Jews left. They made up 10 percent of all immigration to the United States during those years. Almost all stayed and brought their families, often one by one. They had few choices. As one Jewish immigrant wrote of his Russian homeland, "Am I not despised? Am I not urged to leave? . . . Do I not rise daily with the fear lest the hungry mob attack me?"

The Shape of the City

In colonial days, Benjamin Franklin could walk from one end of Boston to the other in an hour. Only Franklin's adopted home, Philadelphia, spilled into suburbs. Over the years these colonial "walking cities" developed ringed patterns of settlement. Merchants, professionals, and the upper classes lived near their shops and offices in the city center. As one walked outward, the income and status of the residents gradually declined.

Cities of the late nineteenth century still exhibited this ringed pattern, except that industrialization had reversed the order of settlement and increased urban sprawl. As the middle and upper classes moved out of a growing industrial core, the poor, some immigrants, African Americans, and lower-class laborers filled the void. They took over old factories and brownstones, shanties and cellars. By sheer weight of numbers they transformed these areas into the slums of the central city. *Patterns of settlement*

Curled around the slums was the "zone of emergence," an income-graded band of those on their way up. It contained second-generation city dwellers, factory workers, skilled laborers, and professional mechanics. They lived in progressively better tenements and neater row houses as the distance from center city increased. Poverty no longer imprisoned them, but they could still slip back in hard times.

Farther out was the suburban fringe, home to the new class of white-collar managers and executives. They lived in larger houses with individual lots on neat, tree-lined streets. The very wealthy still maintained mansions on fashionable city avenues, but by the 1870s and 1880s, they too began to keep suburban homes.

Urban Transport

For all their differences, the circles of settlement held together as a part of a massive and interdependent whole. One reason was an evolving system of urban transporta-

GROWTH OF NEW ORLEANS TO 1900
Streetcars helped cities spread beyond business districts while still functioning as organic wholes. By 1900, streetcar lines in New Orleans reached all the way to Audubon Park and Tulane University, bringing these once distant points within the reach of city dwellers and creating "streetcar suburbs."

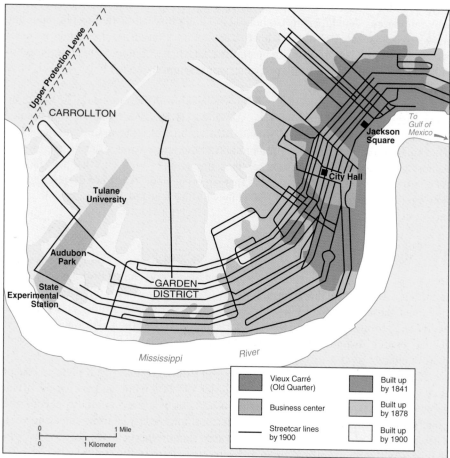

tion. By the mid-nineteenth century horse-drawn railways were conveying some 35 million people a year in New York. Still, the problems were legendary: so slow, a person could walk faster; so dirty, tons of horse manure were left daily in the streets; so crowded, according to Mark Twain, you "had to hang on by your eyelashes and your toenails."

Civic leaders came to understand that the modern city could not survive, much less grow, without improved transportation. San Francisco installed trolley cars pulled by steam-driven cables. It worked so well in San Francisco that Chicago, Seattle, and other hilly cities installed cable systems in the 1880s. Other cities experimented with elevated trestles to carry steam locomotives or cable lines high above crowded streets. But none of the breakthroughs quite did the trick. Cables remained slow and unreliable; the elevated railways, or "els," were dirty, ugly, and noisy.

Electricity rescued city travelers. In 1888 Frank Julian Sprague, a naval engineer who had once worked for Thomas Edison, installed the first electric trolley line in Richmond, Virginia. Electrified streetcars were soon speeding along at 12 miles an hour, twice as fast as horses. By 1902 electricity drove nearly all city railways. Sprague's innovations also meant that "subways" could be built without having to worry about tunnels filled with a steam engine's smoke and soot. Between 1895 and 1897 Boston built the first underground electric line. New York followed in 1904 with a subway that ran from City Hall on the southern tip of Manhattan north to Harlem. Once considered too far afield, Harlem soon became dotted with new apartment and tenement developments. When the white middle class of New York refused to move so far uptown, Philip A. Peyton convinced landlords to allow his Afro-American Realty Company to handle the properties. Within a decade Harlem had become the black capital of America.

Role of electricity

The rich had long been able to keep homes outside city limits, traveling to and fro in private carriages. New systems of mass transit freed the middle class and even the poor to live miles from work. For a nickel or two, anyone could ride from central shopping and business districts to the suburban fringes and back. A network of moving vehicles held the segmented and sprawling city together and widened its reach out to "streetcar suburbs."

Bridges and Skyscrapers

Since cities often grew along rivers and harbors, their separate parts sometimes had to be joined over water. The principles of building large river bridges had already been worked out by the railroads. It remained for a German immigrant and his son, John and Washington Roebling, to make the bridge a symbol of urban growth.

The Brooklyn Bridge, linking New York City with Brooklyn, took 13 years to complete. It cost $15 million and 20 lives, including that of designer John. When it opened in 1883, it stretched more than a mile across the East River, with passage broad enough for a footpath, two double carriage lanes, and two railroad lines. Its arches were cut like giant cathedral windows, and its supporting cables hung, said an awestruck observer, "like divine messages from above." Soon other suspension bridges were spanning the railroad yards in St. Louis and the bay at Galveston, Texas.

Brooklyn Bridge

Even as late as 1880 church steeples dominated the urban landscape. They towered over squat factories and office buildings. But growing congestion and the increasing value of land pushed architects to search for ways to make buildings taller.

In place of thick walls of brick that restricted factory floor space, builders used cast iron columns. The new "cloudscrapers" were strong, durable, and fire-resistant. Their open floors were ideal for warehouses and also for office buildings and department stores.

Steel, tougher in tension and compression, turned cloudscrapers into skyscrapers. William LeBaron Jenney first used steel in his 10-story Home Insurance Building (1885) in Chicago. By the end of the century steel frames and girders raised buildings to 30 stories or more. New York City's triangular Flatiron building (at left) used the new technology to project an angular yet remarkably delicate elegance. In Chicago, Daniel Burnham's Reliance Building (1890) relied so heavily on new plate glass windows that contemporaries called it "a glass tower fifteen stories high."

It was no accident that many of the new skyscrapers arose in Chicago, for the city had burned nearly to the ground in 1871. The "Chicago school" of architects helped rebuild it. The young maverick Louis H. Sullivan promised a new urban profile in which the skyscraper would be "every inch a proud and soaring thing." In the Wainwright Building (1890) in St. Louis and the Carson, Pirie, and Scott department store (1889–1904) in Chicago, Sullivan produced towering structures that symbolized the modern industrial city.

For a building to be a "soaring thing" and remain habitable required solutions to some practical problems. Fireplaces still provided most indoor warmth, but heating with a fireplace in each of hundreds of rooms was costly. A more efficient system of steam or hot water circulating through pipes came into use in the 1870s. When William Baldwin finally perfected the "radiator" in 1874, high-rise buildings became year-round dwellings. To move people to the top of tall buildings, Elisha Graves Otis developed a reliable elevator in 1861. By the 1890s faster electric elevators were whisking passengers into the clouds.

Slum and Tenement

Far below the skyscrapers lay the slums and tenements of the inner city. In cramped rooms and sun-less hallways, along narrow alleys and in flooded basements lived the city poor. They often worked there, too, in "sweaters' shops" where as many as 18 people labored and slept in foul two-room flats.

In New York, whose slums were the nation's worst, almost half the city's population—some 500,000 people—lived in such squalor by the mid-1870s. Slumlords charged rents 25 to 35 percent higher per square foot than in fashionable sections of town. Crime thrived in places called "Bandit's Roost" and "Hell's Kitchen." Bands of young toughs with names like the "Sewer Rats" and the "Rock Gang" stalked the streets in search of thrills and easy money.

Perils of the slum neighborhood

Gambling, prostitution, and alcoholism all claimed their victims most readily in the slums. Some 50,000 unlicensed "blind pigs" and kitchen bars sprang up in slum after slum. In New York City alone, the estimated number of prostitutes quadrupled between 1870 and 1890. Not a few of them walked the streets of city slums. The poor usually turned to such crime in despair. A 20-year-old prostitute supporting a sickly mother and four brothers and sisters made no apologies: "Let God Almighty judge who's to blame most, I that was driven, or them that drove me to the pass I'm in."

The poor diets of slum dwellers left them vulnerable to disease, but it was their close quarters and often filthy surroundings that raised their rates of infection to epidemic levels. Until the 1860s pigs, sheep, and other animals roamed freely in the streets of New York. Tons of manure from horse-drawn carriages and railways covered city streets, furnishing a fertile habitat for deadly microbes. Life indoors was no more sanitary than out. Among the conditions noted in New York tenements by city health inspectors were dirt-filled sinks, stairwells oozing with slop, children urinating on walls, and plumbing pipes leaking gases so noxious that they were flammable.

Tightly packed tenements and streets piled high with refuse were also breeding grounds for microbes. Cholera, typhoid, and an outbreak of yellow fever in Memphis in the 1870s killed tens of thousands. Tuberculosis was deadlier still. As late as 1900, among infectious diseases it ranked only behind influenza and pneumonia *combined* as a killer. Slum children—all city children—were most vulnerable. Almost a quarter of children born in American cities in 1890 never lived to see their first birthday.

The installation of new sewage and water purification systems helped. The modern flush toilet came into use only after the turn of the century. Until then people relied on water closets and communal privies. Some catered to as many as 800. All too often cities dumped waste into old private vaults or rivers used for drinking water. In 1881 an exasperated mayor of Cleveland called the Cuyahoga River "an open sewer through the center of the city."

Slum housing was often more dangerous than the water. The tubercle bacillus flourished in musty, windowless tenements. In 1879 New York enacted a new housing law requiring a window in all bedrooms of new tenements. Architect James E. Ware won a competition with a creative design that contained an indentation on both sides of the building. When two tenements abutted each other, the indentations formed a narrow shaft for air and light. From above, the buildings looked like giant dumbbells. Up to 16 families lived on a floor, with only two toilets in the hall.

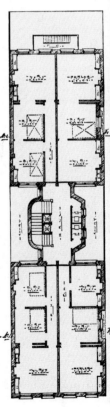

"Dumbbell" tenements were designed to use every inch of available space in the standard 25-by-200-foot city lot while providing ventilation and reducing the spread of disease.

Originally hailed as an innovation, Ware's dumbbell tenement spread over such cities as Cleveland, Cincinnati, and Boston "like a scab," said an unhappy reformer. Ordinary blocks contained 10 such tenements and housed as many as 4000 people. The airshafts became giant silos for trash. They blocked what little light had entered and, worse still, carried fires from one story to the next. When the New York housing commission met in 1900, it concluded conditions were worse than when reformers had started 33 years earlier.

RUNNING AND REFORMING THE CITY

Every new arrival to the city brought dreams and altogether too many needs. Schools and houses had to be built, streets paved, garbage collected, sewers dug, fires fought, utility lines laid. Running the city became a full-time job, and a new breed of professional politician rose to the task. So, too, did a new breed of reformer, determined to help the needy cope with the ravages of urban life.

The Weaknesses of City Government

Those running the new industrial cities struggled to develop a more efficient way to govern their diverse populations. Many city charters dating from the eighteenth century included a cumbersome system of checks and balances. Mayors vetoed city councils; councils ignored mayors. Jealous state legislatures allowed cities only the most limited and unpopular taxes, such as those on property.

But to the cities more than the states fell responsibility for providing services. Municipal government grew into a tangle of little governments—fragmented, scattered, at odds with one another. By 1890, Chicago had 11 branches of government. Each was a tiny kingdom with its own regulations and taxing authority.

Just as such decentralization paralyzed city governments, the traditional sources of political leadership evaporated. The middle and upper classes were being drawn into business and moving to the suburbs. They lost interest in governing the city (though not in how the city was governed). As immigrants and rural newcomers flocked to factories and tenements, the structures of urban government strained to adapt.

Boss Rule

"Why must there be a boss," journalist Lincoln Steffens asked Boss Richard Croker of New York, "when we've got a mayor—and a city council?" "That's why," Croker broke in. "It's because we've got a mayor and a council and judges—*and*—a hundred other men to deal with." The boss was right. He and his system furnished cities with the centralization, authority, and services they sorely needed.

Bosses ruled through the political machine. Often, like New York's Tammany Hall, machines dated back to the late eighteenth and early nineteenth centuries. They began as fraternal and charitable organizations. Over the years they became centers of political power. In New York the machine was Democratic; in Philadelphia,

Republican. Some were less centralized, as in Chicago; some less ethnically mixed, like Detroit. Machines could be found even in rural areas. In Duval County, Texas, for instance, the Spanish-speaking Anglo boss Archie Parr molded a powerful alliance with Mexican American landowners.

In an age of enterprise, the political machine operated similarly to a corporation. *The boss as* Like a corporate executive, the boss looked on politics as a business. His office might *entrepreneur* be a saloon, a funeral home, or, like George Washington Plunkitt, a shoeshine stand. His managers were party activists, connected in a corporate-style chain of command. Local committeemen reported to district captains, captains to district leaders, district leaders to the boss or bosses who directed the machine. And like a business entrepreneur, the boss wanted to absorb the competition or destroy it.

The stock in trade of the machine was simple: a Christmas turkey, a load of coal for the winter, jobs for the unemployed, English language classes for the recently arrived. Bosses sponsored fun, too—sports teams, glee clubs, balls and barbecues with bands playing and drink flowing. "You can't do nothin' with the people unless you do somethin' for 'em," one boss concluded. This system, rough and uneven as it was, *A crude* served as a form of public welfare at a time when private charity could not cope with *welfare* the crush of demands. To the unskilled, the boss doled out jobs in public construc- *system* tion. For bright, ambitious young men, he had places in city offices or in the party. These represented the first steps into the middle class.

This stereotyped depiction of the "party boss" as a larger-than-life thug has him handing out "special privilege" and "immunity from arrest," among other gifts. Cartoons like this one could be powerful weapons. The political cartoons of Thomas Nast, which appeared in the *New York Times,* especially angered Boss William Tweed. His supporters might not have been able to read, but they surely could understand pictures. Tweed offered Nast $100,000 to "study art" in Europe. Nast refused the bribe.

In return, citizens were expected to show their gratitude at the ballot box. Sometimes the grateful were not enough, so bosses turned elsewhere. "Little Bob" Davies of Jersey City was adept at mobilizing the "graveyard vote." He drew names from tombstones to pad lists of registered voters and hired "repeaters" to vote under the phony names. When reformers introduced the Australian (secret) ballot in the 1880s to prevent fraud, bosses pulled the "Tasmanian dodge" by premarking election tickets. Failing that, they dumped whole ballot boxes into the river or drove unpersuaded voters from the polls with hired thugs.

Rewards, Costs, and Accomplishments

Boss William Tweed

Why did bosses go to such lengths? Some simply loved the game of politics. More often bosses loved money. Their ability to get it was limited only by their ingenuity or the occasional success of reform. The record for brassiness must go to Boss William Tweed. During his reign in the 1860s and 1870s, Tweed swindled the city of New York out of a fortune. His masterpiece was a chunky three-story courthouse in lower Manhattan originally budgeted at $250,000. When Tweed was through, the city had spent more than $13 million—and the building was still not finished! Tweed died in prison, but with such profits to be made, it was small wonder that bosses rivaled the pharaohs of Egypt as builders.

In their fashion bosses played a vital role in the industrial city. Rising from the bottom ranks, they guided immigrants into American life and helped some of the underprivileged up from poverty. They changed the urban landscape with massive construction programs and modernized city government by uniting it and making it perform. Choosing the aldermen, municipal judges, mayors, and administrative officials, bosses exerted new control to provide the contracts and franchises to run cities. Such accomplishments fostered the notion that government could be called on to help the needy. The welfare state, still decades away, had some of its roots here.

The toll was often outrageous. Inflated taxes, extorted revenue, and unpunished vice and crime were only the obvious costs. A woman whose family enjoyed Plunkitt's Christmas turkey might be widowed by an accident to her husband in a sweatshop kept open by timely bribes. Filthy buildings might claim her children, as corrupt inspectors ignored serious violations. Buying votes and selling favors, bosses turned democracy into a petty business—as much a "business," said Plunkitt, "as the grocery or dry-goods or the drug business." Yet they were the forerunners of the new breed of full-time, professional politicians who would soon govern the cities and the nation as well.

Nativism and the Social Gospel

Urban blight and the condition of the poor inspired social as well as political activism, especially within churches. Not all of it was positive. The popular Congregationalist minister Josiah Strong concluded that the city was "a menace to society." Along with anxious economists and social workers, he held immigrants responsible for everything from corruption to unemployment and urged restrictions on their entry into the country.

The Sawdust Trail, painted by George Bellows in 1916, depicts one of the revival meetings of William Ashley ("Billy") Sunday in Philadelphia. Sunday, a hard-drinking professional baseball player turned evangelist, began his religious revivals in the 1890s and drew thousands. Here, Sunday leans down from the platform to shake the hand of an admirer. In the foreground, a swooning woman, overcome with a sense of her sins, is carried away.

In the 1880s and 1890s, two depressions sharpened such anxieties. Nativism, a defensive and fearful nationalism, peaked as Americans blamed their economic woes on foreign competition and immigration. New organizations like the Immigration Restriction League attacked Catholics and the foreign-born for subverting democracy, taking jobs, and polarizing society. Already the victims of racial prejudice, the Chinese were an easy target. In 1882 Congress enacted the Chinese Exclusion Act. It banned the entry of Chinese laborers and represented an important step in the drive to restrict immigration. In 1897 the first bill requiring literacy tests for immigrants passed Congress, but President Grover Cleveland vetoed it.

Nativist restrictions

Some clergy took their missions to the slums to bridge the gap between the middle class and the poor. Beginning in 1870 Dwight Lyman Moody, a 300-pound former shoe salesman, joined gospel singer and organist Ira David Sankey to win armies of lowly converts with revivals in Boston, Chicago, and other cities. Evangelists helped to found American branches of the British Young Men's Christian Association and the Salvation Army. By the end of the century the Salvation Army had grown to

647

700 corps staffed by some 3000 officers. They ministered to the needy with food, music, shelter, and simple good fellowship.

The Social Gospel

A small group of ministers rejected the old ethos that weak character explained sin and that society would be perfected only as individual sinners were converted. They spread a new "Social Gospel" that focused on improving the conditions of society in order to save individuals. In *Applied Christianity* (1886), the influential Washington Gladden preached that the church must be responsible for correcting social injustices, including dangerous working conditions and unfair labor practices. Houses of worship, such as William Rainford's St. George's Episcopal Church in New York, became centers of social activity, with boys' clubs, gymnasiums, libraries, glee clubs, and industrial training programs.

The Social Settlement Movement

The settlement house

Church-sponsored programs often repelled the immigrant poor, who saw them as thinly disguised missionary efforts. Immigrants and other slum dwellers were more receptive to a bold experiment called the settlement house. Often situated in the worst slums, these early community centers were run by middle-class women and men to help the poor and foreign-born. At the turn of the century there were more than 100 of them, the most famous being Jane Addams's Hull House in Chicago. When Hull House opened in 1889, it occupied a crumbling mansion on South Halstead Street. Slowly it grew to a dozen buildings over more than a city block. In 1898 the Catholic church sponsored its first settlement house in New York, and in 1900 Bronson House opened its doors to the Latino community in Los Angeles.

High purposes inspired settlement workers. They left comfortable middle-class homes to live in settlement houses and dedicated themselves (like the "early Christians," said one) to service and sacrifice. Teaching immigrants American ways and creating a community spirit would foster "right living through social relations." But immigrants were also urged to preserve their heritages through festivals, parades, and museums. Like political bosses, settlement reformers furnished help, from day nurseries to English language and cooking classes to playgrounds and libraries. Armed with statistics and personal experiences, they also lobbied for social legislation to improve housing, women's working conditions, and public schools.

CITY LIFE

Urban social stratification

City life reflected the stratified nature of American society in the late nineteenth century. Every city had its tenements and slums but also its fashionable avenues for the rich. They constituted barely 1 percent of the population but owned a fourth of all wealth. In between tenement and mansion lived most city dwellers, in neat row houses, in modest "laborers' cottages" and bungalows, in boardinghouses and apartment buildings, and in the homes of others as lodgers. Such families made up the vast and ill-defined middle of urban society—educated professionals, white-collar clerks and salespeople, shopkeepers, corporate managers and executives, public employees, and their families. They composed nearly a third of the population and owned about half the nation's wealth. With more money and more leisure time, their power and influence were growing.

In the impersonal city of the late nineteenth century, class distinctions continued to be based on wealth and income. But no longer were dress and manners enough to distinguish one class from another. Such differences were more often reflected in where people lived, what they bought, which organizations they joined, and how they spent their time.

The Immigrant in the City

When the ship put into port, the first thing an immigrant was likely to see was a city. Perhaps it was Boston or New York or Galveston, Texas, where an overflow of Jewish immigrants was directed after the turn of the century. Enough of the newcomers traveled inland so that by 1900 three-quarters of the residents of Minnesota and Wisconsin and nearly two-thirds in Utah had at least one foreign-born parent.° Most immigrants, exhausted physically and financially, settled in cities.

Cities developed a well-defined mosaic of ethnic communities, since immigrants usually clustered together on the basis of old world villages or provinces. But these neighborhoods were constantly changing. As many as half the residents moved every 10 years, often because they got better-paying jobs or had more family members working. Though one nationality usually dominated a neighborhood, there were always others. Despite popular misconceptions, no other immigrants lived like the Chinese, in urban ghettos of just one ethnic group. Racial prejudice forced the Chinese together, and local ordinances kept them from buying their way out. *Ethnic neighborhoods*

Ethnic communities served as havens from the strangeness of American society and as springboards to a new life. From the moment they stepped off the boat, newcomers felt pressed to learn English, don American clothes, and drop their "greenhorn" ways. Yet in their neighborhoods they also found comrades who spoke their language, theaters that performed their plays and music, restaurants that served their food. Houses of worship were always at the center of neighborhood life, often reflecting the practices of individual towns or provinces.

The *Jewish Daily Forward* and scores of other foreign-language newspapers reported events from the homeland but also gave eager readers profiles of local leaders, advice on voting, and tips on adjusting to America. Immigrant aid societies like the Polish National Alliance and the Society for the Protection of Italian Immigrants furnished fellowship and assistance in the newcomers' own languages. They fostered assimilation by sponsoring baseball teams, insurance programs, libraries, and English classes. *Adapting to America*

Sometimes immigrants combined the old and new in creative adaptations. Italians developed a pidgin dialect called "Italglish." It permitted them to communicate quickly with Americans and to absorb American customs. So the Fourth of July became *"Il Forte Gelato"* (literally "The Great Freeze"), a play on the sound of the words. Other immigrant groups invented similar idioms, like *Chuco*, a dialect that developed among border Mexicans in El Paso.

The backgrounds and cultural values of immigrants often influenced the jobs they took. Because Chinese men did not scorn washing or ironing, more than 7500 of them could be found in San Francisco laundries by 1880. Sewing ladies' garments

---

°Mormons serving as missionaries in Europe and Great Britain especially swelled Utah's population with converts.

seemed unmanly to many native-born Americans but not to Russian and Italian tailors. Slavs tended to be physically robust and valued steady income over education. They worked in the mines for better pay than in factories and pulled their children from school to send them to work.

Family life   On the whole, immigrants married later and had more children than the native-born. Greeks and eastern European Jews prearranged marriages according to tradition. They imported "picture brides," betrothed by mail with a photograph. After marriage men ruled the household, but women managed it. Although child-rearing practices varied, immigrants resisted the relative permissiveness of American parents. Youngsters were expected to contribute like little adults to the welfare of the family.

In these "family economies" of working-class immigrants, key decisions—over whether and whom to marry, over work and education, over when to leave home—were made on the basis of collective rather than individual needs. Though boys were more likely to work outside the home than girls, daughters in immigrant families went to work at an early age so sons could continue their education. It was customary for one daughter to remain unmarried so she could care for younger siblings or aged parents.

Special situation of the Chinese   The Chinese were an exception to the pattern. The ban on the immigration of Chinese laborers in the 1880s (page 647) had frozen the sex ratio of Chinese communities into a curious imbalance. Like other immigrants, most Chinese newcomers had been single men. In the wake of the ban, those in the United States could not bring over their wives and families. Nor by law in 13 states could they marry whites. With few women, Chinese communities suffered from high rates of prostitution, large numbers of gangs and secret societies, and low birth totals. When the San Francisco earthquake and fire destroyed birth records in 1906, resourceful Chinese immigrants created "paper sons" (and less often "paper daughters") by forging American birth certificates and claiming their China-born children as American citizens.

Assimilation   Caught between past and present, immigrants clung to tradition and assimilated slowly. Their children adjusted more quickly. They soon spoke English like natives, married whomever they pleased, and worked their way out of old neighborhoods. Yet the process was not easy. Children faced heartrending clashes with parents and rejection from peers. Sara Smolinsky, the immigrant heroine of Anzia Yezierska's novel

---

Entertainment in immigrant neighborhoods often resulted in a cross-fertilization of cultures. The New Cathay Boys Club Band, a marching band of Chinese Americans (shown here), was formed in San Francisco's Chinatown in 1911. It was inspired by the Columbia Park Boys Band of Italians from nearby North Beach and played American music only.

Bread Givers (1925), broke away from her tyrannical family, only to discover a terrible isolation: "I can't live in the old world and I'm yet too green for the new. I don't belong to those who gave me birth or to those with whom I was educated."

The "new" immigrants: Who came and why?

With so many immigrants coming to America, it is no wonder that historians have disagreed over who came and why. Early historians of immigration focused on those arriving in the United States. These newcomers are depicted as an undifferentiated mass of European peasants, striking out on their own, often poverty-stricken, sometimes persecuted, sometimes eager for opportunity. The march of so many immigrants into American life, these historians argue, both reflected and helped to create the uniqueness of the American experience.

Recent historians have fashioned a broader, more textured rendering of immigration by looking beyond the borders of the United States. In an international framework, the United States moves from the center of action to a point on the periphery of an expanding world economy. American immigration becomes part of a global migration driven not so much by individual immigrants as by an international labor market. The American experience is therefore less exceptional and more comparable to that of other "host countries" such as Argentina and Australia. And by examining "sending nations," these historians have underscored the diversity of immigrants and their motives. Landless young men from Italy hoped to return home to buy plots in Italy, while the sons of cattle farmers from western Norway left the old world for good because inheritance laws kept them from owning farms at home. Others came not from Europe but from Latin America, Africa, the Caribbean, and Asia. In no case (in contrast to the picture painted by early historians of immigration) could the poverty-stricken even afford to make the journey.

Urban Middle-Class Life

The home as haven and status symbol

Life and leisure for the urban middle class centered on home and family. By the turn of the century just over a third of middle-class urbanites owned their homes. Often two or three stories, made of brick or brownstone, these houses were a measure of their owners' social standing. The plush furniture, heavy drapes, antiques, and curios all signaled status and refinement.

Such homes, usually on their own lots, served as havens to protect and nourish the family. Seventeenth-century notions of children as inherently sinful had given way to more modern theories about the shaping influence of environment. Calm and orderly households with nurturing mothers would launch children on the right course. "A clean, fresh, and well-ordered house," stipulated a domestic adviser in 1883, "exercises over its inmates a moral, no less than physical influence, and has a direct tendency to make members of the family sober, peaceable, and considerate of the feelings and happiness of each other."

Advertisement for scouring soap

The middle-class homemaker

A women was judged by the state of her home. The typical homemaker prepared elaborate meals, cleaned, laundered, and sewed. Each task took time. Baking bread alone required nearly 24 hours, and in 1890, four of five loaves were still made at home. Perhaps 25 percent of urban households had live-in servants to help with the work. They were on call about 100 hours a week, were off just one evening and part of Sunday, and averaged $2 to $5 a week in salary.

By the 1890s a host of new consumer products eased the burdens of housework. Brand names trumpeted a new age of commercially prepared food—Campbell's soup, Quaker oats, Pillsbury flour, Jell-O, and Cracker Jacks, to name a few. New appliances such as "self-working" washers offered mechanical assistance, but shredded shirts and aching arms testified to how far short mechanization still fell.

Toward the end of the century, Saturday became less of a workday and more of a family day. Sunday mornings remained a time for church, still an important center of family life. Afternoons had a more secular flavor. There were shopping trips (city stores often stayed open) and visits to lakes, zoos, and amusement parks (usually built at the end of trolley lines to attract more riders). Outside institutions of all kinds—fraternal organizations, uplift groups, athletic teams, and church groups—were becoming part of middle-class urban family life.

Victorianism and the Pursuit of Virtue

Middle-class life reflected a code of behavior called Victorianism, named for Britain's long-reigning Queen Victoria (1837–1901). It emerged in the 1830s and 1840s as part of an effort to tame the turbulent urban-industrial society developing in Europe.

Victorianism dictated personal conduct based on orderly behavior and disciplined moralism. It stressed sobriety, industriousness, self-control, and sexual modesty and taught that demeanor, particularly proper manners, was the backbone of society. According to its rules, women were "pure vessels," devoid of sexual desire. Their job was to control the "lower natures" of their husbands by withholding sex except for procreation.

Women's fashion mirrored Victorian values. Strenuously laced corsets ("an instrument of torture," one woman called them) pushed breasts up, stomachs in, and rear-ends out. Internal organs pressed unnaturally against one another; ribs occasionally cracked; uteruses sagged. Fainting spells and headaches were all too common. But the resulting wasplike figure accentuated the image of women as child bearers. Ankle-length skirts were draped over bustles, hoops, and petticoats to make hips look larger and suggest fertility. Such elegant dress symbolized wealth, status, and modesty. It also set off middle- and upper-class women from those below, whose plain clothes signaled lives of drudgery and want.

Women's Christian Temperance Union

When some Americans failed to follow Victorian cues in behavior and dress, reformers helped them to pursue virtue. It seemed natural to Francis Willard that women, who cared for the moral and physical well-being of their families, should lead the charge. She resigned her position as dean of women at Northwestern University and in 1874 founded the Women's Christian Temperance Union to combat the ill effects of alcohol. Under her leadership the WCTU worked relentlessly to stamp out alcohol and promote sexual purity but also to reform prisons, end prostitution, and establish woman suffrage. By the turn of the century it was the largest women's organization in the world.

Anthony Comstock crusaded with equal vigor against what he saw as moral pollution, the pollution ranging from pornography and gambling to the use of nude art models. In 1873 President Ulysses S. Grant signed the so-called Comstock Law, a statute banning from the mails all materials "designed to incite lust." Two days later Comstock went to work as a special agent for the Post Office. In his 41-year career, he claimed to have made more than 3000 arrests and destroyed 160 tons of vice-ridden books and photographs.

Comstock Law

Victorian crusaders like Comstock were not simply missionaries of a stuffy morality. They were apostles of a middle-class creed of social control and discipline who responded to growing alcoholism, venereal disease, gambling debts, prostitution, and unwanted pregnancies. No doubt they overreacted in warning that the road to ruin lay behind the door of every saloon, pool hall, or bedroom. Yet the new urban environment did indeed reflect the disorder of a rapidly industrializing society.

The insistence with which moralists warned against "impropriety" suggests that many people did not heed their advice. Three-quarters of women surveyed toward the turn of the century reported that they enjoyed sex. The growing variety of contraceptives—including spermicidal douches, sheaths made of animal intestines, rubber condoms, and forerunners of the diaphragm—testified to the desire for pregnancy-free intercourse. Abortion, too, was prevalent. According to one estimate, a third of all pregnancies were aborted, usually with the aid of a midwife. (By the 1880s abortion had been made illegal in most states, following the lead of the first antiabortion statute in England in 1803.) Despite Victorian marriage manuals, middle-class Americans became more conscious of sexuality as an emotional dimension of a satisfying union.

Challenges to Convention

Bold men and women challenged convention more openly. Victoria Woodhull, publisher of *Woodhull & Claflin's Weekly,* divorced her husband, ran for president in 1872 on the Equal Rights party ticket, and pressed the case for sexual freedom. "I am a free lover!" she shouted to a riotous audience in New York. "I have the inalienable, constitutional, and natural right to love whom I may, to love as long or as short a period as I can, to change that love every day if I please!" Woodhull made a strong public case for sexual freedom. But in private she believed in strict monogamy and romantic love for herself.

Victoria Woodhull

The same cosmopolitan conditions that provided protection for Woodhull's unorthodox beliefs also made possible the growth of self-conscious communities of homosexual men and women. Earlier in the century, Americans had idealized romantic friendships among members of the same sex, without necessarily attributing to them sexual overtones. A Victorian book of manners published in 1860, for example, saw nothing wrong with female friends holding hands, kissing, and caressing, so long as such acts were reserved "for hours of privacy, and never indulged in before gentlemen."

Urban homosexual communities

For friendships with an explicitly sexual dimension, the anonymity of large cities provided new meeting grounds. Single factory workers and clerks, living in furnished rooms rather than with their families in small towns and on farms, were freer to seek others who shared their sexual orientation. Homosexual men and women began forming social networks: on the streets where they regularly met or at specific restaurants and clubs, which, to avoid controversy, sometimes passed themselves off as athletic associations or chess clubs. Such places could be found in New York City's Bowery, around the Presidio military base in San Francisco, and at Lafayette Square in Washington, D.C.

Only toward the end of the century did physicians begin to remark upon the new subcultures, and then primarily to condemn homosexual behavior as a disease or an inherited infirmity. (Indeed, not until the turn of the century did the term *homosexual* come into existence.) Certainly homosexual love itself was not new. But for the first time in the United States, the conditions of urban life allowed gay men and lesbians to define themselves in terms of a larger, self-conscious community, even if they were stoutly condemned by the prevailing Victorian morality.

CITY CULTURE

"We cannot all live in cities," reformer Horace Greeley lamented just after the Civil War, "yet nearly all seemed determined to do so. . . ." Economic opportunity drew people to the teeming industrial city. But so, too, did a vibrant urban culture, boasting temples of entertainment, electrified trolleys and lights, the best schools, stores and restaurants, the biggest newspapers, and virtually every museum, library, art gallery, bookshop, and orchestra in America. In the beckoning cities of the late nineteenth century, Americans sought to realize their dreams of success.

Public Education in an Urban Industrial World

For those in the bottom and middle ranks, one path to success in the industrial city lay in public education. Although the campaign for public education began in the Jacksonian era, it did not make real headway until after the Civil War, when industrial cities began to mushroom and business sought more educated workers. As late as 1870 half the children in the country received no formal education at all, and one American in five could not read.

Between 1870 and 1900, an educational awakening occurred. As more and more businesses required workers who could read, write, and figure sums, attendance in public schools more than doubled. The length of the school term rose from 132 to 144 days. Illiteracy fell by half. At the turn of the century, nearly all the states outside the South had enacted mandatory education laws. Almost three of every four school-age children were enrolled. Even so, the average American adult still attended school for only about five years, and less than 10 percent of those eligible ever went to high school.

The average school day started early, but by noon most girls were released under the assumption that they needed less formal education. Curricula stressed the fundamentals of reading, writing, and arithmetic. Courses in manual training, science, and physical education were added as the demand for technical knowledge grew and opportunities to exercise shrank. Students learned by rote, sitting in silent study with hands clasped or standing erect while they repeated phrases and sums. Few schools encouraged creative thinking. "Don't stop to think," barked a Chicago teacher to a class of terrified youngsters in the 1890s, "tell me what you know!"

Educational reformers in the 1870s pushed elementary schools to include drawing as a required subject. Their goal was not to turn out gifted artists but to train students in the practical skills needed in an industrial society. Winslow Homer's portrait of a teacher by her blackboard shows the geometric shapes behind practical design.

A rigid social philosophy underlay the harsh routine. In an age of industrialization, massive immigration, and rapid change, schools taught conformity and values as much as facts and figures. Teachers acted as drillmasters, shaping their charges for the sake of society. "Teachers and books are better security than handcuffs and policemen," wrote a New Jersey college professor in 1879. In *McGuffey's Reader,* a standard textbook used in grammar schools throughout the nineteenth century, students learned not only how to read but also how to behave. Hard work, Christian ethics, and obedience to authority would lead boys to heroic command, girls to blissful motherhood, and society to harmonious progress.

As Reconstruction faded, so did the impressive start made in black education. Most of the first generation of former slaves had been illiterate. So eager were they to learn that by the end of the century nearly half of all African Americans could read. But discrimination soon took its toll. For nearly 100 years after the Civil War, the doc-

African American education

trine of "separate but equal," upheld by the Supreme Court in *Plessy v. Ferguson* (1896), kept black and white students apart but scarcely equal (page 680). By 1882 public schools in a half dozen southern states were segregated by law, the rest by practice. Underfunded and ill-equipped, black schools served dirt-poor families whose every member had to work. In fact, only about a third of the South's black children attended and rarely for the entire school year.

Immigrant education

Like African Americans, immigrants saw education as a way of getting ahead. Some educators saw it as a means of Americanizing newcomers. "Education will solve every problem of our national life, including that of assimilating our foreign element," declared a New York principal. Educators assumed that immigrant and native-born children would learn the same lessons in the same language and turn out the same way. Only toward the end of the century, as immigration mounted, did eastern cities begin to offer night classes that taught English, along with civics lessons for foreigners. When public education proved inadequate, immigrants established their own schools. Catholics, for example, started an elaborate expansion of their parochial schools in 1884. Here, too, education served social purposes: teaching fundamentals while promoting citizenship through wholesome values.

By the 1880s educational reforms were helping schools respond to the needs of an urban society. Opened first in St. Louis in 1873, American versions of innovative German "kindergartens" put four- to six-year-olds in orderly classrooms while parents went off to work. "Normal schools" multiplied to provide teachers with more professional training. By 1900 almost one teacher in five had a professional degree. In the new industrial age, science and manual training supplemented more conventional subjects in order to supply industry with better-educated workers. And vocational education reduced the influence of unions. Now less dependent on a system of training controlled by labor, new workers were also less subject to being recruited into unions.

Higher Learning and the Rise of the Professional

Colleges served the urban industrial society, too, not by controlling mass habits but by providing leaders and managers. Early in the nineteenth century, most Americans had regarded higher learning as unmanly and irrelevant. The few who sought it often preferred the superior universities of Europe to those in the United States.

Postgraduate education

As American society grew more organized, mechanized, and complex, the need for professional, technical, and literary skills brought greater respect for college education. The Morrill Act of 1862 generated a dozen new state colleges and universities, eight mechanical and agricultural colleges, and six black colleges. Private charity added more. Railroad barons like Johns Hopkins and Leland Stanford used parts of their fortunes to found colleges named after them (Hopkins in 1873, Stanford in 1890). John D. Rockefeller reestablished the University of Chicago (1890). The number of colleges and universities nearly doubled between 1870 and 1910, though less than 5 percent of college-age Americans used them.

A practical impulse inspired the founding of several black colleges. In the late nineteenth century, few institutions mixed races. Church groups and private foundations, such as the Peabody and Slater funds (supported by white donors from the North), underwrote black colleges after Reconstruction. By 1900, a total of 700 black students were enrolled. About 2000 had graduated. Through hard work and persistence, some even received degrees from institutions normally reserved for whites.

In keeping with the new emphasis on practical training, professional schools multiplied to provide training beyond a college degree. American universities adopted the German model requiring young scholars to perform research as part of their training. The number of law and medical schools more than doubled between 1870 and 1900; medical students almost tripled. Ten percent of them were women, though their numbers shrank as the medical profession became more organized and exclusive.

Professionals of all kinds—in law, medicine, engineering, business, academics—swelled the ranks of the middle class. Slowly they were becoming a new force in urban America, replacing the ministers and gentlemen freeholders of an earlier day as community leaders.

Higher Education for Women

Before the Civil War women could attend only three private colleges. After the war they had new ones all their own, among them Smith (1871), Wellesley (1875), and Bryn Mawr (1885). Many land-grant colleges, chartered to serve all people, admitted women from the start. By 1910 some 40 percent of college students were women, almost double the 1870 figure. Only one college in five refused to accept them.

Potent myths continued to make college life hard for women. As Dr. Edward Clarke of the Harvard Medical School told thousands of students in *Sex in Education* (1873), the rigors of a college education could lead the "weaker sex" to physical or mental collapse, infertility, and early death. Women's colleges therefore included a strict program of physical activity to keep students healthy. Many also offered an array of courses in "domestic science"—cooking, sewing, and other such skills—to counter the claim that higher education would be of no value to women.

College students, together with office workers and female athletes, became role models for ambitious young women. These "new women," impatient with custom, cast off Victorian restrictions. Fewer of them married, and more were self-supporting. They shed their corsets and bustles and donned lighter, more comfortable clothing, including "shirtwaist" blouses (styled after men's shirts) and lower-heeled shoes. Robust and active, they could be found ice-skating in the winter, riding bicycles in the fall and spring, playing golf and tennis in the summer.

A Culture of Consumption

The city spawned a new material culture built around consumption. As standards of living rose, American industries began providing "ready-made" clothing to replace garments that had once been made at home. Similarly, food and furniture were mass-produced in greater quantities. The city became a giant marketplace for these goods, where new patterns of mass consumption took hold. Radiating outward to more rural areas, this urban consumer culture helped to level American society. Increasingly city businesses sold the same goods to farmer and clerk, rich and poor, native-born and immigrant.

Well-made, inexpensive merchandise in standard sizes and shapes found outlets in new palaces of consumption called "department stores" because they displayed their goods in separate sections or departments. The idea was imported from France, where shopping arcades had been built as early as the 1860s. Unlike the small exclu-

Department stores

Middle-class Americans began to include bananas in their diets during the 1880s. To accommodate the new trend, stores offered consumers a new table accessory: the banana bowl or banana boat.

sive shops of Europe, department stores were palatial, public, and filled with inviting displays of furniture, housewares, and clothing.

The French writer Emile Zola claimed that department stores "democratized luxury." Anyone could enter free of charge, handle the most elegant and expensive goods, and buy whatever was affordable. When consumers found goods too pricey, department stores pioneered layaway plans with deferred payments. Free delivery and free returns or exchanges were available to all, not just the favored customers of exclusive fashion makers. The department store also educated people by showing them what "proper" families owned and the correct names for things like women's wear and parlor furniture. This process of socialization was taking place not only in cities but in towns and villages across America. Mass consumption was giving rise to a mass culture.

Chain stores and mail-order houses
"Chain stores" (a term coined in America) spread the culture of consumption without frills. They catered to the working class, who could not afford department stores, and operated on a cash-and-carry basis. Owners kept their costs down by buying in volume to fill the small stores in growing neighborhood chains. Founded in 1859, the Great Atlantic and Pacific Tea Company was the first of the chain stores. By 1876 its 76 branch stores had added groceries to its original line of teas.

Far from department and chain stores, rural Americans joined the community of consumers by mail. In 1872, Aaron Montgomery Ward sent his first price sheet to farmers from a livery stable loft in Chicago. Ward eliminated the middleman and promised savings of 40 percent on fans, needles, trunks, harnesses, and scores of other goods. By 1884, his catalog boasted 10,000 items, each illustrated by a woodcut. Similarly, Richard W. Sears and Alvah C. Roebuck built a $500 million mail order business by 1907. Schoolrooms that had no encyclopedia used a Ward's or Sears' catalog instead. Children were drilled in reading and spelling from them. When asked the source of the Ten Commandments, one farm boy replied that they came from Sears, Roebuck.

Leisure

As mechanization slowly reduced the number of hours on the job, factory workers found themselves with more free time. So did the middle class, with free weekends, evenings, and vacations. And these changes were occurring at just the moment when freedom on the job was shrinking. Where artisans earlier in the century stopped for brief diversions whenever they pleased, the discipline of factory and office allowed no such luxury. A new, stricter division between work and leisure developed. Exhausted after hours of work but eager for escape and excitement, city dwellers turned their free time into a consumer item that often reflected differences in class, gender, and ethnicity.

Sports and class distinctions
Sports, for example, had been a traditional form of recreation for the rich. They continued to play polo, golf, and the newly imported English game of tennis. Croquet had more middle-class appeal because it required less skill and special equipment.

In towns small and large, cockfighting remained a popular spectator sport well into the twentieth century, even though it was outlawed in most states by the end of the nineteenth century. Cockfighting attracted men from a wide range of classes and races, as seen in Horace Bonham's *Nearing the Issue at the Cockpit,* painted in 1878. Journalists and cartoonists often used the cockpit to symbolize the political arena. By focusing on the racially mixed crowd, Bonham may well have been underscoring the new diversity of the American electorate.

Perhaps as important, it could be enjoyed in mixed company, like the new craze of bicycling. Bicycles evolved from unstable contraptions with large front wheels into "safety" bikes with equal-sized wheels, a dropped middle bar, pneumatic tires, and coaster brakes. A good one cost about $100, far beyond the reach of a factory worker but within the grasp of a mechanic or a well-paid clerk. On Sunday afternoons city parks became crowded with cyclists. Women also rode the new safety bikes, although social convention forbade them from riding alone. But cycling broke down conventions too. It required looser garments, freeing women from corsets. Lady cyclists demonstrated that they were hardly too fragile for physical exertion.

Organized spectator sports attracted crowds from every walk of life. Baseball overshadowed all others. For city dwellers with dull work, tight quarters, and isolated lives, baseball offered the chance to join thousands of others for an exciting outdoor spectacle. By the 1890s it was attracting crowds of 60,000. Baseball began to take its modern form in 1869, when the first professional team, the Cincinnati Red Stockings, appeared. Slowly the game evolved: umpires began to call balls and strikes, the overhand replaced the underhand pitch, and fielders put on gloves. Teams from eight cities formed the National League of Professional Baseball Clubs in 1876, followed by the American League in 1901. League players were distinctly working class.

Spectator sports for the urban masses

POPULAR ENTERTAINMENT

The Vaudeville Show

It looked like a palace or some high-toned concert hall. Patrons walked through a richly ornamented arched gateway to gold-domed, marble ticket booths. Ushers guided them through a stately lobby cushioned with velvet carpets. Large mirrors and brass ornaments hung on brocaded walls. There were "gentlemen's smoking and reading rooms" and suites with dressing cases and free toiletries for the ladies. The house seats were thick and comfortable and positioned well back from the stage. Thousands of electrical fixtures set the place aglow. When the lights dimmed, the audience sank into polite silence as the show began.

Benjamin Franklin Keith, who had worked in circuses, tent shows, and dime museums, opened the New Theatre in Boston in 1894. Seeing housewives with children as a source of new profits, resourceful theater owners like Keith had cleaned up the bawdy variety acts of saloons and music halls, borrowed the animal and acrobat acts from circuses and Wild West shows and the comedy acts of minstrel shows, and moved them to plusher surroundings. They called the new shows "vaudeville," after the French "pieces de vaudeville" developed in eighteenth-century street fairs. In 1881 Tony Pastor opened the first vaudeville theater on Fourteenth Street in New York City. Within a decade more elegant palaces like Keith's New Theatre were opening in cities across the country.

For anywhere from a dime to two dollars, a customer could see up to nine acts—singers, jugglers, acrobats, magicians, trained animals, and comics. The mix of performers reflected the urban tempo and new urban tastes. Skits often drew on the experience of immigrants, and early comedy teams had names like "The Sport and the Jew" and "Two Funny Sauerkrauts." Divided into acts that came in rapid-fire succession, "continuous shows" ran one after another, from early morning until late at night. "After breakfast go to Proctor's," trumpeted one advertisement for F. F. Proctor's vaudeville show, "after Proctor's go to bed."

Saloon music halls had catered to a rowdy all-male, working-class clientele, who smoke, drank, stomped, and jeered at the players. Vaudeville was aimed at middle-class and wealthier working-class families who could no longer afford "legitimate" theater and light opera. Keith worked diligently to make each of his theaters "as 'homelike' an amusement resort as it was possible to make it." Backstage he tacked signs warning performers not to say "slob" or "son-of-a-gun" or "'hully-gee' . . . unless you want to be canceled peremptorily." In the interest of good taste, all of his chorus girls wore stockings. Within a few years Keith was producing the kind of show, as one comedian put it, "to which any child could bring his parents."

The audience, too, was instructed on

At first, teams featured a few black players. When African Americans were barred in the 1880s, black professionals formed their own team, the Cuban Giants of Long Island, New York. The name was chosen with care. In an age of racial separation, the all-black team hoped to increase its chances of playing white teams by calling itself "Cuban."

Balconies at vaudeville shows, like this one depicted by Charles Dana Gibson, attracted a wide variety of customers. Most seats cost $1, and theater owners scheduled performances from morning until night.

proper behavior. No liquor was served. No cigars or cigarettes were permitted. Printed notices directed patrons to "kindly avoid the stamping of feet and pounding of canes on the floor. . . . Please don't talk during acts, as it annoys those about you, and prevents a perfect hearing of the entertainment."

Enjoying its heyday from 1890 to 1920, vaudeville became big business. Nearly one in five city dwellers went to a show once every seven days. Headliners earned $1,000 a week, theaters $20,000. Owners like Keith and Edward Albee merged their operations into gigantic circuits. By the time of Keith's death in 1914, the Keith-Albee circuit had built an empire of 29 theaters in more than seven cities.

Vaudeville became middle-class mass entertainment. Moderate and moral, it furnished cheap recreation that also reinforced genteel values. Skits encouraged audiences to pursue success through hard work. An emerging star system made American heroes out of performers like Will Rogers and George M. Cohan and American models out of Fanny Brice and Mae West. Ethnic comics defused tensions among immigrants with spoofs that exaggerated stereotypes and stressed the common foibles of all humanity. And theatergoers learned how to behave. Order and decorum replaced the boisterous atmosphere of saloons and music halls. Vaudeville audiences adopted the middle-class ideal of behavior—passive and polite. Americans were learning to defer to experts in the realms of public conduct and popular entertainment, as elsewhere in the new urban, industrial society.

Horse racing, bicycle tournaments, and other sports of speed and violence helped to break the monotony, frustration, and routine of the industrial city. In 1869, without pads or helmets, Rutgers beat Princeton in the first intercollegiate football match. By the 1890s the service academies and state universities fielded teams. Not everyone cheered. Cornell University forbade its team from playing the University of

Michigan. "I will not permit 30 men to travel 400 miles to agitate a bag of wind," said President White. Despite protests against rising death tolls (18 players died in 1905), football soon attracted crowds of 50,000 or more. Beginning in 1891 when Dr. James Naismith nailed a peach basket to the gymnasium wall at the YMCA Training School in Springfield, Massachusetts, "basketball" became the indoor interlude between the outdoor sports of spring and fall.

Arts and Entertainment

Variety also marked social life in the city. For the poor and working class, the streets offered a social carnival of vendors, neighbors and friends, games of chance and physical prowess. The saloon served as a workingman's club, a male preserve to enjoy a drink or a free lunch and uninhibited talk. Rougher saloons offered prostitutes, gambling, drugs, or almost any illicit desire. Young working women escaped the drudgery of factory, office, or sweatshop at vaudeville shows, dance halls, and the new amusement parks. Coney Island's Luna Park, opened in 1903, drew 5 million customers in a single season.

Workingmen took their dates to dance halls and boxing exhibitions staged in small rings used for variety acts between fights. Bare-knuckled prizefighting, illegal in some states, took place secretly in saloons and commercial gyms. In the rough-and-tumble world of the industrial city, the ring gave young men from the streets the chance to stand out from the crowd and to prove their masculinity. "Sporting clubs" of German, Irish, and African American boxers sprouted up in cities along the East Coast. *The National Police Gazette* and other magazines followed the bouts with sensational stories chronicling matches in detail. When the sport adopted the Marquis of Queensbury rules in the 1880s, including the use of gloves, boxing gained new respectability and appeal. Soon boxing, like other sports, was being commercialized with professional bouts, large purses, and championship titles.

Wealthier couples went to concerts given by local symphony orchestras, which played a mixture of popular tunes, John Philip Sousa marches, and the music of classical European composers. At the theater, popular melodramas gave patrons a chance to avoid the ambiguities of modern life. Theatergoers booed villains and cheered heroes, as in the illustration on page 661; they shuddered for heroines and marveled at tricky stage mechanics that made ice floes move and players float upward to heaven.

In villages and cities music of every tempo and style filled the air. Organ grinders churned out Italian airs on street corners. Steam-powered calliopes tooted spirited waltzes from amusement parks and riverboat decks. In bandstands brass ensembles played German-style concerts. By 1900 the sale of phonograph records had reached 3 million. Popular music became a big business as companies hawked sentimental ballads like "My Mother Was a Lady" or topical tunes celebrating the discovery of oil or the changing styles of women's clothing. In Scott Joplin's "Maple Leaf Rag" (1899) the lively syncopation of ragtime heralded the coming of jazz.

As the nineteenth century drew to a close the city was reshaping the country, just as the industrial system was creating a more specialized, diversified, and interlocking national and even international economy. Most Americans were ambivalent about this process. Cities beckoned migrants from the countryside and immigrants from abroad with unparalleled opportunities for work and pleasure. The playwright Israel Zangwill celebrated the city's transforming power in his 1908 Broadway hit *The Melting Pot.* "The real American," one of his characters explained, "is only in the Crucible, I tell you—he will be the fusion of all the races, the coming superman."

Where Zangwill saw a melting pot with all its promise for a new super race, champions of traditional American values, such as the widely read Protestant minister Josiah Strong, saw "a commingled mass of venomous filth and seething sin, of lust, of drunkenness, of pauperism, and crime of every sort." Both the champions and the critics of the late nineteenth century had a point. Corruption, crudeness, and disorder were no more or less a part of the cities than the vibrancy, energy, and opportunities that drew people to them. The gap between rich and poor yawned most widely in cities. As social critic Henry George observed, progress and poverty seemed to go hand in hand.

In the end moral judgments, whether pro or con, missed the point. Cities stood at the hubs of the new industrial order. All Americans, whatever they thought about the new urban world, had to search for ways to make that world work.

CHAPTER SUMMARY

The modern city was the product of industrialization. It lay at the center of the new integrated systems of transportation, manufacturing, and communications and the mass distribution of goods and culture. Skyscrapers, electric railways, and other urban technologies increased both urban density and size. Cities began to assume their modern shape of ringed residential patterns around central business districts: slum cores, zones of emergence, and suburban fringes. Yet that rapid growth proved treacherous. The disorder of cities beset by global migration and an inrush of labor from rural areas threatened the very systems that helped bring them into being.

For the political system, the challenge was to find within its democratic traditions a way to bring order out of this seeming chaos. More would be needed than moralistic warnings to the privileged few to observe the desperate plight of the poor. Those who lived and worked in cities found themselves divided by wealth, race, ethnicity, religion, region, social class, age, cultural habits, and gender. The creation of settlement houses, the Salvation Army, and the work of Social Gospel churches were among the responses to urban disorder, but they were only a start. Somehow, the makeshift, arbitrary rule of the bosses would have to give way to government that met the industrial order's need for efficiency, the public's need for services, and the need of the poor for compassion and respect, all at a price society could afford.

As cities grew, the lives of the urban middle classes were shaped by a Victorian code of sobriety, hard work, self-control, and modesty. Such values served the new industrial society and also helped protect against turbulent city life. Reformers pressed for an educational system that would school citizens to adapt to the new industrial culture. Yet for all the emphasis on skills, discipline, and order, the vibrancy of the city was attractive as well: in sports and amusements, concerts and beer halls, at social clubs, and in books and newspapers. These too were a part of the new industrial city.

SIGNIFICANT EVENTS

1869 — Cincinnati Red Stockings become first professional baseball team; Rutgers beats Princeton in first intercollegiate football game

1870 — Elevated railroad begins operation in New York City

1872 — William "Boss" Tweed convicted of defrauding city of New York

1873 — Comstock Law enacted

1874 — Women's Christian Temperance Union founded

1875 — Dwight Moody begins urban evangelical revivals

1876 — Central Park completed in New York City; Johns Hopkins University opens nation's first graduate school

1882 — Chinese Exclusion Act

1883 — Brooklyn Bridge opens

1885 — Home Life Insurance Building, world's first skyscraper, built in Chicago; first all-black professional baseball team, the Cuban Giants, organized

1888 — Nation's first electric trolley line begins operation in Richmond, Virginia

1889 — Hull House opens in Chicago

1892 — Ellis Island opens as receiving station for immigrants

1894 — Immigration Restriction League organized

1896 — *Plessy v. Ferguson* lays down doctrine legitimizing segregation

1897 — Boston opens nation's first subway station

ADDITIONAL READINGS

The best treatment of the rise of cities is Howard B. Chudacoff, *The Evolution of American Urban Society* (rev. ed., 1981). John Stilgoe's *Borderland: The Origins of the American Suburb, 1820–1929* (1988) chronicles the growth of suburban America. William Cronon's *Nature's Metropolis: Chicago and the Great West* (1991) looks at Chicago as part of the ecological landscape. In *Boss Cox's Cincinnati: Urban Politics in the Progressive Era* (1968), Zane Miller reassesses the urban political machine, while Paul Boyer explores efforts at controlling city life in *Urban Masses and Moral Order in America, 1820–1920* (1978). John F. Kasson's *Rudeness & Civility: Manners in Nineteenth-Century Urban America* (1990) and Lawrence Levine's *Highbrow/Lowbrow: The Emergence of Cultural Hierarchy in America* (1988) investigate the emerging urban culture.

Marcus Lee Hanson's classic *The Atlantic Migration, 1607–1860* (1940) began the shift in immigration history away from the national and toward a more global perspective. For richly detailed comparative examinations of the immigrant experience, see Roger Daniels, *Coming to America: A History of Immigration and Ethnicity in American Life* (1990) and Ronald Takaki's *A Different Mirror: A History of*

Multicultural America (1993). Susan A. Glenn's *Daughters of the Shtetl: Life and Labor in the Immigrant Generation* (1990) throws light on the issue of gender by probing the lives and labor of immigrant women, with particular attention to the shaping effect of old world Jewish culture. Virginia Yans-McLaughlin, ed., *Immigration Reconsidered: History, Sociology, and Politics* (1990), offers a collection of penetrating essays that places American immigration in its international context. For a fuller list of readings, see the Bibliography.

20

The New South and the Trans-Mississippi West

he news spread across the South during the late 1870s. Perhaps a man came around with a handbill telling of cheap land, or a letter might arrive from friends or relatives and be read aloud at church. The news spread in different ways, but in the end, the talk always spelled Kansas.

Few black farmers had been to Kansas themselves. But more than a few knew that the abolitionist Old John Brown had lived there before coming east to raid Harpers Ferry. Black folks, it seemed, might be able to live more freely in Kansas. "You can buy land at from a dollar and a half to two dollars an acre," wrote one settler to his friend in Louisiana. There was another distinct advantage: "They do not kill Negroes here for voting."

In 1878 such prospects excited hundreds of black families already stretched to their limits by hardship and violence. With Rutherford Hayes president, Reconstruction was at an end. Southern state governments had been "redeemed" by conservative whites, and the future seemed uncertain. "COME WEST," concluded *The Colored Citizen*, a newspaper in Topeka. "COME TO KANSAS."

St. Louis learned of these rumblings in the first raw days of March 1879, as steamers from downriver began unloading freedmen in large numbers. Some came with belongings and money; others, with only the clothes on their backs. While the weather was still cold, they sought shelter beneath tarpaulins along the river levee, built fires by the shore, and got out frying pans to cook meals while their children jumped rope nearby. By the end of April, more than 6000 had arrived; by the end of 1879, more than 20,000.

When the crowds overwhelmed the wharves and temporary shelters, the city's black churches banded together to house the "refugees," feed them, and help them continue toward Kansas. Repeated rumors that rail passage would not be free failed to shake their hopes. "We's like de chilun ob Israel when dey was led from out o' bondage by Moses," one explained, referring to the Bible's tale of exodus from Egypt. "If we sticks togeter an' keeps up our faith we'll git to Kansas and be out o' bondage for shuah." So the "Exodusters," as they became known, pressed westward.

The Exodusters

Adjusting to the new land was not easy for black emigrants or white settlers. Both northerners and southerners were accustomed to country where lumber was plentiful for building and cooking. Almost no wood could be found on the Kansas

666

Blasting away with pressurized water jets, miners loosen gold-bearing gravel. Such techniques damaged the environment in the rush to exploit western resources. The artist, Mrs. Jonas Brown, lived in Idaho City during the height of its gold rush.

plains. Nor were the Exodusters prepared for the Kansas winters. "Kansas has the roughest wind you ever run across in *your* life," commented one; another was dismayed to find that cotton did not flourish in prairie soil: "If I were back home I might get in a crop of cotton; but I cannot make enough here."

In the end, more black emigrants settled in growing towns like Topeka, Lincoln, and Kansas City. Men worked as hired hands; women did laundry. With luck, couples made $350 a year, saved a bit for a home, and put down roots. Bill Sims, an emigrant who settled in Ottawa, Kansas, put down roots literally—working at tree husbandry for a living. By the 1930s, when he was in his nineties, he could boast that his oldest daughter had been the "first colored girl to ever graduate" from Ottawa University. On the courthouse grounds at the center of town, the trees he had planted years before were still standing, a silent monument to his place in the community.

Sims and the host of Exodusters who poured into Kansas were part of a human flood westward. It had many sources—played-out farms of New England and the South, crowded cities, all of Europe. In 1879, as African Americans traveled up the Mississippi to St. Louis, 1000 white emigrants arrived in Kansas every week. Special trains brought settlers to the plains, all eager to start anew. During the 1880s the number of Kansans jumped from a million to a million and a half. "We have plenty of room for all creation," boasted a newspaper in Olathe, Kansas. Other western states experienced similar booms.

Relations between the South, West, and Northeast

Yet the boomers' optimistic spirits could not mask serious strains in the rapidly expanding nation, especially in the South and West. The boom economies of cotton, cattle, and grain all depended on city markets. The market for cotton lay with the textile mills of New England (and, increasingly, the "New South"), while the demand for beef and western grains came from metropolitan centers. Especially during hard times, westerners and southerners saw themselves as the victims of a colonial economic system, in which their fortunes were controlled by the industries of northeastern cities and their hardships were ignored by Washington.

But these self-styled victims themselves exploited both people and land. Whether locking former slaves into new forms of economic bondage or taking land from Indians and Latinos, both the South and the West built societies of racial caste. Violence became a common means of carving out and sustaining these societies. Imbalances emerged as drought, exhausted mines, overcut timberlands, and overproduction strained these regional economies to their limits. Even in boom times, such stresses required a response from the national political system. When the economy went bust, the inevitable adjustments were often wrenching, as people seeking opportunity and independence turned to government for help.

THE SOUTHERN BURDEN

Henry Grady, the editor of the *Atlanta Constitution*, often liked to tell the story of the poor cotton farmer buried in a pine coffin in the pine woods of Georgia. Except the coffin hadn't been made in Georgia but in Cincinnati. The nails in the coffin had been forged in Pittsburgh, though an iron mine lay near the cemetery. Even the farmer's cotton coat was made in New York and his trousers in Chicago. The "South didn't furnish a thing on earth for that funeral but the corpse and the hole in the ground!" fumed Grady. The irony of the story was the tragedy of the South. The region had human and natural resources aplenty but, alas, few factories to manufacture the goods it needed.

In the 1880s Grady campaigned to bring about a "New South" based on bustling industry, cities, and commerce. The business class and its values would displace the old planter class as southerners raced "to out-Yankee the Yankee." Grady and other publicists recognized the South's potential. Extending from Delaware south to Florida and west to Texas, the region took in a third of the nation's total area. It held a third of its arable farmlands, vast tracts of lumber, and rich deposits of coal, iron, oil, and fertilizers. To overcome the destruction of the Civil War and the loss of slave-holding wealth, apostles of the New South campaigned to catch up with the industrial North.

The gospel of a "New South"

Yet no amount of hopeful talk could change the economic structure of southern society that had emerged from the Civil War—decentralized, isolated, and agricultural. As late as 1890 the census counted less than 10 percent of all southerners as urban dwellers, compared with more than 50 percent in the North Atlantic states. The South had not only fewer large cities but also fewer small towns, which had become an important source of economic diversification and development in the Midwest. Well into the twentieth century, Grady's New South remained the poorest section of the country despite urban growth and gains in mining, textiles, lumber, and railroad building that equaled or surpassed other regions of the country. And the South suffered as well the burden of an unwieldy labor system that was often unskilled, usually underpaid, and always divided along lines of race.

Agriculture in the New South

For all the talk of industry, the economy of the postwar South remained agricultural, tied to crops like tobacco, rice, sugar, and especially cotton. By using fertilizers, planters were able to introduce cotton into areas once considered marginal. The number of acres planted in cotton more than doubled between 1870 and 1900. Some southern farmers sought prosperity in crops other than cotton. George Washington Carver, of Alabama's Tuskegee Institute (page 735), persuaded many poor black farmers to plant peanuts. But most southern soils were too acidic and the spring rains too heavy for other legumes and grains to flourish. Parasites and diseases plagued cattle herds. Work animals like mules were raised more cheaply in other regions. Try as southerners might to diversify, cotton still dominated their economy. "When southern cotton prices drop, every man feels the blow," noted one observer: "when southern cotton prices advance, every industry thrives with vigor."

A cotton-dominated economy

From 1880 to 1900 world demand for cotton grew slowly, and prices fell. As farms in other parts of the country were becoming larger and more efficient and were tended by fewer workers per acre, southern farms decreased in size. This reflected the breakup of large plantations, but it also resulted from a high birthrate. Across the country, the number of children born per mother was dropping, but in the South, large families remained common because more children meant more farmhands. Each year, fewer acres of land were available for each person to cultivate. Even

After the Civil War African Americans marked their freedom by ending field labor for most women and children. The women instead played a vital role in the domestic economy. Home garden plots supplemented the family food supply. (Metropolitan Museum of Art, New York)

though the southern economy kept pace with national growth, per capita income fell behind.

Sharecropping

To freedpeople across the South, the end of slavery brought hopes of economic independence. John Solomon Lewis was one such farmer. After the war Lewis rented land to grow cotton in Tensas Parish, Louisiana. A depression in the 1870s dashed his dreams. "I was in debt," Lewis explained, "and the man I rented land from said every year I must rent again to pay the other year, and so I rents and rents and each year I gets deeper and deeper in debt."

Tenantry   Lewis was impoverished like most small farmers in the cotton South. The South's best lands remained in the hands of large plantation owners. Few freedmen or poor white southerners had money to acquire property. Like Lewis, most rented shares of land—seldom more than 15 to 20 acres—as tenants. Since cotton was king and money scarce, rents for such shares were generally set in pounds of cotton rather than dollars. Usually the amount added up to between one-quarter and one-half the value of the crop.

The practice of farming on shares, or sharecropping, would not have proved so ruinous if the South had possessed a fairer system of credit. Before selling their crop in the fall, farmers without cash had to borrow money in the spring to buy seeds, tools, and other necessities. Most often, the only source of supplies was the local store. When John Solomon Lewis and other tenants entered the store, they saw two prices, one for cash and one for credit. The credit price might be as much as 60 percent higher. (By contrast, merchants in New York City seldom charged over 6 percent to buy on credit.) As security for the merchant's credit, the only asset most sharecroppers could offer was a mortgage or "lien" on their crops. The lien gave the shopkeeper first claim on the crop until the debt was paid off. The practice was known as the crop-lien system.

Sharecropping and crop liens

Many planters recognized that running a store was a way to increase profits. They would rent the land and then sell the goods needed to farm it. At the same time store owners without land often held mortgages on nearby farms. As farms failed, the merchants took them through foreclosure, thereby becoming larger and larger landholders. Most tenants found themselves twice indebted: they owed part of the crop to the landlord and the remainder to the shopkeeper. Often landlord and shopkeeper were the same person.

Sharecropping and crop liens reduced many farmers to virtual slavery by shackling them to debt. Year after year, they rented land and borrowed against their harvests. This economic dependence, known as debt peonage, robbed small farmers of their freedom. The landlord or shopkeeper could insist that sharecroppers grow profitable crops like cotton rather than things they could eat. Most landlords also insisted that raw cotton be ginned, baled, and marketed through their mills—at a rate they controlled. For African Americans the system was not just onerous but dangerous as well. "The white people do not allow us to sell our own crops," one black sharecropper remarked. "When we do, we do it at risk of our lives, getting whipped, shot at, and often some get killed." Sharecropping, crop liens, and monopolies on ginning and

Debt peonage

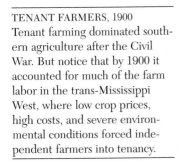

TENANT FARMERS, 1900
Tenant farming dominated southern agriculture after the Civil War. But notice that by 1900 it accounted for much of the farm labor in the trans-Mississippi West, where low crop prices, high costs, and severe environmental conditions forced independent farmers into tenancy.

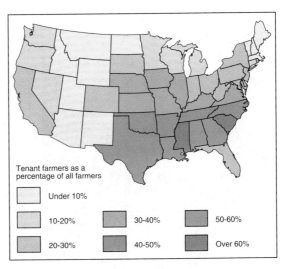

Tenant farmers as a percentage of all farmers

Under 10%

10-20%   30-40%   50-60%

20-30%   40-50%   Over 60%

marketing added up to inequality and crushing poverty for the South's small farmers, black or white.

Southern Industry

By the 1880s many southerners came to believe that industrialization was the only way the South could shed the yoke of poverty. The gospel of the New South swept some localities with the fervor of a religious camp meeting. By soaking up unemployed farm workers, new industries would become as much social as business enterprises. "People were urged to take stock . . . for the town's sake, for the poor people's sake, literally for God's sake," one writer explained.

Boom in textiles

The crusade for a New South did bring change. From 1869 to 1909, industrial production grew faster than the national rate. So did productivity for southern workers. A boom in railroad building after 1879 furnished the region with good transportation. In two areas, cotton textiles and tobacco, southern advances were striking. With cotton fiber and cheap labor close at hand, 400 cotton mills were humming by 1900, when they employed almost 100,000 workers.

Most new textile workers were poor white southerners escaping competition from black farm laborers or fleeing the hardscrabble life of the mountains. Entire families worked in the mills. Older men had the most trouble adjusting. They lacked the experience, temperament, and dexterity to tend spindles and looms in cramped mills. Only over time, as farm folk adapted to the tedious rhythm of factories, did southerners become competitive with workers from other regions of the United States and western Europe.

Tobacco and cigarettes

The tobacco industry also thrived in the New South. Before the Civil War, American tastes had run to cigars, snuff, and chewing tobacco. In 1876, James Bonsack, an 18-year-old Virginian, invented a machine to roll cigarettes. That was just the device Washington Duke and his son James needed to boost the fortunes of their growing tobacco business. Cigarettes suited the new urban market in the North. Unlike chewing tobacco and snuff, they were, according to one observer, "clean, quick, and potent."

The growth of the textile industry was critical to the industrial expansion of the South. Mill towns often attracted entire families, most of them white. The mill floors were generally cramped, noisy, and unsafe. These women at the White Oak Mills in Greensboro, North Carolina, are measuring and sewing denim.

Between 1860 and 1900, the annual rate of tobacco consumption nearly quadrupled. Americans spent more money on tobacco than on clothes or shoes. The sudden interest in smoking offered southerners a rare opportunity to control a national market. But the factories were so hot, the stench of tobacco so strong, and the work so exhausting that native-born white southerners generally refused the jobs. Duke solved the labor problem by hiring Jewish immigrants, expert cigar makers, to train black southerners in the techniques of tobacco work. Then he promoted cigarettes in a national advertising campaign, using gimmicks like collectible picture cards. By the 1890s his American Tobacco Company led the industry.

Timber and Steel

The growth of the textile and tobacco industries encouraged urbanization and investment in regional development. But investment and urbanization could not by themselves lift the region from poverty. Low wages reflected the pattern of southern agriculture rather than the higher wage patterns of industries in the Northeast and upper Midwest. As immigrants flooded into those regions, they created skilled workforces and expanded markets. Low wages discouraged them from settling in the South. Isolated from the international labor pool, the southern labor force grew almost exclusively from natural increase.

The realities of southern economic life were more accurately reflected in lumber and steel than in tobacco and textiles. After the Civil War, the South possessed over 60 percent of the nation's timber resources. With soaring demand from towns and cities, lumber and turpentine became the South's chief industries and employers. If anything, however, aggressive lumbering left the South far poorer. Corruption of state officials and a relaxed federal timber policy allowed northerners and foreigners to acquire huge forest tracts at artificially low prices. The timber was then sold as raw lumber rather than finished products such as cedar shingles or newsprint (or the coffins Henry Grady liked to mention). Only in North Carolina did the manufacture of furniture flourish.

Aggressive lumbering added little to local economies. Logging camps were isolated and temporary. Visitors described the lumberjacks as "single, homeless, and possessionless." Once loggers leveled the forests around their camps, they moved on to other sites. Most sawmills operated for only a few years before the owners followed the loggers to a new area. Thus loggers and millers had little time to put down roots and invest their cash in the community.

The environmental costs were equally high. In the South as elsewhere, overcutting and other logging practices stripped hillsides bare. As spring rains eroded soil and unleashed floods, forests lost their capacity for self-renewal. By 1901 a Georgian complained that "from most of the visible land the timber is entirely gone." With it went the golden eagles, the peregrine falcons, and other native species.

Environmental costs

Turpentine mills, logging, and lumbering provided young black southerners with their greatest source of employment. Occasionally an African American rose to be a supervisor, though most were white. Because the work was dirty and dangerous and required few skills, turnover was high and morale low. Southerners often blamed the workers, not the operators, for the industry's low standards. As one critic complained, "The sawmill negro is rather shiftless and is not inclined to stay in any one location and consequently there is little incentive on the part of the owner or operator to carry

This railroad served a lumber mill. The lumber industry in the South exploited large stands of timber, but overcutting led to erosion and tended to impoverish the region.

on welfare work in any extensive manner." In fact, most black workers left the mills in search of higher wages or to settle down to sharecropping in order to marry and support families.

Birmingham steel

The iron and steel industry most disappointed promoters of the New South. The availability of coke as a fuel made Chattanooga, Tennessee, and Birmingham, Alabama, major centers for foundries. By the 1890s the Tennessee Coal, Iron, and Railway Company (TCI) of Birmingham was turning out iron pipe for gas, water, and sewer lines vital to cities. Unfortunately Birmingham's iron deposits were ill-suited for the kinds of steel in demand. In 1907 the financially strapped TCI was sold to the giant U.S. Steel Corporation, controlled by northern interests.

The pattern of lost opportunity was repeated in other southern industries—mining, chemical fertilizers, cottonseed oil, and railroads. Under the campaign for a New South, all grew dramatically in employment and value, but not enough to end poverty or industrialize the region. The South remained largely rural, agricultural, and poor.

The Sources of Southern Poverty

Why did poverty persist in the New South? Many southerners claimed that the region was exploited by outside interests. In effect, they argued, the South became a colonial economy controlled by business interests in New York or Pittsburgh rather than Atlanta or New Orleans. Raw materials such as minerals, timber, and cotton were shipped to other regions, which earned larger profits by turning them into finished goods. Profits that might have been used to foster development in the South were thereby siphoned off to other regions.

Late start in industrializing

Three factors peculiar to the South offer a better explanation for the region's poverty. First, the South began to industrialize later than the Northeast, so northerners had a head start on learning new manufacturing techniques. Northern workers produced more not because they were more energetic or disciplined but because they were more experienced. Once southern workers overcame their inexperience, they competed well. Second, the South commanded only a small technological community to guide its industrial development. Northern engineers and mechanics seldom followed northern capital into the region. Few people were available to adapt modern technology to southern conditions or to teach southerners how to do it themselves.

Education might have overcome the problem by upgrading the region's workforce. But no region in the nation spent less on schooling than the South. Southern leaders, drawn from the ranks of the upper class, cared little about educating ordinary white residents and openly resisted educating black southerners. Education, they contended, "spoiled" otherwise contented workers by leading them to demand higher wages and better conditions. In fact, the region's low wages encouraged educated workers to leave the South in search of higher pay. Few southern states invested in technical colleges and engineering schools, and so none could match those of the North. *Under-educated labor*

Lack of education aggravated the third and central source of southern poverty, the isolation of its labor force. In 1900 agriculture still dominated the southern economy. It required unskilled, low-paid sharecroppers and wage laborers. Southerners feared outsiders, whether capitalists, industrialists, or experts in technology, who might spread discontent among workers. So southern states discouraged social services and opportunities that might have attracted human and financial resources. The South remained poor because it received too little, not too much, outside investment. *The isolated southern labor market*

LIFE IN THE NEW SOUTH

Many a southern man, noted a son of the region, loved "to toss down a pint of raw whiskey in a gulp, to fiddle and dance all night, to bite off the nose or gouge out the eye of a favorite enemy, to fight harder and love harder than the next man, to be known far and wide as a hell of a fellow. . . ." Life in the New South was a constant struggle to balance this love of the vigorous life with an equally powerful pull: Christian piety.

Divided in its soul, the South was also divided by race. Even after the Civil War ended slavery, some 90 percent of African Americans continued to live in the rural South. Without slavery, however, southerners lost the system of social control that had defined race relations. Over time they substituted a new system of racial separation that eased, but never eliminated, white fear of African Americans.

Rural Life

Pleasure, piety, race—all divided southern life, in town and country alike. And life separated along lines of gender as well in rural areas especially, where most southerners lived.

Southern males found one outlet for their vigor in hunting. Hunting offered a welcome taste of freedom from heavy farm work. One South Carolinian recalled that possum hunting "gave you a wild feeling of being free, of standing alone against darkness and all the forces that cramped you." For rural people a successful hunt could also add meat and fish to a scanty diet. And through hunting many boys found a path to manhood. Seeing his father and brothers return with wild turkeys, young Edward *Hunting*

McIlhenny longed "for the time when I would be old enough to hunt this bird." The prospect of danger, perhaps a fall from a horse, only added to the excitement.

The thrill of illicit pleasure also drew many southern men to events of violence and chance, including cockfighting. They valued combative birds and were convinced that their champions fought more boldly than northern bantams. The longer blades or gaffs attached to the birds' heels cut more deeply, producing more blood and quicker deaths. Gambling between bird owners and among spectators doubtless heightened the thrills. Such sport offended churchgoing southerners. They condemned as sinful "the beer garden, the base ball, the low theater, the dog fight and cock fight and the ring for the pugilist and brute."

Farm entertainments

Many southern customs involved no such disorderly behavior. Work-sharing festivals celebrated the harvest and offered relief from the daily burdens of farm life. A Mississippian spoke of "neighborhood gatherings such as house raisings, log rollings, quiltings, and road workings." These events, too, were generally segregated along gender lines. Men did the heavy chores and competed in contests of physical prowess. Women shared more domestic tasks. Quilting was a favorite, for it brought women an opportunity to work together and enjoy one another's company. Community gatherings also offered young southerners a relaxed place for courtship. In one courting game, the young man who found a rare red ear of corn "could kiss the lady of his choice"—although in the school, church, or home under adult supervision, such behavior was discouraged.

Town

For rural folk, a trip to town brought special excitement, along with a bit of danger. Saturdays, court days, and holidays provided an occasion to mingle. Once again, there were male and female domains. For men the saloon, the blacksmith shop, or the storefront was a place to do business and to let off steam. Few men went to town without participating in social drinking. When they turned to roam the streets, the threat of brawling and violence drove most women away. One woman from Germantown, Tennessee, claimed that "it was never considered safe for a lady to go down on the streets on Saturdays." And with drunkenness came the usual outbursts of violence as men settled old grudges or new ones with their fists.

Court week drew the biggest crowds when a district judge arrived to mete out justice. Some people came to settle disputes; most came to enjoy the spectacle or do some business like horse trading. Given the importance of draft animals to farmers, skill at bargaining commanded great respect. Peddlers and entertainers worked the crowds with magic tricks, patent medicines, and other wares. Town also offered a chance to attend the theater or a traveling circus. Famous European actors and musicians sometimes brought Shakespeare and opera to remote towns. Most children loved the circus parade, which "gave us a feeling of gay exotic abandon," one southerner recalled.

The Church

At the center of southern life stood the church as a great stabilizer and custodian of social order. "When one joined the Methodist church," a southern woman remembered, "he was expected to give up all such things as cards, dancing, theatres, in fact all so called worldly amusements." Many devout southerners pursued these ideals, although such restraint asked more of people, especially men, than most were willing to show, except perhaps on Sunday.

Congregations were often so small and isolated that they could attract a *Rural religion* preacher only once or twice a month. "Living in the country one almost becomes a heathen," one planter confessed. Evangelicals counted on the Sunday sermon to steer them from sin. In town, a sermon might last 30 to 45 minutes, but in the country, a preacher could go on for two hours or more, whipping up his congregation until "even the little children wept."

By 1870 southern churches were segregated by race (see page 580). Within them, the congregation, particularly in rural areas, was separated by gender, too. Upon seeing a man and woman seated together, a Virginia Baptist claimed "they were from Richmond or Lynchburg, or some other city where folks did not know any better." As a boy entered manhood, he moved from the female to the male section. Yet churches were, at base, female domains. Considered guardians of virtue, more women were members, attended services, and ran church activities.

Church was a place to socialize as well as worship. Many of the young went simply to meet those of the opposite sex. Church picnics and all-day sings brought as many as 30 or 40 young people together for hours of eating, talk, services, and hymn singing. Still, these occasions could not match the fervor of a weeklong camp meeting. In the late summer or early fall, town and countryside alike emptied as folks set up tents in shady groves and listened to two or three ministers preach day and night in the largest event of the year. The camp meeting refired evangelical faith while celebrating traditional values of home and family.

For Baptists in the South, both white and black, the ceremony of adult baptism included total immersion, often in a nearby river. The ritual symbolized the waters of newfound faith washing away sins that had been forgiven by God's free grace. Here, a black congregation looks on, some holding umbrellas to protect against the sun.

Segregation

Nothing challenged tradition in the New South more than race. With the abolition of slavery and the end of Reconstruction, white northerners and southerners achieved sectional harmony by sacrificing the rights of black citizens. White southerners were assured that in matters of race they would be "left alone" by the federal government.

Laissez-faire race relations

The hands-off, or laissez-faire, approach suited even the white northerners who once championed black rights. The editor of one magazine published in New York told northern readers that he doubted whether former slaves were capable of participating in "a system of government for which you and I have much respect." In the New South, African Americans would remain free but scarcely equal.

During the 1880s, Redeemer governments (pages 587–589) moved to formalize a new system of segregation or racial separation. Redeemers were Democratic politicians who came to power in southern states to end the Republican rule established during Reconstruction. They were eager to reap the benefits of economic expansion and to attract the business classes—bankers, railroad promoters, industrial operators. As their part of the bargain, the Redeemers assured anxious northerners that Redeemer rule would not mean political disfranchisement of the freedmen. That promise they would not keep.

Pressure to reach a new racial accommodation in the South increased as more African Americans moved into southern towns and cities, competing for jobs with poor whites. One way to preserve the social and economic superiority of white southerners, poor as well as rich, was to separate blacks as an inferior caste. But federal laws designed to enforce the Civil Rights Act of 1866 and the Fourteenth Amendment

A long line of African American voters waits to cast ballots in Caddo Parish, Louisiana, in 1894. Clearly, interest in voting remained high among black citizens. Two years later Louisiana followed the lead of other Southern states in disfranchising most of its black voters (as well as many poor whites).

The cultures of western Indians were remarkably varied, ranging from the nomadic Plains tribes to the more settled peoples of the northwest coast who lived off the sea. This Sioux woman gathers firewood; the photograph was taken by Edward Curtis, who spent many years recording the faces and lives of native peoples of the West.

Hohokams and later the Pima and other tribes in New Mexico and Arizona developed irrigation to allow farming of beans, squash, and corn in the arid climate.

Despite their diversity, Indian peoples shared certain values. Most tribes were *Shared values* small, extended kinship groups of 300 to 500 people in which the well-being of all outweighed the needs of each member. Although some tribes were better off than others, the gap between rich and poor within tribes was seldom large. Such small material differences often promoted communal decision making. The Cheyenne, for example, employed a council of 44 to advise the chief.

Most of all, Indians shared a reverence for nature, whatever their actual impact on the natural world. They believed human beings were not transcendent but part of an interconnected world of animals, plants, and other natural elements. All had souls of their own but were bound together, as if by contract, to live in balance through the ceremonial life of the tribe and the customs related to specific plants and animals. The Taos of New Mexico thought that each spring the pregnant earth issued new life. To avoid disturbing "mother" earth, they removed the hard shoes from their horses, while they themselves walked in bare feet or soft moccasins. Whites were mystified by the attitude of Chief Smohalla of the Wanapun tribe, who explained why his people refused to farm: "You ask me to plow the ground! Shall I take a knife and tear my mother's bosom? . . . You ask me to cut grass and make hay and sell it, and be rich like white men! But how dare I cut off my mother's hair?"

Regard for the land endowed special places with religious meaning. The Taos centered their spiritual and economic life on Blue Lake in northwest New Mexico,

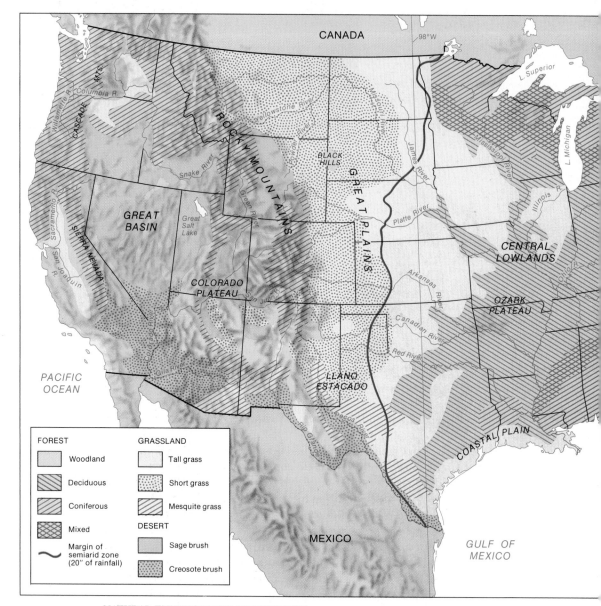

NATURAL ENVIRONMENT OF THE WEST
With the exception of the Pacific Northwest in Oregon and Washington, few areas west of the 20-inch rainfall line receive enough annual precipitation to support agriculture without irrigation. Consequently, water has been the key to growth and development in the area west of the 98th meridian, encompassing over half the land area of the continental United States. The dominance of short grasses and coniferous (evergreen) trees reflects the rainfall patterns.

the source of life and the revelations of the great spirit of the universe. The Shoshone in eastern California came to Coso Hot Springs for healing and worship. Such notions were utterly foreign to most whites. Where the Sioux saw in the Black Hills the sacred home of Wakan Tanka, the burial place of the dead, and the site of their "vision quests," whites saw grass for grazing and gold for the taking. From such contrasting views came conflict.

Whites and the Western Environment: Competing Visions

For white Americans after the Civil War, the new industrial order created both the means and the motive to close the final western frontiers. Transcontinental rail lines, standardized rail gauges and freight systems, telegraph lines to coordinate communications, systems of large-scale finance and military power, and rapidly growing urban markets all made it easier to accelerate white settlement in the West.

As discoveries of gold and silver lured white settlers into Indian territory, many adopted the confident outlook of Missouri politician William Gilpin. Only a lack of vision prevented the opening of the West for exploitation, Gilpin told an Independence, Missouri, audience in 1849. What was most needed were cheap lands and a railroad linking the two coasts "like ears on a human head." Distance, climate, and even the Indians were just impediments to overcome. *William Gilpin, a western booster*

By 1869 a generous Congress had granted western settlers their two greatest wishes: free land under the Homestead Act of 1862 and a transcontinental railroad. As the new governor of Colorado, Gilpin crowed about the region's limitless resources. One day, he believed, the West would support more than a billion people. Scarce rainfall and water did not daunt him, for in his eyes the West was an Eden-like garden, not "the great American Desert." Once the land had been planted, Gilpin assured listeners, the rains would develop naturally. He subscribed to the popular myth that "rain follows the plow."

Unlike the visionary Gilpin, John Wesley Powell knew something about water and farming. After losing an arm in the Civil War, geologist Powell went west. In 1869 and 1871 he led scientific expeditions down the Green and Colorado rivers through the Grand Canyon. No white man had ever made the trip, and most doubted that it could be done at all. Navigating the swirling rapids that blocked his way, he returned to warn Congress that developing the West required more scientific planning. Much of the region had not yet been mapped or its resources identified. *John Wesley Powell*

In 1880 Powell became director of the recently formed U.S. Geological Survey. He, too, had a vision of the West, but one based on the limits of its environment. The key was water, not land. In the water-rich East, the English legal tradition of river rights prevailed. Whoever owned the banks of a river or stream controlled as much water as they might take, regardless of the consequence for those downstream. Such a practice in the West, Powell recognized, would enrich the small number with access to water while spelling ruin for the rest. *Water as a key resource*

The alternative was to treat water as community property. The practice would benefit many rather than a privileged few. To that end Powell suggested that the federal government establish political boundaries defined by watersheds and regulate the distribution of the scarce resource. But his scientific realism could not overcome the popular vision of the West as the American Eden. Powerful interests ensured that development occurred with the same helter-skelter, laissez-faire credo that had captivated the East. The first to feel the effects of this unrestrained expansion would be the Indian and Latino residents of the region.

THE WAR FOR THE WEST

So marginal did federal officials consider the Great Plains that they left the lands to the Indians. By the end of the Civil War, some two-thirds of all Indian peoples lived on the Great Plains. Even before the war, a series of gold and silver discoveries beginning in 1848 signaled the first serious interest by white settlers in the arid and semiarid lands beyond the Mississippi. To open more land, federal officials introduced in 1851 a policy of "concentration," pressuring tribes to sign treaties limiting the boundaries of their hunting grounds—the Sioux to the Dakotas, the Crows to Montana, the Cheyenne to the foothills of Colorado.

Policy of concentration

Such treaties often claimed that their provisions would last "as long as waters run," but time after time, land-hungry pioneers broke the promises of their government by squatting on Indian lands and demanding federal protection. The government, in turn, forced more restrictive agreements on the western tribes. This cycle of promises made and broken continued, until a full-scale war for the West raged between whites and Indians.

Contact and Conflict

In the Pacific Northwest many Indians had welcomed the first white Overlanders, but by the 1850s, in an oft-repeated pattern, the pressures from the newcomers had become disruptive. Territorial governor Isaac Stevens persuaded representatives of the Cayuse, Yakima, Walla Walla, and Nez Percé to cede millions of acres of land on which they had once freely hunted.

In similar fashion, by 1862 the lands of the Santee Sioux had been whittled down to a strip 10 miles wide and 150 miles long along the Minnesota River. Lashing out in frustration, the tribe attacked several undefended white settlements along the Minnesota frontier. In response, General John Pope arrived in St. Paul declaring his intention to wipe out the Sioux. "They are to be treated as maniacs or wild beasts and by no means as people," he instructed his officers. When Pope's forces captured 1800 Sioux, white Minnesotans were outraged that President Lincoln ordered only 38 hanged.

Chivington massacre

The campaign under General Pope was the opening of a guerrilla war that continued on and off for some 30 years. The conflict gained momentum in 1864, when Governor John Evans of Colorado sought to end all land treaties with Indian peoples in eastern Colorado. In November, a force of 700 Colorado volunteers under Colonel John Chivington fell upon a band of friendly Cheyenne gathered at Sand Creek under army protection. Chief Black Kettle raised an American flag to signal friendship, but Chivington would have none of it. "Kill and scalp all, big and little," he told his men. The troops massacred at least 150, including children holding white flags of truce and mothers with babies in their arms. A joint congressional investigation later condemned Chivington. In 1865 virtually all Plains Indians joined in the First Sioux War to drive whites from their lands.

Among those who fought the Plains Indians were African American veterans of the Civil War. In 1866 two regiments of black soldiers were organized into the Ninth and Tenth Calvary under the command of white officers. Their Indian foes dubbed them "buffalo soldiers," reflecting the similarity they saw between the hair of African Americans and that of the buffalo. It was also a sign of hard-won respect. The buffalo soldiers fought Indians across the West for more than 20 years. They also subdued bandits, cattle thieves, and gunmen—from the rugged country of Big Bend to the badlands of South Dakota. And they helped to prepare the way for white settlement by laying the foundations for posts such as Fort Sill in Oklahoma and by locating water, wood, and grasslands for eager homesteaders.

Buffalo soldiers

War was only one of several ways in which white settlement undermined tribal cultures. Over the course of centuries only an estimated 4000 Indians (and about 7000 whites) were killed in direct warfare—a paltry few compared to the casualty lists of the Civil War. Far more devastating forces were at work. Disease, including smallpox, measles, and cholera, killed more Indians than combat. Liquor furnished by white traders entrapped many a brave in a deadly cycle of alcoholism. Trading posts altered traditional ways of life with metal pots and pans, traps, coffee, and sugar but furnished no employment and thus few ways for their Indian customers to pay for these goods. Across the West mines, crops, grazing herds, and fences disturbed traditional hunting and farming lands of many tribes.

On the Great Plains the railroad disrupted the migratory patterns of the buffalo and thus the patterns of the hunt. When buffalo robes became popular in the East in the 1870s and hides became a source of leather for industrial belts, commercial companies hired hunters, who could kill more than 100 bison an hour. Military commanders promoted the butchery as a way of undermining Indian resistance. By 1883 bison had nearly disappeared from the plains. (See After the Fact: "Where Have All the Bison Gone?" on pages 708–711.). With them went a way of life that left the Plains Indians more vulnerable to white expansion.

Custer's Last Stand—And the Indians'

The Sioux War ended in 1868 with the signing of the Treaty of Fort Laramie. It established two large Indian reservations, one in Oklahoma and the other in the Dakota Badlands. Only six years later, however, in the summer of 1874, Colonel George Armstrong Custer led an expedition into *Pa Sapa*, the sacred Black Hills of the Sioux. In doing so, he flagrantly disregarded the treaty of 1868. Custer, a Civil War veteran, already had a reputation as a "squaw killer" for his cruel warfare against Indians in western Kansas. To open the Black Hills to whites, his expedition spread rumors of gold "from the grass roots down." Prospectors poured into Indian country. Once again, federal authorities tried to force a treaty to gain control of the Black Hills. When negotiations failed, President Grant ordered all "hostiles" in the area rounded up and driven onto the reservations.

In reaction the Cheyenne for the first time allied with the Sioux, who were led by a young war chief named Crazy Horse and medicine man Sitting Bull. Against them marched several army columns, including Custer's Seventh Cavalry, a force of about 600 troops. Custer, eager for glory, arrived at the Little Big Horn River a day earlier than the other columns. Hearing of a native village nearby, he attacked, only to discover that he had stumbled onto an encampment of more than 12,000 Sioux and

Battle of Little Big Horn

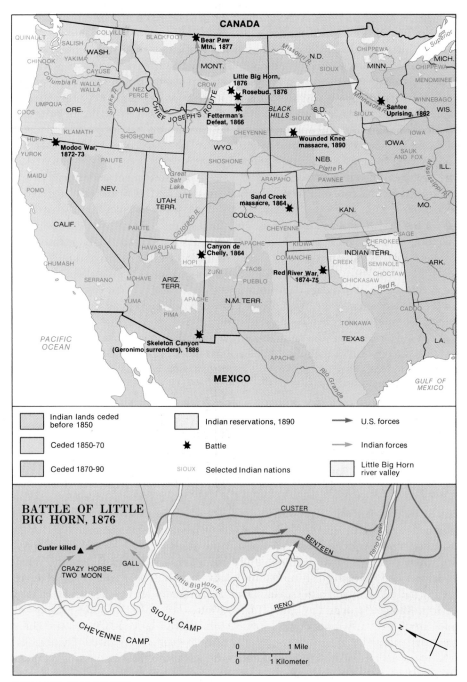

THE INDIAN FRONTIER

As conflict erupted between Indian and white cultures in the West, the government sought increasingly to concentrate tribes on reservations. Resistance to the reservation concept helped unite the Sioux and Cheyenne, traditionally enemies, in the Dakotas during the 1870s. Along the Little Big Horn River, the impetuous Custer underestimated the strength of his Indian opponents and attacked before the supporting troops of Reno and Benteen were in a position to aid him.

Cheyenne extending for almost 3 miles. From a deep ravine Crazy Horse charged Custer, killing him and some 250 soldiers.

As he led the attack, Crazy Horse yelled "It is a good day to die!"—the traditional war cry. Even in the midst of victory he spoke truly. Although Custer had been conquered, railroads stood ready to extend their lines, prospectors to make fortunes, and soldiers to protect them. By late summer the Sioux were forced to split into small bands in order to evade the army. While Sitting Bull barely escaped to Canada, Crazy Horse and 800 with him surrendered in 1876 after a winter of suffering and starvation.

The battles along the Platte and upper Missouri rivers did not end the war between whites and Indians, but never again would it reach such proportions. Even peaceful tribes like the Nez Percé of Idaho found no security once whites began to hunger for their land. The Nez Percé had become breeders of livestock, rich in horses and cattle that they grazed in the meadows west of the Snake River canyon. That did not prevent the government from trying to force them onto a small reservation in 1877.

Rather than see his people humiliated, Chief Joseph led almost 600 Nez Percé *Chief Joseph* toward Canada, pursued by the U.S. Army. In just 75 days they traveled more than 1300 miles. Every time the army closed to attack, Chief Joseph and his warriors drove them off. But before the Nez Percé could reach the border, they were trapped and forced to surrender. Chief Joseph's words still ring with eloquence: "Hear me, my chiefs, I am tired; my heart is sick and sad. From where the sun now stands I will fight no more forever." The government then shipped the defeated tribe to the bleak Indian Country of Oklahoma. There disease and starvation finished the destruction begun by the army.

Killing with Kindness

Over these same years Indians saw their legal sovereignty being whittled away. Originally, federal authorities had treated various tribes as autonomous nations existing within the United States, with whom treaties could be made. That tribal status began shrinking in 1831, when the Supreme Court declared Indians "domestic dependent nations." While the United States continued to negotiate treaties with the tribes, government officials began treating Indians as wards, with as little regard for them as for inept children. In 1869 President Grant created the Board of Indian Commissioners, whose members were chosen by Protestant churches to help settle conflicts with local tribes and to spread Christian values and white styles of living. Finally, in 1871, Congress abandoned the treaty system altogether and with it the legal core of Indian autonomy.

Some whites and Indians spoke out against the tragedy taking place on the Great Plains. In the 1870s, Susette La Fleche, daughter of an Omaha chief, lectured east- *La Fleche and* ern audiences about the mistreatment of Indian peoples and inspired reformers to *Jackson* action. Similarly moved, the poet Helen Hunt Jackson turned her energies to lobbying for Indian rights and attacking government policy. In 1881, she published *A Century of Dishonor.* The best-selling exposé detailed government fraud and corruption in dealing with Indians, as well as the many treaties broken by the United States.

Reformers began pressing for assimilation of Indians into white society, ironically as the only means of preserving Indians in a society that seemed bent on destroying them. The Women's National Indian Association, created in 1874, and the later Indian Rights Association, joined by Helen Hunt Jackson, sought to end the Indian way of life by suppressing communal activities, reeducating Indian children, and establishing individual homesteads.

Reformers also recognized that the policy of concentrating Indians on reservations had failed. Deprived of their traditional lands and culture, reservation tribes became dependent on government aid. In any case, whites who coveted Indian lands were quick to violate treaty terms. With a mix of good intentions and unbridled greed, Congress adopted the Dawes Severalty Act in 1887. It ended reservation policy by permitting the president to distribute land to Indians who had severed their attachments to their tribes. The goals of the policy were simple: to draw Indians into white society as farmers and small property owners and (less high-mindedly) to bring Indian lands legally into the marketplace.

The Dawes Act

In practice, the Dawes Act was more destructive than any blow struck by the army. It undermined the communal structure upon which Indian tribal life was based. Lands held by tribes would now be parceled out to individuals: 160 acres to the head of a family and 80 acres to single adults or orphans. But as John Wesley Powell had warned, small homestead farms in the West could not support a family—white or Indian—unless the farms were irrigated. Most Indians, moreover, had no experience with farming, managing money, or other white ways.

The sponsors of the Dawes Act, knowing that whites might swindle Indians out of their private holdings, arranged for the government to hold title to the land for 25 years. That did not stop unscrupulous speculators from "leasing" lands. Furthermore, all reservation lands not allocated to Indians were opened to non-Indian homesteaders. In 1881, Indians held over 155 million acres of land. By 1890 the figure had dropped to 104 million and by 1900 to just under 78 million.

Against such a dismal future, some Indians sought solace in the past. In 1890 a religious revival swept the Indian nations when word came from the Nevada desert that a humble Paiute named Wovoka had received revelations from the Great Spirit. Wovoka preached that if his followers adopted his mystical rituals and lived together in love and harmony, the Indian dead would come back, disrespectful whites would be driven from the land, and game would be thick again. As the rituals spread, alarmed settlers called the strange shuffling and chanting the "Ghost Dance." The army moved to stop the proceedings among the Sioux for fear of another uprising. At Wounded Knee in South Dakota the cavalry fell upon one band and with devastating machine-gun fire killed some 146 men, women, and children, including the great chief Sitting Bull.

Wounded Knee

Wounded Knee was a final act of violence against an independent Indian way of life. After 1890 the battle was over assimilation, not extinction. The system of markets, rail networks, and extractive industries was linking the Far West with the rest of the nation. Free-roaming bison were being replaced by herded cattle and sheep, nomadic tribes by prairie sodbusters, and sacred hunting grounds with gold fields. Reformers relied on education, citizenship, and allotments to move Indians from their communal lives into white society. Most Indians were equally determined to preserve their tribal ways and separateness as a people.

Borderlands

The coming of the railroad in the 1880s and 1890s brought wrenching changes to the Southwest as well, especially to the states and territories along the old border with

Western cities attracted ethnically diverse populations. This chili stand in San Antonio served the city's large Hispanic population.

Mexico. But here there was a twist. As new markets and industries sprang up, new settlers poured in from the East but also from the South, across the Mexican border. Indians like the Navajo and the Apache thus faced the hostility of newcomers—Anglos and Mexicans alike—as well as Hispanos, those settlers of Spanish descent already in the region. Before the Mexican War of 1846, the governors of northern Mexico had offered bounties for Indian scalps.

Like Indians, Hispanos discovered that they had either to accommodate or to resist the flood of new Anglos. The elite, or *Ricos*, often aligned themselves with Anglos against their countryfolk to protect their status and property. Others, including Juan José Herrera, resisted the newcomers. When Anglo cattle ranchers began forcing Hispanos off their lands near Las Vegas, Herrera assembled a band of masked nightriders known as *Las Gorras Blancas* (the White Caps). In 1889 and 1890 as many as 700 White Caps burned Anglo fences, haystacks, and occasionally barns and houses. Herrera's followers also set thousands of railroad ties afire when the Atchison, Topeka and Santa Fe Railroad refused to raise the low wages it paid Hispano workers.

Juan José Herrera and the White Caps

New Anglos frequently fought Hispanos. But it was western lawyers and politicians, using legal tactics, who deprived Hispanos of most of their property. Thomas Catron, an ambitious New Mexico lawyer, squeezed out many Hispanos by contesting land titles so aggressively that his holdings grew to 3 million acres. In those areas of New Mexico and California where they remained a majority, Hispanos continued to play a role in public life. During the early 1890s Herrera and his allies formed a "People's Party," swept local elections, and managed to defeat a bid by Catron to represent the territory in Congress.

With the railroads came more white settlers, as well as Mexican laborers from south of the border. Just as the southern economy depended on African American labor, the Southwest grew on the labor of Mexicans. Mexican immigrants worked mostly as contract and seasonal laborers for railroads and large farms. Many of them

Mexican immigrants

settled in the growing cities along the rail lines: El Paso, Albuquerque, Tucson, Phoenix, and Los Angeles. They lived in segregated *barrios*, Spanish towns, where their cultural traditions persisted. But by the late nineteenth century, most Hispanics, whether in barrios or on farms and ranches, had been excluded from power.

Formation of regional communities

Yet to focus attention on any one of those sites distorts the experience of south-westerners of Spanish descent. As a market economy dominated by Anglos advanced across the region, Hispanic villagers turned to seasonal migration to adapt. While women labored in the old villages, men traveled from job to job in mining, in farm-ing, and on the railroads. The money they made helped preserve the communal cul-ture of the village and diversify its economy. The village, in turn, helped sustain the migrants with a base from which to operate and to which they could return in protest if working conditions proved too harsh.

The resulting "regional community" stretched over hundreds of square miles of northern New Mexico and Colorado. Relying only in part on wage labor, the network of villages and migrant workers retained some independence from white domination, incorporating just those aspects of Anglo culture that suited their needs, such as sewing machines. After the turn of the century, the regional community found itself under seige by powerful corporations bent on creating a docile labor force. Eventually it collapsed as a strategy of adaptation and resistance.

BOOM AND BUST IN THE WEST

Opportunity in the West lay in land and resources, but wealth also accumulated in the towns and cities. Each time a speculative fever hit a region, new communities sprouted to serve those who rushed in. The western boom began in mining—with the California gold rush of 1849 and the rise of San Francisco (see page 469). In the decades that followed, new hordes threw up towns in Park City in Utah, Tombstone in Arizona, Deadwood in the Dakota Territories, and other promising sites. All too often, busts followed booms, transforming many boom towns into ghost towns.

Mining Sets a Pattern

The gold and silver strikes of the 1840s and 1850s set a pattern followed by other booms. Stories of easy riches attracted single prospectors with their shovels and wash pans. Almost all were male, and nearly half were foreign-born. Someone entering the local saloon could expect to hear English, the Irish brogue, German, French, Spanish, Chinese, Italian, Hawaiian, and various Indian dialects. Muddy mining camps sprang up where a prospector could register a claim, get provisions, bathe, and buy a drink or a companion.

Prostitution

Prostitution flourished openly in mining towns (as it did in cattle towns). They provided ideal conditions: large numbers of rootless men, few women, and money enough to buy sexual favors. In the booming towns of Gold Hill and Virginia City near the Comstock Lode of Nevada, men outnumbered women by a ratio of 2 to 1 in 1875. Almost 1 woman in 12 was a prostitute. Usually they were young, in their teens and twenties. They walked the streets and plied their trade in one-room shacks called "cribs." If young and in demand, they worked in dance halls, saloons, and brothels.

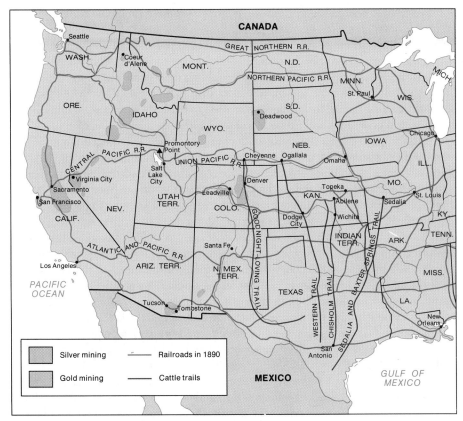

THE MINING AND CATTLE FRONTIERS
In the vast spaces of the West, railroads, cattle trails, and gold mining usually preceded the arrival of enough settlers to establish towns and cities. The railroads forged a crucial link between the region's natural resources and urban markets in the East and in Europe, but by transecting the plains they also disrupted the migratory patterns of the buffalo herds, undermining Plains Indian cultures while opening the land to cattle grazing and farming.

Pay varied by race, with Anglos at the top of the scale, followed by African Americans, Mexicans, and Indians. But even in the best of times earnings were scanty, perhaps $30 a week for whites. All told, as many as 50,000 women worked as prostitutes in the trans-Mississippi West before the turn of the century.

A few succeeded well enough at their trade to accumulate property. In Helena, Montana, Josephine Hensley (known among her patrons as "Chicago Jo") started as a madame. By the 1880s, she controlled most of the tenderloin district of saloons and brothels. Throughout the town, prostitutes earned from $179 to $339 a month at a time when saleswomen made no more than $65 a month. But in a common pattern, independent prostitutes in Helena became renters rather than property owners. Hard times and competition undermined their relative prosperity, and by the 1890s, men had seized control of the business. Most prostitutes found themselves mired in a life of alcoholism, drug addiction, disease, and violence. Many ended as suicides.

Prostitution was one source of revenue, but a far more profitable one came from outfitting these boom societies with the equipment they needed. Such sales siphoned riches into the pockets of store owners and other suppliers. Once the quick profits were gone, a period of consolidation brought more order to towns. Police departments replaced vigilantes. Brothels, saloons, and gambling dens were limited to certain districts. And larger scale came to regional businesses. In the mine fields, that meant corporations with the capital for hydraulic water jets to blast ore loose and for other heavy equipment to crush rock and extract silver and gold from deeper veins.

Environmental costs of mining

In their quest for quick profits, such operations often led to environmental disaster. With each snow melt and rain, the gravel from hydraulic mining worked its way down into river systems. The resulting floods, mudslides, and dirty streams threatened the livelihood of farmers in the valleys below. Outside of Sacramento, 39,000 acres of farmland lay under the debris by the 1890s, while another 14,000 acres were nearly ruined. In 1893 Congress created the Sacramento River Commission to eliminate flooding with series of dams and canals, effectively ending free-flowing rivers in California. Meanwhile underground mining consumed so much timber that one observer called the Comstock Lode in Nevada "tomb of the forest of the Sierras." In Butte, Montana, the smoke from sulfur-belching smelters turned the air so black that by the 1880s townsfolk had trouble seeing even in daylight.

In corporate mining operations, paid laborers replaced the independent prospectors of earlier days. As miners sought better wages and working conditions, shorter hours, and the right to unionize, management fought back. In Coeur d'Alene, Idaho, troops crushed a strike in 1892, killing seven miners. The miners then created the Western Federation of Miners. In the decade after 1893 the union attracted some 50,000 members and gained a reputation for militancy. In a cycle repeated elsewhere, the rowdy mining frontier of small-scale prospectors was integrated into the industrial system of wage labor, large-scale resource extraction, and high-finance capital.

The Transcontinental Railroad

As William Gilpin predicted in 1849, the development of the West awaited the railroads. Before the Central and Union Pacific railroads were joined to span the continent in 1869, travel across the West was slow and dusty. Vast distances and sparse population gave entrepreneurs little chance to follow the eastern practice of building local railroads from city to city.

But such difficulties put no end to dreaming, especially for the likes of Collis P. Huntington. A transplanted New Yorker, Huntington soon discovered that the way to make a fortune was not in the hunt for gold but by supplying the boom society that came with the rush. Huntington often strapped bags of gold to his waist and rowed out into San Francisco harbor to meet incoming supply ships. Before they could land, he had bought up the entire cargo, which he then sold at highly inflated prices. Huntington understood all too well the credo of the West in those early days: "It pays to be shifty in a new land." He and three other Sacramento business leaders, Mark Hopkins, Leland Stanford, and Charles Crocker, incorporated the Central Pacific Railroad. Known as the "Big Four," all of them happened to be ample in girth as well as in wealth.

Railroad land grants

In 1862 Congress granted the Central Pacific Railroad the right to build the western link of the transcontinental railroad eastward from Sacramento. To the

Union Pacific Corporation fell responsibility for the section from Omaha westward. Generous loans and gifts of federal and state lands made the venture wildly profitable. For every mile of track completed, the rail companies received between 200 and 400 square miles of land—some 45 million acres by the time the route was completed. Fraudulent stock practices, corrupt accounting, and wholesale bribery (involving a vice president of the United States and at least two members of Congress) swelled profits even more. More than 75 western railroads eventually benefited from such government generosity.

General Grenville Dodge, an army engineer on leave to the Union Pacific, recruited his immense labor force from Irish and other European immigrants. He drove them with ruthless army discipline, completing as much as 10 miles of track in a single day. Charles Crocker of the Central Pacific had no similar source of cheap labor in California. Worse yet, he faced the formidable task of cutting through the Sierra Nevadas. When his partner Leland Stanford suggested importing workers from China, Crocker dismissed him with a laugh—at first. But it was some 10,000 Chinese laborers who accomplished the feat. With wheelbarrows, picks, shovels, and baskets they inched eastward, building trestles like the one at Secrettown at right and chipping away at the Sierras' looming granite walls. On the worst stretches they averaged only eight inches a day.

Once Chinese crews had broken into the flat country of the desert basin, the two railroads raced to claim as much federal land as possible. In the resulting scramble, both sides passed each other, laying more than 200 miles of parallel track before the government ordered them to join. On May 10, 1869, at Promontory Point, Utah, a silver hammer pounded a gold spike into the last tie. East and West were finally linked by rail.

As the railroads pushed west in the 1860s, they helped to spawn cities like Denver and later awakened sleepy communities such as Los Angeles. Railroads opened the Great Plains to cattle drives that in the 1870s brought great herds to "cow towns" like Sedalia, Missouri, and Cheyenne, Wyoming, where cattle could be shipped to market. Fast behind the cattle boom came the "sodbusters" in the late 1870s to till the hard prairie soils left open by the destruction of the buffalo. By the 1890s the once barren

Great Plains were crisscrossed by rails, dotted with towns, and divided into farms, ranches, and Indian reservations.

The power of
the railroads

The rail companies recognized early the strategic value of their enterprise. If a key to profiting from the gold rush was supplying miners, one way to prosper from the West was to control transportation. Just by threatening to bypass a town, a railroad could extract concessions on rights of way, taxes, and loans. When Los Angeles resisted Charles Crocker's demands for major concessions, he and his partners in the Central Pacific Railroad threatened to ruin the town by leaving it off their route. After acquiring waterfront land in Oakland, the Central Pacific eventually commanded all railroad, ferry, and dock land around the rim of San Francisco Bay. That was why westerners developed such mixed feelings toward the railroads.

Cattle Kingdom

Westerners recognized that railroads were crucial components of the cattle industry. Cow towns like Abilene, Denver, and Cheyenne flourished from the business of the growing cattle kingdom. By 1860, some 5 million head of longhorn cattle were wandering the grassy plains of Texas. Ranchers allowed their herds to roam the unbroken or "open" range freely, identified only by a distinctive mark on their hides. Each spring cowboys rounded up the herds, branded the calves, and selected the steers to send to market.

Clara Williamson painted this herd on the long drive north from Texas. Cowboys normally worked in pairs, opposite each other, as shown here; the chuck wagon can be seen at the rear of the train. So strenuous was the work that each cowboy brought with him about eight horses so that fresh mounts would always be available.

Anglo Americans who came to Texas readily adopted the Mexican equipment: the tough mustangs and broncos (horses suited to managing mean-spirited long-horns), the branding iron for marking the herds, the corral for holding cattle, and the riata, or lariat, for roping. The cowboys also wore Mexican chaps, spurs, and broad-brimmed sombreros, or "hats that provide shade." After the Civil War, veterans of the Confederate army made up the majority of the cowhands in Texas. But at least a third of all cowboys were Mexicans and black freedmen. *Mexican ranching techniques*

In 1866, as rail lines swept west, Texas ranchers began driving their herds north to railheads for shipment to market. These "long drives" lasted from two to three months and sometimes covered more than 1000 miles. When early routes to Sedalia, Missouri, proved unfriendly, ranchers scouted alternative paths. The Chisholm Trail led from San Antonio to Abilene and Ellsworth in Kansas. More westerly routes soon ran to Dodge City and even Denver and Cheyenne.

Since cattle grazed on the open range, early ranches were primitive. Most had a house for the rancher and his family, a bunkhouse for the hired hands, and about 30 to 40 acres of grazing land per animal. Women were scarce in the masculine world of the cattle kingdom. Most were ranchers' wives, strong and resourceful women who cooked, nursed the sick, and helped run things. Some women ranched themselves. When Helen Wiser Stewart of Nevada learned in July 1884 that her husband had been murdered, she took over the ranch. Her life was an endless round of buying and selling cattle, managing the hands, and tending to family and crops. *Home on the range*

Farmers looking for their own homesteads soon became rivals to the cattle ranchers. The "nesters," as ranchers disdainfully called them, fenced off their lands, thus shrinking the open range. Vast grants to the railroads also limited the area of free land, while ranchers intent on breeding heavier cattle with more tender beef began to fence in their stock to prevent them from mixing with inferior strays.

Conflicts also arose between cattle ranchers and herders of another animal intro-duced by the Mexicans—sheep. Cattlemen had particular contempt for the sheep raiser and his "woolies." Sheep cropped grasses so short that they ruined land for cat-tle grazing. To protect the range they saw as their own from the "hooved locust," cat-tlemen attacked shepherds and their flocks. On one occasion enraged cattlemen clubbed 8000 sheep to death along the Green River in Wyoming. The feuds often burst into range wars, some more violent than those between farmers and ranchers.

The cattle boom that began with the first long drive of 1866 reached its peak from 1880 to 1885. Ranchers came to expect profits of 25 to 40 percent a year. Millions of dollars poured into the West from eastern and foreign interests eager to cash in on soaring cattle prices. Ranching corporations extended the open range from Texas into Wyoming and Montana. *Western boom and bust*

As in all booms, forces were at work bringing the inevitable bust. High profits soon swelled the size of the herds and led to overproduction. Increased competition from cattle producers in Canada and Argentina caused beef prices to fall. And nature imposed its own limits. On the plains, nutritious buffalo and gamma grasses were eaten to the nub, only to be replaced by unpalatable species. In the Great Basin, overgrazing destroyed the delicate balance between sagebrush and an understory of perennial bunch grasses. In their place came Russian thistle and cheatgrass that could support only small herds. When overgrazing combined with drought, as in New Mexico in the 1880s and 1890s, the results could be disastrous. In all these regions, as vegetation changed, erosion increased, further weakening the ecosystem. In 1870,

5 acres of plains land were needed to feed a steer. By the mid-1880s, 50 acres were required.

There was, moreover, simply not enough grass along the trails to support the millions of head on their way to market. Diseases like "Texas fever" sometimes wiped out entire herds. Then in 1886 and 1887 came two of the coldest winters in recorded history. The winds brought blizzards that drove wandering herds up against fences, where they either froze or starved to death. Summer brought no relief. Heat and drought scorched the grasslands and dried up waterholes. In the Dakotas, Montana, Colorado, and Wyoming, losses ran as high as 90 percent.

By the 1890s the open range and the long drives had largely vanished. What prevailed were the larger cattle corporations like the King Ranch of Texas. Only they had enough capital to acquire and fence vast grazing lands, hire ranchers to manage herds, and pay for feed during winter months. As for the cowboy, most became wage laborers employed by the ranching corporations. As with mining, the eastern pattern of economic concentration and labor specialization was being applied in the West.

THE FINAL FRONTIER

In the 1860s they had come in a trickle; in the 1870s they became a torrent. They were farmers from the East and Midwest, black freedmen from the rural South, and peasant-born immigrants from Europe. What bound them together was a craving for land. They had read railroad and steamship advertisements and heard stories from friends about millions of free acres in the plains west of the 98th meridian. Hardier strands of wheat like the "Turkey Red" from Russia, improved machinery, and new farming methods made it possible to raise crops in what once had been called the "Great American Desert." The number of farms in the United States jumped from around 2 million on the eve of the Civil War to almost 6 million in 1900.

A Rush for Land

So intense was the desire for land that in the spring of 1889 nearly 100,000 people made their way by wagon, horseback, carriage, buckboard, mule, and on foot to a line near present-day Oklahoma City, in the center of land once reserved for the Indians. These were "Boomers," gathered for the last great land rush in the trans-Mississippi West. At noon on April 22, 1889, the Boomers raced across the line to claim some 2 million acres of Indian territory just opened for settlement. Beyond the line lay the "Sooners"—those who had jumped the gun and hidden in gullies and thickets, ready to leap out an instant after noon to claim a stake in prosperity.

Boomers and Sooners

Yet even as the hopefuls lined up in Oklahoma, thousands of other settlers were abandoning their farms to escape mounting debts. The dream of the West as a garden paradise was already being shaken by harsh weather, overproduction, and competition from abroad. Wheat sold for $1.60 a bushel during the Civil War. It fell to 49 cents in the 1890s. Holding on as best they could, plains farmers braved a harsh climate in isolation.

Farming on the Plains

Farmers looking to plow the plains faced a daunting task. Under the Homestead Act (1862), government land could be bought for $1.25 an acre or claimed free if a homesteader had worked it for 5 years. But the best parcels—near a railroad line, with access to eastern markets—were owned by the railroads themselves or by speculators and sold for around $25 an acre. Furthermore, successful farming on the plains demanded expensive machinery. Steel-tipped plows and harrows (which left a blanket of dust to keep moisture from evaporating too quickly) permitted "dry farming" in arid climates. Threshers, combines, and harvesters brought in the crop, while powerful steam tractors pulled the heavy equipment.

Homestead Act

With little rain, many farmers had to install windmills and pumping equipment to draw water from deep underground. The threat of cattle trampling the fields forced farmers to erect fences. Lacking wood, they found the answer in barbed wire, first marketed by Illinois farmer Joseph Glidden in 1874. When all was said and done, the average farmer spent what was for the poor a small fortune, about $785 on machinery and another $500 for land. Bigger operators invested 10 or 20 times as much.

Tracts of 160 acres granted under the Homestead Act might be enough for eastern farms, but in the drier West more land was needed to produce the same harvest. Farms of more than 1000 acres, known as "bonanza farms," were most common in the wheat lands of the northern plains. A steam tractor working a bonanza farm could plow, harrow, and seed up to 50 acres a day—20 times more than a single person could do without machinery. Against such competition, small-scale farmers could scarcely survive. As in the South, many westerners became tenants on land owned by others. Bonanza farmers hired as many as 250 laborers to work each 10,000 acres in return for room, board, and 50 cents a day in wages.

Bonanza farms

A Plains Existence

For poor farm families, life on the plains meant sod houses or dugouts carved from hillsides for protection against the wind. Tough, root-bound sod was cut into bricks a

---

Sod houses could often make living difficult. It might be dry in a downpour, but afterward, the soaked roof would begin to drip and rain for hours. This Kansas sod house, built in 1899, looks simple enough from the outside, but the four windows hint that it was better furnished than most. For its interior, turn the page.

foot wide and three feet long and laid edgewise to create walls. Sod bricks covered rafters for a roof. The average house was seldom more than 18 by 24 feet, and in severe weather it had to accommodate animals as well as people. One door and often a single window provided light and air. The thick walls kept the house warm in winter and cool in summer, but a heavy, soaking rain or snow could bring the roof down or drip mud and water into the living area. As soon as a home was established, armies of flies, gnats, mosquitoes, and fleas moved in. Katherine Gibson of the Dakota territories went to light her stove one cold morning only to be attacked by a rattlesnake and its offspring.

Plains women   The heaviest burdens fell to women. With stores and supplies scarce, they spent long days over hot tubs preparing tallow wax for candles or soaking ashes and boiling lye with grease and pork rinds to make soap. In the early years of settlement wool was in such short supply that resourceful women used hair from wolves and other wild animals to make cloth. Buttons had to be fashioned from old wooden spoons. Without doctors, women learned how to care for the hurt and sick, treating anything from frostbite to snakebite and from sore throats to burns and rheumatism. Cobwebs could bandage small wounds; turpentine served as a disinfectant.

Nature added its hardships. In summer, searing winds blasted the plains for weeks. Grasses grew so dry that a single spark could ignite thousands of acres. Farmers in the Southwest lived in dread of stinging centipedes and scorpions that inhabited wall cracks. From Missouri to Oregon, nothing spelled disaster like locusts. They descended without warning in swarms 100 miles long. Beating against houses like hailstones, they stripped all vegetation, including the bark of trees. An entire year's labor might be destroyed in a day.

Winter held special horrors. Blizzards swept the plains, piling snow to the rooftops and halting all travel. Settlers might awaken to find their food frozen and snow on their beds. Weeks would pass before farm families saw an outsider. To prepare for the lean winter months women stocked their cellars with jarred preserves and made wild fruits into leathery cakes eaten to ward off the scurvy caused by vitamin deficiency.

The interior of the sod house shown on page 699. Mr. and Mrs. Bartholomew sit proudly amidst their possessions, including two ample bookcases, a pedal organ (note the fancy swiveled seat), wallpapered walls, pictures, and rugs on the floor.

In the face of such hardships many westerners found comfort in religion. Indians *Religion*
turned to traditional spiritualism and Hispanics to the Catholic church as a means of
coping with nature and change. Though Catholics and Jews came West, evangelical
Protestants dominated the Anglo frontier in the mining towns and in other western
communities. Worship offered an emotional outlet and some intellectual stimulation,
as well as a means of preserving old values and sustaining hope. As in the rural South,
circuit riders compensated for the shortage of preachers, while camp meetings offered the chance to socialize. Both brought contact with a world beyond the prairie.
In many communities it was the churches that first instilled order on public life.
Through church committees westerners could deal with local problems like the need
for schools or charity for the poor.

The Urban Frontier

Not all westerners lived in isolation. By 1890 the percentage of those in cities of
10,000 or more was greater than in any other section of the country except the
Northeast. Usually unruly, often chaotic and unplanned, western cities were mostly
the products of history, geography, technology, and commerce.

Some western cities—San Antonio, El Paso, and Los Angeles—were old
Spanish towns whose growth had been sparked by the westward march of Anglo migrants, the northward push of Mexican immigrants, and the spread of railroad lines.
Other cities profited from their location near commercial routes, like Portland on the
Columbia River in Oregon. Still others, such as Witchita, Kansas, arose to serve the
cattle and mining booms of the West. And as technology freed people from the need
to produce their own food and clothing, westerners turned to the business of supplying goods and services, enterprises that required the labor of more densely populated
cities.

Most newer cities had wide streets and large blocks. Where the streets of eastern cities measured 30 to 60 feet across, street widths of 80 feet or more were typical in the West. They had to be broad enough to allow ox-drawn wagons to turn, but
they also bespoke the big plans of town promoters. "Every town in the West," marveled one European, "is laid out on a plan as vast as though it were destined, at no
distant future, to contain a million of inhabitants."

Denver, Colorado, was typical. Founded in 1859, Denver's growth was boosted
by the discovery of gold at the mouth of Cherry Creek. It catered largely to miners
with a mix of supply stores, saloons, gambling parlors, and brothels. As it grew, so did
its reputation for violence. "A city of demons," said one disgusted visitor, where "a
man's life is of no more worth than a dog's." Until the early 1860s, when the city hired
its first police force, vigilante committees kept the peace with "the rope and the re-
volver."

The Bishop Is Coming!

LET US ALL TURN OUT AND
HEAR THE BISHOP

*Services in George and Human's Hall
tomorrow, Sunday, at 11 A.M. and 8 P.M.*

PLEASE LEAVE YOUR GUNS
WITH THE USHER

Wallace, Idaho, Miner Print.

The town of Wallace, Idaho, in the Coeur d'Alene mining region, illustrates the difficult
transition from a raw frontier community to a settled town with churches and family life.
("Please leave your guns with the usher," notes the 1890 circular.) When the first church was
finally built, it was competing for attention with over 60 saloons.

Daily Lives

FOOD/DRINK/DRUGS

The Frontier Kitchen of the Plains

Out on the treeless plains the Indians had adjusted to scarcity of food, water, and other necessities by adopting a nomadic way of life. Their small kinship groups moved each season to wherever nature supplied the food they needed. Such mobility discouraged families from acquiring extensive material possessions. Tools and housing had to be light and portable. Even tribes that raised crops as part of their subsistence cycle often moved with the seasons.

White settlement was different. Farmers, ranchers, and townspeople rooted themselves to a single place. What the surrounding countryside could not supply had to be brought from afar, generally at great effort and expense. In areas distant from the railroad or other transportation links, families generally had to learn either to do without or to improvise from materials at hand. Keeping food on the table was nearly impossible some seasons of the year. Coffee and sugar were staples in such short supply that resourceful women invented a variety of substitutes. "Take a gallon of bran, two tablespoonsful of molasses, scald and parch in an oven until it is somewhat browned and charred," one woman suggested. Something as simple as finding water suitable for drink-

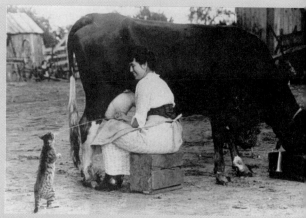

Just as on southern farms, women in the West played an essential role in the family economy. This woman has found a rather remarkable way to feed her cat.

ing or cooking became a problem in many western areas, where the choice might be between "the strong alkaline water of the Rio Grande or the purchase of melted manufactured ice (shipped by rail) at its great cost."

Gardening, generally a woman's responsibility, brought variety to the diet and color to the yard. The legume family of peas and beans, in particular, provided needed protein. Flowers were much prized but seldom survived the winds, heat, and dry periods. Dishwater and laundry water helped keep them alive. One woman was so excited

In the 1870s Denver embarked on a new phase of growth. The completion of the Denver Pacific and Kansas Pacific railroads made it the leading city on the eastern slope of the Rocky Mountains. Its economy diversified, and its population soared from about 5000 in 1870 to over 100,000 by 1890. It soon ranked only behind Los Angeles and Omaha among western cities.

Like much of the urban West, Denver grew outward rather than upward, spreading across the open landscape. Such spawling patterns of growth produced a by the discovery of a hardy dandelion that she cultivated it with care and planted its seeds each spring. To prepare for the lean winter months, women stocked their cellars and made wild fruits into leathery cakes eaten to ward off the scurvy that resulted from vitamin deficiency.

Until rail lines made the shipment of goods cheap and Sears, Roebuck "wishbooks" brought mail order to the frontier, a woman's kitchen was fairly modest. A cast iron stove, which sold for $25 in the East, was in such demand and so expensive to ship that it fetched $200 in some areas of the West. One miner's wife in Montana during the 1870s considered her kitchen "well-furnished" with two kettles, a cast iron skillet, and a coffeepot. A kitchen cupboard might be little more than a box nailed to a log. One "soddie" recalled that her kitchen remained snug and dry during a rainstorm, but after the sun came out, the water trapped in the thick sod roof seeped slowly down. She ended up frying pancakes on her stove under the protection of an umbrella while the sun shone brightly outside.

Without doctors, women learned how to care for the hurt and sick. Most folk remedies did little more than ease pain. Whiskey and patent medicines were often more dangerous than the disease, but they were used to treat a range of ills from frostbite to snakebite and from sore throats to burns and rheumatism. Settlers believed that onions and gunpowder had valuable medicinal properties. Cobwebs could bandage small wounds; turpentine served as a disinfectant. Mosquitoes were repelled with a paste of vinegar and salt. Most parents thought the laxative castor oil could cure any childhood malady. And if a family member had a fever, one treatment was to bind the head with a cold rag, wrap the feet in cabbage leaves, and then force down large doses of sage tea, rhubarb, and soda. Some women adapted remedies used on their farm animals. Sarah Olds, a Nevada homesteader whose family was plagued by fleas and lice, recalled that "we all took baths with plenty of sheep dip in the water. . . . I had no disinfectant . . . so I boiled all our clothing in sheep dip and kerosene."

Gradually, as the market system penetrated the West, families had less need to improvise in matters of diet and medicine. Through catalogs one might order spices like white pepper or poultry seasoning and appliances like grinders for real coffee. If a local stagecoach passed by the house, a woman might send her eggs and butter to town to be exchanged for needed store-bought goods like thread and needles. It took a complex commercial network to bring all that the good life required to a land that produced few foods and necessities in abundance.

city with sharply divided districts for business, government, and industry. Workers lived in one section of town—managers, owners, and other wealthier citizens in another.

Development was so rapid that Denver struggled to keep up with itself. Within a decade of plotting its initial tracts, the city began construction of the first of several horse-drawn railways. In 1891 the electrified trolley made its first appearance. By 1900, the city contained 800 miles of streets, but only 24 of them were paved. A

British observer marveled at "how [Denver's] future vast proportions seem to exist already in the minds of its projectors. Instead of its new streets and buildings being huddled as with us in our urban beginnings, they are placed here and there at suitable points, with confidence that the connecting links will soon be established." So, too, with the rest of the urban West.

Examining the census records of 1890, the superintendent of the census noted that landed settlements stretched so far that "there can hardly be said to be a frontier line." One after another, territories became states: Nebraska in 1867; Colorado in 1876; North Dakota, South Dakota, Montana, and Washington in 1889; Wyoming in 1890; Utah in 1896; Oklahoma in 1907; and New Mexico and Arizona in 1912. A new West was emerging as a mosaic of ethnicities, races, cultures, and climates but with the shared identity of a single region.

That sense of a regional identity was heightened, for both westerners and southerners, because so many of them felt isolated from the mainstream of industrial America. Ironically, it was not their isolation from northern industry but their links to it that marginalized them. The campaign for a New South to out-Yankee the industrial Yankee could not overcome the low wages and high fertility rates of an older South. The promoters of the West had greater success in adapting large-scale industry and investment to mining, cattle ranching, and farming. Still, they too confronted the limits of their region, whose resources were not endless and whose rainfall did not follow the plow. Like easterners, citizens of the West found that large corporations with near-monopoly control over markets and transportation bred inequality, corrupt politics, and resentment.

These conflicts of class, race, and region inevitably affected the political system. By the 1890s, an agrarian revolt was sweeping the South and West. In both sections disillusionment and despair turned to bitterness as more small farmers, black and white, found themselves enslaved to debt and driven toward bankruptcy, tenantry, and wage labor. It was small wonder, then, that the South and West gave rise to a "People's party" determined to end the "business-as-usual" approach of the Democratic and Republican parties.

CHAPTER SUMMARY

As different as the West and South might be in geography, certain features united them in the late nineteenth century. Both were major sources of agricultural goods and raw materials that fed urban and industrial growth. Both were racially divided societies in which whites often used violence to assert dominance. And both looked to human and finance capital beyond the region to boost their economies.

After the Civil War many southerners embraced the "New South" gospel that industrialization would bring prosperity. Certain industries did flourish, especially textiles, tobacco, steel, and timber. But the exploitation of local resources did not bring wealth to the region. And the southern economy remained wedded to cotton. Short of cash and credit, southern landowners resorted to sharecropping as a way to find labor to farm the land. Poor black and white southerners found themselves ever deeper in debt, due to high interest rates and low crop prices. Race, too, remained a divisive issue. As northerners accepted a laissez-faire policy on race relations, Redeemer governments introduced a Jim Crow policy of segregation. Socially, the South's rural culture reflected a division along lines of gender. Men loved to hunt, gamble, and drink together socially. Women's recreations more often had a domestic flavor. In the communities of both black and white southerners, the church provided spiritual uplift and social discipline, though religion was also segregated by race.

The West, too, was a largely rural society, though its population was far more ethnically and racially diverse. Two impediments limited growth: poor transportation and scarce water. The railroad boom eased the transportation problem, but powerful interests blocked John Wesley Powell's plan for cooperative water development. As eastern newcomers migrated into the region, white immigrants and Indians waged a sporadic guerrilla war for almost 30 years. Even more devastating for Indian culture were efforts under the Dawes Act to turn Indians into farmers. The pressure of white settlement also forced many Hispanics off their lands. Some integrated into Anglo society; others resisted. Along with a new influx of Mexicans, most Hispanics by the turn of the century worked as farm or railroad laborers or at other low-paying jobs. The booms in minerals, cattle, and farmlands during this era shared a common pattern. Small operators at first grabbed quick profits, but large corporations amassed the capital to produce wealth. For the small farm families who came in search of land, life on the plains was often lonely and harsh. Despite such difficulties, the West prospered more than the South because it attracted more human and finance capital.

SIGNIFICANT EVENTS

1849–1859	Gold and silver strikes open western mining frontier
1862	Homestead Act; Minnesota Sioux uprising begins Plains Indian wars
1864	Chivington massacre
1866	Drive to Sedalia, Missouri, launches cattle boom
1869	Completion of first transcontinental railroad; Powell explores the Grand Canyon
1872–1874	The great buffalo slaughter
1874	Black Hills gold rush; barbed wire patented
1876	Battle of Little Big Horn; Nez Percé resist relocation
1877	Compromise of 1877 ends Reconstruction; Crazy Horse surrenders
1879	Height of Exoduster migration to Kansas
1880	Bonsack cigarette-rolling machine invented
1883	*Civil Rights Cases*
1886–1887	Severe winter and drought cycle in the West
1887	Dawes Severalty Act
1889	Oklahoma opened to settlement
1890	Ghost Dance Indian religious revival; Wounded Knee
1892	Union violence at Coeur d'Alene, Idaho; Wyoming range wars
1896	*Plessy v. Ferguson* upholds separate but equal doctrine

ADDITIONAL READING

The themes of change and continuity have characterized interpretations of southern history after Reconstruction. For years C. Vann Woodward's classic, *The Origins of the New South* (1951), dominated thinking about the region with its powerful argument for a changing South. Edward Ayers, *The Promise of the New South* (1992) offers a fresh, comprehensive synthesis that sees both change and continuity. Gavin Wright, *Old South, New South* (1986) destroys the myth of the southern colonial economy. Ted Ownby, *Subduing Satan* (1990) provides a valuable discussion of southern social life, especially the role of religion. On the issue of race relations see Joel Williamson, *The Crucible of Race: Black–White Relations in the South since Emancipation* (1984).

The contours of western history were first mapped by Fredrick Jackson Turner in his famous address "The Significance of the Frontier in American History" (1893) but have been substantially reshaped by Richard White, *"It's Your Own Misfortune and None of My Own": A New History of the American West* (1992); Patricia Limerick, *A Legacy of Conquest: The Unbroken Past of the American West* (1987); and Donald Worster, *Rivers of Empire* (1985). Each describes the history of the West less as a traditional saga of frontier triumphs than as an analysis of how the region and its resources have been exploited by various peoples and cultures. Sarah Deutsch, *No Separate Refuge: Culture, Class and Gender on an Anglo-Hispanic Frontier in the American Southwest, 1880–1940* (1987) develops the concept of regional community to depict the interpenetration of cultures and their impact on gender in New Mexico and Colorado, while Robert M. Utley offers an excellent survey of American Indians in *The Indian Frontier of the American West 1846–1890* (1984). For a fuller list of readings, see the Bibliography.

Where Have All the Bison Gone?

In late summer of 1875 a herd of great American bison—the largest animals in North America—grazed lazily along a shallow creek bed. Summering on the highlands of the southern plains, they fed on the mid- and tall grasses of early spring and the late-sprouting shortgrasses of summer. They groomed, played, and mated before beginning their slow trek down to the river bottoms, where naturally cured shortgrasses and cottonwood bark nourished them during the winter months.

So the cycle had spun for thousands of years. But on this day in 1875 the bison of this herd began mysteriously to die. One by one, they dropped to the ground as if swatted by a huge, invisible hand. Those at the herd's edges went

first. Occasionally the animals gathered about a carcass and sniffed at the warm blood. Or they raised their heads to scent the wind for trouble. With the poorest eyesight on the plains, the bison could see little—certainly not the puff of smoke that appeared downwind as each new bison staggered and fell.

The hunter lay perfectly still. No need to move; his powerful .50-caliber Sharps rifle could drop a "shaggy" at 600 feet. No need for horses; they would only spook the herd. The man lay quietly downwind, ideally firing one, maybe two rounds a minute, keeping the pace of killing slow and steady. With care, a good hunter might bag as many as a hundred bison a day. And Tom Nixon was a good hunter, a professional in it for profit.

On this day in 1875, legend has it, Nixon killed 120 bison in 40 minutes. The barrel of his Sharps grew so hot that his bullets wobbled in flight. He forgot about the slow and steady kill, forgot even about his rifle, which was ruined in the hunt. That day he was out for a record, and he got it. The season was as profitable as the day. From September 15 to October 20, Nixon killed 2127 bison.

Other hunters fared well too. A buffalo robe fetched as much as $5 in the East. Operating in bands of three or four—a shooter, two skinners, and a cook—professional hunters wreaked havoc with the southern herd of the Great Plains in the 1870s. And within a decade, the northern herd had nearly vanished. By some counts, the 30 million bison that roamed the plains in the early nineteenth century shrank to 5000 by the mid-1880s.

Where had all the bison gone? Popular historical accounts have focused almost entirely on the gun-toting white hunters of legend and the smoke-belching railroad: symbols of a market economy penetrating the West. Without doubt, the market economy played a role in eliminating the vast herds. As far back as the 1830s and 1840s, fur trappers and traders were eating buffalo meat; so too were the railroad crews who extended tracks west. More to the point, the new rail lines provided easy transport of bulky robes and skins to the East. Railroad companies also brought whole trainloads of tourists to shoot at the herd from open windows

or atop the cars. In all, the great hunts brought about 10 million bison hides to market.

Ten million is an immense number. But even conservative estimates have suggested that 30 million buffalo had been roaming the plains. What other factors can account for the precipitous drop?

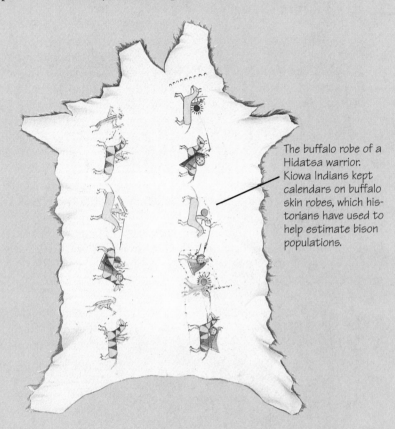

The buffalo robe of a Hidatsa warrior. Kiowa Indians kept calendars on buffalo skin robes, which historians have used to help estimate bison populations.

Understanding the fate of the bison herds has required historians to analyze the entire ecology of the plains, of which the bison were an integral part. In many ways, the decades of the 1870s and 1880s represent the end of a process begun much earlier. In reconstructing that process, historians have assembled evidence ranging from traditional accounts of traders and trappers to Indian oral traditions, agricultural census data for livestock, and meteorology reports. They have even found ingenious ways to evaluate the rings of trees and pollen sediment.

One piece of the bison puzzle appears in the 1850s, nearly 20 years before the great white hunts. Starving Indians began to appear across the central and southern plains. Traders reported that the Cheyenne were eating their treasured horses, and other tribes were raiding Mexico for stock. Historians are also able to catch a glimpse of these hard times in the painted robe calenders of the Kiowa. The calendars show the sign for "few or no bison" for four successive years beginning in 1849.

Contemporaries blamed white emigrants headed overland to the Pacific coast. But the pressures of overland migration alone were not enough to bring the Indians to starvation. From accounts in their diaries and letters, Overlanders themselves admitted to being poor hunters of bison. Few recorded ever killing more than a handful at a time. More puzzling, many Overlanders reported seeing the "blanched skulls and bones" of bison in the early 1840s, *before* the height of the overland migration. Most puzzling, bison were disappearing first from the western portion of the central plains, where whites were most scarce.

This Blackfoot robe records the history of one warrior's exploits. It also shows the importance in plains culture of the horse, which competed with the bison for food, especially during the winter.

Dozens of horseshoes record animals stolen from enemies.

Here, in the western plains, was precisely where Indians were plentiful. Since the seventeenth century, Indian peoples had been lured to the bison-rich plains. The bison became a staple of Indian life, providing a "grocery store on the hoof," hides for clothing and shelter, and a source of powerful religious symbols. Most Plains Indians followed the herds for their subsistence, but as the commercial trade in buffalo robes grew in the 1870s, tribes such as the Blackfeet were being drawn into the hunt for profit. In the first half of the nineteenth century, moreover, new Indian peoples had come to the plains, pushed by the westward advance of Euro-Americans and by hostile tribes from the Great Lakes region. The Indian population in the central plains grew from perhaps 8000 in 1820 to as many as 20,000 in the 1850s.

For a time, the competition between tribes actually helped protect the bison. Warring groups created buffer zones between them. These contested spaces served as refuges for bison, since hunting could be conducted only sporadically for fear of enemy attack. But after 1840 Indian diplomacy brought peace among many rival tribes. The bison began to disappear as Indians stepped up the hunt across the former buffer zones of the western range. They especially favored two- to five-year-old bison cows for their tender meat and their thinner, more easily processed hides. The death of these cows, the most fertile members of the herd, sharply reduced the number of new births.

Yet more was at work on the plains than the onslaught of hunters, white or Indian. A broader biotic invasion was under way. Incoming whites and Indians carried animals with them. Indians brought tens of thousands of horses, while the Pacific-bound Overlanders brought oxen, cattle, mules, and sheep. These ungulates carried diseases new to the plains—brucellosis, tuberculosis, and a variety of parasites. Later in the century, bison in refuges were found to be riddled with these deadly ailments. The new species also competed for grazing land. So Overlanders and

Indians were weakening the herds less through slaughter than by occupying the *habitats* of the bison and consuming their food.

Then, beginning in the late 1840s, two decades of unusually heavy rainfall were followed by years of drought. Scientists can deduce these conditions using the science of dendrochronology, which focuses on reading tree rings to provide clues about the weather of a particular era. Around 1850 tree rings began to shrink, indicating the onset of a cycle with more frequent droughts. As highland springs and creeks dried up and summer shortgrasses grew poorly, more bison began to disappear.

Earlier cycles of drought had led to the virtual disappearance of bison from the plains. No bison bones appear, for example, at archaeological levels that match pollen data indicating droughts between 5000 and 2500 B.C. and A.D 500 to 1300 . Thereafter a cycle of above-average rainfall and cooler weather created a more hospitable climate for bison. Unusually abundant rains in the early nineteenth century allowed the herds to grow much larger than normal, as Indian calendars also noted. When drought set in, the herds started to shrink.

In the end, the bison were brought low not by one factor but many. Drought, Indian population increases, and Indian market hunting weakened the great herds. The disturbances created by Overlanders and their animals, the appearance of new bovine diseases, and the increased competition for grazing land only made matters

By comparing the rings from this pine tree taken from the Grand Canyon, historians can date the years of its growth. The widest ring, indicating the wettest year, was 1767.

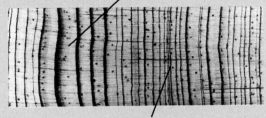

In contrast, 1754 was extremely dry.

worse. By the time the great white hunts began, the bison, though still numerous, were already in crisis.

BIBLIOGRAPHY. Maria Sandoz, *The Buffalo Hunters: The Story of the Hide Men* (1954) provides a vivid description of white hunters in the 1870s and 1880s. Dan Flores sets that traditional tale in a broader context in his pathbreaking article "Bison Ecology and Bison Diplomacy: The Southern Plains from 1800 to 1840," *Journal of American History* (September 1991): 465–485. Flores focuses on the southern plains, but more recently, Elliott West has come to similar conclusions about the central plains in *The Way to the West: Essays on the Central Plains* (1995). His essays move beyond the bison and include broader discussions of the interplay of climate, animals, plants, and people in the region.

21

The Political System Under Strain

World's Columbian Exposition

t was May 1, 1893. An eager crowd of nearly half a million people jostled into a dramatic plaza fronted on either side by gleaming white buildings overlooking a sparkling lagoon. Named the Court of Honor, the plaza was the center of a strange ornamental city that was at once awesome and entirely imaginary. At one end stood a building whose magnificent white dome exceeded even the height of the capitol in Washington. Unlike the marble-built capitol, however, this building was all surface: a stucco shell plastered onto a steel frame and then sprayed with white oil paint to make it glisten. Beyond the Court of Honor stretched thoroughfares encompassing over 200 colonnaded buildings, piers, islands, and watercourses. Located five miles south of Chicago's central business district, this city of the imagination proclaimed itself the "World's Columbian Exposition." Over the previous 2 years it had been erected in honor of the 400th anniversary of Columbus's voyage to America.

President Grover Cleveland opened the world's fair in a way that symbolized the nation's industrial transformation. He did not cut any simple ceremonial ribbon. Instead, Cleveland pressed a telegrapher's key. Instantly electric current set 7000 feet of shafting into motion—motion that in turn unfurled flags, set fountains pumping, and lit 10,000 electric bulbs. All told, 7000 arc lamps and 120,000 incandescent bulbs illuminated the fair, banishing darkness from the grounds. The lights played over an array of exhibition buildings soon known far and wide as the "White City."

In Cleveland's judgment the neoclassical architecture was both "magnificent" and "stupendous." Surely the sheer size was astonishing, for the buildings had been laid out not by the square foot but by the acre. The Illinois Building covered three acres and was a pygmy among giants. Transportation, Mines, Horticulture, and the U.S. Government were all bigger. The largest building, the Hall of Manufactures and Liberal Arts, spread its roof over 30 acres, twice the area of Egypt's Great Pyramid.

One English visitor dismissed the displays within as little more than "the contents of a great dry goods store mixed up with the contents of museums." In a sense he was right. Visitors paraded by an unending collection of typewriters, pins, watches, agricultural machinery, cedar canoes, and refrigerators, to say nothing of a 22,000-pound cheese and a map of the United States fashioned entirely out of pickles. But this riot of mechanical marvels, gewgaws, and bric-a-brac was symbolic, too, of the nation's industrial transformation. The fair resembled nothing so much as a tangible version of the new mail-order catalogues whose pages were now introducing the goods of the city to the hinterlands. By the time the fair closed on October 30, over 12 million people had come to gawk.

In 1893 the World's Columbian Exposition set the night ablaze with a towering searchlight visible 60 miles away. Here it spotlights the fair's theme, "the World United," just as the giant exhibition halls demonstrated how the new industrial order was reshaping the globe.

The connections made by the fair were international as well. This was the *World's Columbian Exposition*, with exhibits from 36 nations. Visitors could admire chinaware from England and a four-story high cross section of a modern new ocean liner that was making international travel easier. Germany's famous manufacturer of armaments, Krupp, had its own separate building. It housed a 120-ton rifled gun, 46 feet long, "said to be able to throw a projectile weighing one ton a distance of twenty miles." Easily within the range of its gunsights was a replica of the U.S. battleship *Illinois*, whose own bristling turrets stood just offshore of the exposition, on Lake Michigan. At the fair's amusement park, visitors encountered exotic cultures—and not just temples, huts, and totems, but exhibits in the living flesh. The Arabian village featured Saharan camels, veiled ladies, elders in turbans, and beggar children. Nearby, Irish peasants boiled potatoes over turf fires while Samoan men threw axes.

Like all such fairs, the Columbian Exposition created a fantasy: the best of all possible worlds enfolded into a single 583-acre park. Yet beyond the boundaries of the White City, the new industrial order was showing signs of strain. Early in 1893 the Philadelphia and Reading Railroad had gone bankrupt, setting off a financial panic. By the end of the year, nearly 500 banks and 15,000 businesses had failed. Although tourists continued to marvel at the fair's wonders, crowds of worried and unemployed workers also gathered elsewhere in Chicago. In August 25,000 listened to speeches by labor leader Samuel Gompers. On Labor Day, Governor John Altgeld of Illinois told another crowd that the government was powerless to avoid the "long dark day" of "suffering and distress" brought by this latest economic downturn. There would be no public works program to cushion the effects of the depression, he warned. People would simply have "to face it squarely and bear it with that heroism and fortitude with which an American citizen should face and bear calamity."

Strains on the political system

In truth, the political system was ill equipped to cope with the economic and social revolutions reshaping America. Those changes had created industrial and financial systems of remarkable power, as well as cities whose social diversity and stratification had increased sharply. The regional economies of the South and West had seen their raw materials being drawn into national and international markets over which farmers and workers had little control. Yet by and large, the political system had not taken part in a similar transformation. The executive branch remained weak, while members of Congress and the courts found themselves easily swayed by the financial interests of the industrial class. The crises of the 1890s strained the political order and forced it to confront such inequities.

International consequences

The political system also had to take into account developments abroad. Industrialization had sent American businesses around the world in search of raw materials and new markets. As that search intensified, many influential Americans argued that the United States needed to compete with European nations in acquiring territory overseas. By the end of the century, the nation's political system had taken its first steps toward modernization. That included a major political realignment at home and a growing empire abroad. The changes launched the United States into the twentieth century and an era of prosperity and global power.

THE POLITICS OF PARALYSIS

During the 1880s and 1890s, as the American political system came under strain, the Russian political scientist Moisei Ostrogorski visited the United States. Part of a flood of foreign observers, Ostrogorski also had come to see the American experiment in democracy firsthand. His verdict was as blunt as it was widely shared: "the constituted authorities are unequal to their duty." It seemed that the glorious experiment had fallen victim to greed, indifference, and political mediocrity.

In fact, there were deeper problems. Beyond simple "greed," the process of industrialization had created an increasing gulf between the very rich and poor of both city slums and depressed rural areas. The gap was deepened by the unpredictable cycle of boom and bust that periodically wrung out the economy. Finally, long-standing social inequalities continued to handicap African Americans, Indians, and women. The political system had scarcely addressed these problems, and it was grinding into a dangerous stalemate.

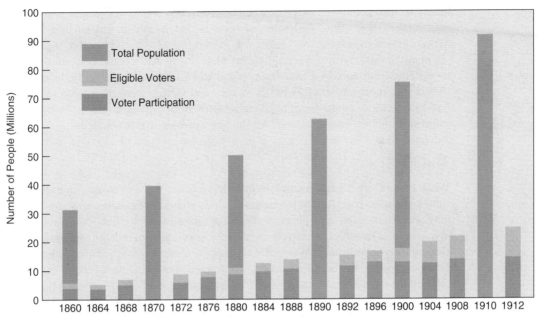

THE VOTING PUBLIC, 1860–1912

Between 1860 and 1910 the population and the number of eligible voters increased nearly threefold. As reforms of the early twentieth century reduced the power of political machines and parties, the percentage of voter participation actually declined.

Political Stalemate

From 1877 to 1897 American politics rested on a delicate balance of power that left neither Republicans nor Democrats in control. Republicans inhabited the White House for 12 years; Democrats, for 8. Margins of victory in presidential elections were paper thin. No president could count on having a majority of his party in both houses of Congress for his entire term. Usually Republicans controlled the Senate and Democrats the House of Representatives.

With elections so tight, both parties worked hard to turn out the vote. Brass bands, parades, cheering crowds of flag-wavers "are the order of the day and night from end to end of the country," reported a British visitor. In cities party workers handed out leaflets and pinned campaign buttons on anyone who passed. When Election Day rolled around, stores closed and businesses shut down. At political clubs and corner saloons men lined up to get voting orders (along with free drinks) from ward bosses. In the countryside, fields went untended as farmers took their families to town, cast their ballots, and bet on the outcome.

An average of nearly 80 percent of eligible voters turned out for presidential elections between 1860 and 1900, a figure higher than at any time since. In that era, however, the electorate made up a smaller percentage of the population. Strict voting qualifications limited participation. Only one American in four qualified to vote, and only one in five actually voted in presidential elections from 1876 to 1892. Most were white

Voter turnout

males. Women could vote in national elections only in a few western states, and beginning in the 1880s, the South erected barriers that eventually disfranchised many African American voters.

Party loyalty rarely wavered. In every election, 16 states could be counted on to vote Republican and 14 Democratic (the latter mainly in the South). In only six states—the most important being New York and Ohio—were the results in doubt. National victories often hung on their returns. Both parties courted these pivotal states with money, attention, and, not the least, presidential candidacies.

The Parties

What inspired such party loyalty? While Republicans and Democrats shared broad values, they also had clear differences that drew voters. Both parties supported business and condemned radicalism, and neither offered embattled workers or farmers much help. Democrats believed in states' rights and limited government, while Republicans favored federal activism to foster economic growth. The stronghold of Democrats lay in the South, where they reminded voters that they had led the states of the Old Confederacy, "redeemed" them from Republican Reconstruction, and championed white supremacy. Republicans dominated the North with strong support from industry and business. They, too, invoked memories of the Civil War to secure voters, black as well as white. "Not every Democrat was a rebel," they chanted, "but every rebel was a Democrat."

"For three months processions, usually with brass bands, flags, badges, crowds of cheering spectators, are the order of the day and night from end to end of the country," commented a British observer. Here, Denver Republicans celebrate the election of Benjamin Harrison in the presidential contest of 1888.

Ethnicity and religion also cemented voter loyalty. Republicans relied on old-stock Protestants, who feared new immigrants and put their faith in promoting pious behavior throughout society. In the Republican party, they found support for immigration restriction, prohibition, and English-only schools. In the North, the Democratic party attracted urban political machines, their immigrant voters, and the working poor. Often Catholic, these voters saw salvation in following their own religious rituals, not in dictating the conduct of the rest of society. For them, the Democratic party defended liberty because it opposed the very restrictions aimed at them by native-born, Protestant Americans.

Ethnic and religious factors

Region, religion, and ethnicity thus bound voters to each party. So too did the ordinary concerns of daily life. Some citizens weighed their purses and calculated the effect of their vote on their incomes. More thought of their parents, their children, or their communities when they went to the polls. Year after year, these familial and cultural loyalties shaped political allegiances.

Outside the two-party system, reformers often fashioned political organizations of their own. Some formed groups that aligned themselves behind issues rather than parties. Opponents of alcohol created the Women's Christian Temperance Union (1874) and the Anti-Saloon League (1893). Champions of women's rights joined the National Woman Suffrage Association (1890), a reunion of two branches of the women's suffrage movement that had split in 1869.

Third political parties also crystallized around a single concern or a particular group. Advocates of prohibition rallied to the Prohibition party (1869). Those who sought inflation of the currency formed the Greenback party (1874). Angry farmers in the West and South created the Populist, or People's, party (1892). All drew supporters from both conventional parties, but as largely single-interest groups they mobilized minorities, not majorities.

Third parties

The Issues

In the halls of Congress, attention focused on well-worn issues: veterans' benefits, appointments, tariffs, and money. The presidency had been weakened by the impeachment of Andrew Johnson, the scandals of Ulysses S. Grant, and the contested victory of Rutherford B. Hayes in 1876 (see pages 588–589). So Congress enjoyed the initiative in making policy. Time after time, legislators squandered it amid electioneering and party infighting.

Some divisive issues were the bitter legacy of the Civil War. Republicans and Democrats waved symbolic "bloody shirts," each tarring the other with responsibility for the war. The politics of the Civil War also surfaced in the lobbying efforts of veterans. The Grand Army of the Republic, an organization of more than 400,000 Union soldiers, petitioned Congress for pensions to make up for poor wartime pay and to support the widows and orphans of fallen comrades. By the turn of the century Union army veterans and their families were receiving $157 million annually. It was one of the largest public assistance programs in American history, which at its peak accounted for nearly half of the federal budget. It was also one of the first government programs to offer benefits to African Americans, although many black veterans were unable to cash in because they lacked the documentation required to prove they had served during the Civil War.

Pension system as forerunner of welfare state

The Civil War pension system, in fact, was more comprehensive than most of the fledgling social insurance programs begun in Europe during these same years. Nearly a

For all the voter turnout in the Gilded Age, politicians were often considered untrustworthy opportunists, out for the spoils of office. In this cartoon from the Gilded Age, entitled "Our Stumbling Block," Thomas Nast depicts corrupt politics and the spoils system as blocking the path of business and keeping Americans from prosperity. "One might search for the whole list of Congress, Judiciary, and Executive during the years 1870–1895 and find little but damaged reputations," concluded historian Henry Adams of the politicians of his era.

majority of aging men in northern states received benefits, as did a good many widows and children of veterans. (Confederate veterans were excluded.) Unlike the European systems, however, Congress did not extend benefits beyond veterans. Still, the veterans' assistance program was an important forerunner of the modern welfare state.

COUNTERPOINT

Origins of the welfare state

Historians disagree over the origins of the welfare state. Some maintain that the United States looked to Europe for initiatives and continually lagged behind industrial nations across the Atlantic in developing social welfare programs. In Europe the first social security and insurance laws were passed in the 1880s and 1890s. It was not until the Great Depression of the 1930s and the New Deal, when popular outcries for public assistance reached a fevered pitch, that the U.S. government introduced significant welfare legislation (see Chapter 26). Marxist historians add that such social policies originated less from public demands than from capitalists interested in controlling the working class and heading off more radical change.

More recently, historians and social scientists have focused on how public policies have been created or shaped by political organizations—not only conventional political parties but also politically active unions, veterans groups, and voluntary women's organizations. These scholars mark the birth of the modern welfare state in the Civil War pension program of the late nineteenth century. They see in the lobbying efforts of such groups as the General Federation of Women's Clubs and the National Congress of Mothers more pressure for government to aid women and children. (The efforts of these and other groups would bear fruit in the first two decades of the twentieth century, when some 40 states enacted programs for mothers' or widows' pensions.) Rather than lagging behind Europe in these realms, the United States had more elaborate and comprehensive programs than those abroad.

Equally important as an issue of reform was the campaign for a new method of staffing federal offices. Since the early nineteenth century, political victors had awarded government jobs to loyal followers, regardless of their qualifications. After elections, winners faced an army of office seekers, "lying in wait . . . like vultures for a wounded bison." Yet the federal bureaucracy had increased sharply, from barely 53,000 employees at the end of the Civil War to 166,000 by the early 1890s. Far more of these new jobs required special skills.

But dismantling this "spoils system" proved difficult for politicians who had rewarded faithful supporters with government jobs. Reacting to the scandals of the Grant administration, a group of independents formed the National Civil Service Reform League in 1881. The league promoted the British model of civil service based on examination and merit. Most members of Congress were predictably unenthusiastic, before their minds were changed in July of that year by a frustrated office seeker named Charles Guiteau. As President James Garfield hurried to catch a train, Guiteau jumped from the shadows and shot him twice. Garfield's death finally produced reform. In 1883 the Civil Service Act, or Pendleton Act, created a bipartisan civil service commission to administer competitive examinations for some federal jobs. Later presidents expanded the jobs covered. By 1896 almost half of all federal workers came under civil service jurisdiction. Whether the new system actually improved the quality of bureaucrats was hotly debated.

Pendleton Act

As much as any issue, the protective tariff stirred emotions in Congress. As promoters of economic growth and protectors of American industry, Republicans usually championed the tax on manufactured imports. Democrats, with their strength in the agrarian South, generally sought tariff reduction to encourage foreign trade, cut the federal surplus, and reduce the price of manufactured goods. In 1890, when Republicans controlled the House, Congress enacted the McKinley Tariff. It raised schedules to an all-time high. The McKinley Tariff also contained a novel twist known as reciprocity: the president could lower rates if other countries did the same. In 1894 House Democrats succeeded in reducing rates, only to be thwarted by some 600 Senate amendments restoring most cuts. In 1897 the Dingley Tariff raised rates still higher but soothed reductionists by broadening reciprocity.

McKinley Tariff

Just as divisive was the issue of currency. For most of the nineteenth century, currency was backed by both gold and silver. The need for more money during the Civil War had led Congress to issue "greenbacks"—currency printed on paper with a green back and not convertible to gold or silver. For the next decade and a half Americans argued over whether to print more such paper money or take it out of circulation. Farmers and other debtors favored printing greenbacks as a way of inflating prices and thus reducing their debts. For the opposite reasons, bankers and creditors stood for "sound money" backed by gold. Fear of inflation led Congress first to reduce the number of greenbacks and then in 1879 to make all remaining paper money convertible into gold.

A more heated battle was developing over silver-backed money. By the early 1870s so little silver was being used that Congress officially stopped coining it in 1873, touching off a steep economic slide as the supply of money contracted. With it came charges that a conspiracy of bankers had been responsible for "demonetizing" silver and wrecking the economy in what was widely referred to as the "Crime of '73." In 1878 the Bland–Allison Act inaugurated a limited form of silver coinage. But pressure for unlimited coinage of silver—coining all silver presented at U.S. mints— mounted as silver production quadrupled between 1870 and 1890. In 1890 pressure for silver peaked in the Sherman Silver Purchase Act. It obligated the government to buy 4.5 million ounces of silver every month. Paper tender called "treasury notes," redeemable in either gold or silver, would pay for it. The compromise satisfied both sides only temporarily.

Bland–Allison Act

The White House from Hayes to Harrison

From the 1870s through the 1890s a string of nearly anonymous presidents presided over the country. Not all were mere caretakers. Some tried to energize the office, but Congress continued to bridle the executive.

In this cartoon, Uncle Sam sits securely behind a locked door, protected by the Dingley tariff bill from the riotous clamor of foreigners seeking entry into U.S. markets. Whenever reformers tried to reduce tariffs, political support for protection made the task nearly impossible. In 1882 Congress created a commission to consider lowering tariffs, but it was quickly captured by the interests who stood to gain most from high tariffs. Complained one senator: "There was a representative of the wool growers on the commission; . . . of the iron interest . . . of the sugar interest. . . . And those interests were very carefully looked out for."

Republican Rutherford B. Hayes was the first of the "Ohio dynasty," which in-cluded three presidents from 1876 to 1900. As president, Hayes moved quickly to end Reconstruction and tried unsuccessfully to woo southern Democrats with promises of economic support. His pursuit of civil service reform ended only in split-ting his party between "Stalwarts" (who favored the old spoils systems) and "Half-Breeds" (who opposed it and favored reform). Hayes left office after a single term, happy to be "out of a scrape."

In 1880, Republican James Garfield, another Ohioan, succeeded Hayes by a handful of votes. He spent his first hundred days in the White House besieged by of-fice hunters, trying and failing to placate the rival sections of his party. After Garfield's assassination only six months into his term, Chester A. Arthur, the "spoilsman's spoilsman," became president. To everyone's surprise, the dapper Arthur turned out to be an honest president. He broke with machine politicians, including his mentor and Stalwart leader Roscoe Conkling of New York. He worked to lower the tariff, warmly endorsed the new Civil Service act, and reduced the federal surplus by be-ginning construction of a modern navy. Such evenhandedness left him little chance for renomination from divided party leaders.

The election of 1884 was one of the dirtiest ever recorded. Senator James Blaine, the beloved "Plumed Knight" from Maine and leader of the reform-minded Half-Breeds, ran against Democrat Grover Cleveland, the former governor of New York. Despite superb talents as a leader and vote-getter, Blaine was haunted by old charges of illegal favoritism for the Little Rock and Fort Smith Railroad. For his part, "Grover the Good" had built a solid reputation for honesty by fighting corruption and the spoils system in New York. So hard a worker was the portly Cleveland, sighed a reporter, that he "remains within doors constantly, eats and works, eats and works, and works and eats." Still, the bachelor Cleveland spent enough time away from his desk to father an illegitimate child. The country rang with Republican taunts of "Ma, ma, where's my pa?"

The dirty election of 1884

In the last week of the tight race, Cleveland supporters in New York circulated the statement of a local Protestant minister that labeled Democrats the party of "Rum, Romanism, and Rebellion" (alcohol, Catholicism, and the Civil War). The Irish-Catholic vote swung to the Democrats. New York went to Cleveland, and with it, the election. Democrats crowed with delight over where to find the bachelor "pa": "Gone to the White House, ha, ha, ha!"

Cleveland was the first Democrat elected to the White House since James Buchanan in 1856, and he was more active than many of his predecessors. He pleased reformers by expanding the civil service, and his devotion to gold-backed currency, economy, and efficiency earned him praise from business. He supported the growth of federal power by endorsing the Interstate Commerce Act (1887), new agricultural research, and federal arbitration of labor disputes.

Cleveland's presidential activism nonetheless remained limited. He vetoed two of every three bills brought to him, more than twice the number of all his predeces-sors. Toward the end of his term, embarrassed by the large federal surplus, Cleveland finally reasserted himself by attacking the tariff, but to no avail. The Republican-con-trolled Senate blocked his attempt to lower it.

In 1888 Republicans nominated a sturdy defender of tariffs, Benjamin Harrison, the grandson of President William Henry Harrison. President Cleveland won a plu-rality of the popular vote but lost in the Electoral College. The "human iceberg" (as

A Chinese laborer, queue in hand, proudly displays patches in support of the 1888 Democratic presidential candidate Grover Cleveland and his running mate, Allen B. Thurman. Cleveland and Thurman lost to Benjamin Harrison and Levi P. Morton, a wealthy New York banker. After his victory, Harrison, a pious Presbyterian, grabbed the hand of Senator Matthew Quay and crowed, "Providence has given us the victory." "Providence hadn't a damn thing to do with it," Quay said later, irked that Harrison seemed to have no idea how many Republicans "were compelled to approach the gates of the penitentiary to make him President."

Harrison's colleagues called him) worked hard, rarely delegated management, and turned the White House into a well-regulated office. He helped to shape the Sherman Silver Purchase Act (1890), kept up with the McKinley Tariff (1890), and accepted the Sherman Antitrust Act (1890) to limit the power and size of big businesses.

By the end of Harrison's term in 1892, Congress had completed its most productive session of the era, including the first billion-dollar peacetime budget. To Democratic jeers of a "Billion Dollar Congress," Republican House Speaker Thomas Reed shot back, "This is a billion-dollar country!"

Ferment in the States and Cities

Despite its growing expenditures and more legislation, most people expected little from the federal government. Few newspapers even bothered to send correspondents to Washington. Public pressure to curb the excesses of the new industrial order mounted closer to home, in state and city governments. Experimental and often effective, state programs began to grapple with the problems of corporate power, discriminatory shipping rates, political corruption, and urban decay.

State commissions   Starting in 1869 with Massachusetts, states established commissions to investigate and regulate industry, especially railroads, America's first big business. By the turn of the century, almost two-thirds of the states had them. These early commissions gathered and publicized information on shipping rates and business practices and furnished advice about public policy.

In the Midwest, on the Great Plains, and in the Far West, merchants and farmers pressed state governments to rein in high railroad rates and stop the rebates given to large shippers. In California, one newspaper published a schedule of freight rates to Nevada, showing that lower rates had been charged by wagon teams before the railroads were built. On the West Coast and in the Midwest, state legislatures empowered commissions to end rebates and monitor freight rates. In 1870 Illinois became the first of several states to define railroads as public highways subject to regulation, including setting maximum rates.

Concern over political corruption and urban blight led to state municipal conventions, the first in Iowa in 1877. Philadelphia sponsored a national conference on good city government in 1894. A year later reformers founded the National Municipal League. It soon had more than 200 branches. Its model city charter advanced such farsighted reforms as separate city and state elections, limited contracts for utilities, and more authority for mayors. Meanwhile cities and states in the Midwest enacted laws closing stores on Sundays, prohibiting the sale of alcohol, and making English the language of public schools—all in an effort to standardize social behavior and control the habits of new immigrants.

National Municipal League

THE REVOLT OF THE FARMERS

In 1890, the politics of stalemate cracked as the patience of farmers across the South and the western plains reached an end. Beginning in the 1880s, a sharp depression drove down agricultural prices and forced thousands from their land. "We went to work and plowed and planted," recalled one woman, ". . . and we raised the big crop they told us to; and what came of it? Eight cent corn, ten cent oats, two cent beef and no price at all for butter and eggs. . . . Then the politicians said we suffered from overproduction."

Plummeting prices and overproduction had taken their toll, but farmers suffered from a great deal more, including heavy mortgages, widespread poverty, and railroad rates that sometimes discriminated against them. In 1890 their resentment boiled over. An agrarian revolt—called Populism—swept the political landscape. It stirred first on the southern frontier, spread eastward from Texas through the rest of the Old South, then west across the Great Plains until it reached the Rockies, where silver miners were touched by its magic promise of empowering "toilers" like themselves. By the end of the century, Populism had run its course, but not before helping to break the political stalemate of the previous 20 years.

The Harvest of Discontent

The harvest of discontent was first reaped by farmers. Manufacturers protected by the tariff, railroads with sky-high shipping rates, wealthy bankers who held their mounting debts, expensive middlemen who stored and processed their commodities—all seemed to profit at the expense of farmers.

Targets of farm anger

The true picture was a good deal fuzzier. The tariff protected industrial goods but also supported some farm commodities. Railroad rates, however high, actually fell from 1865 to 1890. And while mortgages were heavy, most were short, no more

Mary Shelley's novel of a man-made monster who turns against its creator strikes the theme for this 1874 cartoon entitled "The American Frankenstein." As pictured here, the railroad is a monstrous creation that crushes the common people in its path. It carries the symbols of wealth and might—a cloak of ermine and a club of capital. "Agriculture, commerce, and manufacture are all in my power," the monster bellows in the caption. Figures of authority, like the policeman at the lower right, can only snap to attention and salute.

than four years. Farmers often refinanced them and used the money to buy more land and machinery, thus increasing their debts. Millers and operators of grain elevators or storage silos earned handsome profits, yet every year more of them came under state regulation.

Credit crunch   In hard times, of course, none of this mattered. And in the South many poor farmers seemed condemned forever to hard times. Credit lay at the root of their problem, since most southern farmers had to borrow money to plant and harvest their crops. The inequities of sharecropping and the crop–lien system (pages 670–671) forced them into debt. When the prices for their crops fell, they borrowed still more, stretching the financial resources of the South beyond their meager limits. Within a few years after the Civil War, Massachusetts's banks had five times as much money as all the banks of the Old Confederacy.

Beginning in the 1870s, nearly 100,000 debt-ridden farmers a year picked up stakes across the Deep South and fled to Texas to escape this ruinous system of credit, only to find it waiting for them. Others stood and fought, as one pamphlet exhorted in 1889, "not with glittering musket, flaming sword and deadly cannon, but with the silent, potent and all-powerful ballot."

The Origins of the Farmers' Alliance

Before farmers could vote together, they had to get together. Life on the farm was harsh, drab, and isolated. Such conditions shocked Oliver Hudson Kelley as he traveled across the South after the Civil War. In 1867 the young government clerk founded the Patrons of Husbandry to brighten the lives of farmers and broaden their

Patrons of Husbandry

horizons. Local chapters, called "granges," brought farmers and their families together to pray, sing, and learn new farming techniques. The Grangers sponsored fairs, picnics, dances, lectures—anything to break the bleakness of farm life. After a slow start the Grange grew quickly. By 1875 there were 800,000 members in 20,000 locals, most in the Midwest, South, and Southwest.

At first the Grangers swore off politics. But in a pattern often repeated, socializing led to economic and then political action. By pooling their money to buy supplies and equipment to store and market their crops, Grangers could avoid the high charges of middlemen. By the early 1870s they also were lobbying midwestern legislatures to adopt "Granger laws" regulating rates charged by railroads, grain elevator operators, and other middlemen.

Eight "Granger cases" came before the Supreme Court in the 1870s to test the new regulatory measures. *Munn v. Illinois* (1877) upheld the right of Illinois to regulate private property (in this case, the giant elevators for storing grain) so long as it was "devoted to a public use." Later decisions allowed state regulation of railroads, but only within state lines. Congress responded in 1887 by creating the Interstate Commerce Commission, a federal agency that could regulate commerce across state boundaries. In practice, it had little power, but it was a key step toward establishing the public right to oversee private corporations. *Granger cases*

Slumping prices in the 1870s and 1880s bred new farm organizations. Slowly they blended into what the press called the "Alliance Movement." The Southern Alliance, formed in Texas in 1875, spread rapidly after Dr. Charles W. Macune took command in 1886. A doctor and lawyer as well as a farmer, Macune planned to expand Texas's network of local chapters, or suballiances, into a national network of state Alliance Exchanges. Like the Grangers, the exchanges pooled their resources in cooperatively owned enterprises for buying and selling, milling and storing, banking and manufacturing. *Southern Alliance*

Soon the Southern Alliance was publicizing its activities in local newspapers, publishing a journal, and sending lecturers across the country. By 1890 it claimed more than a million members. Hoping to stay within the framework of the two-party system, the Southern Alliance tried to win over the Democratic party. Alliance advocates "Pitchfork" Ben Tillman in South Carolina and Tom Watson in Georgia successfully challenged party regulars and won office as Democrats.

For a brief period, between 1886 and 1892, the Alliance cooperatives multiplied throughout the South and challenged accepted ways of doing business. Macune claimed that his new Texas Exchange saved members 40 percent on plows and 30 percent on wagons. But most Alliance cooperatives were managed by farmers without the time or experience to succeed. Usually opposed by irate local merchants, the ventures eventually failed.

Although the Southern Alliance admitted no African Americans, it encouraged them to organize. A small group of black and white Texans founded the Colored Farmers' National Alliance and Cooperative Union in 1886. By 1891 a quarter of a million farmers had joined. Its operations were largely secret, since public action often brought swift retaliation from white supremacists. When the Colored Farmers' Alliance organized a strike of black cotton pickers near Memphis in 1891, white mobs hunted down and lynched 15 strikers. The murders went unpunished, and the Colored Alliance began to founder.

The Alliance Peaks

Farmer cooperation reached northward to the states of the Midwest and Great Plains in the National Farmers' Alliance, created in 1880. In June 1890 Kansas organizers formed the first People's party to compete with Democrats and Republicans. Meanwhile the Southern Alliance changed its name to the National Farmers' Alliance and Industrial Union, incorporated the strong Northern Alliances in the Dakotas and Kansas, and made the movement truly national.

The key to Alliance success was not organization but leadership, both at the top and in the middle. Alliance lecturers fanned out across the South and the Great Plains, organizing suballiances and teaching new members about finance and cooperative businesses. Women were often as active as men. Membership lists, recorded in the rough script of a farmer-secretary, showed that at least one-quarter of Alliance members were women. Families had formed an essential part of the Grange, and the Alliance movement continued the practice of sponsoring family-oriented activities: songfests; parades; picnics; even burial services. Although Alliance members remained sharply divided over woman suffrage, more than a few women became speakers and organizers. "Wimmin is everywhere," noted one observer of the Alliance. The comment seemed to apply literally to Mary Elizabeth Lease, who in the summer of 1890 alone gave 160 speeches.

Ocala Demands

In 1890 members of the Alliance met in Ocala, Florida, and issued the "Ocala Demands." The manifesto reflected the Populists' deep distrust of "the money power"—large corporations and banks whose financial power gave them the ability to manipulate the "free" market. The Ocala Demands called on government to correct such abuses by reducing tariffs, abolishing national banks, regulating railroads, and coining silver money freely. The platform also demanded a federal income tax and the popular election of senators to make government more responsive to the public.

The most innovative feature of the platform came from Charles Macune. His "subtreasury system" would require the federal government to furnish warehouses for harvested crops and low-interest loans to tide farmers over until prices rose. Under such a system farmers would no longer have to sell in a glutted market, as they did under the crop–lien system. And they could exert control over the money supply, expanding it simply by borrowing at harvest time.

In the elections of 1890 the old parties faced hostile farmers across the nation. In the South, the Alliance continued to work within the Democratic party and elected 4 governors, won 8 legislatures, and sent 44 members of Congress and 3 senators to Washington. In the Great Plains, Alliance candidates drew farmers from the Republican party. Newly created farmer parties elected five representatives and two senators in Kansas and South Dakota and took over both houses of the Nebraska legislature.

Mary Elizabeth Lease, the "Kansas Pythoness," was admitted to the bar as a young woman but soon turned to radical activism. A charismatic speaker, she campaigned for Populist candidates in the 1890s, on one occasion warning the industrial Northeast that "the people are at bay, let the bloodhounds of money beware."

In the West especially, Alliance organizers began to dream of a national third party that would be free from the corporate influence, sectionalism, and racial tensions that split Republicans and Democrats. It would be a party not just of farmers but of the downtrodden, including industrial workers.

In February 1892, as the presidential election year opened, a convention of 900 labor, feminist, farm, and other reform delegates (100 of them black) met in St. Louis. They founded the People's, or Populist, party and called for another convention to nominate a presidential ticket. Initially southern Populists held back, clinging to their strategy of working within the Democratic party. But when newly elected Democrats failed to support Alliance programs, southern leaders like Tom Watson of Georgia abandoned the party and began recruiting black and white farmers for the Populists.

The national convention of Populists met in Omaha, Nebraska, on Independence Day, 1892. Their impassioned platform promised to return government "to the hands of 'the plain people.'" More conservative southern Populists succeeded in blocking a plank for woman suffrage, though western Populists joined the campaign that would win women the right to vote in Colorado in 1893. Planks advocated the subtreasury plan, unlimited coinage of silver and expansion of the money supply, direct election of senators, an income tax, and government ownership of railroads, telegraph, and telephone. To attract wage earners the party endorsed the eight-hour workday, restriction of immigration, and a ban on the use of Pinkerton detectives in labor disputes—for the Pinkertons had engaged in a savage gun battle with strikers that year at Andrew Carnegie's Homestead steel plant. Delegates rallied behind the old greenbacker and Union general James B. Weaver, carefully balancing their presidential nomination with a one-legged Confederate veteran as his running mate.

The Election of 1892

The Populists enlivened the otherwise dull campaign of 1892, as Democrat Grover Cleveland and Republican incumbent Benjamin Harrison refought the election of 1888. This time, however, Cleveland won, and for the first time since the Civil War, Democrats gained control of both houses of Congress. The Populists, too, enjoyed success. Weaver polled over a million votes, the first third-party candidate to do so. Populists elected 3 governors, 5 senators, 10 representatives, and nearly 1500 members of state legislatures.

Despite these victories, the election revealed dangerous weaknesses in the People's party. Across the nation thousands of voters did change political affiliations, but most often from the Republicans to the Democrats, not to the Populists. No doubt the Democratic campaign of intimidation and repression hurt the People's party in the South, where white conservatives had been appalled by Tom Watson's open courtship of black southerners. ("You are kept apart that you may be separately fleeced of your earnings," Watson had told his racially mixed audiences.) In the North, Populists failed to win over labor and most city dwellers. Both were more concerned with family budgets than with the problems of farmers and the downtrodden.

Longer-term weaknesses of the Populists

The darker side of Populism also put off many Americans. Its rhetoric was often violent; it spoke ominously of conspiracies and stridently in favor of immigration restriction. In fact, in 1892 the Alliance lost members, an omen of defeats to come. But for the present, the People's party had demonstrated two conflicting truths. It showed how far from the needs of many ordinary Americans the two parties had drifted and how difficult it would be to break their power.

THE NEW REALIGNMENT

President Cleveland took office in March 1893, only a month after a British banking firm had suddenly gone bankrupt. Nervous investors there quickly sold millions of shares of American stock, depressing those prices and giving U.S. financiers the jitters. Four days after the president opened the Columbian Exposition, a wave of bankruptcies destroyed major firms across the country, and stock prices sank to all-time lows. The chain reaction was not as instantaneous as Cleveland's flick of an electric switch, but the consequences quickly rippled through the economy. In the months that followed, some 600 banks and 15,000 businesses across the nation failed. The depression of 1893 was the worst the nation had yet experienced.

At first Chicago staved off the downturn, thanks in part to the business generated by the exposition. But when it closed in October, thousands of laborers found themselves out of a job. Chicago's mayor estimated the number of unemployed in the city to be near 200,000. He had some firsthand experience on which to base his calculations, for every night desperate men slept on the floors and stairways of City Hall, while every police station in the city put up 60 to 100 additional homeless. Children as well as their parents rifled the city's garbage dumps for food.

The Depression of 1893

The sharp contrast between the exposition's White City and the nation's economic misery demonstrated the inability of the political system to smooth out the economic cycle of boom and bust. In the slow recovery from the depression of 1873, the economy had overexpanded. Railroads, at the center of boom, overbuilt. Businesses borrowed heavily to finance new projects. Farmers increased their production by purchasing expensive machinery on credit. In March 1893 the inevitable contraction began, sparked by the collapse first of the Philadelphia and Reading Railroad, then of the giant National Cordage Company.

The price of interdependence

The new industrial order had brought prosperity by increasing production, opening markets, and tying Americans closer together. But in 1893, the price of interdependence became obvious. A major downturn in one area affected the other sectors of the economy. With no way to control swings in the business cycle, depression came on a scale as large as the booming prosperity had been. Four years would pass before the economy began to revive.

Railroad baron and descendant of two presidents Charles Francis Adams, Jr., called the depression a "convulsion," but the country experienced it as crushing idleness. In August 1893, unemployment stood at 1 million; by the middle of 1894, it was 3 million. At the end of the year nearly one worker in five was out of a job, and one survey revealed that as late as 1901 half the heads of working-class households still had no jobs. Lining the streets of Washington stood "a vast army of unemployed, and men pleading for food who have never before been compelled to seek aid."

Charles Dana Gibson, the Massachusetts-born illustrator famous for his portraits of well-bred young women in the 1890s, tackles a different subject in this ink drawing, a bread line of mixed classes during the depression of 1893.

Working and middle-class families took in boarders, laundry, and sewing to make ends meet. With so many fathers and husbands unemployed, more and more wives and children left home to work. In the 1890s the number of laboring women actually increased, from 4 million to 5.3 million, but mainly in the exploitative fields of domestic and clerical work. In the South, where half the nation's working children were employed, child labor rose by 160 percent in textile mills during the decade. Concern for the young became so acute that middle-class women created the League for the Protection of the Family in 1896. Among other things it advocated compulsory education to keep children out of factories and mines.

League for the Protection of the Family

The federal government had no program at all to combat the effects of the depression. "While the people should patriotically and cheerfully support their Government," President Cleveland had said at his inauguration, "its functions do not include the support of the people." The states offered little more. Relief, like poverty, was considered a private matter. The burden fell on local charities, benevolent societies, churches, labor unions, and ward bosses. In city after city, citizens organized relief committees to distribute bread and clothing until their meager resources gave out.

Others were less charitable. As the popular preacher Henry Ward Beecher told his congregation, "No man in this land suffers from poverty unless it be more than his fault—unless it be his sin." But the scale of hardship was so great, its targets so random, that anyone could be thrown out of work—an industrious neighbor, a factory foreman with 20 years on the job, a bank president. Older attitudes about personal guilt and responsibility for poverty began to give way to new ideas about its social origins and the obligation of public agencies to help.

The Rumblings of Unrest

Even before the depression, rumblings of unrest had begun to roll across the country. The Great Railroad Strike of 1877 had ignited nearly two decades of labor strife (pages 628–629). After 1893 discontent mounted as wages were cut, employees laid off, and factories closed. During the first year of the depression, 1400 strikes sent more than half a million workers from their jobs.

Uneasy business executives and politicians saw radicalism and the possibility of revolution in every strike. But the depression of 1893 had unleashed another force: simple discontent. In the spring of 1894, it focused on government inaction. On Easter Sunday, "General" Jacob Coxey, a 39-year-old Populist and factory owner, *Coxey's Army*   launched the "Tramps' March on Washington" from Massillon, Ohio. His "Commonweal Army of Christ"—some 500 men, women, and children—descended on Washington at the end of April to offer "a petition with boots on" for a federal program of public works. President Cleveland's staff tightened security around the White House as other "armies" of unemployed mobilized: an 800-person contingent left from Los Angeles; a San Francisco battalion of 600 swelled to 1500 by the time it reached Iowa.

On May 1, Coxey's troops, armed with "clubs of peace," massed at the foot of the capitol. When Coxey entered the capitol grounds, 100 mounted police routed the demonstrators and arrested the general for trespassing on the grass. Nothing came of the protest, other than to signal a growing demand for federal action.

Federal help was not to be found. Grover Cleveland had barely moved into the White House when the depression struck. The country blamed him; he blamed silver. In his view the Sherman Silver Purchase Act of 1890 had shaken business confidence by forcing the government to use its shrinking reserves of gold to purchase (though not coin) silver. Repeal of the act, Cleveland believed, was the way to build gold reserves, restore confidence, and achieve recovery. After bitter debate, Congress complied. But this economic tinkering only strengthened the resolve of "silverites" in the Democratic party to overwhelm Cleveland's conservative "gold" wing.

Worse for the president, repeal of silver purchases brought no economic revival. In the short run abandoning silver hurt the economy by shrinking the money supply just when expansion might have stimulated it by providing needed credit. As panic and unemployment spread, Cleveland's popularity wilted. Democrats were buried in the congressional elections of 1894. Dropping moralistic reforms and stressing national activism, Republicans won control of both the House and the Senate. With the Democrats now confined to the South, the politics of stalemate was over. All that remained for the Republican party was to capture the White House in 1896.

The Battle of the Standards

The campaign of 1896 quickly became known as the "battle of the standards"—a reference to the burning question of whether gold alone or gold and silver should become the nation's monetary standard. Most Republicans saw gold as the stable base for building business confidence and economic prosperity. They adopted a platform calling for "sound money" supported by gold alone. Their candidate, Governor William McKinley of Ohio, cautiously supported the gold plank and firmly believed in high tariffs to protect American industry.

Free silver   Silverites, on the other hand, campaigned for "free and independent" coinage of silver, in which the Treasury freely minted all the silver presented to it, independent of other nations. The supply of money would increase, prices would rise, and the economy would revive—or so their theory held. But the free silver movement was more than a monetary theory. It was a symbolic protest of region and class—of the

William Jennings Bryan made the first of his three presidential bids in 1896, when he ran on both the Democratic and Populist tickets. Passionate in his convictions and devoted to the plain people, the "Great Commoner" is depicted in this hostile cartoon as a Populist snake devouring the Democratic party.

agricultural South and West against the commercial Northeast, of debt-ridden farm folk against industrialists and financiers. Silverites pressed their case like preachers exhorting their flocks, nowhere more effectively than in William Harvey's best-selling pamphlet, *Coin's Financial School* (1894). It reached tens of thousands of readers with the common sense of Coin, its young hero, fighting for silver.

At the Democratic convention in Chicago, William Jennings Bryan of Nebraska was ready to fight, as well. Just 36 years old, Bryan looked "like a young divine"— "tall, slender, handsome," with a rich melodic voice that reached the back rows of the largest halls (no small asset in the days before electric amplification). He had served two terms in Congress and worked as a journalist. He favored low tariffs, opposed Cleveland, and came out belatedly for free silver. "I don't know anything about free silver," he confessed in 1892, but "the people of Nebraska are for free silver and I am for free silver. I will look up the arguments later." Systematically, he coordinated a quiet fight for his nomination.

Silverites controlled the convention from the start. They paraded with silver banners, wore silver buttons, and wrote a plank into the anti-Cleveland platform calling for free and unlimited coinage of the metal. The high point came when Bryan stepped to the lectern, threw back his head, and offered himself to "a cause as holy as the cause of liberty—the cause of humanity." The audience rose as one, cheered wildly, then listened as Bryan spoke for "the plain people of this country," for "our farms" and against "your cities," for silver and against gold. The crowd was in a near frenzy as he reached the dramatic climax and spread his arms in mock crucifixion: "You shall not crucify mankind upon a cross of gold." The next day the convention nominated him for the presidency.

Populists were in a quandary. They had expected the Democrats to stick with Cleveland and gold, sending unhappy silverites headlong into their camp. Instead, the Democrats had stolen their thunder. "If we fuse [with the Democrats] we are sunk," complained one Populist. "If we don't fuse, all the silver men we have will leave us for the more powerful Democrats." At a bitter convention, fusionists nominated Bryan for president. The best antifusionists could do was drop the Democrats' vice presidential candidate in favor of the agrarian rebel who had set Georgia aflame in 1892, Tom Watson.

Campaign and Election

Bryan knew he faced an uphill battle. Adopting a more active style that would be imitated in future campaigns, he tried to "educate" voters. He traveled 18,000 miles by train, gave as many as 30 speeches a day, and reached perhaps 3 million people in 27 states. The nomination of the People's party actually did more harm than good by labeling Bryan a Populist (which he was not) and a radical (which he definitely was not). Devoted to the "plain people," the Great Commoner spoke for rural America and Jeffersonian values: small farmers, small towns, small government.

McKinley knew he could not compete with Bryan's barnstorming, so he contented himself with sedate speeches from his front porch in Canton, Ohio. The folksy appearance of the campaign belied its reality. From the beginning, it had been engineered by Marcus Alonzo Hanna, a talented Ohio industrialist. Hanna relied on modern techniques of organization and marketing. He advertised McKinley, said Theodore Roosevelt, "as if he were patent medicine." His well-oiled campaign brought to Canton tens of thousands, who cheered the candidate's promises of a "full dinner pail." Hanna also saturated the country with millions of leaflets, along with 1400 speakers attacking free trade and free silver. Frightened conservatives poured some $4 million into McKinley's war chest.

ELECTION OF 1896

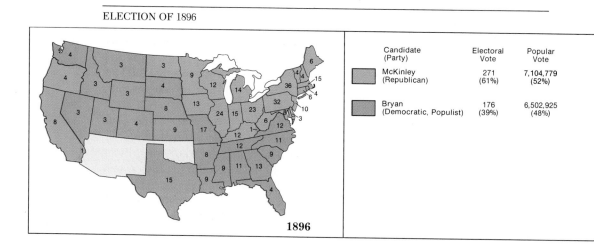

Candidate (Party)	Electoral Vote	Popular Vote
McKinley (Republican)	271 (61%)	7,104,779 (52%)
Bryan (Democratic, Populist)	176 (39%)	6,502,925 (48%)

1896

On election night, Bryan sat at home in Lincoln, Nebraska, as three telegraph operators brought him bulletin after bulletin spelling defeat. He soon conceded to the Republican McKinley. Still, the election had captivated the electorate. Both candidates tallied more votes than any of their predecessors: Bryan, 6.5 million; McKinley, 7.1 million (making him the first president since Grant to receive a popular majority).

The election also proved to be one of the most critical in the republic's history.° Over the previous three decades, political life had been characterized by vibrant campaigns, slim party margins, high voter turnout, and low-profile presidents. The election of 1896 signaled a new era of dwindling party loyalties and voter turnout, stronger presidents, and Republican rule. McKinley's victory broke the political stalemate and forged a powerful coalition that dominated politics for the next 30 years. It rested on the industrial cities of the Northeast and Midwest and combined old support from business, farmers, and Union army veterans with broader backing from industrial wage earners. The Democrats controlled little but the South.

Republican coalition

The Rise of Jim Crow Politics

In 1892, despite the stumping of Populists like Tom Watson, African Americans had cast their ballots for Republicans, when they were permitted to vote freely. But increasingly, their voting rights were being curtailed across the South.

As the nineteenth century drew to a close, a long-standing racialism—categorizing people on the basis of race—deepened. The arrival of "new" immigrants from eastern and southern Europe and the acquisition of new overseas colonies highlighted differences among races and also helped to encourage prejudices that stridently justified segregation and other forms of racial control (see page 680). In the South racialism was enlisted into a political purpose—preventing an alliance of poor blacks and whites that might topple white conservative Democrats. The white supremacy campaign, on the face of it directed at African Americans, also had a broader target in the world of politics: rebellion from below, whether black or white.

Sometimes disfranchisement laws relied on the complicated procedure of charging poll taxes and demanding receipts at the polls. (To trick voters who had paid, local politicians arranged for circuses to tour black districts before elections and collect poll tax receipts as the price of admission. Without them, black voters could not cast their ballots.) Sometimes literacy tests were used as a barrier. Where African American voters were concentrated in large numbers, some states gerrymandered, or remapped the boundaries of election districts, to split up black votes. "Grandfather clauses" allowed citizens to vote only if their grandfathers had voted in elections held before 1860 (or 1866 in some cases). The provision excluded most African Americans.

Mississippi, whose Democrats had led the move to "redeem" their state from Republican Reconstruction, in 1890 took the lead in disfranchising African Americans. A new state constitution required voters to pay a poll tax and pass a literacy test, requirements that eliminated the great majority of black voters.

Disfranchisement

°Five elections, in addition to the contest of 1896, are often cited as critical shifts in voter allegiance and party alignments: the Federalist defeat of 1800, Andrew Jackson's rise in 1828, Lincoln's Republican triumph of 1860, Al Smith's Democratic loss in 1928, and—perhaps—Ronald Reagan's conservative tide of 1980.

Conservative Democrats favored the plan because it also reduced voting among poor whites, who were most likely to join opposition parties. Before the new constitution went into effect, Mississippi contained more than 250,000 eligible voters, black and white. By 1892, after its adoption, there were fewer than 77,000. Soon an all-white combination of conservatives and "reformers"—those disgusted by frequent election-stealing with blocs of black votes—passed disfranchisement laws across the South. Between 1895 and 1908, campaigns to limit voting won out in every southern state.

The disfranchisement campaign succeeded in achieving its broad aim of splitting rebellious whites from blacks, as the tragic fate of Tom Watson demonstrated. Only a dozen years after his biracial campaign of 1892, Watson was promoting black disfranchisement and white supremacy in Georgia. Like other southern Populists, Watson returned to the Democratic party still hoping to help poor whites. But under the increased atmosphere of intolerance, only by playing a powerful race card could he hope to win election. "What does civilization owe the negro?" he asked bitterly. "Nothing! Nothing!! NOTHING!!!"

The African American Response

To mount a successful campaign for disfranchisement, white conservatives inflamed racial passions. They staged "White Supremacy Jubilees" and peppered newspaper editorials with complaints of "bumptious" and "impudent" African Americans. The lynchings of blacks peaked during the 1890s, averaging over a hundred a year for the

---

In keeping with Booker T. Washington's emphasis on manual training, the Tuskegee Institute, opened in Alabama in 1881, was training 1400 students in 30 trades by 1900. Academic subjects received attention, too, as evidenced by this photograph of a history class (segregated by gender) learning about Captain John Smith and Pocahontas.

decade. Most took place in the South. White mobs in cities such as Atlanta and New Orleans terrorized blacks for days in the new, heightened atmosphere of tension.

African Americans worked out their own responses to the climate of intolerance. One came from Booker T. Washington, a former slave and founder of an industrial and agricultural school for blacks in Tuskegee, Alabama. "I love the South," he reassured an audience of white and black southerners in Atlanta in 1895. He conceded that white prejudice against blacks existed throughout the region but nonetheless counseled African Americans to accept what was offered them and work for their economic betterment through manual labor. Every laborer who learned a trade, every farmer who tilled the land could increase his savings. And those earnings would amount to "a little green ballot" that "no one will throw out or refuse to count." Thus Tuskegee's curriculum stressed vocational skills for farming, manual trades, and industrial work.

Booker T. Washington

Many white Americans hailed Washington's "Atlanta Compromise," for it struck the note of patient humility they were so eager to hear. For African Americans, it made the best of a bad situation. Washington, an astute politician, discovered that philanthropists across the nation hoped to make Tuskegee an example of their generosity. He was the honored guest of Andrew Carnegie at his imposing Skibo Castle. California railroad magnate Collis Huntington became his friend, as did other business executives eager to discuss "public and social questions."

Throughout, Washington preached accommodation to the racial caste system. He accepted segregation (so long as separate facilities were equal) and qualifications on voting (if they applied to white citizens as well). Above all Washington sought economic self-improvement for common black folk in fields and factories. In 1900 he organized the National Negro Business League to help establish black businessmen as the leaders of their people. The rapid growth of local chapters (320 by 1907) extended his influence across the country.

Not all black leaders accepted Washington's call for accommodation. W. E. B. Du Bois, a professor at Atlanta University, leveled the most stinging attack in *The Souls of Black Folk* (1903). Du Bois saw no benefit for African Americans in sacrificing intellectual growth for narrow vocational training. Nor was he willing to abide the humiliating stigma that came from the South's discriminatory caste system. A better future would come only if black citizens struggled politically to achieve suffrage and equal rights.

W. E. B. Du Bois

Instead of exhorting African Americans to pull themselves up slowly from the bottom, Du Bois called on the "talented tenth," a cultured black vanguard, to blaze a trail of protest. In 1905 he founded what became known as the Niagara movement for political and economic equality. In 1909 a coalition of black and sympathetic whites transformed the Niagara movement into the National Association for the Advancement of Colored People (NAACP). Middle class and elitist, it mounted legal challenges to the Jim Crow system of segregation. But for sharecroppers in southern cotton fields and laborers in northern factories—the mass of African Americans—the strategy offered little relief, at least in the short run.

NAACP

Neither accommodation nor legal agitation would suffice. But in the "Solid South" (as well as an openly racist North) it was Washington's restrained approach that set the agenda for most African Americans. The ferment of the early 1890s, among black Populists and white, was replaced by a lily-white Democratic party that dominated the region but remained in the minority on the national level.

McKinley in the White House

In William McKinley, Republicans found a skillful chief with a national agenda and personal charm. He cultivated news reporters, openly walked the streets of Washington, and courted the public with handshakes and flowers from his own lapel. Firmly but delicately, he curbed the power of old-time state bosses. When need be, he prodded Congress to action. In all these ways, he foreshadowed "modern" presidents, who would act as party leaders rather than as executive caretakers.

Fortune at first smiled on McKinley. When he entered the White House, the economy had already begun its recovery, as the cycle of economic retrenchment hit bottom. Factory orders were slowly increasing, and unemployment dropped. Farm prices climbed. New discoveries of gold in Alaska and South Africa expanded the supply of money without causing "gold bugs" to panic that currency was being destabilized by silver.

Freed from the burdens of the economic crisis, McKinley called a special session of Congress to revise the tariff. In 1897 the Dingley Tariff raised protective rates still higher but allowed the tariffs to come down if other nations lowered theirs. McKinley also sought a solution for resolving railroad strikes, like the Pullman conflict, before they turned violent. The Erdman Act of 1898 set up machinery for government mediation. McKinley even began laying plans for stronger regulation of trusts.

But affairs overseas competed for his attention. The same expansive forces that had transformed the United States were also causing Americans to look increasingly beyond their borders. McKinley found himself facing a crisis with Spain that would force the nation to decide whether a democratic, industrial republic should also become an imperial nation. Regulation—and a true age of reform—would await the next century.

An 1896 Republican campaign poster features presidential hopeful William McKinley. McKinley stands atop a giant gold coin engraved with the words "sound money" and supported by workers and businessmen alike. The poster promises domestic prosperity and respect overseas and touts American commerce and civilization. The links between prosperity and empire as well as commerce and civilization were made not only in McKinley's campaign but also by all subsequent presidents and the electorate.

VISIONS OF EMPIRE

The crisis with Spain was only the affair of the moment that turned American attention abroad. Underlying the conflict were larger forces linking the destiny of the United States with international events. By the 1890s, southern farmers were exporting half their cotton crop to factories worldwide, while western wheat farmers earned some 30 to 40 percent of their income from markets abroad. John D. Rockefeller's Standard Oil Company shipped about two-thirds of its refined products overseas, and Cyrus McCormick supplied Russian farmers with the reaper.

Even when the United States encompassed no more than thirteen small states clustered along the Atlantic seaboard, Thomas Jefferson had dreamed of an American "empire of liberty" that would stretch from sea to sea. Jefferson supposed it might take a thousand generations before American pioneers had vaulted the continent, but it took a mere 40 years before Americans were claiming their "manifest destiny" to form a continental republic. During the last half of the nineteenth century, many influential Americans began dreaming of an empire reaching all the way to the Far East.

The New Imperialism, European-Style and American-Style

The ambition for empire, of course, was as old as history itself. Spain and Portugal still clung to the remnants of their colonial empires, dating from the fifteenth and sixteenth centuries. In the early nineteenth century, England, France, and Russia accelerated their drive to control foreign peoples and lands. But the late nineteenth century became the new age of imperialism because the technology of arms and the networks of communication, transportation, and commerce brought the prospect of effective, truly global empires within much closer reach.

From the very first years of settlement, the success of European expansion into colonial North America benefited from ecological factors. European diseases, animals, *Ecological* and plants often devastated and disrupted the new worlds they entered. The coming *factors* of smallpox and measles; of pigs, cattle, and horses; and of sugar and wheat played equally important roles in opening the Western Hemisphere and the Pacific basin to

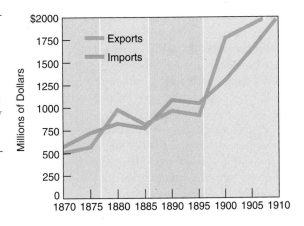

BALANCE OF U.S. IMPORTS AND EXPORTS, 1870–1910 After the Depression of 1893, both imports and exports rose sharply, doubling by 1910. That rise suggests one reason why the age of imperialism was so closely linked with the emerging global industrial economy.

European domination. In areas like the Middle East, Asia, and Africa, where populations already possessed hardy domesticated animals and plants (as well as their own devastating disease pools), European penetration was less complete and sometimes relied on naked force alone.

The speed and efficiency with which Europeans took over in the Niger and Congo basins of Africa in the 1880s prompted many Americans to argue for this European-style imperialism of conquest and possession. Germany, Japan, and Belgium were eagerly joining the hunt for colonies. But other Americans preferred a more indirect imperialism: one that exported products, ideas, and influence. To them, this American imperialism seemed somehow purer, for they could portray Americans as bearers of long-cherished values: democracy, free-enterprise capitalism, and Protestant Christianity.

Forces encouraging imperialism

While Americans tried to justify imperial control in the name of such values, social, economic, and political forces were drawing them rapidly into the imperial race. The growth of industrial networks linked them to international markets as never before. This was true whether they were Arkansas sharecroppers dependent on world cotton prices or Pittsburgh steelworkers whose jobs were made possible by orders for Singer sewing machines for Europe, China, and the Hawaiian Islands. As economic systems became more tightly knit and political systems more responsive to industrialists and financiers, a rush for markets and distant lands was perhaps unavoidable.

The Shapers of American Imperialism

Although the climate for expansion and imperialism was present at the end of the nineteenth century, the small farmer or steelworker was little concerned with how the United States advanced its goals abroad. An elite group—Christian missionaries, intellectuals, business leaders, and commercial farmers—joined navy careerists to shape a more active American imperialism.

By 1880 the once-proud Civil War fleet of more than 600 warships was rotting with neglect. The U.S. Navy ranked twelfth in the world, behind Denmark and Chile. The United States had a coastal fleet but no functional fleet to protect its interests overseas. Discontented navy officers combined with trade-hungry business leaders to lobby Congress for a modern navy.

Mahan calls for a strong navy

Alfred Thayer Mahan, a Navy captain and later admiral, formulated their ideas into a widely accepted theory of navalism. In *The Influence of Sea Power Upon History* (1890), Mahan argued that great nations were seafaring powers that relied on foreign trade for wealth and might. In times of overproduction and depression, as had occurred repeatedly in the United States after the Civil War, overseas markets assumed even greater importance. The only way to protect foreign markets, Mahan reasoned, was with large cruisers and battleships. These ships, operating far from American shores, would need coaling stations and other resupply facilities throughout the world.

Mahan's logic was so persuasive and the profits to be reaped by American factories so great that in the 1880s Congress launched a program to rebuild the navy with steam vessels made of steel rather than the wooden sailing ships of old. By 1900, the U.S. Navy ranked third in the world. With a modern navy, the country had the means to become an imperial power.

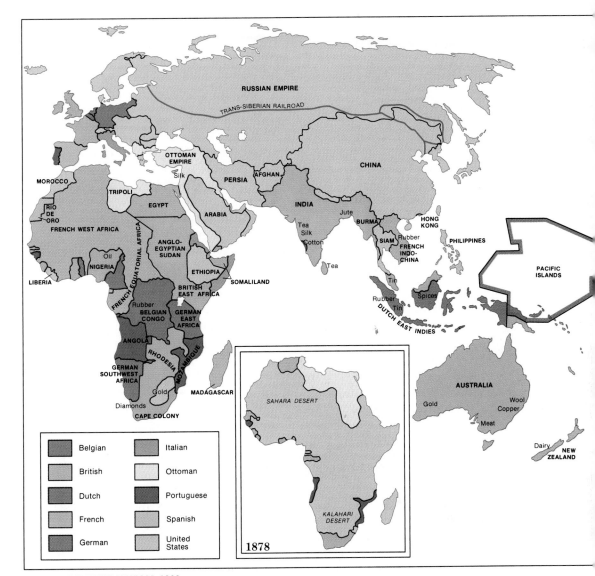

IMPERIALIST EXPANSION, 1900
A comparison of Africa in 1878 (inset) and 1900 shows how quickly Europeans extended their colonial empires. Often resource-poor countries like Japan and England saw colonies as a way to acquire raw materials, such as South African diamonds and tin from Southeast Asia. Closer scrutiny shows that four of the most rapidly industrializing countries—Germany, Japan, Russia, and the United States—had few if any overseas possessions, even in 1900. And while China appears to be undivided, all the major powers were eagerly establishing spheres of influence there.

Daily Lives

TIME AND TRAVEL

The New Navy

Early on February 3, 1874, a fleet of chunky monitors, steam frigates, and sloops lumbered out of Key West at a slow 4.5 knots. It was the largest assembly of American naval power since the Civil War. To the officers watching from shore, this fleet was an embarrassment. "Two modern vessels of war would have done us up in thirty minutes," a future admiral later observed.

In the era after the Civil War technology transformed the navies of Europe. Compound engines, improved armor plating, self-propelled torpedoes, and large rifled guns revolutionized naval warfare. The U.S. Navy, by contrast, sailed into the past. With 3000 miles of ocean as protection and no colonies to defend, a large blue-water fleet seemed unnecessary. Even steamships seemed impractical. The United States had no coaling stations in foreign waters to fuel them. By 1878 the navy had just 6000 sailors, the smallest force since the presidency of Andrew Jackson.

In 1873, as the U.S. Navy fell into disrepair, the British launched the *Devastation,* a single-masted, steam-driven vessel with heavy armor and powerful twin turrets. A forerunner of the modern battleship, it could steam across the Atlantic and back without stopping for coal. Less than a decade later, a British fleet smashed Alexandria, Egypt, whose fortifications were sturdier than those of American ports. That battle convinced Congress that the American coast was no longer safe. In 1883 it appropriated $1.3 million for four modern, steel-hulled vessels—the cruisers *Atlanta, Boston,* and *Chicago,* each 3000 to 4500 tons, and the 1500-ton dispatch boat *Dolphin.* These early "protected" cruisers (so named for the armored deck built over boilers, engines, and other machinery) were an odd mix of old and new. All three had full sail rigs yet were completely electrified and contained watertight compartments and double bottoms. The *Chicago* had twin propellers but engines and boilers so antiquated that one observer compared them to a sawmill. The steel breech-loading guns were vast improvements over the iron muzzle loaders, yet gunners still aimed them the old-fashioned way, by looking down the barrels through open sights.

The naval program that began as a halfhearted effort had become a major commitment by the turn of the century. The fleet included additional protected cruisers, larger armored cruisers, and its first full-sized battleships—the *Indiana, Massachusetts,* and *Oregon,* each displacing more than 10,000 tons. (Soon after 1900 giant battleships were displacing 20,000 tons; on the eve of World War I they reached more than 30,000 tons.) With five more first-class battleships commissioned by 1896, the U.S. Navy rose to fifth place in the world. The prestige of naval service had risen, too, and with it the number of sailors: nearly 10,000 in uniform.

The new navy, unlike the civilian world, was not a democratic culture. Privileges of rank were everywhere appar-

---

Missionaries   Protestant missionaries provided a spiritual rationale for imperialism that complemented Mahan's military and economic arguments. As devout Americans sought to convert "heathen" unbelievers in the faraway lands of China, the Middle East, and the western Pacific, they encountered people whose cultural differences often made them unreceptive to the Christian message. Many missionaries came to believe that

Daily Lives

Passengers on riverboats and yachts saluted the new steel-hulled, steam-powered American fleet as it steamed triumphantly up the Hudson River after naval victories in the Spanish-American War. Within a few years, these modern ships would be obsolete as an international arms race forced rapid innovation in naval design.

ent. Commanders lived in wood-paneled luxury and dined on specially prepared cuisine, capped by coffee, brandy, and cigars. The crew ate salted meats, beans, and potatoes. Officers had private quarters, while enlisted men, so the saying went, lived under the place where they slept and slept under the place where they ate. At night the tables and benches used for dining in the common quarters were stowed between overhead beams from which hammocks were hung.

Battery drill was held twice a day, but under fire American marksmanship proved poor. During one battle in the Spanish-American War, Americans fired more than 8000 shells at fleeing Spanish cruisers. An examination of their hulls later revealed only 120 hits.

By 1907 President Theodore Roosevelt decided to put American naval power on display. He sent 16 battleships on a 46,000-mile, 14-month world tour. Ironically, the Great White Fleet (named for the gleaming white hulls of its ships) was already out of date. In 1906 Great Britain had commissioned the *Dreadnought*, a warship whose new guns rendered all its competitors obsolete. Unlike conventional battleships with guns of varying sizes, the *Dreadnought* carried guns so powerful that the ship had twice the firepower of anything else afloat. In a single stroke the new American navy, the proud product of a quarter century of effort, was outclassed—but not for long. The United States would match the British, for it had joined a naval arms race that would lead the world down the path to war.

natives first had to become Western in culture before turning Christian in belief. Although most opposed expansion through direct military or political intervention, they eagerly took up what British poet Rudyard Kipling called "the White Man's Burden" of "civilizing" the nonwhite world. Missionaries introduced Western goods, education, and systems of government administration—any "civilizing medium," as

Missionaries often viewed the Chinese as uncivilized "heathen" whose souls needed saving and whose culture needed civilizing. This cartoon, published around 1900, pokes fun at the common stereotype by suggesting what the Chinese must think of American "heathen." "Contributions Received Here to Save the Foreign Devils," reads the sign of the Chinese "preacher," who laments the uncivilized behavior of corrupt American city governments, feuding backwoodsmen, rioting laborers, and mobs tormenting Chinese and black Americans.

one minister remarked when he encouraged Singer to bring his sewing machines to China. Implanting Western civilization would surely "uplift" native populations but also open the way for American economic expansion.

Social Darwinism

From scholars, academics, and scientists came racial theories to justify European and American expansion. Charles Darwin's *On the Origin of Species* (1859) had popularized the notion that among animal species, the fittest survived through a process of natural selection. Social Darwinists like Herbert Spencer in England and William Graham Sumner in the United States argued that the same laws of survival governed the social order. By natural as well as divine law, the fittest people (those descended from Anglo-Saxon and Teutonic stock, said Spencer and Sumner) would assert their dominion over lesser peoples of the world.

Commercial factors

Perhaps more compelling than either religious or racial motives for American expansion was the need for trade. The business cycle of boom and bust reminded

Americans of the unpredictability of their economy. In hard times, people sought salvation wherever they could, and one obvious road to recovery lay in markets abroad. With American companies outgrowing the home market, "expansion of our foreign trade is [the] only promise of relief," explained the National Association of Manufacturers. In and out of government, leading public figures called for a campaign to "find markets in every part of the habitable globe."

William Henry Seward

No one did more to initiate the idea of a "New Empire" for the United States than William Henry Seward, secretary of state under Lincoln and Andrew Johnson. Seward's expansive dreams rested on two central assumptions. The first was that "empire has . . . made its way constantly westward . . . until the tides of the renewed and decaying civilizations of the world meet on the shores of the Pacific Ocean." The United States must thus be prepared to win supremacy in the Far East. Seward's second premise underscored how the battle could be won: the great empires of the future would be commercial, not military. The American empire required not colonies but markets. Equal access to foreign markets, often called the "open door," guided American policy in Asia.

Seward's focus on Asia

    While he pursued ties to Japan, Korea, and China, Seward promoted a transcontinental railroad at home and a canal across the Central American isthmus. Link by link, he was trying to connect eastern factories to western ports in the United States and, from there, to markets in the Far East. But his dreams of opening Asia to American commerce produced little result in his lifetime.

    Still, Seward made two notable territorial acquisitions. An American naval officer raised the Stars and Stripes over the Pacific island of Midway in 1867 as a result of his efforts. Unimportant by itself, the value of Midway lay as a way station to Asia and a Pacific toehold near Hawaii, where missionary planters were already establishing an American presence. Seward also engineered the purchase of Alaska in 1867. Critics called it "Seward's Folly" and the "Polar Bear Garden," but the Alaskan purchase turned out to be a bargain. The United States paid Russia $7.2 million, or about 2 cents an acre, for a mineral-rich territory twice the size of Texas.

Alaska purchase

The United States and Latin America

Many Americans did not accept Seward's conviction that their future lay in Asia. After the Civil War, some expansionists renewed talk of annexing Canada or provoking a border war with Mexico to gain territory. By the early 1870s, however, most Americans had decided that it was more profitable to trade with their northern neighbor than to possess it. Similarly, commercial and business interests pushed for friendly economic ties with Mexico. In 1881 Secretary of State James G. Blaine made clear that the United States was not looking for the chance to acquire new territory there, only the opportunity to invest its "large accumulation of capital."

    Elsewhere in Latin America, Blaine looked for ways to expand American trade and influence. One obstacle was the British presence in Central America. Blaine launched a campaign to cancel the Clayton–Bulwer Treaty (1850) sharing rights with Great Britain to any canal built in the region. At the same time, he tried to shift Central American imports from British to American goods by promoting hemispheric

Blaine's Pan-American Congress

cooperation and stability. He helped organize the Pan-American Congress and presided over the opening session as representatives from 18 nations gathered in October 1889. Blaine immediately proposed a "customs union" to reduce trade barriers in the Americas and a set of arbitration procedures to prevent disputes from erupting into war. Deep suspicions over American motives hamstrung delegates, who in the end established only the weak Pan-American Union to foster peaceful understanding in the hemisphere.

Blaine thus found himself forced to pursue separate talks and sometimes to strong-arm his way to the tariff reductions he wanted. If Latin American nations refused to lower their tariffs, he threatened to ban the products of their often single-crop economies under provisions of the 1890 McKinley Tariff. Only three nations—Colombia, Haiti, and Venezuela—had the will to resist.

Venezuelan dispute

American influence in Latin America reached a new peak in the boundary dispute that erupted between Venezuela and Great Britain. The two nations had bickered over the boundary line of British Guiana since 1814, when the British took over that possession from the Dutch. The discovery of gold in the contested territory in the 1880s turned the dispute bitter and led Venezuela to ask the United States to arbitrate the matter. For nearly a decade Great Britain refused despite angry assertions by President Cleveland that the United States was "practically sovereign on the continent" and would regard British pressure on Venezuela as a violation of the Monroe Doctrine. Finally Britain accepted arbitration and signed a treaty with Venezuela in 1897. The British had little choice, for in Europe they faced a powerful Germany and, in Asia, Japan and Russia. Granting the United States supremacy in the Western Hemisphere seemed a small price to pay for cementing Anglo-American relations.

Prelude in the Pacific

In the Pacific, the United States confronted Great Britain and Germany as they vied for control of the strategically located islands of Samoa. In 1878 a treaty gave America the rights to the fine harbor at Pago Pago. When the Germans sent marines to secure their interests in 1889, the British and Americans sent gunboats. As tensions rose, a typhoon struck, sinking the rival fleets and staving off conflict. Ten years later the three powers finally carved up the islands, with the United States retaining Pago Pago.

Ambitions in Hawaii

If American expansionists wanted to extend trade across the Pacific to China, Hawaii was the crucial link. It afforded a fine naval base and a way station along the route to Asia. The archipelago had been settled some 2000 years earlier by visitors from the Polynesian Islands. In the 1780s an American merchant ship had stopped there, and by the 1840s merchants and missionaries dominated the port at Honolulu.

Whereas the missionaries had been God-fearing idealists, their descendants were a practical lot: they saw the possibilities for a harvest in sugarcane, not Polynesian souls. Thus they acquired thousands of acres on which they produced sugar for export to the United States. In 1879 the total value of sugar estates in Hawaii was less than $10 million. By 1898 the figure had jumped to over $40 million. Planters imported cheap laborers from China, Japan, the Philippines, Korea, and Puerto Rico to work the sugarcane fields. Soon Japanese immigrants made up a fourth of the population. Native Hawaiians were rapidly becoming a minority on their own islands.

Sugar was the key to Hawaii's English- and American-dominated plantations. Polynesians were culturally ill suited to the backbreaking labor sugar cultivation demanded. Planters filled their labor needs by recruiting Japanese workers like this one.

By the 1880s the United States had asserted virtual control over the islands, including naval rights to a base at Pearl Harbor. European imperialists found themselves hopelessly outmaneuvered. The Hawaiian sugar planters had forged particularly close ties with the United States because a treaty in 1875 allowed Hawaiian sugar to enter the states duty-free.

In 1890, the planters received a jolt when the McKinley Tariff added sugar to its duty-free list but also gave a bounty of 2 cents a pound to home-growers of sugarcane. Of course, if the Hawaiian Islands were annexed by the United States, their growers would gain this advantage—a thought that set more than a few planters to scheming. Unfortunately for them, Queen Liliuokalani ascended to the Hawaiian throne the very next year. A strong nationalist, she tried to limit foreign influence and restore the power of the monarchy.

McKinley Tariff

As a nationalist, Queen Liliuokalani believed that Hawaii should remain in the hands of its native peoples. And as a monarchist, she believed those hands should be hers, not those of sugar planters who might dominate a constitutional legislature. In 1893, the planters overthrew her. Their success was ensured when a contingent of U.S. marines arrived ashore on the pretext of protecting American lives. In the face of heavily armed opposition, the queen capitulated. A commission of planters—four American and one British—took over.

Planters plot a revolt

Eager to dampen any British designs on the islands, President Benjamin Harrison signed an annexation treaty with the American-dominated commission early in 1893. But before the Senate could ratify it, Grover Cleveland took office and put the treaty on hold. Cleveland was no foe of expansion but was, as his secretary of state noted, "unalterably opposed to stealing territory, or of annexing people against their consent, and the people of Hawaii do not favor annexation." The idea of incorporating the nonwhite population also troubled Cleveland. For a time, matters stood at a stalemate.

THE IMPERIAL MOMENT

In 1895, after almost 15 years of planning from exile in the United States, José Martí returned to Cuba to renew the struggle for independence from Spain. With cries of "Cuba libre," Martí and his rebels cut railroad lines, destroyed sugar mills, and set fire to the cane fields. Within a year, rebel forces controlled more than half the island. But even as they fought the Spanish, the rebels worried about the United States. *Cuba in* Their island, just 90 miles off the coast of Florida, had long been a target of American *revolt* expansionists and business interests. Martí had no illusions. "I have lived in the bowels of the monster," he explained, "and I know it."

The Spanish overlords struck back at Martí and his followers with brutal force. Governor-General Valeriano Weyler herded half a million Cubans from their homes into fortified camps where filth, disease, and starvation killed perhaps 200,000. Outside these "reconcentration" camps, Weyler chased the rebels across the countryside, polluting drinking water, killing farm animals, burning crops.

Mounting Tensions

President Cleveland had little sympathy for the Cuban revolt. He doubted that the mostly black population was capable of self-government and feared that independence from Spain might lead to chaos on the island. Already the revolution had caused widespread destruction of American-owned property. The president settled on a policy that would throw American support neither to Spain nor to the rebels: opposing the rebellion but pressing Spain to grant Cuba some freedoms.

Republican   In the Republican party, expansionists such as Theodore Roosevelt and Massa-
imperialism   chusetts Senator Henry Cabot Lodge urged a more forceful policy. In 1896 they succeeded in writing an imperial wish list into the Republican national platform: annexation of Hawaii, construction of a Nicaraguan canal, purchase of the Virgin Islands, and more naval expansion. They also called for recognition of Cuban independence, a step that, if taken, would likely provoke war with Spain. When the victorious William McKinley entered the White House, however, his Republican supporters found only a moderate expansionist. Cautiously, privately, he lobbied Spain to stop cracking down on the rebels and destroying American property.

In October 1897 Spain promised to remove the much-despised Weyler, end the reconcentration policy, and offer Cuba greater autonomy. The shift encouraged McKinley to resist pressure at home for more hostile action. But leaders of the Spanish army in Cuba had no desire to compromise. Although Weyler was removed, the military renewed efforts to quash the rebellion and encouraged pro-army riots in the streets of Havana. Early in 1898, McKinley dispatched the battleship *Maine* to show that the United States meant to protect its interests and its citizens.

Then in February 1898 the State Department received a stolen copy of a letter to Cuba sent by the Spanish minister in Washington, Enrique Dupuy de Lôme. So did William Randolph Hearst, a pioneer of sensationalist, or "yellow," journalism who was eager for war with Spain. "WORST INSULT TO THE UNITED STATES IN ITS HISTORY," screamed the headline of Hearst's *New York Journal*. What had de Lôme actually written? After referring to McKinley as a "would-be politician," the letter admitted that Spain had no intention of changing policy in Cuba. The Spanish planned to crush the rebels. Red-faced Spanish officials immediately recalled de Lôme, but most Americans now believed that Spain had deceived the United States.

The de Lôme letter

On February 15, 1898, as the *U.S.S. Maine* lay peacefully at anchor in the Havana harbor, explosions ripped through the hull. Within minutes the ship sank to the bottom, killing some 260 American sailors. The cause of the blasts remains unclear, but most Americans, inflamed by hysterical news accounts, concluded that Spanish agents had sabotaged the ship. McKinley sought a diplomatic solution but also a $50 million appropriation "to get ready for war."

Sinking of the Maine

Pressures for war proved too great, and on April 11, McKinley asked Congress to authorize "forceful intervention" in Cuba. Nine days later Congress recognized Cuban independence, insisted on the withdrawal of Spanish forces, and gave the president authority to use military force. In a flush of idealism, Congress also adopted the Teller Amendment, renouncing any aim to annex Cuba. Certainly both idealism and moral outrage led many Americans down the path to war. But in the end, the

Teller Amendment

President McKinley sent the battleship *Maine* to Havana in January 1898. Despite a thorough investigation, the causes of the explosion that sank it remain a mystery. Nonetheless, fervent patriots turned the event into a call for war.

"splendid little war" (as Secretary of State John Hay called it) resulted from less lofty ambitions—empire, trade, glory.

The Imperial War

For the 5462 men who died, there was little splendid about the Spanish-American War. Only 379 gave their lives in battle. The rest suffered from accidents, disease, and the mismanagement of an unprepared army. As war began, the American force totaled only 30,000, none of whom had been trained for fighting in tropical climates. The sudden expansion to 60,000 troops and 200,000 volunteers overtaxed the Army's graft-ridden system of supply. Rather than tropical uniforms, some troops were issued winter woolens and fed on rations that were diseased, rotten, or even lethally spoiled. Others found themselves fighting with weapons from the Civil War.

Dewey at Manila

The Navy fared better. Decisions in the 1880s to modernize the fleet now paid handsomely. Naval battles largely determined the outcome of the war. As soon as war was declared, Admiral George Dewey ordered his Asiatic battle squadron from China to the Philippines. Just before dawn on May 1, he began shelling the Spanish ships in Manila Bay. ("You may fire when ready, Gridley," was his laconic command.) Five hours later the entire Spanish squadron lay at the bottom of the bay. Three hundred eighty-one Spaniards were killed but only one American, a ship's engineer who died of a heart attack. Dewey had no plans to follow up his stunning victory with an invasion. His fleet carried no marines with which to take Manila. So ill prepared was President McKinley for war, let alone victory, that only after learning of Dewey's success did he order 11,000 American troops to the Philippines.

Halfway around the globe, another Spanish fleet had slipped into Santiago harbor in Cuba just before the arrival of the U.S. Navy. The Navy, under Admiral William Sampson, blockaded the island, expecting the Spanish to flee under the cover of darkness. Instead, on July 3, the Spanish fleet made a desperate dash for the open seas in broad daylight. So startled were the Americans that several of their ships nearly collided as they rushed to attack their exposed foes. All seven Spanish ships were sunk, with 474 casualties. Only one American was killed and one wounded. With Cuba now cut off from Spain, the war was virtually won.

War in Cuba

Few Americans had heard of the Philippine Islands; fewer still could locate them on a globe. McKinley himself followed news from the Pacific front on an old textbook map. But most Americans knew the location of Cuba and how close it lay to the Florida coast.

Racial tensions

Before the outbreak of hostilities, Tampa, Florida, was a sleepy coastal town with a single railroad line. As the port of embarkation for the Cuban expeditionary force, some 17,000 troops arrived in the spring of 1898 alone. Tampa's overtaxed facilities soon broke down, spawning disease, tension, and racial violence. President McKinley had authorized the army to raise five volunteer regiments of black soldiers. By the time war was declared, over 8000 African Americans had signed up, half of them stationed around segregated Tampa. They found that while they could sail off to die freeing the peasants of Cuba, they were forbidden to buy a soda at the local drugstore. "Is America any better than Spain?" one dismayed black chaplain wondered.

Black veterans of the western Indian wars along with volunteers, segregated and commanded by white officers, made up almost a quarter of the American force that invaded Cuba. Members of the Tenth Cavalry, shown here, were clearly in no mood to be subjected to the harassment they and other black troops encountered around Tampa. Later the Tenth Cavalry supported a charge by Colonel Teddy Roosevelt's Rough Riders at the battle of San Juan Hill.

After drunken white troops shot at a black child, black troops in Tampa rioted. Three white and 27 black Americans were wounded in the melee.

Matters were scarcely less chaotic as 17,000 disorganized troops and hundreds of reporters finally scrambled aboard ships. There they sat for a week, until sailing on June 14 for Santiago and battle. By June 30, the Americans had landed to challenge some 24,000 Spanish, many equipped with modern rifles. The following day 7000 Americans—including the black soldiers of the Ninth and Tenth Cavalry regiments—stormed up heavily fortified San Juan and nearby Kettle hills. Their objective was the high ground north and east of Santiago.

Among them Lieutenant Colonel Theodore Roosevelt thrilled at the experience of battle. He had raised a cavalry troop of cowboys and college polo players, originally called "Teddy's Texas Tarantulas." By the time they arrived in Cuba, the volunteers were answering to the nickname "Rough Riders." As they charged toward the high ground, Roosevelt yelled: "Gentlemen, the Almighty God and the just cause are with you. Gentlemen, charge!" The withering fire drowned out his shrill, squeaky voice, so he repeated the call. Charge they did and conquer the enemy, though the battle cost more than 1500 American casualties.

The Rough Riders

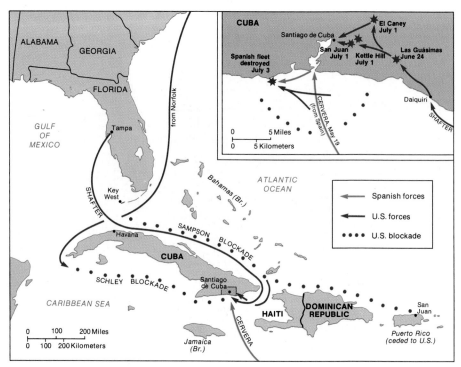

THE SPANISH-AMERICAN WAR
Had the Spanish-American War depended largely on ground forces, the ill-prepared U.S. Army might have fared poorly. But the key to success, in both Cuba and the Philippines, was naval warfare, in which the recently modernized American fleet had a critical edge. Proximity to Cuba also gave the United States an advantage in delivering troops and supplies and in maintaining a naval blockade that isolated Spanish forces.

Without a fleet for cover or any way to escape, the Spanish garrison surrendered on July 17. In the Philippines, a similar brief battle preceded the American taking of Manila on August 13. The "splendid little war" had ended in less than four months.

Peace and the Debate over Empire

Conquering Cuba and the Philippines proved easier than deciding what to do with them. The Teller Amendment had renounced any American claim to Cuba. But clearly the United States had not freed the island to see chaos reign or American business and military interests excluded. And what of the Philippines—and Spanish Puerto Rico, which American forces had taken without a struggle? Powerful public and congressional sentiment pushed McKinley to claim empire as the fruits of victory.

The president himself favored such a course. The battle in the Pacific highlighted the need for naval bases and coaling stations. "To maintain our flag in the Philippines, we must raise our flag in Hawaii," the New York *Sun* insisted. On July 7

McKinley signed a joint congressional resolution annexing Hawaii, as planters had wanted for nearly a decade.

Annexing Hawaii

The Philippines presented a more difficult problem. Filipinos had greeted the American forces as liberators, not new colonizers. The popular leader of the rebel forces fighting Spain, Emilio Aguinaldo, had returned to the islands on an American ship. But to the rebels' dismay, McKinley insisted that the islands were under American authority until the peace treaty settled matters.

Aguinaldo

Such a settlement, McKinley knew, would have to include American control of the Philippines. He had no intention of leaving Spain in charge or of seeing the islands fall to other European rivals. American military advisers warned that without control of the entire island of Luzon, its capital, Manila, would be indefensible as the naval base McKinley wanted. Nor, McKinley felt certain, were the Filipinos capable of self-government. Aguinaldo and his rebels thought otherwise, and in June he declared himself president of a new Philippine republic.

THE UNITED STATES IN THE PACIFIC

In the late nineteenth century both Germany and the United States emerged as major naval powers and as contestants for influence and commerce in China. The island groups of the central and southwest Pacific, though of little economic value, had potential strategic significance as bases and coaling stations along the routes to Asia. Rivalry (as in the case of Samoa) sometimes threatened to erupt into open conflict. Control of Hawaii, Midway, Samoa, Guam, and the Philippines gave the United States a string of strategic stepping-stones to the Orient.

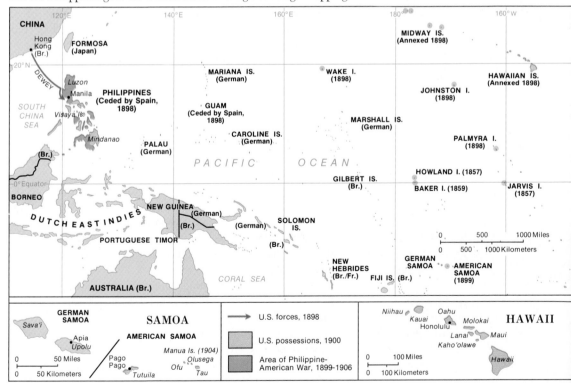

Anti-imperialists

Many influential Americans—former president Grover Cleveland, steel baron Andrew Carnegie, novelist Mark Twain—opposed annexation of the Philippines. Yet even these anti-imperialists favored expansion, if only in the form of trade. Business leaders especially believed that the country could enjoy the economic benefits of the Philippines without the costs of maintaining it as a colony. Annexation would mire the United States too deeply in the quicksands of Asian politics, they argued. More important, a large, costly fleet would be necessary to defend the islands. To the imperialists that was precisely the point: a large fleet was crucial to the interests of a powerful commercial nation.

The role of race

Racial ideas shaped both sides of the argument. Imperialists believed that the racial inferiority of nonwhites made occupation of the Philippines necessary, and they were ready to assume the "White Man's Burden" and govern. Filipinos, they argued, would gradually be taught the virtues of Western civilization, Christianity, democracy, and self-rule. (In fact, most Filipinos were already Catholic after many years under Spanish rule.) Anti-imperialists, on the other hand, feared racial intermixing and the possibility of Asian workers flooding the American labor market. They also maintained that dark-skinned people would never develop the capacity for self-government. An American government in the Philippines could be sustained only at the point of bayonets—yet the U.S. Constitution made no provision for governing people without representation or equal rights. Such a precedent abroad, the anti-imperialists warned, might one day threaten American liberties at home.

Still, when the Senate debated the Treaty of Paris ending the Spanish-American War in 1898, the imperialists had the support of the president, most of Congress, and the majority of public opinion. Even an anti-imperialist like William Jennings Bryan, defeated by McKinley in 1896, endorsed the treaty. In it Spain surrendered title to Cuba, ceded Puerto Rico and Guam to the United States, and in return for $20 million turned over the Philippines as well.

Eager to see war ended, Bryan and other anti-imperialists believed that once the United States possessed the Philippines, it could free them. The imperialists had other notions. Having acquired an empire and a modern navy to protect it, the United States could now assert its new status as one of the world's great powers.

America's First Asian War

Managing an empire turned out to be even more devilish than acquiring one. As the Senate debated annexation of the Philippines in Washington, rebels fought with an American patrol outside of Manila. The few Americans who paid attention to the ensuing clash called it the "Filipino insurrection," but to those who fought, it was a brutal war. When it ended more than three years later, nearly 5000 Americans, 25,000 rebels, and perhaps as many as 200,000 civilians lay dead.

Racial antagonism spurred the savage fighting. American soldiers tended to dismiss Filipinos as nearly subhuman. Their armed resistance to American occupation often transformed the frustrations of ordinary troops into brutality and torture. To avenge a rebel attack, one American officer swore he would turn the surrounding countryside into a "howling wilderness." Before long the American force was resorting to a garrison strategy of herding Filipinos into concentration camps, while destroying their villages and crops. The policy was embarrassingly reminiscent of the tactics of "Butcher" Weyler in Cuba. In 1902, only after the Americans captured Aguinaldo himself, did the war end.

In contrast to the bitter guerrilla war, the United States ruled the Philippines with relative benevolence. Under William Howard Taft, the first civilian governor, the Americans built schools, roads, sewers, and factories and inaugurated new farming techniques. The aim, said Taft, was to prepare the island territory for independence, and in keeping with it, he granted great authority to local officials. These advances—social, economic, and political—benefited the Filipino elite and thus earned their support. Decades later, on July 4, 1946, the Philippines were finally granted independence.

The United States played a similar role in Puerto Rico. As in the Philippines, executive authority resided in a governor appointed by the U.S. president. Under the Foraker Act of 1900 Puerto Ricans received a voice in their government, as well as a nonvoting representative in the U.S. House of Representatives and certain tariff advantages. All the same, many Puerto Ricans chafed at the idea of such second-class citizenship. Some favored eventual admission to the United States as a state; others advocated independence, a division of opinion that persists even today.

Puerto Rico

An Open Door in China

Like a reciprocal equation, interest in Asia drove the United States to annex the Philippines, and annexation of the Philippines only whetted American interest in Asia. As ever, the possibility of markets in China—whether for Christian souls or consumer goods—proved an irresistible lure.

Both the British, who dominated China's export trade, and the Americans, who wanted to, worried that China might soon be carved up by other powers. Japan had

---

The American decision to occupy the Philippines rather than give it independence forced Filipino nationalists to fight U.S. troops, as they had already been fighting the Spanish since 1896. Forces like the ones pictured at the right were tenacious enough to require more than 70,000 Americans (left) to put down the rebellion. Sporadic, bloody guerrilla fighting continued until 1902, and other incidents persisted until 1906.

defeated China in 1895, encouraging Russia, Germany, and France to join in demanding trade concessions. Each nation sought to establish an Asian "sphere of influence" in which its commercial and military interests reigned. Often this ended in commercial and other restrictions against rival powers. Since Britain and the United States wanted the benefits of trade rather than actual colonies, they tried to limit foreign demands while leaving China open to all commerce.

The open door notes   In 1899, at the urging of the British, Secretary of State John Hay circulated the first of two "open door" notes among the imperial powers. He did not ask them to give up their spheres of influence in China, only to keep them open to free trade with other nations. The United States could hardly have enforced even so modest a proposal, for it lacked the military might to prevent the partitioning of China. Still, Japan and most of the European powers agreed in broad outline with Hay's policy out of fear that the Americans might tip the delicate balance by siding with a rival. Hay seized on the tepid response and brashly announced that the open door in China was international policy.

Boxer Rebellion   Unrest soon threatened to close the door. Chinese nationalists, known to Westerners as Boxers for their clenched fist symbol, formed secret societies to drive out the *fon kwei*, or foreign devils. Encouraged by the Chinese empress, Boxers murdered hundreds of Christian missionaries and their followers and set siege to foreign diplomats and citizens at the British Embassy in Beijing. European nations quickly dispatched troops to quell the uprising and free the diplomats, while President McKinley sent 2500 Americans to join the march to the capital city. Along the way, the angry foreign armies plundered the countryside and killed civilians before reaching Beijing and breaking the siege.

Hay feared that once in control of Beijing the conquerors might never leave. So he sent a second open-door note in 1900, this time asking foreign powers to respect China's territorial and administrative integrity. They endorsed the proposal in principle only. In fact, the open-door notes together amounted to little more than an announcement of American desires to maintain stability and trade in Asia. Yet they reflected a fundamental purpose to which the United States dedicated itself across the globe: to open closed markets and to keep open those markets that other empires had yet to close. The new American empire would have its share of colonies, but in Asia as elsewhere it would be built primarily on trade.

Sense of mission   To expansionists like Alfred Thayer Mahan, Theodore Roosevelt, and John Hay, American interests would be secure only when they had been established worldwide, a course of action they believed to be blessed by divine providence. "We will not renounce our part in the mission of the race, trustee under God of the civilization of the world," declared Senator Albert Beveridge. But to one French diplomat, more accustomed to wheeling and dealing in the corridors of international power, it seemed that the Americans had tempted fate. With a whiff of Old World cynicism or perhaps a prophet's eye, he remarked, "The United States is seated at the table where the great game is played, and it cannot leave it."

On New Year's Eve at the State House in Boston a midnight ceremony ushered in the twentieth century. The crowd celebrated with psalms and hymns. There was a flourish of trumpets, and in the absence of a national anthem everyone sang "America."

that girls have been burned alive in the city. Every year thousands of us are maimed." A special state commission investigated the tragedy. Over the next four years its recommendations produced 56 state laws regulating fire safety, hours, machinery, and home work. They amounted to the most far-reaching labor code in the country.

The Triangle fire shocked the nation and underscored a widespread fear: modern industrial society had created profound strains, widespread misery, and deep class divisions. Corporations grew to unimagined size, bought and sold legislators, dictated the terms of their own profit. Men, women, and children worked around the clock in unsafe factories for wages that barely supported them. In cities across America, tenement-bred diseases took innocent lives. Criminals threatened people and property, while saloons tied the working poor to dishonest political bosses. Even among the middle class, inflation was shrinking wallets at the rate of 3 percent a year. "It was a world of greed," concluded one garment worker; "the human being didn't mean anything."

In 1911 the fiery deaths of 146 people at the Triangle Shirtwaist Company shocked the nation. Firefighters arrived within minutes, but their ladders could not reach the top stories. Trapped by locked doors, those who failed to escape perished within or leaped to their deaths on the streets below. Following the horrifying episode, New York enacted the most ambitious labor code in the country.

But human beings did mean something to followers of an influential reform movement sweeping the country. Progressivism had emerged as a political force in the mid-1890s and would continue to shape politics through World War I. The movement sprang from many impulses, mixing both a liberal concern for the poor and working class with conservative efforts to stabilize business and avoid social chaos. But liberal or conservative, most progressives shared a desire to soften the harsher aspects of industrialization, urbanization, and immigration.

Progressivism thus began in the cities, where the wellspring of misery was fullest, political corruption deepest, and social division clearest. It was organized by an angry, idealistic middle class and percolated up from neighborhoods to city halls, state capitals, and, finally, to Washington. Though usually pursued through politics, the goals of progressives were broadly social—to create a "good society" where people could live decently, harmoniously, and prosperously, along middle-class lines.

Unlike past reformers, progressives saw government as a protector, not an oppressor. Only government possessed the resources for the broad-based reforms they sought. Progressivism spawned the modern activist state, with its capacity to regulate the economy and manage society. And because American society had become so interdependent, progressivism became the first nationwide reform movement. No political party monopolized it; no single group controlled it. It flowered in the presidencies of Republican Theodore Roosevelt and Democrat Woodrow Wilson. In 1912 it even gave birth to its own party, the Progressive, or "Bull Moose," party. But by then progressivism had filtered well beyond politics into every realm of American life.

THE ROOTS OF PROGRESSIVE REFORM

Families turned from their homes; an army of unemployed on the roads; hunger, strikes, and bloody violence across the country—the wrenching depression of 1893 forced Americans to take a hard look at their new industrial order. They found common complaints that cut across lines of class, religion, and ethnicity. If streetcar companies raised fares while service deteriorated, if food processors doctored their canned goods with harmful additives, if politicians skimmed money from the public till, everyone suffered. And no one could stop it alone.

The result was not a coherent progressive movement but a set of loosely connected goals. Some progressives fought to make government itself efficient and honest. Others called for greater regulation of business and a more orderly economy. Some sought social justice for the poor and working classes; others, social welfare to protect children, women, and consumers. Still other progressives looked to purify society by outlawing alcohol and drugs, stamping out prostitution and slums, and restricting the flood of new immigrants.

Aims of progressives

Paternalistic by nature, progressives often imposed their solutions, no matter what the less "enlightened" poor or oppressed saw as their own best interests. Then, too, reformers acted partly out of nostalgia. In a rapidly changing world, they wanted to redeem such traditional American values as democracy, opportunity for the individual, and the spirit of public service. Yet if the ends of progressives were traditional, their means were distinctly modern. They used the systems and methods of the new industrial order—the latest techniques of organization, management, and science—to fight its excesses.

COUNTERPOINT

Embracing such diversity, progressivism has spawned a host of interpretations. Early historians of the movement saw progressives as they saw themselves—as idealistic representatives of the "good people," checking the power of big business, ending political corruption, and promoting democracy and social justice. A later generation of historians questioned the idealism of progressives as well as their commitment to democracy. By examining individual progressives, they concluded that these "reformers" were a small group of business leaders and professionals anxious about the status and influence they had lost to industrialists and corporate executives. Far from representing "the people," progressives were bent on reestablishing their own authority in the new industrial order.

What was progressivism?

Neither the democratic nor the status-anxiety interpretation explains the strong support progressivism often received from corporations. Historians on the "New Left," writing as critics of corporate capitalism, have depicted progressivism instead as the "triumph of conservatism." Progressive reform was less an instrument for guarding the people than for protecting corporations, either from stricter regulation or from competition. Still other historians have employed an "organizational" approach by looking at progressivism as a broad-based effort by businessmen, professionals, and other members of the "new middle class" to bring order and efficiency to politics and the economy by restructuring such institutions as government.

Historians with specialized interests have examined the role of women, African Americans, and consumers. In each case, progressive reform afforded an opportunity for these groups to advance their separate, sometimes conflicting goals in the public sphere. Perhaps the most helpful interpretation in explaining the diversity and conflict within progressivism is one advanced by historians examining the structure and interplay of politics and culture. They have underscored the weakening of political parties during the progressive era and the rising influence of organized groups, whether of workers, industrialists, consumers, or others. Lobbying legislatures, mounting publicity campaigns, marshaling voters, these interest groups pressed for reform as part of the broad process of adjustment to the new industrial order.

The Progressive System of Beliefs

Progressives were moderate modernizers—reformers, not revolutionaries. They accepted the American system as sound, only in need of adjustment. Many drew on the increasingly popular Darwinian theories of evolution to buttress this gradual approach to change. With its notion of slowly changing species, evolution undermined the acceptance of fixed principles that had guided social thought in the Victorian era. Progressives saw an evolving landscape and ever-shifting values. They denied the old Calvinist doctrine of inborn sinfulness and instead saw people as having a greater potential for good than for evil.

Yet progressives had seen the mean side of industrialism and somehow had to explain the existence of evil and wrongdoing. Most agreed that they were "largely, if not wholly, products of society or environment." People went wrong, wrote one progressive, because of "what happens to them." By changing what happened, the human potential for good could be released. As reformer Jane Addams explained, "what has been called 'the extraordinary pliability of human nature'" made it "impossible to set any bounds to the moral capabilities which might unfold under ideal civic and educational conditions."

Pragmatism   With an eye to results, progressives asked not "Is it true?" but "Does it work?" Philosopher Charles Peirce called this new way of thinking "pragmatism." William James, the Harvard psychologist, became its most famous popularizer. For James, pragmatism meant "looking towards last things, fruits, consequences, facts."

The Pragmatic Approach

Pragmatism led educators, social scientists, and lawyers to adopt new approaches to reform. John Dewey, the master educator of the progressive era, believed that environment shaped the patterns of human thought. Instead of demanding mindless memorization of abstract and unconnected facts, Dewey tried to "make each one of our schools an embryonic community life." At his School of Pedagogy, founded in 1896 with his wife, Alice, he let students unbolt their desks from the floor, move about, and learn by doing so they could train for real life.

Behaviorism   Psychologist John B. Watson believed that human behavior could be shaped at will. "Give me a dozen healthy infants," he wrote, ". . . and my own specified world to bring them up in, and I'll guarantee to take any one at random and train him to become any specialist I might select, doctor, lawyer, artist, merchant, chief, and yes, even beggarman and thief." "Behaviorism" swept the social sciences and later advertising, where Watson himself eventually landed.

Lawyers and legal theorists applied their own blend of pragmatism and behaviorism. Justice Oliver Wendell Holmes, Jr., appointed to the Supreme Court in 1902, rejected the idea that the traditions of law were constant and universal. "Long ago I decided I was not God," said Holmes. Law was a living organism to be interpreted according to experience and the needs of a changing society.

John Dewey, progressive philosopher and educator

That was what Denver Judge Ben Lindsey did when he handed down a verdict. Presiding over one of the first juvenile courts in the country, the "Kids' Judge" examined the home life of youthful offenders before he ruled. Often he discovered poverty, illness, and joblessness. So he used the new authority of his court to remove delinquents from dysfunctional homes and make them wards of the state. In several states, supervised probation replaced suspended sentences to ensure that bad habits stayed broken.

This environmental view of the law, known as "sociological jurisprudence," found a skilled practitioner in Louis Brandeis. Shaken by the brutal suppression of the Homestead steel strike of 1892, Brandeis quit his corporate practice and proclaimed himself the "people's lawyer." The law must "guide by the light of reason," he wrote, by which he meant bringing everyday life to bear in any court case. *Sociological jurisprudence*

Brandeis had a chance to test his practical principles when laundry owner Curt Muller challenged an Oregon law that limited his laundresses to working 10 hours a day. Brandeis defended the statute before the Supreme Court in 1908. His famous legal brief in *Muller v. Oregon* contained 102 pages describing the damaging effects of long hours on working women and only 2 pages of legal precedents. The Supreme Court upheld Oregon's right to limit the working hours of laborers and thus legitimized the "Brandeis Brief." *Brandeis Brief*

The Progressive Method

Seeing the nation riven by conflict, progressives tried to restore a sense of community through the ideal of a single public interest. Christian ethics were the guide, to be applied after using the latest scientific methods to gather and analyze data about a social problem. The modern corporation furnished an appealing model for organization. Like corporate executives, progressives relied on careful management, coordinated systems, and specialized bureaucracies to carry out reforms.

Between 1902 and 1912 a new breed of journalists investigated wrongdoers, named them in print, and described their misdeeds in vivid detail. Most exposés began as articles in mass-circulation magazines. *McClure's* magazine stirred controversy and boosted circulation when it sent reporter Lincoln Steffens to uncover the crooked ties between business and politics. Steffens's "Tweed Days in St. Louis" appeared in the October 1902 issue of *McClure's* and was followed in the November issue by Ida M. Tarbell's *History of the Standard Oil Company*, another stinging, well-researched indictment. Soon a full-blown literature of exposure was covering every ill from unsafe food to child labor.

A disgusted Theodore Roosevelt thought the new reporters had gone too far and called them "muckrakers," after the man who raked up filth in the seventeenth-century classic *Pilgrim's Progress*. But by documenting dishonesty and blight, muckrakers not only aroused people but educated them. No broad reform movement of American institutions would have taken place without them. *Muckrakers*

To move beyond exposure to solutions, progressives stressed volunteerism, civic responsibility, and collective action. They drew on the organizational impulse that seemed everywhere to be bringing people together in new interest groups. Between 1890 and 1920 nearly 400 organizations were founded, many to combat the ills of industrial society. Some, like the National Consumers' League, grew out of efforts to promote general causes—in this case protecting consumers and workers from ex- *Voluntary organizations* ploitation. Others, such as the National Tuberculosis Association, aimed at a specific problem.

When voluntary action failed, progressives looked to government to protect the public welfare. They mistrusted legislators, who might be controlled by corporate interests or political machines. So they strengthened the executive branch by increasing the power of individual mayors, governors, and presidents. Then they watched those executives carefully.

Professionals   Progressives also drew on the expertise of the newly professionalized middle class. Confident, cosmopolitan professionals—doctors, engineers, psychiatrists, city planners—mounted campaigns to stamp out venereal disease and dysentery, to reform prisons and asylums, and to beautify cities. At all levels—local, state, federal— new agencies and commissions staffed by impartial experts began to investigate and regulate lobbyists, insurance and railroad companies, public health, even government itself.

THE SEARCH FOR THE GOOD SOCIETY

If progressivism ended in politics, it began with social reform: the need to reach out, to do something to bring the "good society" a step closer. Ellen Richards had just such ends in mind in 1890 when she opened the New England Kitchen in downtown Boston. Richards, a chemist and home economist, designed the Kitchen to sell cheap, wholesome food to the working poor. For a few pennies, customers could choose from a nutritious menu, every dish of which had been tested in Richards's laboratory at the Massachusetts Institute of Technology.

The New England Kitchen promoted social as well as nutritional reform. Women freed from the drudgery of cooking could seek gainful employment. And as a "household experiment station" and center for dietary information, the Kitchen tried to educate the poor and Americanize immigrants by showing them how the middle class prepared meals. According to philanthropist Pauline Shaw, it was also a "rival to the saloon." A common belief was that poor diets fostered drinking, especially among the lower classes.

Pattern of   In the end, the New England Kitchen served more as an inexpensive eatery for middle-class working women and students than as a resource for the poor or an agency of Americanization. Still, Ellen Richards's experiment reflected a pattern typical of progressive social reform: the mix of professionalism with uplift of the poor and needy, socially conscious women entering the public arena, the hope of creating a better world along middle-class lines.

Poverty in a New Light

During the 1890s crime reporter and photographer Jacob Riis launched a campaign to introduce middle-class audiences to urban poverty. Writing in vivid detail in *How the Other Half Lives* (1890), Riis brought readers into the teeming tenement. Accompanying the text were shocking photos of poverty-stricken Americans—Riis's "other Half." He also used slide shows to publicize their plight. His pictures of slum life appeared artless, merely recording the desperate poverty before the camera. But

Riis used them to tell a moralistic story, much the way the earlier English novelist Charles Dickens had used his melodramatic tales to attack the abuses of industrialism in England. People began to see poverty in a new, more sympathetic light, the result less of flawed individuals than of environment.

A haunting naturalism in fiction and painting followed the tradition introduced by Riis's gritty photographic essays. In *McTeague* (1899) and *Sister Carrie* (1900), novelists like Frank Norris and Theodore Dreiser spun dark tales of city dwellers struggling to keep body and soul intact. The "Ashcan school" painted urban life in all its grimy realism. Photographer Alfred Stieglitz and painters such as John Sloan and George Bellows chose slums, tenements, and dirty streets as subjects. Poverty began to look less ominous and more heartrending. *Naturalism*

Between 1908 and 1914 the Russell Sage Foundation produced six large volumes of facts and figures documenting a vicious cycle of urban poverty that trapped its victims for generations. The children of paupers were likely to be paupers themselves, the reports explained, not because of heredity or sin but because of deprivation.

A new profession—social work—proceeded from this new view of poverty. Social work developed out of the old settlement house movement (page 648). Like the physicians from whom they drew inspiration, social workers studied hard data to diagnose the problems of their "clients." Unlike nineteenth-century philanthropists, the new social workers refused to do things to or for people. Instead they worked with their clients, enlisting their help to solve their own problems. A social worker's "differential casework" attempted to treat individuals case by case, each according to the way the client had been shaped by environment. *Social work*

In reality poverty was but a single symptom of many personal and social ills. Most progressives continued to see it as a by-product of political and corporate greed, slum neighborhoods, and "institutions of vice" like the saloon. Less clear to them was how deeply rooted poverty had become. Simple middle-class goodwill or even the era's most up-to-date scientific treatments were not enough to banish the alcoholism, drug addiction, and mental illness associated with poverty.

Expanding the "Woman's Sphere"

Progressive social reform attracted a great many women seeking what Jane Addams called "the larger life" of public affairs. In the late nineteenth century, women found that protecting their traditional sphere of home and family forced them to move beyond it. Bringing up children, making meals, keeping house, and caring for the sick now involved community decisions about schools, public health, and countless other matters.

Many middle- and upper-middle-class women received their first taste of public life from women's organizations, including mothers' clubs, temperance societies, and church groups. By the turn of the century, some 500 women's clubs boasted over 160,000 members. Through the General Federation of Women's Clubs, they funded libraries and hospitals and supported schools, settlement houses, compulsory education, and child labor laws. Eventually they moved beyond the concerns of home and family to endorse such controversial causes as woman suffrage and unionization. To that list the National Association of Colored Women added the special concerns of African Americans, none more urgent than the fight against lynching. *Women's organizations*

By 1900 one-fourth of the nonfarm labor force was female. On average, women industrial workers made $3 less a week than did unskilled men. Here, at a Labor Day parade in San Diego in 1910, women demand equal pay for equal work.

New woman

The dawn of the century saw the rise of a new generation of women. Longer lived, better educated, and less often married than their mothers, they were also willing to pursue careers for fulfillment. Usually they turned to professions that involved the traditional role of nurturer—nursing, library work, teaching, and settlement house work.

Custom and prejudice still restricted these new women. The faculty at the Massachusetts Institute of Technology, for example, refused to allow Ellen Richards to pursue a doctorate. Instead they hired her to run the gender-segregated "Woman's Laboratory" for training public school teachers. At the turn of the century, only about 1500 women lawyers practiced in the whole country, and in 1910 women made up barely 6 percent of licensed physicians. That figure rapidly declined as male-dominated medical associations grew in power and discouraged the entry of women.

Despite the often bitter opposition of families, some feminists tried to destroy, not widen, the boundaries of the woman's sphere. In *Women and Economics* (1898) Charlotte Perkins Gilman condemned femininity, marriage, maternity, and domesticity as enslaving and obsolete. She argued for a radically restructured society with large apartment houses, communal child rearing and housekeeping, and cooperative kitchens to free women from economic dependence on men.

Margaret Sanger

Margaret Sanger sought to free women from the bonds of chronic pregnancy. Sanger, a visiting nurse on the Lower East Side of New York, had seen too many poor women overburdened with children, pregnant year after year, with no hope of escaping the cycle. The consequences were sometimes deadly but always crippling. "Women cannot be on equal footing with men until they have complete control over their reproductive functions," she argued.

The insight came as a revelation one summer evening in 1912 when Sanger was called to the home of a distraught immigrant family on Grand Street. Sadie Sachs, mother of three, had nearly died a year earlier from a self-induced abortion. In an effort to terminate another pregnancy, she had accidentally killed herself. Sanger vowed that night "to do something to change the destiny of mothers whose miseries were as vast as the sky." She became a crusader for what she called "birth control." By distributing information on contraception, she hoped to free women from unwanted pregnancies and the fate of Sadie Sachs.

Single or married, militant or moderate, professional or lay, white or black, more and more middle-class urban women thus became "social housekeepers." From their own homes they turned to the homes of their neighbors and from there to all of society.

Social Welfare

In the "bigger family of the city," as one woman reformer called it, settlement house workers found that they could not care for the welfare of the poor alone. If industrial America, with its sooty factories and overcrowded slums, was to be transformed into the good society, individual acts of charity would have to be supplemented by government. Laws had to be passed and agencies created to promote social welfare, including improved housing, workplaces, parks, and playgrounds; the abolition of child labor; and the enactment of eight-hour-day laws for working women.

By 1910 the more than 400 settlement houses across the nation had organized into a loose affiliation, with settlement workers ready to help shape government policy. Often it was women who led the way. Julia Lathrop, a Vassar College graduate, spent 20 years at Jane Addams's Hull House before becoming the first head of the new federal Children's Bureau in 1912. By then two-thirds of the states had adopted some child labor legislation, although loopholes exempted countless youngsters from coverage. Under Lathrop's leadership, Congress was persuaded to pass the Keating–Owen Act (1916), forbidding goods manufactured by children to cross state lines.[*]

Keating–Owen Act

Florence Kelley, who had also worked at Hull House, spearheaded a similar campaign in Illinois to protect women workers by limiting their workday to eight hours. As general secretary of the National Consumers' League, she also organized boycotts of companies that treated employees inhumanely. Eventually most states enacted laws restricting the number of hours women could work.

Woman Suffrage

Ever since the conference for women's rights held at Seneca Falls in 1848, women reformers had pressed for the right to vote on the grounds of equal opportunity and simple justice. Progressives embraced women's suffrage by stressing what they saw as the practical results: reducing political corruption, protecting the home, and increasing the voting power of native-born whites. The "purer sensibilities" of women—an ideal held by Victorians and progressives alike—would help cleanse the political process of selfishness and corruption, while their sheer numbers would keep the political balance tilted away from immigrant newcomers.

---

[*]The Supreme Court struck down the law in 1918 as an improper regulation of local labor; nonetheless, the law focused greater attention on the abuses of child labor.

" BEAN HIM ! "*

*Note for ignorami—Hit him in the head

The campaign for women's suffrage was waged on many fronts. In this cartoon from a 1914 issue of *Life* magazine, a burly feminist catcher tells a suffragist pitcher to "bean" the male batter at the plate.

The suffrage movement benefited, too, from new leadership. In 1900 Carrie Chapman Catt became president of the National American Woman Suffrage Association, founded by Susan B. Anthony in 1890. Politically astute and a skilled organizer, Catt mapped a grass-roots strategy of education and persuasion from state to state. She called it "the winning plan." As the map (page 769) shows, victories came first in the West, where women and men had already forged a more equal partnership to overcome the hardships of frontier life. By 1914, 10 western states (and Kansas) had granted women the vote in state elections, as Illinois had in presidential elections.

Catt's "winning plan"

The slow pace of progress drove some women to militancy. In England, turn-of-the-century suffragists chained themselves to lampposts, refused to eat when imprisoned, and assaulted politicians. A young American Quaker named Alice Paul had been with them and brought the aggressive tactics to America. In 1913 she organized 5000 women to parade in protest at President Woodrow Wilson's inauguration. Half a million people watched as a near riot ensued. The suffragists were hauled to jail, stripped naked, and thrown into cells with prostitutes.

Militant suffragists

A year later Paul formed the Congressional Union, dedicated to enacting a suffrage amendment at any cost. She soon allied her organization with western women voters in the militant National Woman's party. In 1917, they picketed the White House. When Paul was thrown into jail, she refused to eat in protest. "This is a spirit like Joan of Arc," concluded the doctor who examined her. Prison officials declared her insane.

Finally, public anger over such treatment, along with the need for broad-based support for World War I, led the House of Representatives to pass a woman suffrage amendment in 1918. In 1920 it became the Nineteenth Amendment.

Nineteenth Amendment

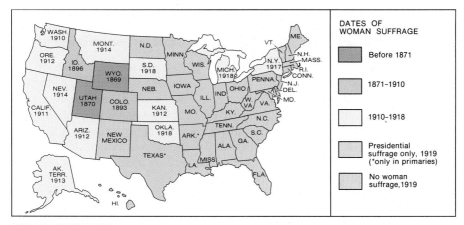

WOMAN SUFFRAGE

Western states were the first to grant women the right to vote. Sparsely populated and more egalitarian than the rest of the nation, the West was used to women participating fully in settlement and work. Other sections of the country, notably the Midwest, granted women partial suffrage that included voting for school boards and taxes. Suffragists encountered the most intractable resistance in the South, where rigid codes of social conduct elevated women symbolically but shackled them practically.

CONTROLLING THE MASSES

"Observe immigrants," wrote one American in 1912; "you are struck by the fact that from ten to twenty percent are hirsute, low-browed, big-faced persons of obviously low mentality. . . . They clearly belong in skins, in wattled huts at the close of the Ice Age." The writer was neither an uneducated fanatic nor a stern opponent of change. He was Professor Edward A. Ross, a progressive from Madison, Wisconsin, who prided himself on his scientific study of sociology.

Faced with the chaos and corruption of urban life, more than a few progressives feared they were losing control of their country. Saloons and dance halls lured youngsters and impoverished laborers; prostitutes walked the streets; vulgar amusements pandered to the uneducated. Strange Old World cultures clashed with "all-American" customs, and races jostled uneasily. The city challenged middle-class reformers to convert this riot of diversity into a more uniform society. To maintain control progressives sometimes moved beyond education and regulation and sought restrictive laws to control the masses.

Stemming the Immigrant Tide

A rising tide of nonwhite and immigrant Americans, many settling in cities, aggravated the fears of more than a few progressives and other native-born whites. During the 1890s, segregation laws had already begun to restrict the opportunities of African

Daily Lives

PUBLIC SPACE/PRIVATE SPACE

"Amusing the Million"

On a sunny May morning in 1903, 45,000 people poured through the gates of Luna Park at Coney Island, just south of Brooklyn. What they saw on opening day amazed them: "a storybook land of trellises, columns, domes, minarets, lagoons, and lofty aerial flights." A huge dolphin fountain gushed water from the base of the main tower. Barkers beckoned them into a Venetian city, a Japanese garden, and a bustling Asian Indian celebration. They could hop aboard the "Switchback" Railroad, a forerunner of the roller coaster, or career on flat-bottom boats down a steep incline into the "Shoot-the-Chutes" lagoon. They could even witness a disaster. In "Fire and Flames," mock firefighters doused a four-story blaze as mock residents jumped from top floors to safety nets below—all on cue. Those who spent their days in crowded tenements rolling cigars or sleeping nights in stuffy apartments might well blink in awe as a quarter of a million electric lights, strung like glittering pearls across the buildings, turned night into enchanted day. This was "a world removed—shut away from the sordid clatter and turmoil of the streets," such a place "as Aladdin never dreamed."

Coney Island was but one of a host of similar parks that popped up across the country at the turn of the century. Soaring urban populations, increases in leisure time, more spending money, and new trolley systems that made for cheap excursions from the city led to the opening of Boston's Paragon Park, Cleveland's Euclid Beach, Atlanta's Ponce de Leon Park, and Los Angeles's Venice Beach.

All traded in entertainment, but of a sort new to city dwellers. Earlier Victorian reformers had promoted two models of public entertainment: the spacious city park and the grand public exposition. Both were meant to instruct as well as amuse. Their planners hoped to reduce urban disorder by raising public taste and refining public conduct. When it opened in 1858, New York City's Central Park became a model pastoral retreat in the midst of the city. Its rustic paths, tranquil lakes, and woodsy views were designed as respites from the chaos of urban life. According to designer Frederick Law Olmstead, such vistas would have "a distinctly harmonizing and refining influence" on even the rudest fellow.

The World's Columbian Exposition of 1893 in Chicago also reflected an elevating vision of society. Its neoclassical buildings were designed to instruct citizens about

Americans in the South. After 1900, the rhetoric of reform was used to support white supremacy. Southern progressives won office by promising to disfranchise black southerners, in order to break the power of corrupt political machines that rested on the black vote, much as northern machines marshaled the immigrant vote.

The South was hardly the only region in which discrimination flourished. Asians, Latinos, and Indians faced similar curbs in the West, as did the new arrivals from southern and eastern Europe in the North. The sharp increase in immigration especially troubled native-born Americans, including reformers anxious over the changing ethnic complexion of the country. In northern cities progressives often succeeded in reducing immigrant voting power by increasing residency requirements.

Daily Lives

ndoias in Venice Canal, Venice, California

The Venice Amusement Park in California was meant to conjure up Venice, Italy, complete with a network of canals. (Note the gondola in the foreground.) The founders dubbed Venice Park "the Coney Island of the Pacific."

ened. At the Columbian Exposition, the amusements section, a mile-long strip of theaters, restaurants, sideshows, and rides, had easily lured more people than the free public exhibits. As one owner put it, parks were in the business of "amusing the million." Coney Island's Luna Park drew 5 million paying customers in a single season.

Jostling with crowds, eating ice cream and hot dogs, riding "Shoot-the-Chutes," young working men and women, single, in couples, or married, even the newest immigrant could feel gloriously free and independent, gloriously American. A sense of solidarity drew the mostly working-class crowds together, and the zaniness of the setting loosened social restraints. "I have heard some of the high people with whom I have been living say that Coney Island is not tony," reported one 20-year old servant girl. "The trouble is that these high people don't know how to dance. I have to laugh when I see them at their balls and parties. If only I could get out on the floor and show them how—they would be astonished." In this girl's mind, the Victorian values of sober industry, thrift, and orderly conduct could hardly compete with the democratic abandon and gaiety of the new amusement parks. They heralded the rise of mass culture, invading public space with the private dreams of ordinary people.

their country's marvelous wealth and industry (see pages 712–713). At the center of the exposition stood a 100-foot statue, "The Republic," a toga-draped figure holding an eagle perched on a globe. Some amusement parks, like Venice Beach's, mimicked the style of the exposition.

But it did not escape the amusement park operators that people wanted to have fun more than they wished to be enlight-

A new science called "eugenics" lent respectability to the idea that newcomers were *Eugenics* biologically inferior. Eugenicists believed that heredity largely shaped all human behavior, and they therefore advocated selective breeding for human improvement. By 1914 more magazine articles discussed eugenics than slums, tenements, and living standards combined. In *The Passing of the Great Race* (1916), upper-crust New Yorker and amateur zoologist Madison Grant helped popularize the notion that the "lesser breeds" threatened to "mongrelize" America. So powerful was the pull of eugenics that it captured the support of many reformers, including birth control advocate Margaret Sanger.

More enlightened reformers such as Jane Addams stressed the cultural "gifts" immigrants brought with them: folk rituals, dances, music, and handicrafts. With

Americani-
zation

characteristic paternalism, these reformers hoped to "Americanize" the foreign-born (the term was newly coined) by teaching them middle-class ways. Education was one key. Progressive educator Peter Roberts, for example, developed a lesson plan for the Young Men's Christian Association that taught immigrants to dress, tip, buy groceries, and vote.

Less tolerant citizens sought to restrict immigration as a way of reasserting control and achieving social harmony. Though white, Protestant, and American-born, these nativists were usually not progressives themselves, but they did employ progressive methods of organization, investigation, education, and legislation. Active since the 1890s, the

Literacy test

Immigration Restriction League pressed Congress in 1907 to require a literacy test for admission into the United States. Presidents Taft and Wilson vetoed it in 1913 and 1915, but Congress overrode Wilson's second veto in 1917, when war fever raised defensive nationalism to a new peak.

The Curse of Demon Rum

Tied closely to concern over immigrants was an attack on saloons. Part of a broader crusade to clean up cities, the antisaloon campaign drew strength from the century-old drive to lessen the consumption of alcohol. Women made up a disproportionate number of alcohol reformers. The temperance movement reflected their growing campaign to storm male domains—in this case the saloon—and to contain male violence, particularly the wife and child abuse associated with drinking.

By 1900 the dangers of an alcoholic republic seemed all too real. Alcohol consumption had risen to an annual rate of more than two gallons per person. Over half of Boston and Chicago visited a bar at least once a day. Often political bosses owned saloons or conducted their business there. To alcohol reformers, taverns and saloons thus seemed at the center of many social problems—gambling and prostitution, political corruption, drug trafficking, unemployment, and poverty. Few reformers recognized the complex cycle of social decay that produced such problems, fewer still the role of saloons as "workingmen's clubs." The saloon was often the only place to cash a check, find out about jobs, eat a cheap meal, or take a bath.

Reformers considered a national ban on drinking unrealistic and intrusive. Instead they concentrated on prohibiting the sale of alcohol at local and state levels

Anti-Saloon
League

and attacked businesses that profited from it. Led by the Anti-Saloon League (1893), a massive publicity campaign bombarded citizens with pamphlets and advertisements. Doctors cited scientific evidence linking alcohol to cirrhosis, heart disease, and insanity. Social workers connected drink to the deterioration of the family; employers, to accidents on the job and lost efficiency.

By 1917 three out of four Americans lived in "dry" counties. Nearly two-thirds of the states had adopted laws outlawing the manufacture and sale of alcohol. Not all progressives were prohibitionists, but the many who were sighed with relief at having taken the profit out of human pain and corruption.

Prostitution

No urban vice worried reformers more than prostitution. In their eyes it was a social evil that threatened young city women with a fate much worse than death. The Chicago Vice Commission of 1910 estimated that 5000 full-time and 10,000 occa-

The "Inebriate's Express," loaded with drunken riders, is heading straight for hell. This detail from a chromolithograph, published around 1900, was typical of Victorian-era responses to the problems posed by alcohol. To the all-seeing eye of the omnipotent God, faith, hope, charity, and the Bible are sufficient to cure the problems of drinking.

sional prostitutes plied their trade in the city. Other cities, small and large, reported similar numbers.

An unlikely group of reformers united to fight the vice: feminists who wanted husbands to be as chaste as their wives, public health officials worried about the spread of sexually transmitted disease, and immigration restrictionists who regarded the growth of prostitution as yet another sign of corrupt newcomers. Progressives condemned prostitution but saw the problem in economic and environmental terms. "Poverty causes prostitution," concluded the Illinois Vice Commission in 1916. On average, prostitutes earned five times the income of factory workers.

Some reformers saw more active agents at work. Rumors spread of a vast and profitable "white slave trade." Men armed with hypodermic needles were said to be lurking about streetcars, amusement parks, and dance halls in search of young women. Although the average female rider of the streetcar was hardly in danger of abduction, in every city there could be found cribs with locked doors where women were held captive and forced into prostitution. By conservative estimates they comprised some 10 percent of all prostitutes.

White slave trade

As real abuses blended with sensationalism, Congress passed the Mann Act (1910), prohibiting the interstate transport of women for immoral purposes. By 1918 reformers succeeded in banning previously tolerated "red light" districts in most cities. As with the liquor trade, progressives went after those who made money from misery.

THE POLITICS OF MUNICIPAL AND STATE REFORM

Reform the system. In the end, so many urban problems seemed to come back to the premise that government had to be overhauled. Jane Addams learned as much outside the doors of her beloved Hull House in Chicago. For months during the early 1890s, garbage had piled up in the streets. The filth and stench drove Addams and her fellow workers to city hall in protest—700 times in one summer—but to no avail. In Chicago, as elsewhere, corrupt city bosses had made garbage collection a plum to be awarded to the company that paid them the most for it.

In desperation, Addams herself submitted a bid for garbage removal in the ward. When it was thrown out on a technicality, she won an appointment as garbage inspector. For almost a year she dogged collection carts, but boss politics kept things

Jane Addams founded her settlement at Hull House in Chicago because she was convinced, like many progressives, that reform must be practical, arising out of the needs of individuals within a community. As Addams continued her campaigns, she also looked beyond the local neighborhood to reform political structures of municipal and state governments.

dirty. So Addams ran candidates in 1896 and 1898 against local ward boss Johnny Powers. They lost, but Addams kept up the fight for honest government and social reform—at city hall, in the Illinois legislature, and finally in Washington. Politics turned out to be the only way to clean things up.

The Reformation of the Cities

For middle-class reformers, the urban battleground furnished the first test of political reform. And a series of colorful and independent mayors demonstrated that cities could be run humanely without changing the structure of government.

In Detroit, shoe magnate Hazen Pingree turned the mayor's office into an instrument of reform when elected in 1889. By the end of his fourth term, Detroit had new parks and public baths, fairer taxes, ownership of the local light plant, and a work-relief program for victims of the depression of 1893. In 1901, Cleveland Mayor Tom Johnson launched a similar reform campaign. Before he was through, municipal franchises had been limited to a fraction of their previous 99-year terms and the city ran the utility company. By 1915 nearly two out of three cities in the nation had copied some form of this "gas and water socialism" to control the runaway prices of utility companies. *Gas and water socialism*

Tragedy dramatized the need to alter the very structure of government. On a hot summer night in 1900 a tidal wave from the Gulf of Mexico smashed the port city of Galveston, Texas. Floods killed one of every six residents. The municipal government sank into confusion and political wrangling. In reaction business leaders won approval of a new charter that replaced the mayor and city council with a powerful commission. Each of five commissioners controlled a municipal department, and together they ran the city. By 1920 nearly 400 cities had adopted the plan. Expert commissioners enhanced efficiency and helped to check party rule in municipal government. *Commission plan*

In other cities, elected officials appointed an outside expert or "city manager" to run things. The first was hired in Staunton, Virginia, in 1908. Within a decade, 45 cities had them. At lower levels experts took charge of services: engineers oversaw utilities; accountants, finances; doctors and nurses, public health; specially trained firefighters and police, the safety of citizens. Broad civic reforms attempted to break the corrupt alliance between companies doing business with the city and the bosses who controlled the wards. Citywide elections replaced the old ward system, and civil service laws helped to create a nonpartisan bureaucracy. Political machines and ethnic voters lost power, while city government gained efficiency. *City-manager plan*

Progressivism in the States

"Whenever we try to do anything, we run up against the charter," complained the reform mayor of Schenectady, New York. Charters granted by state governments defined the powers of cities. The rural interests that generally dominated state legislatures rarely gave cities adequate authority to levy taxes, set voting requirements, draw up budgets, or legislate reforms. State legislatures, too, found themselves under the influence of business interests, party machines, and county courthouse rings. Reformers therefore tried to place their candidates where they could do some good— in the governors' mansions. *Weaknesses of city government*

State progressivism enjoyed its greatest success in the Midwest, under the leadership of Robert La Follette of Wisconsin. La Follette first won election to Congress in 1885 by toeing the Republican line of high tariffs and the gold standard. When a Republican boss offered him a bribe in a railroad case, LaFollette pledged to break "the power of this corrupt influence." In 1900 he won the governorship of Wisconsin as an uncommonly independent Republican.

La Follette's Wisconsin idea

Over the next six years "Battle Bob" La Follette made Wisconsin, in the words of Theodore Roosevelt, "the laboratory of democracy." La Follette's "Wisconsin idea" produced the most comprehensive set of state reforms in American history. There were new laws regulating railroads, controlling corruption, and expanding the civil service. His direct primary weakened the hold of party bosses by transferring nominations from the back rooms of party conventions and caucuses to the voters at large. Among La Follette's notable "firsts" were a state income tax, a state commission to oversee factory safety and sanitation, and a Legislative Reference Bureau at the University of Wisconsin. University-trained experts poured into state government.

Other states copied the Wisconsin idea or hatched their own. By 1916 all but three had direct primary laws. To cut the power of party organizations and make officeholders directly responsible to the public, progressives worked for three additional reforms: initiative (voter introduction of legislation), referendum (voter enactment or repeal of laws), and recall (voter-initiated removal of elected officials). By

Initiative, referendum, recall

1912 a dozen states had adopted initiative and referendum, seven recall. A year later the Seventeenth Amendment to the Constitution permitted the direct election of senators, previously selected by state legislatures.

Almost every state established regulatory commissions with the power to hold public hearings, and examine company books and question officials. Some could set maximum prices and rates. Yet it was not always easy to define, let alone serve, the

La Follette

believes in the American people. He believes that YOU should know the TRUTH about the inside workings of YOUR government and the records of your representatives at Washington.

So with the help and approval of a score of other fighters for the common good, Senator La Follette established

La Follette's Magazine

devoted to fearless discussion of the most important public questions, and has departments for the home, special articles, stories, a Farm Department, fiction, humor, important news of the world.

Published monthly. Regular price $1.00 per year. To permit you to get acquainted with the magazine we will send it to you on trial

3 Months for 25c.

Simply send a quarter with your name and address to

LA FOLLETTE'S, Box 45, Madison, Wis.

On the state level, progressives made their greatest impact in Wisconsin, where Robert LaFollette led the fight to regulate railroads, control corruption, and expand the civil service. In trying to do an end-run around political party bosses, he used his publication, *LaFollette's Magazine*, to reach ordinary Americans directly.

"public good." All too often commissioners found themselves refereeing battles within industries—between carriers and shippers, for example—rather than between what progressives called "the interests" and "the people." Regulators had to rely on the advice of experts drawn from the business community itself. Many commissions thus became captured by the industries they regulated.

Social welfare received special attention from the states. The lack of workers' compensation for injury, illness, or death on the job had long drawn fire from reformers and labor leaders. American courts still operated on the common-law assumption that employees accepted the risks of work. Workers or their families could collect damages only if they proved employer negligence. Most accident victims received nothing. In 1902 Maryland finally adopted the first workers' compensation act. By 1916, most states required insurance for factory accidents and over half had employer liability laws. Thirteen states also provided pensions for widows with dependent children.

More and more it was machine politicians and women's organizations that pressed for working-class reforms. Despite the progressive attack on machine politics, political bosses survived, in part by adapting the climate of reform to the needs of their working-class constituents. After the Triangle fire of 1911, for example, it was Tammany Democrats Robert F. Wagner and Alfred E. Smith who led the fight for a new labor code.

This working-class "urban liberalism" also found advocates among women's associations, especially those concerned with mothers, children, and working women. The Federation of Women's Clubs led the fight for mothers' pensions (a forerunner of aid to dependent children). When in 1912 the National Consumers' League and other women's groups succeeded in establishing the Children's Bureau, it was the first federal welfare agency and the only female-run national bureau in the world. At a time when women lacked the vote, they nonetheless sowed the seeds of the welfare state as they helped to make urban liberalism a powerful instrument of social reform.

Seeds of the welfare state

PROGRESSIVISM GOES TO WASHINGTON

On September 6, 1901, at the Pan-American Exposition in Buffalo, New York, Leon Czolgosz stood nervously in line. He was waiting among well-wishers to met President William McKinley. Unemployed and bent on murder, Czolgosz shuffled toward McKinley. As the president reached out, Czolgosz fired two bullets into his chest. McKinley slumped into a chair. Eight days later the president was dead. The mantle of power passed to Theodore Roosevelt. At 42 he was the youngest president ever to hold office.

Roosevelt's entry into the White House was a political accident, as he himself acknowledged. Party leaders had seen the weak office of vice president as a way of removing him from power, but the tragedy in Buffalo foiled their plans. "It is a dreadful thing to come into the presidency this way," he remarked, "but it would be a far worse thing to be morbid about it." Surely progressivism would have come to Washington without Theodore Roosevelt, and while there he was never its most daring advocate. In many ways he was quite conservative. He saw reform as a way to avoid more radical change. Yet without Roosevelt progressivism would have had neither the broad popular appeal nor the buoyancy he gave it.

TR

TR, as so many Americans called him, was the scion of seven generations of wealthy, aristocratic New Yorkers. A sickly boy, he built his body through rigorous exercise, sharpened his mind through constant study, and pursued a life so strenuous that few could keep up. He learned to ride and shoot, roped cattle in the Dakota Badlands, mastered judo, and later in life climbed the Matterhorn, hunted African game, and explored the Amazon.

In 1880, driven by an urge to lead and serve, Roosevelt won election to the New York State Assembly. In rapid succession he became a civil service commissioner in Washington, New York City police commissioner, assistant secretary of the navy, and the Rough Rider hero of the Spanish-American War. At the age of 40 he won election as reform governor of New York and two years later as vice president. Through it all, TR remained a solid Republican, personally flamboyant but committed to mild change only.

To the Executive Mansion (he renamed it the "White House"), Roosevelt brought a passion for order, a commitment to the public, and a sense of presidential possibilities. Most presidents believed the Constitution set specific limits on their power. Roosevelt thought that the president could do anything not expressly forbidden in the document. Recognizing the value of publicity, he gave reporters the first press room in the White House and favored them with all the stories they wanted. He was the first president to ride in an automobile, fly an airplane, and dive in a submarine—and everyone knew it.

To dramatize racial injustice, Roosevelt invited black educator Booker T. Washington to lunch at the White House in 1901. White southern journalists called

Bull-necked and barrel-chested, Theodore Roosevelt was "pure act," said Henry Adams. TR may have had the attention span of a golden retriever, as one critic charged, but he also embodied the great virtues of his day—honesty, hard work, constancy, courage, and, while in power, self-control.

such mingling with African Americans treason, but for Roosevelt the gesture served both principle and politics. His lunch with Washington was part of a "black and tan" strategy to build a biracial coalition among southern Republicans. He denounced lynching and appointed black southerners to important federal offices in Mississippi and South Carolina.

Sensing the limits of political feasibility, Roosevelt went no further. Perhaps his own racial narrowness stopped him too. In 1906, when Atlanta exploded in a race riot that left 12 people dead, he said nothing. Later that year he discharged "without honor" three entire companies of African American troops because some of the soldiers were unjustly charged with having "shot up" Brownsville, Texas. All lost their pensions, including six winners of the Medal of Honor. The act stained Roosevelt's record. (Congress acknowledged the wrong in 1972 by granting the soldiers honorable discharges.)

Brownsville incident

A Square Deal

By temperament, Roosevelt was not inclined to follow the cautious course McKinley had charted. He had more energetic plans in mind. He accepted growth—whether of business, labor, or government—as natural. In the pluralistic system he envisioned, big labor would counterbalance big capital, big farm organizations would offset big food processors, and so on. Standing astride them all, mediating when needed, was a big government that could ensure fair results for all. Later, as he campaigned for a second term in 1904, Roosevelt named this program the "Square Deal."

Philosophy of the Square Deal

In a startling display of presidential initiative, Roosevelt in 1902 intervened in a strike that idled 140,000 miners and paralyzed the anthracite (hard) coal industry. As winter approached, public frustration with the mine owners mounted. They refused even to recognize the miners' union, let alone negotiate worker demands for higher

Anthracite coal strike

wages and fewer hours. Roosevelt summoned both sides to the White House. John A. Mitchell, the young president of the United Mine Workers, agreed to arbitration, but management balked. Roosevelt leaked word to Wall Street that the army would take over the mines if the owners did not yield.

Seldom had a president acted so boldly, and never on behalf of strikers. In late October 1902 the owners settled by granting miners a 10 percent wage hike and a nine-hour day in return for increases in coal prices and no recognition of the union. Roosevelt was equally prepared to intervene on the side of management, as he did when he sent federal troops to end strikes in Arizona in 1903 and Colorado in 1904. His aim was to establish a vigorous presidency ready to deal squarely with all sides.

Roosevelt especially needed to face the issue of economic concentration. Financial power had become consolidated in giant trusts following a wave of mergers at the end of the century. As large firms swallowed smaller ones, Americans feared that monopoly would destroy individual enterprise and free competition. A series of government investigations revealed a rash of corporate abuses—rebates, collusion, "watered" stock, payoffs to government officials. The conservative courts showed little willingness to break up the giants or blunt their power. In *United States v. E. C. Knight* (1895), the Supreme Court crippled the Sherman Antitrust Act by ruling that the law applied only to commerce and not to manufacturing. The decision left the American Sugar Refining Company in control of 98 percent of the nation's sugar factories.

U.S. v. E. C. Knight

In his first State of the Union message, Roosevelt told Congress that he did not oppose business concentration. As he saw it, large corporations were not only inevitable but more productive than smaller operations. He wanted to regulate, not destroy them, to make them fairer and more efficient. Only then would the economic order be humanized, its victims protected, and class violence avoided. Like individuals, trusts had to be held to strict standards of morality. Conduct, not size, was the yardstick TR used to measure "good" and "bad" trusts.

With a progressive's faith in the power of publicity and a regulator's need for the facts, Roosevelt moved immediately to strengthen the federal power of investigation. He called for the creation of a Department of Commerce with a Bureau of Corporations that could force companies to hand over their records. Congressional conservatives shuddered at the prospect of putting corporate books on display. Finally, in 1903, after Roosevelt charged that John D. Rockefeller was orchestrating the opposition, Congress enacted the legislation and provided the Justice Department with additional staff to prosecute antitrust cases.

Northern Securities

In 1902, to demonstrate the power of government, Roosevelt had Attorney General Philander Knox file an antitrust suit against the Northern Securities Company. The mammoth holding company virtually monopolized railroads in the Northwest. Worse still, it had bloated its stock with worthless certificates. Here, clearly, was a symbol of the "bad trust."

J. P. Morgan, one of the company's founders, rushed to the White House. "Send your man [the attorney general] to my man [Morgan's lawyer] and they can fix it up," he told Roosevelt and Knox. "We don't want to fix it up," replied the attorney general. "We want to stop it." A trust-conscious nation cheered as the Supreme Court ordered the company to dissolve in 1904. Ultimately, the Roosevelt administration brought suit against 44 giants, including the Standard Oil Company, the American Tobacco Company, and the Du Pont Corporation.

Despite his reputation for trustbusting, Roosevelt always preferred regulation. *Railroad* The problems of the railroads, for example, were newly underscored by a recent *regulation* round of consolidation that had contributed to higher freight rates. Roosevelt pressed Congress to strengthen the weak Interstate Commerce Commission (ICC) (page 721). In 1903 Congress enacted the Elkins Act, which gave the ICC power to end rebates. Even the railroads supported the act because it saved them from the costly practice of granting special reductions to large shippers.

By the election of 1904 the president's boldness had won him broad popular support. He trounced his two rivals, Democrat Alton B. Parker, a jurist from New York, and Eugene V. Debs of the Socialist party. No longer was he a "political accident," Roosevelt boasted.

Conservatives in his own party opposed Roosevelt's meddling in the private sector. But progressives, goaded by Robert La Follette, demanded still more regulation of the railroads, in particular a controversial proposal for making public the value of all rail property. In 1906, the president finally reached a compromise typical of his restrained approach to reform. The Hepburn Railway Act allowed the ICC to set ceilings on rates and to regulate sleeping car companies, ferries, bridges, and terminals. La Follette did not gain his provision to disclose company value, but the Hepburn Act drew Roosevelt nearer to his goal of continuous regulation of business.

Bad Food and Pristine Wilds

Extending the umbrella of federal protection to consumers, Roosevelt belatedly threw his weight behind two campaigns for healthy foods and drugs. In 1905 Samuel Hopkins Adams of *Collier's Weekly* wrote that in its patent medicines "Gullible America" would get "huge quantities of alcohol, an appalling amount of opiates and narcotics," and worse—axle grease, acid, glue. Adams sent the samples he had collected to Harvey Wiley, chief chemist at the Agriculture Department. Wiley's "Poison Squad" produced scientific evidence of Adams's charges.

Several pure food and drug bills had already died at the hands of lobbyists, despite a presidential endorsement. The appearance of Upton Sinclair's *The Jungle* in 1906 spurred Congress to act. Sinclair intended to recruit people to socialism by exposing the plight of workers in the meat-packing industry. His novel contained a brief but vivid description of the slaughter of cattle infected with tuberculosis, of meat covered with rat dung, and of men falling into cooking vats and being served to the public as "Durham's Pure Leaf Lard." Readers paid scant attention to the workers, but their stomachs turned at what they might be eating for breakfast. The Pure Food and Drug Act of 1906 sailed through Congress, and the Meat Inspection Act soon followed.

Roosevelt had come late to the consumer cause, but on conservation he led the *Conservation* nation. An outdoors enthusiast, he galvanized public concern over the reckless use of *through* natural resources. His chief forester, Gifford Pinchot, persuaded him that planned *planned* management under federal guidance was needed to protect the natural domain. *management* Cutting trees must be synchronized with tree plantings, oil pumped from the ground under controlled conditions, and so on.

In the western states water was the problem. Economic growth, even survival, depended on it. As fragmented local and state water policies sparked controversy, violence, and waste, many progressives campaigned for a federal program to replace the chaotic web of rules. Democratic Senator Frederick Newlands of Nevada introduced the Reclamation Act of 1902 to set aside proceeds from the sale of public lands for irrigation projects. The Reclamation Act signaled a progressive step toward the conservationist end of rational resource development.

John Muir and preservation

Conservation often conflicted with the more radical vision of preservationists, led by naturalist and wilderness philosopher John Muir. Muir founded the Sierra Club in 1892 in hopes of maintaining such natural wonders as Yosemite and its neighboring Hetch-Hetchy valley in a state "forever wild" to benefit future generations. Many conservationists saw such valleys only as sites for dams and reservoirs. Controversy flared after 1900 when San Francisco announced plans to create a reservoir in the Hetch-Hetchy valley. For 13 years Muir waged a publicity campaign against the "devotees of ravaging commercialism." Pinchot enthusiastically backed San Francisco's claim. Roosevelt, torn by his friendship with Muir, did so less loudly. Not until 1913 did President Woodrow Wilson finally decide the issue in favor of San Francisco. Conservation had won over preservation.

Roosevelt nonetheless advanced many of Muir's goals. Over the protests of cattle and timber interests, he added nearly 200 million acres to government forest reserves; placed coal and mineral lands, oil reserves, and water-power sites in the public domain; and enlarged the national park system. When Congress balked, he appropriated another 17 million acres of forest before the legislators could pass a bill limiting him. Roosevelt also set in motion national congresses and commissions on conservation and mobilized governors across the country. Like a good progressive, he sent hundreds of experts to work applying science, education, and technology to environmental problems.

The Sierra Club, founded by naturalist John Muir, believed in the importance of preserving wilderness in its natural state. "In God's wildness," Muir wrote in 1890, "lies the hope of the world—the great fresh unblighted, unredeemed wilderness." Muir helped to persuade President Theodore Roosevelt to double the number of national parks. Here some Sierra Club members lounge at the base of a giant redwood in Big Basin in 1905.

As Roosevelt acted more forcefully, conservatives lashed back. So far his record had been modest, but his chief accomplishment—invigorating the presidency—could lead to deeper reform. When another dip in the business cycle produced financial panic on Wall Street in 1907, business leaders and conservative politicians blamed the president. Roosevelt blamed the "speculative folly and the flagrant dishonesty of a few men of great wealth."

Clearly shaken, however, Roosevelt assured business leaders that he would do nothing to interfere with their efforts at recovery. That included a pledge not to file an antitrust suit if the giant U.S. Steel bought the Tennessee Coal and Iron Company. The economy recovered, and having declared he would not run in 1908, the 50-year-old Roosevelt prepared to give over his office to William Howard Taft.

The Troubled Taft

On March 4, 1909, as snow swirled outside the White House, William Howard Taft readied himself for his inauguration. Over breakfast with Roosevelt, he warmed in the glow of recent Republican victories. Taft had beaten Democrat William Jennings Bryan in the "Great Commoner's" third and last bid for the presidency. Republicans had retained control of Congress, as well as a host of northern legislatures. Reform was at high tide, and Taft was eager to continue the Roosevelt program.

"Will," as Roosevelt called him, was his handpicked successor. A distinguished jurist and public servant, the first American governor-general of the Philippines, and Roosevelt's secretary of war, Taft had great administrative skill and personal charm. But he disliked the political maneuvering of Washington and preferred conciliation to confrontation. Even Roosevelt had doubts. "He's all right," TR had told a reporter on inauguration day. "But he's weak. They'll get around him. They'll"—and here Roosevelt pushed the reporter with his shoulder—"lean against him."

William Howard Taft—big, good-natured, and modest—was reluctant to run for the presidency in 1908. At the outset of the campaign, President Roosevelt sent him pointed advice: "Photographs on horseback, yes, tennis, no, and golf is fatal." But Taft played anyway. He loved golf despite its reputation as a "dude's game."

Trouble began early when progressives in the House moved to curb the near-dictatorial power of the conservative Speaker, Joseph Cannon. Taft waffled, first supporting them, then abandoning them to preserve the tariff reductions he was seeking. When progressives later broke Cannon's power without Taft's help, they scorned the president. And Taft's compromise was wasted. Senate protectionists peppered the tariff bill with so many amendments that rates jumped nearly to their old levels.

Ballinger–
Pinchot affair

Late in 1909, the rift between Taft and the progressives reached the breaking point in a dispute over conservation. Taft had appointed Richard Ballinger secretary of the interior over the objections of Roosevelt's old friend and mentor Chief Forester Pinchot. When Ballinger opened a million acres of public lands for sale, Pinchot rebelled openly. He charged that shady dealings had led Ballinger to transfer Alaskan public coal lands to a syndicate that included J. P. Morgan. Early in 1910, Taft fired him for insubordination. Angry progressives saw the Ballinger–Pinchot controversy as another betrayal by Taft. They began to look longingly across the Atlantic, where TR was stalking big game in Africa.

Taft's accomp-
lishments

Despite his failures, Taft was no conservative pawn. He ended up protecting more land than Roosevelt, and he pushed Congress to enact a progressive program regulating safety standards for mines and railroads, creating a federal children's bureau, and setting an eight-hour workday for federal employees. Taft's support of a graduated income tax—sometimes fiery, sometimes mild—was finally decisive. Early in 1913 it became the Sixteenth Amendment. Historians view it as one of the most important reforms of the century, for it eventually generated the revenue for many new social programs.

Yet no matter what Taft did, he managed to alienate conservatives and progressives alike. That spelled trouble for the Republicans as the presidential election of 1912 approached.

Roosevelt Returns

In June 1910 Roosevelt had come home laden with hunting trophies and exuberant as ever. He found Taft unhappy and progressive Republicans threatening to defect. Party loyalty kept Roosevelt quiet through most of 1911, but in October Taft pricked him personally on the sensitive matter of busting trusts. Like TR, Taft accepted trusts as natural, but he failed to make Roosevelt's distinction between "good" and "bad" ones. He demanded, more impartially, that all trusts be prevented from restraining trade. In four years as president, Taft had brought nearly twice the antitrust suits Roosevelt had in seven years.

In October 1911 the Justice Department charged U.S. Steel with having violated the Sherman Antitrust Act by acquiring the Tennessee Coal and Iron Company. Roosevelt regarded the action as a personal rebuke, since he himself had allowed U.S. Steel to proceed with the acquisition. Taft "was playing small, mean, and foolish politics," complained TR.

New
Nationalism

Roosevelt decided to play big, high-minded, and presidential. Already, in a speech at Osawatomie, Kansas, in 1910, he had outlined a program of sweeping reform. His "New Nationalism" stressed the interests of the nation as a whole and the value of government as an agent of reform. It accepted consolidation in the economy—whether big business or big labor—but insisted on protecting the interests of individuals through big government. The New Nationalism promised government planning and efficiency under a powerful executive, "a steward of the public welfare." It promoted taxes on incomes and inheritances and greater regulation of industry. And it embraced social justice, specifically workers' compensation for accidents, minimum wages and maximum hours, child labor laws, and "equal suffrage"—a nod to women and loyal black Republicans. Roosevelt, a cautious reformer as president, grew daring as he set his sights again on the White House.

The Election of 1912

"My hat is in the ring!" Roosevelt announced in February 1912, to no one's surprise. Taft responded by claiming that the New Nationalism had won support only from "radicals," "emotionalists," and "neurotics." In fact, the enormously popular Roosevelt won most of the primaries, but by the time Republicans met in Chicago in June 1912, Taft had used presidential patronage and promises to secure the nomination. A frustrated Roosevelt bolted and took progressive Republicans with him. Two months later, amid choruses of "Onward Christian Soldiers," delegates to the newly formed Progressive party nominated Roosevelt for the presidency. "I'm feeling like a bull moose!" he bellowed. Progressives suddenly had a symbol for their breakaway party.

Progressive, or "Bull Moose," party

The Democrats met in Baltimore, jubilant over the prospect of a divided Republican party. Delegates chose as their candidate Woodrow Wilson, the progressive governor of New Jersey. Wilson wisely concentrated his fire on Roosevelt. He countered the New Nationalism with his "New Freedom." It rejected the economic consolidation that Roosevelt embraced. Bigness in itself was a sin, no matter how big corporations acted, because it crowded out competition, promoted inefficiency, and

Woodrow Wilson's New Freedom

REPUBLICAN AND DEMOCRATIC PARTIES' SHARE OF POPULAR VOTE, 1860–1912
In the last quarter of the nineteenth century the Republican and Democratic parties were deadlocked until the Republicans became the majority party in 1896. In 1912 the parties splintered. TR ran as a Progressive, and Republican fortunes plummeted.

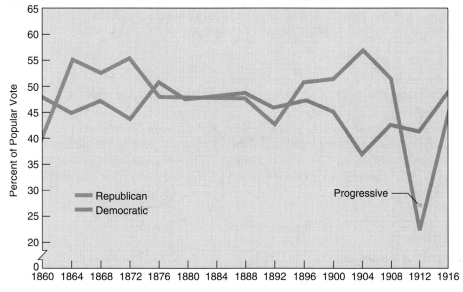

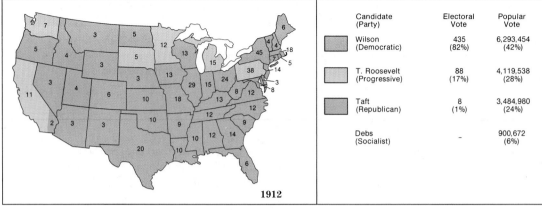

Candidate (Party)	Electoral Vote	Popular Vote
Wilson (Democratic)	435 (82%)	6,293,454 (42%)
T. Roosevelt (Progressive)	88 (17%)	4,119,538 (28%)
Taft (Republican)	8 (1%)	3,484,980 (24%)
Debs (Socialist)	–	900,672 (6%)

ELECTION OF 1912

reduced economic opportunity. Only by strictly limiting the size of business enterprises could the free market be preserved and Americans be released from the control of the wealthy and powerful. And only by keeping government small could individual liberty be protected. "Liberty," Wilson cautioned, "has never come from government," only from the "limitation of governmental power."

Increasingly voters found Taft beside the point. In age of reform, even the Socialists looked good. Better led, financed, and organized than ever, the Socialist party had enlarged its membership to nearly 135,000 by 1912. Socialist mayors ran 32 cities. The party also had an appealing candidate in Eugene V. Debs, a homegrown Indiana radical. He had won 400,000 votes for president in 1904. Now, in 1912, he summoned voters to make "the working class the ruling class."

On Election Day voters gave progressive reform a resounding endorsement. Wilson won 6.3 million votes, Roosevelt 4.1 million, Taft just 3.6 million. Debs received almost a million votes. Together the two progressive candidates amassed a three to one margin. The Republican split, moreover, had broken the party's hold on national politics. For the first time since 1896, a Democrat would sit in the White House—and with his party in control of Congress.

WOODROW WILSON AND THE POLITICS OF MORALITY

Woodrow Wilson was not shy about his good fortune. Soon after the election he confessed to William McCombs, chairman of the Democratic National Committee: "God ordained that I should be the next President of the United States." To the White House Wilson brought a passion for reform and the conviction that he was meant to accomplish great things. Under him, progressivism peaked.

Early Career

From the moment of his birth in 1856, Thomas Woodrow Wilson could not escape a sense of destiny. It was all around him. In the family's Presbyterian faith, in the sermons of his minister father, in dinnertime talk ran the unbending belief in a world predetermined by God and ruled by saved souls, the "elect." Wilson ached to be one of them and behaved as if he were.

To prepare to lead, young Tommy Wilson studied the fiery debates of the British Parliament and wandered the woods reciting them from memory. Like most southerners, he grew up loving the Democratic party, hating the tariff, and accepting racial separation. (Under his presidency, segregation would return to Washington for the first time since Reconstruction.)

An early career in law bored him, so he turned to political science and became a professor. His studies persuaded him that a modern president must act as a "prime minister," directing and uniting his party, shaping legislation and public opinion, exerting continuous leadership. In 1910, after a stormy tenure as head of Princeton University, Wilson was helped by Democratic party bosses to win the governorship of New Jersey. In 1912 they helped him again, this time to the presidency of the country.

The Reforms of the New Freedom

As governor, Wilson had led New Jersey on the path of progressive reform. As president, he was a model of executive leadership. More than Theodore Roosevelt, he shaped policy and legislation. He went to Congress to let members know he intended to work personally with them. He kept party discipline tight and mobilized public opinion when Congress refused to act.

Lowering the high tariff was Wilson's first order of business. Progressives had long attacked the tariff as another example of the power of trusts. By protecting American manufacturers, Wilson argued, such barriers weakened the competition he cherished. When the Senate threatened to raise rates, the new president appealed directly to the public. "Industrious" and "insidious" lobbyists were blocking reform, he cried to reporters. A "brick couldn't be thrown without hitting one of them."

Woodrow Wilson came to the White House with promises to reform government. In this 1913 cartoon entitled "A New Captain in the District," the newly elected president strides through corrupt Washington, ready to police such abuses as easy land grants and pork barreling, the much-criticized congressional practice of voting for projects that benefit home districts and constituents.

Underwood–
Simmons
Tariff

The Underwood–Simmons Tariff of 1913 marked the first downward revision of the tariff in 19 years and the biggest since before the Civil War. To compensate for lost revenue, Congress enacted a graduated income tax under the newly adopted Sixteenth Amendment. It applied solely to corporations and the tiny fraction of Americans who earned more than $4000 a year. It nonetheless began a momentous shift in government revenue from its nineteenth-century base—public lands, alcohol taxes, and customs duties—to its twentieth-century base—personal and corporate incomes.

Wilson turned next to the perennial problems of money and banking. Early in 1913 a congressional committee under Arsene Pujo revealed that a few powerful banks controlled the nation's credit system. They could choke Wilson's free market by raising interest rates or tightening the supply of money. As a banking reform bill moved through Congress in 1913, Wall Street conservatives lobbied for a privately controlled, centralized banking system that could issue currency and set interest rates. Rural Democrats favored a decentralized system of regional banks run by local bankers. Populists and progressives—including William Jennings Bryan and Robert La Follette—wanted government control.

Federal
Reserve Act

Wilson split their differences in the Federal Reserve Act of 1913. The new Federal Reserve System contained 12 regional banks scattered across the country. But it also created a central Federal Reserve Board in Washington, appointed by the president, to supervise the system. The board could regulate credit and the money supply by setting the interest rate it charged member banks, by buying or selling government bonds, and by issuing paper currency called Federal Reserve notes. Thus the Federal Reserve System sought to stabilize the existing order by increasing federal control over credit and the money supply.

Federal Trade
Commission

When Wilson finally took on the trusts, he moved closer to the New Nationalism of Theodore Roosevelt. The Federal Trade Commission Act of 1914 created a bipartisan executive agency to oversee business activity. The end—to enforce orderly competition—was distinctly Wilsonian, but the means—an executive commission to regulate commerce—were pure Roosevelt.

Clayton
Antitrust Act

Roosevelt would have stopped there, but Wilson made good on his campaign pledge to attack trusts. The Clayton Antitrust Act (1914) barred some of the worst corporate practices—price discrimination, holding companies, and interlocking directorates (directors of one corporate board sitting on others). Yet despite Wilson's bias against size, the advantages of large-scale production and distribution were inescapable. In practice his administration chose to regulate rather than break up bigness. Under Wilson the Justice Department filed fewer antitrust suits than under the Taft administration and negotiated more "gentlemen's agreements" (voluntary agreements by companies to change practices) than under Roosevelt.

Labor and Social Reform

For all of Wilson's impressive accomplishments, voters turned lukewarm toward the New Freedom. In the elections of 1914 Republicans cut Democratic majorities in the House and won important industrial and farm states. To strengthen his hand in the presidential election of 1916, Wilson began edging toward the social reforms of the New Nationalism he had once criticized as paternalistic and unconstitutional. Early in 1916 he signaled the change when he nominated his close adviser Louis D. Brandeis to the Supreme Court. The progressive Brandeis had fought for the social reforms lacking in Wilson's agenda. His appointment also broke the tradition of anti-Semitism that had previously kept Jews off the Court.

In a host of other ways, Wilson revealed his willingness to intervene more actively in the economy. He helped pass laws improving the working conditions of merchant seamen and setting an eight-hour day for workers on interstate railroads. He endorsed the Keating–Owen Child Labor Act (page 767) and threw his support to legislation providing farmers with low-interest loans. And just before the election Wilson intervened to avert a nationwide strike of rail workers.

The Limits of Progressive Reform

Woodrow Wilson's administration capped a decade and a half of heady reform. Seeing chaos in the modern industrial city, progressive reformers had worked to reduce the damage of poverty and the hazards of industrial work, control the rising immigrant tide, and spread a middle-class ideal of morality. In city halls and state legislatures, they tried to break the power of corporate interests and entrenched political machines. In Washington, they enlarged government and broadened its mission from caretaker to promoter of public welfare.

Progressivism did not always succeed. Reformers sometimes betrayed their high ideals by denying equality to African Americans, Asians, and other minorities. They preferred to Americanize foreigners rather than accept the contributions of their cultures. Too often government commissions that were designed to be "watchdog" agencies found themselves captured by the interests they were supposed to oversee. Well-meaning but cumbersome regulation crippled industries like the railroads for decades. Although the direct primary, the popular election of senators, and other reforms weakened the power of political machines, boss rule survived.

For all its claims of sweeping change, progressivism left the system of market capitalism intact. Neither the New Nationalism of Theodore Roosevelt, with its emphasis on planning and regulation, nor Woodrow Wilson's New Freedom, which promoted competition through limits on corporate size, aimed to do more than improve the system. But the Gilded Age philosophy of laissez faire—of giving private enterprise a free hand—had clearly been rejected. Both state and federal governments established their right to regulate the actions of private corporations for the public good.

The reforms thus achieved, including the eight-hour day, woman suffrage, direct election of senators, graduated income taxes, and public ownership of utilities, began to address the problems of an urban industrial society. Under progressive leadership, the modern state—active and interventionist—was born.

American confidence was restored as the new century unfolded. A golden age of peace, prosperity, and human advancement seemed within reach, at least to progressives. But in 1914, as progressivism crested in America, the guns of a hot August shattered the uneasy calm in Europe and plunged the world into war. Few people anywhere were prepared for the bloodbath that followed.

CHAPTER SUMMARY

Progressivism was as much a set of attitudes and a method as a reform movement. It sprang from many impulses: desires to curb the advancing power of corporations and end widespread political corruption; efforts to bring order and efficiency to economic and political life; attempts by new interest groups to make business and government more responsive to the needs of ordinary citizens; moralistic urges to rid society of such perceived evils as drink and prostitution. Progressivism began in the cities of the Midwest, where it was first promoted by middle-class reformers who sought to apply expertise, professionalism, the newest techniques of social science, and the force of law to the problems of an industrial society.

Galvanized by the depression of 1893, progressive reformers became moderate modernizers, at once nostalgic and innovative. They aimed at redeeming such traditional American values as democracy, Judeo-Christian ethics, individual opportunity, and the spirit of public service. But they used the newest techniques of management and planning, coordinated systems, and specialized bureaucracies of experts. The twin drives for social welfare and social justice often relied upon women, who extended women's traditional sphere of home and family to all of society to become "social housekeepers."

Increasingly politics seemed the only way to clean things up, but first politics itself had to be cleaned up. New structures of government such as the city-manager plan, colorful and independent reform mayors, and finally governors like Wisconsin's Robert La Follette attacked corruption in politics and extended the scope of government regulation. In the presidency of Theodore Roosevelt, progressivism moved to Washington, and an era of federal reform and regulation began. Under Woodrow Wilson progressivism peaked. Rejecting Roosevelt's "New Nationalism" of private consolidation and government planning, Wilson promised a "New Freedom" of regulated competition and strict limits on business and government. In the end the weaknesses of progressivism—the narrowness of its social vision; its exclusion of African Americans and other minorities; the fuzziness of its concept of the public interest; the ease with which its regulatory agencies were captured by industry—were counterbalanced by its accomplishments in establishing the modern, activist state.

ADDITIONAL READINGS

The long interpretive debate over progressivism is best covered in Arthur Link and Richard L. McCormick, *Progressivism* (1985). Benchmarks in that debate include George Mowry's *The California Progressives* (1951) and Richard Hofstadter's *The Age of Reform: From Bryan to FDR* (1955), both of which see progressives as a small elite seeking to recapture its fading status and influence. Gabriel Kolko's *The Triumph of Conservatism: A Reinterpretation of American History 1900–1916* (1963) makes the controversial case of the New Left for business capture of reform to control competition and stave off stricter federal regulation. Richard McCormick stresses the transformation of political culture accompanying the decline of political parties and the rise of interest groups in *From Realignment to Reform: Political Change in New York State, 1893–1910* (1981).

John M. Blum's *The Republican Roosevelt* (1954) remains the most incisive rendering of TR, while Lewis L. Gould's *The Presidency of Theodore Roosevelt* (1991) is the best single-volume study of the White House years. Unsurpassed for its detail and depth is Arthur Link, *Woodrow Wilson*, 5 vols. (1947–1965). Robert Crunden's *Ministers of Reform: The Progressives' Achievements in American Civilization, 1889–1920* (1982) emphasizes the cultural origins and impact of progressivism, while Ellen Chesler's *Woman of Valor: Margaret Sanger and the Birth Control Movement in America* (1992) looks through a feminist lens at the life and times of social reformer Margaret Sanger. For a fuller list of readings, see the Bibliography.

SIGNIFICANT EVENTS

1890	New England Kitchen opens; General Federation of Women's Clubs organized
1892	Sierra Club founded
1893	Illinois legislature enacts eight-hour workday law for women; Anti-Saloon League created
1895	*United States v. E. C. Knight*
1899	National Consumers League founded
1900	Robert La Follette elected governor of Wisconsin; Galveston, Texas, creates first commission form of government
1901	Leon Czolgosz assassinates President McKinley; Theodore Roosevelt becomes president; Socialist Party of America founded
1902	Bureau of the Census created; Northern Securities Company dissolved under Sherman Antitrust Act; anthracite coal miners strike in Pennsylvania; Maryland adopts first workers' compensation law
1903	Department of Labor and Commerce created; Elkins Act ends railroad rebates; Wisconsin first state to enact direct primary
1904	Lincoln Steffens's *The Shame of the Cities* published; Theodore Roosevelt elected president
1906	Hepburn Act strengthens Interstate Commerce Commission; Upton Sinclair's *The Jungle* published; Meat Inspection and Pure Food and Drug acts passed
1907	William James's *Pragmatism* published
1908	*Muller v. Oregon* upholds the right of states to regulate working hours of women; William Howard Taft elected president
1909	Ballinger–Pinchot controversy
1910	Mann Act passed
1911	Triangle Shirtwaist fire
1912	Progressive ("Bull Moose") party nominates Theodore Roosevelt for presidency; Woodrow Wilson elected president
1913	Sixteenth and Seventeenth amendments allow for federal income taxes and direct election of senators; Underwood–Simmons Tariff enacted; Federal Reserve Act passed
1914	Clayton Antitrust Act passed; Federal Trade Commission created
1916	Margaret Sanger organizes New York Birth Control League; Keating–Owen Child Labor Act passed; Woodrow Wilson reelected president
1917	Congress enacts literacy test for new immigrants
1920	Nineteenth Amendment grants women the right to vote

23

The United States and the Old World Order

ar! War! WAR!" The news had flashed across the country in the spring of 1898. As tens of thousands of eager young men signed up to fight the Spanish in Cuba, the USS *Oregon* left San Francisco Bay on a roundabout route toward its battle station in the Caribbean. It first headed south through the Pacific, passing Central America and leaving it thousands of miles behind. Then, in the narrow Strait of Magellan at South America's tip, the ship encountered a gale so ferocious, the shore could not be seen. All communication ceased, and Americans at home feared the worst. But the *Oregon* passed into the Atlantic and steamed north until finally, after 68 days and 13,000 miles at sea, it helped win the Battle of Santiago Bay.

The daring voyage electrified the nation but worried its leaders. Since the defeat of Mexico in 1848, the United States had stretched from the Atlantic to the Pacific without enough navy to go around. As an emerging power, the country needed a quicker way to get its ships from one coast to the other, not only to defend itself but to promote its growing trade. It needed, in short, a path between the seas—a canal across Central America.

The strategic and commercial possibilities of a canal had long inspired dreamers. Ferdinand de Lesseps, a French diplomat involved in building the Suez Canal, had also begun a route across the Central American isthmus in the 1880s. After 10 years of construction, 20,000 men lay dead of yellow fever and mishaps in the steamy jungles. Only a third of the canal had been dug. Theodore Roosevelt was equally visionary about the possibility of a canal and even more energetic at mustering resources. "With Roosevelt," said one engineer, "anything is possible."

"I took the isthmus," TR later told a cheering crowd. In a way he did. As president, in 1903 he bought up the old de Lesseps Company's equipment and negotiated an agreement with Colombia to lease the needed strip of land, which stretched across Colombia's province of Panama. Holding out for more money and greater control over the canal, the Colombian senate refused to ratify the agreement.

Privately, TR talked of seizing Panama. (The Colombians were "highwaymen" and blackmailers," he fumed.) But when he learned of a budding independence movement in Panama, he let it be known that he would welcome a revolt. On schedule and without bloodshed, the Panamanians rebelled late in 1903. The next day a
U.S. cruiser dropped anchor offshore to prevent Colombia from landing troops. The

African American artist Horace Pippin lost the use of his right arm in the First World War. In 1930, after three years of work, he completed The End of the War: Starting Home. *It shows black troops, bayonets at the ready, forcing a German surrender.*

United States quickly recognized the new Republic of Panama and signed a treaty for a renewable lease on a canal zone 10 miles wide. Panama received $10 million plus an annual rent of $250,000 (the same terms offered to Colombia). One of the few critics called it "a rough-riding assault upon another republic." Roosevelt never apologized, but in 1921, after oil had been discovered in the Canal Zone, Congress voted $25 million to Colombia. One historian later dubbed it "canalimony."

In November 1906 Roosevelt pulled into port at Panama City aboard the USS *Louisiana*, newly launched and the biggest battleship in the fleet. He spent the next three days traveling the length of the canal site in the pouring rain. Soaked from head to toe, his huge panama hat and white suit sagging about his body, he splashed through labor camps and asked workers for their complaints. He toured the hospital at Ancon and met Dr. William Gorgas, the sanitation engineer in charge of eradicating the yellow-fever-bearing mosquito. He walked railroad ties at the cuts and made

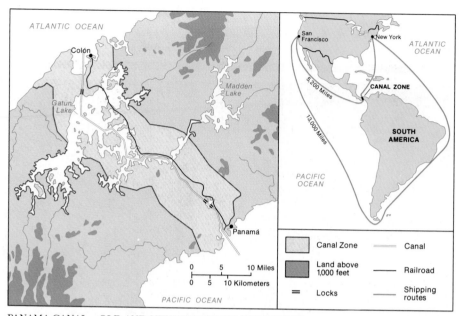

PANAMA CANAL—OLD AND NEW TRANSOCEANIC ROUTES
Tropical forests cover three-fourths of Panama, including the Canal Zone. Vegetation is denser at high elevations but tightly packed even below 1000 feet. The terrain is rugged, but the distance saved by the canal (nearly 8000 miles) made the ordeal of construction worthwhile.

speeches in the mud. "This is one of the great works of the world," he told an assembly of black diggers.

Indeed, the workers appreciated all too well the back-breaking effort that had gone into digging the largest trench yet cut into the earth's surface. Some 30,000 laborers were brought from the West Indies to accomplish the task. Paid 10 cents an hour, they worked 10 hours a day, 6 days a week. When completed, the canal stretched some 50 miles across the Isthmus of Panama. At $352 million, its final cost was four times that of the Suez Canal. The giant locks used to raise and lower water levels were deeper than a six-story building.

The Panama Canal embodied Roosevelt's muscular foreign policy of respect through strength. He modernized the army and tripled its size, created a general staff for planning and mobilization, and established the Army War College. As a pivot point between the two hemispheres, his canal allowed the United States to flex its strength across the globe.

These expanding horizons came about largely as an outgrowth of American commercial and industrial expansion, just as the imperialist empires of England, France, Germany, Russia, and Japan reflected the spread of their own industrial and commercial might. The Americans, steeped in democratic ideals, frequently seemed uncomfortable with the naked ambitions of European empire-builders. Roosevelt's embrace of the canal, however, showed how far some progressives had come in being willing to shape the world.

Theodore Roosevelt visited the site of the Panama Canal in 1906. Relentlessly curious, he had to know everything, from the salary of engineers to the proper techniques for operating this giant Bucyrus steam shovel. "It is greater work than you, yourselves, at the moment realize," he told workers.

Expansionist diplomats at home and abroad assured each other that global order could be maintained by balancing power through a set of carefully crafted alliances. But that system and the spheres of influence it spawned did not hold. In 1914, the year the Panama Canal opened, the old world order shattered in a terrible war.

PROGRESSIVE DIPLOMACY

As the Panama Canal was being built, progressive diplomacy was taking shape. Like progressive politics, it stressed moralism and order as it stretched executive power to new limits in an effort to mold and remake the international environment. It rested on faith in the superiority of Anglo-American stock and institutions. "Of all our race, [God] has marked the American people as His chosen nation to finally lead in the redemption of the world," said one senator in 1900. Every western leader assumed that northern Europeans were superior in other ways, too. The darker peoples of the tropical zones, observed a progressive educator, dwelled in "nature's asylum for degenerates." In this global vision of Manifest Destiny, few progressives questioned the need to uplift those whose destiny placed them below.

Foundations of progressive diplomacy

Economic expansion underlay the commitment to a "civilizing" mission. The depression of 1893 had encouraged American manufacturers and farmers to look overseas for markets, and that expansion continued after 1900. By 1918, at the end of World War I, the United States had become the largest creditor in the world, with networks of commerce that reached as far away as the deserts of Arabia and river valleys of central China. Every administration committed itself to opening doors of trade and keeping them open.

Big Stick in the Caribbean

Theodore Roosevelt liked to invoke the old African proverb "Walk softly and carry a big stick." But in the Caribbean he moved both loudly and mightily. The Panama

Canal gave the United States a commanding position in the Western Hemisphere. Its importance required the country to "police the surrounding premises," explained Secretary of State Elihu Root. Before granting Cuba independence in 1902, the United States reorganized its finances and attached the Platt Amendment to the Cuban constitution. The amendment gave American authorities the right to intervene in Cuba if the independence or internal order of the country were threatened. Claiming that power, U.S. troops occupied the island twice between 1906 and 1923.

Platt Amendment

In looking to enforce a favorable environment for trade in the Caribbean, Roosevelt also worried about European intentions. The Monroe Doctrine of 1823 declared against further European colonization of the Western Hemisphere, but in the early twentieth century the rising debts of Latin Americans to Europeans invited intrusion. "If we intend to say hands off to the power of Europe, then sooner or later we must keep order ourselves," Roosevelt warned. In his balance-of-power system, it was the obligation of great powers to avoid the spheres of others while keeping order in their own. Across the globe, great powers would thus check each other, much as big government held big business in check at home.

Going well beyond Monroe's concept of resisting foreign intrusions into the Western Hemisphere, Roosevelt tightened his grip on the region. He convinced Britain and Germany to arbitrate a debt dispute with Venezuela in 1902. Two years later, when the Dominican Republic defaulted on its debts, he added the "Roosevelt Corollary" to the Monroe Doctrine by claiming the right to intervene directly if Latin Americans failed to keep their own households in order. Invoking its sweeping (and self-proclaimed) power, the United States assumed responsibility for several Caribbean states—sometimes by force—including the Dominican Republic, Cuba, and Panama.

Roosevelt Corollary to the Monroe Doctrine

A "Diplomatist of the Highest Rank"

In the Far East Roosevelt exercised ingenuity rather than force, since he considered Asia beyond the American sphere of influence. In any event, few Americans would have supported armed intervention half a world away. Like McKinley before him, TR committed himself only to maintaining an "open door" of equal access to trade in China and to protecting the Philippines, a Pacific stepping-stone to Asia. Roosevelt called it "our heel of Achilles."

The key to success lay in offsetting Russian and Japanese ambitions in the region. When Japan attacked Russian holdings in the Chinese province of Manchuria in 1904, Roosevelt offered to mediate. Privately he cheered the audacity of the Japanese, but he also worried that if unchecked, Japan might threaten American interests in China and the Philippines. At the U.S. Naval Base near Portsmouth, Maine, Roosevelt guided the Russians and the Japanese to the Treaty of Portsmouth in 1905. It recognized the Japanese victory (the first by an Asian power over a European country) and ceded to Japan Port Arthur, the southern half of Sakhalin Island, and, in effect, control of Korea. Japan promised to leave Manchuria as part of China and keep trade open to all foreign nations. The balance of power in Asia and the open door in China thus had been preserved. For his contributions, Roosevelt received the Nobel Peace Prize in 1906.

Treaty of Portsmouth

Japanese nationalists resented the peace treaty. Their anger surfaced in a protest *Gentlemen's*
lodged, of all places, against the San Francisco school board. In 1906, rising Japanese *agreement*
immigration led San Francisco school authorities to place the city's 93 Asian students
in a separate school. In Japan citizens talked of war over the insult. Roosevelt, fuming
at the "infernal fools in California," summoned the mayor of San Francisco and seven
school board members to the White House. In exchange for an end to the segregation
order Roosevelt offered to arrange a mutual restriction of immigration between Japan
and the United States. In 1907 all sides accepted his "gentlemen's agreement."

The San Francisco school crisis sparked wild rumors that Japan was bent on taking Hawaii, or the Philippines, or the Panama Canal. In case Japan or any other nation thought of upsetting the Pacific balance, Roosevelt sent 16 gleaming white battleships on a world tour. "By George, isn't it magnificent!" he crowed as the "Great *Great White*
White Fleet" steamed out of Hampton Roads, Virginia, in 1907. *Fleet*

The fleet made its most conspicuous stop in Japan. Some Europeans predicted
disaster. Instead, cheering crowds turned out in Tokyo and Yokohama, where a group
of Japanese children sang "The Star-Spangled Banner" in English. The show of force
heralded a new age of American naval might but had an unintended consequence
that haunted Americans for decades: it spurred Japanese admirals to expand their
own navy.

Watching Roosevelt in his second term, an amazed London *Morning Post* honored him as a "diplomatist of the highest rank." Abroad as at home, his brand of progressivism was grounded in an enthusiastic nationalism that mixed force with finesse
to achieve balance and order.

Dollar Diplomacy

Instead of force or finesse, William Howard Taft stressed private investment to promote economic stability, keep peace, and tie debt-ridden nations to the United
States. "Dollar diplomacy" simply amounted to "substituting dollars for bullets," Taft
explained. He and Philander Knox, his prickly secretary of state, treated the restless
nations of Latin America like ailing corporations, injecting capital and reorganizing
management. By the time Taft left office in 1913, half of all American investments
abroad were in Latin America.

In Nicaragua dollar diplomacy was not enough. In 1909, when the Nicaraguan
legislature balked at American demands to take over its customshouse and national
bank, a U.S. warship dropped anchor off the coast. The lawmakers hastily changed
their minds, but in 1912 a revolution led Taft to dispatch 2000 marines to protect
American lives and property. Sporadic American intrusions lasted more than a dozen
years.

Failure dogged Taft overseas as it did at home. In the Caribbean his dollar diplomacy was linked so closely with unpopular regimes, corporations, and banks that
Woodrow Wilson scrapped it as soon as he entered the White House. Taft's efforts to
strengthen China with investments and trade only intensified rivalry with Japan and
made China more suspicious of all foreigners, including Americans. In 1911 the
southern Chinese provinces rebelled against foreign intrusion and overthrew the
monarchy. Only persistent pressure from the White House kept dollar diplomacy in
Asia alive at all.

WOODROW WILSON AND MORAL DIPLOMACY

The Lightfoot Club had been meeting in the Reverend Wilson's hayloft for months when the question of whether the pen was mightier than the sword came up. Young Tommy Wilson, who had organized the debating society, jumped at the chance to argue that written words were more powerful than armies. But when the boys drew lots, Tommy ended up on the other side. "I can't argue that side," he protested. "I can't argue for something I don't believe in." Thomas Woodrow Wilson eventually dropped his first name, but he never gave up his boyhood conviction that morality, at least as he defined it, should guide all conduct. To the diplomacy of order, force, and finance, Wilson added a missionary's commitment to spreading his system of beliefs—justice, democracy, and the Judeo-Christian values of harmony and cooperation.

Missionary Diplomacy

As president, Woodrow Wilson revived and enlarged Jefferson's notion of the United States as a beacon of freedom. The country had a mission: "We are chosen, and prominently chosen, to show the way to the nations of the world how they shall walk in the paths of liberty." Such paternalism only thinly masked Wilson's assumption of Anglo-American superiority and his willingness to force others to accept American-style democracy and Christian morality.

Wilson's missionary diplomacy had a practical side. In the twentieth century foreign markets would serve as America's new frontier. In 1893, the historian Frederick Jackson Turner alerted Americans to the dangers of the closing of the western frontier of landed settlement (see page 681.) Without expansion commerce would stifle. American industries "will burst their jackets if they cannot find free outlets in the markets of the world," Wilson cautioned in 1912. His special genius lay in reconciling this commercial self-interest with a global idealism. In his eyes, exporting American democracy and capitalism would promote peace, prosperity, and human advancement throughout the world.

Solitary and self-assured, Wilson conducted foreign policy on his own. Bypassing the State Department, he sent personal emissaries to foreign leaders and often typed his own dispatches. Sometimes Secretary of State William Jennings Bryan had no idea of what was happening. In rare moments of doubt, Wilson turned to his trusted friend, Edward M. House. The honorary "Colonel" House had hooked himself to Wilson in the early days of his political career and wielded power behind the scenes.

In William Jennings Bryan, Wilson found the perfect preacher for the gospel of democracy and Christianity. Bryan quoted Scripture chapter and verse, had unshakable faith in the common people, and was devoted to peace. But like Wilson, he had no experience in foreign affairs and ran the State Department as if it were a temperance club. At diplomatic receptions, he served only mineral water and grape juice. To the diplomatic corps he appointed not experts but politically "deserving Democrats." They were often as ill equipped and unsophisticated as Bryan himself.

Cooling-off treaties   In 1913, Bryan set in motion a plan for world peace. He negotiated treaties of conciliation with some 30 nations, including Great Britain, France, and Italy.

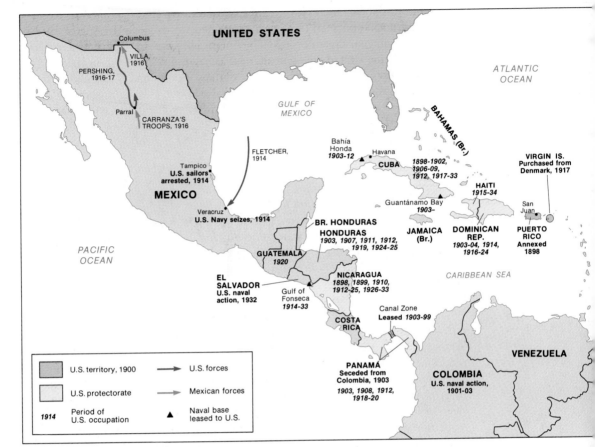

AMERICAN INTERVENTIONS IN THE CARIBBEAN, 1898–1930
In the first three decades of the twentieth century, U.S. diplomacy transformed the Caribbean into an American lake as armed and unarmed intervention became part of the country's diplomatic arsenal.

(Ominously, Germany refused to sign one.) Completed in 1914, these "cooling-off" agreements placed disputes before international commissions of investigation, usually for a year. Neither side could further arm itself or declare war until the commission rendered an opinion. Peace groups applauded the treaties, but Theodore Roosevelt and the champions of military strength dismissed them, since they had no means of enforcement.

In Asia and the Pacific Wilson moved to put "moral and public considerations" ahead of the "material interests of individuals." He pulled American bankers out of a six-nation railroad project in China backed by President Taft. The scheme encouraged foreign intervention and undermined Chinese sovereignty, said Wilson. The United States became the first major power to recognize the new Republic of China in 1911 when nationalists overthrew the last Manchu emperor. And in 1915 Wilson strongly opposed Japan's "Twenty-One Demands" for control of China. At the end of Wilson's first administration the Philippines gained limited self-government, the first step toward the eventual independence finally granted in 1946.

Twenty-One Demands

In the Caribbean and Latin America, Wilson discovered that interests closer to home could not be pursued through high-minded words alone. In August 1914 he convinced Nicaragua, already occupied by American troops, to yield control of a naval base and grant the United States an alternate canal route. Upheavals in Haiti and the Dominican Republic brought in the U.S. Marines. By the end of his administration American troops were still stationed there and also in Cuba. All four nations were economically dependent on the United States and virtual protectorates. Missionary diplomacy, it turned out, could spread its gospel with steel and cash.

Intervention in Mexico

Mexican Revolution

A lingering crisis in Mexico turned Wilson's "moral diplomacy" into a mockery. A common border, 400 years of shared history, and millions of dollars in investments made what happened in Mexico of urgent importance to the United States. In 1910 a revolution overthrowing the aged dictator, Porfirio Díaz, plunged the country into turmoil. Just as Wilson was entering the White House in 1913, the ruthless general Victoriano Huerta emerged as head of the government. Wealthy landowners and foreign investors endorsed Huerta, a conservative militarist who was likely to protect their holdings. Soon a bloody civil war was raging between Huerta and his rivals.

Most European nations recognized the Huerta regime immediately, but Wilson refused to accept the "government of butchers." (Huerta had murdered the popular leader Francisco Madera with the approval of the Taft administration.) When Huerta proclaimed himself dictator, Wilson banned arms shipments to Mexico. He threw his support to rebel leader Venustiano Carranza, on the condition that Carranza participate in American-sponsored elections. Wilson wanted to extend into Mexico the same principles progressivism fostered at home: orderly government and a democratic rule of law. "They say the Mexicans are unfitted for self-government," Wilson told a reporter. "And to this I reply that, when properly directed, there is no people not fitted for self-government." No Mexican was ready to tolerate the foreign interference embodied in American-sponsored elections. Carranza and his "constitutionalists" rejected the offer. With few options, Wilson armed the rebels anyway.

Wilson's distaste for Huerta was so great that he used a minor incident as a pretext for an invasion. In April 1914 the crew of the USS *Dolphin* landed without permission in the Mexican port city of Tampico. Local police arrested the sailors, only to release them with an apology. Unappeased, their squadron commander demanded a 21-gun salute to the American flag. Agreed, replied the Mexicans, but only if American guns returned the salute to Mexico. Learning of a German shipload of weapons about to land at Veracruz, Wilson broke the impasse by ordering American troops to take the city. Instead of the bloodless occupation they expected, U.S. marines encountered stiff resistance as they stormed ashore; 126 Mexicans and 19 Americans were killed before the city fell. The intervention accomplished little, except the unlikely feat of uniting the rival Mexican factions against the United States.

Pancho Villa

Only the combined diplomacy of Argentina, Brazil, and Chile (the "ABC powers") staved off war between Mexico and the United States. When a bankrupt Huerta resigned in 1914, Carranza formed a new constitutionalist government but refused to follow Wilson's guidelines. Wilson turned to Francisco "Pancho" Villa, a wily, peasant-born general who had broken from Carranza. Together with Emiliano Zapata, another peasant leader, Villa kept a rebellion flickering.

General John J. "Black Jack" Pershing led U.S. forces into Mexico on a "punitive action" to catch rebel leader Pancho Villa "dead or alive." Villa (pictured here) eluded the Americans for several months before they abandoned the expedition. Audacious and ruthless, he was worshiped by Mexican peasants, who extolled his exploits in folktales and ballads after his assassination in 1923.

A year later, Wilson finally recognized the Carranza regime, which only turned Villa against the United States. In January 1916 Villa abducted 18 Americans from a train in Mexico and slaughtered them. In March, he galloped into Columbus, New Mexico, killed 19 people, and left the town in flames. Wilson ordered 6000 troops into Mexico to capture Villa "dead or alive." A reluctant Carranza agreed to yet another American invasion.

For nearly two years, General John "Black Jack" Pershing (nicknamed for the all-black unit he commanded in the Spanish-American War) chased Villa on horseback, by automobile, and in airplanes. There were bloody skirmishes with government troops but not a single one with Villa and his rebels. As the chase grew wilder and wilder, Carranza withdrew his consent for U.S. troops on Mexican soil. Early in 1917 Wilson pulled Pershing home. The "punitive expedition," as the president called it, poisoned Mexican–American relations for the next 30 years, while Villa became a folk hero at home, his exploits celebrated in folk tales and *corridos,* or ballads.

THE ROAD TO WAR

In early 1917, around the time Wilson recalled Pershing, the British liner *Laconia* was making a voyage across the Atlantic. As the ship steamed through the black night, passengers below decks talked almost casually of the war raging in Europe since

1914. "What do you think are our chances of being torpedoed?" asked Floyd Gibbons, an American reporter who was aboard. Since Germany had stepped up its submarine attacks, the question was unavoidable. "I should put our chances at 250 to 1 that we don't meet a sub," replied a British diplomat.

"At that minute," recalled Gibbons, "the torpedo hit us." Suddenly whistle blasts echoed through the corridors and the passengers were forced to abandon ship, watching in horror from lifeboats as a second torpedo struck its target. The *Laconia*'s bow rose straight in the air as its stern sank; then the entire ship slid silently beneath icy waters. After a miserable night spent bobbing in the waves, Gibbons was rescued. But by 1917 other neutral Americans had already lost their lives at sea. And in April, despite Woodrow Wilson's best efforts at peace, the United States declared war on Germany and her allies.

The Guns of August

Causes of World War I

For a century, profound strains had been pushing Europe toward war. Its population tripled, its middle and working classes swelled, discontent with industrial society grew. The United States had experienced many of the same strains, of course, yet in Europe these pressures played out on a field that was at once more stratified socially and more divided ethnically and culturally. As the continent's political systems adjusted to the new industrial order, both imperialism and nationalism gained sway. Abroad, European nations competed for empire, acquiring colonies that could supply industrial raw materials and cheap manpower. At home, nationalism proved an equally useful political card to play. It papered over internal division and dissent by focusing ambitions and rivalries toward other nations. By 1914 empires jostled uneasily against one another across the globe.

Europe responded to the increased competition with an arms race. Great Britain became convinced that its mastery of the seas depended on maintaining a navy equal in power to the combined navies of its closest two rivals. France and Germany both doubled the size of their standing armies between 1870 and 1914. Led by Kaiser Wilhelm II, Germany aligned itself with two other nations eager for empire, Turkey and Austria–Hungary. The established imperial powers of England and France looked to contain Germany by supporting its foe, Russia. Soon Europe bristled with weapons, troops, and armor-plated navies. All of these war machines were linked to one another through a web of diplomatic alliances—all of them committed to war should someone or some nation set chaos in motion.

That moment came in 1914, in the unstable Balkan region of southeastern Europe. Since the 1870s the Ottoman, or Turkish, empire had been slowly disintegrating, allowing a host of smaller, ethnically based states to emerge. Serbia was one of them, and many Serbs dreamed of uniting other Slavic peoples in a "Pan-Slavic" nation. Their ambitions had been blocked in 1908, when Austria–Hungary annexed neighboring Bosnia. Tensions in the region were high when the Archduke Franz Ferdinand, heir to the Austro–Hungarian throne, visited Sarajevo, Bosnia's capital. On June 28, 1914, the Archduke and his wife were gunned down by a Serbian nationalist.

Assassination of Archduke Franz Ferdinand

As anti-Serbian riots erupted in Sarajevo, Austria–Hungary mobilized to punish Serbia. In response, rival Russia called up its 6-million-man army to help the Serbs. Germany joined with Austria–Hungary, France with Russia. On July 28, after a

Fervent nationalism heightened the imperial rivalries that pulled European nations into World War I. Flags became important patriotic symbols, masses of morale-boosting color deployed above parades of marching troops and cheering citizens. The American artist Childe Hassam demonstrated that Americans shared this patriotic penchant. Here, flags of the Allies are featured.

month of insincere demands for apologies, Austria–Hungary declared war on Serbia. On August 1, Germany issued a similar declaration against Russia and, two days later, against France. Following a battle plan drawn up well in advance, German generals pounded neutral Belgium with siege cannons the size of freight cars. Within days, five German columns were slicing west through the Belgian countryside, determined to overrun France before Russia could position its slow-moving army on the eastern front.

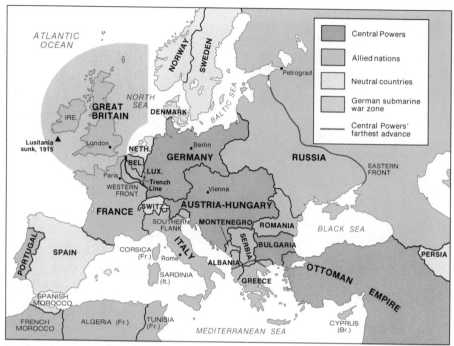

THE COURSE OF WAR IN EUROPE, 1914–1917
When World War I erupted between the Central and Allied Powers in 1914, few countries in Europe remained neutral. The armies of the Central Powers penetrated as far west as France and as far east as Russia, but by 1917, the European war had settled into a hideous standoff along the deadly line of trenches on the western front.

The guns of August heralded the first global war. Like so many dominoes, the industrialized nations fell into line: Britain, Japan, Romania, and later Italy to the side of "Allies" France and Russia; Bulgaria and Turkey to the "Central Powers" of Germany and Austria–Hungary. Armies fought from the deserts of North Africa to the plains of Flanders in Belgium. Fleets battled off the coasts of Chile and Sumatra. Soldiers came from as far away as Australia and India. Nearly 8 million never returned.

Neutral But Not Impartial

The outbreak of war in Europe shocked most Americans. Few knew Serbia as anything but a tiny splotch on the map of Europe. Fewer still were prepared to go to war in its defense. President Wilson issued an immediate declaration of neutrality and approved a plan for evacuating Americans stranded in Belgium. "The more I read about the conflict," he wrote a friend, "the more open it seems to me to utter condemnation."

Wilson's neutral ideals   Wilson came to see the calamity as an opportunity. Neutral America could lead warring nations to "a peace without victory" and a new world order. Selfish nationalism would give way to cooperative internationalism, power politics to collective security and Christian charity. Progressive faith in reason would triumph over violence. Everything hinged on maintaining American neutrality. Only if the United States stood above the fray could it lead the way to a higher peace. Americans must remain "impartial in thought as well as action," Wilson insisted in 1914.

True impartiality was impossible. Americans of German and Austrian descent naturally sympathized with the Central Powers, as did Irish-Americans, on the grounds of England's centuries-old domination of Ireland. But the bonds of language, culture, and history tied most Americans to Great Britain. Even Wilson, long an admirer of British institutions, could not escape the tug of loyalty. And gratitude for French aid during the American Revolution still lived. When the first American division marched through Paris years later, its commander stopped to salute Lafayette's tomb with the cry, "Nous voilà, Lafayette!"—Lafayette, we are here!

Germany aroused different sentiments. Although some progressives admired German social reforms, Americans generally saw Germany as an iron military power bent on conquest. For years newspapers had featured photographs of the uniformed Kaiser, a monocle clutched in his eye, looking like an imperial robber baron. Americans read British propaganda about spike-helmeted "Huns" raping Belgian women, bayoneting their children, pillaging their towns. Some of the stories were true, some embellished, some manufactured, but all worked against Germany.

American economic ties to Britain and France created an investment in Allied victory. After faltering briefly in 1914, the American economy boomed with the flood of war orders. The commanding British navy ensured that the Atlantic trade went mostly to the Allies. Between 1914 and 1916 trade with the Allies rocketed from $800 million to $3 billion. The Allies eventually borrowed more than $2 billion from American banks to finance their purchases. By contrast, a British naval blockade reduced American "contraband" commerce with the Central Powers to a trickle.

The Diplomacy of Neutrality

Though Wilson insisted that all warring powers respect the right of neutrals to trade with any nation, he hesitated to retaliate against Great Britain's blockade. Embargoing arms, he feared, would weaken Britain's most powerful weapon—the navy—and tip the balance toward Germany, a land power. Meanwhile, Great Britain enforced its blockade with caution and shrewdness where the Americans were concerned. When Britain forbade the sale of cotton to the Central Powers in 1915, the British government bought American surpluses. It also agreed to compensate American firms for their losses when the war was over. By the end of 1915 the United States had all but accepted the British blockade of Germany, while American supplies continued to flow to England. True neutrality was dead as America became the quartermaster of the Allies.

Early in 1915, Germany turned to a dreadful new weapon to even the odds at sea. It mounted a counterblockade of Great Britain with two dozen submarines, or *Unterseebootes*, called U-boats. Before submarines, sea raiders usually gave crews and passengers the chance to escape. But if thin-skinned U-boats surfaced to obey these conventions, they risked being rammed or blown from the water. So submarines attacked without warning and spared no lives. Invoking international law and national honor, President Wilson threatened to hold Germany to "strict accountability" for any American losses. Germany promised not to sink any American ships, but soon a new issue grabbed the headlines: the safety of American passengers on belligerent vessels.

Submarine warfare

On the morning of May 7, 1915, the British passenger liner *Lusitania* appeared out of a fog bank off the coast of Ireland on its way from New York to Southampton. The commander of the German U-20 could hardly believe his eyes: the giant ship filled the viewfinder of his periscope. He fired a single torpedo. A tremendous roar followed as one of the *Lusitania*'s main boilers exploded. The ship stopped dead in the water and listed so badly that lifeboats could barely be launched before the vessel sank. Nearly 1200 men, women, and children perished, including 128 Americans.

Former President Theodore Roosevelt charged that such an "act of piracy" demanded war against Germany. Wilson, though horrified at this "murder on the high seas," urged restraint. "There is such a thing as a nation being so right that it does not need to convince others by force," he said a few days later. He sent notes of protest but did little more.

Secretary of State Bryan, an advocate of what he called "real neutrality," wanted equal protests lodged against both German submarines and British blockaders. He suspected that the *Lusitania* carried munitions as well as passengers and was thus a legitimate target. (Much later, evidence proved him right.) Relying on passengers for protection against attack, Bryan argued, was "like putting women and children in front of an army." Rather than endorse Wilson's policy, Bryan resigned.

Battling on two fronts in Europe, Germany wanted to keep the United States out of the war. But in February 1916 a desperate Germany declared submarine warfare on all *armed* vessels, belligerent or neutral. A month later a U-boat commander mistook the French steamer *Sussex* for a mine layer and torpedoed the unarmed vessel as it ferried passengers and freight across the English Channel. Several Americans were injured.

In mid-April, Wilson issued an ultimatum. If Germany refused to stop sinking nonmilitary vessels, the United States would break off diplomatic relations. War would surely follow. Without enough U-boats to control the seas, Germany agreed to Wilson's terms, all but abandoning its counterblockade. This *Sussex* pledge gave Wilson a great victory but carried a grave risk. If German submarines resumed unrestricted attacks, the United States would have to go to war. "Any little German [U-boat] commander can put us into the war at any time," Wilson admitted to his cabinet.

Sussex pledge

Peace, Preparedness, and the Election of 1916

While hundreds of young Yanks slipped across the border to enlist in the Canadian army, most Americans agreed neutrality was the wisest course. Before the war a peace movement had taken seed in the United States, nourished in 1910 by a gift of $10 million from Andrew Carnegie. In 1914 social reformers Jane Addams, Charlotte Perkins Gilman, and Lillian Wald founded the Women's International League for Peace and Freedom and the American Union Against Militarism. Calling on Wilson to convene a peace conference, they lobbied for open diplomacy, disarmament, an end to colonial empires, and an international organization to settle disputes. In time these aims would become the core of Wilson's peace plan.

Pacifists might condemn the war, but Republicans and corporate leaders argued that the nation was woefully unprepared to keep peace. The army numbered only 80,000 men in 1914, the navy just 37 battleships and a handful of new "dreadnoughts," or supercruisers. Advocates of "preparedness" called for a navy larger than Great Britain's, an army of millions of reservists, and universal military training.

By the end of 1915, frustration with German submarines led Wilson to join the preparedness cause. He toured the country promoting preparedness and promised a "navy second to none." In Washington, he pressed Congress to double the army, increase the National Guard, and begin construction of the largest navy in the world. To foot the bill progressives pushed through new graduated taxes on higher incomes and on estates as well as additional levies on corporate profits.

Whoever paid for it, most Americans were thinking of preparedness for peace, not war, in 1916. The Democrats discovered the political power of peace early in the presidential campaign. As their convention opened in St. Louis in June, the keynote speaker began what he expected to be a dull description of Wilson's recent diplomatic maneuvers—only to have the crowd roar back in each case, "What did we do? What did we do?" The speaker knew the answer and shouted it back: "We didn't go to war! We didn't go to war!" The next day Wilson was renominated by acclamation. "He Kept Us Out of War" became his campaign slogan.

The Republicans had already nominated Charles Evans Hughes, the former governor of New York. He endorsed "straight and honest" neutrality and peace. But despite his moderate stand, Democrats succeeded in painting Hughes as a warmonger, partly because Theodore Roosevelt had rattled his own sabers so loudly. As the election approached, Democrats took full-page advertisements in newspapers across the country: "If You Want WAR, Vote for HUGHES! If You Want Peace with Honor VOTE FOR WILSON!"

As the polls closed on election day, the race was still too close to call. Hughes went to bed thinking he was president. When a reporter phoned around midnight, he was told, "The president cannot be disturbed." The reporter shot back, "When he wakes up, just tell him he isn't president." Wilson squeaked out a paper-thin victory. He carried the South and key states in the Midwest and West on a tide of prosperity, progressive reform, and, most of all, promises of peace. As the British ambassador reported, "Americans desire nothing so much as to keep out of war."

ELECTION OF 1916

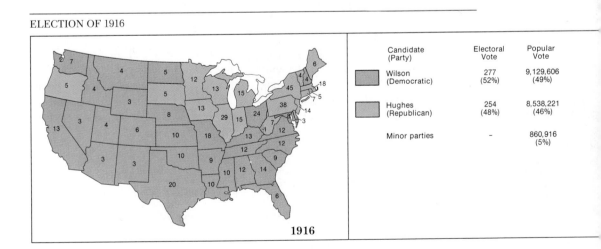

Candidate (Party)	Electoral Vote	Popular Vote
Wilson (Democratic)	277 (52%)	9,129,606 (49%)
Hughes (Republican)	254 (48%)	8,538,221 (46%)
Minor parties	–	860,916 (5%)

1916

Wilson's Final Peace Offensive

Twice since 1915 Wilson had sent Colonel House to Europe to negotiate a peace between the warring powers, and twice he had failed. With the election over, Wilson opened his final peace offensive. But when he asked the belligerents to state their terms for a cease-fire, neither side responded. Frustrated, fearful, and genuinely agonized, Wilson called for "peace without victory:" no victor, no vanquished, no embittering division of the spoils of war, only "a peace among equals," the president told the Senate in January 1917.

As Wilson spoke, a fleet of U-boats was cruising toward the British Isles. Weeks earlier German military leaders had persuaded the Kaiser to take one last gamble to starve the Allies into submission. On January 31, 1917, the German ambassador in Washington announced that unrestricted submarine warfare would resume the next day.

Zimmermann telegram

Wilson's dream of keeping the country from war collapsed. He asked Congress for authority to arm merchant ships and early in February severed relations with Germany. Then British authorities handed him a bombshell—an intercepted telegram from the German foreign secretary, Arthur Zimmermann, to the Kaiser's ambassador in Mexico. In the event of war, the ambassador was instructed to offer Mexico guns, money, and its "lost territory in Texas, New Mexico, and Arizona" to attack the United States. Hot with rage, Wilson released the Zimmermann telegram to the press. Soon after, he ordered gun crews aboard merchant ships and directed them to shoot U-boats on sight.

The logic of events now propelled a reluctant United States toward war. On March 12 U-boats torpedoed the American merchant vessel *Algonquin*. On March 15, a revolution in Russia toppled Czar Nicholas II. A key ally was crumbling from within. By the end of the month U-boats had sunk nearly 600,000 tons of Allied and neutral shipping. For the first time reports came to Washington of cracking morale in the Allied ranks.

On April 2, 1917, accompanied by armed cavalry, Wilson rode down Pennsylvania Avenue and trudged up the steps of the capitol. He delivered to Congress a stirring war message, full of idealistic purpose. "We shall fight for the things we have always carried nearest our hearts—for democracy, for the right of those who submit to authority to have a voice in their own governments, for the rights and liberties of small nations."

Pacifists held up the war resolution until it finally passed on April 6, Good Friday. Six senators and 50 House members opposed it, including the first woman in Congress, Jeannette Rankin of Montana. Cultural, economic, and historical ties to the Allies, along with the German campaign of submarine warfare, had tipped the country toward war. Wilson had not wanted it, but now the battlefield seemed the only path to a higher peace.

Jeannette Rankin

Because the United States was never attacked, the question of why the country **COUNTERPOINT**
went to war has sparked heated debate among historians. Within a decade of victory, *Why did the*
scholars began challenging the official explanation that for moral and pragmatic rea- *United States*
sons, Germany's campaign of submarine warfare compelled the United States to *go to war?*
enter. An early generation of "revisionists" pointed instead to a conspiracy of greedy
financiers, munitions makers, and others who sought to protect their investments in
the Allies by ensuring an Allied victory with the help of the United States. A school
of "realists," interested in demonstrating the importance of strategic, diplomatic, and
other practical considerations in American foreign policy, maintained that Wilson had
rightly gone to war in 1917 but for the wrong reasons—abstract moral principles such
as "making the world safe for democracy."

Other historians have painted a more complex portrait, stressing that the pressures from all sides limited Wilson's choices. Interventionists, preparedness groups,
and advocates of continued trade, especially with the Allies, as well as pressure from
German submarines and the British blockade—all combined to restrict the president's options. So, too, did the American economic system, at least according to a
group of New Left historians writing in the 1960s and 1970s. As they saw it, the
German campaign of submarine warfare was only a precipitating cause for American
entry into the war. The underlying cause was the desire for an international order in
which the United States could exert its economic supremacy through unimpeded
commerce.

WAR AND SOCIETY

In 1915 the German zeppelin LZ-38, hovering at 8000 feet, dropped a load of bombs
that killed seven Londoners. For the first time in history, civilians died in an air attack. Few aerial bombardments occurred during the First World War, but they signaled the growing importance of the home front in modern combat. Governments
not only fielded armies, they mobilized industry, controlled labor, even rationed food.
In the United States, traditions of cooperation and volunteerism helped government
to organize the home front and the battle front, often in ways that were peculiarly
progressive.

The Slaughter of Stalemate

While the United States debated entry into the Great War, the Allies were coming
perilously close to losing it. Following the German assault in 1914, the war had settled into a grisly stalemate. A continuous, immovable front stretched from Flanders
in the north to the border of Switzerland in the south. Troops dug ditches, six to eight *Trench*
feet deep and four to five feet wide, to escape bullets, grenades, and artillery. Twenty- *warfare*
five thousand miles of these "trenches"—enough to circle the globe—slashed a
muddy scar across Europe. Men lived in them for years, prey to disease, lice, and a
plague of rats.

The ideal of neat, sharply defined spaces for living and fighting is exemplified by these model trenches in northern France (left). Trench warfare, wrote one general, was "marked by uniform formations, the regulation of space and time by higher commands down to the smallest details . . . fixed distances between units and individuals." The reality (below) was something else again.

War in the machine age gave the advantage to the defense. When soldiers bravely charged "over the top" of the trenches, they were shredded by machine guns that fired 600 rounds a minute. Poison gas choked them in their tracks. Giant howitzers lobbed shells on them from positions too distant to see. "The advantage is all with the shell and you have no comeback," one veteran wrote. Even in quiet times 7000 British soldiers died or were wounded every day. In the Battle of the Somme River in 1916 a million men were killed in just four months of fighting, all to enable the British army to advance barely seven miles. Only late in the war did new armored "landships"—code-named "tanks"—return the advantage to the offense by surmounting the trench barriers with their caterpillar treads.

By then Vladimir Lenin was speeding home to Russia aboard a special train provided by the Germans. Lenin had been exiled to Switzerland during the early stages of the Russian Revolution but returned to lead his Bolshevik ("majority" in Russian) party to power in November 1917. Soon the Bolshevik-controlled government negotiated a separate peace with Germany, which promptly transferred a million of its soldiers to the western front for the coming spring offensive. A dispirited Allied army settled in for another cold winter. "We will wait for the tanks and the Americans," said a French commander.

"You're in the Army Now"

The Allies' plight forced the army into a crash program to send a million men to Europe by the spring of 1918. The United States had barely 180,000 men in uniform. Volunteers rushed to recruitment offices, especially in ethnic communities, where

With hostility remaining high between Mexico and the United States after President Wilson sent U.S. troops into Mexico, many Mexican laborers returned to Mexico rather than be drafted into a foreign army whose goals they did not share. On the other hand Mexican Americans, especially those whose families had long lived in the United States, enlisted in the U.S. Army. Felix Sanchez of New Mexico was one such recruit.

Mexican Americans enlisted in numbers proportionately higher than any other group. But they were not enough.

Selective Service Act

To raise the necessary force, Congress passed the Selective Service Act in May 1917. Young men between the ages of 20 and 30 would be conscripted into the armed forces. During the Civil War, discontent over the draft had ignited riots in New York, and feelings against pressing men into service still ran high. "There is precious little difference between a conscript [draftee] and a convict," protested the House Speaker in 1917. Progressives were more inclined to see military service as an opportunity to unite America and promote democracy: "Universal [military] training will jumble the boys of America all together, . . . smashing all the petty class distinctions that now divide, and prompting a brand of real democracy."

When the first number was drawn in the new draft lottery in July 1917, some 24 million men were already registered. Almost 3 million were drafted; another 2 million volunteered. Most were white and young, between the ages of 21 and 31. Several thousand women served as clerks, telephone operators, and nurses. In a nation of immigrants, nearly one draftee in five was born in another country. Training often aimed at educating and Americanizing ethnic recruits. In special "development battalions" drill sergeants barked out orders while volunteers from the YMCA taught American history and English.

Like Mexican Americans, African Americans volunteered in disproportionately high numbers. They quickly filled the four all-black army and eight National Guard units already in existence. They were also granted fewer exemptions from the draft than white Americans. Only 10 percent of the population, they comprised 13 percent of all draftees. Abroad, where 200,000 black troops served in France, some 42,000 were permitted in combat, or just one in five (compared with two of every three whites). Southern Democrats in Congress had opposed training African Americans to arms, fearful of the prospect of putting "arrogant, strutting representatives of black soldiery in every community." But four regiments of the all-black 93rd Division, brigaded with the French army, were among the first Americans in the trenches and among the most decorated units in the U.S. Army.

Houston riot

Racial violence sometimes flared among the troops, notably in Houston in the summer of 1917. Harassed by white soldiers and by the city's Jim Crow laws, seasoned black regulars rioted and killed 17 white civilians. Their whole battalion was disarmed and sent under arrest to New Mexico. Thirteen troopers were condemned to death and hanged within days, too quickly for appeals even to be filed.

Progressive reformers did not miss the chance to put the social sciences to work in the army. Most recruits had fewer than seven years of education, yet they had to be classified and assigned quickly to units. Psychologists saw the chance to use new intelligence tests to help the army and prove their own theories about the value of "IQ" (intelligence quotient) in measuring the mind. In fact, these new "scientific" IQ tests often measured little more than class and cultural origins. Questions such as "Who wrote 'The Raven'?" exposed background rather than intelligence. More than half the Russian, Italian, and Polish draftees and almost 80 percent of blacks showed up as "inferior." The army stopped the testing program in January 1919, but schools across the country adopted it after the war, reinforcing many ethnic and racial prejudices.

On the home front, moral crusaders waged a war against sin, often pursuing old reforms with the help of mushrooming patriotism. Temperance leaders pressured the War Department to prohibit the sale of liquor to anyone in uniform in the vicinity of training camps. Alcohol would only impair a soldier's ability to fight. The army also declared war on venereal disease. "A Soldier who gets a dose is a Traitor!" warned one poster. The Commission on Training Camp Activities produced thousands of pamphlets, films, and lectures on the dangers of sexual misconduct. The drive constituted the first serious sex education many young Americans had ever received.

Most of the 2 million American troops who landed in Europe looked forward to service. "Here was our one great chance for excitement and risk," wrote a volunteer later. Some people opposed the war and military service. A handful of tenant farmers, blacks, and Indians in two Oklahoma counties protested in the "Green Corn Rebellion." Official reports put the number of draft evaders at 300,000. Many more went unreported. Others, including some 4000 conscientious objectors, simply requested exemptions.

Mobilizing the Economy

To equip, feed, and transport an army of nearly 5 million demanded a national effort. The production of even a single ammunition shell brought components from every section of the country (plus vital nitrates from Chile) to assembly plants in New Jersey, Virginia, and Pennsylvania and from there to military installations or Atlantic ports.

At the Treasury Department, Secretary William Gibbs McAdoo fretted over how to finance the war, which cost, finally, $32 billion. New taxes paid about a third of the war costs. The old revenue base of excise (luxury) taxes and customs duties gave way to a new one of taxes on incomes and profits. And by reducing the minimum level of taxable income to $1000, the number of Americans paying taxes jumped tenfold, from 437,000 in 1916 to 4,425,000 in 1918.

The rest of war financing came from loans in the form of "Liberty" and "Victory" bonds and war savings certificates. Bond drives served a dual purpose. They raised national fervor as well as money. "We capitalized on the profound impulse called patriotism," McAdoo explained. All five bond issues were oversubscribed—and no wonder. "Every person who refuses to subscribe," McAdoo told a crowd in California, ". . . is a friend of Germany." The Federal Reserve System expanded the money supply to make borrowing easier. The national debt, which had stood at $2 billion in 1917, jumped to $20 billion only three years later.

With sweeping grants of authority provided by Congress, President Wilson constructed a massive bureaucracy to manage the home front. What emerged was a managed economy, ironically similar to the New Nationalism envisioned by Theodore Roosevelt. Under the leadership of Wall Street wizard Bernard Baruch, a War *War* Industries Board (WIB) coordinated production through networks of industrial and *Industries* trade associations. Though it had the authority to order firms to comply, the WIB re- *Board* lied instead on persuasion through publicity and "cost-plus" contracts that covered all costs, plus a guaranteed profit. But when businessmen balked—as when Henry Ford refused to accept government curbs on the manufacture of civilian automobiles— Baruch could twist arms. In this case, he threatened to have the army run Ford's factories. Ford quickly reversed himself. Overall, corporate profits tripled and production soared during the war years.

The Food Administration encouraged farmers to grow more and citizens to eat less wastefully. Herbert Hoover, who had saved starving refugees as chairman of the Commission for Relief in Belgium in 1914, was appointed administrator. Like the WIB, the Food Administration mobilized what Hoover called "the spirit of self-sacrifice." Huge publicity campaigns promoted "wheatless" and "meatless" days each week and encouraged families to plant "victory" gardens. "Do not permit your child to take a bite or two from an apple and throw the rest away; nowadays even children must be taught to be patriotic to the core," joked *Life* magazine. Stirred by high commodity prices, farmers brought more marginal lands into cultivation, and their real income increased 25 percent. When in later years prices fell and rain did not, both farmers and their land would suffer from the rush to maximize profits and production.

A Fuel Administration met the army's energy needs by increasing production and limiting domestic consumption. Transportation snarls required more drastic action. In December 1917 the U.S. Railroad Administration took over rail lines for the duration of the war. Government coordination, together with a new system of permits, got freight moving and kept workers happy. Federally imposed "daylight savings time" stretched the workday and saved fuel as well. Rail workers saw their wages grow by $300 million. Railroad unions won recognition, an eight-hour day, and a grievance procedure. For the first time in decades labor unrest subsided, and the trains ran on schedule.

Bureaucratic state

The modern bureaucratic state received a powerful boost during the 18 months of American participation in the war. Speeding trends that were already under way, some 5000 new federal agencies centralized authority as they cooperated with business and labor to mount an unprecedented war effort. The number of federal employees more than doubled between 1916 and 1918, to over 850,000, and thousands of business executives entered government service for a nominal dollar a year. The wartime bureaucracy was quickly dismantled at the end of the war, but it set an important precedent for the growth of government.

War Work

The war benefited working men and women, though not as much as it benefited their employers. Government contracts guaranteed high wages, an eight-hour day, and equal pay for comparable work. To encourage people to stay on the job, federal contracting agencies set up special classes to teach employers the new science of personnel management in order to supervise workers more efficiently and humanely. American industry moved one step closer to the "welfare capitalism" of the 1920s, with its promises of profit-sharing, company unions, and personnel departments to forestall worker discontent.

National War Labor Board

Personnel management was not always enough to guarantee industrial peace. In 1917 American workers called over 4000 strikes, the largest annual outbreak in American history. To keep factories running smoothly, President Wilson created the National War Labor Board (NWLB) early in 1918. The NWLB arbitrated more than 1000 labor disputes, helped to increase wages, established overtime pay, and supported the principle of equal pay for women. In return for pledges not to strike, the board guaranteed the rights of unions to organize and bargain collectively. Membership in the American Federation of Labor jumped from 2.7 million in 1914 to nearly 4 million by 1919.

The constraints of war brought more women than ever into the job market. These women work on a production line manufacturing bullets. The novelty of the situation seems evident from the fashionable high-heeled high-button shoes that they wear—ill suited to the conditions in an armaments plant.

As doughboys went abroad, the war brought nearly a million new women into the labor force. Most were young and single. Sometimes they took over jobs once held by men as railroad engineers, drill press operators, and electric lift truck drivers. Here, too, government tried to mediate between labor and management. In 1917 the Labor Department opened the Women in Industry Service (WIS) to recommend guidelines for using female labor. Among the most important were an eight-hour day, rest periods and breaks for meals, and equal pay for equal work. Most women never worked under such conditions, but for the first time, the federal government tried to upgrade their working conditions. *Women in the workforce*

The prewar trend toward higher-paying jobs for women intensified. Most still earned less than the men they replaced as they switched from domestic and clerical work to industrial work. And some of the most spectacular gains in defense and government work evaporated after the war as male veterans returned and the country demobilized. Tens of thousands of army nurses, defense workers, and war administrators lost their jobs. Agencies such as the Women's Service Section of the Railroad Administration, which fought sexual harassment and discrimination, simply went out of business.

Great Migrations

War work sparked massive migrations of laborers. As the fighting abroad choked off immigration and the draft depleted the workforce, factory owners scoured the country and beyond for willing workers. Pressed by railroads and large-scale farmers, Congress waived immigration requirements in 1917 for agricultural workers from Mexico. A year later, the waiver was extended to workers on railroads, in mines, and on government construction projects. *Latino migrations*

815

Industrial cities, no matter how small, soon swelled with newcomers, many of them Mexican and Mexican American. Between 1917 and 1920, some 50,000 Mexicans legally crossed the border into Texas, California, New Mexico, and Arizona. At least another 100,000 entered illegally. Some Mexican Americans left the segregated *barrios* and farmlands of the West, pushed out by cheaper labor from Mexico, and migrated to Chicago, Omaha, and other midwestern cities. Mexican *colonias*, or communities, sprang up across the industrial heartland. But most Mexicans and Mexican Americans continued to work on the farms and ranches of the Southwest, where they were freed from military service by the deferment granted to all agricultural labor.

African Americans Northern labor agents fanned out across the rural South to recruit young African Americans, while black newspapers like the Chicago *Defender* summoned them up to the "Land of Hope." Over the war years more than 400,000 moved to the booming industrial centers of the North. Largely unskilled and semiskilled, they worked in the steel mills of Pennsylvania, the war plants of Massachusetts, the brickyards of New Jersey. Southern towns were decimated by the drain. Finally, under pressure from southern politicians, the U.S. Employment Service suspended its program to assist blacks moving north.

These migrations—of African Americans into the army as well as into the city— aggravated racial tensions. Lynching parties murdered 38 black southerners in 1917 and 58 in 1918. In 1919, after the war ended, more than 70 African Americans were hung, some still in uniform. Housing shortages and job competition helped to spark race riots across the North.

In almost every city black citizens, stirred by war rhetoric of freedom and democracy, showed new militancy by fighting back. In mid-1917 some 40 black and 9 white Americans died when East St. Louis erupted in racial violence. During the "red summer" of 1919, blood flowed in the streets of Washington, D.C., Omaha, Nebraska, New York City, and Chicago, where thousands of African Americans were burned out of their homes and hundreds injured. "The Washington riot gave me the *thrill that comes onces in a life time,*" wrote a young black woman in 1919; ". . . at last our men had stood like men, struck back, were no longer dumb driven cattle."

Propaganda and Civil Liberties

"Once lead this people into war," President Wilson warned before American entry into the First World War, "and they'll forget there ever was such a thing as tolerance." *Committee on* Americans succumbed to war hysteria, but they had help. Wilson knew how reluctant *Public* Americans had been to enter the war, and he created the Committee on Public *Information* Information (CPI) to boost American commitment to the war.

Under George Creel, a California journalist, the CPI launched "a fight for the *minds* of men, for the 'conquest of their convictions.'" A zealous publicity campaign produced 75 million pamphlets, patriotic "war expositions" attended by 10 million people in two dozen cities, and colorful war posters, including James Flagg's famous, "I Want *You* for the U.S. Army." Seventy-five thousand fast-talking "Four-Minute Men" invaded movie theaters, lodge halls, schools, and churches to keep patriotism at "white heat" with four minutes of war tirades. The CPI organized "Loyalty Leagues" in ethnic communities and sponsored parades and rallies, among them a much-publicized immigrant "pilgrimage" to the birthplace of George Washington.

The division between patriotism and intolerance proved impossible to maintain. As war fever rose, voluntary patriotism blossomed into an orgy of "100 percent Americanism" that distrusted all aliens, radicals, pacifists, and dissenters. German Americans became special targets. In Iowa the governor made it a crime to speak German in public. Hamburgers were renamed "Salisbury steak"; German measles, "liberty measles." When a mob outside of St. Louis lynched a naturalized German American who had tried to enlist in the navy, a jury found the leaders not guilty.

100 percent Americanism

Congress gave hysteria more legal bite by passing the Espionage and Sedition acts of 1917 and 1918. Both set out harsh penalties for any actions that hindered the war effort or that could be viewed as even remotely unpatriotic. Following their passage, 1500 citizens were arrested for offenses that included denouncing the draft, criticizing the Red Cross, and complaining about wartime taxes.

Espionage and Sedition acts

Radical groups received especially severe treatment. The Industrial Workers of the World (IWW), a militant labor union centered in western states, saw the war as a battle among capitalists and threatened to strike mining and lumber companies in protest. Federal agents raided the Chicago headquarters of the IWW—familiarly known as the "Wobblies"—and arrested 113 of its leaders in September 1917. The crusade destroyed the union. Similarly, the Socialist party stridently opposed the "capitalist" war. In response, the postmaster general banned a dozen Socialist publications from the mail, though the party was a legal organization that had elected mayors, municipal officials, and members of Congress. In June 1918 government agents arrested Eugene V. Debs, the Socialist candidate in the presidential election of 1912, for attacking the draft. A jury found him guilty of sedition and sentenced him to 10 years in jail. Running for the presidency from his jail cell in 1920, Debs received nearly 1 million votes.

The Supreme Court condoned the wartime assault on civil liberties. In *Schenck v. United States* (1919), the Court unanimously affirmed the use of the Espionage Act to convict a Socialist party officer who had mailed pamphlets urging resistance to the draft. Free speech had limits, wrote Justice Oliver Wendell Holmes, and the pamphlets created "a clear and present danger" to a nation at war. In *Abrams v. United States* (1919) the Court upheld the verdict against Russian immigrant Jacob Abrams, whose pamphlets had denounced an American intervention in Russia to fight the Bolsheviks. Although Holmes saw no "clear and present danger," the majority ruled that the pamphlets tended to discourage the American war effort and thus violated the Sedition Act.

Schenck v. United States

Over There

The first American doughboys landed in France in June 1917, but they saw no battle. Not until November would the first Americans die in action. General John Pershing held back his raw troops until they could receive more training. He also separated them in a distinct American Expeditionary Force to preserve their identity and avoid Allied disagreements over strategy.

In the spring of 1918, as the Germans pushed within 50 miles of Paris, Pershing rushed 70,000 American troops to the front. American units helped block the Germans both at the town of Chateau-Thierry and a month later, in June, at Belleau Wood. At Belleau, it cost half their force to drive the enemy from the woods. Two more German attacks, one at Amiens, the other just east of the Marne River, ended

In September 1918 half a million Americans moved against the German stronghold at the strategic Saint-Mihiel salient. Four days of fighting produced some 8000 casualties and netted the Allied victors 15,000 German prisoners. Here, John Singer Sargent's painting *Gassed* depicts the horrid results of a poison gas attack on Allied soldiers.

in costly German retreats. On September 12, 1918, half a million American soldiers and a smaller number of French troops overran the German stronghold at Saint-Mihiel in four days.

With their army in retreat and civilian morale low, Germany's leaders sought an armistice. They hoped to negotiate terms along the lines laid out by Woodrow Wilson in a speech to Congress in January 1918. Wilson's bright vision of peace had encompassed "Fourteen Points." The key provisions called for open diplomacy, free seas and free trade, disarmament, democratic self-rule, and an "association of nations" to guarantee collective security. It was nothing less than a new world order to end selfish nationalism, imperialism, and war.

Wilson's Fourteen Points

Allied leaders were not impressed. "President Wilson and his Fourteen Points bore me," French Premier Georges Clemenceau said. "Even God Almighty has only ten!" But Wilson's idealistic platform was also designed to save the Allies deeper embarrassment. Almost as soon as it came to power in 1917, the new Bolshevik government in Moscow began publishing secret treaties from the czar's archives. They revealed that the Allies had gone to war for territory and colonies, not the high principles they claimed. Wilson's Fourteen Points now gave their cause a nobler purpose.

His ideals also stirred German liberals. On October 6 Wilson received a telegram from Berlin requesting an immediate truce. Within a month Turkey and Austria surrendered. Early in November the Kaiser was overthrown and fled to neutral Holland. On November 11, 1918, just before dawn, German officers filed into Allied headquarters in a converted railroad car near Compiègne, France, and signed the armistice.

Of the 2 million Americans who served in France, 50,000 were killed in combat, fewer than had died in the influenza pandemic of 1918. Over 200,000 were wounded. By comparison, the war claimed 1.8 million Germans, 1.7 million Russians, 1.4 million French, 1.2 million Austro-Hungarians, and nearly a million Britons. The American contribution had nonetheless been crucial, providing vital convoys at sea and fresh, confident troops on land. The United States emerged from the war

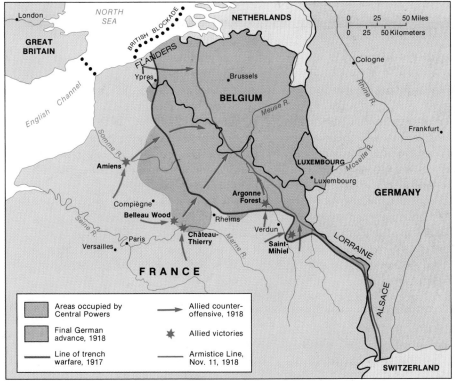

THE FINAL GERMAN OFFENSIVE AND ALLIED COUNTERATTACK, 1918
On the morning of March 21, 1918, the Germans launched a spring offensive designed to cripple the Allies. Sixty-three German divisions sliced through Allied lines for the first time since 1914 and plunged to within 50 miles of Paris. The tide turned in July, when the Germans were stopped at the Marne. The Allied counterattack, with notable American successes at Château-Thierry, Belleau Wood, Saint-Mihiel, and Meuse-Argonne, broke the German war effort.

stronger than ever. Europe, on the other hand, looked forward—as one newspaper put it—to "Disaster . . . Exhaustion . . . Revolution."

THE LOST PEACE

As the USS *George Washington* approached the coast of France in mid-December 1918 the mist suddenly lifted in an omen of good hope. Woodrow Wilson had come to represent the United States at the Paris peace conference at Versailles, once the glittering palace of Louis XIV. A world of problems awaited him and the other Allied leaders. Europe had been shelled into ruin and scarred with the debris of war. Fifty million people lay dead or maimed from the fighting. Throughout the Balkans and the old Turkish empire, ethnic rivalries, social chaos, and revolution loomed.

Daily Lives

TIME AND TRAVEL

The Doughboys Abroad

At ten in the morning on July 20, 1917, Secretary of War Newton Baker tied a blindfold over his eyes, reached into a huge glass bowl at the Senate Office Building, and drew the first number in a new draft lottery. The United States, with barely 180,000 men in the service, had begun to raise an army. By the time the conflict ended in November 1918, nearly 2 million men had donned uniforms, learned the manual of arms and close order drill, and gone off to fight in Europe. For the first time the New World was invading the Old, and for most of those who went, it was their first trip from home.

Armed against the enemy, scrubbed and clothed, drilled until they dropped, the "doughboys" marched out of their training camps and up the gangplanks of the "Atlantic Ferry"—the ships that conveyed them to Europe. (Infantrymen were called "doughboys" for the "dough" of clay that soldiers had used to clean their white belts in the 1850s.) Each man was outfitted with a pack, a weapon, a set of uniforms, and a "safety" razor, a new device that quickly altered American shaving habits.

Almost half the soldiers sailed on British vessels. Some were fortunate enough to ship out on refitted luxury liners, but most made the voyage below decks in converted freighters, "the blackest, foulest, most congested hole that I ever set foot into," reported one private. A few died from anthrax in the horsehair of their new shaving brushes. It was a poignant taste of things to come. Disease killed more Americans than enemy fire. Some 62,000 troops died of influenza and other diseases.

The first American troops, a division of army regulars and a battalion of marines, arrived in France at the end of June 1917. Two months later the first volunteers landed, wearing spring parade uniforms and carrying just 10 rounds of ammunition apiece. They were squeezed into "40-and-8's"—French freight cars designed to hold 40 men and 8 horses—and carried inland to training areas.

With the United States at war for such a short time, most American soldiers spent more time in training and on leave than in the trenches. To keep the men from becoming restless, company commanders marched their troops against imaginary enemies in never-ending exercises. "Every hill in this vicinity has been captured or lost at least ten times," wrote one weary infantryman who had to keep training even after the armistice. Soldiers complained about

---

With the old world order so evidently in shambles, Wilson felt the need to take vigorous action. Thus the president handpicked the Peace Commission of experts that accompanied him. It included economists, historians, geographers, and political scientists—but not a single member of the Republican-controlled Senate. What promised to make peace negotiations easier, however, created a crippling liability in Washington, where Republicans cast a hostile eye on the mirrored halls of Versailles.

The Treaty of Versailles

Everywhere he went, cheers greeted the president. In Paris 2 million people showered him with flowers. In Italy they hailed him as the "peacemaker from America."

Daily Lives

After months of training stateside, the American Expeditionary Force sailed to Europe on the troop ships of the "Atlantic Ferry." Most soldiers departed from Hoboken, New Jersey, and almost half made the journey aboard British vessels.

"cooties" (lice) and food (so bad that many reported a 10 percent weight loss within weeks of arriving). Used to freewheeling individualism and equality, they positively hated military discipline.

Enlisted men groused about army life, but the Old World awed them. Paris was titillating, with women who danced the "Can-Can" and cried "oo-la-la." The antiquity of Europe struck the doughboys even more: "The church here is very, very old, probably built sometime in the 12th or 13th century. Saint Louis the Crusader, King of France, attended a service there on three occasions and Jeanne d'Arc was there several times." The Europeans seemed old and old-fashioned, too. Elderly women in black shawls of mourning often were the only ones left in shattered villages. "They still harvest with cradles and sickles," noted one soldier. Everything endorsed the American myth of the Old World as hidebound and worn and the New as modern and vital.

It was as if they had become crusaders, off on what one doughboy called "a glorious adventure" to save beleaguered Europe. Disillusion and discontent overcame British and French troops after years in the trenches, but most doughboys never fought long enough to lose their sense of wonder and delight. A year after the war ended a veteran wrote: "I know how we all cried to get back to the States. But now that we are here, I must admit for myself at least that I am lost and somehow strangely lonesome. These our own United States are truly artificial and bare. There is no romance or color here, nothing to suffer for and laugh at."

And everywhere he went, Wilson believed what he heard, unaware of how determined the victors were to punish the vanquished Germans. David Lloyd George of England, Georges Clemenceau of France, Vittorio Orlando of Italy, and Wilson comprised the Big Four at the conference that included some 27 nations. War had united them; now peacemaking threatened to divide them.

Wilson's sweeping call for reform had taken Allied leaders by surprise. Hungry for new colonies, eager to see Germany crushed and disarmed, their secret treaties had already divided up the territories of the Central Powers. Germany had offered to surrender on the basis of Wilson's Fourteen Points, but the Allies refused to accept them. When Wilson threatened to negotiate peace on his own, Allied leaders finally agreed—but only for the moment.

Noticeably absent when the peace conference convened in January 1919 were the Russians. None of the Western democracies had recognized the Bolshevik regime in Moscow out of fear that the communist revolution might spread. Instead, France and Britain were helping to finance a civil war to overthrow the Bolsheviks. Even Wilson had been persuaded to send a small number of American troops to join the Allied occupation of Murmansk in northern Russia and Vladivostok on the Sea of Japan. The Soviets would neither forget nor forgive this invasion of their soil.

Grueling peace negotiations forced Wilson to yield several of his Fourteen Points. Britain, with its powerful navy, refused even to discuss the issues of free trade and freedom of the seas. Wilson's "open diplomacy" was conducted behind closed doors by the Big Four. The only mention of disarmament involved Germany, which was permanently barred from rearming. Wilson's call for "peace without victory" gave way to a "guilt clause" that saddled Germany with responsibility for the war. Worse still, the victors imposed on the vanquished a impoverishing debt of $33 billion in reparations.

Wilson did achieve some successes. His pleas for national self-determination led to the creation of a dozen new states in Europe, including Yugoslavia, Hungary, and Austria. (Newly created Poland and Czechoslovakia, however, contained millions of ethnic Germans.) Former colonies gained new status as "mandates" of the victors, who were obligated to prepare them for independence. The old German and Turkish empires in the Middle East and Africa became the responsibility of France and England, while Japan took over virtually all German possessions in the Pacific north of the equator.

League of Nations   Wilson never lost sight of his main goal—a League of Nations. He had given so much ground precisely because he believed this new world organization would correct any mistakes in the peace settlement. As constituted, the League was composed

Allied leaders convened the peace conference in the Old World palace of Louis XIV at Versailles, just outside Paris. Woodrow Wilson faces the painter, as British Prime Minister David Lloyd George and French Premier Georges Clemenceau discuss matters. On June 28, 1919, representatives of the new German republic were herded into the famed Hall of Mirrors, where they glumly signed the peace treaty they had no hand in writing. The Germans, observed one reporter, suffered a "horrible humiliation."

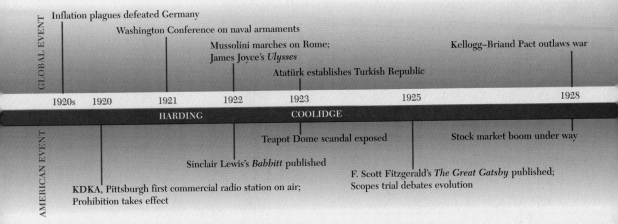

GLOBAL EVENT

Inflation plagues defeated Germany

Washington Conference on naval armaments

Mussolini marches on Rome;
James Joyce's *Ulysses*

Atatürk establishes Turkish Republic

Kellogg–Briand Pact outlaws war

1920s   1920   1921   1922   1923   1925   1928

HARDING   COOLIDGE

AMERICAN EVENT

Teapot Dome scandal exposed

Stock market boom under way

Sinclair Lewis's *Babbitt* published

F. Scott Fitzgerald's *The Great Gatsby* published;
Scopes trial debates evolution

KDKA, Pittsburgh first commercial radio station on air;
Prohibition takes effect

perity. In the second half of the 1920s the world economy expanded. Some optimists suggested that innovations in manufacturing, like Henry Ford's moving assembly line, would usher in an era in which plenty would replace want. Increased earnings encouraged a democratic culture of consumption, whether it was buying radios in France or Western-style fashions in Tokyo (at right). Products like the automobile, once available only to the rich, were increasingly accessible to people of all classes. Ford himself became an international hero, and German and Russian engineers used the term *Fordismus* to characterize modern industrial techniques.

Along with the automobile the mass media introduced a revolution in world culture. The impact of movies, radio, and mass circulation magazines, while greatest in the United States, was felt around the globe. Once-remote people and places became accessible and familiar. Stories, names, phrases, images, and ideas could become the common property of all. "In short, it seems to be the nature of radio to encourage people to think and feel alike," two prominent psychologists concluded. Consumption of culture as well as manufactured goods seemed to walk hand in hand with the democracy of the masses.

But the foundations upon which democracy rested were fragile. In the new Soviet Union, communists led by Lenin and the young Joseph Stalin demonstrated how readily talk of "the masses" and "democratic socialism" could mask an iron totalitarianism. In Japan, democracy was hampered by that nation's persistent feudal traditions and the rise of militarism. Although its parliamentary government was controlled for a time by liberal, westernized factions, nationalists from the old samurai class joined with the nation's economically powerful families in quest of a Japanese East Asian empire.

Fear of communist revolution led some nationalists in Europe to reject democracy. With Italy's parliamentary government seemingly paralyzed by postwar unrest,

831

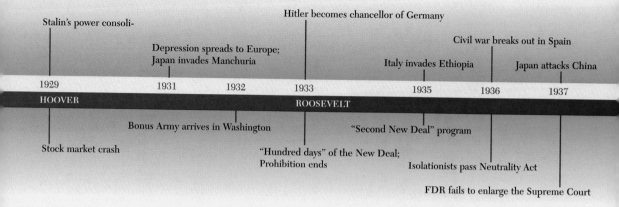

Stalin's power consoli-

Hitler becomes chancellor of Germany

Civil war breaks out in Spain

Depression spreads to Europe;
Japan invades Manchuria

Italy invades Ethiopia

Japan attacks China

| 1929 | 1931 | 1932 | 1933 | 1935 | 1936 | 1937 |

HOOVER   ROOSEVELT

Bonus Army arrives in Washington

"Second New Deal" program

Stock market crash

"Hundred days" of the New Deal;
Prohibition ends

Isolationists pass Neutrality Act

FDR fails to enlarge the Supreme Court

Benito Mussolini and his *Fasci di Combattimento,* or fascists, used terrorism, murder, and intimidation to create an "all-embracing" single-party state, outside which "no human or spiritual values can exist, let alone be desirable." They rejected both the liberals' belief in political parties and the Marxist concept of class solidarity. Instead, they glorified the nation-state dominated by the middle class, small businesspeople, modest property owners, and small farmers.

Fascism thus gave a sinister twist to the liberal ideal of national solidarity, but one that others embraced as a no-nonsense means of blunting Marxism. Adolf Hitler, like many Germans, resented the stinging defeat that war brought in 1919 and blamed communists, among others, for the sorry state of German life. Like Mussolini, Hitler used the politics of discontent to rise to power. Having achieved it in 1933, his Nazi party destroyed democracy. Under one-party rule, the Gestapo secret political police ensured that Germans expressed only those

ideas that conformed to the views of their national leader, the Führer.

Hitler succeeded partly because the prosperity of the 1920s was shattered worldwide by the corrosive hardships of the Great Depression. Farmers were particularly hard hit: during the 1920s the opening of new lands to cultivation had already led to overproduction. In Java, for example, the use of scientific agricultural techniques created a glut in the sugar market. By 1930 the price of wheat, measured in gold, reached its lowest point in 400 years. And those urban unemployed who walked the street in search of a job ("I seek work of any sort," reads the German's sign at left) were often ready to believe that only the forceful leadership of one could unite the many. Even in the United States, the business newspaper *Barron's*

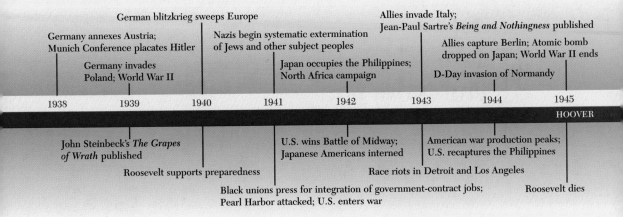

German blitzkrieg sweeps Europe

Allies invade Italy;
Jean-Paul Sartre's *Being and Nothingness* published

Germany annexes Austria;
Munich Conference placates Hitler

Nazis begin systematic extermination
of Jews and other subject peoples

Allies capture Berlin; Atomic bomb
dropped on Japan; World War II ends

Germany invades
Poland; World War II

Japan occupies the Philippines;
North Africa campaign

D-Day invasion of Normandy

| 1938 | 1939 | 1940 | 1941 | 1942 | 1943 | 1944 | 1945 |

HOOVER

John Steinbeck's *The Grapes
of Wrath* published

U.S. wins Battle of Midway;
Japanese Americans interned

American war production peaks;
U.S. recaptures the Philippines

Roosevelt supports preparedness

Race riots in Detroit and Los Angeles

Black unions press for integration of government-contract jobs;
Pearl Harbor attacked; U.S. enters war

Roosevelt dies

voiced the thoughts of more than a few when it mused that "a mild species of dictatorship" might "help us over the roughest spots in the road ahead."

Still, the rise of Hitler and Mussolini shook those who had faith in the possibilities of mass politics. While Franklin Roosevelt had used his radio "fireside chats" to bring government closer to the people, Hitler's fiery speeches and mass rallies seemed bent on encouraging racist fears and manipulating public opinion. While Hollywood produced films that affirmed popular faith in democratic government, a capitalist economy, and the success ethic, the German director Leni Riefenstahl used her cinematic gifts to combine myth, symbolism, and documentary into an evocation of the Führer as a pagan god of strength and a Christian savior. The "mass" aspects of the media were a two-edged sword. Perceptive critics recognized that even in democracies, mass culture was devoted primarily to the entertainment and escapism of light comedy and melodrama rather than serious social criticism.

Thus the Depression shook both the political and the material pillars of democratic culture. On the eve of World War II the number of European democracies had been reduced from 27 to 10. Latin America was ruled by a variety of dictators and military juntas that differed little from the dictatorships of Europe. China suffered not only from invasion by Japan's militarists and civil war but also from the corrupt and ineffectual one-party dictatorship of Chiang Kai-shek. Almost alone, the New Deal attempted to combat the Depression through the methods of parliamentary democracy. The totalitarian states that had promised stability, national glory, and an end to the communist menace instead led the world to chaos and war, from which both communism and democracy emerged triumphant.

24

The New Era

Just before Christmas 1918 the "Gospel Car" pulled into Los Angeles. Bold letters on one side announced: "JESUS IS COMING—GET READY." Aimee Semple McPherson, the ravishing redheaded driver, had completed a cross-country drive to seek her destiny as "the world's most pulchritudinous evangelist." With only "ten dollars and a tambourine" to her name, Sister Aimee at first found destiny elusive. After three years of wandering the state, she landed in San Diego. With the highest rates of illness and suicide in California, it was the perfect place for Sister Aimee to preach the healing message of her "Foursquare Gospel." Her revival attracted 30,000 people, who witnessed her first proclaimed miracle: a paralytic walked.

Sister Aimee had a Pentecostal message for her flock: "Jesus is the healer. I am only the little office girl who opens the door and says, 'Come in.'" As news of the dramatic healing in San Diego spread, so did Sister's fame. She returned triumphantly to Los Angeles, where nearly three-quarters of a million people, many from the nation's heartland, had migrated in search of opportunity, sun, and perhaps salvation. In heading west, most had lost touch with the traditional Protestant denominations at home. Sister Aimee put her traveling gospel tent away. She would minister to the lost flock at her doorstep.

To the blare of trumpets on New Year's Day, 1923, she unveiled the $1.5 million Angelus Temple, graced by a 75-foot, rotating electronic cross. It was visible at night from 50 miles away. Inside was a 5000-seat auditorium, radio station KFSG (Kall Four Square Gospel), a "Cradle Roll Chapel" for babies, and a "Miracle Room" filled with the many crutches, canes, and other aids discarded by the cured faithful. Services were not simply a matter of hymn, prayer, and sermon. Sister added pageants, Holy Land slide shows, circuses, and healing sessions.

Aimee Semple McPherson succeeded because she was able to blend old and new. Her lively sermons carried the spirit of what people were calling the "New Era" of productivity and glittering consumerism. Where country preachers menaced their congregations with visions of eternal damnation, Sister Aimee, wrote a reporter, offered "flowers, music, golden trumpets, red robes, angels, incense, nonsense, and sex appeal." Her approach revealed a nose for publicity and a sophisticated understanding of the booming media industries of the 1920s. Here was one brand of evangelism suited to a new consumer age.

Aimee Semple McPherson was hardly the only evangelist to use technology. In Fort Worth, Texas, the Reverend J. Frank Norris of the First Baptist Church built a

Blues, painted in 1929 by African American artist Archibald Motley, Jr., evokes the improvised rhythms of the Jazz Age. New Orleans–born Motley was one of a group of black genre painters in the 1920s who became part of the Harlem Renaissance.

6000-seat amphitheater, set aglow by spotlights. If the lights failed to bring the faithful to Christ, advertising would. Bruce Barton, founder of a major advertising agency, became concerned that Christ no longer had the proper "image." In *The Man Nobody Knows* (1925), he portrayed Jesus as the thoroughly modern businessman and a bibulous socializer. The Lord was no teetotaler: He had, after all, changed water into wine at the wedding feast at Cana. His parables of wisdom were the "most powerful advertisements of all times," Barton explained. Christ "picked up twelve men from the bottom ranks of business and forged them into an organization that conquered the world." With the Savior himself said to be blessing mass marketing, it was small wonder that so many Americans embraced a consumer culture. Half a million of them bought Barton's book before the end of the decade.

Sister Aimee Semple McPherson, billed as "the world's most pulchritudinous evangelist," in her robe

Modernizing the gospel was just one symptom of the "New Era." Writing in 1931, journalist Frederick Lewis Allen found the changes of the preceding decade so breathtaking that he could not believe that 1919 was *Only Yesterday,* as he titled his book. To give a sense of the transformation, Allen followed an average American couple, the fictitious "Mr. and Mrs. Smith," through the 1920s. Among the most striking changes was the revolution in women's fashions and behavior. By the end of the decade, Mrs. Smith's corset—a staple of her wardrobe in 1919—had vanished, her hemline had jumped from her ankle to her knee, and she now donned flesh-colored, rayon stockings (which fashionable young "flappers" rolled down at the top). Mrs. Smith "bobbed," or cut, her long hair to the popular, near-boyish length and flattened her breasts for greater freedom of movement.

Urban role in the New Era

With Prohibition in full force, Mrs. Smith and other women of her day walked into illegal "speakeasy" saloons as readily as men. In the trendy hotels she and her husband danced to jazz. Modern couples like the Smiths sprinkled their conversations with references to "repressed sexual drives" and the best methods of contraception. But perhaps the most striking change about these "average" Americans was that they lived in the city. The census of 1920 showed that for the first time just over half of the population were urbanites. Here, in urban America, the New Era worked its changes and sent them rippling outward.

Yet the city-dwelling Smiths of Frederick Allen's imagination were hardly average. Nearly as many Americans still lived on isolated farms, in villages, and in small towns as in cities. In fact, many "city" dwellers lived there, too. By defining cities as incorporated municipalities with 2500 people or more, the Census Bureau had created hundreds of statistical illusions. New York with its millions of inhabitants ranked in the census tables alongside Sac Prairie, Wisconsin, whose population hovered barely above the mystical mark of 2500, and tiny Hyden, along the Cumberland plateau of eastern Kentucky.

Most citizens, the Smiths aside, dwelled in an earlier America and clung to its traditions. Even the technology of the New Era had yet to penetrate many urban American homes, let alone the hinterlands. As late as 1927, two-thirds of American households had no washing machines or vacuum cleaners and half had no telephones; 95 percent were without refrigerators; and despite the amazing growth of the medium, 70 percent had no radio. Nearly all American farms lacked electricity.

The poet August Derleth grew up under just such conditions in Sac Prairie. As a 10-year-old in 1919 he could hear the "howl of wolves" at night. The town observed changing seasons not with new fashions but by the appearance and disappearance of plants and animals. In Hyden, Kentucky, Main Street was still unpaved. By 1930 there were still only 10 automobiles in the county. God-fearing Baptists worshiped together as their parents had before them and still repaired to the Middle Fork of the Kentucky River for an open-air baptism when they declared their new birth in Christ. They would have nothing to do with flapper girls or the showy miracles of Aimee McPherson.

As much as some Americans resisted the transforming forces of modern life—technology, corporatism, bureaucratization, suburbanism, and consumerism—the New Era could not be walled out. Industrial breakthroughs led to a host of new consumer goods, while large corporations developed more "modern" bureaucracies to make production more efficient and profitable. Automobiles had come to Hyden, no matter how few in number, and in Tennessee, a few hundred miles away, the mass media flocked to a spectacular trial involving Darwinian evolution. Whether Americans embraced the New Era or condemned it, change came nonetheless, in the form of a mass-produced consumer economy, a culture shaped by mass media, and a more materialistic society.

THE ROARING ECONOMY

In the 1920s, Americans found themselves in the midst of a revolution in production. Manufacturing rose 64 percent; output per workhour, 40 percent. With factories humming, the sale of electricity doubled; the consumption of fuel oil more than doubled. Between 1922 and 1927 the economy grew by 7 percent a year—the largest peacetime rate ever. If anything roared in the "Roaring Twenties," it was industry and commerce.

Technology and Consumer Spending

Technology was partly responsible. Steam turbines and shovels, electric motors, belt and bucket conveyors, and countless other new machines became commonplace at work sites. Machines replaced 200,000 workers each year, and a new phrase—"technological unemployment"—entered the vocabulary. Even so, rising demand, especially for new consumer goods, kept the labor force growing at a faster rate than the population. And for the larger percentage of the population that worked, pay improved. Between 1919 and 1927, average income climbed nearly $150 for each industrial worker.

As the industrial economy matured, more consumer goods appeared on store shelves—cigarette lighters, wristwatches, radios, panchromatic film. Under their impact, American customs changed, sometimes with unintended results. Electric washing machines and vacuum cleaners lightened the load of a "Blue Monday" spent washing clothes by hand and reduced the drudgery of cleaning house. At the same time these innovations boosted standards of household cleanliness and meant hours more of work for homemakers. Commercial laundries disappeared, and the long-term trend toward fewer domestic servants intensified.

The improvement in productivity helped keep down prices. The cost of a tire and an inner tube, for example, dropped by half between 1914 and 1929. Meanwhile, the purchasing power of wage earners jumped by 20 percent. Americans enjoyed the highest standard of living any people had ever known. Yet for all the prosperity, a dangerous imbalance in the economy developed. Most Americans were putting very little of their savings into the bank. Personal debt was rising two and a half times faster than personal income, an unhealthy sign of consumers scrambling to spend.

The Booming Construction Industry

Along with technology and consumer spending, new "boom industries" promoted economic growth. In a rebound after the war years, construction boomed. Even cities the size of Beaumont, Texas, Memphis, Tennessee, and Syracuse, New York, were erecting buildings of 20 stories or more. New York got a new skyline of tall towers, topped in 1931 when the Empire State Building rose to the world-record height of 86 stories.

Residential construction doubled as people moved from cities to suburbs. Near Detroit, suburban Grosse Point grew by 700 percent, and Beverly Hills, on the outskirts of Los Angeles, by 2500 percent. Road construction made suburban life possible and pumped millions of dollars into the economy. In 1919 Oregon, New Mexico, and Colorado hit on a novel idea for financing roads—a tax on gasoline. Within a decade every state had one. By 1928 a tourist could drive from New York as far west as Kansas and never leave a paved highway.

Construction stimulated other businesses: steel, concrete, lumber, home mortgages, and insurance. It even helped change the nation's eating habits. The limited storage space of small "kitchenettes" in new apartments boosted supermarket chains and the canning industry. As shipments of fresh fruits and vegetables sped across new roads, interest in nutrition grew. Vitamins, publicized with new zeal, appeared on breakfast tables.

The Automobile

No industry boomed more than automobile manufacturing. Although cars had first appeared on streets at the turn of the century, for many years they remained little more than expensive toys. By 1920 there were 10 million in America, a sizable number. But by 1929 the total had jumped to 26 million, one for every five people (compared to one for every 43 in Britain and one for every 7000 in Russia). Automakers bought one-seventh of the nation's steel and more rubber, plate glass, nickel, and lead than any other industry. By the end of the decade, one American in four somehow earned a living from automobiles.

Henry Ford

Henry Ford helped to make the boom possible by pushing standardization and mass production to such ruthless extremes that the automobile became affordable. At the age of 16, Ford walked away from the family farm in Dearborn, Michigan. In 1902, after a decade of tinkering and building autos, he saw his flame-shooting "999" race car roar to a world speed record of 70 miles per hour. Trading on his fame as a race-car manufacturer, he founded the Ford Motor Company in 1903 with the dream of building a "motor car for the multitude." "Everybody wants to be somewhere he ain't," Ford observed. The way to succeed was to drive down costs by making all the cars alike, "just like one pin is like another pin." In 1908 Ford perfected the Model T. It had a 20-horsepower engine and a body of steel. It was high enough to ride the worst roads, and it came in only one color: black.

Henry Ford at the turn of the century

Priced at $845, the Model T was cheap by industry standards but still too costly and too time-consuming to build. Two Ford engineers suggested copying a practice of Chicago meat-packing houses, where beef carcasses were carried on moving chains past meat dressers. In 1914 Ford introduced the moving assembly line. A conveyor belt, positioned waist high to eliminate bending or walking, propelled the chassis at six feet per minute as stationary workers put the cars together. The process cut assembly time in half. In 1925 new Model Ts were rolling off the line every 10 seconds. At $290, almost anybody could buy one. By 1927 Ford had sold 15 million of his "tin lizzies."

Ford was also a social prophet. Breaking with other manufacturers, he preached a "doctrine of high wages." According to it, workers with extra money in their pockets would buy enough to sustain a booming prosperity. In 1915 Ford's plants in Dearborn established the "Five-Dollar Day," twice the wage rate in Detroit. He reduced working hours from 48 to 40 a week and cut the workweek to five days. By 1926 he also employed 10,000 African Americans, many of whom had advanced far enough to hire and fire their white subordinates. Ford's methods simplified each operation so much that he could employ even the disabled.

Doctrine of high wages

Yet Ford workers were not happy. Ford admitted that the repetitive operations on his assembly line made it scarcely possible "that any man would care to continue long at the same job." The Five-Dollar Day was designed, in part, to reduce the turnover rate of 300 percent a year at Ford plants. And Ford recouped his profits by speeding up the assembly line and enforcing ruthless efficiencies. Ford workers could not talk, whistle, smoke, or sit on the job. They wore frozen expressions called "Fordization of the Face" and communicated in the "Ford Whisper" without moving their lips. A "Sociological Department" spied on workers in their homes, and the "Education Department" taught plant procedures but also "Americanization" classes where immigrant workers learned English, proper dress, and even etiquette.

General Motors copied Ford's production techniques but not his business strategies. While Ford tried to sell everyone the same car, GM created "a car for every purse and purpose." There were Cadillacs for the wealthy, Chevrolets for the modest. GM cars were painted in a rainbow of colors, and every year the style changed. In a standardized society, such details made automobiles symbols of distinction as well as prestige. Only in 1927 did Ford finally drop the Model T, retool his factories, and introduce a year later the upscale Model A in an array of colors.

By making automobiles available to nearly everyone, the industry changed the face of America. The spreading web of paved roads fueled urban sprawl, real estate booms in California and Florida, and a new roadside culture of restaurants, service stations, and motels. Thousands of "auto camps" opened to provide tourists with tents and crude toilets. "Auto clubs" like the Tin Can Tourists Association (named for the tin can tied to the radiator cap of a member's car) sprang up to aid travelers. Automobile travel broke down rural isolation and advanced common dialects and manners. By 1930 almost two farm families in three had cars.

A car culture

Across the country the automobile gave the young unprecedented freedom from parental authority. After hearing 30 cases of "sex crimes" (19 had occurred in cars), an exasperated juvenile court judge declared that the automobile was "a house of prostitution on wheels." It was, of course, much more. The automobile was to the 1920s what the railroad had been to the nineteenth century: the catalyst for economic growth, a transportation revolution, and a cultural symbol.

ONLY
PACKARD
CAN BUILD A
PACKARD

A MAN IS KNOWN BY THE CAR HE KEEPS

In the old days men were rated by the homes in which they lived

and few but their friends saw them.

Today, men are rated by the cars they drive

and everybody sees them—

for the car is mobile and the home is not.

To own a Packard is an evidence of discriminating taste.

Woman, with her observing eye, has known this for twenty-five years.

And woman, proverbial for her greater thrift, will insist upon the family motor car being a Packard once she learns that the Packard Six costs less to own, operate and maintain than the ordinary car the family has been buying every year or two.

Packard Six and Packard Eight both furnished in ten body types, open and enclosed. Packard's extremely liberal monthly payment plan makes possible the immediate enjoyment of a Packard, purchasing out of income instead of capital.

ASK   THE   MAN   WHO   OWNS   ONE

In the 1920s, automobile advertising shifted gears by broadening its audience and making the automobile a symbol of social success. Earlier advertisements had stressed the technical advantages of automobiles and were aimed strictly at men. Here an automobile advertisement from 1925 emphasizes the subliminal rewards of owning a luxury car. Prestige, power, wealth, and romantic love belong to a man who owns a Packard automobile. And women are not ignored. The advertisement points out to women that owning a Packard is not only "evidence of discriminating taste" but also a sign of cost-consciousness for family-minded females.

The Business of America

In business, said Henry Ford, the "fundamentals are all summed up in the single word, 'service.'" President Calvin Coolidge echoed the theme of service to society in 1925: "The business of America is business. The man who builds a factory builds a temple. The man who works there worships there." A generation earlier, progressives had criticized business for its social irresponsibility. But the wartime contributions of business managers and the return of prosperity in 1922 gained them a renewed respect. When Harvard established a graduate school of business administration in 1924, it was a sign that business had become a "profession," whose mastery required special training.

Encouraged by federal permissiveness, a wave of mergers swept the country. *Corporate* Between 1919 and 1930, some 8000 firms disappeared as large gobbled small. *consolidation* Oligopolies (where a few firms dominated whole industries) flourished in steel, meat packing, cigarettes, and other businesses. National chains began to replace local "mom and pop" stores. By 1929, one bag of groceries in ten came from the 15,000 red-and-gold markets of the Great Atlantic and Pacific Tea Company.

This expansion and consolidation meant that the capital of the nation was being controlled not by individuals or even by a few wealthy tycoons. The model of mod- *Managerial* ern business was the large, bureaucratic corporation, in which those who actually *elite* managed the company had little to do with those who owned it—the shareholders. Stocks and bonds were becoming so widely dispersed that few individuals held more than 1 or 2 percent of any company.

A salaried bureaucracy of executives and plant managers formed a new elite, which no longer set their sites on becoming swashbuckling entrepreneurs like the Carnegies and Rockefellers of old. The new managers looked to work their way up a corporate ladder. They were less interested in risk than in productivity and stability. Managers subdivided operations and put experts in charge. Corporate leaders learned the techniques of "scientific management" taught at Harvard and other new schools of business through journals, professional societies, and consulting firms. And they channeled earnings back into their companies to expand factories, carry on research, and grow in size and wealth. By the end of the decade, more than a thousand firms had research laboratories and half the total industrial income was concentrated in 100 corporations.

Welfare Capitalism

The new "scientific management" also stressed smooth relations between managers and employees. It had good reason to, for the rash of postwar strikes had left business leaders suspicious as ever of labor unions and determined to find ways to limit their influence.

Some tactics were more strong-armed than scientific. In 1921 the National Association of Manufacturers, the Chamber of Commerce, and other employer groups launched the "American Plan," aimed at opening "closed shops," factories *The American* where only union members could work. Employers made workers sign agreements *Plan* disavowing union membership. Labor organizers called them "yellow dog contracts." Companies infiltrated unions with spies, locked union members out of factories if they protested, and boycotted firms that hired union labor.

The benevolent side of the American Plan involved a social innovation called "welfare capitalism." Companies like General Electric and Bethlehem Steel pledged to care for their employees and give them incentives for working hard. They built clean, safe factories, installed cafeterias, hired trained dietitians, formed baseball teams and glee clubs. Several hundred firms encouraged perhaps a million workers to buy company stock. Millions more enrolled in company unions. Called "Kiss-Me Clubs" for their lack of power, they offered what few independent unions could match: health and safety insurance; a grievance procedure; and representation for African Americans, women, and immigrants.

But welfare capitalism embraced barely 5 percent of the workforce and often gave benefits only to skilled laborers, the hardest to replace. Most companies cared more for production than for contented employees. In the 1920s a family of four could live in "minimum health and decency" on $2000 a year. The average industrial wage was $1304, and almost one family in six was labeled as "chronically destitute." Thus working-class families often needed more than one wage earner just to get by. Over a million children, ages 10 to 15, still worked full-time in 1920. Some received as little as 20 cents an hour. In the textile town of Gastonia, North Carolina, parents and children worked side by side for 10- to 12-hour shifts in 90-degree heat. To wring more production from the mill, managers imposed "stretch-outs," the textile equivalent of assembly-line speedups.

In 1927, the most famous strike of the decade idled 2500 mill hands in Gastonia, North Carolina. Even strikebreakers walked out. Eventually, however, authorities broke the strike, presaging a national trend. A year later there were a record-low 629 strikes. Union membership sank from almost 5 million in 1921 to less than 3.5 million in 1929. "The AF of L [American Federation of Labor] machinery has practically collapsed," reported one union official.

The Consumer Culture

During the late nineteenth century the economy had boomed, too, but much of its growth had gone into producer goods: huge steel factories and rail, telephone, and electric networks. By World War I, these industrial networks had penetrated enough of the country to create mass markets for consumer goods such as refrigerators, bicycles, and other products for ordinary Americans. As an increasing percentage of the nation's industries turned out consumer goods, prosperity hinged more and more on consumption. If consumers purchased more goods, production would increase, and with it employment. At the same time economies of scales or the savings afforded by large-scale production would bring down costs. Lower production costs would allow for lower prices, which would lift sales, production, and employment still higher.

Everything in this cycle of prosperity depended on consumption. Business leaders began to look at their fellow citizens as "consumers." Wives ceased to be homemakers and became purchasers of processed food and manufactured goods. Husbands were not merely workers but, equally important, consumers of mortgages and other forms of credit. Even vacationers became consumers—in this case, consumers of leisure time as more employees got two-week (unpaid) vacations. Consumption was the key to prosperity, and increased consumption rested on two innovations: advertising to help people buy and credit to help them pay.

A shop steward

Before World War I advertising had been a grubby business, hawking the often *Role of* exaggerated virtues of products. Around the turn of the century, advertisers began a *advertising* critical shift from emphasizing *products* to stressing a consumer's *desires:* health, popularity, social status. During the First World War the Committee on Public Information, the federal propaganda agency, demonstrated the power of emotional appeals as an instrument of mass persuasion. Like the war propaganda, advertising copy aimed at emotions and cynically regarded the "average normal American," in the words of one executive, as having the "literate capacity of a 12- or 14-year-old." Behavioral psychologists like John B. Watson, who left Johns Hopkins University for an advertising agency in the 1920s, helped advertisers develop more sophisticated techniques for attracting customers.

Earlier in the century Albert Lasker, the owner of Chicago's largest advertising firm, Lord and Thomas, created modern advertising in America. His eye-catching ads were hard-hitting, positive, and often preposterous. To expand the sales of Lucky Strike cigarettes Lord and Thomas advertisements claimed smoking made people slimmer and more courageous. "Lucky's" became one of the most popular brands in America. Bogus doctors and dentists endorsed all kinds of products, including toothpaste containing potassium chloride—eight grams of which was lethal. "Halitosis" was plucked from the pages of an obscure medical dictionary and used to sell Listerine mouthwash. Lifebuoy soap thrived on fears of "B.O." ("body odor").

Advertisers encouraged Americans to borrow against tomorrow to purchase what advertising convinced them they wanted today. Installment buying had once *Installment* been confined to sewing machines and pianos. In the 1920s it grew into the tenth *buying as* biggest business in the United States. In 1919 Alfred Sloan created millions of new *credit* customers by establishing the General Motors Acceptance Corporation, the nation's first consumer credit organization. By 1929 Americans were buying most of their cars, radios, and furniture on the installment plan. Consumer debt jumped 250 percent, to $7 billion, almost twice the federal budget.

A MASS SOCIETY

In the evening after a day's work in the fields—perhaps in front of an adobe house built by one of the western sugar-beet companies—Mexican American workers might gather to chat or sing a *corrido* or two. The *corrido,* or ballad, was an old Mexican folk tradition. The subjects changed over time, to match the concerns of the day. One *corrido* during the 1920s told of a field laborer distressed that his family had rejected old Mexican customs in favor of new American fashions. His wife, he sang, now had "a bob-tailed dress of silk" and, wearing makeup, went about "painted like a *piñata.*" As for his children:

> My kids speak perfect English
> And have no use for our Spanish
> They call me "fader" and don't work
> And are crazy about the Charleston.

It was enough to make him long for Mexico.

CLOTHING AND FASHION

The Beauty Contest

On a sunlit day early in September 1921 eight young women stood nervously on the boardwalk at Atlantic City, New Jersey. For a week the seaside resort had presented a succession of swimming exhibitions, dance contests, and automobile races. A giant parade featured clowns, bands, and a float carrying King Neptune escorted by mermaids. All the marchers except the clowns wore bathing suits, even the mayor and members of the chamber of commerce. They had been instrumental in organizing the week's central event—a national beauty contest to select the first "Miss America."

The American beauty contest drew on an old heritage. In colonial times the traditional May Day celebration crowned a Queen of the May as a symbol of fertility. Queens embodied fruitfulness and community. Though physical beauty mattered in the selection, qualities such as civic leadership and popularity also counted. By the middle of the nineteenth century many cities began holding such festivals to publicize their virtues.

In 1854 showman P. T. Barnum conceived of a competition among women to judge their beauty at his American Museum in New York. Because Victorian codes prohibited such displays, Barnum attracted only contestants of "questionable reputation." To lure middle-class women, he announced that "daguerreotypes," or photographs, could be submitted. Participants did not even have to send their names. The idea spread to newspapers and later to the new mass circulation dailies. When the promoters of the St. Louis Exposition advertised a beauty contest in 1905, some 40,000 women applied.

Promoters had conceived of the Miss America pageant as a way of extending the summer season past September 1. The contest measured physical beauty alone, with the high point being a bathing suit competition. (Only later did the pageant add a talent show.) After the turn of the century, bathing suits had grown alarmingly scant, exposing arms and discarding billowy bloomers in favor of revealing tights. Organizers worried that straitlaced visitors might balk at the sight of middle-class women strutting seminude before a panel of judges.

Aware of such perils, pageant officials depicted entrants as wholesome, conventional, and unsophisticated. None of the contestants was permitted to wear short "bobbed" hair or makeup—both symbols of the racy modern woman. Models, theatrical performers, and other "professional beauties" competed separately. Famous women's illustrators lent legitimacy by serving as judges. To underscore the lightheartedness

For Americans from all backgrounds, the New Era was witness to "a vast dissolution of ancient habits," commented columnist Walter Lippmann. Mass marketing and mass distribution led not simply to a higher standard of living but to a life less regional and diverse. In the place of moral standards set by local communities and churches came "modern" fashions and attitudes, spread by the new mass media of movies, radio, and magazines. In the place of "ancient habits" came the forces of mass society: independent women, freer love, standardized culture, urban energy and impersonality, and deep alienation.

Margeret Gorman of Washington, D.C., crowned in 1921 as the first Miss America

innocence and athletic vigor. "She represents the type of womanhood America needs," observed Samuel Gompers of the American Federation of Labor, "—strong, red-blooded, able to shoulder the responsibilities of home-making and motherhood."

The Miss America pageant was an immediate success. Newspapers across the country reported the results. In 1922 representatives of 58 cities competed, and a crowd of 200,000 watched the opening parade. The much-feared protests nonetheless materialized. In 1928 organizers were forced to cancel the pageant when hotel owners objected that their middle-class clientele found the display offensive. The pageant was revived again in 1935, and a Miss America has reigned ever since.

Miss America and other beauty contests evolved as commercialism and advertising took hold and Victorianism declined in the early twentieth century. But the lengths to which pageant organizers went to gain respect demonstrated the strength of the older social ideals. The Miss America pageant in particular came to symbolize the middle-class ideal of womanhood. Physical beauty remained the chief component, marriage and motherhood the chief ends. The message was graphic: men competed in sports gear, business attire, and professional garb; women, in bathing suits. That fashion would be slow to change.

of the pageant, local police dressed like Keystone Kops, the bumbling heroes of Mack Sennett's comedy films.

As the contestants waited anxiously, officials announced the winner—Margaret Gorman of Washington, D.C. She radiated

The New Woman

The "New Woman," charged critics, was at the bottom of what Frederick Lewis Allen called the "revolution in manners and morals" of the twenties. The term was first used in the 1890s to describe the small cohort of women who had attended college and entered the professions. They often rejected the restrictions of Victorianism on dress and behavior and pushed the boundaries of the "woman's sphere" well beyond the home.

By the 1920s, the most flamboyant of the "New Women" wore close-fitting felt hats and makeup, long-waisted dresses and few undergarments, strings of beads, and unbuckled galoshes (which earned them the nickname "flappers"). Cocktail in hand, cigarette in mouth, footloose and economically free, the New Woman became a symbol of liberation and sexuality to some. To others she represented the decline of civilization.

World War I had served as a social catalyst, while the decade before it had stimulated changes for women workers. Single and married women poured into the workforce after the turn of the century. From a fifth of the labor force in 1900, women jumped to a quarter by 1930, with the greatest gains coming before the war. But most female workers remained in poor-paying jobs, and few found new freedom after quitting time. Daughters often turned their checks over to their parents. Wives returned from the factory or office to face a second shift of house cleaning and cooking. And all women confronted barriers outside the home. Before the war women were arrested for smoking cigarettes openly, using profanity, appearing on public beaches without stockings, and driving automobiles without men beside them. Wartime America ended many of these restrictions. With women bagging explosives, running locomotives, and drilling with rifles, the old taboos often seemed silly.

Margaret Sanger

Disseminating birth control information by mail had also been a crime before the war. By the armistice there was a birth control clinic in Brooklyn, a National Birth Control League, and later an American Birth Control League led by Margaret Sanger. Sanger's crusade had begun as an attempt to save poor women from the burdens of unwanted pregnancies (pages 766–767). In the 1920s her message found a

"Street selling was torture for me," Margaret Sanger recalled of her efforts to promote the *Birth Control Review.* Hecklers often taunted Sanger and her colleagues. "Have you never heard God's word to 'be fruitful and multiply and replenish the earth'?" one asked. The reply came back, "They've done that already."

receptive middle-class audience. Surveys showed that by the 1930s nearly 90 percent of college-educated couples practiced contraception.

Being able to a degree to control the matter of pregnancy, women felt less guilt about enjoying sex and less fear over the consequences. In 1909 Sigmund Freud had come to America to lecture on his theories of coping with the unconscious and overcoming harmful repressions. Some of Freud's ideas, specifically his emphasis on childhood sexuality, shocked Americans, while most of his complex theories sailed blissfully over their heads. As popularized in the 1920s, however, Freudian psychology stamped sexuality as a key to health. Sears, Roebuck began listing such books as *Ten Thousand Dreams Interpreted* and *Sex Problems Solved.* For a price, anybody could learn to free suppressed desires and enjoy a richer, sexually fulfilled life. *Freudian psychology*

Such changes in the social climate were real enough, but the life of a "flapper girl" hardly mirrored the lives and work routines of most American women. Over the decade, the female labor force grew by only 1 percent. As late as 1930 nearly 60 percent of all working women were African American or foreign-born and generally held low-paying jobs in domestic service or the garment industry. At home, women found that even new, "labor-saving" appliances could increase their burdens by raising standards of household cleanliness. Electric washing machines lightened the load of a "Blue Monday" spent washing clothes by hand but often resulted in more laundry. Women began changing sheets every week instead of moving the top sheet to the bottom and adding only a single fresh one. *Women and labor*

The New Era did spawn new careers for women. The consumer culture capitalized on a preoccupation with appearance and led to the opening of some 40,000 beauty parlors staffed by hairdressers, manicurists, and cosmeticians. "Women's fields" carved out by progressive reformers expanded opportunities in education, libraries, and social welfare. Women earned a higher percentage of doctoral degrees (from 10 percent in 1910 to 15.4 percent in 1930) and held more college teaching posts than ever (32 percent). But in most areas, professional men resisted the "feminization" of the workforce. The number of female doctors dropped by half. Medical schools imposed restrictive quotas, and 90 percent of all hospitals rejected female interns.

In 1924 two women—Nellie Ross in Wyoming and Miriam ("Ma") Ferguson in Texas—were elected governors, the first female chief executives. For the most part, women continued to be marginalized in party politics while remaining widely involved in educational and welfare programs. Operating outside male-dominated political parties, women activists succeeded in winning passage of the Sheppard–Towner Federal Maternity and Infancy Act in 1921 to fight infant mortality with rural prenatal and baby-care centers. It was the first federal welfare statute. Yet by the end of the decade the Sheppard–Towner Act had lapsed. And even the most flamboyant flapper, if she wed, found herself defined by home and family.

In the wake of its greatest success, the hard-won vote for women, feminists splintered. The National Woman Suffrage Association disbanded in 1920. In its place the new League of Women Voters encouraged informed voting with nonpartisan publicity. For the more militant Alice Paul and her allies, that was not enough. Their National Woman's party pressed for a constitutional Equal Rights Amendment (ERA). Social workers and others familiar with the conditions under which women labored opposed it. Death and injury rates for women were nearly double those for men. To them the ERA meant losing the protection as well as the benefits women *Equal Rights Amendment*

The vibrant energy of the New Woman is reflected in the geometric designs of this fashionable evening wrap (1928), whose jagged lines also suggest the era's newest vaulting skyscrapers. The beaded handbag (1925) conveys a similar excitement.

derived from mothers' pensions and maternity insurance. Joined by most men and a majority of Congress, they fought the amendment to a standstill.

Mass Media

In balmy California, where movies could be made year-round, Hollywood helped give the New Woman notoriety as a temptress and trendsetter. When sexy Theda Bara (the "vamp") appeared in *The Blue Flame* in 1920, crowds mobbed theaters. And just as Hollywood dictated standards of physical attraction, it became the judge of taste and fashion in countless other ways because motion pictures were a virtually universal medium. There was no need for literacy or fluency, no need even for sound, given the power of the pictures parading across the screen.

Motion pictures   Motion pictures, invented in 1889, had first been shown in tiny neighborhood theaters called "nickelodeons." For only a nickel, patrons watched a silent screen flicker with moving images as an accompanist played music on a tinny piano. The audience was anything but silent. The theater reverberated with the cracking of Indian nuts, the day's equivalent of popcorn, while young cowboys shot off their Kilgore repeating cap pistols during dramatic scenes. Often children read the subtitles aloud to their immigrant parents, translating into Italian, Yiddish, or German.

After the first feature-length film, *The Great Train Robbery* (1903), productions became rich in spectacle, attracted middle-class audiences, and turned into America's favorite form of entertainment. By 1926 more than 20,000 movie houses offered customers lavish theaters with overstuffed seats, live music, and a celluloid dream world—all for 50 cents or less. At the end of the decade, they were drawing over 100 million people a week, roughly the equivalent of the national population.

In the spring of 1920 Frank Conrad of the Westinghouse Company in East Pittsburgh rigged up a research station in his barn and started transmitting phonograph music and baseball scores to local wireless operators. An ingenious Pittsburgh newspaper began advertising radio equipment to "be used by those who listen to Dr. Conrad's programs." Six months later Westinghouse officials opened the first licensed broadcasting station in history, KDKA, to stimulate sales of their supplies. By 1922 the number of licensed stations had jumped to 430. And by 1930 nearly one home in three had a radio ("furniture that talks," comedian Fred Allen called it). *Radio*

At first radio was seen as a civilizing force. "The air is your theater, your college, your newspaper, your library," exalted one ad in 1924. But with the growing number of sets came commercial broadcasting, catering to more common tastes. By 1931 advertisers were paying $10,000 an hour for a national hookup, and the most popular show on radio was "Amos 'n' Andy," a comedy about African Americans created by two white vaudevillians in 1926. It borrowed its style from black comedians Aubrey Lyles and Flournoy Miller, who occasionally wrote dialogue for the show. People refused to answer their telephones during the program, and in towns across America, movie theaters stopped their shows to tune in so their audiences would not leave. A slice of black culture, often stereotyped, sometimes mocked, nonetheless entered mainstream American life.

At night families gathered around the radio instead of the hearth, listening to a concert, perhaps, rather than going out to hear music. Ticket sales at vaudeville theaters collapsed. The aged, the sick, and the isolated, moreover, could be "at home but never alone," as one radio ad declared. Linked by nothing but airwaves, Americans were finding themselves part of a vast new community of listeners.

Print journalism also broadened its audience during the 1920s. In 1923 Yale classmates Henry R. Luce and Briton Hadden rewrote news stories in a snappy style, mixed them with photographs, and created the country's first national weekly, *Time* magazine. Fifty-five giant newspaper chains distributed 230 newspapers with a combined circulation of 13 million by 1927. Though they controlled less than 10 percent of all papers, the chains pioneered modern mass news techniques. Editors relied on central offices and syndicates to prepare editorials, sports, gossip, and Sunday features for a national readership. *Mass circulation weeklies*

A Youth Culture

By the 1920s, the drive for public education had placed a majority of teenagers in high school for the first time in American history. College enrollment reached 10 percent of the eligible population by 1928; in 1890 it had been less than 3 percent. A full-blown "peer culture" emerged as children and adolescents spent more time outside the family among people their own age. Revolving around school and friends, its components were remarkably modern—athletics, clubs, sororities and fraternities, dating, proms, "bull sessions," and moviegoing.

Tolerance for premarital sex among young adults seems to have grown in the 1920s ("necking" and "petting" parties replaced sedate tea parties), but the new subculture of youth still tied sexual relations to love. Casual sex remained rare; what

The Roxy, the largest theater in the world when it opened in 1926, in all its palatial glory. Such lavish movie houses sought to attract more prosperous middle-class audiences with splendor reminiscent of European cathedrals. On the night the Roxy opened, pealing chimes marked the beginning of the show, whereupon a man dressed as a monk strode onto center stage, pointed to the balcony, and declared, "Let there be light!" Blazing spotlights then set the orchestra aglow. "Does God live here?" asked a little girl in a *New Yorker* cartoon.

changed was the point at which sexual intimacy occurred. A growing minority of young women reported having premarital intercourse, for example, but only with their future husbands. Unsupervised dating and "going together" replaced chaperoned courting. A boy picked up his "date" without meeting her parents just by honking the horn of his car. And once on the road the couple were completely free of control by adults.

For all the frivolity and rebelliousness it promoted, the new youth culture tended to fuse the young to the larger society by promoting widely held values—competitiveness, merit through association, service, prestige. Even notorious young "flappers," who wore short skirts and short hair and rouged their cheeks, ended their courting days with marriages that emphasized the conventional roles of wife and mother.

"Ain't We Got Fun?"

"Ev'ry morning, ev'ry evening, ain't we got fun?" ran the 1921 hit song. As the average hours on the job each week decreased from 47.2 in 1920 to 42 by 1930, spending on *Spectator sports* amusement and recreation tripled. Spectator sports came of age. In 1921, some 60,000 fans paid $1.8 million to see Jack Dempsey, the "Manassas Mauler," knock out French champion Georges Carpentier. Millions more listened as radio took them ringside for the first time in sports history. Universities constructed huge stadiums for football—a 60,000-seater at Berkeley, a 64,000-seater at Ohio State. By the end of the decade college football games were outdrawing major league baseball.

Baseball remained the national pastime but became a bigger business. An ugly World Series scandal in 1919 led owners to appoint Judge Kenesaw Mountain Landis as "czar" of the sport early in the decade. His strict rule reformed the game. In 1920 the son of immigrants revolutionized it. George Herman "Babe" Ruth hit 54 home runs and made the New York Yankees the first club to attract a million fans in one season. A heroic producer in an era of consumption, Ruth was also baseball's bad boy. He smoked, drank, cursed, and chased every skirt in sight. Under the guidance of the first modern sports agent, Christy Walsh, Ruth became the highest paid player in the game and made a fortune endorsing everything from clothing to candy bars.

At parties old diversions—charades, card tricks, recitations—faded in popularity as dancing took over. The ungainly camel walk, the sultry tango, and in 1924 the frantic Charleston were the urban standards. Country barns featured a revival of square dancing with music provided by Detroit's WBZ, courtesy of Henry Ford. And from the turn-of-the-century brothels and gaming houses of New Orleans, Memphis, and St. Louis came a rhythmic, compelling music that swept into nightclubs and over the airwaves: jazz.

Jazz was a remarkably complex blend of several older African American musical *Jazz* traditions, combining the soulfulness of the blues with the brighter syncopated rhythms of ragtime music. The distinctive style of jazz bands came from a marvelous improvising as the musicians embellished melodies and played off one another. The style spread when the "Original Dixieland Jazz Band" (hardly original but possessed of the advantage of being white) recorded a few numbers for the phonograph. The music became a sensation in New York in 1917 and spread across the country. Black New Orleans stalwarts like Joe "King" Oliver's Creole Jazz Band began touring, and in 1924 Paul Whiteman inaugurated respectable "white" jazz in a concert at Carnegie Hall. When self-appointed guardians of good taste denounced such music as "intellectual and spiritual debauchery," Whiteman disagreed: "Jazz is the folk music of the machine age."

The Art of Alienation

Before World War I a generation of young writers had begun to rebel against Victorian purity. The savagery of the war drove many of them even farther from any faith in reason or progress. Instead they embraced a "nihilism" that denied all meaning in life. When the war ended, they turned their resentment against American life, especially its small towns and big businesses, its conformity, technology, and materialism. Some led unconventional lives in New York City's Greenwich Village. Others, called expatriates, left the country altogether for the artistic freedom of London and *Expatriates* Paris. Their alienation helped produce a literary outpouring unmatched in American history.

On the eve of World War I the poet Ezra Pound had predicted an "American Risorgimento" that would "make the Italian Renaissance look like a tempest in a teapot." From Europe the expatriate Pound began to make it happen. Abandoning rhyme and meter in his poetry, he decried the "botched civilization" that had produced the war. Another voluntary exile, T. S. Eliot, bemoaned the emptiness of modern life in his epic poem *The Waste Land* (1922). Ernest Hemingway captured the disillusionment of the age in *The Sun Also Rises* (1926) and *A Farewell to Arms* (1929), novels where resolution came as it had in war—by death.

At home Minnesota-born Sinclair Lewis, the first American to win a Nobel Prize in literature, sketched a scathing vision of midwestern small-town life in *Main Street* (1920). The book described "savorless people . . . saying mechanical things about the excellence of Ford automobiles, and viewing themselves as the greatest race in the world." His next novel, *Babbitt* (1922), dissected small-town businessman George Follansbee Babbitt, a peppy realtor from the fictional city of Zenith. Faintly absurd and supremely dull, Babbitt was the epitome of the average.

The novels of another Minnesotan, F. Scott Fitzgerald, glorified youth and romantic individualism but found redemption nowhere. Fitzgerald's heroes, like Amory Blaine in *This Side of Paradise* (1920), spoke for a generation "grown up to find all Gods dead, all wars fought, all faiths in man shaken." Like most writers of the decade, Fitzgerald saw life largely as a personal affair—opulent, always self-absorbing, and ultimately tragic.

John Dos Passos aimed at a different target. The child of Portuguese immigrants, Dos Passos drew a hard bead on politics as usual. He embraced individualism and communism equally, fought entrenched power, and saw the country as divided along class, ethnic, and racial lines between haves and have-nots. "All right," he declared in *The Big Money* (1936), "we are two nations."

A "New Negro"

As World War I seared white intellectuals, so too did it galvanize black Americans. Wartime labor shortages had spurred a migration of over a million African Americans out of the rural South into northern industrial cities. But postwar unemployment and racial violence quickly dashed black hopes for equality. Common folk in these urban *Marcus* enclaves found an outlet for their alienation in a charismatic nationalist from Jamaica *Garvey* named Marcus Garvey.

Garvey brought his organization, the Universal Negro Improvement Association (UNIA), to America in 1916 in hopes of restoring black pride by returning African Americans to Africa and Africa to Africans. "Up you mighty race," he told his followers, "you can accomplish what you will." When Garvey spoke at the first national UNIA convention in 1920, over 25,000 supporters jammed Madison Square Garden in New York to listen. Even his harshest critics admitted there were at least half a million members in more than 30 branches of his organization. It was the first mass movement of African Americans in history. But in 1925 Garvey was convicted of mail fraud and sentenced to prison for having oversold stock in his Black Star Line, the steamship company founded to return African Americans to Africa. In 1927 he was deported. Deprived of his home base, Garvey watched his dream shatter.

Born in Jamaica in 1887, Marcus Garvey founded his "Back to Africa" movement in 1914. He went to prison for mail fraud in 1925, but it was like "jailing a rainbow," said one observer. President Coolidge pardoned Garvey in 1927, then deported him to Jamaica.

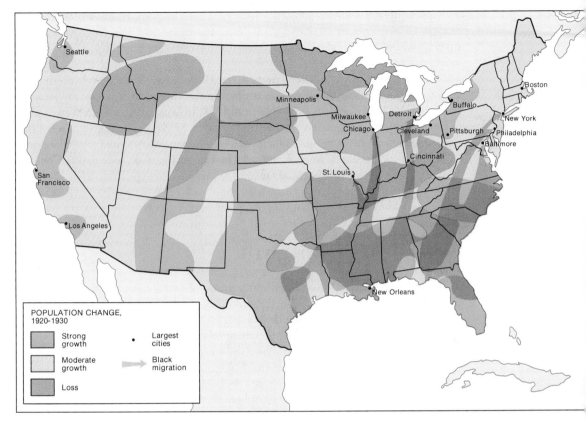

AREAS OF POPULATION GROWTH
In the 1920s the population of urban America grew by some 15 million people, at the time the greatest 10-year jump in American history. Spurred first by the industrial demands of World War I and then by declining farm income, cities grew largely by depopulating rural areas. The biggest gains were in the South and West, where farmers followed opportunity to cities in climates similar to their own. In the most dramatic manifestation of the overall trend, more than a million African Americans migrated from the rural South to the urban North in hopes of escaping poverty and discrimination.

Harlem Renaissance

As Garvey rose to prominence a renaissance of black literature, painting, and sculpture was brewing in Harlem. Since the completion of Manhattan's subway system in 1904, Harlem had grown increasingly black as eagerly expected white renters never appeared, despite millions of dollars invested in new apartment developments. By the end of World War I, Harlem had become the cultural capital of black America.

The first inklings of a renaissance in Harlem came in 1922 when Claude McKay, another Jamaican immigrant, published a book of poems entitled *White Shadows*. In his most famous, "If We Must Die," McKay mixed defiance and dignity: "Like men we'll face the murderous, cowardly pack/Pressed to the wall, dying but fighting back!" Often supported by white patrons, or "angels," the young black writers and artists of Harlem found their subjects in the street life of cities, the folkways of the rural South, and the primitivism of preindustrial cultures. Poet Langston Hughes reminded his readers of the ancient heritage of African Americans in "The Negro Speaks of Rivers," while Zora Neale Hurston collected folktales, songs, and prayers of black southerners.

Though generally not a racial protest, the Harlem Renaissance drew on the new assertiveness of African Americans as well as on the alienation of white intellectuals. In 1925 Alain Locke, a black professor from Howard University, collected a sampling of their works in *The New Negro*. The New Negro, Locke wrote, was "not a cultural foundling without his own inheritance" but "a conscious contributor . . . collaborator and participant in American civilization." The title of the book reflected not only an artistic movement but a new racial consciousness.

DEFENDERS OF THE FAITH

As mass society pushed the country into a future of machines, organization, middle-class living, and cosmopolitan diversity, not everyone approved. Dr. and Mrs. Wilbur Crafts, the authors of *Intoxicating Drinks and Drugs in All Lands and Times*, set forth a litany of sins that tempted young people in this "age of cities." "Foul pictures, corrupt literature, leprous shows, gambling slot machines, saloons, and Sabbath breaking. . . . *We are trying to raise saints in hell.*"

The changing values of the New Era seemed especially threatening to traditionalists like the Crafts. Their deeply held beliefs reflected the rural roots of so many Americans: an ethic that valued neighborliness, small communities, and a homogeneity of race, religion, and ethnicity. Opponents of the new ways could be found among not only countryfolk but also rural migrants to cities as well as an embattled Protestant elite. All were determined to defend the older faiths against the modern age.

Nativism and Immigration Restriction

Sacco and Vanzetti

In May 1920 Nicola Sacco and Bartolomeo Vanzetti, two Italian aliens and admitted anarchists, were arrested for a shoe company robbery and murder in South Braintree, Massachusetts. Most of the evidence linking them to the crime was circumstantial. In July 1921, after a jury found them guilty, Judge Webster Thayer sentenced them to death. For the next six years they appealed the decision. Each time Thayer denied their motions, even when a Rhode Island gang member confessed to the crime.

Critics charged that Sacco and Vanzetti were innocent and convicted only for being foreign-born radicals. Whatever the merits of the charges, the two never received a fair hearing. Testimony often focused on their radical beliefs, draft evasion, and foreign birth. In private, even Judge Thayer had scorned them as "anarchist bastards." For protesters around the world, Sacco and Vanzetti were symbols of bigotry and prejudice. Following their August 1927 execution 50,000 mourners marched in the funeral procession for eight miles to bid them a final farewell.

By then, nativism—a rabid hostility to foreigners—had produced the most restrictive immigration laws in American history. In the aftermath of World War I im-

Chicago and a professed agnostic, acted as cocounsel for Scopes. Opposing him was William Jennings Bryan, the three-time presidential candidate who had recently joined the antievolution crusade. It was urban Darrow against rural Bryan in what Bryan described as a "duel to the death" between Christianity and evolution.

The presiding judge ruled that scientists could not be used to defend evolution. He considered their testimony "hearsay" because they had not been present at the Creation. The defense virtually collapsed, until Darrow called Bryan to the stand as an "expert on the Bible." Under withering examination Bryan admitted, to the horror of his followers, that the Earth might not have been made "in six days of 24-hours." Even so, the Dayton jury took only eight minutes to find Scopes guilty of violating the law and fine him $100.

By then the excesses of the Scopes trial had transformed it into more of a national joke than a confrontation between darkness and light. Yet the debate over evolution raised a larger issue that continued to reverberate across the twentieth century. As scientific, religious, and cultural standards clashed, how much should religious beliefs influence public education in a nation where church and state were constitutionally separated?

REPUBLICANS ASCENDANT

"The change is amazing," wrote a Washington reporter shortly after the inauguration of Warren G. Harding on March 4, 1921. Woodrow Wilson had been ill, reclusive, and austere. Harding was handsome, warm, lovable. Wilson had kept his own counsel; Harding promised to bring the "best minds" into the cabinet and let them run things. Sentries disappeared from the gates of the White House, tourists again walked the halls, and reporters freely questioned the president. The reign of "normalcy," as Harding called it, had begun. "By 'normalcy,'" he explained, ". . . I mean normal procedure, the natural way, without excess."

The Politics of "Normalcy"

"Normalcy"—Harding's misreading of normality—turned out to be anything but normal. After eight years of Democratic rule, Republicans controlled the White House from 1921 to 1933 and both houses of Congress from 1918 to 1930. Fifteen years of bold reform gave way to eight years of cautious governing. A strengthened executive fell into weak hands. The cabinet and the Congress set the course of the nation, increasingly toward business leadership and economic growth.

Harding and his successor, Calvin Coolidge, were content with delegating power. Harding appointed to the cabinet some men of quality, as he promised: jurist Charles Evans Hughes as secretary of state, farm leader Henry C. Wallace as secretary of agriculture, and Herbert Hoover, savior of Belgian war refugees and former head of the Food Administration, as secretary of commerce. He also made, as one critic put it, some "unspeakably bad appointments": his old crony Harry Daugherty as attorney general and New Mexico Senator Albert Fall as interior secretary. Daugherty sold influence for cash and resigned in 1923. Only a divided jury saved him from jail. In 1929 Albert Fall became the first cabinet member to be convicted of a felony. In 1922 he

Warren G. Harding

had accepted bribes of more than $400,000 for secretly leasing naval oil reserves at Elk Hill, California, and Teapot Dome, Wyoming, to private oil companies.

Harding died suddenly in August 1923, before most of the scandals came to light, and Coolidge was left to clean up the mess. Though Harding would be remembered as lackluster, his tolerance and moderation had a calming influence on the strife-ridden nation. Slowly he had even begun to lead. In 1921 he created a new Bureau of the Budget that brought modern accounting techniques to the management of federal revenues. Toward the end of his administration he cleared an early scandal from the Veterans' Bureau and set an agenda for Congress that included expanding the merchant marine.

Calvin
Coolidge

To his credit Calvin Coolidge handled Harding's sordid legacy with skill and dispatch. He created a special investigatory commission, prosecuted the wrongdoers, and restored public confidence. Decisiveness, when he chose to exercise it, was one of Coolidge's hallmarks. As governor of Massachusetts, he had ended the Boston police strike in 1919 with a firm declaration: "There can be no right to strike against the public safety by anybody, anywhere, anytime." He believed in small-town democracy and minimalist government. "One of the most important accomplishments of my administration has been minding my own business," he boasted. Above all Coolidge worshiped wealth. "Civilization and profits," he once said, "go hand in hand."

Coolidge had been in office barely a year when voters returned him to the White House by a margin of nearly two to one in the election in 1924. Coolidge credited "Divine Providence" for his victory, but it was another sign that Americans had wearied of reform and delighted in surging prosperity. Whether the business-dominated policies served the economy or the nation well in the long term was open to question.

The Policies of Mellon and Hoover

Coolidge retained most of Harding's cabinet, including his powerful Treasury Secretary Andrew Mellon. The former president of aluminum giant Alcoa, Mellon believed that prosperity "trickled down" from rich to poor. If the rich made enough money, they would invest, which would raise production, employment, and the wages of lowlier workers. For more than a decade Mellon devoted himself to encouraging investment by reducing taxes on high incomes. In 1921 he persuaded Congress to repeal the excess-profits tax on corporations; under Coolidge he convinced them to end all gift taxes, halve estate and income taxes, and reduce corporation and consumption taxes even further.

Business leaders applauded the Mellon tax program for reversing the progressive tax policies of the Wilson era. They profited most from the tax cuts and also from the protectionism of a new tariff. In 1922 the Fordney–McCumber Tariff increased rates on manufactured and farm goods.

Associa-
tionalism

Unlike Mellon, Commerce Secretary Herbert Hoover (another Harding holdover) was not a traditional Republican. Dedicated to efficiency, distribution, cooperation, and service, Hoover promoted a progressive capitalism called "associationalism." It sought to bring order to the economy through the industrywide trade associations that had helped government to organize war production. Government provided advice, statistics, and forums. Business leaders exchanged ideas, set industry standards, and developed markets. For labor Hoover promoted the ideals of welfare capitalism by encouraging firms to sponsor company unions, pay employees de-

Andrew Mellon, secretary of the treasury and the millionaire head of an aluminum monopoly, is flanked by Grace and Calvin Coolidge on the lawn of the White House. A disciple of business, President Coolidge believed that what was of "real importance to wage-earners was not how they might conduct a quarrel with their employers but how the business of the country might be so organized as to insure steady employment at a fair rate of pay. If that were done there would be no occasion for a quarrel, and if it were not done a quarrel would do no good."

cent wages, and protect workers from factory hazards and unemployment. Meanwhile the Commerce Department worked to expand foreign markets and fight international cartels.

Both Hoover and Mellon, each in his own way, placed government in the service of business. For all their talk of limiting government, the role of government in the economy grew. And so did its size, by more than 40,000 employees between 1921 and 1930. Building on their wartime partnership, government and business dropped all pretense of a laissez-faire economy and joined in a powerful partnership. "Never before, here or elsewhere, has a government been so completely fused with business," noted the *Wall Street Journal*.

Distress Signals

Some economic groups remained outside the magic circle of Republican prosperity. Ironically, they included those people who made up the biggest business in America: farmers. In 1920 farming still had an investment value greater than manufacturing, all utilities, and all railroads combined. A third of the population relied on farming for a living.

Yet the farmers' portion of the national income shrank by almost half during the 1920s. The government withdrew wartime price supports for wheat and ended its practice of feeding refugees with American surpluses. As European farms began producing again, the demand for American exports dropped. New dietary habits meant that average Americans of 1920 ate 75 fewer pounds of food annually than they had 10 years earlier. New synthetic fibers drove down demand for natural wool and cotton fibers.

McNary–
Haugenism

In 1921 a group of southern and western senators organized the "farm bloc" in Congress to coordinate relief for farmers. Over the next two years they succeeded in bringing stockyards, packers, and grain exchanges under federal supervision. Other legislation exempted farm cooperatives from antitrust actions and created a dozen banks for low-interest farm loans. But regulation and credit were not enough, and in 1924, Senator Charles McNary and Representative Gilbert Haugen proposed a radical plan to raise American farm prices by selling staple crop surpluses abroad. Since it did not address the central problem of overproduction and would have sent agricultural prices plummeting overseas, "McNary–Haugenism" was doomed to fail. When Congress passed the bill in 1927 and again in 1928, President Coolidge vetoed it. Farmers' purchasing power continued to slide.

The distressing signals from America's heartland resulted, in part, from the emphasis of government on business. Farmers stood outside the magic circle, as did workers, who reaped few gains in wages, purchasing power, and bargaining rights. Although welfare capitalism promised workers profit-sharing and other benefits, only a handful of companies put it into practice. Those that did often used it to weaken independent unions. As dangerous imbalances in the economy developed, Coolidge ignored them.

COUNTERPOINT

Were the
1920s a sharp
break with
the past?

Historians have long argued over the significance of the 1920s. Initially most concluded that the decade represented a sharp break from the past as well as from the future. Wedged between two eras of reform, demarcated by a world war at one end and a world depression at the other, the 1920s was depicted as a discrete era, often frivolous and irresponsible, that represented a period of decline in the history of the nation. Prevailing institutions and standards began to disintegrate as an orgy of consumption and speculation fueled a society bent on pleasure. Government fell into the hands of conservatives who reflected the narrow interests of business, retreated from progressive activism, and ignored danger signals in the economy. Like a morality play, the decade ended with retribution—the greatest depression the country had ever experienced.

Other historians see the 1920s as more continuous with the past, more complex, and more important. Business historians have pointed to the trade association movement as an innovative attempt to achieve the old progressive goals of efficiency and equity in the modern industrial economy. Political historians have emphasized the remnant progressives who continued to fight for social justice and social welfare in the form of such legislation as the Shepard–Towner Act for maternal and infant care.

Some social historians, interested in examining complex social structures, have stressed the search for continuity amid change by fastening on the theme of shared anxiety over the future and nostalgia for a mythic past. Linking nativism, religion, and such reforms as Prohibition and creationism, these historians argue that groups like the Ku Klux Klan, religious fundamentalists, and prohibitionists represented a reaction to the encroachments of secularism, science, and social pluralism on an older, more homogeneous America. Cultural historians also have emphasized the importance of both change and continuity. Some see the origins of the intellectual revolt of the 1920s a decade earlier, while others have highlighted the emergence of a new American culture radiating outward from "mongrel Manhattan," with its hybrid mix of ethnicities, races, and sexes.

Economic Unrest and an Arms Race Abroad

If most Americans paid little attention to the distress signals at home, they ignored economic unrest abroad. At the end of World War I, Europe's victors had forced Germany to take on $33 billion in war costs or reparations, partly to repay their own war debts to the United States. When Germany defaulted in 1923, French forces occupied the Ruhr valley, the center of German industry. Germany struck back by printing more money to cope with the crushing burden of debt. Runaway inflation soon wiped out the savings of the German middle class, shook confidence in the new democratic Weimar Republic, and eventually threatened the economic structure of all Europe.

In 1924 American business leader Charles G. Dawes persuaded the victorious Europeans to scale down reparations. In return the United States promised to help stabilize the German economy. Encouraged by the State Department, American bankers made large loans to Germany, with which the Germans paid their reparations. The European victors then used those funds to repay *their* war debts to the United States. It amounted to taking money out of one American vault and depositing it in another. In 1926 the United States also reduced European war debts. Canceling them altogether would have made more sense, but few Americans were that forgiving.

The Dawes plan

Despite Europe's debt problems, an arms race continued among the great powers. The United States vied with Britain, France with Italy, and Japan with nearly everyone for naval supremacy. Within the United States two factions sought to end military escalation, but for different reasons. Pacifists and peace activists blamed the arms race between Germany and England for having brought the world to war in 1914. They believed disarmament would secure a permanent peace. Saber-rattling Republicans had few qualms about military rivalry but worried about the high cost of maintaining navies in the Pacific as well as the Atlantic Ocean.

To cut the budget and still protect Pacific interests, Secretary of State Charles Evans Hughes invited eight nations to a naval disarmament conference in November 1921 in Washington, where he presented an electrifying proposal. Scrap 2 million tons of battleships and cruisers, he said, and cancel those under construction. A "tornado of cheering" welled up as delegates whooped and embraced each other. Hughes was proposing to save their treasuries from bankruptcy.

Washington Naval Conference

The Five-Power Agreement that emerged from the Washington Naval Conference was the first disarmament treaty in modern history. It froze battleship construction by the United States, Great Britain, France, Italy, and Japan for 10 years and set ratios controlling the tonnage of each navy. What seemed bold on paper, however, proved ineffective in practice. The French, resenting the lower limits set on their battleships, began building smaller warships such as submarines, cruisers, and destroyers. The arms race now concentrated on these vessels.

An extravagant peace gesture came in 1928, when the major nations of the world (except the Soviet Union) signed an agreement outlawing war. Originally French Foreign Minister Aristide Briand had proposed a pact between France and the United States, but Secretary of State Frank Kellogg transformed it into an international treaty. "Peace is proclaimed," said Kellogg as he signed the document with a foot-long pen made of gold. But with no means of enforcement, the Kellogg–Briand pact remained a hollow proclamation.

Kellogg– Briand Pact

The Election of 1928

On August 2, 1927, in a small classroom in Rapid City, South Dakota, Calvin Coolidge handed a terse, typewritten message to reporters: "I do not choose to run for President in nineteen twenty-eight." Republicans honored the request and nominated Herbert Hoover. Hoover was not a politician but an administrator who had never once campaigned for public office. It did not matter. Republican prosperity made it difficult for any Democrat to win. Hoover, perhaps the most admired public official in America, made it impossible.

The Democratic party continued to be polarized between its rural supporters in the South and West and urban laborers in the Northeast. The two factions had clashed during the 1924 convention, scuttling the presidential candidacy of New York Governor Al Smith. By 1928 the shift in population toward cities had given an edge to the party's urban wing. Al Smith won the nomination on the first ballot, even though his handicaps were evident. For one, he sounded like a city slicker. When the New York City–bred Smith spoke "poisonally" on the "rha-dio," voters across America winced. Though he pledged to enforce Prohibition, Smith campaigned against it and even took an occasional drink (which produced the false rumor that he was a hopeless alcoholic). Most damaging of all, Smith was Catholic at a time when anti-Catholicism remained strong in many areas of the country.

In the election of 1928, nearly 60 percent of the eligible voters turned out to give all but eight states to Hoover. The solidly Democratic South cracked for the first time. Still, the stirrings of a major political realignment lay hidden in the returns for those who cared to look. The 12 largest cities in the country had gone to the Republicans in 1924; in 1928 the Democrats won them. Western farmers, ignored by Republicans for a decade, also voted for Smith. The Democrats were becoming the party of the cities and of immigrants, a core around which they would build the most powerful vote-getting coalition of the twentieth century.

Just as important, a new kind of electorate was emerging. No longer were voters part of a vast partisan army whose loyalties were tied to the party, year in, year out, by barbecues, rallies, and torchlight parades. The reforms of the progressive era had restricted the power of machines and the discipline they could exert over voters. The culture of consumption that had shaped American life in the 1920s also worked to shape politics. Increasingly, parties courted voters with newspaper advertisements and persuaded them with radio "spots." In 1929 the Democrats created the first public relations department in American politics. Paradoxically, the twentieth century would witness a growing lack of political loyalty, as the growing reliance on the media to communicate with "consumer/voters" weakened traditional party networks.

Early on a May morning in 1927, a silver monoplane streaked into the skies above Long Island and headed east. At the controls sat the young pilot, Charles Lindbergh. Thirty-three hours and thirty minutes later, he landed just outside of Paris. An ecstatic mob swamped him and nearly tore his plane to pieces in search of souvenirs. Eight other flyers had died trying to cross the ocean. Lindbergh alone succeeded.

Lindbergh, dubbed the "Lone Eagle," and his plane, the *Spirit of St. Louis,* returned home aboard the warship *Memphis.* As he sailed up the Potomac, he received an honor previously reserved only for heads of state, a 21-gun salute. Lindbergh,

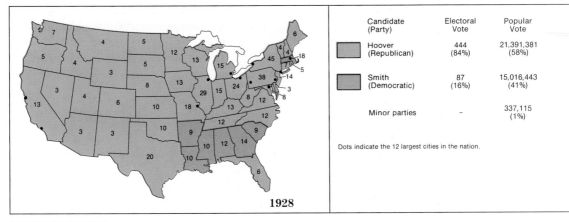

Candidate (Party)	Electoral Vote	Popular Vote
Hoover (Republican)	444 (84%)	21,391,381 (58%)
Smith (Democratic)	87 (16%)	15,016,443 (41%)
Minor parties	–	337,115 (1%)

Dots indicate the 12 largest cities in the nation.

1928

ELECTION OF 1928

Historians still debate whether the election of 1928 was a pivotal one that produced a significant political realignment. Hoover cracked the solidly Democratic South, which returned to the Democratic fold in 1932. On the other hand, Democrat Al Smith won the twelve largest cities in the country, all of which had voted Republican in 1924 but stayed in the Democratic fold in 1932.

wrote one reporter, "fired the imagination of mankind." Never had one person mastered a machine so completely or conquered nature so heroically. To Americans ambivalent about mass production and mass consumption here was a sign. Perhaps they could control the New Era without losing their cherished individualism. For a brief moment it seemed possible.

CHAPTER SUMMARY

Modern times came to America in the 1920s. The economy boomed as the transforming forces of modern life—bureaucracy, productivity, technology, mass advertising, suburbanization, and consumerism—vastly accelerated. Despite Harding's pledge to return to "normalcy," Americans faced much that was anything but normal. Economic concentration grew as fewer corporations controlled more enterprise. A strong state became more involved in fostering business growth and monitoring personal habits such as drinking. During the economy's greatest peacetime growth rate ever, a new "modern" ethic of high spending and high consumption worked its way into American society.

Modern systems of mass distribution and mass marketing led not simply to a higher standard of living but to a mass culture and a mass society. New, more self-sufficient women and new modes of behavior appeared. Automobiles gave people new mobility and independence and in doing so undermined the family and the community. Public education loosened family control by creating competing centers of authority for children, including a new peer culture of students. Modern life unsettled the older ways with its mass culture, mass media of radio and film, spectator sports, jazz music, and literary culture centered around alienated intellectuals.

In the face of modern mass society, traditional culture hardened. Immigration restriction, the rise of religious fundamentalism, and the rebirth of the Ku Klux Klan were only a few signs of an assertive but fearful traditionalism. But by the end of the decade city-bred modernism dominated American life, and the growing strength of the urban vote began to realign American politics.

SIGNIFICANT EVENTS

1903	First feature-length film, *The Great Train Robbery*, released
1909	Sigmund Freud comes to America
1914	Henry Ford introduces moving assembly line
1915	Modern Ku Klux Klan founded
1916	Marcus Garvey brings Universal Negro Improvement Association to America
1919	Eighteenth Amendment outlawing alcohol use ratified
1920	First commercial radio broadcast; Nineteenth Amendment grants women right to vote; Warren Harding elected president
1921	Congress enacts quotas on immigration; Sheppard–Towner Federal Maternity and Infancy Act; American Birth Control League organized
1921–1922	Washington Naval Disarmament Conference
1922	Fordney–McCumber Tariff raises rates; Sinclair Lewis's *Babbitt* published; T. S. Eliot's *The Waste Land* published
1923	*Time* magazine founded; Harding dies; Calvin Coolidge becomes president; Harding scandals break
1924	Dawes plan to stabilize German inflation; Coolidge elected president
1925	John T. Scopes convicted of teaching evolution in Tennessee; Alain Locke's *The New Negro* published
1927	Charles Lindbergh's solo flight across the Atlantic; Sacco and Vanzetti executed; first "talking" film, *The Jazz Singer*, released
1928	Herbert Hoover elected president

ADDITIONAL READING

For years, Frederick Lewis Allen's *Only Yesterday: An Informal History of the 1920s* (1931) shaped the stereotyped view of the decade as a frivolous interlude between World War I and the Great Depression. William Leuchtenburg's *The Perils of Prosperity, 1914–1932* (1958) began an important reconsideration by stressing the serious conflict between urban and rural America and the emergence of modern mass society. Ann Douglas's *Terrible Honesty: Mongrel Manhattan in the 1920s* (1995) puts Manhattan at the core of the cultural transformation in the 1920s, especially its success at bringing African American folk and popular art into the mainstream.

Roland Marchand's *Advertising the American Dream: Making Way for Modernity, 1920–1940* (1985) analyzes the role of advertising in shaping mass consumption, values, and culture, while Ellis Hawley's *The Great War and the Search for a Modern Order* (1979) emphasizes economic institutions. Three recent studies explore continuity and change for women in the 1920s: Kathleen M. Blee, *Women of the Klan: Racism and Gender in the 1920s* (1991); Virginia Scharff, *Taking the Wheel: Women and the Coming of the Motor Age* (1991); and Jacqueline Jones, *Labor of Love, Labor of Sorrow: Black Women, Work, and Family, From Slavery to the Present* (1985). For a fuller list of readings, see the Bibliography.

25

Crash and Depression

igh above Columbus Circle in New York City a gigantic electric sign blinked out the happy decree: "You should have $10,000 at the age of 30; $25,000 at the age of 40; $50,000 at the age of 50." In the pages of the *Ladies Home Journal* John J. Raskob, who had run the Finance Committee at General Motors and listed his profession as "capitalist," told people how. "Everyone ought to be rich," he declared: $15 a month, "wisely invested," would be worth $80,000 in 20 years. In the 1920s, when 4 families in 10 earned less than $1500 a year, that was rich.

Possibilities for profit seemed to be everywhere, including far-off Florida. In 1929 the Marx Brothers broke into films with *The Cocoanuts*, a zany farce about real estate scams in the Sunshine State. "You can get stucco," says Groucho as he pitches *Florida land* a land deal. "Oh, can you get stucco!" Thousands of investors had gotten "stucco" *boom* when land fever hit southern Florida in the mid-1920s. Before World War I Miami sat on mangrove jungle and bug-infested swamp. Attracted by 80-degree temperatures in winter, developers cleared the jungle, drained the swamp, put up a sea wall, and built a three-mile causeway from the beach to the mainland. Miami became the fastest growing city in America.

Land prices skyrocketed, as greedy speculators bought and sold on the hope of realizing quick profits. No one cared about the true value of the land, only its price. By 1925 lots were selling for $20,000 apiece, sight unseen. So many people arrived in the summer of 1925 that famine threatened the state, and ice could be obtained only by doctor's prescription.

One mid-September night in 1926, Miami barometers dropped to 27.75—the lowest reading North America had ever recorded. Wind howled through the city at 130 miles per hour. Twenty-foot waves pounded sea walls and washed away beaches. Flooded swamps reclaimed landfills. In one night 100 Miamians drowned; 40,000 lost their homes. Speculators discovered an awful truth: southern Florida lay in the middle of the hurricane belt. Reality punctured the vast speculative bubble. The value of oceanfront lots dropped from $2000 to $700 a foot. Hundreds went bankrupt; thousands lost their land to foreclosures.

If the Florida land boom of the 1920s made only a few people rich, at least it laid the foundation for the region's later development. By contrast, the era's stock market scams and speculative fever did nothing except turn the financial center of the nation into a gambling den. Outright swindles in phony stocks (oil wells and mines were the most popular) netted con artists more than $600 million a year. Some stock maneu-

In the 1930s Dorothea Lange pioneered a new realism in photography—grim, unvarnished, and poignant. Nowhere did she better capture the shattering effects of the Great Depression than in these pictures of a heavily mortgaged Georgia cotton farmer.

vering was legal but deceptive. Favored "insiders" (including President Calvin Coolidge) were placed on "preferred lists" at brokerage houses and tipped off about impending issues. Some insiders formed "stock pools" to drive up prices so they could make a killing. In 1928 a group that included John Raskob pushed Radio Corporation of America stock from $90 to $109 a share. They made $5 million by selling the stock one week later.

The dream of riches obsessed the nation. The volume of sales on the New York Stock Exchange jumped 400 percent from 1923 to 1928. Other exchanges in Chicago, St. Louis, San Francisco, and Los Angeles registered similar gains. Buyers were less concerned about wise investments—about profit-and-loss statements and market shares of a company—than about rising stock prices. A simple dictum governed the market: buy low, sell high; buy high, sell higher.

The stock market dominated the news. Millions watched it as closely as they watched their favorite baseball team. In Saginaw, Michigan, and Amarillo, Texas, people shook open their morning papers to the financial pages. In Steubenville, Ohio, and Storm Lake, Iowa, they gathered at brokerage houses to watch the daily ups and downs of stocks. Perhaps as many as 9 million Americans bought and sold stock in the 1920s; a few got rich quick, and most shoveled their profits into the market again. Even if they lost money, it did not matter. "Everybody ought to be rich"—and anyone could be.

So it seemed in the late 1920s, as the New Era careened toward disaster. Behind electric signs directing the pursuit of wealth and slogans exhorting it, beneath land booms and stock deals, the economy was honeycombed with weaknesses. In 1929 it collapsed.

THE GREAT BULL MARKET

Strolling across the felt-padded floor of the New York Stock Exchange, Superintendent William Crawford greeted the New Year with swaggering confidence. Nineteen twenty-eight had been a record-setter, with more than 90,500,000 shares traded. The "bulls"—buyers of stock—had routed the bears—those who sell. It was the greatest bull market in history as eager purchasers drove prices to new highs. At the end of the last business day of 1928, Crawford surveyed the floor and declared flatly, "The millennium's arrived."

Veteran financial analyst Alexander Noyes knew better. Speculation—buying and selling on the expectation that rising prices will yield quick gains—had taken over the stock market. "Something has to give," said Noyes in September 1929. Less than a month later, the Great Bull Market fell in a heap.

The Rampaging Bull

New blood

No one knows exactly what caused the wave of speculation that boosted the stock market to dizzying heights. Driven alternately by greed and fear, the market succumbed to greed in a decade that considered it a virtue. A new breed of aggressive outsiders helped to spread the speculative fever. William Durant of General Motors, the Fisher brothers from Detroit, and others like them bought millions of shares, crowded out more conservative investors from the East, and helped to send prices soaring.

ing costs dropped almost 25 percent, but family incomes tumbled by 40 percent. Homemakers watched family budgets with a closer eye than ever. They substituted less expensive fish for red meat or dropped meat from their menus altogether. Jell-O, the cheapest all-purpose dessert, surged in popularity. Corn, tomatoes, and pole beans sprang up in backyards and vacant city lots. Families took in relatives and boarders. Some homemakers sold baked goods, made dresses, or opened kitchen beauty parlors. Returning to Muncie, Indiana, where they had studied the habits of a typical American "Middletown" in the 1920s, sociologists Robert and Helen Lynd discovered an increase in prostitution. Working-class wives were selling themselves to keep their families going.

After a decade of being drawn from home by automobiles and mass entertainment, the middle-class family turned inward. Church attendance declined. A third of the Grange and rural women's clubs vanished. Home and family emerged as the center of recreation and companionship. People dreamed of the outdoors—playing tennis, swimming, or boating—but surveys showed that they spent their free time indoors, reading, listening to the radio, and going to the movies, in that order.

The Great Depression was like an "earthquake," wrote one journalist, and it sent ordinary Americans scurrying for the reassuring shelter of the past. The middle-class dream of a wife freed from working for wages, which had weakened in the 1910s and 1920s, reasserted itself, as many women came to associate working outside the home with financial distress. Whether in the renewed importance of homemaking and family life or the reemergence of home industries, Americans retreated into traditionalism.

The Fate of Women and Children

Just at the moment when the cult of domesticity was reasserting itself, the Depression was forcing more and more women from their homes to supplement meager family incomes. Some critics claimed they took jobs from men, and one offered a simple solution: "Fire the women, who shouldn't be working anyway, and hire the men. Presto! No unemployment. No relief rolls. No depression." *Working outside the home*

Such thinking was nonsense, a reflection of the prejudice still dogging female wage earners. Past discrimination had relegated many women to jobs as secretaries, schoolteachers, and social workers. Over half the female labor force worked in domestic service or the garment trades. Live-in maids, the elite of domestic servants, earned $8 a week; pieceworkers in the textile mills of Lawrence, Massachusetts, $4. Most unemployed men were reluctant to take such "women's work," even when it was available.

Married women who sought employment faced special obstacles. Opinion polls showed that more than three in four Americans believed wives belonged at home. Few school districts would hire them, and half had a policy of firing them first. Between 1932 and 1937 federal regulations prohibited more than one family member from holding a civil service job. Three-quarters of those forced to resign were women. The proportion of women in the workforce rose anyway because they were willing to take almost any job. By 1940 it approached 25 percent. Wages for women rose too, until they were 63 percent of men's.

The nation's 21 million children could not escape anxiety. Teachers reported even kindergartners being "excitable and high-strung." Many of them were as uncertain of their future as they were of their next meal. Perhaps 250,000 children took to *Childhood anxiety*

Daily Lives

FOOD/DRINK/DRUGS

The Control of Narcotics

When Franklin Roosevelt entered the White House in 1933, narcotics had been under federal control for two decades. But it had taken a half century before that to recognize the social costs of addiction.

In the nineteenth century, a host of drugs offered Americans control over tension and pain. Laudanum, or tincture of opium, had been used since the Renaissance to calm nerves, induce sleep, and relieve gastrointestinal illnesses such as cholera and food poisoning. Chloroform and ether had anesthetized patients since the 1850s. Chloral hydrate (the famed "knockout drops" of sensational novels) was isolated in 1868. Derived from opium in 1898, heroin promised to be a "heroic" painkiller and sedative. Cocaine had been made commercially from the South American coca leaf since the 1850s. By the 1880s Sigmund Freud and former surgeon general of the army William Hammond were praising it as an anesthetic and stimulant, even a cure for opiate addiction.

Such drugs were available in many products. The exhilarating qualities of cocaine made it a favorite ingredient in medicines, wines, tonics, and (until 1903) the soft drink Coca-Cola. Morphine and other opiates had worked their way into popular over-the-counter medicines like Mrs. Winslow's Soothing Syrup. Still, with drug use on the rise, the detrimental effects soon became obvious. By the turn of the century, an estimated million Americans were abusing drugs nationwide.

As early as 1860 some states had begun regulating pure narcotics. Strong traditions of individualism and privacy made control difficult and uneven. The emergence of the United States as a world power at the end of the nineteenth century gave reformers a powerful boost. They had depicted addiction as a foreign contagion. In the early years of the twentieth century they called on the United States to lead an international war on drugs. Naturally such moral leadership abroad required moral rectitude at home.

Concern for public health and individual morality peaked during the progressive era. New laws brought narcotics under federal control. The federal government had regulated opium through import taxes since the late nineteenth century. In 1909 Congress excluded the importation of opium for other than medical uses. Finally, in 1914 it enacted the more comprehensive Harrison Anti-Narcotic Act. The Harrison Act permitted only federally registered dealers to dispense morphine, cocaine, opium, and heroin. Physicians were allowed to issue the substances for medicinal purposes but had to file records with federal authorities.

the road, some to relieve families of their support, others just to wander. School enrollments grew as prospects for employment shrank. By 1940 three of four high school–aged children were attending, compared with fewer than half in 1930. Extended schooling kept children out of the labor force, and the Depression fed the long-term trend toward a highly educated public.

Play

Somber faces fill the photographs of the Depression decade, but there still was time for fun. Play was often conditioned by the crisis. In the midst of fear and uncertainty,

Daily Lives

The fruits of a drug raid in the 1920s. Until 1930, when the Federal Bureau of Narcotics was created, drug agents operated under the Treasury Department's Narcotics Division.

Once the prohibition of alcohol went into effect in 1920, the Treasury Department (given authority over enforcement) created a special Narcotics Division. As alcohol prohibition declined in popularity, supporters of the Harrison Act succeeded in establishing a separate Federal Bureau of Narcotics in 1930. In 1937, over opposition from the understaffed Bureau, Congress enacted the Marijuana Tax Act. Possession of cannabis became illegal.

A pattern of nativism runs through the history of narcotics control. Campaigners often believed that certain drugs would make feared minorities unmanageable. In the late nineteenth century opium had been linked to the Chinese, raising alarm that its use would promote sexual contact with white women. At the turn of the century, cocaine was believed to endow blacks with cunning, hostility, and superhuman strength. (The fear that "cocainized" blacks could not be stopped by .32-caliber bullets is said to have led many southern police departments to arm themselves with .38-caliber pistols.) Heroin was used to explain the violence and promiscuity of adolescents in urban gangs in the 1920s. And in the 1930s, as pressure mounted for federal control of cannabis, or marijuana, local officials in southwestern states said smoking it increased crime among Mexican immigrants.

In each instance anxieties peaked amid social crisis: a glut of low-paid Chinese workers in the depression-filled 1890s; a battle for political control of blacks at the turn of the century; the rise of an unruly youth culture in the 1920s; and high unemployment among Mexican immigrants in the Great Depression of the 1930s. "America is a nation of drug-takers," wrote one authority in 1881. By the 1930s the nation had taken steps to change its habits.

games built on rationality captured middle-class imaginations: contract bridge with its systematic bidding and play; Parker Brothers' board game Monopoly, which rewarded orderly investing in real estate; pinball, the ultimate machine-age game that carried the injunction "Do Not Tilt." All relied on rules and skill as well as luck. In more physical games, endurance became a virtue. Six-day bicycle races staged a comeback. Dance marathons, another contest for survival, kept partners on the floor 45 minutes out of every hour, 24 hours a day, sometimes for weeks on end.

The Depression produced more sober fashions for women: longer skirts and hair and more curves. A desire to escape the here-and-now helped to make bestsellers of *The Good Earth* (1931), Pearl Buck's saga of China, and Margaret Mitchell's Civil

War epic, *Gone with the Wind* (1936). New skepticism about business led Fred Schlink to write *100,000,000 Guinea Pigs*, a sequel to *Your Money's Worth* (1927), his earlier exposé of false advertising. By 1935 the two books had sold half a million copies. A new tightfistedness led to a tenfold increase in consumer cooperatives during the decade.

Hungry for diversions, people still flocked to spectacles, as they had in the 1920s. A world's fair in Chicago in 1933 and another in New York in 1939 drew millions. Families living on a limited budget took up cheaper pursuits, such as stamp collecting, knitting, and jigsaw puzzles. Boxtop contests and other games of chance held out hope of turning bad luck good. Inaugurated in 1930, the Irish Sweepstakes became the most successful lottery in the world within five years.

With a wider audience than ever, record sales jumped a hundredfold between 1934 and 1937. Classical music enjoyed new popularity as tastes turned to a more controlled, full-bodied sound. By 1939 there were more than 270 symphony orchestras in the country; only 17 had existed in 1915. More than 10 million families listened to symphonic music and opera each weekend on radio. Popular music became more melodic and cheerful. "Swing," a commercialized jazz, dominated the charts, and big-band orchestras played popular favorites at nightclubs and theaters. In 1937 Benny Goodman, the "King of Swing," drew an audience of nearly 4000 when he opened at the Paramount Theater in New York City.

The Golden Age of Radio and Film

By the end of the decade almost 9 out of 10 families owned radios. (The cost of one had dropped from $100 in 1929 down to about $50 by the mid-1930s.) People de-

Programming pended on them for nearly everything—news, sports, and weather; music and entertainment; advice on how to bake a cake or find God. Radio entered a golden age of commercialism as sponsors hawked their products on variety programs like "Major Bowes' Amateur Hour" and comedy shows with George Burns and Gracie Allen. Daytime melodramas, called "soap operas" because they were sponsored by soap companies, aimed at women with stories of the personal struggles of ordinary folk. By 1939 the hair-raising adventures of "The Lone Ranger" were being heard three times a week on 140 stations.

Radio continued to bind the country together. A teenager in Splendora, Texas, could listen to the same wisecracks from Jack Benny, the same music from Guy Lombardo, as kids in New York and Los Angeles. In 1938 Orson Welles broadcast H. G. Wells's classic science fiction tale, *The War of the Worlds*. Americans everywhere listened to breathless reports of an "Invasion from Mars," and many believed it. In Newark, New Jersey, cars jammed roads as families rushed to evacuate the city. The nation, bombarded with continual reports of impending war in Europe and used to responding to radio advertising, was prepared to believe almost anything, even invaders from Mars.

Art Deco radio, 1930. Art Deco, popularized in the 1920s, relied on the geometrical shapes of machines arranged in decorative patterns.

Lunatic social jesters, the Marx brothers turned convention topsy-turvy in the 1930s. Their antics made the Depression-spawned prospect of social disorder fun. *Monkey Business* (1931), their first Hollywood film, unleashed Groucho, Chico, Harpo, and Zeppo on a gang of crooks.

In Hollywood an efficient but autocratic "studio system" churned out a record number of feature films. Eight motion picture companies produced more than two-thirds of them. Color, first introduced in features in *Becky Sharp* (1935), soon complemented sound, which had debuted in the 1927 version of *The Jazz Singer.* Neither alone could keep movie theaters full. As attendance dropped early in the Depression, big studios like Metro-Goldwyn-Mayer and Universal lured audiences back with films that shocked, titillated, and just plain entertained. *Studio system*

Popular movies often played upon deep national emotions. Early Depression gangster movies like *Little Caesar* (1931) and *Scarface* (1932) allowed Americans ambivalent about the ethic of success to root for misfits who challenged it and still applaud their just demise. The Marx Brothers made fun of social disorder in *Monkey Business* (1931) and *Duck Soup* (1933), while the elaborately choreographed musicals of Busby Berkeley and the dancing duo of Fred Astaire and Ginger Rogers stressed teamwork and cooperation. *She Done Him Wrong* (1933) catapulted Mae West to the top of box-office favorites by mixing sex with West's bawdy humor. ("Haven't you ever met a man who could make you happy?" Cary Grant asks. "Sure, lots of times," West replies.) Only toward the end of the decade did Hollywood develop a social conscience in such films as *Dead End* (1937) and *The Grapes of Wrath* (1941).

By the mid-1930s more than 60 percent of Americans were going to the movies at least once a week. They saw tamer films as the industry regulated movie content in the face of growing criticism. In 1933 the Catholic church created the Legion of Decency to monitor features. To avoid censorship and boycotts, studios stiffened

Production code

their own regulations. "Evil and good are never to be confused," stated the Motion Picture Production Code of 1934. In case producers had any trouble distinguishing between the two, codemakers drew up a list of do's and don't's. Producers could not depict homosexuality, abortion, drug use, or sex. (Even the word "sex" was banned, as was all profanity.) If couples were shown in bed, they had to be clothed and at least one foot of each had to touch the floor. Traditional middle-class morality reigned on the screen, and most Depression movies, like most of popular culture, preserved the basic social and economic tenets of American culture.

"Dirty Thirties": An Ecological Disaster

On Armistice Day 1933, the wind began to blow through Beadle County, South Dakota: not just briskly but at 60 miles an hour. "By noon," reported R. D. Lusk from a local farmhouse, "it was darker than night." When the wind finally died down, the farm, like the rest of Beadle County, was transformed. Lusk saw no fields, "only sand drifting into mounds. . . . Fences, machinery, and trees were gone, buried. The roofs of sheds stuck out through drifts deeper than a man is tall."

Dust Bowl

Between 1932 and 1939 an average of nearly 50 "black blizzards" a year turned 1500 square miles between the Oklahoma panhandle and western Kansas into a gigantic "Dust Bowl." It was one of the worst ecological disasters in modern history. Nature played its part, scorching the earth and whipping the winds. But the "dirty thirties"

"Black blizzards" dwarfed all man-made structures. The drought that gave rise to the huge dust storms lasted from 1932 until 1936, and few who lived through one ever forgot. "Noon was like night," reported a conductor on the Santa Fe railroad. "There was no sun, and, at times, it was impossible to see a yard. The engineer could not see the signal lights." In a single day in 1934, 12 million tons of western dirt fell on Chicago.

were mostly man-made. The semiarid lands west of the 98th meridian were not suitable for agriculture or livestock. Sixty years of intensive farming and grazing had stripped the prairie of its natural vegetation and rendered it defenseless against the elements. When the dry winds came, one-third of the Great Plains just blew away.

The dust storms lasted anywhere from hours to days. Walking into one, as R. D. Lusk discovered when he stepped outside, was like walking into "a wall of dirt." "This is the ultimate darkness," despaired a Kansan in the midst of a dust storm. "So must come the end of the world." As far east as Memphis citizens dared not step outdoors without handkerchiefs to filter the air they breathed. Yellow grit from Nebraska collected on the windowsills of the White House.

For protection people wore gauze masks, swabbed their nostrils with Vaseline, covered their windows with paraffin-soaked rags. Nothing worked. Tiny particles of dust covered everything, and food crunched to the bite. An epidemic of respiratory infections and a new disease called "dust pneumonia" broke out among farm families. Even fish died from lack of oxygen in dust-coated rivers.

Some 3.5 million plains people abandoned their farms. Landowners or corporations forced off about half of them as large-scale commercial farming slowly spread into the heartland of America. Huge "factories in the field," these commercial farms advanced east from California, where 10 percent of the farms grew more than 50 percent of the crops. As in industrial America, the strategy was to consolidate and mechanize. As farms grew in size, so did the number of tenants. In most Dust Bowl counties people owned less than half the land they farmed. American agriculture was turning from a way of life into an industry. American farmers were becoming common laborers. And as the economy contracted, owners cut costs by cutting workers.

The Great Plains contained the only states that suffered a net loss of residents during the decade. No one knows how many of these rural refugees became migrants, but relief offices around the country reported a change in migrant families. No longer black or brown, more and more were white and native-born, typically a young married couple with one child.

Most did not travel far, perhaps to the next county. Long-distance migrants—the "exodusters" from Oklahoma, Arizona, and Texas—usually set their sights on California. Handbills and advertisements promised jobs picking fruit and harvesting vegetables. If they were like the Joad family in John Steinbeck's classic novel *The Grapes of Wrath* (1939), they drove west along Route 66 through Arizona and New Mexico, their belongings piled high atop rickety jalopies, heading for the west coast, their Promised Land of jobs and opportunity.

Exodusters

More than 350,000 Oklahomans migrated like the Joads to California, so many that "Okie" came to mean any Dust Bowler, even though most of Oklahoma lay outside the Dust Bowl. The poor were only a small minority of new arrivals, but enough came to make Californians edgy. By the middle of the decade Los Angeles police had formed "bum blockades" to keep migrants out. "Negroes and Okies upstairs," read one sign in a San Joaquin Valley theater. Native-born whites had never encountered such discrimination before.

Only one in two or three migrants actually found work. The labor surplus allowed growers to set their own terms. A migrant family earned about $450 a year, less than a third the subsistence level. Those that did not work formed wretched enclaves called "little Oklahomas." The worst were located in the fertile Imperial Valley. There

William Gropper specialized in social realism, an art style prominent in many American paintings of the 1930s. In *Migration,* one of thousands of farm families from the Great Plains heads west with its belongings. The desperation of the family's flight is underscored by the flat landscape, the brown tones and bent figures, and the ominous sky.

at the end of the decade relief officials discovered a family of 10 living in a 1921 Ford. When told to leave, the mother responded vacantly, "I wonder where."

Mexican Americans and African Americans

Cesar Chavez

The Chavez family lost their farm in the North Gila River valley of Arizona in 1934. They had owned a small homestead near Yuma for two generations, but the Depression pushed them out. Cesar, barely six years old at the time, remembered only images of the departure: a "giant tractor" leveling the corral; the loss of his room and bed; a beat-up Chevy hauling the family west; his father promising to buy another plot in Arizona someday.

The elder Chavez could never keep his promise. Instead he and his family lived on the road, "following the crops" in California. In eight years Cesar went to 37 schools. The family was forced to sell their labor to unscrupulous "enganchistas," or contractors, for less than $10 a week. The father joined strikers in the Imperial Valley in the mid-1930s, but they were crushed. "Some people put this out of their minds and forget it," said Cesar Chavez years later. "I don't." Thirty years later he founded the United Farm Workers of America, the first union of migratory workers in the country.

The Chavezes resembled the Joads in every way but one: they were Mexican Americans. The Joads had encountered a few sympathetic store clerks on their way west. When the Chavezes found a roadside restaurant, the sign outside read: "White trade only." In an America still strictly segregated, the owner never thought twice about refusing service to Americans who were brown or black. "Every time we thought of it, it hurt us," remembered Cesar.

A deep ambivalence had always characterized American attitudes toward Mexicans, but the Great Depression turned most Anglo communities against them. Cities like Los Angeles, fearing the burden of relief, found it cheaper to ship Mexican migrants home. Some left voluntarily. Others were driven out by frustrated officials or angry neighbors. Beginning in 1931 the federal government launched a series of deportations, or "repatriations," of Mexicans back to Mexico. These included their American-born children, who by law were citizens of the United States. *Repatriation*

During the decade the Latino population of the Southwest dropped by 500,000. In a city like Chicago, the Mexican community shrank almost by half. Staying in the United States often turned out to be as difficult as leaving. The average income of Mexican American families in the Rio Grande valley of Texas was $506 a year. The sum represented the combined income of parents and children. Following the harvest made schooling particularly difficult: fewer than 2 Mexican American children in 10 completed five years of school.

Hard times were nothing new to African Americans. "The Negro was born in depression," opined one black man. "It only became official when it hit the white man." Still, when the Depression struck, black unemployment surged. By 1932 it reached 50 percent, twice the national level. In 1933 several cities reported between 25 and 40 percent of their black residents with no support but relief payments. Even skilled black workers who retained their jobs saw their wages cut in half, according to one study of Harlem in 1935.

Migration out of the rural South, up 800,000 over the 1920s, dropped by 50 percent during the 1930s. As late as 1940 three of four African Americans still lived in poor rural areas, yet conditions there were just as bad as in cities. Forty percent of all black workers in the United States were farm laborers or tenants. In 1934 one study estimated the average income for black cotton farmers at under $200 a year. Millions of African Americans made do by stretching meager incomes as they had for years. "Our wives could go to the store and get a bag of beans or a sack of flour and a piece of fat meat, and they could cook this. And we could eat it," explained another man. "Now you take the white fella, he couldn't do this."

Like many African Americans, George Baker refused to be victimized by the Depression. Baker had moved from Georgia to Harlem in 1915. He changed his name to M. J. Divine and founded a religious cult that promised followers an afterlife of full equality. In the 1930s "Father Divine" preached economic cooperation and opened shelters, or "heavens," for regenerate "angels," black and white. In Detroit, Elijah Poole changed his name to Elijah Muhammad and in 1931 established the Black Muslims, a blend of Islamic faith and black nationalism. He exhorted African Americans to celebrate their African heritage, to live a life of self-discipline and self-help, and to strive for a separate all-black nation. *Father Divine and Elijah Muhammad*

The Depression inflamed racial prejudice. "Dust has been blown from the shotgun, the whip, and the noose," reported *The New Republic* in 1931, "and Ku Klux Klan practices were being resumed in the certainty that dead men not only tell no tales but create vacancies." Lynchings tripled between 1932 and 1933. In 1932 the Supreme Court ordered a retrial in the most celebrated racial case of the decade. A year earlier nine black teenagers had been accused of raping two white women on a train bound for Scottsboro, Alabama. Within weeks all-white juries had sentenced eight of them to death. The convictions rested on the testimony of the women, one of whom later admitted the boys had been framed. Appeals kept the case alive for almost a decade. In the end charges against four of the "Scottsboro boys" were dropped. The other five received substantial prison sentences.

Scottsboro boys

Elsewhere the Depression divided black and white Americans, but in the Arkansas delta hard times drew them together. In Arkansas poor black and white farmers joined forces to organize the Southern Tenant Farmers Union in 1934. "The landlord is always betwixt us," an old black man advised the founders. "There ain't but one way for us to get him where he can't help himself and that's for us to get together and stay together." The union published its own newspaper, the *Sharecropper's Voice,* and attracted national support from Socialists and other radicals. Landlords became uneasy with union demands for federal subsidies and an end to arbitrary evictions. Planters and riding bosses broke up union meetings and horsewhipped organizers. Although they won few concessions, union members stuck together.

THE TRAGEDY OF HERBERT HOOVER

A cold, gray morning sent shivers through the crowd huddled in front of the capitol on March 4, 1929. Herbert Hoover had just been sworn in as the thirty-first president of the United States. His monotone came booming over the loudspeakers: "I have no fears for the future of our country. It is bright with hope." Engineer, millionaire businessman, secretary of commerce for eight years, Herbert Hoover embodied competence, efficiency, and success. No one seemed better suited to anticipate trouble or resolve it. "We were in a mood for magic," recalled journalist Anne McCormick. "We had summoned a great engineer to solve our problems for us; now we sat back comfortably and confidently to watch the problems being solved."

Within seven months a "depression" had struck. (Hoover coined the term himself to minimize the crisis.) Try as he might, he could not beat it and the nation turned against him. "People were starving because of Herbert Hoover," sputtered an angry mother in 1932. "Men were killing themselves because of Herbert Hoover, and their fatherless children were being packed away to orphanages . . . because of Herbert Hoover."

The charge was unfair, but it stuck. Hoover's presidency, which had begun with such bright hope, became the worst ordeal of his life. Near the end of his term in 1932 he lamented that "all the money in the world could not induce me to live over the last nine months." He nonetheless felt duty-bound to accept his party's renomination for the presidency. His ordeal soon turned into a tragic and humiliating rejection.

The Failure of Relief

Private charity

By the winter of 1931–1932 the story was the same everywhere: relief organizations found themselves with too little money and too few resources to make any significant headway against the Depression. Once-mighty private charity had dwindled to 6 percent of all relief funds. Hull House in Chicago, the model of progressive benevolence, was overwhelmed by the needs of its neighbors. New York City employees had

Louis Ribak's *Home Relief Station* is a grim portrait of the failing relief efforts of private charities. The painting depicts the humiliation and degradation of applying for relief. A crowd of broken men and women sits anxiously as a burly administrator interrogates a frail relief applicant.

been donating 1 percent of their salaries to feed the needy since 1930, yet many New Yorkers were starving to death, over two dozen in 1931 alone.

Ethnic charities made similar efforts to stave off disaster. Mexican Americans and Puerto Ricans turned to *mutualistas,* traditional societies that provided members with social support, life insurance, and sickness benefits. The stress of the Depression quickly bankrupted most *mutualistas.* In San Francisco, the Chinese Six Companies offered food and clothing to needy Chinese Americans. But as the head of the Federation of Jewish Charities warned, private efforts were failing. The government would be "compelled, by the cruel events ahead of us, to step into the situation and bring relief on a large scale."

An estimated 30 million needy people nationwide quickly depleted city trea- *City services* suries, already pressed because nearly 30 percent of city taxpayers had already fallen behind in paying the taxes they owed. In Philadelphia relief payments to a family of four totaled $5.50 a week, the highest in the country. Some cities gave nothing to unmarried people or childless couples, no matter how impoverished they were. New Orleans refused all new applications for aid in 1931. Oklahoma City began arresting unemployed men, charging them with vagrancy, and ordering them out of town. Roads went unpaved in summer, snow unplowed in winter. By the end of 1931, Detroit, Boston, Buffalo, and scores of other cities were bankrupt.

Cities clamored for help from state capitals, but after a decade of extravagant spending and sloppy bookkeeping, many states were already running in the red. As businesses and property values collapsed, tax bases shrank and with them state revenues. Michigan, one of the few states to provide any relief, reduced funds by more than half between 1931 and 1932. Until New York established its Temporary *TERA*

Emergency Relief Administration (TERA) in 1931, no state had any agency at all to handle the problem of unemployment.

Some people refused to accept help even when they qualified. To go on relief, said one man, was to endure a "crucifixion." Before applications could even be considered, all property had to be sold, all credit exhausted, all relatives declared flat broke. After a half-hour grilling about his family, home, and friends, one applicant left, "feeling I didn't have any business living any more." Hostile officials attached every possible stigma to aid. In 1932 residents of Lewiston, Maine, voted to bar all welfare recipients from the polls. Ten states wrote property requirements for voting into their constitutions. The destitute were being disfranchised.

Herbert Hoover

Glittering trumpets blared, servants bowed, and the president of the United States sat down to dinner. One after another, seven full courses were set before him. When he finished, the uniformed buglers sounded his departure. Every night he stayed at the White House during the Great Depression Herbert Hoover dined in such splendor.

It was not that Herbert Hoover was insensitive—far from it. He never visited a bread line or a relief shelter because he could not bear the sight of suffering. He had even thought about economizing himself but decided against it. If the president changed his habits one bit, it might be taken as a sign of lost confidence. He was doing all he could to promote recovery, more than any of his predecessors, and still the public scorned him. His credibility collapsed. Journalist Edward Angley published all of the president's sunny forecasts in 1931 and called the book *Oh Yeah!* Hoover's natural sullenness turned to self-pity. Calvin Coolidge advised patience: "You can't expect to see calves running in the field the day after you put the bull to the cows." "No," said an exasperated Hoover, "but I would expect to see contented cows."

Hoover's frustration was understandable. He had never failed before. Orphaned at nine, he became one of the first graduates of Stanford University in 1895, an expert engineer, and the owner of one of the most successful mining firms in the world. Before he turned 40, he was a millionaire. As a good Quaker he balanced private gain with public service. He saved starving refugees in war-torn Europe and flood victims at home. He became known as the greatest humanitarian of his generation. The people of Finland added a new word to their vocabulary: to "hoover" meant to help.

The Hoover Depression Program

From the fall of 1930 onward, Hoover took responsibility for ending the crisis—and as humanely as possible. He understood the vicious cycle of rising unemployment and falling demand and knew the necessity for investment. His unprecedented depression program rested on his associational philosophy, with its commitment to voluntary efforts (see pages 860–861). The president firmly believed that capitalism

Herbert Hoover

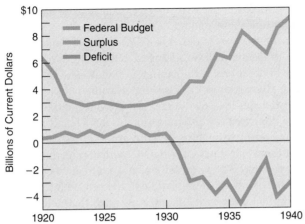

FEDERAL BUDGET AND SURPLUS/DEFICIT, 1920–1940
During the 1920s, the federal government ran a modest surplus as federal spending shrank in the wake of the massive spending during the First World War. Beginning in the early 1930s, spending for Hoover's cautious Depression program led to a small deficit, which grew steadily as Franklin Roosevelt's New Deal spent boldly and revenues from taxes and tariffs continued to sink. In 1937 federal spending cuts to balance the budget reduced the deficit but brought on a recession that was quickly followed by renewed federal spending and increasing deficits.

would spur a recovery and worried that too much government action would undermine freedoms and initiative.

Despite Hoover's best efforts, the program failed. As a good associationalist, he rallied business leaders, who pledged to maintain employment, wages, and prices—only to have them back down as the economy sputtered. In 1930 Hoover succeeded in pushing a tax cut through Congress in order to increase the purchasing power of consumers. But when the cuts produced an unbalanced federal budget, Hoover followed with tax increases in 1932, further undermining investment and consumption. Presidential commissions to discover the number of unemployed and spark local relief did neither. Hoover's Federal Farm Board, created to stimulate the sale of farm commodities, lacked the funds to make it effective. The president endorsed the Smoot–Hawley Tariff (1930) to protect the United States from cheap foreign goods, but that bill ended up bringing a wave of retaliation that choked world trade and reduced American sales abroad. Even Hoover's spending on public works—at $1 billion, more than all of his predecessors—did not approach the $10 billion needed to employ only half the unemployed. (At the time, the entire federal budget was only $3.2 billion.)

Under pressure from Congress, Hoover took his boldest action to save the banks. Without them, there could be no recovery. Between 1930 and 1932 some 5100 banks failed as panicky depositors withdrew their funds. Losses amounted to more than $3.2 billion. Hoover convinced Congress to create the Reconstruction Finance Corporation (RFC) in 1932, an agency that could lend money to banks and their chief corporate debtors—insurance companies and railroads. Modeled on a similar agency

Reconstruction Finance Corporation

that had been created during World War I, the RFC had a capital stock of $500 million and the power to borrow four times that amount. Within three months bank failures dropped from 70 a week to 1 every two weeks. The Glass–Steagall Banking Act (1932) made it easier for banks to loan money by adding $2 billion of new currency to the money supply, backed by Federal Reserve government bonds.

Yet in spite of this success, Hoover drew criticism for rescuing banks and not people. From the start he rejected the idea of direct federal relief for the unemployed. He feared that a "dole" or giveaway program (of the kind being used in Britain) would damage the character of recipients. Federal experiments with relief could have unhealthy results for the whole nation, he argued, perhaps creating a permanent underclass. The program would also be expensive, and a bureaucracy would be needed to police recipients. Inevitably it would meddle in the private lives of citizens and bring a "train of corruption and waste." Hoover assumed that neighborliness and cooperation would be enough.

In 1930, as unemployment topped 4 million, Americans sent a new Congress to Washington. The off-year elections reduced the Republican majority to one in the Senate and gave Democrats a slim lead in the House. After rejecting Democratic proposals for more public works and a federal employment service, Hoover slowly softened his stand on federal relief. In 1932 he dictated the terms of his surrender in the Emergency Relief and Construction Act. It authorized the RFC to lend up to $1.5 billion for "reproductive" public works that paid for themselves—like toll bridges and slum clearance. Another $300 million went to states as loans for the direct relief of the unemployed. The funds were hardly adequate: when the governor of Pennsylvania requested loans to furnish the destitute with 13 cents a day for a year, the RFC sent only enough for 3 cents a day.

Unemployment relief

Stirrings of Discontent

Hoover had given ground on relief, but like the rest of his Depression program it was too little and came too late. "The word revolution is heard at every hand," one writer warned in 1932. Some wondered if capitalism itself had gone bankrupt.

Here and there the desperate took matters into their own hands in 1932. In Wisconsin the Farm Holiday Association, under the leadership of Milo Reno, dumped thousands of gallons of milk on highways in a vain attempt to raise prices. Ten thousand striking miners formed a 48-mile motor car "Coal Caravan" that worked its way in protest across southern Illinois. In March a demonstration turned violent when communist sympathizers led a hunger march on Henry Ford's Rouge Assembly Plant in Dearborn, Michigan. As 3000 protesters surged toward the gates, Ford police drenched them with hoses, then opened fire at point-blank range. Four marchers were killed and more than 20 wounded.

Farm Holiday Association

For all the stirrings of discontent, revolution was never a danger. By 1932 the Communist party of the United States had only 20,000 members, up from 6500 in 1929 but hardly a political force. Under the slogan "Starve or Fight!" the Communists staged dozens of food, unemployment, and eviction protests. They led unionizing drives and courted intellectuals and the oppressed with rhetoric that stressed the rights of labor and minorities.

Communist party

Deeply suspicious of Marxist doctrine, most Americans were unsympathetic. Fewer than 1000 African Americans joined the party in the early 1930s. In the election of 1932 Communist presidential candidate William Z. Foster polled just over 100,000 votes. At first hostile to established politics, the Communists adopted a more cooperative strategy to contain Adolf Hitler when his Nazi party won control of Germany in 1933. The Soviet Union ordered Communist parties in Europe and the United States to join with liberal politicians in a "popular front" against Nazism. Thereafter party membership peaked in the mid-1930s at about 80,000.

Hoover sympathized with the discontented, but only to a point. When 1600 Communist-led hunger marchers came to Washington in December 1931, Hoover was determined to protect their right to protest. The president ordered blankets, tents, a field kitchen, and medical aid for them. Washington police stood guard over their parade. Hoover himself received their petitions at the White House. In January 1932 James Cox, a Catholic priest from Pittsburgh, led 10,000 unemployed men through Washington in a motorcade eight miles long. Hoover listened as the priest pleaded for public works and a tax on the rich. But the following summer, the "Bonus Army" received a far different reception.

The Bonus Army

The army, a ragtag collection of World War I veterans, was looking to cash in certificates they had received from Congress in 1924 as a reward for wartime service. Called "bonuses," the certificates were due to mature at an average of $1000 each in 1945. Walter Waters, one of the leaders, was typical of the Bonus Army's recruits. He had

Protests mounted as the Great Depression deepened. Labor pickets, such as the one shown in Joe Jones's *We Demand*, highlighted the failures of industrial capitalism. Here, workers and their children, white and black alike, show a new militancy as they march in protest.

served overseas with the 146th Field Artillery. By 1930 he was married, assistant super-intendent of a cannery in Portland, and happy. A year later he was jobless and destitute. The only thing of value he owned was his Adjusted Compensation Certificate. Penniless and hungry, veterans like Waters wanted their bonuses now, whatever they were worth.

In May 1932 Congressman Wright Patman of Texas introduced a bill for imme-diate payment of bonuses. Three hundred veterans set out from Portland, Oregon, on a march to press their case and support the bonus bill. By the time they reached Washington in June, the "Bonus Expeditionary Force" had swelled to 15,000, the largest protest in the city's history. Bonus Army leaders met with congressional rep-resentatives, but the president refused to see them. For the first time since the armistice ending World War I the gates of the Executive Mansion were chained shut.

Hoover dismissed the veterans as a special-interest lobby eager to feather their already soft nest. Veterans' benefits accounted for 25 percent of the federal budget, the largest single item. At a cost of $2.3 billion, bonus payments would have nearly doubled the deficit. The Senate spared Hoover the trouble of vetoing the bonus bill by blocking it.

Some veterans went home, but about 10,000 stayed to dramatize their plight, drilling and parading peacably. When Washington police tried to evict the veterans from buildings in the Federal Triangle in July, Hoover called in the army to help. He wanted nothing more than unarmed military support. Instead Army Chief of Staff General Douglas MacArthur arrived dressed in jodhpurs and all his medals, with four troops of saber-brandishing cavalry, six tanks, and a column of infantry. At dusk on July 28, 1932, soldiers cleared the Federal Triangle with bayonets and tear gas. Major George S. Patton, Jr., rode down a crowd of marchers in the last mounted charge of the U.S. Cavalry. Despite Hoover's orders to halt, MacArthur then burned down the Bonus encampment across the Potomac River. By the time the smoke was drifting over the capitol the next morning, the Bonus marchers had vanished, except for some 300 wounded veterans. Among them was Joseph T. Angelino. In 1918 he had received the Distinguished Service Cross for saving the life of a young officer named George S. Patton, Jr.

Hoover took responsibility for the army's actions, claiming that Bonus marchers were "not veterans" but "Communists and persons with criminal records" bent on in-surrection. An exhaustive survey conducted by the Veterans Administration belied the claim. In Albany, New York, Governor Franklin Roosevelt exploded at the presi-dent's performance: "There is nothing inside the man but jelly." Hoover's fear of big government and commitment to the associational formula of private initiative and voluntarism overcame his humanitarian impulses. Like the hero of a classical tragedy, Herbert Hoover came tumbling down.

The Election of 1932

The Republicans refused to abandon Hoover. In June 1932 their national convention opened in Chicago and endorsed his Depression program to the last detail. Hoover was renominated and, rather thoughtlessly, the band struck up "California, here I come/Right back where I started from."

With an opportunity to recapture the White House for the first time since 1920, buoyant Democrats also gathered in Chicago. Their platform blamed the Depression on the Republicans, called for a 25 percent cut in federal spending, and promised a bal-anced budget. It also vowed somehow to provide federal public works and unemployment relief. When the convention heard the plank calling for repeal of Prohibition, the cheering lasted for 25 minutes.

New York Governor Franklin D. Roosevelt swept all challengers aside on the fourth ballot. Effervescent and inspiriting, Roosevelt broke tradition by accepting the nomination in person: "I pledge you, I pledge myself, to a new deal for the American people." In that instant, Roosevelt found his slogan—"the New Deal." Moments later, an organ blared out "Happy Days Are Here Again," and he had a theme song.

The campaign was over before it began, and Hoover knew it. "I had little hope of re-election, but it was incumbent on me to fight it out to the end," he explained. Hoover saw the contest as a battle between two philosophies of government: the dangerous federal activism of Democrats against the voluntarism and prudent leadership of Republicans. Roosevelt, Hoover warned, would increase federal spending, inflate the currency, reduce the tariff, and "build a bureaucracy such as we have never seen in our history."

Without a national following, Roosevelt tailored his appeal to as broad a constituency as possible. In Iowa he said he was a "farmer"; in San Francisco, an economic planner. He called for a balanced budget one minute, more unemployment relief the next. He attacked Hoover as a "profligate spender," then went on to describe his own costly program for expanding public works. It didn't matter. As one shrewd reporter noted: "Mr. Roosevelt did not look or sound like a Messiah," only "the one sure means of rebuking the party in power."

Election Day brought a thundering rejection of Hoover and the Republicans. Roosevelt received nearly 58 percent of the popular vote. Norman Thomas won for the Socialists proportionately fewer votes than in 1912 or 1920. Democrats held majorities in both houses of Congress.

As telling as the margin of victory were the sources of the returns. Roosevelt carried the South and West and almost all the industrial states. Dissatisfaction with Republican rule was galvanizing immigrants, Catholics and Jews, farmers and industrial laborers, city dwellers and the rural poor into a broad coalition. The Democrats' campaign had been vague, certainly. But in the decade to come, the new president would move vigorously to involve the federal government in relieving the burdens of

Roosevelt coalition

ELECTION OF 1932

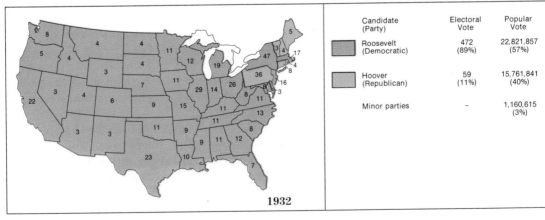

the unemployed and the poor. He would come to recognize that in a modern industrial state, it was no longer enough to rally round business and hope that capitalism would take care of itself. Citizens who voted for Roosevelt had experienced firsthand the savage effects of the boom-and-bust business cycle. For decades to come, they would vote their support of the Democratic party's newly active and interventionist welfare state.

But for the moment, even the cheers of victory could not hide the difficulty of the task. When Franklin Roosevelt returned to his town house after the celebrations at the Biltmore Hotel in New York, he could not suppress a rare moment of doubt. As his son James helped him to bed, he confessed, "I am afraid I may not have the strength to do this job. After you leave me tonight, Jimmy, I am going to pray. . . . I hope you will pray for me, too."

The challenge was daunting: more than 12 million unemployed; 30 banks a week failing; factories idle; farms on the auction block; prices plummeting. People who had scorned government, including businessmen, were baffled and now looked to Washington. The nation awaited Roosevelt, but not even Roosevelt knew whether he would be equal to the job. All he knew was that he would try anything to help. In the progressive tradition, he would rely on the power of government to regulate and plan, to protect the welfare of the public. In one of his first acts, Roosevelt ordered that no one telephoning the White House for aid should be shut off. Someone in the administration would be found to answer every call.

CHAPTER SUMMARY

Although the prosperity of the 1920s was real enough, the economy was honeycombed with weaknesses. Few Americans noticed them because of the hot pursuit of material wealth, whether in speculative real estate ventures or in the booming stock market. The stock market crash of 1929 did not bring about the Great Depression that followed. It only accelerated the slide. Overexpansion of industry, uneven distribution of income, a decline in mass purchasing power, a weak banking and corporate structure, "sick" industries, and economic errors caused the Great Depression.

The Great Depression leveled the nation economically and socially. Unemployment skyrocketed as spending plummeted. Common need reduced differences in class, ethnicity, and race. With hard times also came shame, self-doubt, and a loss of confidence. Birth and marriage rates dropped, and troubled marriages broke apart. More and more women worked outside the home to supplement meager family incomes. Popular culture rallied to reinforce basic tenets of American life: middle-class morality, family, capitalism, democracy.

An ecological disaster transformed 1500 square miles from the Oklahoma panhandle to western Kansas into a gigantic "Dust Bowl." Hardship was acute among the 3.5 million farm migrants and especially among Latinos and African Americans. Private, municipal, and state resources proved unequal to the task of providing relief. President Herbert Hoover did more than any of his predecessors had ever done to combat a downturn, but he could not bring himself to do enough. In 1932 Hoover suffered a humiliating rebuke as Democrat Franklin Roosevelt won a landslide victory. The powerful Roosevelt coalition ushered in the New Deal and kept a Democrat in the White House for the next 20 years.

SIGNIFICANT EVENTS

1926 ┼ Miami real estate bust
1928 ┼ Great Bull Market begins to peak
1929 ┼ Herbert Hoover inaugurated; stock market crash; Federal Farm Board created
1930 ┼ Smoot–Hawley Tariff raises rates
1931 ┼ Repatriation of Mexicans; Scottsboro boys arrested; New York establishes Temporary Emergency Relief Administration
1932 ┼ Glass–Steagall Banking Act; Reconstruction Finance Corporation established; Emergency Relief and Construction Act; Farm Holiday Association formed; Bonus Army marches on Washington, D.C.; Franklin Roosevelt elected president
1933 ┼ Legion of Decency formed; Motion Picture Production Code; "black blizzards" begin to create Dust Bowl
1934 ┼ Southern Tenant Farmers Union organized
1935 ┼ *Becky Sharp*, first color film; Communist party announces popular front
1936 ┼ Margaret Mitchell's *Gone with the Wind* published
1938 ┼ Orson Welles's radio broadcast of "Invasion from Mars"
1939 ┼ John Steinbeck's *The Grapes of Wrath* published

ADDITIONAL READING

The best books on the disintegration of the American economy are Lester Chandler, *America's Greatest Depression, 1929–1941* (1970) and, from the global perspective, Charles Kindleberger, *The World in Depression* (1973). The Keynesian perspective on the causes of the Great Depression is lucidly discussed in economist John Kenneth Galbraith's *The Great Crash* (rev. ed., 1988). For the monetarist argument, see Milton Friedman and Anna Jacobson Schwartz, *Monetary History of the United States* (1963) and Peter Temin, *Did Monetary Forces Cause the Great Depression?* (1976).

For a comparative look at responses to the Great Depression, see John A. Garraty's *The Great Depression* (1987). Robert Sobel's *The Great Bull Market: Wall Street in the 1920s* (1968) is a brief, evenhanded study of the stock market and Republican fiscal policies in the 1920s. Caroline Bird's *The Invisible Scar* (1966) remains the most sensitive treatment of the human impact of the Great Depression, but it should not be read without Studs Terkel's *Hard Times: An Oral History of the Great Depression* (1970) and Robert McElvaine's *The Great Depression: America, 1929–1941* (1984), which are especially good on Depression culture and values. Joan Hoff Wilson's *Herbert Hoover: Forgotten Progressive* (1975) traces Hoover's progressive impulses before and during his presidency. For a fuller list of readings, see the Bibliography.

26

The New Deal

Winner, South Dakota, November 10, 1933. "Dammit, I don't WANT to write to you again tonight. It's been a long, long day, and I'm tired." All the days had been long since Lorena Hickok began her cross-country trek. Four months earlier Harry Hopkins, the new federal relief administrator, had hired her to report on the relief efforts of the New Deal. Forget about statistics or the "social worker angle," he told her. "Talk with the unemployed, those who are on relief and those who aren't, and when you talk to them," he added, "don't ever forget that but for the grace of God you, I, any of our friends might be in their shoes."

Traveling 7000 miles, interviewing people in 32 states, driving along roads with ruts so deep she had trouble telling them from plowed fields, Hickok often felt tired. Sometimes she was plain out-of-sorts, as when *Time* magazine had run that "damned article" about her appointment. "I suppose I am 'a rotund lady with a husky voice' and 'baggy clothes,'" she admitted as she quoted the article. But to say she had gotten her job because of her friendship with the president's wife—that was too much! Knowing Eleanor Roosevelt hadn't hurt, but Hickok's talent and experience as a journalist put her on the federal payroll. She was the first woman hired by the Associated Press. In the days when female reporters were routinely handed delicate assignments, the hard-nosed "Hick" covered politics, kidnappings, and worse.

As she toured the country in 1933 and 1934, Hickok found that Roosevelt's relief program was falling short. Its half-billion-dollar subsidy to states, localities, and charities was still leaving out too many Americans, like the sharecropper Hickok discovered near Raleigh, North Carolina. He and his daughters had been living in a tobacco barn for two weeks on little more than weeds and table scraps. "Seems like we just keep goin' lower and lower," said the blue-eyed 16-year-old. To Hickok's surprise, hope still flickered in those eyes. She couldn't explain it until she noticed a pin on the girl's chest. It was a campaign button from the 1932 election—"a profile of the President." Hope sprang from the man in the White House.

Before Franklin D. Roosevelt and the New Deal, the federal government was far removed from ordinary citizens. In 1932 most Americans paid no federal income taxes. Federal welfare payments and public works had yet to be begun. Social security did not exist, and federal deposit insurance, the sole protection for the funds of depositors, would not be enacted for another year. The old order was widely perceived to have failed, and nothing, least of all government, seemed capable of reviv-

Franklin Roosevelt was inaugurated on March 4, 1933. Skies were overcast, but the previous day's rain had stopped. Washington, wrote a reporter, "welcomes the 'new deal,' even though it is not sure what the new deal is going to be."

Lorena Hickok (left) met Eleanor Roosevelt (right) in 1928 and thereafter served as her unofficial press adviser. She traveled with Eleanor during Franklin's campaign for the presidency in 1932, arranged her women-only press conferences, and became her closest friend. (In the center of this photograph is Paul Person, governor of the Virgin Islands.)

ing it. The only federal agency with which Americans had any contact at all was the post office. And after 1929, it usually delivered bad news.

As Lorena Hickok traveled the country in 1933, she detected a change. People were talking about government programs. Perhaps it was long-awaited contributions to relief or maybe reforms in securities and banking or the new recovery programs for industry and agriculture. Just as likely it was Franklin Roosevelt. Hickok seldom heard voters call themselves "Republicans" or "Democrats" anymore. Instead, she wrote, they were "for the president."

The mail to Washington carried other signs that plain people were looking to Washington and the president as at no time since the Civil War. During the first weekend after the inauguration nearly half a million letters and telegrams poured into the White House. For years the average remained a record 5000 to 8000 a day. Over half the letters came from those at the bottom of the economic heap. Most sought help, offered praise, or just expressed their gratitude.

Whatever the individual messages, their collective meaning was clear: Franklin D. Roosevelt and the New Deal had begun to restore hope. Though it never brought about a full recovery, the New Deal did improve economic conditions and provided relief to thousands of Americans. It reformed the economic system and committed the federal government to managing its ups and downs. Finally it extended the progressive drive to soften the impact of industrialization and translated decades of growing concern for the disadvantaged into a federal aid program. For the first time, Americans believed Washington would help them through a terrible crisis. The liberal state came of age: active, interventionist, and committed to social welfare.

THE EARLY NEW DEAL (1933–1935)

On March 4, 1933, as the clocks struck noon, Eleanor Roosevelt wondered if it were possible to "do anything to save America now." One-fourth of the workforce was unemployed. Thirty million families had no means of support. There wasn't enough money in the Treasury to meet the federal payroll.

Eleanor looked at her husband, who had just been sworn in as thirty-second president of the United States. Franklin Roosevelt removed his hand from the 300-year-old family Bible, turned to the podium, and solemnly addressed the crowd of over 100,000: "Let me assert my firm belief that the only thing we have to fear is fear itself—nameless, unreasoning, unjustified terror." Heeding the nation's call for "action, and action now," he promised to exercise "broad Executive power to wage a war against the emergency." The crowd cheered. Eleanor was terrified: "One has the feeling of going it blindly because we're in a tremendous stream, and none of us know where we're going to land."

The early New Deal unfolded in the spring of 1933 with a chaotic 100-day burst of legislation. It stressed recovery through planning and cooperation with business. But it also tried to furnish relief for the unemployed and to reform the economic system. Above all, the early New Deal revived national confidence. With Roosevelt in the White House, most Americans believed that they were in good hands, wherever they landed.

The Democratic Roosevelts

From the moment they entered it in 1933, Franklin and Eleanor—the Democratic Roosevelts—transformed the White House. No more footmen; no more buglers; above all, no more seven-course meals as Hoover had served. Instead White House guests got fare fit for a boardinghouse. Roosevelt's lunches of hash and a poached egg cost 19 cents. With millions of Americans tightening their belts, the president joined them in a symbolic gesture that nonetheless made his point of ending business as usual.

Such belt-tightening was new to Franklin Roosevelt. Born of an old Dutch family in New York, he grew up rich and pampered. He idolized his Republican cousin Theodore Roosevelt and mimicked his career, except as a Democrat. Like Theodore, Franklin was graduated from Harvard University (in 1904), won a seat in the New York State legislature (in 1910), secured an appointment as assistant secretary of the navy (in 1913), and ran for the vice presidency (in 1920). Then disaster struck. On vacation in the summer of 1921, Roosevelt fell ill with poliomyelitis. The disease paralyzed him from the waist down. For the rest of his life, he walked only with the aid of crutches and heavy steel braces, by rocking his torso from side to side.

Franklin Roosevelt

Roosevelt emerged from the ordeal with greater patience, deeper conviction, and more empathy for the unfortunates of the world. The disease probably enhanced his appeal to Depression America. When they saw Roosevelt, voters imagined not a spoon-fed aristocrat but a man who had triumphed over adversity. He won the governorship of New York in 1928. When the Depression struck, he created the first state relief agency in 1931, the Temporary Emergency Relief Administration. Aid to the jobless "must be extended by Government, not as a matter of charity, but as a matter of social duty," he explained.

Most photographers acceded to White House wishes that President Roosevelt never be shot from the waist down. After coming down with polio, Roosevelt helped to transform the ramshackle resort at Warm Springs, Georgia (where this picture was taken), into a treatment center for victims of the disease.

Roosevelt considered himself a progressive, especially in his concern for the protection of human and physical resources. But he adopted no single ideology and was wed to no particular method. A conventional budget balancer, he could abandon convention and be bold with sometimes costly social programs. He cared little about political principles or philosophical consistency. What he wanted were results. "Take a method and try it," he instructed his staff. "If it fails, try another. But above all try something." Experimentation became a hallmark of the New Deal. And so did effervescence. Meeting Franklin Roosevelt, Winston Churchill once said, was like "uncorking a bottle of champagne." Roosevelt bubbled with enthusiasm and good cheer. He simply loved being president. "Wouldn't you be president, if you could?" he asked a visitor to the White House. "Wouldn't anybody?"

Having followed a political path to the presidency, Roosevelt understood the value of public relations. As president, he held an unequaled number of press conferences (998) and hired the first press secretary. His famous "fireside chats" on radio brought him into American homes. When Roosevelt's reassuring voice came over the airwaves ("My friends, I want to tell you what has been done in the last few days, why it was done, and what the next steps are going to be."), people felt as if he had each of them in mind. "It was a sacred time," explained one women, "as if a father was talking to his children who were afraid."

Eleanor Roosevelt

Eleanor Roosevelt redefined what it meant to be First Lady. Never had a president's wife been so visible, so much of a crusader, so cool under fire. She was the first First Lady to hold weekly press conferences. Her column, "My Day," appeared in 135 newspapers, and her twice-weekly broadcasts made her a radio personality rivaling her husband. She became his eyes, ears, and legs, traveling 40,000 miles a year. Secret Service men code-named her "Rover."

Anna Eleanor Roosevelt was a distant cousin of Franklin and the niece of Theodore. Eleanor had known Franklin as a child, and the two married in 1905. By the 1920s, they had raised five children, endured a near divorce (as the result of Franklin's affair), and forged what would become the most potent political partnership in American history. Eleanor believed that she was only a spur to her husband. But she was an activist in her own right, as a teacher and social reformer before Franklin became president and after as a tireless advocate of the underdog. In the White House, she pressed her husband to hire more women and minorities. She supported antilynching and anti–poll tax measures when he would not and experimental towns for the homeless. By 1939 more Americans approved of her than of her husband.

Launching the New Deal

"This nation asks for action and action now," Roosevelt had said in his inaugural address. In his first hundred days in office he called Congress into emergency session and launched a record 15 major pieces of legislation. (The record stood until Lyndon Johnson's Great Society of the 1960s.) Congress shaped the programs, but with an urgency and speed rarely seen on Capitol Hill. So rapidly were bills sent from the White House and enacted that even Roosevelt confessed to being "a bit shell-shocked." Government began to dominate American economic life so much that conservatives feared the end of capitalism. But Roosevelt's aim was to save capitalism, even if that meant modifying it.

Before the election Roosevelt had gathered a group of lawyers and university professors called the "Brains Trust" to advise him on economic policy. Out of their recommendations came the early or "first" New Deal of government planning, intervention, and experimentation. Brains Trusters rejected Hoover's conclusion that the Great Depression was spawned overseas. Like Roosevelt, they saw it as the homegrown product of corporate greed, Republican mismanagement, and failed purchasing power. *The Brains Trust*

Brains Trusters disagreed over the means of achieving their goals but shared the broad aims of economic recovery, relief for the unemployed, and sweeping reform to soften the industrial order and to guard against another depression. All concurred that the first step was to save the banks. Without a sound credit structure, there could be no borrowing; without borrowing, no investment; without investment, no recovery. *Recovery, relief, and reform*

Saving the Banks

By the eve of the inauguration governors in 38 states had temporarily closed their banks to stem the withdrawal of deposits by worried customers. Since the crash of 1929, 5500 banks had failed as mortgages, securities, and other bank investments fell to a fraction of their former value. On March 5, the day after his inauguration, Roosevelt ordered every bank in the country closed for four days (later extended to eight). He called it a "bank holiday." Instead of panicking, Americans acted as if it were a holiday, using homemade currencies called "scrip" and bartering their services. On March 9, the president introduced emergency banking legislation. The House passed the measure, sight unseen, and the Senate endorsed it later in the day. Roosevelt signed it that night.

Emergency Banking Act

Rather than nationalizing the banks as radicals wanted, the Emergency Banking Act followed the modest course of extending federal assistance to them. Sound banks would reopen immediately with government support. Troubled banks would be handed over to federal "conservators," who would guide them to solvency. On Sunday, March 12, Roosevelt explained what was happening in the first of his fireside chats. When banks reopened the next day, deposits exceeded withdrawals. "Capitalism was saved in eight days," crowed one Roosevelt adviser.

To restore confidence in government, Roosevelt pushed through the Economy Act in March 1933, slashing $400 million in veterans' payments and $100 million in salaries from the federal budget. To guard against future stock crashes, financial reforms gave government greater authority to manage the currency and regulate stock transactions. In April 1933, Roosevelt dropped the gold standard and began experimenting with the value of the dollar to boost prices. Later that spring the Glass–Steagall Banking Act restricted speculation by banks and, more important, created

---

UNEMPLOYMENT RELIEF, 1934

The percentage of those receiving unemployment relief differed markedly throughout the nation. The farm belt of the plains was especially hard-hit, with 41 percent of South Dakota's citizens receiving federal benefits. In the East, the percentage dropped as low as 8 percent in some states.

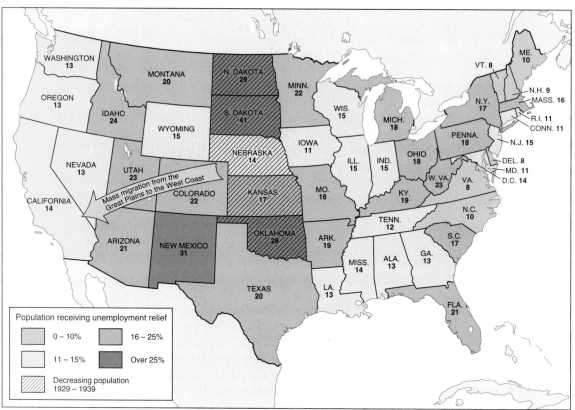

federal insurance for bank deposits of up to $2500. Under the Federal Deposit *Federal* Insurance Corporation, fewer banks failed for the rest of the decade than in the best *Deposit* year of the 1920s. The Securities Exchange Act (1934) established a new federal *Insurance* agency, the Securities and Exchange Commission, to oversee the stock market.

Relief for the Unemployed

Saving the banks and financial markets meant little if human suffering could not be relieved. Mortgage relief for the millions who had lost their homes came eventually in 1934 in the Home Owners' Loan Act. But to meet the urgent need to alleviate starvation, Congress created the Federal Emergency Relief Administration (FERA) in May 1933. Sitting amid unpacked boxes, gulping coffee and chain-smoking, former social worker Harry Hopkins spent $5 million of a $500 million appropriation in his first two hours as head of the new agency. In its two-year existence, FERA furnished more than $1 billion in grants to states, local areas, and private charities.

As much as Hoover, Roosevelt feared that public assistance might become a "narcotic," but he recognized that short-term need took precedence over long-term dangers. As the winter of 1933–1934 approached, Hopkins persuaded the president to expand relief with an innovative shift from government giveaways to a work pro- *Work relief* gram. Paying someone "to do something socially useful preserves a man's morale," Hopkins explained.

The Civil Works Administration (CWA) employed 4 million Americans. Many had useful jobs repairing schools, laying sewer pipes, building roads. Others, like the balloon brigade that rousted starlings from the eaves of federal buildings, gave rise to

Despite the popularity of Roosevelt and the New Deal, there were critics. New federal agencies, designated by their initials, became easy targets of satirists and cartoonists. In this 1934 cartoon, a wincing Uncle Sam receives an unwelcomed set of tattoos, each signifying a New Deal agency.

the stereotype of the worthless government "boondoggle." Alarmed at the high cost of the program, Roosevelt disbanded the CWA in the spring of 1934. It nonetheless furnished a new weapon against unemployment and an important precedent for future relief programs.

Another work relief program established during the hundred days proved even more creative. The Civilian Conservation Corps (CCC) was Roosevelt's pet project. It combined his concern for conservation with compassion for youth. The CCC took unmarried, 18- to 25-year-olds from relief rolls and sent them into the woods and fields to plant trees, build parks, and fight soil erosion. During its 10 years, the CCC provided 2.5 million young men with jobs (which prompted critics who felt women were being neglected to chant, "Where's the she, she, she?").

Tennessee Valley Authority

New Dealers intended relief programs to last only through the crisis. But the Tennessee Valley Authority (TVA)—a massive public works project created in 1933—made a continuing contribution to regional planning. For a decade, planners had dreamed of transforming the flood-ridden basin of the Tennessee River, one of the poorest areas of the country, with a program of regional development and social engineering. The TVA constructed a series of dams along the seven-state basin to control flooding, improve navigation, and generate cheap electric power. In cooperation with state and local officials, it also launched social programs to stamp out malaria, provide library bookmobiles, and create recreational lakes.

Like many New Deal programs, the TVA left a mixed legacy. It saved 3 million acres from erosion, multiplied the average income in the valley tenfold, and repaid its original investment in federal taxes. Its cheap electricity helped to bring down the rates of private utility companies and to increase usage. By the 1980s, the Tennessee Valley region was using 100 billion kilowatt-hours of electricity annually, some 65 times the number used before the TVA. But the experiment in regional planning also pushed thousands of families from their land, failed to end poverty, and created an agency that became one of the worst polluters in the country.

Planning for Industrial Recovery

Planning, not just for regions but for the whole economy, seemed to many New Dealers the key to recovery. If businesses were allowed to plan and cooperate over production, distribution, pricing, and wages, the ruthless competition that was driving down the economy might be controlled and the riddle of industrial recovery solved. Business leaders had been urging such a course since 1931. In June 1933, under the National Industrial Recovery Act (NIRA), Roosevelt put planning to work for industry.

Public Works Administration

The legislation created two new agencies. The Public Works Administration (PWA) was designed to boost consumer spending with a $3.3 billion public works program. The workers it hired would spend their paychecks and stimulate production, while its orders for factory and other goods would send waves of capital rippling through the economy. Harold Ickes, the prickly interior secretary who headed PWA, built the Triborough Bridge and Lincoln Tunnel in New York, the port city of Brownsville, Texas, and two aircraft carriers. But he was so fearful of waste and corruption that he never spent funds quickly enough to jump-start the economy.

National Recovery Administration

A second federal agency, the National Recovery Administration (NRA), aimed directly at controlling competition. Originally designed to work in tandem with the

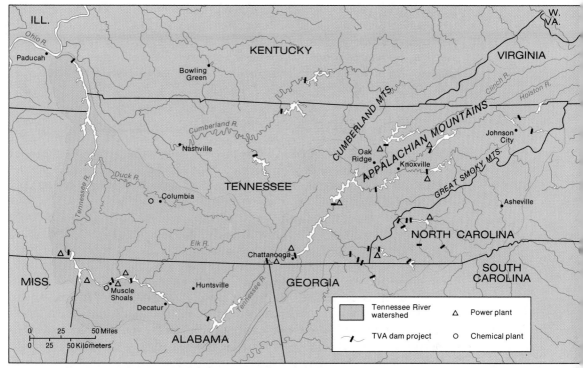

THE TENNESSEE VALLEY AUTHORITY
The Tennessee River basin encompassed parts of seven states. Rivers honeycombed the area, which received some of the heaviest rainfall in the nation. A long-time dream of Senator George Norris, the Tennessee Valley Authority, created in 1933, constructed some 20 dams and improved 5 others over the next 20 years to control chronic flooding and erosion and to produce cheap hydroelectric power and fertilizers.

PWA, the NRA soon found itself operating alone, without the incentives to businesses furnished by prized PWA projects. Under NRA chief Hugh Johnson, representatives from government and business (and also from labor and consumer groups) drew up "codes of fair practices." Industry by industry, the codes established minimum prices and wages and maximum hours. No company could seek a competitive edge by cutting prices or wages below certain levels or by working a few employees mercilessly and firing the rest.

Roosevelt cast the NRA as a "partnership in planning" between government and business modeled on the War Industries Board of the First World War. To permit such cooperation, NIRA suspended antitrust laws but in return required business to accept key demands of labor. Section 7a of the NIRA guaranteed union rights to organize and bargain with management (thus ensuring that if prices jumped, so too might wages). And each code promised improved working conditions and outlawed such practices as child labor and sweatshops.

Eventually more than 600 codes governed almost every industry in America, from building cars to making dog food. No business was forced to comply, for fear that government coercion might be ruled unconstitutional. The NRA relied instead on voluntary participation. A publicity campaign of parades, posters, and massive public pledges exhorted businesses to join the NRA and consumers to buy only NRA-sanctioned products. More than 2 million employers eventually signed up. In store windows and on merchandise, shiny decals with blue-eagle crests alerted customers that "We Do Our Part."

The NRA in Trouble

For all the hoopla, the NRA failed to bring recovery. Big businesses shaped the codes to their advantage. Often they limited production and raised prices, sometimes beyond what they normally might have been. Not all businesses joined the NRA, and those that did often found the codes too complicated or costly to follow. The NRA also tried to cover too many businesses. The relatively few NRA inspectors had trouble keeping up with all the complaints. Even NRA support for labor tottered, for Section 7a guaranteeing union rights had no mechanism for enforcement.

Business survived under the NRA, but without increasing production there was no incentive for expansion, employment, and investment. "This was scarcity economics, and it meant reduced purchasing power," concluded one historian. Under such conditions hard times could last indefinitely. And in the short run, despite an enthusiastic start, the NRA was soon spawning little but evasion and criticism. Labor leaders began calling it the "National Run Around," while consumers complained about "NRA prices and Hoover wages."

On May 27, 1935, the Supreme Court struck down the floundering NRA in *Schecter Poultry Corp. v. United States.* The justices unanimously ruled that the NRA had exceeded federal power over commerce among the states by regulating the Schecter brothers' poultry business within the state of New York. Privately Roosevelt was relieved to be rid of the NRA. It had become an "awful headache." But he and other New Dealers were plainly shaken by the grounds of the decision. They were relying on federal power to regulate commerce as a means of fighting the Depression. Their distress only grew when Justice Benjamin Cardozo added a chilling afterthought: the NRA's code-making represented "an unconstitutional delegation of legislative power" to the executive branch. Without the ability to make rules and regulations, all the executive agencies of the New Deal might flounder.

Planning for Agriculture

Like planning for industry, New Deal planning for agriculture relied on private interests—the farmers—to act as the principal planners. Under the Agricultural Adjustment Act of 1933, producers of basic commodities agreed to limit their own production. The AAA, in turn, paid farmers for not planting crops, while a tax on millers, cotton ginners, and other processors financed the payments. In theory, production quotas would reduce surpluses, demand for farm commodities would rise, as would prices, and agriculture would recover.

Agricultural Adjustment Administration

In practice the Agricultural Adjustment Administration (AAA) did help to increase prices. Unlike the code-ridden NRA, the AAA wisely confined coverage to seven major commodities and paid close attention to them. As a way to push prices even higher, the new Commodity Credit Corporation gave loans to farmers who stored their crops rather than sold them—a modification of the Populists' old sub-treasury plan (see page 726). Farm income rose from $5.5 billion in 1932 to $8.7 billion in 1935.

Not all the gains in farm income were the result of government actions or free of problems. In the mid-1930s dust storms, droughts, and floods helped reduce harvests and push up prices. The AAA, moreover, failed to distribute its benefits equally. Large landowners controlled decisions over which plots would be left fallow. In the South this frequently meant cutting the acreage of tenants and sharecroppers or forcing them out. Even when they reduced the acreage that they themselves plowed, big farmers could increase yields, since they had the money and equipment to cultivate more intensively. And just at the moment the AAA was working to have farmers grow less, the Department of Agriculture was performing its traditional job of teaching farmers how to grow more. Not for the first time or the last would New Dealers find themselves working at cross-purposes with their own government.

In 1936 the Supreme Court voided the AAA. In *Butler v. U.S.*, the six-justice majority concluded that the government had no right to regulate agriculture either by limiting production or by taxing processors. A hastily drawn replacement, the Soil Conservation and Domestic Allotment Act (1936), addressed the complaints. Farmers were now subsidized for practicing "conservation"—taking soil-depleting crops off the land—and paid from general revenues instead of a special tax. A second Agricultural Adjustment Act in 1938 returned production quotas.

Other agencies tried to help impoverished farmers. The Farm Credit Administration refinanced about a fifth of all farm mortgages. In 1935 the Resettlement Administration gave marginal farmers a fresh start by moving them to better land. Beginning in 1937 the Farm Security Administration furnished low-interest loans to help tenants buy family farms. In neither case did the rural poor have enough political leverage to obtain sufficient funds from Congress. Fewer than 5000 families (of a projected 500,000) were resettled, and less than 2 percent of tenant farmers received loans.

After years of Hoover paralysis, Roosevelt's first hundred days nonetheless broke national despair. The economic depression proved more resistant. Though Roosevelt regarded recovery as his primary goal, the New Deal never achieved it. Conditions improved, but the economy only limped along. As late as 1939 industrial production had yet to reach 1929 levels. Nearly 10 million Americans walked the streets in search of work, and displaced farm families still huddled around campfires on western highways. Perhaps no one could have solved the riddle of recovery, but Roosevelt tried and in 1935 he began boldly to address a second riddle: how to reform the system so that the Great Depression did not return.

A SECOND NEW DEAL (1935–1936)

"Boys—this is our hour," crowed Harry Hopkins in the spring of 1935. A year earlier voters had broken precedent by returning the party in power to office, giving the Democrats their largest majorities in decades. With the presidential election of 1936 only a year away, Hopkins figured that time was short: "We've got to get everything we want—a works program, social security, wages and hours, everything—now or never."

Hopkins calculated correctly. In 1935 politics, swept along by a torrent of protest, helped to produce a "second hundred days" of lawmaking and a "Second New Deal." The emphasis shifted from planning and cooperation with business to greater regulation of business, broader relief, and bolder reform. A limited welfare state emerged, in which government was finally committed—at least symbolically—to guaranteeing the well-being of needy Americans. Roosevelt justified this not only as a practical matter of maintaining the purchasing power of consumers. In his words, it was a matter of "social duty."

Voices of Protest

In 1934 a mob of 6000 stormed the Minneapolis city hall, demanding more relief and higher pay for government jobs. In San Francisco, longshoremen walked off the job. Soon a general strike paralyzed the city. Before the year was over, 1.5 million workers had joined in 1800 strikes. Conditions were improving but not quickly enough, and across the country voices of protest gathered strength.

From the right came the charges of a few wealthy business executives and conservatives that Roosevelt was an enemy of private property and a dictator in the making. His welfare measures were ruining the country. "Five Negroes on my place in South Carolina refused work this Spring . . . saying they had easy jobs with the government," reported a retired Du Pont executive. Moved by his predicament, a group

Liberty League of corporate leaders and conservative Democrats founded the American Liberty League in August 1934. Despite spending $1 million in anti–New Deal advertising, the League won little support and only helped to convince the president that cooperation with business was failing.

In California discontented voters took over the Democratic party and turned sharply to the left by nominating novelist Upton Sinclair, a Socialist, for governor.

End Poverty in California Running under the slogan "End Poverty in California" (EPIC), Sinclair proposed to confiscate idle factories and land and permit the unemployed to produce for their own use. Republicans mounted a no-holds-barred counterattack, including fake newsreels depicting Sinclair as a Bolshevik, atheist, and free-lover. Sinclair lost the election but won nearly 1 million votes.

Huey Long Huey P. Long, the flamboyant senator from Louisiana, had ridden to power on a wave of rural discontent against banks, corporations, and machine politics as usual. As governor of Louisiana, he pushed through reforms regulating utilities, building roads and schools, even distributing free schoolbooks. By turns comical and ruthless, Long used his power to feather his own financial nest, and his private police force was not above kidnapping political opponents. Detractors called him "dictator"; most Louisianans affectionately called him the "Kingfish," after a character in the popular "Amos 'n' Andy" radio show.

Louisiana Governor and Senator Huey Long promised to make "every man a king," but critics predicted that only Long would wear the crown. Power-hungry and charismatic, the "Kingfish" made no secret of his presidential aspirations.

In the early years of the Depression, demonstrations of the unemployed, some organized by Communists and other radicals, broke out all over the country. On March 6, 1930, a Communist-led protest at Union Square in New York turned into an ugly riot. In 1935 Communist parties, under orders from Moscow, adopted the more cooperative strategy of allying with democratic and socialist groups against fascism, proclaiming in the United States that "Communism is twentieth century Americanism."

Breaking with Roosevelt in 1933, Long pledged to bring about recovery by making "every man a king." His plan to "Share Our Wealth" was drastic but simple: the government would limit the size of all fortunes and confiscate the rest. Every family would then be guaranteed an annual income of $2500 and an estate of $5000, enough to buy a house, an automobile, and a radio (over which Long had already built a national following).

Despite wild underestimates of subsidies for the have-nots, Long was addressing a real problem, the uneven distribution of wealth. By 1935, one year after his Share Our Wealth organization was begun, it boasted 27,000 clubs with files containing nearly 8 million names. Democratic National Committee members shuddered at polls showing that Long might capture up to 4 million votes in 1936, enough to put a Republican in the White House. But late in 1935, in the corridors of the Louisiana capitol, Long was shot to death by a disgruntled constituent whose family had been wronged by the Long political machine.

Father Charles Coughlin was Long's urban counterpart. Where Long explained the Depression as the result of bloated fortunes, Coughlin blamed the banks. In weekly broadcasts from the Shrine of the Little Flower in suburban Detroit, the "Radio Priest" conjured up old devils to his working-class, largely Catholic audience: international bankers (many of them Jewish, Coughlin also charged) had toppled the world economy by manipulating gold-backed currencies.

Charles Coughlin

911

Across the urban North, 30 to 40 million Americans gathered around their radios to listen to Coughlin's message. Like Long, Coughlin promised to solve a real problem—the inadequate money supply—with specious solutions. He would end the Depression with simple strokes: nationalizing banks, inflating the currency with silver, spreading work. (None would have worked because each would have dampened investment, the key to recovery.) When Roosevelt refused to adopt Coughlin's schemes, the priest broke with the president. In 1934 Coughlin organized the National Union for Social Justice to pressure both parties. As the election of 1936 approached, the Union loomed ominously as a third-party threat.

Francis Townsend

A less ominous challenge came from Dr. Francis Townsend, a California physician who had recently retired from the public health service. Moved by the plight of elderly Americans without pension plans or medical insurance, Townsend set up Old Age Revolving Pensions, Limited, in 1934. He proposed to have the government pay $200 a month to those 60 years or older who quit their jobs and spent the money within 30 days. For funding, the government would levy a 2 percent tax on commercial transactions. The Townsend plan was thus a means of furnishing aid to the elderly, jobs to the unemployed (who would fill the slots vacated by retirees), and purchasing power to consumers, since recipients would have to spend their government checks immediately.

As much as the elderly needed help, the Townsend plan—like the plans of Long and Coughlin—was economic hokum. Townsendites expected to spend more than half the national income to compensate less than one-tenth of the population. The plan would create no new jobs, and its 2 percent sales tax would fall on everyone, including impoverished American consumers. By 1936 Townsend clubs counted 3.5 million members, most of them small businessmen and farmers at or beyond retirement age.

For all their differences, Sinclair, Long, Coughlin, Townsend, and other critics struck a few of the same notes. Although the cures they proposed were simplistic, the problems they addressed were serious: a maldistribution of goods and wealth, inadequacies in the money supply, the plight of the elderly. They attacked the growing control of corporations, banks, and government over individuals and communities. And they created mass political movements based on social as well as economic dissatisfaction. When Sinclair supporters pledged to produce for their own use and Long's followers swore to "share our wealth," when Coughlinites damned the "monied interests" and Townsendites thumped their Bibles at foul-ups in Washington, they were also trying to protect their freedom and their communities from the intrusions of big business and big government.

The Second Hundred Days

By the spring of 1935, the forces of discontent were pushing Roosevelt to bolder action. So was Congress. With Democrats accounting for more than two-thirds of both houses, they were prepared to outspend even the president in extending the New Deal. The 100 days from April through mid-July, the "second hundred days," produced a legislative barrage that moved the New Deal toward Roosevelt's ultimate destination—"a little to the left of center," where government would permanently seek to soften the impact of industrial excesses, protect the needy, and compensate for swings in the economy.

speech and expression, freedom of worship, freedom from want, and freedom from fear. In effect, the Atlantic Charter was an unofficial statement of war aims.

By the time of the Argentia meetings, American destroyers in the North Atlantic were stalking German U-boats and reporting their whereabouts to British commanders. Given the harsh weather and aggressive American policy, incidents were inevitable. In October a U-boat sank the destroyer *Reuben James* with the loss of more than 100 American sailors. That act increased public support for the Allied cause. Yet when interventionists criticized Roosevelt for being too cautious, isolationists attacked him for being too provocative. As late as September 1941 eight of ten Americans opposed entering the hostilities. Few in the United States suspected that an attack by Japan, not Germany, would bring a unified America into the war.

Disaster in the Pacific

Worried most by the prospect of a German victory in Europe, Roosevelt avoided a showdown with Japan. The navy, the president told his cabinet, had "not got enough ships to go round, and every little episode in the Pacific means fewer ships in the Atlantic." But precisely because American and European attention lay elsewhere, Japan was emboldened to expand militarily into Southeast Asia.

Japanese leaders were able to justify their expansion easily enough. They viewed their Greater East Asia Co-Prosperity Sphere as simply an Asian version of the Monroe Doctrine. Japan, the preeminent power in the region, would replace the Europeans as a promoter of economic development. To American leaders, however, Japan's actions threatened the principles of the open-door policy and the survival of Chinese independence. By the summer of 1941 Japanese forces controlled the China coast and all major cities. When its army marched into French Indochina (present-day Vietnam) in July, Japan stood ready to conquer all of the Southeast Asian peninsula and the oil-rich Dutch East Indies. *Japanese expansion*

Japan's thrust into Indochina forced Roosevelt to act. He embargoed trade, froze Japanese assets in American banks, and barred shipments of vital scrap iron and petroleum. When the Dutch slapped a similar embargo on their oil from the East Indies, Japan faced a turning point. If the United States would not supply needed petroleum, it would be forced to attack the Dutch East Indies. Prime Minister Fumimaro Konoye still hoped to negotiate a settlement and proposed a summit meeting with Roosevelt. In fact, the two nations' goals were so at odds that no diplomatic resolution was possible. The Japanese ambassador pressed the United States to recognize recent conquests and Japanese dominance in Asia. Secretary of State Cordell Hull replied that Japan must renounce the Tripartite Pact with Italy and Germany and withdraw from China before any summit talks could begin.

In October the militant General Hideki Tojo replaced the more moderate Prime Minister Konoye. With the war party firmly in control, Japan began preparing surprise attacks on American positions in Guam, the Philippines, and Hawaii. They planned one final round of diplomacy before striking.

For their part, American military leaders urged Roosevelt to avoid conflict until the United States had built up its national defenses. Massive Japanese troop movements southward indicated an assault on British and Dutch holdings. If the Japanese attacked American possessions, most expected the blow to fall on Guam or the Philippines. In late November American intelligence located, and then lost, a Japanese armada in Hitokappu Bay in Japan. Observing strict radio silence, the six carriers and their escorts steamed across the North Pacific toward the American base at Pearl Harbor in Hawaii. On Sunday morning, December 7, 1941, the first wave of Japanese planes roared down on the Pacific Fleet lying at anchor. For more than an hour the Japanese pounded the harbor and nearby airfields. Altogether 19 ships— the heart of the Pacific Fleet—were sunk or battered. Practically all of the 200 American aircraft were damaged or destroyed. Only the aircraft carriers, by chance on maneuvers, escaped the worst naval defeat in American history.

In Washington, Secretary of War Henry Stimson could not believe the news. "My God! This can't be true, this must mean the Philippines." Later that day the Japanese did attack the Philippines, along with Guam, Midway, and British forces in Hong Kong and the Malay peninsula. On December 8, Franklin Roosevelt told a stunned nation that "yesterday, December 7, 1941" was "a date which will live in infamy." America, the "reluctant belligerent," was in the war at last. Three days later Hitler declared war on the "half Judaized and the other half Negrified" people of the United States. Italy quickly followed suit.

COUNTERPOINT

Did Roosevelt deliberately invite war?

Had Roosevelt known the attack on Pearl Harbor was coming? Some critics have charged that the president deliberately contrived to bring war about. For months, American intelligence had been cracking some of Japan's secret codes. Much information indicated that Pearl Harbor was at risk. Yet Roosevelt left the fleet exposed, seeming almost to provoke an attack to bring the United States into the war. Was it mere coincidence that the vital aircraft carriers were at sea? That only the obsolete battleships were left at Pearl Harbor?

This argument, however, is based on circumstantial, not documentary, evidence. Roosevelt's defenders (and they include most historians) have countered that he wanted to fight Germany more than Japan. If he really had wished to provoke an incident leading to war, one in Atlantic waters would have served him far better. More important, the intelligence signals intercepted by American code-breakers were confusing. Analysts lost track of the Japanese fleet as it moved toward Hawaii. Secretary of War Stimson had good reason to be astonished when the fleet attacked Pearl Harbor."

In the end, it seems equally plausible to argue that cultural misperceptions explained the coming of war better than any conspiracy theory. American leaders were surprised by the attack on Pearl Harbor because they could not quite believe that the Japanese were daring or resourceful enough to attack an American stronghold some 4000 miles from Japan. Japanese militarists counted on a surprise attack to give them time to build a line of defense strong enough to discourage weak-willed Westerners from continuing the war. As it turned out, both calculations were wrong.

A GLOBAL WAR

British Prime Minister Winston Churchill greeted the news of Pearl Harbor with shock but, even more, elation. Great Britain would no longer stand alone in the North Atlantic and the Pacific wars. "We have won the war," he thought, and that night he slept "the sleep of the saved and thankful."

More than Franklin Roosevelt ever could, Japan's shocking triumph over U.S. forces united Americans. And as Churchill recognized, only with the Americans fully committed to war could the Allies make full use of the enormous material and human resources of the United States. Still, the Allies needed to secure an alliance between the Anglo-American democracies and the Soviet Communist dictatorship. And they needed to find a strategy to win both the war and the peace to follow.

Strategies for War

Within two weeks, Churchill was in Washington, meeting with Roosevelt to coordinate production schedules for ships, planes, and armaments. The numbers they announced were so high that some critics openly laughed—at first. A year later combined British, Canadian, and American production boards not only met but exceeded the schedules.

Roosevelt and Churchill also planned grand strategy. Outraged by the attack on Pearl Harbor, many Americans thought Japan should be the war's primary target. But the two leaders had always agreed that Germany posed the greater threat. The Pacific war, they decided, would be fought as a holding action, while the Allies concentrated on Europe. In a global war, in which arms and resources had to be allocated carefully, these long-range decisions would prove important. But in the short term, the Allies faced a daunting future indeed.

Defeat Germany first

Gloomy Prospects

By summer's end in 1942 the Allies faced defeat. The Nazis were massed outside the Soviet Union's three major cities—Leningrad, Moscow, and Stalingrad. In North Africa General Erwin Rommel, the famed "Desert Fox," swept into Egypt with his Afrika Korps and stood within striking distance of the Suez Canal—a crucial link to the resources of the British empire. German U-boats in the North Atlantic threatened to break the ocean link between the United States and Britain. U-boat sailors called the first six months of 1942 "the American hunting season," as they sank 400 Allied ships in U.S. territorial waters. So deadly were these "Wolfpacks" that merchant sailors developed a grim humor about sleeping. Those on freighters carrying iron ore slept above decks, since the heavily laden ships could sink in less than a minute. On flammable oil tankers, however, sailors closed their doors, undressed, and slept soundly. If a torpedo hit, no one would survive anyway.

U-boat war

In the Far East the Allies fared no better. Japanese forces had invaded the Philippines, British Malaya, and the Dutch East Indies. The supposedly impregnable British bastion of Singapore fell in just one week, and at the Battle of Java Sea, the Japanese navy destroyed almost the entire remaining Allied naval force in the western Pacific. In April 1942 General Douglas MacArthur, commander of American forces in the Philippines, fled to Australia. In what appeared to be an empty pledge, he vowed, "I shall return." Left behind with scant arms and food, American and Philippine troops on Bataan and Corregidor put up a heroic but doomed struggle. By summer no significant Allied forces stood between the Japanese and India or Australia.

Fall of the Philippines

The chain of spectacular victories disguised fatal weaknesses within the Axis alliance. Japan and Germany were fighting separate wars, each on two fronts. They

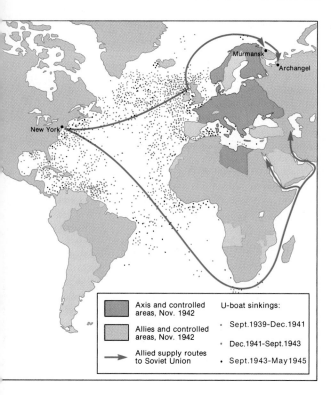

never coordinated strategies. Vast armies in China and Russia drained them of both manpower and supplies. Brutal occupation policies made enemies of conquered populations. Axis armies had to use valuable forces to maintain control and move supplies. The Nazis were especially harsh. They launched a major campaign to exterminate Europe's Jews, Slavs, and Gypsies. Resistance movements grew as the victims of Axis aggression fought back. At the war's height 50 countries joined the Allies, who referred to themselves as the United Nations.

A Grand Alliance

Defeat at first obscured the Allies' strengths. Chief among these were the human resources of the Soviet Union and the industrial capacity of the United States. During World War II Americans would develop a global economy. Safe from the fighting, American farms and factories could produce enough food and war materials to supply two separate wars at once. By the end of the war American factories had turned out 300,000 airplanes, 87,000 ships, 400,000 artillery pieces, 102,000 tanks and self-propelled guns, and 47 million tons of ammunition.

The Big Three   The Allies benefited too from exceptional leadership. The "Big Three"—Joseph Stalin, Winston Churchill, and Franklin Roosevelt—all had shortcomings but were able to maintain a unity of purpose that eluded Axis leaders. All three understood the global nature of the war. To a remarkable degree they managed to set aside their differences in pursuit of a common goal—the defeat of Nazi Germany. The arch–anti-Communist Churchill pledged Britain's resources to assist the defense of the world's largest Communist state. The anti-imperialist Roosevelt poured American resources into the war effort of two of Europe's major imperial powers.

To be sure, each nation had its own needs. Russian forces faced 3.5 million Axis troops along a 1600-mile front in eastern Europe. To ease the pressure on those troops, Stalin repeatedly called upon the Allies to open a second front in western Europe. So urgent were his demands that one Allied diplomat remarked that Stalin's foreign minister knew only four words in English: *yes, no,* and *second front.* But Churchill and Roosevelt felt compelled to turn Stalin down. In August 1942 the western Allies lacked the massive, well-trained force needed for a successful invasion of Europe. Churchill himself flew to Moscow to give Stalin the bad news: no second front in Europe until 1943. Postponed again until mid-1944, the second front became a source of festering Russian discontent.

Yet after an initial surge of anger over the postponement, Stalin accepted Churchill's rationale for a substitute action. British and American forces would invade North Africa by the end of 1942. Code-named Operation Torch, the North African campaign could be mounted quickly. Equally important, it could bring British and American troops into direct combat with the Germans and stood an excellent chance of succeeding. Here was an example of how personal contact among the Big Three ensured Allied cooperation. The alliance sometimes bent but never broke. *Operation Torch*

The Naval War in the Pacific

Despite the Allied decision to concentrate on defeating Germany first, the earliest successes came in the Pacific. At the Battle of Coral Sea in May 1942 planes from the aircraft carriers *Yorktown* and *Lexington* stopped a large Japanese invading force headed for Port Moresby in New Guinea (see the map, page 968). For the first time in history two fleets fought without seeing each other. The age of naval aviation had arrived. The Japanese fleet actually inflicted greater damage but decided to turn back to nurse its wounds. Had they captured Port Moresby, the Japanese could have severed Allied shipping routes to Australia.

To extend Japan's defenses, Admiral Yamamoto ordered the capture of Midway, a small island guarding the approach west of Hawaii. The Americans, in possession of decoded Japanese transmissions, were ready. On June 3, as the Japanese main fleet bore down on Midway, a patrol plane from the American carrier task force spotted smoke from the ships. Aircraft from the carriers *Hornet, Enterprise,* and *Yorktown* sank four enemy carriers, a cruiser, and three destroyers. The United States lost only the *Yorktown.* More important, the Japanese lost many of their best carrier pilots, who were more difficult to replace than planes. The Battle of Midway broke Japanese naval supremacy in the Pacific and stalled Japan's offensive. In August 1942 American forces launched their first offensive—on the Solomon Islands, east of New Guinea. With the landing of American marines on the key island of Guadalcanal, the Allies started on the bloody road to Japan and victory. *Midway*

Turning Points in Europe

By the fall of 1942 the Allies had their first successes in the European war. At El Alamein, 75 miles from the Suez Canal, British forces under General Bernard Montgomery broke through Rommel's lines. Weeks later, the Allies launched Operation Torch, the invasion of North Africa. Under the command of General Dwight D. Eisenhower, Allied forces swept eastward through Morocco and Algeria. They were halted in February 1943 at the Kasserine Pass in Tunisia, but General George S. Patton regrouped them and masterminded an impressive string of victories. By May 1943 Rommel had fled from North Africa, leaving behind 300,000 German troops.

Stalingrad   Success in North Africa provided a stirring complement to the Russian stand at Stalingrad. From August 1942 until February 1943 Axis and Soviet armies pounded each other with more than a million troops. In one of the bloodiest engagements in history, each side suffered more casualties than the Americans did during the entire war. When it was over, the Germans had lost an army and their momentum. Stalin's forces went on the offensive, moving south and west through the Ukraine toward Poland and Romania. By the fall of 1942 the Allies had also gained the edge in the war for the Atlantic. Supplies moved easily after antisubmarine forces sank 785 out of the nearly 1200 U-boats the Germans built.

The Battle of Midway proved the importance of naval airpower. The Japanese suffered major losses of aircraft carriers and pilots. Never again after Midway would the Japanese navy offer a major threat.

THOSE WHO FOUGHT

Mobilizing for war brought together Americans from all regions, social classes, and ethnic backgrounds. "The first time I ever heard a New England accent," recalled a midwesterner, "was at Fort Benning. The southerner was an exotic creature to me. The people from the farms. The New York street smarts." More than any other social institution the army acted as a melting pot. It also offered educational opportunities and job skills or suggested the need for them. "I could be a technical sergeant only I haven't had enough school," reported one Navajo soldier in a letter home to New Mexico. "Make my little brother go to school even if you have to lasso him."

In waging the world's first global war, the U.S. armed forces swept millions of Americans into new worlds and new experiences. When Pearl Harbor came, the army had 1.6 million men in uniform. By 1945 it had more than 7 million; the navy, 3.9 million; the army air corps, 2.3 million; and the marines, 600,000. Nineteen-year-olds who had never left home found themselves swept off to Europe or to the South Pacific. At basic training new recruits were subjected to forms of regimentation—the army haircut, foul-mouthed drill sergeants, and barracks life—they had seldom experienced in other areas of America's democratic culture.

As with most wars, the infantry bore the brunt of the fighting and dying. They *A GI's life* suffered 90 percent of the battlefield casualties. In all, almost 400,000 Americans

Many young GIs at first looked forward to going into battle. "I was going to gain my manhood," recalled one soldier. But combat soon hardened such troops. The same soldier, after taking part in an assault on the French coast, concluded that war was "a nightmare." Looking at newly arrived troops, he now had but one thought: "You poor innocents." Donald Dickson's portrait of one such war-weary GI (left) is titled *Too Many, Too Close, Too Long.*

died and more than 600,000 were wounded. But service in the military did not mean constant combat. Most battles were reasonably short, followed by long periods of waiting and preparation. The army used almost 2 million soldiers just to move supplies. Yet even during the lull in battle, the soldiers' biggest enemy, disease, stalked them: malaria, dysentery, typhus, and even plague. In the Pacific theater, the thermometer sometimes rose to over 110 degrees Fahrenheit.

Wherever they fought, American soldiers usually lived in foxholes dug by hand with small shovels. Whenever possible they turned a hole in the ground into a home. "The American soldier is a born housewife," observed war correspondent Ernie Pyle. Between battles, movies were about the only entertainment many troops had. Each film was a tenuous link to a more comfortable world at home, a place American soldiers yearned for with special intensity. It was not a country or an idea for which they fought so much as a set of memories—a house, a car, Mom and Pop.

Uneasy Recruits

African Americans at war

Minorities enlisted in unusually large numbers because the services offered training and opportunities unavailable in civilian life. Still, prejudice against African Americans and other minorities remained high. The army was strictly segregated and generally assigned black soldiers to noncombatant roles. The navy accepted them only as cooks and servants. At first the air corps and marines would not take them at all. The American Red Cross even kept "black" and "white" blood plasma separated, as if there were a difference. (Ironically, a black physician, Charles Drew, had invented the process allowing plasma to be stored.)

Despite the persistence of prejudice, more than a million black men and women served. As the war progressed, leaders of the black community pressured the military

In *Shipping Out,* black artist Jacob Lawrence, a veteran of the New Deal's Federal Arts Project, commemorated black troops heading overseas in the crowded confines of a troop ship. African Americans in segregated units served more often in service roles than in combat. It was ironic that, in a war against Nazi racism, race remained a central issue among Americans. Lawrence was certainly aware of such ironies; the portrayal of soldiers crowded onto their bunks recalls eerily the packing of slave transport ships from earlier centuries.

to ease segregation and allow black soldiers a more active role. The army did form some black combat units, usually led by white officers, as well as a black air corps unit. By mid-1942 black officers were being trained and graduated from integrated officer candidate schools at the rate of 200 a month. More than 80 black pilots won the Distinguished Flying Cross.

Choices for homosexuals

Homosexuals who wished to join the military faced a dilemma. Would their sexual orientation be discovered during the screening process? And if they were rejected and word got back to their parents or communities, would they be stigmatized? Many took that chance. Charles Rowland, from Arizona, recalled that he and other gay friends "were not about to be deprived the privilege of serving our country in a time of great national emergency by virtue of some stupid regulation about being gay." Those who did pass the screening test found themselves in gender-segregated bases, where life in an overwhelmingly male or female environment allowed many, for the first time in their lives, to meet like-minded gay men and women. Like other servicemen and -women, they served in a host of different roles, fighting and dying on the battlefield or doing the unglamorous jobs that kept the army going.

Women at War

World War II brought an end to the military as an exclusive male enclave that women entered only as nurses. During the prewar mobilization, Eleanor Roosevelt and other female leaders had campaigned for a regular military organization for women. The War Department came up with a compromise that allowed women to join the Women's Army Auxiliary Corps (WAAC), but only with inferior status and lower pay.

WACs By 1943 the "Auxiliary" had dropped out of the title: WAACs became WACs, with full army status, equal ranks, and equal pay. (The navy had a similar force called the WAVEs.)

Women could look with a mixture of pride and resentment on their wartime military service. Thousands served close to the battlefields, working as technicians, mechanics, radio operators, postal clerks, and secretaries. Although filling a vital need, these were largely traditional female jobs that implied a separate and inferior status. Until 1944 women were prevented by law from serving in war zones, even as noncombatants. There were female pilots, but they were restricted to shuttling planes behind the lines. At many posts WAVEs and WACs lived behind barbed wire and could move about only in groups under armed escort.

WAR PRODUCTION

When Pearl Harbor brought the United States into the war, Thomas Chinn sold his publishing business and devoted full time to war work. Like many other Chinese Americans, it was the first time he had worked outside of Chinatown. He served as a supervisor in the Army Quartermaster Market Center, which was responsible for supplying the armed forces with fresh food as it was harvested across California. Chinn found himself coordinating a host of cold storage warehouses all the way from the Oregon border as far south as Fresno. "At times," he recalled, "in order to catch seasonal goods such as fresh vegetables, as many as 200 or 300 railroad cars would be shuttling in and out" of the warehouses.

Food production and distribution was only one of many areas that demanded attention from the government. After Pearl Harbor, steel, aluminum, and electric power were all in short supply, creating bottlenecks in production lines. Roosevelt recognized the need for more direct government control of the economy.

Although the conversion from peace to war came slowly at first, the president used a mix of compulsory and voluntary programs to control inflation and guarantee an ever-increasing supply of food, munitions, and equipment. In the end the United States worked a miracle of production that proved every bit as important to victory as any battle fought overseas. From 1939 to 1945 the gross national product grew from $91 billion to $166 billion. (In World War I it had not changed significantly.) So successful was war production that civilians suffered little deprivation.

Finding an Industrial Czar

Roosevelt's first attempt at coordinating the production effort was to set up a War Production Board (WPB) under the direction of former Sears, Roebuck president

When war cut off the United States from its rubber supply in Malaysia, old tires were recycled to help meet the shortage. Most Americans were unable to replace their car tires during the four years the United States was at war. The manufacturers of synthetic rubber eventually eased the crisis.

Donald M. Nelson. On paper, Nelson's powers were impressive. The WPB had authority to allocate resources and organize factories in whatever way promoted national defense. In one of its first acts, the WPB ordered an end to all civilian car and truck production. The American people would have no new cars until the war ended.

In practice, Nelson was scarcely the dictator the economy needed. Other federal agencies with their own czars controlled petroleum, rubber, and labor resources, while military agencies continued their own procurement. To end the bottlenecks once and for all, the president in 1943 installed Supreme Court Justice James F. Byrnes as director of the new Office of War Mobilization (OWM). A canny political facilitator, Byrnes became the dictator the economy needed. His authority was so great and his access to Roosevelt so direct that he became known as the "assistant president." By assuming control over vital materials such as steel, aluminum, and copper, OWM was able to allocate them more systematically. The bottlenecks disappeared. Such centralized planning helped ease the conversion to war production of industries both large and small. While the "Big Three" automakers—Ford, General Motors, and Chrysler—generated some 20 percent of all war goods, small business also played a vital role. A manufacturer of model trains, for example, made bomb fuses.

The career of Henry J. Kaiser, a California industrialist, illustrates how the war inspired creative financing and management. Kaiser sent his lobbyists to Washington, where they rustled up generous government loans for building factories. And since Kaiser needed steel to build new factories, they found ways around wartime restrictions. To attract workers to his new West Coast shipyards, Kaiser offered high wages and benefits, including day care for the children of working mothers. His innovative application of assembly line techniques reduced the time required to build cargo vessels, known as Liberty ships, from almost a year to only 56 days. His yards finished one in a record 14 days. Speed had its price: one Liberty ship actually split in half at its launching. Despite such occasional missteps, Kaiser built ships in the quantity the war effort demanded.

West Coast war industries

The aircraft industry also transformed the industrial landscape of the West Coast. When production of aircraft factories peaked in 1944, the industry had 2.1 million workers producing almost 100,000 planes. Most of the new factories were located around Los Angeles, San Diego, and Seattle, where large labor pools, temperate climates, and available land made the locations attractive. The demand for workers opened opportunities for many Asian workers who had been limited to jobs within their own ethnic communities. In Los Angeles about 300 laundry workers closed their shops so that they could work on the construction of the ship *China Victory*. By 1943, 15 percent of all shipyard workers around San Francisco Bay were Chinese.

The military relied on large, established firms in part because they had more experience producing in large volume. At the same time lucrative war contracts helped big corporations increase their dominance over the economy. Workers in companies with more than 10,000 employees amounted to just 13 percent of the workforce in 1939; by 1944 they made up more than 30 percent. In agriculture a similar move toward bigness occurred. The number of people working on farms dropped by a fifth, yet productivity increased 30 percent, as small farms were consolidated into larger ones. Large commercial farming by corporations rather than individuals (later called "agribusiness") came to dominate farming.

Productivity increased for a less tangible but equally important reason: pride in work done for a common cause. Civilians volunteered for civil defense, hospitals, and countless scrap drives. Children became "Uncle Sam's Scrappers" and "Tin-Can Colonels" as they scoured vacant lots for valuable trash. One 13-year-old in Maywood, Illinois, collected more than 100 tons of paper between Pearl Harbor and D-Day. Backyard "victory" gardens added 8 million tons of food to the harvest in 1943; car pooling conserved millions of tires. As citizens put off buying new consumer goods, they helped limit inflation. Morale ran high because people believed that every contribution, no matter how small, helped defeat the Axis.

Science Goes to War

The striking success of aircraft against ships at Coral Sea and Midway demonstrated how science and technology changed the way war was fought. The air war in Europe spurred the development of a new generation of fighter planes and long-range bombers. To combat enemy bombers and submarines, English and American scientists rushed to perfect electronic detection devices such as radar and sonar.

Without sonar the Allies might never have won the submarine war in the North Atlantic. At the same time, improved American submarines crippled Japanese shipping in the western Pacific. By 1944 the home islands faced serious shortages of vital raw materials. Above the water, the newly developed techniques of radar-controlled naval and antiaircraft gunnery gave American ships a decided edge in crucial sea battles. It was possible to hit targets obscured by darkness, fog, or smoke. One of the most critical technical advances was also one of the best kept secrets of the war, the proximity fuse. By placing a small radio device in a warhead, scientists created a shell that did not need to hit a target to destroy it. Proximity fuses accounted for the success of American antiaircraft guns against Japanese planes and German V-1 bombs.

Scientific advances saved lives as well as destroying them. Insecticides, pesticides, and drugs limited the spread of infectious diseases like malaria and syphilis. Penicillin had its first widespread use in World War II. The health of the nation actually improved during the war. Life expectancy rose by three years overall and by five years for African Americans. Infant mortality was cut by more than a third, and in 1942 the nation recorded its lowest death rate in history. Still, such discoveries sometimes had unforeseen consequences. While the pesticide DDT helped control malaria and other insect-borne diseases, its harmful effects on the environment became clear only years later.

Science made its most dramatic advances in atomic research. In 1938 German scientists discovered the process of fission, in which atoms of uranium-235 were split, releasing an enormous amount of energy. Leading European physicists who had come to America to escape the Nazis understood all too well the military potential of the German discovery. In 1939 Enrico Fermi, Albert Einstein, and Leo Szilard warned President Roosevelt "that extemely powerful bombs of a new type may thus be constructed."

Roosevelt initiated what soon became the largest research and development effort in history, code-named the Manhattan Project. More than 100,000 scientists, engineers, technicians, and support workers from the United States, Canada, and England worked at 37 installations across the country to build an atomic bomb. The key to success was not so much secret discoveries but money (the project cost $2 billion) and industrial, scientific, and technical resources to produce nuclear fuels and a bomb design. Yet even with increased funding, scientists feared they might not win the race to produce an atomic bomb. *The Manhattan Project*

War Work and Prosperity

War production revived prosperity, but not without stress. As late as 1940 unemployment stood at almost 7 million. By 1944, it had virtually disappeared. Jeff Davies, president of Hoboes of America, reported in 1942 that 2 million of his members were "off the road." In retirement communities like San Diego nearly 4 retirees in 10 returned to work. Employers, eager to overcome the labor shortage, welcomed handicapped workers. The hearing impaired found jobs in deafening factories; dwarfs became aircraft inspectors because they could crawl inside wings and other cramped spaces. By the summer of 1943 nearly 3 million children aged 12 to 17 were working.

Roosevelt had to find some means to pay the war's enormous cost without undermining prosperity. His approach attempted to mix conservative and liberal elements. The Treasury Department tried to raise money voluntarily, by selling war bonds through advertising campaigns. To raise more funds, Secretary of the Treasury *Tax reform*

The Manhattan Project required complex facilities to produce small amounts of nuclear materials for the first atom bombs. This plant at Oak Ridge, Tennessee, took advantage of abundant electricity from the Tennessee Valley Authority as well as the expertise of scientists from universities and private industry.

Henry Morgenthau also proposed a tax structure that was highly progressive—that is, it taxed higher income at a higher rate. Conservatives in Congress balked at sweeping tax reforms. After six months of wrangling, Congress passed a compromise, the Revenue Act of 1942, which levied a flat 5 percent tax on all annual incomes over $624. That provision struck hardest at low-income workers: in 1942 almost 50 million citizens paid taxes compared with 13 million the year before. The most innovative feature of the bill was a payroll deduction system. No longer would taxpayers have to set aside money to pay their total tax bill to the Internal Revenue Service at the end of the year.

Organized Labor

War Labor Board

Wartime prosperity did not end the tug-of-war between business and labor. In 1941 alone more than 2 million workers walked off their jobs in protest. To end labor strife Roosevelt established the War Labor Board in 1942. Like the similar agency Woodrow Wilson had created during World War I, the new WLB had authority to impose arbitration in any labor dispute. Its most far-reaching decision established a compromise between employers and unions that gave workers 15 days to leave the union after a contract was signed. Any worker who remained a member had to pay union dues for the life of the contract. That policy led to an almost 40 percent growth in union membership between 1941 and 1945, when a record 14.75 million workers held union cards.

Despite the efforts of the WLB, strikes did occur. Dissatisfied railroad workers tied up rail lines in a wildcat strike in 1943. General George C. Marshall cursed it as

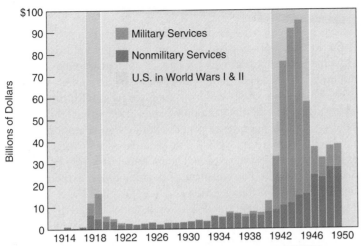

THE IMPACT OF WORLD WAR II ON GOVERNMENT SPENDING
This chart shows that World War II more than the New Deal spurred government spending, even on nonmilitary sectors. Note that after both world wars, nonmilitary spending was higher than in the prewar years.

the "damnedest crime ever committed against America." To break the impasse, the government seized the railroads and then granted wage increases. That same year the pugnacious John L. Lewis allowed his United Mine Workers to go on strike. "The coal miners of America are hungry," he charged. "They are ill-fed and undernourished." Roosevelt seized the mines and ran them for a time; he even considered arresting union leaders and drafting striking miners. But as Secretary of the Interior Harold Ickes noted, a "jailed miner produces no more coal than a striking miner." In the end the government negotiated a settlement that gave miners substantial new benefits.

Lewis leads a coal strike

Most Americans were unwilling to forgive Lewis or his miners. A huge coal shortage along the East Coast had left homes dark and cold. "John L. Lewis—Damn your coal black soul," wrote the military newspaper *Stars and Stripes*. In reaction, Congress easily passed the Smith–Connolly Act of 1943. It gave the president more authority to seize vital war plants shut by strikes and required union leaders to observe a 30-day "cooling-off" period before striking. Roosevelt vetoed the bill, only to be overridden in both houses.

Despite these incidents, most workers remained dedicated to the war effort. Stoppages actually accounted for only about one-tenth of one percent of total work time during the war. When workers did strike, it was usually in defiance of their union leadership, and they left their jobs for just a few days.

John L. Lewis

Women Workers

The demands of war placed a double demand for labor: not only soldiers to fight but workers to increase production. With as many as 12 million men in uniform, women (especially married women) became the nation's largest untapped source of labor. During the high-unemployment years of the Depression, both government and business had discouraged women from competing with men for jobs. With the onset of war, magazines and government bulletins suddenly began trumpeting "the vast resource of womanpower." The percentage of female workers grew from around a quarter in 1940 to more than a third by 1945. These women were no longer mostly young and single, as female workers of the past had been. A majority were either married or between 55 and 64 years old. Patriotism alone could not explain their willingness to leave families and homes for the factories.

Many women preferred the relative freedom of work and wages to the confines of home. With husbands off at war, millions of women needed additional income and had more free time. Black women in particular realized dramatic gains. Once concentrated in low-paying domestic and farm jobs with erratic hours and tedious labor, some 300,000 rushed into factories that offered higher pay and more regular hours. Given the chance to learn skills like welding, aircraft assembly, and electronics, women shattered many stereotypes about their capabilities. The diary of a ship welder in Oregon recorded both amazement and pride at what she accomplished:

> I, who hates heights, climbed stair after stair after stair till I thought I must be close to the sun. I stopped on the [tanker's] top deck. I, who hate confined spaces, went through narrow corridors, stumbling my way over rubber-coated leads. . . . I welded in

Between 1940 and 1945 the female labor force increased more than 50 percent. Many women performed jobs once restricted exclusively to males. Lionized with nicknames such as "Rosie the Riveter," women like this airplane factory worker dispelled stereotypes about the work women were able to do.

the poop deck lying on the floor while another welder spattered sparks from the ceiling and chippers like giant woodpeckers shattered our eardrums. . . . I did overhead welding, horizontal, flat, vertical. . . . I made some good welds and some frightful ones. But now a door in the poop deck of an oil tanker is hanging, four feet by six of solid steel, by my welds. Pretty exciting!

Although the demand for labor improved the economic status of women, it did not alter conventional views about gender roles. Most Americans assumed that when the war ended veterans would pick up their old jobs and women would return to the home. Surveys showed that the vast majority of Americans, whether male or female, continued to believe that child rearing was a woman's primary responsibility. The birthrate, which had fallen during the Depression, began to rise in 1943 as prosperity returned. And other traditional barriers continued to limit women's opportunities, even in wartime. Most professions admitted few women into graduate programs or other career paths. As women flooded into government bureaucracies, factory production lines, and corporate offices, few became managers. Supervision remained men's work. *Restraints on women's roles*

The social stresses of wartime placed additional pressures on women. Alcohol abuse, teenage prostitution, divorce, and juvenile delinquency all were on the rise. Some observers blamed such trends on working mothers, who were said to neglect their families. In fact, studies showed that the families of mothers who stayed home fared no better than did those where mothers held outside jobs. The real problem lay with the extraordinary mobility created by the war. Crowded into new communities with inadequate schools and recreational facilities, young people had few outlets for their energies. Rather than build new recreational facilities, concerned public agencies were just as likely to recommend rules restricting mothers from work. Only labor shortages prevented the acceptance of such rules. The war inspired a change in economic roles for women without fomenting a revolution in attitudes about gender. That would come later.

A QUESTION OF RIGHTS

Franklin Roosevelt had been a government official during World War I. Now, presiding over a bigger world war, he was determined to avoid many of the patriotic excesses he had witnessed then: mobs menacing immigrants, the patriotic appeals to spy on neighbors, the raids on pacifist radicals. Even so, the conflicts arising over race, ethnic background, and class differences could not simply be ignored. In a society in which immigration laws discriminated against Asians by race, the war with Japan made life difficult for loyal Asian Americans of all backgrounds. Black and Hispanic workers faced discrimination in shipyards and airplane factories as much as they had in peacetime industries.

Little Italy

Aliens from enemy countries fared far better in World War II than in World War I. When the war began about 600,000 Italian aliens and 5 million Italian Americans lived in the United States. Most still resided in Italian neighborhoods centered around churches, fraternal organizations, and clubs. Some had been proud of Mussolini and supported *Fascismo.* "Mussolini was a hero," recalled one Italian American, "a superhero. He made us feel special." Those attitudes changed abruptly after Pearl Harbor. During the war, Italian Americans pledged their loyalties to the United States.

At first the government treated Italians without citizenship (along with Japanese and Germans) as "aliens of enemy nationality." They could not travel without permission, enter strategic areas, or possess shortwave radios, guns, or maps. By 1942 few Americans believed that German Americans or Italian Americans posed any kind of danger. Eager to keep the support of Italian voters in the 1942 congressional elections, Roosevelt chose Columbus Day, 1942, to lift restrictions on Italian aliens. The segregation of Italian Americans ended. Henceforth they would maintain their ethnic unity as a matter of choice, not necessity.

Concentration Camps

Americans did not show similar tolerance toward the 127,000 Japanese living in the United States, whether they were aliens or citizens. Ironically, tensions were least high in Hawaii, where the war with Japan had begun. Local newspapers there expressed confidence in the loyalty of Japanese Americans, who in any case were crucial to Hawaii's economy. General Delos Emmons, the military governor of the islands, rebuffed pressures from Washington to evacuate as many as 20,000 "dangerous" Japanese. He branded a Justice Department report warning of widespread sabotage to be "so fantastic it hardly needs refuting."

The situation was quite different on the mainland, where Japanese Americans remained largely separated from the mainstream of American life. State laws and local custom threw up complex barriers to integration. In the western states, where they were concentrated around urban areas, most Japanese could not vote, own land, or live in decent neighborhoods. Approximately 47,000 Japanese aliens, known as *Issei* "Issei," were ineligible for citizenship under American law. Only their children could become citizens. Despite such restrictions, some Japanese achieved success in small businesses like landscaping, while many others worked on or owned farms that supplied fruits and vegetables to growing cities.

West Coast politicians pressed the Roosevelt administration to evacuate the Japanese from their communities. It did not seem to matter that about 80,000 were *Nisei* American citizens, called "Nisei," and that no evidence indicated that they posed any threat. "A Jap's a Jap. . . ." commented General John De Witt, commander of West Coast defenses. "It makes no difference whether he is an American citizen or not." In response, the War Department in February 1942 drew up Executive Order 9066, which allowed the exclusion of any person from designated military areas. Under De Witt's authority, the order was applied only on the West Coast against Japanese Americans. By late February Roosevelt had agreed that both Issei and Nisei would be evacuated. But where would they go?

The army began to ship the entire Japanese community to "assembly centers." Most Nisei incurred heavy financial losses as they sold property at far below market value. Their distress became a windfall for people who had long resented their economic competition. "We've been charged with wanting to get rid of the Japs for self-

The bleak landscape of the internment camp at Manzanar, California, was typical of the sites to which the government sent Japanese Americans. In such a harsh environment the Japanese had no real opportunity to create productive farm communities, as government officials had promised.

ish reasons," admitted the Grower–Shipper Vegetable Association. "We might as well be honest. We do. It's a question of whether the white man lives on the Pacific Coast or the brown man." At the assembly centers—racetracks, fairgrounds, and similar temporary locations—the army had not prepared basic sanitation, comfort, or privacy. "We lived in a horse stable," remembered one young girl. "We filled our cheesecloth with straw—for our mattress." The authorities at least had the decency to keep families together.

Most Japanese were interned in 10 camps in remote areas of seven western states. Notions that the camps might become self-sufficient communities proved wishful thinking. Even resourceful farmers could not raise food in arid desert soil. No claim of humane intent could change the reality—these were concentration camps. Internees were held in wire-enclosed compounds by armed guards. Temporary tarpapered barracks housed families or small groups in single rooms. Each room had a few cots, some blankets, and a single light bulb. That was home.   *Internment camps*

Some Japanese within the camps protested, especially when government officials circulated a loyalty questionnaire that asked Nisei citizens if they would be willing to serve in the armed forces. "What do they take us for? Saps?" asked Dunks Oshima, a camp prisoner. "First, they change my army status to 4-C [enemy alien] because of my ancestry, run me out of town, and now they want me to volunteer for a suicide squad so I could get killed for this damn democracy. That's going some, for sheer brass!" Yet thousands of Nisei did enlist, and many distinguished themselves in combat.

Korematsu and Hirabayashi

Other Japanese Americans challenged the government through the legal system. Fred Korematsu in California and Gordon Hirabayashi in Washington State were arrested when they refused to report for relocation. "As an American citizen, I wanted to uphold the principles of the Constitution," recalled Hirabayashi. But the Supreme Court let stand military policies aimed specifically at Japanese Americans. The majority opinion stated that "residents having ethnic affiliations with an invading enemy may be a greater source of danger than those of different ancestry," even though the army had never demonstrated that any danger existed. And in *Korematsu v. United States* (1944), the Court upheld the government's relocation program as a wartime necessity. Three justices dissented, criticizing relocation as the "legalization of racism."

Concentration camps in America did not perpetuate the horror of Nazi death camps, but they were built on racism and fear. Worse, they violated the traditions of civil rights and liberties for which Americans believed they were fighting.

Minorities on the Job

Minority leaders saw the irony of fighting a war for freedom in a country in which civil rights were still limited. "A jim crow army cannot fight for a free world," the NAACP declared. Such ideas of racial justice had been the driving force in the life of A. Philip Randolph, long an advocate of greater militancy. Randolph had demonstrated his gifts as an organizer and leader of the Brotherhood of Sleeping Car Porters, the most powerful black labor organization. He was determined to break down the wall of discrimination that kept minority workers out of jobs in defense industries and segregated in government agencies, unions, and the armed forces. "The Administration leaders in Washington will never give the Negro justice," Randolph argued, "until they see masses—ten, twenty, fifty thousand Negroes on the White House lawn." In 1941 he began to organize a march on Washington.

A. Philip Randolph

President Roosevelt had the power to issue executive orders ending segregation in the government, defense industries, unions, and the armed forces, as Randolph demanded. It took the threat of the march to make him act. He issued Executive Order 8802 in June, which forbade discrimination by race in hiring either government or defense industry workers. To carry out the policy, the order established the Fair Employment Practices Commission (FEPC). In some ways creating the FEPC was the boldest step toward racial justice taken since Reconstruction. Even so, the new agency had only limited success in breaking down barriers against black and Hispanic Americans. It was one thing to ban discrimination, quite another to enforce that ban in a society still deeply divided by racial prejudice.

Fair Employment Practices Commission

Still, efforts by the FEPC did open industrial jobs in California's shipyards and aircraft factories, which had previously refused to hire Hispanic Americans. Thousands migrated from Texas, where job discrimination was most severe, to California, where war work created new opportunities. Labor shortages led the southwestern states to join with the Mexican government under the bracero program to recruit Mexican labor under specially arranged contracts. In Texas, by contrast, antagonism to braceros ran so deep that the Mexican government tried to prevent workers from going there. With support from labor unions, officials in the oil and mining

Bracero program

industries routinely blocked Hispanics from training programs and job advancement. Not until late 1943 did the FEPC investigate the situation.

Black Americans experienced similar frustrations. More than half of all defense jobs were closed to minorities. For example, with 100,000 skilled and high-paying jobs in the aircraft industry, blacks held about 200 janitorial positions. The federal agency charged with placing workers honored local "whites only" employment practices. Unions segregated black workers or excluded them entirely. One person wrote to the president with a telling complaint: "Hitler has not done anything to the colored people—it's people right here in the United States who are keeping us out of work and keeping us down."

Eventually the combination of labor shortages, pressure from black leaders, and initiatives from government agencies opened the door to more skilled jobs and higher pay. Beginning in 1943, the United States Employment Service rejected requests with racial stipulations. Faced with a dwindling labor pool, many employers finally opened their doors. By 1944 African Americans, who accounted for almost 10 percent of the population, held 8 percent of the jobs.

At War with Jim Crow

At the beginning of World War II three-quarters of the 12 million black Americans lived in the South. Hispanic Americans, whose population exceeded a million, were concentrated in a belt along the United States–Mexico border. When jobs for minorities opened in war centers, blacks and Hispanics became increasingly urban. In cities, too, they encountered deeply entrenched systems of segregation that denied them basic rights to decent housing, jobs, and political participation. Competition with whites for housing and the use of public facilities like parks, beaches, and transportation produced explosive racial tensions.

To ease crowding the government funded new housing. In Detroit, federal authorities had picked a site for minority housing along the edge of a Polish neighborhood. One such project, named in honor of the black abolitionist Sojourner Truth, included 200 units for black families. When the first of them tried to move in, they faced an angry mob of whites. Local officials had to send several hundred National *Detroit riots* Guardsmen to protect the newcomers from menacing Ku Klux Klan members. Tensions increased with the approaching hot summer, and riots broke out in June 1943, as white mobs beat up African Americans riding public trolleys or patronizing movie theaters, and black protesters looted white stores. Six thousand soldiers from nearby bases finally imposed a troubled calm, but not before the riot had claimed the lives of 24 black and 9 white residents. Although wartime labor shortages gradually improved the situation for African Americans in Detroit, local officials refused to accept responsibility. Instead, they blamed the NAACP and the "militant" Negro press for stirring up trouble.

Hispanics in southern California suffered similar indignities. By 1943 overt Anglo hostility had come to focus on the pachucos, or "zoot suiters." These young Hispanic men and boys had adopted the stylish fashions of Harlem hipsters: greased hair swept back into a ducktail; broad-shouldered, long-waisted suit coats; baggy pants, pegged at the ankles, polished off with a swashbuckling keychain. The Los Angeles city council passed an ordinance making it a crime even to wear a zoot suit.

Zoot suit riots

For most "zooters" this style was a modest form of rebellion; for a few it was a badge of criminal behavior; for some white servicemen it was a target for racism.

In June 1943 sailors from the local navy base invaded Hispanic neighborhoods in search of zooters who had allegedly attacked servicemen. The self-appointed vigilantes grabbed innocent victims, tore their clothes, cut their hair, and beat them. When Hispanics retaliated, the police arrested them, ignoring the actions of white sailors. Irresponsible newspaper coverage made matters worse. "ZOOTERS THREATEN L.A. POLICE," charged one Hearst paper. A citizens committee created at the urging of California Governor Earl Warren rejected Hearst's inflammatory accusations. Underlying Hispanic anger were the grim realities of filthy housing, unemployment, disease, and white racism. All that added up to a level of poverty that wartime prosperity eased but did not end.

Minority leaders acted on the legal as well as the political front. The Congress of Racial Equality (CORE), a nonviolent civil rights group inspired by the Indian leader Mohandas K. Gandhi, used sit-ins and other peaceful tactics to desegregate some restaurants and movie theaters. In 1944 the Supreme Court outlawed the "all-white primary," an infamous device used by southerners to exclude blacks from voting in primary elections within the Democratic party. Because Democratic candidates in the South often ran unopposed in the general elections, the primary elections were usually the only true political contests. In *Smith v. Allwright* the Court ruled that since political parties were integral parts of public elections, they could not deny minorities the right to vote in primaries. Thus the war sowed the seeds of future protest and reform. Hispanic, black, and Indian veterans would play leading roles in the postwar struggle for equality.

The New Deal in Retreat

After Pearl Harbor Roosevelt told reporters that "Dr. New Deal" had retired so that "Dr. Win-the-War" might go about his business. Political opposition, however, could not be eliminated even during a global conflict. The increasingly powerful anti–New Deal coalition of Republicans and rural Democrats saw in the war an opportunity to attack programs they had long resented. The president, for his part, never lost sight of the election returns. When war came, New Deal foes moved quickly. They ended the Civilian Conservation Corps, the National Youth Administration, and the largely ineffective National Resources Planning Board. They reduced the powers of the Farm Security Administration and blocked moves to extend social security and unemployment benefits. Seeming to approve such measures, voters in the 1942 elections sent an additional 44 Republicans to the House and another 9 to the Senate. The GOP began eyeing the White House.

FDR wins a fourth term

By the spring of 1944 no one knew whether Franklin Roosevelt would seek an unprecedented fourth term. The president's health had declined noticeably. Pallid skin, sagging shoulders, and shaking hands seemed open signs that he had aged too much to run. In July, one week before the Democratic convention, Roosevelt announced his decision: "All that is within me cries out to go back to my home on the Hudson River. . . . But as a good soldier . . . I will accept and serve." Conservative Democrats, however, made sure that FDR's liberal vice president, Henry Wallace, would not remain on the ticket. In his place they settled on Harry S Truman of Missouri, a loyal New Dealer and party stalwart. The Republicans chose the moderate governor of New York, Thomas E. Dewey, to run against Roosevelt, but Dewey never had much of a chance. The increasing reports of victory in Europe and the Pacific undermined his charges that Roosevelt had mismanaged the war. Always pragmatic, Roosevelt made his domestic policies more conservative as well.

At the polls, voters gave Roosevelt 25.6 million popular votes to Dewey's 22 million, a clear victory, although the election was tighter than any since 1916. Like its aging leader, the New Deal coalition was showing signs of strain.

WINNING THE WAR AND THE PEACE

To impress upon newly arrived officers the vastness of the war theater in the Pacific, General Douglas MacArthur laid out a map of the region. Over it, he placed an outline map of the United States. Running the war from headquarters in Australia, MacArthur pointed out, the distances were about the same as if, in the Western Hemisphere, the center was located in South America. On the same scale, Tokyo would lie far up in northern Canada, Iwo Jima somewhere in Hudson Bay, Singapore in Utah, Manila in North Dakota, and Hawaii off the coast of Scotland.

In a war that stretched from one end of the globe to the other, the Allies had to coordinate their strategies on a grand scale. Which war theaters would receive equipment in short supply? Who would administer conquered territories? Inevitably, the questions of fighting a war slid into discussions of the peace that would follow. What would happen to occupied territories? How would the Axis powers be punished? If a more stable world order could not be created, the cycle of violence might never end. So as Allied armies struggled mile by mile to defeat the Axis, Allied diplomacy concentrated just as much on winning the peace.

The Fall of the Third Reich

After pushing the Germans out of North Africa in May 1943, Allied forces looked to drive Italy from the war. Late in July, two weeks after a quarter of a million British and American troops had landed on Sicily, Mussolini fled to German-held northern Italy. Although Italy surrendered early in September, Germany continued to pour in reinforcements. It took the Allies almost a year of bloody fighting to reach Rome, and at the end of the campaign they had yet to break German lines. Along the eastern front, Soviet armies steadily pushed the Germans out of Russia and back toward Berlin.

General Dwight D. Eisenhower, fresh from battle in North Africa and the Mediterranean, took command of Allied preparations for Operation Overlord, a massive invasion of Europe striking from across the English Channel. By June 1944 all attention focused on the coast of France, for Hitler, of course, knew the Allies were preparing. He suspected they would hit Calais, the French port city closest to the British Isles. Allied planners did their best to encourage this belief, even deploying fake armaments across the Channel. On the morning of June 6, 1944, the invasion began—not at Calais but on the less fortified beaches of Normandy (see the map, page 942). Almost 3 million men, 11,000 aircraft, and more than 2000 vessels took part in D-Day.

D-Day

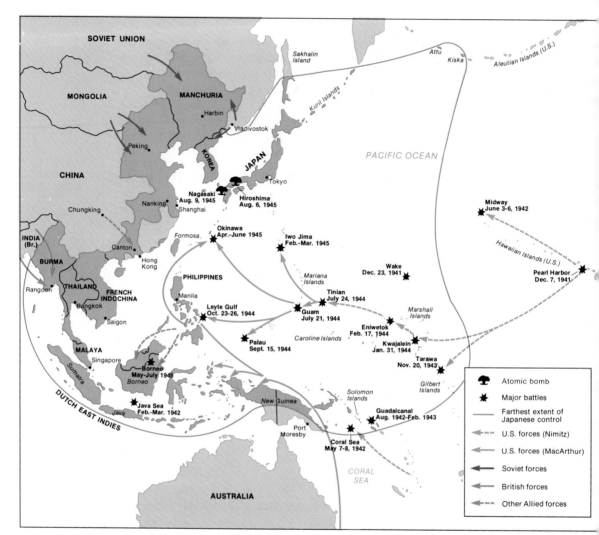

THE PACIFIC CAMPAIGNS OF WORLD WAR II
The extraordinary distances of the Pacific spurred the United States to devise a two-front strategy to defeat Japan. MacArthur's army forces used Australia as a base of operations, aiming for the Philippines and the southeast coast of China. Once those areas were secured, forces could then launch air attacks on Japan. The navy, under command of Admiral Nimitz, set out to destroy the Japanese fleet and to conduct a series of amphibious landings on island chains in the central Pacific. Meanwhile, British forces launched separate operations in Burma, forces under Chiang Kai-shek occasionally engaged Japanese forces on China's mainland, and in August 1945 Soviet troops attacked northern China.

As Allied forces hit the beaches, luck and Eisenhower's meticulous planning favored their cause. Persuaded that the Allies still wanted Calais, Hitler delayed sending in two reserve divisions. His indecision allowed the Allied forces to secure a foothold. Over the next few days more than 1.5 million soldiers landed on the beaches—but they still had to move inland. Slowed by difficult conditions, the Allied advance from Normandy took almost two months, not several weeks as expected. Once Allied tanks broke through German lines their progress was spectacular. In August Paris was liberated, and by mid-September the Allies had driven the Germans from France and Belgium.

All went well until December 1944, when Hitler threw his reserves into a last, desperate gamble. The unexpected German onslaught drove the Allied lines back along a 50-mile bulge. There the Germans trapped the 101st Airborne Division. When asked to surrender, General Tony MacAuliffe sent back a one-word reply: "Nuts!" His troops held, General George Patton raced to the rescue, and the last German offensive collapsed. Little stood between the Allies and Berlin. *Battle of the Bulge*

Two Roads to Tokyo

In the bleak days of 1942 General Douglas MacArthur—flamboyant and jaunty with his dark sunglasses and corncob pipe—had emerged as America's only military hero. MacArthur believed that the future of America lay in the Far East. The Pacific theater, not the European, should have top priority, he argued. In March 1943 the Combined Chiefs of Staff agreed to his plan for a westward advance along the northern coast of New Guinea toward the Philippines and Tokyo. Naval forces directed by Admiral Chester Nimitz used amphibious warfare to move up the island chains of the Central Pacific (see the map, page 968).

The Normandy landing involved complex problems of moving troops and matériel. These awkward craft allowed the landing forces to improvise docking facilities soon after the invasion forces landed. Sailors described the Rhino ferry as "ugly as hell, cranky as hell—but efficient as hell."

In the face of Japanese occupation, many Filipinos actively supported the American war effort. Valentine Untalan survived capture by the Japanese and went on to serve in the American army's elite Philippine Scouts. Like a growing number of Filipinos, he moved to the United States once the war was over.

MacArthur returns

By July 1944 the navy's leapfrogging campaign had reached the Marianas, east of the Philippines. From there B-29 bombers could reach the Japanese home islands. As a result, Admiral Nimitz proposed bypassing the Philippines in favor of a direct attack on Formosa (present-day Taiwan). MacArthur insisted instead on keeping his personal promise "to eighteen million Christian Filipinos that the Americans would return." President Roosevelt himself came to Hawaii to resolve the impasse, giving MacArthur the green light. Backed by more than 100 ships of the Pacific Fleet, the general splashed ashore on the island of Leyte in October 1944 to announce his return.

Battle of Leyte Gulf

The decision to invade the Philippines led to savage fighting until the war ended. As retreating Japanese armies left Manila, they tortured and slaughtered tens of thousands of Filipino civilians. The United States suffered 62,000 casualties redeeming MacArthur's pledge to return. A spectacular U.S. Navy victory at the Battle of Leyte Gulf spelled the end of the Japanese Imperial Navy as a fighting force. MacArthur and Nimitz prepared to tighten the noose around Japan's home islands.

Big Three Diplomacy

While the Allies cooperated to gain military victories in both Europe and the Pacific, negotiations over the postwar peace proved knottier. Churchill believed that only a stable European balance of power, not an international agency, could preserve peace.

In his view the Soviet Union was the greatest threat to upsetting that balance of power. Premier Joseph Stalin left no doubt that an expansive notion of Russian security defined his war aims. For future protection Stalin expected to annex the Baltic states, once Russian provinces, along with bits of Finland and Romania and about half of prewar Poland. In eastern Europe and other border areas such as Iran, Korea, and Turkey, he wanted "friendly" neighbors. It soon became apparent that "friendly" meant regimes dependent on Moscow.

Early on, Franklin Roosevelt had promoted his own version of an international balance of power, which he called the "Four Policemen." Under its framework, the Soviet Union, Great Britain, the United States, and China would guarantee peace through military cooperation. But by 1944 Roosevelt had rejected both this scheme and Churchill's wish to return to a balance of power that safely hemmed in the Russians. Instead, he looked to bring the Soviet Union into a peacekeeping system based on an international organization similar to the League of Nations. This time, Roosevelt intended that the United States, as well as all the great powers, would participate. Whether Churchill and Stalin—or the American people as a whole—would accept the idea was not yet clear.

The Road to Yalta

The outlines—and the problems—of a postwar settlement became clearer during several summit conferences among the Allied leaders. In November 1943, with Italy's surrender in hand and the war against Germany going well, Churchill and Roosevelt agreed to make a hazardous trip to Teheran, Iran. There, the Big Three leaders met together for the first time and had a chance to take a personal measure of each other. ("Seems very confident," Roosevelt said of Stalin, "very sure of himself, moves slowly—altogether quite impressive.") The president tried to charm the Soviet premier, teasing Churchill for Stalin's benefit, keeping it up "until Stalin was laughing with me, and it was then that I called him 'Uncle Joe.'"

Teheran Conference

Teheran proved to be the high point of cooperation among the Big Three. It was there that FDR and Churchill committed to the D-Day invasion Stalin had so long sought. In return he promised to launch a spring offensive to keep German troops occupied on the eastern front. He also reaffirmed his earlier pledge to declare war against Japan once Germany was beaten.

But thorny disagreements over the postwar peace had not been resolved. That was clear in February 1945, when the Big Three met one last time at the Russian resort city of Yalta, on the Black Sea. By then, Russian, British, and American troops were closing in on Germany. Roosevelt arrived tired, ashen. At 62, limited by his paralysis, he had visibly aged. He came to Yalta mindful that although Germany was all but beaten, Japan still held out in the Pacific. Under no circumstances did he want Stalin to withdraw his promise to enter the fight against Japan or to join a postwar international organization. Churchill remained profoundly mistrustful of Soviet intentions. As Germany and Japan disintegrated, he saw power vacuums opening up in both Europe and Asia. These the Russians appeared only too eager to fill. Most diplomats in the American State Department and a growing number of military officers and politicians shared Churchill's fears.

Yalta Conference

Daily Lives

Air Power Shrinks the Globe

During World War I, the popular imagination thrilled to the stories of aerial dogfights and "flying aces." In reality, airplanes played only a secondary role in that war's military strategy. Short flying ranges and an inability to carry heavy loads limited what planes could do. Between the two wars, however, airframes grew stronger, engines more powerful, and payloads greater. Air-power strategists began to suggest that concerted waves of planes could attack industrial and military targets deep in enemy territory. Hitler grasped the strategic possibilities and insisted that Germany's air force as well as its army rearm and modernize.

During the blitzkriegs against Poland and France in the opening campaigns of the war, Hitler's air attacks terrorized civilian populations and disrupted enemy forces. Air Marshal Hermann Goering predicted that bombers from the German *Luftwaffe* would soon bring England to its knees. The Battle of Britain, fought during the winter of 1940–1941, signaled the start of the age of modern air warfare. For the first time in history, one nation tried to conquer another from the skies. Goering's boast failed as England continued doggedly to resist.

Despite the *Luftwaffe's* failure, Allied air-power strategists believed heavy bombers could cripple Germany and Japan. The first test of such "strategic bombing" came in 1942, when more than 1100 planes of the British Royal Air Force (RAF) destroyed some 20,000 homes, 1500 stores and offices, and about 60 factories around Cologne, Germany. Horrific as that sounds, the attack did not level the city, as RAF planners had predicted. Indeed, later studies indicated that for all the damage done, Axis productivity actually increased until the last months of the war. Still, strategic bombing disrupted Japanese and German industry, brought the war home to the civilian population, and diverted enemy forces from the front to home defense.

Raids on Dresden and on Tokyo dramatized the horrors of the new technology. Dresden, a charming German city almost untouched by the twentieth century, had largely been ignored until February 1945. The RAF hit it first; then, with fires still raging, the American bombing wave struck. A huge inferno drew all the oxygen out of the center city, so that victims who did not burn suffocated. The city and its 60,000 people died. In March 340 American bombers hit Tokyo with incendiary bombs. The resulting firestorms, whipped by strong winds, leveled 16 square miles, destroyed 267,000 homes, left 83,000 dead, and injured 41,000. The heat was so intense that the water in canals boiled.

To ensure the success of aerial warfare, aircraft designers on both sides raced to make their planes bigger and faster. The first English raids used the Wellington

Dispute over Poland

Allied differences were most clearly reflected in the disagreements over Poland. For Britain, Hitler's invasion of Poland had been the flashpoint for war. It was fighting, in part, to ensure that Poland survived as an independent nation. For Stalin, Poland was the historic corridor of invasion used by Russia's enemies. After Soviet troops reentered Poland, he insisted that he would recognize only the Communist-controlled government at Lublin. Stalin also demanded that Russia receive territory

Daily Lives

The B-29 bombers gave the American air force much greater range, speed, and bomb loads. The *Enola Gay* (above), named after the pilot's mother, was modified to carry the first atom bomb dropped on Hiroshima.

bomber, a plane 65 feet long with a wing span of 86 feet and a bomb load of 1500 pounds. By contrast, the American B-29s that bombed Hiroshima and Nagasaki carried up to 10 tons on a plane that was about 50 percent larger. The Wellington flew 255 miles an hour and cruised as high as 12,000 feet, with a range of 2200 miles, whereas the new B-29s could travel more than 350 miles an hour, at altitudes up to 30,000 feet, with a range of up to 5000 miles—more than double the Wellington's. German scientists took an even more radical step. To increase the speed and range of their

weaponry they produced a new V-1 pilotless "buzz bomb" (named for the sound of its jet engine) and the V-2 rocket, the first true missile used as a weapon. Launched from bases in Europe, V-1s and V-2s easily reached targets in England. For all the terror they inspired, however, they were inaccurate and the Germans could not launch them in sufficient quantities to mount a decisive threat.

With the development of long-range air power, the "front line" of traditional war vanished. Every civilian became a potential combatant, every village a potential target in a total war. Although air power was not decisive in the war, the creation of longer-range aircraft with heavier payloads forced Americans to rethink their ties to the world. After World War I, Americans had rejected the League of Nations and involvement in the political affairs of Europe. Arthur Vandenberg, a Republican senator from Michigan, became one of the nation's most outspoken isolationists. That was before Pearl Harbor and before Vandenberg visited London during the war. As German V-1 and V-2 missiles brought terror from the skies, the senator came to believe that an isolationist policy no longer made sense. Physical distance would never again be a safeguard from attack, because air power had reshaped the strategic map of the world. The United States was now a matter of hours, not days, away from both friends and potential enemies.

in eastern Poland, for which the Poles would be compensated with German lands. That was hardly the "self-determination" called for in the Atlantic Charter. Roosevelt proposed a compromise. For the time being, Poland would have a coalition government; after the war, free elections would settle the question of who should rule. The Soviets would also receive the territory they demanded in eastern Poland, and the western boundary would be established later.

Similarly, the Allies remained at odds about Germany's postwar future. Stalin was determined that the Germans would never invade Russia again. Many Americans shared his desire to have Germany punished and its war-making capacity eliminated. At the Teheran Conference, Roosevelt and Stalin had proposed that the Third Reich be drastically dismembered, split into five powerless parts. Churchill was much less eager to bring low the nation that was the most natural barrier to Russian expansion. The era after World War I, he believed, demonstrated that a healthy European economy required an industrialized Germany.

Dividing
Germany

As with Poland, the Big Three put off making a firm decision. For the time being, they agreed to divide Germany into separate occupation zones (France would receive a zone carved from British and American territory). These four powers would jointly occupy Berlin while an Allied Control Council supervised the national government.

When the Big Three turned their attention to the Far East, Stalin held a trump card. Roosevelt believed that only a bloody invasion of Japan itself could force a surrender. He thus secured from Stalin a pledge to enter the Pacific war within three months of Germany's defeat. His price was high. Stalin wanted to reclaim territories that Russia had lost in the Russo-Japanese War of 1904–1906, including islands north of Japan as well as control over the Chinese Eastern and South Manchurian railroads.

The agreements reached at Yalta depended on Stalin's willingness to cooperate. In public Roosevelt put the best face on matters. He argued that the new world organization (which Stalin had agreed to support) would "provide the greatest opportunity in all history" to secure a lasting peace. As if to lay to rest the isolationist sentiments that had destroyed Woodrow Wilson's dream, Roosevelt told Congress, "We shall take responsibility for world collaboration, or we shall have to bear the responsibility for another world conflict." Privately the president was less optimistic. He confessed to one friend that he doubted that, "when the chips were down, Stalin would be able to carry out and deliver what he had agreed to."

The Fallen Leader

The Yalta Conference marked one of the last and most controversial chapters of Franklin Roosevelt's presidency. Critics charged that the concessions to Stalin had been too generous and a threat to American national interests. Poland had been betrayed; China sold out; the United Nations crippled at birth. Yet Roosevelt gave to Stalin little that Stalin had not liberated with Russian blood and could have taken anyway. Even Churchill, an outspoken critic of Soviet ambitions, concluded that although "our hopeful assumptions were soon to be falsified . . . they were the only ones possible at the time."

What peace Roosevelt might have achieved can never be known. He returned from Yalta visibly ill. On April 12, 1945, while sitting for his portrait at his vacation home in Warm Springs, Georgia, he complained of a "terrific headache," then suddenly fell unconscious. Two hours later Roosevelt was dead, the victim of a cerebral hemorrhage. Not since the assassination of Lincoln had the nation so grieved. Under Roosevelt's leadership government had become a protector, the president a father and friend, and the United States the leader in the struggle against Axis tyranny. Eleanor recalled how many Americans later told her that "they missed the way the

President used to talk to them. . . . There was a real dialogue between Franklin and the people."

Harry S Truman faced the awesome task of replacing Roosevelt. "Who the hell is Harry Truman?" the chief of staff had asked when Truman was nominated for the vice presidency in 1944. In the brief period he served as vice president, Truman had met with Roosevelt fewer than 10 times. He knew almost nothing about the president's postwar plans and promises. When a reporter now addressed him as "Mr. President," he winced. "I wish you didn't have to call me that," he said. Sensing his own inadequacies, Truman adopted a tough pose and made his mind up quickly. People welcomed the new president's decisiveness as a relief from Roosevelt's evasive style. Too often, though, Truman acted before the issues were clear. He at least knew victory in Europe was near as Allied troops swept into Germany.

Truman becomes president

The Holocaust

The horror of war in no way prepared the invading armies for the liberation of the concentration camps. Hitler, they discovered, had ordered the systematic extermination

---

In April 1945, at the concentration camp in Buchenwald, Germany, Senator Alben Barkley of Kentucky viewed a grisly reminder of the horrors of the Nazis' "final solution." As vice president under Harry Truman, Barkley urged the administration to support an independent homeland in Israel for Jews.

of all European Jews as well as Gypsies, homosexuals, and others considered deviant. The SS, Hitler's security force, had constructed six extermination centers in Poland. By rail from all over Europe the SS shipped Jews to die in the gas chambers.

No issue of World War II more starkly raised questions of human good and evil than what came to be known as the Holocaust. Tragically, the United States could have done more to save at least some of the 6 million Jews killed. Until the fall of 1941 the Nazis permitted Jews to leave Europe, but few countries would accept them—including the United States. Americans haunted by unemployment feared that a tide of new immigrants would make competition for jobs even worse. Tales of persecution from war refugees had little effect on most citizens: opinion polls showed that more than 70 percent of Americans opposed easing quotas. After 1938 the restrictive provisions of the 1924 Immigration Act were made even tighter.

American Jews wanted to help, especially after 1942, when they learned of the death camps. But they worried that highly visible protests might only aggravate American anti-Semitism. They were also split over support for Zionists working to establish a Jewish homeland in Palestine. The British had blocked Jewish emigration to Palestine and, to avoid alienating the Arabs, opposed Zionism. Roosevelt and his advisers ultimately decided that the best way to save Jews was to win the war quickly. That still does not explain why the Allies did not do more. They could have bombed the rail lines to the camps, sent commando forces, or tried to destroy the death factories.

Influence of anti-Semitism

Anti-Semitism offers a partial answer. Assistant Secretary of State Breckinridge Long, the man responsible for immigration policy, personified a tradition of gentlemanly anti-Semitism. Polite on the surface but deeply bigoted, Long used his authority over visas to place obstacles in the way of desperate Jewish refugees. But Long went too far when he blocked a plan that both Treasury Secretary Henry Morgenthau and the president had approved to ransom Jews in Romania and 6000 Jewish children in France. Morganthau, the only Jewish member of Roosevelt's cabinet, had at first shown little interest in the debate over Palestine and the refugees. Long's actions so disturbed him, however, that he sent Roosevelt a report entitled "The Acquiescence of this Government in the Murder of the Jews." The president immediately stripped Long of his authority. He appointed a War Refugee Board charged with saving as many Jews as possible and promised to seek the establishment of a Jewish commonwealth in Palestine. But some 18 precious "long and heartbreaking" months had been lost and with them an untold number of lives.

A Lasting Peace

After 15 years of first depression and then war, the Allies sought a new international framework for cooperation among nations. That system, many believed, needed to be economic as well as political. At a 1944 meeting at Bretton Woods, a resort in New Hampshire, Americans led the way in creating two new economic organizations: the International Monetary Fund (IMF) and the International Bank for Reconstruction and Development, later known as the World Bank. The IMF hoped to promote trade by stabilizing national currencies, while the World Bank was designed to stimulate economic growth by investing in projects worldwide. Later that summer the Allies met at Dumbarton Oaks, a Washington estate, to lay out the structure for the proposed United Nations Organization (UNO, later known simply as the UN). An 11-

Bretton Wood economic strategies

Dumbarton Oaks and the UNO

vasion. The country, after all, was virtually without defense against bombing raids. Later critics have suggested that the Allies should have modified their demand for "unconditional surrender," instead allowing the Japanese to keep their

Truman recalled that General George Marshall, the Army Chief of Staff, had told him in July 1945 that in an invasion of Japan "1/4 of a million casualties would be the cost as well as an equal number of Japanese." But when a White House

power. If the test should fail, then it would be even more important to us to bring about a surrender before we had to make a physical conquest of Japan. General Marshall told me that <u>it might cost half a million American lives</u> to force the enemy's surrender on his home grounds.

Harry S Truman, *Memoirs*, page 417: an estimate of half a million deaths

revered institution of the emperor. (As events turned out, Japan surrendered only after such a guarantee was issued.) Others argue that the United States should have arranged for a demonstration of the bomb's power without actually detonating one over Japan.

Yet as the debates over these alternatives swirled during the 1960s and 1970s, no one challenged the estimates of a million-casualty invasion. That number had been put forward in 1947 by Henry Stimson, the highly respected former secretary of war. In an article for *Harper's* magazine Stimson wrote, "We estimated the major fighting would not end until the latter part of 1946 at the earliest. I was informed that such operations might be expected to cost over a million casualties, to American forces alone."

Stimson's account cast a long shadow. A few years later Harry Truman provided an air force historian with a significantly lower number.

aide checked Truman's memory against Stimson's account, he discovered the discrepancy—one million versus only 1/4 million. "The President's casualty figure [should] be changed to conform with that of Secretary Stimson," the aide advised, "because presumably Stimson got his from Gen. Marshall; the size of the casualty figures is very important."

The last phrase is significant. Why were the numbers so important? Obviously, the higher the potential casualties, the stronger the case that using the

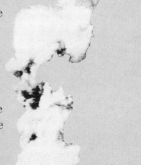

Hiroshima, August 6, 1945

bomb saved lives. So it is worth looking a bit closer at Stimson's article.

In fact, the idea to write an article was not actually Stimson's. It came from another atomic policymaker, James Conant. Conant, the president of Harvard University, had become increasingly concerned about "the spreading accusation that it was unnecessary to use the atomic bomb at all. . . . This type of sentimentalism," he complained privately in 1946, ". . . is bound to have a great deal of influence on the next generation. The type of person who goes into teaching, particularly school teaching, will be influenced a great deal by this type of argument." Conant believed that Stimson had the prestige to counter such criticisms. One of the nation's most distinguished public servants, he had been twice a secretary of war, an ambassador, and secretary of state.

So Simpson agreed to write an article. But where did he get his casualty estimates? During the war a memo from former President Herbert Hoover had been circulated, warning that an invasion could claim anywhere from half a million to a million American lives. At the time, in June 1945, a successful test of an atomic bomb was still a month away and the possibility of an invasion loomed larger. Stimson was convinced that the war might be ended without an invasion if the Allies would only assure the Japanese that the position of emperor would be protected. Hoover's dire warning about the costs of an invasion reinforced Stimson's argument against invading.

Remains of a wristwatch from the atomic blast site at Hiroshima. The bomb exploded at 8:16 a.m.

But contrary to the aide who later helped Truman with his memoirs, Stimson did not get similarly high casualty estimates from General Marshall. Marshall's staff thought Hoover's estimates were way too high. They estimated that the first-stage invasion (of Kyushu Island) might produce American casualties of perhaps 31,000, including about 7000 to 8000 deaths. If the invasion of Japan's main island, Honshu, took place, those numbers would rise to 120,000 casualties and 25,000 deaths. Estimates by General MacArthur were slightly higher, but within the same range. For reasons that remain unclear, however, when Stimson wrote his article after the war, he chose to use the higher estimates.

Thus, intentionally or not, Stimson's article greatly overestimated the number of invasion casualties predicted by the American military. And Conant's private worries show that those who dropped the bomb were more sensitive about their decision than they wished to admit. One of the most telling illustrations of the pressure to keep the estimates high can be seen in the successive drafts of Harry Truman's own memoirs, which were finally published in 1955. The assistants who helped Truman kept revising the figure

Japanese fighting on Okinawa and other Pacific islands produced high casualty and death rates for American forces, reinforcing the notion that an invasion of Japan would claim many American lives.

upward. Truman's recollection, in 1952, mentioned only 250,000 casualties (not deaths); that figure jumped to 500,000 casualties in the first draft; then, in the published version, to a "half-million" *lives* saved.

Do the lower figures mean that historians should condemn Truman, Stimson, and others for preferring to use the bomb rather than invade Japan? Not necessarily. After Japan's surprise attack on Pearl Harbor and its fierce resistance in the Pacific islands, American sentiments against the Japanese ran high. The atomic bomb had cost $2 billion to develop, and officials always as-

understood that the record of the past is always shaped by those who do the telling. "History," he wrote in 1948, "is often not what actually happened but what is recorded as such."

BIBLIOGRAPHY. Stimson's "The Decision to Use the Bomb" appears in the February 1947 issue of *Harper's* magazine. The debate over his casualty estimates and those of Truman and Churchill was launched by Barton J. Bernstein, "A Postwar Myth: 500,000 Lives Saved," *Bulletin of the Atomic Scientists* 42 (June/July 1986) and by Rufus Miles,

And conquering Japan would take a frightful sacrifice of American and Allied lives. Our military estimated no less than <u>half a million casualties with at least 300,000 dead.</u>

We were faced, in addition, with a very serious problem of transporting troops across the Pacific, which was a much bigger job than

Truman, *Memoirs*, first draft: at least 300,000 deaths

sumed that if the bomb were successful, it would be used. Why else develop it? One can argue that even an invasion costing 25,000 lives would have justified using the bomb, in the view of Truman (and most Americans).

Even so, historians must constantly remind themselves that seemingly "impartial" accounts are influenced by the conditions under which they were created. Stimson set out not simply to tell the facts about the decision to drop the bomb. He wished to justify a decision he believed was necessary and proper. Like Conant, he

"Hiroshima: The Strange Myth of Half a Million Lives Saved," *International Security* 10 (Fall 1985). Bernstein provides valuable background on Stimson's 1947 article in "Seizing the Contested Terrain of Nuclear History," *Diplomatic History*, 19 (Winter 1993). Also useful is John Ray Skates, *The Invasion of Japan: Alternative to the Bomb* (Columbia, S.C., 1994). The debate over the projected invasion, of course, is only one aspect of the larger question of whether atom bombs should have been dropped on Japan. For readings on that topic, see the Bibliography.

PART SIX

THE UNITED STATES IN A NUCLEAR AGE

GLOBAL ESSAY

At Los Alamos in July 1945, during the final feverish days of work on the first atom bomb, a few scientists calculated the possible unexpected effects of an atomic blast. The strategic bombings at Dresden and Tokyo showed how a firestorm, once started, sucked oxygen from the surrounding atmosphere, feeding upon itself and enlarging the inferno. No one had ever set off an atomic explosion, and some scientists worried that an even greater chain reaction might follow, one that would not only ignite the atmosphere around it but envelop the earth's atmosphere, leaving the planet in ashes. Members of the team checked and rechecked the calculations before deciding that those fears were unwarranted.

In the half century after Hiroshima, the atomic nightmare returned repeatedly to haunt the world. The threat appeared to be not from the detonation of a single bomb but from an all-too-human chain reaction in which escalating violence leads to atomic strike and counterstrike, followed by a decades-long radioactive "nuclear winter," from which intelligent life could never fully recover.

During the heady victory celebrations of 1945, the threat of nuclear annihilation seemed distant. Although President Truman and other American leaders had become increasingly distrustful of Stalin, the United States preserved a clear atomic monopoly. The dangers from radioactive fallout impressed only a handful of officials and even fewer members of the public, who were treated to cheery fantasies of the peacetime use of atomics. One such whimsy, featured in the May

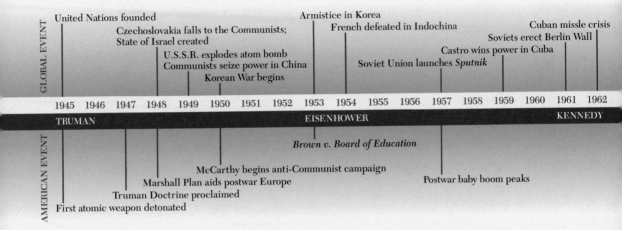

GLOBAL EVENT

United Nations founded
Czechoslovakia falls to the Communists;
State of Israel created
U.S.S.R. explodes atom bomb
Communists seize power in China
Korean War begins
Armistice in Korea
French defeated in Indochina
Soviet Union launches *Sputnik*
Castro wins power in Cuba
Cuban missle crisis
Soviets erect Berlin Wall

1945 1946 1947 1948 1949 1950 1951 1952 1953 1954 1955 1956 1957 1958 1959 1960 1961 1962

TRUMAN   EISENHOWER   KENNEDY

AMERICAN EVENT

Brown v. Board of Education

McCarthy begins anti-Communist campaign
Marshall Plan aids postwar Europe
Truman Doctrine proclaimed
First atomic weapon detonated
Postwar baby boom peaks

1947 *Collier's* magazine, showed a recovered paraplegic emerging from the mushroom cloud of his atomic treatment, his wheelchair almost miraculously left behind. By 1949, when fallout from Russian explosions indicated that the Soviet Union had gained the power of atomic weapons, the grim global realignment was already well established. Two superpowers, the Soviet Union and the United States, had replaced the players in the old "balance of power" politics that had defined European politics for two centuries.

The polarization of the globe into two camps, each dominated by a superpower, would have seemed strange even 20 years earlier. But in the long view, the result was not surprising. Since the sixteenth century, the expansion of European culture and power has been most significant along the continent's peripheries, both west and east. Along the west-facing rim, the Portuguese, Spanish, Dutch, French, and English reached beyond themselves for commercial and colonial empires. By the late nineteenth century England's colonial offshoot, the United States, was coming into its own even farther west. Over these same centuries of expansion, Europe's eastern flank saw Russian settlers pushing across the steppes of Eurasia, turning grasslands into cultivated fields. Farther north, Russian fur traders were bringing the forest and tundra of Siberia into the Russian orbit, just as French and English fur traders were mastering the forests of the Canadian shield.

In area and vastness of resources, the Soviet Union surpassed even the United States, its boundaries encompassing 12 time zones. Given the centuries-long tradition of authoritarian rule (*czar* is the Russian derivative of "caesar"), the Russian Revolution of 1917 took a firmly centralized approach to modernization. At sometimes frightful cost Stalin brought the Soviet Union to its position as superpower by the end of World War II. The peripheral powers of Europe—the United States and Russia—had become dominant. By the 1960s both relied on stockpiles of nuclear weapons to guarantee their security and power.

Deterrence—the knowledge of "mutual assured destruction"—would prevent either side from being the first to launch a missile attack. So, at least, nuclear strate-

987

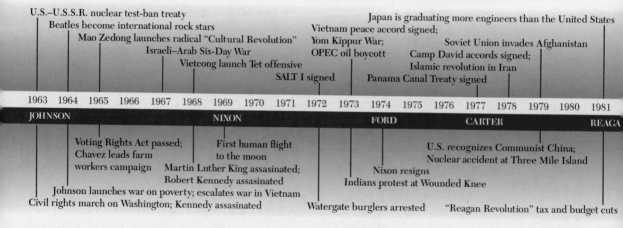

U.S.–U.S.S.R. nuclear test-ban treaty								Japan is graduating more engineers than the United States
Beatles become international rock stars					Vietnam peace accord signed;			
Mao Zedong launches radical "Cultural Revolution"				Yom Kippur War;		Soviet Union invades Afghanistan	
Israeli–Arab Six-Day War			OPEC oil boycott		Camp David accords signed;		
Vietcong launch Tet offensive				Islamic revolution in Iran		
SALT I signed		Panama Canal Treaty signed				

1963 1964 1965 1966 1967 1968 1969 1970 1971 1972 1973 1974 1975 1976 1977 1978 1979 1980 1981

JOHNSON   NIXON   FORD   CARTER   REAGA

Voting Rights Act passed;	First human flight			U.S. recognizes Communist China;
Chavez leads farm	to the moon			Nuclear accident at Three Mile Island
workers campaign	Martin Luther King assasinated;		Nixon resigns	
Robert Kennedy assasinated		Indians protest at Wounded Knee	
Johnson launches war on poverty; escalates war in Vietnam			
Civil rights march on Washington; Kennedy assasinated	Watergate burglars arrested	"Reagan Revolution" tax and budget cuts

gists suggested. Yet that strategy was frightening precisely because the globe could not be cut neatly into communist and noncommunist halves, each with clearly unified political and economic interests. The world was riven by ethnic, religious, and economic rivalries. When the prestige of either superpower became critically involved, such regional conflicts threatened to escalate into a full-scale nuclear war.

Both the Soviets and the Americans discovered the limits of projecting their power in regional conflicts. For more than a decade, the United States sought un-

successfully to win a war against North Vietnam by conventional means, before withdrawing in defeat. For another decade, the Soviet Union waged a similarly unsuccessful war in Afghanistan. In both cases, regional rivalries played a dominant role. In the Vietnam conflict, the Communist Ho Chi Minh was enough of a nationalist to prefer nearly any form of government, including French colonial rule, to domination by Vietnam's traditional enemy, China. It did not matter that China was led by a Communist "comrade," Mao Zedong. During the war in Afghanistan, the Soviets discovered that their rebel opponents were inspired by their Islamic faith. The 1979 revolution in Iran brought the Ayatollah Khomeini to power and further demonstrated that Islamic fundamentalism would play a crucial role in the Middle East and the Saharan subcontinent. Those same religious divisions led increasingly to disputes within the Soviet Union, weakening its own empire.

In the midst of the ongoing cold war, Europe recovered from the devastation of World War II, thanks in part to aid from the United States. Over the next few

988

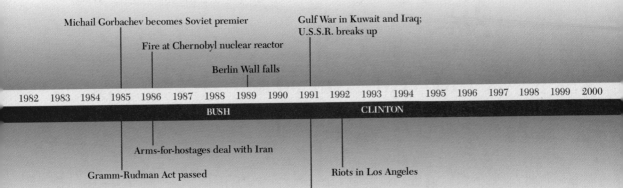

Michail Gorbachev becomes Soviet premier

Fire at Chernobyl nuclear reactor

Berlin Wall falls

Gulf War in Kuwait and Iraq;
U.S.S.R. breaks up

| 1982 | 1983 | 1984 | 1985 | 1986 | 1987 | 1988 | 1989 | 1990 | 1991 | 1992 | 1993 | 1994 | 1995 | 1996 | 1997 | 1998 | 1999 | 2000 |

BUSH   CLINTON

Arms-for-hostages deal with Iran

Gramm-Rudman Act passed

Riots in Los Angeles

Recession: lowest rate of job growth since World War II

decades, the peacetime economic expansion that benefited the Americans also allowed both West Germany and Japan, their former enemies, to grow into modern industrial states with robust consumer economies. That prosperity, in part, helped nurture a new generation of "baby boomers," in Europe as well as America, who became politically active during the 1960s. In Africa and Asia, old colonial regimes gave way to newly independent nations.

But the global industrial economy did not expand indefinitely. In America, the boom and development mentality of the 1950s and 1960s was tempered in the 1970s as the environmental costs of air and water pollutants, strip mining, pesticides, and a host of other abuses became obvious. Similarly, by the mid-1970s major Soviet rivers like the Ural, Volga, and Dnieper had been polluted by industrial wastes. China, possessing coal reserves as great as those of the United States and the Soviet Union combined, had built so many coal-fired electrical plants that its northern cities were heavily polluted and damage from acid rain could be charted in neighboring regions.

By the end of the 1980s the natural limits of global growth and the strains of a nuclear standoff were becoming clear. The Soviet empire, perhaps the last of the old colonial powers, saw its Eastern European satellite nations break away. The Union of Soviet Socialist Republics itself split into a host of nations. Although some Americans cheered at having "won" the cold war, the U.S. economy was suffering from an immense budget deficit run up in large part by military budgets aimed at checking Soviet power.

In the emerging multipolar world of the 1990s, the process of industrialization had created a truly global theater of markets, cultures, and politics. It also created such threats as a hole in the ozone layer and the possibility of a global warming trend. The United States, no longer such a dominant economic power, looked to rebuild its decayed public infrastructure, retrain displaced workers, and restore growth without further degrading the global environment. Half a millennium after the civilizations of two hemispheres achieved sustained contact, their ultimate fates have been indivisibly intertwined.

28

Cold War America

The war had been over for almost five months and still troopships steamed into New York and other ports. Timuel Black was packing his duffel below decks when he heard some of the white soldiers shout, "There she is! The Statue of Liberty!" Black felt a little bitter about the war. He'd been drafted in Chicago in 1943, just after race riots ripped the city. His father, a strong supporter of civil rights, was angry. "What the hell are you goin' to fight in Europe for? The fight is here." He wanted his son to go with him to demonstrate in Detroit, except the roads were blocked and the buses and trains screened to prevent more African Americans from coming in.

Instead, Black went off to fight the Nazis, serving in a segregated army. He'd gone ashore during the D-Day invasion, survived the Battle of the Bulge, and marched through one of the German concentration camps. "The first thing you get is the stench," he recalled. "Everybody knows that's human stench. You begin to realize something terrible had happened. There's quietness. You get closer and you begin to see what's happened to these creatures. And you get—I got more passionately angry than I guess I'd ever been." He thought: if it could happen here, to the Germans, it could happen anywhere. It could happen to black folk in America. So when the white soldiers called to come up and see the Statue of Liberty, Black's reaction was, "Hell, I'm not goin' up there. Damn that." But after all, he went up. "All of a sudden, I found myself with tears, cryin' and saying the same thing [the white soldiers] were saying. Glad to be home, proud of my country, as irregular as it is. Determined that it could be better."

At the same time Betty Basye was working across the continent as a nurse in a burn-and-blind center at Menlo Park, California. Her hospital treated soldiers shipped back from the Pacific: "Blind young men. Eyes gone, legs gone. Parts of the face. Burns—you'd land with a firebomb and be up in flames." She'd joke with the men, trying to keep their spirits up, talking about times to come. She liked to take Bill, one of her favorites, for walks downtown. Half of Bill's face was gone, and civilians would stare. It happened to other patients, too. "Nicely dressed women, absolutely staring, just standing there staring." Some people wrote the local paper, wondering why disfigured vets couldn't be kept on their own grounds and off the streets. Such callousness made Basye indignant. The war was over—"and we're still here." After a time, she started dating a soldier back from the South Pacific. "I got busy after

The mushroom-cloud image captured both the spectacle and the potential horror of atomic warfare. With scant regard for the effects of radioactive fallout, the Defense Department conducted above-ground tests like this one near Las Vegas, Nevada, in 1953.

the war," she recalled, "getting married and having my four children. That's what you were supposed to do. And getting your house in suburbia."

Yet as Basye and Black soon discovered, the return to "normal" life was filled with uncertainties. The first truly global war had left a large part of Europe in ruins and the old balance of power shattered. The dramatic events occurring month after month during 1945 and 1946 made it clear that whatever new world order emerged, the United States would have a central role in building it. Isolation seemed neither practical nor desirable in an era in which the power of the Soviet Union and communism seemed on the rise. To blunt that threat the United States converted not so much to peace as to a "cold war" against its former Soviet ally.

This undeclared war came to affect almost every aspect of American life. Abroad, it justified a far wider military and economic role for the United States in areas like the Middle East and the Pacific rim nations of Asia, from Korea to Indochina. At home it sent politicians scurrying across the land in a search for Communist spies and "subversives." The red hunt led from the State Department to

Effects of the cold war

the movie studios of Hollywood and even into college classrooms. Preparing for war in times of peace dramatically increased the role of the military–industrial–university complex formed during World War II.

Like the return to "normalcy" after the first world war, the new postwar era was notable for what was *not* normal about it. In a time of peace, a cold war produced unprecedented military budgets, awesomely destructive weapon systems, and continued international tension. A nation that had traditionally followed an isolationist foreign policy now possessed military forces deployed across the globe. A people who had once kept government intrusion into the economy at a minimum now voted to maintain programs that ensured an active federal role. That economy produced prosperity beyond anything Americans had known before.

THE RISE OF THE COLD WAR

World War II devastated lands and people almost everywhere outside the Western Hemisphere. Once the war ended the world struggled to rebuild. Power that had once been centered in Europe shifted to nations on its periphery. In place of Germany, France, and England the United States and the Soviet Union emerged as the world's two reigning superpowers—and as enemies. Their rivalry was not altogether an equal one. The United States ended the war with a booming economy, a massive military establishment, and the atomic bomb. By contrast, much of the Soviet Union lay in ruins.

Americans fear Soviet intentions

But the defeat of Germany and Japan left no power in Europe or Asia to block the still formidable Soviet army. And many Americans feared that desperate, warweary peoples would find the appeal of communism irresistible. If Stalin intended to extend the Soviet Union's dominion, only the United States had the economic and military might to block him. Events in the critical years of 1945 and 1946 persuaded most Americans that Stalin did have such a plan. The Truman administration concluded that "the USSR has engaged the United States in a struggle for power, or 'cold war,' in which our national security is at stake and from which we cannot withdraw short of national suicide." What had happened that led Western leaders to such a dire view of their former Soviet allies? How did the breach between the two nations become irreparable?

Cracks in the Alliance

When Truman entered the White House, he lacked Roosevelt's easy confidence that he could manage "Uncle Joe" Stalin. The new president approached the Soviets with a good deal more suspicion. "Stalin is an SOB, but of course he thinks I'm one, too," Truman commented after their meeting at Potsdam in July 1945. Roosevelt had hoped to strike a balance between the idealism of Wilsonian internationalism and the more practical reality that the major powers would continue to guarantee their own security. Spheres of influence would inevitably continue to exist. What was not clear was just how far each sphere would extend. That uncertainty contained the seeds of conflict. Behind all the diplomatic bowing and bluffing, what were the Soviets' real intentions? Their demand that Poland's borders be adjusted was easy to understand. The new boundaries there would strengthen Soviet national security.

Stalin had also asked that Russia join Turkey in assuming joint control of the Dardanelles, the narrow straits linking Soviet ports on the Black Sea with the Mediterranean (see the map, page 998). During the war, both Roosevelt and Churchill had been willing to consider such a change, especially since Turkey had leaned toward the Axis. In the uncertain postwar atmosphere, Stalin's intentions seemed less acceptable. The Russian dictator had also suggested that the Soviet Union become trustee of Libya, Italy's former African colony. As one British diplomat at Potsdam aptly put it, the great debate was "whether Russia [is] peaceful and wants to join the Western Club but is suspicious of us, or whether she is out to dominate the world and is hoodwinking us." Truman and his advisers, like the diplomat, tended to opt for the same answer: "It always seems safer to go on the worse assumption."

What were Soviet ambitions?

American suspicions were not eased when they looked to Greece, where local Communists led the fighting to overturn the traditional monarchy. And in November 1945 Soviet forces occupying northern Iran lent support to rebels seeking to break away from the Iranian government. Asia, too, seemed a target for Communist ambitions. Russian occupation forces in Manchuria were turning over captured Japanese arms to the Chinese Communist forces of Mao Zedong. Russian troops controlled the northern half of Korea. In Vietnam leftist nationalists were fighting against the return of colonial rule. To deal with this combination of menace and disorder Harry Truman and his advisers sought to frame a policy.

The View from West and East

While postwar events heightened American suspicions of the Soviets, that mistrust had deeper roots. A deep ideological gulf had long separated the two nations. After the October Revolution of 1917, most Americans viewed Lenin's Bolshevik revolutionaries with a mixture of fear, suspicion, and loathing. In their grasp for power the Communists had often used violence, terror, and crime to achieve their ends. As Marxists they rejected both religion and the notion of private property, two institutions central to the American dream. Stalin's brutal purges during the late 1930s created a horrifying image of the Soviet Union. This was a totalitarian state ruled by terror. Then in 1939 Stalin had signed a cynical nonaggression pact with Germany, freeing him to divide Poland with Germany and make war on his Finnish neighbors. Would the defeat of Germany and Japan free the Soviet dictator to renew his expansion? If it did, how would the Western powers react?

Roots of the cold war

The events leading to World War II provided one lesson in what a policy of "appeasement" could mean. When Neville Chamberlain attempted to satisfy Hitler's demands in 1938, it only emboldened the Nazis to expand further. After the war, Secretary of the Navy James Forrestal applied the Munich analogy to the new situa-

Joseph Stalin

Munich analogy

tion in Europe. Giving in to Russian claims would only seem like an attempt "to buy their understanding and sympathy. We tried that once with Hitler. . . . There are no returns on appeasement." To many of Truman's advisers, the Soviet dictator seemed to be every bit as much bent on conquest as Hitler.

COUNTERPOINT

What were Stalin's intentions?

What was Stalin's view of the postwar world? Because Soviet records have remained secret for so many decades, historians have lacked sufficient information to explain Stalin's intentions. But revisionist historians have made the case that American policymakers consistently exaggerated Soviet ambitions. Over the previous two centuries, Russians had seen their lands invaded once by Napoleon (in 1812) and twice by Germany, during the two world wars. In 1945, as the Soviets struggled to rebuild their war-ravaged economy, the United States continued to gain influence and power throughout the world. When Stalin looked outward, he saw American occupation forces in Europe and Asia ringing the Soviet Union, their military might backed by a newly developed atomic arsenal. American corporations owned or controlled vast oil fields in the Middle East. Along with the French and British, the United States was a strong presence in Southeast Asia. Given that situation, one could argue that Stalin's actions after the war were primarily defensive, designed to counter what appeared to him a threatening American–European alliance.

More recently, some historians have used evidence from newly opened Russian archives to argue that Stalin's position was hardly as defensive as some scholars had suggested. Despite the ravages of war, Stalin recognized that in 1945 the Soviet Union was emerging as a more powerful state. With Germany and Japan defeated, Soviet borders to the east and west were secure from invasion. Only to the south did Stalin see a problem, along the border with Iran. Further, he recognized that the people of Britain and the United States had tired of fighting. Their leaders were not about to threaten the Soviet Union with war, at least in the near term. Equally significant, Soviet spies had informed Stalin that in late 1946 the United States possessed only a few atom bombs. For the time being, the nuclear threat was more symbolic than real. These historians thus conclude that Stalin was neither a global expansionist nor a leader fearful that his nation would soon be encircled and broken apart by American imperialists. Rather, he was a political realist eager to advance the interests of the Soviet state and his own regime—so long as his actions did not risk war.

Toward Containment

The disagreements arising out of the conflicting Soviet and American points of view came to a head in the first months of 1946. For his part, Stalin announced in February that the Soviet Union would take unilateral steps to preserve its national security. In a world dominated by capitalism, he warned, future wars were inevitable. The Russian people had to ensure against "any eventuality" by undertaking a new five-year plan for economic development.

Some Americans thought Stalin was merely rallying Russian support for his domestic programs. Others saw their worst fears confirmed. *Time* magazine, an early voice for a "get tough" policy, called Stalin's speech "the most warlike pronouncement uttered by any top-rank statesman since V-J day." "I'm tired of babying the Soviets," remarked the president, who in any case seldom wore kid gloves. Even Truman's mother passed along a message: "Tell Harry to be good, be honest, and behave himself, but I think it is now time for him to get tough with someone." In March Winston Churchill warned that the Soviets had dropped an "Iron Curtain" between their satellite nations and the free world.

As policymakers groped for an effective way to deal with these developments, the State Department received a diplomatic cable, extraordinary for both its length (8000 words) and its impact in Washington. The author was George Kennan, chargé d'affaires in Moscow and long a student of Soviet conduct. Kennan argued that Russian leaders, including Stalin, were so paranoid that it was impossible to reach any useful accommodations with them. This temperament could best be explained by "the traditional and instinctive Russian sense of insecurity." That insecurity, when combined with Marxist ideology that viewed capitalism as evil, created a potent force for expansion. Soviet power, Kennan explained, "moves inexorably along a prescribed path, like a toy automobile wound up and headed in a given direction, stopping only when it meets some unanswerable force." *George Kennan's long telegram*

The response Kennan recommended was "containment." The United States must apply "unalterable counterforce at every point where [the Soviets] show signs of encroaching upon the interests of a peaceful and stable world." The idea of containment was not particularly novel, but Kennan's historical analysis provided leaders in Washington with a framework for analyzing Soviet behavior. It also laid out a plan for responding to that behavior. By applying firm diplomatic, economic, and military counterpressure, the United States could block Russian aggression. Eventually, that firmness might even persuade the Soviets to reform their domestic institutions. Only with free speech, a free press, and democratic elections in the Soviet Union would a reasonable accommodation between East and West be possible. Navy Secretary Forrestal was so impressed with Kennan's "long telegram," as it came to be known, that he sent hundreds of copies to high officials in Washington as well as American diplomats abroad. Truman wholeheartedly adopted the doctrine of containment.

The Truman Doctrine

At first it appeared that Iran, lying along the Soviet Union's southern border, would provide the first test for containment. An independent Iran seemed crucial in protecting rich fields of petroleum in the Persian Gulf region. In 1943 an oil mission sent to the area had reported that vast Middle Eastern oil fields would soon displace those in the United States as the center of world production. American oil companies had already taken a major position in the region alongside British fields established earlier in the century. During World War II the United States had adopted a far more active role in the affairs of Iran, Turkey, Saudi Arabia, and other Middle Eastern states.

At war's end, Stalin failed to respect his treaty obligation to withdraw Russian troops. The presence of those troops might force Iran to grant economic and political concessions. In March 1946 Secretary of State James Byrnes went to the United *The Iranian crisis*

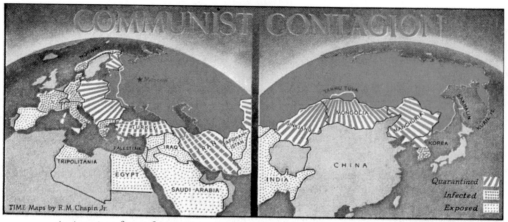

As American fears of Soviet intentions increased, journalists often described communism as though it were a disease, an inhuman force, or a savage predator. In April 1946, *Time* magazine, a particularly outspoken source of anti-Communist rhetoric, portrayed the spread of "infection" throughout Europe and Asia as the "Red Menace."

Nations, determined to force a showdown over continued Soviet occupation of northern Iran. But before he could extract his pound of Russian flesh, the Soviets reached an agreement with Iran to withdraw.

The face-off in Iran only intensified American suspicions. In Europe severe winter storms and a depressed postwar economy threatened to encourage domestic Communist movements. A turning point in the cold war came in early 1947, when *Aid to Greece and Turkey* Great Britain announced that it could no longer support the governments of Greece and Turkey. Without British aid, the Communists seemed destined to win critical victories. Truman decided that the United States should provide $400 million in military and economic aid. He went before Congress in March, determined to "scare hell out of the country." The world was now divided into two hostile camps, the president warned. To preserve the American way of life, the United States must now step forward and help "free people" threatened by "totalitarian regimes." This rationale for aid to Greece and Turkey soon became known as the Truman Doctrine.

Critics pointed out that the president had placed no limits on the American commitment. His was a proposal not simply to contain Communists in Greece and Turkey but to resist Soviet expansion everywhere. Robert Taft, once a leader of congressional isolationists, thought it was a mistake to talk about a bipolar world divided between Communist and anti-Communist camps. Congress, however, supported the new cold war crusade. It voted overwhelmingly to grant aid to Greece and Turkey.

The Truman Doctrine marked a new level of American commitment to a cold war. Just what responsibility the Soviets had for unrest in Greece and Turkey remained unclear. But Truman had linked communism with rebel movements all across the globe. That committed Americans to a relatively open-ended struggle. In the battle between communism and freedom, the president gained expanded powers to act when unrest threatened. Occasionally Congress would regret giving the executive branch so much power, but by 1947 anticommunism had become the dominant theme in American policy, both foreign and domestic.

Yet success brought little comfort. The Soviet Union was not simply a major power seeking to protect its interests and expand where opportunity permitted. In the eyes of many Americans, the Soviets were determined, if they could, to overthrow the United States from either without or within. This was a war being fought not only across the globe but right in America, by unseen agents using subversive means. In this way, the cold war mentality soon came to shape the lives of Americans at home much as it did American policy abroad.

POSTWAR PROSPERITY

At war's end, many business leaders feared that a sudden drop in government purchases would bring back the hard times of the 1930s. Once war production ended, wartime boom towns might become ghost towns. Hard times would offer fertile ground for those, like the Communists, who fed on discontent. But the hard times never came. Instead, Americans entered into the longest period of prosperity in the nation's history, lasting until the 1970s. Even the fear of communism could not dampen the simple joys of getting and spending.

Two forces drove the postwar economic boom. One was unbridled consumer and business spending that followed 16 years of depression and war. High war wages had piled up in savings accounts and war bonds. Eager consumers set off to find the new cars, appliances, and foods unavailable during the war. Despite a sharp drop in government spending (from $83 billion in 1945 to only $31 billion in 1946), the gross national product fell less than 1 percent and employment actually increased. Consumers had taken up the slack.

Sources of prosperity

Government expenditures at the local, state, and federal levels provided another boost to prosperity. The three major growth industries in the decades after World War II were health care, education, and government programs. Each of these was spurred by public spending. Equally important, the federal government poured millions of dollars into the military–industrial sector. The defense budget, which fell to $9 billion in 1947, reached $50 billion by the time Truman left office. Over the longer term, these factors promoting economic growth became clearer. In 1946, though, the road from war to peace seemed much more uncertain, especially for those at the margins of the economy.

Postwar Adjustments

With millions of veterans looking for peacetime jobs, workers on the home front, especially women and minorities, found themselves out of work. Cultural attitudes added to the pressure on these groups to resume more traditional roles. War employment had given many women their first taste of economic independence. As peace came, almost 75 percent of the working women in one survey indicated that they hoped to continue their jobs. But as the troops came home, male social scientists stressed how important it was for women to accept "more than the wife's usual responsibility for her marriage" and offer "lavish—and undemanding—affection" to returning GIs. One marriage counselor urged women to let their husbands know "you are tired of living alone, that you want him now to take charge."

Minority workers

For minorities, the end of the war brought a return of an old labor practice, "last hired, first fired." At the height of the war over 200,000 African Americans and Hispanics had found jobs in shipbuilding. By 1946 that number had dwindled to fewer than 10,000. The influx of Mexican laborers under the bracero program temporarily halted. In the South, where the large majority of black Americans lived, wartime labor shortages had become surpluses, leaving few jobs available.

At the same time, many black and Hispanic veterans who fought during the war had been treated with greater equality and freedom than they had known before enlisting. Thus they often resented returning to a deeply segregated society with limited opportunities. One observer noted that Hispanic veterans in Texas were no longer willing to tolerate discrimination. They "have acquired a new courage, have become more vocal in protesting the restrictions and inequalities with which they are confronted." Benefits received under the GI Bill allowed many Mexican Americans to enter the middle class. When confronted by "haughty, lordly, or unfriendly" businesses, they sometimes organized informal boycotts. Much of the Anglo business community learned to respect this new activism.

Veterans and civil rights

Black veterans exerted a similar impact on the civil rights movement. Angered by violence, frustrated by the slow pace of desegregation, they breathed new energy into civil rights organizations like the NAACP and the Congress of Racial Equality. Voting rights was one of the issues they pushed. Registration drives in the South had the greatest success in urban centers like Atlanta. Other black leaders pressed for improved education. In rural Virginia, for example, a young Howard University lawyer,

---

Having lived through twelve years of depression, Americans placed jobs at the top of their postwar domestic agenda. The Employment Act of 1946 shifted responsibility for a full-employment economy from the private sector to the federal government.

for full employment after the war
REGISTER•VOTE
C I O POLITICAL ACTION COMMITTEE

In San Antonio, Texas, Mexican American veterans helped form the Liga Pro Defensa Escolar, or School Improvement League. The huge crowd at this 1948 meeting demonstrated the interest among Hispanic Americans in tearing down the Jim Crow system of school segregation.

Spottswood Robinson, litigated cases for the NAACP to force improvement in segregated all-black schools. In one county Robinson and the NAACP even won equal pay for black and white teachers.

Out in the countryside, however, segregationists used economic intimidation, violence, and even murder to preserve the "Jim Crow" system. White citizens in rural Georgia lynched several black veterans who had shown the determination to vote. Such instances disturbed President Truman, who saw civil rights as a key ingredient in his reform agenda. The president was especially disturbed when he learned that police in South Carolina had gouged out the eyes of a recently discharged black veteran. Truman responded in December 1946 by appointing a Committee on Civil Rights. A year later it published its report, *To Secure These Rights*.

To Secure These Rights

Discovering inequities for minorities, the committee exposed a racial caste system that denied African Americans employment opportunities, equal education, voting rights, and decent housing. But every time Truman appealed to Congress to implement the committee's recommendations, southern senators threatened to filibuster. That opposition forced the president to resort to executive authority to achieve even modest results. In his most direct attack on segregation, he issued an executive order in July 1948 banning discrimination in the armed forces. Segregationists predicted disaster, but experience soon demonstrated that integrated units fought well and exhibited minimal racial tension.

POPULAR ENTERTAINMENT

Jackie Robinson Integrates Baseball

After World War II, Branch Rickey of the Brooklyn Dodgers was determined to break the color line in baseball. For years he had wanted to give black players the opportunity to play in the majors. Equally to the point, he was convinced that this action would improve his team. "The greatest untapped reservoir of raw material in the history of the game is the black race," he explained, adding, "The Negroes will make us winners for years to come. . . ."

In the early years of professional baseball, African Americans had played on several major league teams. In 1887, however, as Jim Crow laws spread across the South, the threat of a boycott by some white players caused team owners to adopt an unwritten rule barring black players. That ban stood for 60 years. Even the most talented black ballplayers could only barnstorm at unofficial exhibitions or play in the Negro League.

World War II created a new climate. The hypocrisy of fighting racism abroad while promoting it at home was becoming harder for team owners to ignore. "If a black boy can make it on Okinawa and Guadalcanal," Commissioner Albert "Happy" Chandler told reporters in April 1945, "hell, he can make it in baseball." Economic factors played a role as well. The African American migration to northern cities during World War II created a new, untapped audience for major league baseball. Growing cold war tensions added another factor. Even a Mississippi newspaper saw blacks in the major leagues as "a good answer to our communist adversaries who say the Negro has no chance in America."

Rickey recognized the enormous hostility that the first black player would face. He found the ideal prospect in Jackie Robinson, a World War II veteran and a remarkable athlete who had lettered in four sports at UCLA. After the war Robinson had signed with the Kansas City Monarchs in the Negro League. Rickey asked Robinson to a meeting in 1945, where he laid out his proposition. But "I need a man that will take abuse, insults," he warned. Robinson would be carrying "the flag for [his] race."

Robinson was intensely proud of his people and his heritage. He had risked court-martial during the war to fight segregation. "Nobody's going to separate bullets and label them 'for white troops' and 'for colored troops,'" Robinson told a superior officer. But he let Rickey know that he would turn the other cheek. "If you want to take this gamble, I will promise you there will be no incident." Rickey assigned him to Montreal where he led the Dodgers' farm team to a championship.

When the Dodgers invited Robinson to spring training, several southern-born players circulated a petition stating their opposition to playing with a black man. But manager Leo Durocher bluntly warned them they would be traded if they refused to cooperate. Robinson would make them all rich, Durocher insisted.

On April 15, 1947, Robinson made his debut with the Dodgers at Ebbets Field. A black newspaper, the Boston *Chronicle,* proclaimed, "TRIUMPH OF WHOLE RACE SEEN IN JACKIE'S DEBUT IN MAJOR LEAGUE BALL." Half of the fans in the stands that day were African Americans. They cheered wildly at everything Robinson did. Indeed, blacks everywhere instantly adopted the Dodgers as their team, showing up in large numbers when Brooklyn was on the road.

If anything, the abuse heaped on Robinson was worse than Rickey had antic-

Daily Lives

It is not difficult to identify Jackie Robinson in this photo, as the Brooklyn Dodgers celebrate a key win in the 1948 pennant race. Though Robinson had made the Dodgers a much better team, full integration of major league sports took many more years.

ipated. Opposing players shouted vicious racial epithets. Robinson received death threats, his family was harassed, and some hotels barred him from staying with the team. He secretly wore a protective lining inside his hat in case he was beaned (he was hit a record 9 times during the season, 65 times in seven years), and on several occasions he was spiked by opposing players. Through it all, Robinson kept his temper, though not without difficulty. Once when a Cubs' player kicked him, Robinson started to swing, then stopped. "I knew I was kind of an experiment," he recalled; ". . . the whole thing was bigger than me."

Robinson spoke with his glove, his bat, and his feet, not his fists. His daring base running, which he learned in the old Negro League, brought a new excitement to the game (he stole home 19 times in his career). In his first year, the Dodgers won the pen-

nant and he was named Rookie of the Year. Two years later he was named the Most Valuable Player in the National League. After he retired in 1957, the skill and dignity he brought to the game earned him a place in baseball's Hall of Fame.

In the wake of his success other teams added African Americans. Professional basketball and football followed baseball's lead. Still, the pace of integration was slow, and it was not until 1959 that all major league teams had a black member. Nevertheless, for once baseball had led the nation rather than followed it: the armed services were not integrated until 1948, and the Supreme Court would not strike down segregation until seven years after Robinson first played for the Dodgers. Thanks to the vision of Branch Rickey and the courage of Jackie Robinson, America's pastime had become truly a national game.

Several Supreme Court decisions gave added weight to Truman's civil rights initiatives. In cases that indicated a growing willingness to reconsider the doctrine that black facilities could be "separate but equal" (*Plessy v. Ferguson,*1896) the Court struck down several state education laws clearly designed to create separate but inferior facilities.

Organized labor

For organized labor, reconversion brought an abrupt drop in hours worked and overtime paid. As wages declined and inflation ate into paychecks, strikes spread. Autoworkers walked off the job in the fall of 1945; steelworkers, in January 1946; miners, in April. In 1946 some 5 million workers struck, a rate triple that of any previous year. Antiunion sentiment soared. The crisis peaked in May 1946 with a national rail strike, which temporarily paralyzed the nation's transportation network. An angry President Truman asked, "What decent American would pull a rail strike at a time like this?"

At first, Truman threatened to seize the railroads and then requested from Congress the power to draft striking workers into the military. The strike was settled before the threat was carried out, but few people, whether conservative or liberal, approved the idea of using the draft to punish political foes. Labor leaders, for their part, became convinced they no longer had a friend at the White House.

The New Deal at Bay

In September 1945 Harry Truman had boldly claimed his intention to extend the New Deal into the postwar era. He called for legislation to guarantee full employment, subsidized public housing, national health insurance, and a peacetime version of the Fair Employment Practices Commission to fight job discrimination. Instead of promoting his liberal agenda, he found himself fighting a conservative backlash. Labor unrest was just one source of his troubles. The increased demand for consumer goods temporarily in short supply triggered a sharp inflation. For two years prices rose as much as 15 percent annually. Consumers blamed the White House for not doing more to manage the economy.

With Truman's political stock falling, conservative Republicans and Democrats blocked the president's attempts to revive and extend the New Deal. All he achieved was a watered-down full-employment bill, which created the Council of Economic Advisers to guide the president's policies. The bill did establish the principle that the government rather than the private sector was responsible for maintaining full employment. As the congressional elections of 1946 neared, Republicans pointed to production shortages, the procession of strikes, the mismanagement of the economy. "To err is Truman," proclaimed the campaign buttons—or, more simply, "Had Enough?" Evidently many voters had. The Republicans gained control of both houses of Congress. Not since 1928 had the Democrats fared so poorly.

Leading the rightward swing was Senator Robert A. Taft of Ohio, son of former president William Howard Taft. Bob Taft not only wanted to halt the spread of the New Deal—he wanted to dismantle it. "We have to get over the corrupting idea we can legislate prosperity, legislate equality, legislate opportunity," he said in dismissing the liberal agenda. Taft especially wished to limit the power of the unions. In 1947 he

Taft–Hartley Act

pushed the Taft–Hartley Act through Congress, over Truman's veto. In the event of a strike, the bill allowed the president to order workers back on the job during a 90-day "cooling-off" period while collective bargaining continued. It also permitted states to adopt "right-to-work" laws, which banned the closed shop by eliminating union membership as a prerequisite for many jobs. Union leaders criticized the new law as a "slave-labor" act but discovered they could live with it, though it did hurt union efforts to organize, especially in the South.

A Welfare Program for GIs

Despite Republican gains, most Americans did not repudiate the New Deal's major accomplishments: social security, minimum wages, a more active role for government in reducing unemployment. The administration maintained its commitment to setting a minimum wage, raising it again in 1950 from 45 to 75 cents. Social security coverage was broadened to cover an additional 10 million workers. Furthermore, a growing list of welfare programs benefited not only the poor but veterans, middle-income families, the elderly, and students. The most striking of these was the GI Bill of 1944, *The GI Bill* designed to reward soldiers for their service during the war.

For veterans, the "GI Bill of Rights" created unparalleled opportunity. Those with more than two years of service received all tuition and fees plus living expenses for three years of college education. By 1948 the government was paying the college costs of almost 50 percent of all male students as more than 2 million veterans took advantage of the GI Bill. Increased educational levels encouraged a shift from blue- to white-collar work and self-employment. Although the number of jobs in areas like mining and manufacturing increased little if at all, work in areas like insurance, teaching, state and local governments, construction, and retailing all grew rapidly. Veterans also received low-interest loans to start businesses or farms of their own and to buy homes. By the 1950s the Veterans Administration, in charge of the program, was funding the purchase of some 20 percent of all new houses.

The GI Bill accelerated trends that would transform American society into a prosperous, heavily middle-class suburban nation. It also contributed to the economic advantages that white males held over minorities and females. Few women received benefits under the bill. Many lost their jobs or seniority to returning veterans. African Americans and Hispanics, even those eligible for veterans' benefits, were hampered by Jim Crow restrictions in segregated universities and in jobs in both the public and private sectors. The Federal Housing Administration even helped draw up "model" restrictive housing covenants. In order to "retain stability," neighborhoods were allowed to use the covenants to segregate according to "social and racial classes."

The Election of 1948

With his domestic program blocked, Harry Truman faced almost certain defeat in the election of 1948. The New Deal coalition that Franklin Roosevelt had held together for so long seemed to be coming apart. On the left Truman was challenged by Henry *Henry Wallace* Wallace, who had been a capable secretary of agriculture and vice president under *and the* Roosevelt, then secretary of commerce under Truman. Wallace wanted to pursue *progressives* New Deal reforms even more vigorously than Truman did, and he continually voiced his sympathy for the Soviet Union. Disaffected liberals bolted the Democratic party to support Wallace on a third-party Progressive ticket.

Dixiecrats

Within the southern conservative wing of the party, archsegregationists resented Truman's moderate civil rights proposals for a voting rights bill and an antilynching law. When the liberal wing of the party passed a civil rights plank as part of the Democratic platform, delegates from several Deep South states stalked out of the convention. They banded together to create the States' Rights or "Dixiecrat" party, with J. Strom Thurmond, the segregationist governor of South Carolina, as their candidate.

With the Democrats divided, Republicans smelled victory. They sought to control the political center by rejecting the conservative Taft in favor of the more moderate former New York Governor Thomas Dewey. Dewey proved so aloof that he inspired scant enthusiasm. "You have to know Dewey well to really dislike him," quipped one Taft supporter. Such shortcomings aside, it seemed clear to most observers that Dewey would walk away with the race. Pollster Elmo Roper stopped canvassing the voters two months before the election.

Truman fights back

Truman, however, would not roll over and play dead. He launched a stinging attack against the "reactionaries" in Congress: that "bunch of old mossbacks . . . gluttons of privilege . . . all set to do a hatchet job on the New Deal." From the rear platform of his campaign train, he made almost 400 speeches in eight weeks. Over and over he hammered away at the "do-nothing" 80th Congress, which, he told farmers, "had stuck a pitchfork" in their backs. Still, on election day oddsmakers favored Dewey by as much as 20 to 1. Hours before the polls closed the archconservative Chicago *Tribune* happily headlined "Dewey Defeats Truman." But the experts were wrong. Not only did the voters return Truman by over 2 million popular votes, they gave the Democrats commanding majorities in the House and Senate.

The defection of the liberal and conservative extremes had allowed Truman to hold the New Deal coalition together, after all. Jews grateful for his stand on Israel, Catholics loyal to the Democratic party, and ethnics all supported him. He had been the first major presidential candidate to campaign in Harlem. Farmers hurt by falling prices deserted the Republicans. An easing of inflation had reminded middle-income Americans that they had benefited significantly under Democratic leadership. "I

ELECTION OF 1948

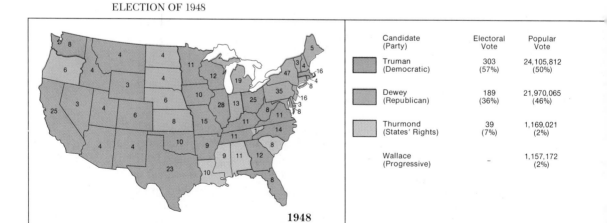

Candidate (Party)	Electoral Vote	Popular Vote
Truman (Democratic)	303 (57%)	24,105,812 (50%)
Dewey (Republican)	189 (36%)	21,970,065 (46%)
Thurmond (States' Rights)	39 (7%)	1,169,021 (2%)
Wallace (Progressive)	–	1,157,172 (2%)

1948

have a new car and am much better off than my parents were. Why change?" one suburban voter remarked.

The Fair Deal

As he began his new term, Harry Truman expressed his conviction that all Americans were entitled to a "Fair Deal" from their government. His agenda called for a vigorous revival of New Deal programs like national health insurance and regional TVA-style projects. Echoing an old Populist idea, Truman hoped to keep his working coalition together by forging stronger links between farmers and labor.

As before, a conservative coalition of Democrats and Republicans in Congress blocked any significant new initiatives. They voted down plans for a St. Lawrence Seaway in the Northeast, rejected national health insurance, and refused to approve federal aid to education. Furthermore, Truman could not forge a working coalition between farmers and labor. The farm bloc would not support labor in its attempts to repeal the Taft–Hartley Act, nor would labor vote to help pass farm price supports designed to encourage family farms at the expense of larger agribusinesses. On the domestic front Truman remained largely the conservator of Franklin Roosevelt's legacy.

THE COLD WAR AT HOME

Bob Raymondi, a mobster serving a prison term in the late 1940s, was no stranger to extortion, racketeering, or gangland killings. In fact, he was so feared that he dominated the inmate population at Dannemora Prison. Raymondi began to make the acquaintance of a group of Communists who had been jailed for advocating the overthrow of the government. He enjoyed talking with people who had some education. When Raymondi's sister learned about his new friends, she was frantic. "My God, Bob," she told him. "You'll get into trouble."

Was something amiss? Most Americans judged it riskier to associate with Communists than with hardened criminals. Out of a population of 150 million, the Communist party in 1950 could claim a membership of only 43,000. (More than a few of those were FBI undercover agents.) But worry about Communists Americans did. In part, conscientious citizens were appalled by party members who excused Stalin's violent crimes against his own people. Millions of Russians had been executed or sent to Siberian labor camps; under those circumstances, most Americans found it outrageous to hear American Communists dismiss civil liberties as "bourgeois."

Conservative Anticommunism

Conservatives were especially outspoken about the Communist menace. Some honestly feared the New Deal as "creeping socialism." The president's advisers, it seemed to them, were either Communist agents or their unwitting dupes. Leftists, they believed, controlled labor unions, Hollywood, and other interest groups sympathetic to the New Deal. Their outrage grew after the war as Stalin extended Soviet control in Eastern Europe and Asia. Many conservatives charged that a conspiracy within Roosevelt's administration had sold out America to its enemies. More cynical conservatives used red baiting simply to discredit people and ideas they disliked.

The Shocks of 1949

Truman won in 1948 in large part because of his strong leadership in foreign affairs. In 1949 a series of foreign policy shocks allowed Republicans to seize the anti-Communist issue. In August American scientists reported that rains monitored in the Pacific contained traces of hot nuclear waste. Only one conclusion seemed possible:

The H-bomb the Soviet Union possessed its own atom bomb. When Truman announced the news, Congress was debating whether to spend $1.5 billion for military aid to the newly formed NATO alliance. The House stopped debating and voted the bill through, while Truman directed that research into a newer, more powerful fusion, or hydrogen, bomb continue. Senator Arthur Vandenberg, a Republican with wide experience in international affairs, summed up the reaction of many to the end of the American nuclear monopoly: "This is now a different world."

China falls to Then in December came more bad news. The long embattled Nationalist gov-
Communists ernment of Chiang Kai-shek fled mainland China to the offshore island of Formosa (present-day Taiwan). By January Communist troops under Mao Zedong swarmed

The fall of China to the Communist forces of Mao Zedong was one of two great cold war shocks of 1949. Anti-Communists joined members of the China Lobby in blaming Truman for "losing China."

into Beijing, China's capital city. Chiang's defeat came as no surprise to State Department officials, who had long regarded the Nationalists as hopelessly corrupt and inefficient. Despite major American efforts to save Chiang's regime and stabilize China, poverty and civil unrest spread in the postwar years. In 1947 full-scale civil war broke out, so Mao's triumph was hardly unexpected.

But Republicans, who had up until 1949 supported the president's foreign policy, now broke ranks. For some time, a group of wealthy conservatives and Republican senators had resented the administration's preoccupation with Europe. Time-Life publisher Henry Luce used his magazines to campaign for a greater concern for Asian affairs and especially more aid to defeat Mao Zedong. Luce and his associates, known as the "China Lobby," were supported in part with funds from the Chinese embassy. When Chiang at last collapsed, his American backers charged Democrats with letting the Communists win.

Worries that subversives had sold out the country were heightened when former State Department official Alger Hiss was brought to trial in 1949 for perjury. Hiss, an adviser to Roosevelt at the Yalta Conference, had been accused by former Communist Whittaker Chambers of passing secrets to the Soviet Union during the 1930s. Though the evidence in the case was far from conclusive, the jury convicted Hiss for lying about his association with Chambers. And in February 1950 the nation was further shocked to learn that in Britain, a high-ranking physicist, Klaus Fuchs, had spied for the Russians while working on the Manhattan Project. Here was clear evidence of conspiracy at work.

The Hiss case

The Loyalty Crusade

President Truman sought to blunt Republican accusations that he was "soft" on communism. Ten days after proposing the Truman Doctrine in March 1947, the president signed an executive order establishing a Federal Employee Loyalty Program designed to guard against the possible disloyalty of "Reds, phonies, and 'parlor pinks.'" Since the FBI could hardly find time to examine all of the 2 million government employees, the order required supervisors to review and certify the loyalties of those who worked below them, reporting to a system of federal loyalty review boards.

The system quickly got out of hand. Seth Richardson, the conservative who headed the Loyalty Review Board, brushed the Bill of Rights aside. In his opinion, the government could "discharge any employee for reasons which seem sufficient to the Government, and without extending to such employee any hearing whatsoever." After several years the difficulty of proving that employees were actually disloyal became clear, and Truman allowed the boards to fire those who were "potentially" disloyal or "bad security risks," such as alcoholics, homosexuals, and debtors. Suspect employees, in other words, were assumed guilty until proven innocent. After some 5 million investigations, the program identified a few hundred employees who, though not Communists, had at one time been associated with suspect groups. Rather than calm public fears, the loyalty program gave credibility to the growing red scare.

Loyalty Review Board

HUAC, Hollywood, and Unions

About the same time Truman established the Loyalty Review Board, the House Committee on Un-American Activities (HUAC) began to investigate Communist influence in the film industry. Hollywood, with its wealth, glamour, and highly visible Jewish and foreign celebrities, had long aroused a mixture of attraction and suspicion among traditional Americans. "Large numbers of moving pictures that come out of Hollywood carry the Communist line," charged committee member John Rankin of Mississippi. Indeed, during the Depression some Hollywood figures had developed ties to the Communist party or had become sympathetic to party causes. To generate support for the Allies during the war Hollywood (with Roosevelt's blessing) produced films with a positive view of the Soviet Union like *Mission to Moscow* and *Song of Russia.*

HUAC called a parade of movie stars, screen writers, and producers to sit in the glare of its public hearings. Some witnesses were considered "friendly" because, like Gary Cooper, Robert Montgomery, and Ronald Reagan, they answered committee questions or supplied names of suspected leftists. Others refused to inform on their colleagues or to answer questions about earlier ties to the Communist party. Eventually 10 uncooperative witnesses, known as the "Hollywood Ten," refused on First Amendment grounds to say whether they were or ever had been Communists. They served prison terms for contempt of Congress.

For all its probing, HUAC never offered convincing evidence that filmmakers were in any way subversive. About the most damning evidence presented was that one eager left-leaning extra, when asked to "whistle something" during his walk-on part, hummed a few bars of the Communist anthem the "Internationale." The investigations did, however, inspire nervous Hollywood producers to turn out films like *The Iron Curtain* (1948), in which a Russian spy ring in the United States is exposed, and *I Was a Communist for the FBI* (1950). The studios also purged anyone sus-

Blacklisting   pected of disloyalty, adopting a blacklist that prevented admitted or accused Communists from finding work. Since no judicial proceedings were involved, victims of false charges, rumors, or spiteful accusations found it nearly impossible to clear their names.

Suspicion of aliens and immigrants led finally to the passage, over Truman's veto,
McCarran Act   of the McCarran Act (1950). It required all Communists to register with the attorney general, forbade the entry of anyone who had belonged to a totalitarian organization, and allowed the Justice Department to detain suspect aliens indefinitely during deportation hearings. It was supported overwhelmingly in Congress. That same year a Senate committee began an inquiry designed to root out homosexuals holding government jobs. Even one "sex pervert in a Government agency tends to have a corrosive influence upon his fellow employees," warned the committee. The campaign had effects beyond government offices: the armed forces stepped up their rates of dismissal for sexual orientation, while city police more frequently raided gay bars and social clubs.

The Ambitions of Senator McCarthy

By 1950 anticommunism had created a climate of fear where legitimate concerns mixed with irrational hysteria. Joseph R. McCarthy, a Senate nonentity from Wisconsin, saw in that fear an issue to rebuild his political fortunes. To an audience in Wheeling, West Virginia, in February 1950 he waved a sheaf of papers in the air and announced that he had a list of 205—or perhaps 81, 57, or "a lot of"— Communists in the State Department. (No one, including the senator, could remember the number, which he continually changed.) In the following months

Godless Communists run wild as the American flag goes up in flames in this comic book distributed by patriotic church groups. Over 4 million copies were printed to try to counter the influence of suspected subversives infiltrating American society.

McCarthy leveled charge after charge. He had penetrated the "iron curtain" of the State Department to discover "card-carrying Communists," the "top Russian espionage agent" in the United States, "egg-sucking phony liberals," and "Communists and queers" who wrote "perfumed notes."

It seemed not to matter that McCarthy never substantiated his charges. When examined, his lists contained names of people who had left the State Department long before or who had been cleared by the FBI. When forced into a corner, McCarthy simply lied and went on to another accusation. No one seemed beyond reach. In the summer of 1950 a Senate committee headed by Millard F. Tydings of Maryland concluded that McCarthy's charges were "a fraud and a hoax." Such candor among those in government did not last long, as "Jolting Joe" (one of McCarthy's favorite macho nicknames) in 1952 helped defeat Tydings and several other Senate critics.

McCarthy served some conservative Republicans as a blunt instrument they used to damage the Democrats. Without their support, he would have had little credibility. Many of his accusations came from information secretly (and illegally) funneled to him by FBI Director J. Edgar Hoover. But McCarthyism was also the bitter fruit Truman and the Democrats reaped from their own attempts to exploit the anti-Communist mood. McCarthy, more than Truman, had tapped the fears and hatreds of a broad coalition of Catholic leaders, conservatives, and neo-isolationists who har-

The appeal of McCarthyism

bored suspicion of things foreign, liberal, internationalist, European, or vaguely intellectual. They saw McCarthy and his fellow witch-hunters as the protectors of a vaguely defined but deeply felt spirit of Americanism.

By the time Truman stepped down as president, 32 states had laws requiring teachers to take loyalty oaths, government loyalty boards were asking employees what newspapers they subscribed to or phonograph records they collected, and a library in Indiana had banned *Robin Hood* because the idea of stealing from the rich to give to the poor seemed rather too leftish. As one historian commented, "Opening the valve of anticommunist hysteria was a good deal simpler than closing it."

FROM COLD WAR TO HOT WAR AND BACK

As the cold war heated up in 1949, the Truman administration searched for a more assertive foreign policy—one that went beyond George Kennan's notion of "containment." The new policy was developed by the National Security Council (NSC), an agency created by Congress in 1947 as part of a plan to help the executive branch respond more effectively to cold war crises. The army, navy, and air force were united under a single Department of Defense. All overseas intelligence gathering and espionage activities became the responsibility of the Central Intelligence Agency. To the National Security Council fell the job of advising the president about foreign and military policy. From the beginning, the NSC had lobbied for an active policy not just to contain the Soviets but also to win the cold war. In April 1950 it sent Truman a document, NSC-68, which came to serve as the framework for American policy over the next 20 years.

NSC-68   NSC-68 argued that rather than merely hold the Soviets at bay, the United States should "strive for victory." To that end NSC-68 called for an immediate increase in defense spending from $13 billion to $50 billion a year, to be paid for with a large tax increase. Most of the funds would go to rebuild conventional forces, but the NSC urged that the hydrogen bomb be developed to offset the Soviet nuclear capacity. At the same time the American people had to be mobilized to make the necessary sacrifices while the United States worked (NSC-68 never explained how) to make "the Russian people our Allies" in undermining their totalitarian government.

Efforts to carry out NSC-68 at first aroused widespread opposition. George Kennan argued that the Soviets had no immediate plans for domination outside the Communist bloc. Thus, NSC-68 was too simplistic and militaristic. Fiscal conservatives, both Democrat and Republican, resisted any proposal for higher taxes. Truman's own secretary of defense, Louis Johnson, warned that the new military budget would bankrupt the country. All such reservations were swept away on June 25, 1950. "Korea came along and saved us," Acheson later remarked.

Police Action

In 1950 Korea was about the last place in the world Americans might have imagined themselves fighting a war. Since World War II the country had been divided along the 38th parallel, the north controlled by the Communist government of Kim Il Sung, the south by the dictatorship of Syngman Rhee. Preoccupied with China and the rebuilding of Japan, the Truman administration's interest had dwindled steadily after the war. When Secretary of State Dean Acheson discussed American policy in Asia before the National Press Club in January 1950, he did not even mention Korea.

On June 24 Harry Truman was enjoying a leisurely break from politics at the family home in Independence, Missouri. In Korea it was already Sunday morning when Acheson called the president. North Korean troops had crossed the 38th parallel, Acheson reported, possibly to fulfill Kim Il Sung's proclaimed intention to "lib-

The North Korean invasion

THE KOREAN WAR

In their opening offensive, North Korean troops almost pushed South Korean and American forces into the sea at Pusan. After MacArthur rallied United Nations forces, he commanded a successful landing at Inchon behind North Korean lines and then crossed the 38th parallel into North Korea. Red Chinese troops counterattacked, inflicting on U.S. troops one of the most humiliating defeats in American military history. Fighting continued for another two years.

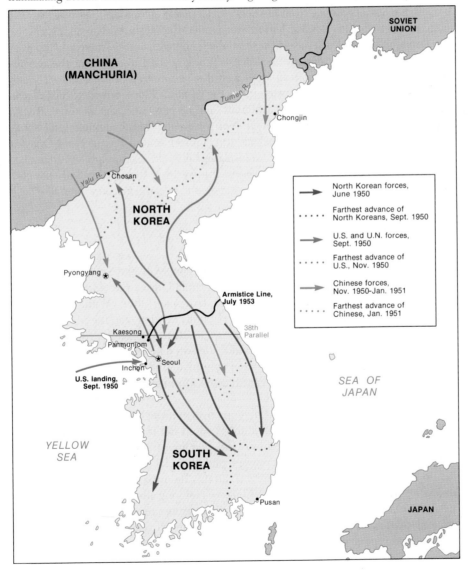

erate" the South. Soon Acheson confirmed that a full-scale invasion was in progress. The United Nations, meeting in emergency session, had ordered a cease-fire, which the North Koreans were ignoring. With that, Truman flew back to Washington, convinced that Stalin and his Chinese Communist allies had ordered the invasion. Kim, Truman reasoned, would hardly have acted on his own. The threat of a third world war, this one atomic, seemed agonizingly real. Truman and his advisers wanted to respond firmly enough to deter aggression but without provoking a larger war with the Soviet Union or China.

Truman did not hesitate; American troops would fight the North Koreans, though the United States would not declare war. The fighting in Korea would be a "police action" supervised by the United Nations. On June 27 the Security Council passed a U.S. resolution to send United Nations forces to Korea. That move succeeded only because the Soviet delegate, who had veto power, was absent. Six months earlier he had walked out in protest over the Council's refusal to seat mainland China. (Indeed, the Soviet absence from the Security Council vote undermines the idea that Stalin, rather than Kim Il Sung, had masterminded the North Korean attack.)

Truman's forceful response won immediate approval across America. Congress quickly voted the huge increase in defense funds needed to carry out the recommendations of NSC-68. American allies were less committed to the action. Though 16 nations contributed to the war effort, the United States provided half of the ground troops, 86 percent of the naval units, and 93 percent of the air force. By the time the UN forces could be marshaled, North Korean forces had pinned the South Koreans within a small defensive perimeter centered around Pusan. Then Douglas MacArthur, commander of the UN forces, launched a daring amphibious attack behind North Korean lines at Inchon, near the western end of the 38th parallel. Fighting eastward, MacArthur's troops threatened to trap the invaders, who fled back to the North.

The Chinese Intervene

MacArthur's success led Truman to a fateful decision. With the South liberated, he gave MacArthur permission to cross the 38th parallel, drive the Communists from the North, and reunite the country under Syngman Rhee. With Senator Joe McCarthy on the attack at home, the 1950 elections nearing, and the McCarran Act just passed, Truman was glad enough for the chance to vanquish the North Koreans. By Thanksgiving American troops had roundly defeated northern forces and were advancing on several fronts toward the frozen Yalu River, the boundary between Korea and China. MacArthur, emboldened by success, promised that the boys would be home by Christmas.

China, however, grew increasingly restive. Throughout the fall offensive, Premier Zhou Enlai warned that his country would not tolerate an American presence on its border. Washington officials did not take the warning seriously. Mao Zedong, they assumed, was a Soviet puppet, and Stalin had declared the Korean conflict to be merely a "civil war" and off limits. Ignoring the Chinese warnings, MacArthur launched his end-the-war offensive. Not long after, American troops captured a Chinese prisoner—as Secretary of State Acheson recalled, "you began to know at that point something was happening." On November 26 some 400,000 Chinese troops poured across the Yalu, smashing through lightly defended UN lines.

Marines in North Korea wait at a roadblock on December 1, 1950. American forces re-treated after the Chinese crossed the Yalu. The harsh weather added to the casualties those forces suffered.

At Chosan they trapped 20,000 American and South Korean troops, inflicting one of the worst defeats in American military history. Within three weeks they had driven UN forces back behind the 38th parallel. So total was the rout that Truman wondered publicly about using the atom bomb. That remark sent a frightened British Prime Minister Clement Attlee flying to Washington to dissuade the president. He readily agreed that the war must remain limited and withdrew his nuclear threat.

Truman versus MacArthur

The military stalemate in Korea brought into the open a simmering feud between MacArthur and Truman. The general had made no secret of his political ambitions or of his differences with Truman over American policy in Asia. He was eager to bomb Chinese and Russian supply bases across the Korean border, to blockade China's coast, and to "unleash" Chiang Kai-shek on mainland China. On March 23 he issued a personal ultimatum to Chinese military commanders demanding total surrender. To his Republican congressional supporters he sent a letter declaring, "We must win. There is no substitute for victory."

To Truman, MacArthur's insubordination threatened the tradition that military policy remained under clear civilian control. Equally alarming, MacArthur's strategy appeared to be an open invitation to another world war. Despite the general's enormous popularity, Truman made plans to discipline him. When Omar Bradley reported that MacArthur threatened to resign before Truman could act, the irate Truman replied, "The son of a bitch isn't going to resign on me. I want him fired!" Military leaders agreed that MacArthur had to go. On April 11 a stunned nation learned that the celebrated military commander had been relieved of his duties. On his return to the states, cheering crowds gave MacArthur one of the largest ticker-tape parades in New York City's history. Truman's move seemed one of the great political mistakes of his career. Congress gave MacArthur the unprecedented opportunity to address a joint session before a national television audience. His rabid supporters tried to impeach Truman and Acheson.

Europe, not Asia first   Behind the scenes, Truman was winning this personal clash. At stake was not simply Truman or MacArthur but the future direction of American foreign policy. MacArthur demanded an all-out effort in Asia. To Secretary of State Dean Acheson, the war had to be fought with Europe always foremost in American strategy. Korea was only one link in a worldwide "collective security system." Inevitably a general war in Asia would threaten American interests in Europe. Or as General Omar Bradley argued, a showdown in Asia would lead to "the wrong war, at the wrong place, at the wrong time, and with the wrong enemy." Congressional leaders were thus persuaded of the need to accompany limited war in Korea with a military buildup in Europe.

MacArthur may have lost the debate, but Korea took its toll on Truman's political fortunes. After July 1951, aimless peace talks dragged on along the border at Panmunjon. While the negotiators argued over how to reunify Korea and what to do with North Korean prisoners of war who refused to go home, the United States suffered another 32,000 casualties in an ugly war of attrition. By March 1952 Truman's popularity had sunk so low that he lost the New Hampshire presidential primary to Senator Estes Kefauver of Tennessee. With that defeat, he announced he would not run for reelection in 1952.

K1C2: The Election of 1952

The Republican formula for victory in 1952 played on the Truman administration's obvious weaknesses. Those did not include the economy, which remained remarkably healthy. Wage and price controls put in place by the administration prevented the sharp inflation that was expected to follow increased wartime spending. But the Republicans could capitalize on the stalemate over Korea. And several of Truman's advisers had been forced to resign for accepting mink coats and large freezers in return for political favors. The campaign strategy was summed up in the formula K1C2: Korea, corruption, and communism.

Moderates like "Ike"   The bigger problem for Republicans lay in choosing a candidate. Once General Dwight Eisenhower formally joined the Republican party, he became the choice of moderates and the northeastern establishment. Party regulars and the conservative wing were heavily committed to Robert Taft, who ran surprisingly well in the party primaries. But Ike was more popular with voters. His backers maneuvered their candidate to a first-ballot nomination. To heal the breach with the Taft delegates, the convention chose the staunch anti-Communist Senator Richard Nixon as Eisenhower's running mate.

With no candidate as popular as Eisenhower, the Democrats drafted Illinois Governor Adlai E. Stevenson. Few candidates could match Stevenson's eloquence, but, like Dewey before him, Stevenson lacked the common touch. Republican strategists turned his intelligence into a liability by dismissing him and his intellectual supporters as "eggheads." The GOP's campaign against communism and corruption, led by Nixon, left the Democratic candidate on the defensive. Eisenhower, meanwhile, took the high road above the mudslinging and promised voters that if elected, he would go to Korea to seek an end to the war.

Righteous indignation over corruption mired the Republicans in a scandal of their own. Newspapers reported that a group of wealthy Californians had provided Richard Nixon with an $18,000 "slush fund" to help cover personal expenses. With his place on the ticket in peril, Nixon made an impassioned television appeal, portraying himself and his wife Pat as ordinary folks. Like other young couples, they had monthly payments to make on a mortgage and a car. Pat had only a sensible "Republican cloth coat," not furs. And yes, his daughter Tricia had received a cocker spaniel puppy named Checkers, but no matter what his enemies might say, his family was going to keep the dog. As soon as Nixon finished, sympathetic viewers deluged GOP headquarters with messages of support. Nixon's survival demonstrated the power of television to influence public opinion. *Nixon's Checkers Speech*

The election outcome was never much in doubt. Eisenhower's broad smile and confident manner won him more than 55 percent of the vote. "The great problem of America today," Ike had said during the campaign, "is to take that straight road down the middle." Most Americans who voted for him were comforted to think that was just where they were headed.

Even before taking office, Eisenhower's first priority was to end the stalemated Korean War. As president-elect, he fulfilled his campaign promise "to go to Korea" and appraise the situation firsthand. Once in office, he renewed negotiations with North Korea but warned that unless the talks made speedy progress, the United States might retaliate "under circumstances of our choosing." The carrot-and-stick approach worked. On July 27, 1953, the Communists and the United Nations forces signed an armistice ending a "police action" in which 54,000 Americans had died. Korea remained divided, almost as it had been in 1950. Communism had been "contained," but at a high price in human lives. *Eisenhower and Korea*

The Fall of McCarthy

It was less clear, however, whether domestic anticommunism could be contained. Eisenhower boasted that he was a "modern" Republican, distinguishing himself from what he called the more "hidebound" members of the GOP. Their continuing anti-Communist campaigns caused him increasing embarrassment. Senator McCarthy's reckless antics, at first directed at Democrats, began to hit Republican targets as well.

By the summer of 1953 the senator was on a rampage. He dispatched two young staff members, Roy Cohn and David Schine, to investigate the State Department's overseas information agency and the Voice of America radio stations. Behaving more like college pranksters, the two conducted a whirlwind 18-day witch-hunt through Western Europe. To the chagrin of the administration, they insisted on purging government library shelves of "subversive" books, including those by John Dewey and Foster Rhea Dulles, a conservative historian and cousin of Eisenhower's secretary of

The energetic and opportunistic Roy Cohn (left) served as a key strategist in the inquisition that made Senator Joseph McCarthy a figure to fear. Together with fellow staffer David Schine (right) they helped McCarthy turn a minor Senate subcommittee into a major power center.

state. Some librarians, fearing for their careers, burned a number of books. That drove President Eisenhower to denounce "book burners," though soon after he reassured McCarthy's supporters that he did not advocate free speech for Communists.

The administration's own behavior contributed to the hysteria on which McCarthy thrived. The president launched a loyalty campaign, which he claimed resulted in 3000 firings and 5000 resignations of government employees. It was a godsend to McCarthyites: What further proof was needed that subversives were lurking in the federal bureaucracy? Furthermore, a well-publicized spy trial had led to the conviction of Ethel and Julius Rosenberg, a couple accused of passing atomic secrets to the Soviets. Although the evidence was not conclusive, the judge sentenced both Rosenbergs to the electric chair, an unusually harsh punishment even in cases of espionage. When asked to commute the death sentence to life imprisonment, Eisenhower refused, and the Rosenbergs were executed in June 1953.

The case of J. Robert Oppenheimer

A year later the Atomic Energy Commission turned its investigative eyes on physicist J. Robert Oppenheimer. During World War II it was Oppenheimer's administrative and scientific genius that had led to the development of the atom bomb. Widely respected by his colleagues, he had raised the hackles of many politicians in 1949 when he opposed the construction of a hydrogen bomb. Despite a few left-wing associations from the 1930s (which army officials had known about), no one had ever accused him of passing on national security information. Nonetheless, the Atomic

Once the Soviet Union developed its own nuclear capability, Americans felt vulnerable to a surprise atomic attack. This advertisement from the *New York Times* in 1954 promised consumers that their valuables could be stored deep in a mountain vault.

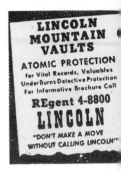

Energy Commission in effect suggested Oppenheimer was a traitor by barring him from sensitive research.

In such a climate—where Democrats remained silent for fear of being called leftists and Eisenhower cautiously refused to "get in the gutter with *that* guy"— McCarthy lost all sense of proportion. When the army denied his aide David Schine a commission, McCarthy decided to investigate communism in the army. The new American Broadcasting Company network, eager to fill its afternoon program slots, televised the hearings. For three weeks, the public had an opportunity to see McCarthy badger witnesses and make a mockery of Senate procedures. Soon after, his popularity began to slide and the anticommunist hysteria ebbed as well. The Senate finally moved to censure him. He died three years later, destroyed by alcohol and the habit of throwing so many reckless punches.

McCarthy vs. the Army

With the Democrats out of the White House for the first time since the Depression and with right-wing McCarthyites in retreat, Eisenhower did indeed seem to be leading the nation on a course "right down the middle." Still, it is worth noting how much that sense of "middle" had changed.

Both the Great Depression and World War II made most Americans realize that the nation's economy was firmly tied to the international order. The crash in 1929, with its worldwide effects, illustrated the closeness of the links. The New Deal demonstrated that Americans were willing to give the federal government power to influence American society in major new ways. And the war led the government to intervene in the economy even more actively.

So when peace came in 1945, it became clear that the "middle road" did not mean a return to the laissez-faire economics of the 1920s or the isolationist politics of the 1930s. "Modern" Republicans supported social welfare programs like social security and granted that the federal government had the power to lower unemployment, control inflation, and manage the economy in a variety of ways. Furthermore, the shift from war to peace demonstrated that it was no longer possible to make global war without making a global peace. Under the new balance of power in the postwar world, the United States and the Soviet Union stood alone as "superpowers," with the potential capability to annihilate each other and the rest of the world.

CHAPTER SUMMARY

After fighting an exhausting global war, Americans discovered themselves in the midst of a cold war against their former ally, the Soviet Union. The roots of the cold war lay partly in traditional American suspicion of Russian communism and Soviet suspicion of newfound American power. But Stalin's aggressive posture toward Eastern Europe and the Persian Gulf region raised new fears. The Truman Doctrine, the Marshall Plan, NATO, and the policies of NSC-68 were all part of Truman's efforts to apply the doctrine of containment.

At home, the end of World War II brought readjustments as the government, industry, and private citizens converted from war to peace. Inflation, shortages, layoffs, and strikes led voters to take their revenge against Democratic candidates in the 1946 elections. The new Congress resisted any attempts to revive the New Deal. Only through executive action such as desegregating the armed forces could Truman advance his civil rights agenda. On the other hand, fear of a renewed depression soon gave way to a prosperity fueled by consumer and government spending. The GI Bill helped launch a shift from blue- to white-collar work, giving veterans a chance to pursue a college education. Postwar prosperity, however, was tinged with anti-Communist fears. The House Un-American Activities Committee investigated Hollywood, while anti-Communist conservatives pointed to the Hiss, Fuchs, and Rosenberg cases as evidence of subversion in government. Truman responded with his own loyalty program, but Senator McCarthy most effectively exploited the anti-Communist hysteria.

In 1949 the Soviet detonation of an atom bomb and the fall of China to Mao Zedong's Communists underlined a growing sense of cold war crisis. With North Korea's invasion of South Korea, the cold war turned hot. Once China entered and the war became stalemated, the Republicans and the popular Dwight Eisenhower captured the White House, promising to end the war. Eisenhower's moderate Republicanism eased the communist hysteria somewhat, although not before Senator McCarthy fell from his own excesses. The cold war abroad would continue to cast its shadow over prosperity at home.

SIGNIFICANT EVENTS

1945 — Iran crisis; civil war in Greece

1946 — Labor unrest; Kennan's "long telegram"; Stalin and Churchill "cold war" speeches; Republican congressional victories; McMahon Bill creates Atomic Energy Commission; Baruch plan fails at United Nations

1947 — Truman Doctrine; Taft–Hartley Act; Marshall announces European recovery plan; federal loyalty oath; HUAC investigates Hollywood; National Security Act creates Defense Department and CIA; Truman's Committee on Civil Rights issues *To Secure These Rights*

1948 — Marshall Plan adopted; Berlin blockade; Truman upsets Dewey; Truman recognizes Israel

1949 — Soviet A-bomb test; China falls to the Communists; NATO established; Truman orders work on H-bomb

1950 — McCarthy's Wheeling, West Virginia, speech; Korean War begins; McCarran Act; NSC-68 adopted; Alger Hiss convicted

1951 — Truman fires MacArthur; peace talks in Korea

1952 — Richard Nixon's Checkers speech; Eisenhower defeats Stevenson

1953 — U.N. armistice ends police action in Korea; Rosenbergs executed

1954 — Army–McCarthy hearings; McCarthy censured; Robert Oppenheimer denied security clearance

ADDITIONAL READING

On the cold war Daniel Yergin, *Shattered Peace* (2d ed., 1989) is both readable and balanced, as are Thomas Paterson, *On Every Front* (3d ed., 1996) and Walter LaFeber, *America, Russia, and the Cold War* (8th ed., 1997). David McCullough, *Truman* (1992) combines the best of good history and popular biography. Alonzo Hamby, *Liberalism and Its Challengers* (1992) and Donald Coy, *The Presidency of Harry S Truman* (1984) are useful on the Fair Deal.

Much of the domestic red scare was fought out in and over the media. Stephen Whitfield, *The Culture of the Cold War* (1991) and John Diggins, *The Proud Decades* (1988) both provide good introductions to the tensions between popular and intellectual culture and McCarthyism. James Gilbert, *A Cycle of Outrage: America's Reaction to Juvenile Delinquency in the 1950s* (1986) shows that some critics found other forms of subversion in comic books and movies aimed at teen audiences. The special problems of Hollywood are explored in Robert Sklar, *Movie Made America: A Cultural History of American Movies* (rev. ed., 1994); Nora Sayre, *Running Time: Films of the Cold War* (1982); and Peter Biskind, *Seeing Is Believing: How Hollywood Taught Us to Stop Worrying and Love the Fifties* (1983). Erik Barnouw, *Tube of Plenty: The Evolution of American Television* (1975) argues that the same cold war tensions inhibited television programming. For a most vivid dramatic view of the "brown scare" in television see the 1976 movie, *The Front*, starring Woody Allen and Zero Mostel, a blacklist victim. For a fuller list of readings, see the Bibliography.

29

The Suburban Era

he company that epitomized the corporate culture of the 1950s was General Motors. GM executives sought to blend in rather than to stand out. They chose their suits in drab colors—dark blue, dark gray, or light gray—to increase their anonymity. Not head car designer Harley Earl. Earl brought a touch of Hollywood into the world of corporate bureaucrats. He had a closet filled with colorful suits. His staff would marvel as he headed off to a board meeting dressed in white linen with a dark blue shirt and *blue suede shoes,* the same shoes that Elvis Presley sang so protectively about.

Mr. Earl—no one who worked for him ever called him Harley—could afford to be a maverick. He created the cars that brought customers into GM showrooms across the country. Before he came to Detroit, engineering sold cars. Advertising stressed mechanical virtues—the steady ride, reliable brakes, or, perhaps, power steering. Earl made style the distinctive feature. Unlike the boxy look other designers favored, an Earl car had a low, sleek look, suggesting motion even when the car stood still. No feature stood out more distinctively than the fins he first put on the 1948 Cadillac. By the mid-1950s jet planes inspired Earl to design ever more outrageous fins, complemented by huge, shiny chrome grills and ornaments. These features served no mechanical purpose. Some critics dismissed Earl's designs as jukeboxes on wheels.

To Earl and GM that did not matter. Design sold cars. "It gave [customers] an extra receipt for their money in the form of visible prestige marking for an expensive car," Earl said. The "Big Three" auto manufacturers—General Motors, Ford, and Chrysler—raced one another to redesign their annual models, the more outrageous the better. Earl once joked, "I'd put smokestacks right in the middle of the sons of bitches if I thought I could sell more cars." In the lingo of the Detroit stylists, these designs were "gasaroony," an adjective *Popular Mechanics* magazine translated as "terrific, overpowering, weird." The goal was not a better car but what Earl called "dynamic obsolescence" or simply change for change's sake. "The 1957 Ford was great," its designer remarked, "but right away we had to bury it and start another." Even a successful style had to go within a year. "We would design a car to make a man unhappy with his 1957 Ford 'long about the end of 1958." Even though the mechanics of cars changed little from year to year, dynamic obsolescence persuaded Americans in the 1950s to buy new cars in record numbers.

In Easter Morning, *Norman Rockwell satirized the contrasting conformities of suburban life. This sheepish father, no doubt forced to wear suits all week, prefers a shocking red bathrobe, a cigarette, and the Sunday paper to the gray flannel lockstep of his churchbound family.*

Fins, roadside motels, "gaseterias," drive-in burger huts, interstate highways, shopping centers, and, of course, suburbs—all these were part of a culture of mobility in the 1950s. Americans continued their exodus from rural areas to cities and from the cities to the suburbs. African Americans left the South, heading for industrial centers in the Northeast, Midwest, and West Coast. Mexican Americans concentrated in southwestern cities, while Puerto Ricans came largely to New York. And for Americans in the Snowbelt, the climate of the West and South (at least when civilized by air-conditioning) made the Sunbelt irresistible to ever larger numbers.

Consensus in the 1950s

The mobility was social, too. As the economy continued to expand, the size of the American middle class grew. In an era of prosperity and peace, some commentators began to speak of a "consensus"—a general agreement in American culture, based on values of the broad middle class. In a positive light consensus reflected the agreement among most Americans about fundamental democratic values. Most citizens embraced the material benefits of prosperity as evidence of the virtue of "the American way." And they opposed the spread of communism abroad.

But consensus had its dark side. Critics worried that consensus bred a mindless conformity. Were Americans becoming too homogenized? Was there a depressing sameness in the material goods they owned, in the places they lived, and in the values they held? Besides, wasn't any notion of consensus hollow so long as racism and segregation prevented African Americans and other minorities from fully sharing in American life?

The baby boomers born into this era seldom agonized over such issues. In the White House President Eisenhower radiated a comforting sense that the affairs of the nation and the world were in capable hands. That left teenagers free to worry about what really mattered: a first date, a first kiss, a first job, a first choice for college, and whether or not to "go all the way" in the back seat of one of Harley Earl's fin-swept Buicks.

THE RISE OF THE SUBURBS

The lure of the suburbs was hardly new to Americans. From the mid-nineteenth century onward, suburbs had been growing up around cities as new modes of transportation made traveling to work easier. But suburban growth accelerated sharply at the end of World War II. During the 1950s suburbs grew 40 times faster than cities, so that by 1960 half the American people lived in them. Urbanites escaping the crowding of large cities were drawn to more pastoral communities with names like Park Forest or Pacific Palisades.

Other changes in postwar society shaped the character of suburban life. With the end of the war came a baby boom and a need for new housing. With the return of prosperity came a boom in automobiles that made the suburbs accessible. But the spurt in suburban growth took its toll on the cities, which suffered as the middle class fled urban areas.

A Boom in Babies and in Housing

The Depression forced many couples to delay beginning a family. In the 1930s birthrates had reached the low point of American history, about 18 to 19 per thousand. As

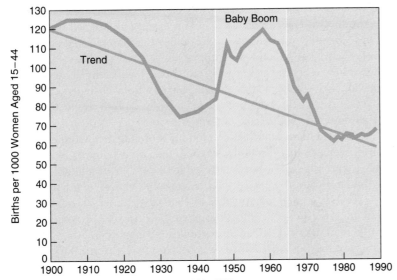

THE UNITED STATES BIRTHRATE, 1900–1989
Despite periods of rapid rise and fall, the nation's birthrate has shown a steady downward trend. The Depression years showed an even sharper decline as financially strapped couples deferred child rearing. Younger marriages and postwar prosperity triggered the baby boom, but in general, affluence encourages lower birthrates. (*Sources:* U.S. Bureau of the Census, *Historical Statistics of the United States* and *Statistical Abstract of the United States,* various years.)

prosperity returned during the war, birthrates began to rise. By 1952 they had passed 25 per thousand, one of the highest fertility rates in the world. In 1946 Americans married in record numbers, twice as many as in 1932. The new brides were also younger, which translated into unusual fertility. Americans chose to have larger families, as the number with three children tripled and those with four or more quadrupled. "Just imagine how much these extra people, these new markets, will absorb—in food, in clothing, in gadgets, in housing, in services," one journalist predicted.

The boom in marriage and families created a need for housing. At war's end, 5 million families were searching, eager to find anything, tired of living doubled up with other families, in basements, or even in coal cellars. With the help of the GI Bill and the rising prosperity, the chance to own a house rather than rent became a reality for over half of American families. And it was the suburbs that offered the residence most idealized in American culture: a detached single-family house with a lawn and garden.

After World War II inexpensive, suburban housing became synonymous with the name of William Levitt. From building houses for war workers, Levitt learned how to use mass production techniques. In 1947 he began construction of a 17,000-house community in the New York City suburb of Hempstead. All the materials for a Levittown house were precut and assembled at a factory, then moved to the site for assembly. If all went according to schedule, a new house was erected on a cement slab every 16 minutes. Buoyed by his success in Hempstead, Levitt later built developments in Bucks County, Pennsylvania, and Willingboro, New Jersey.

Levittown, U.S.A.

The typical early Levitt house, a "Cape Codder," had a living room, kitchen, bath, and two bedrooms on the ground floor and an expansion attic, all for $7990. None had custom features, insulation, or any amenities that complicated construction. "The reason we have it so good in this country," Levitt said, "is that we can produce lots of things at low prices through mass production." Uniformity in house style extended to behavior as well. Levitt discouraged owners from changing colors or adding distinctive features to the house or yard. Buyers promised to cut the grass each week of the summer and not to hang out wash on weekends. African Americans were expressly excluded. Other suburban communities excluded Jews and ethnics through restrictive covenants that dictated who could take up residence.

In California, a state with three cars registered for every four residents, suburbs bloomed across the landscape. By 1962 it had become the nation's most populous state. Growth was greatest around Los Angeles. In 1940 city planners began building a freeway system to lure shoppers into downtown Los Angeles. Instead, white Angelinos saw the road network as an opportunity to migrate to the suburbs. Eventually one-third of the Los Angeles area was covered by highways, parking lots, and interchanges, increasing to two-thirds in the downtown areas.

Cities and Suburbs Transformed

Single-family houses on their own plots of land required plenty of open land, unlike the row houses built side by side in earlier suburban developments. That meant Levitt and other builders chose vacant areas outside of major urban areas. With the new houses farther away from factories, offices, and jobs, the automobile became more indispensible than ever.

Almost all suburban activities depended on the availability of cars, cheap gasoline, and accessible roads. Shopping centers, the predecessors of more elaborate malls, exemplified the new auto-centered life. At the end of World War II the United States had just eight of these retail complexes, their clusters of stores attracting customers with convenient parking. Even a few churches and funeral homes provided drive-in facilities to attract people committed to life behind the wheel. By 1960 more than 3840 shopping centers covered as much land as the nation's central business districts.

As the population shifted to suburbs, traffic choked old country roads. To ease this congestion, the Eisenhower administration proposed a 20-year plan to build a massive interstate highway system of some 41,000 miles. Eisenhower addressed cold war fears to build support, arguing that the new system would ease evacuation of cities in case of nuclear attack. In 1956 Congress passed the Interstate Highway Act, setting in motion the largest public works project in history. The federal government picked up 90 percent of the cost through a Highway Trust Fund, financed by special taxes on cars, gas, tires, lubricants, and auto parts.

Interstate Highway Act of 1956

The Interstate Highway Act had an enormous impact on American life. Average annual driving increased by 400 percent. Shopping centers, linked by the new roads, sprang up to provide suburbanites with an alternative to the longer trip downtown. Almost every community had at least one highway strip dotted with drive-in movies, stores, bowling alleys, gas stations, and fast-food joints.

For cities, the interstates created other problems. The new highway system featured beltways—ring roads around major urban areas. Instead of leading traffic

Like a freak of evolution run riot, automotive tailfins metamorphosed from the modest stubs of a 1948 Cadillac into the monstrous protrusions of the 1959 Cadillac. With a return of prosperity, the suburban era celebrated a culture of mobility.

downtown, the beltways allowed motorists to avoid the center city altogether. As people took to their cars, intercity rail service and mass transit declined. Seventy-five percent of all government transportation dollars went to subsidize travel by car and truck; only one percent was earmarked for urban mass transit. At the same time that middle-class home owners were moving to the suburbs, many low-paying, unskilled jobs disappeared from the cities. That forced the urban poor into reverse commuting from city to suburb. All of these trends made cities less attractive places to live or do business. With fewer well-to-do taxpayers to draw upon, city governments lacked the tax base to finance public services. A vicious cycle ensued that proved most damaging to the urban poor, who had few means of escape.

Declining cities

Much of the white population that moved to the suburbs was replaced by African Americans and Hispanics. They were part of larger migrations, especially of millions of black families leaving the South to search for work in urban centers. Most headed for the Middle Atlantic, Northeast, and Upper Midwest regions. While central cities lost 3.6 million white residents, they gained 4.5 million African Americans. Indeed, by 1960 half of all black Americans were living in central cities.

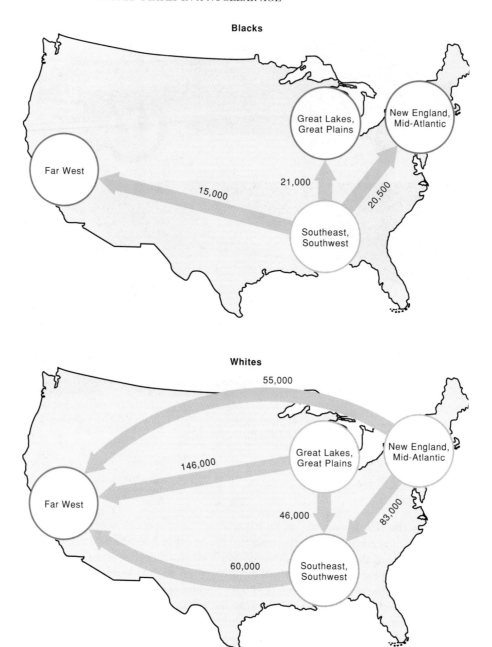

AVERAGE ANNUAL REGIONAL MIGRATION, 1947–1960
In this period, African Americans were moving in significant numbers to urban centers in the Northeast, the Midwest, and the Far West. Whites were being drawn to the increasingly diversified economy of the South as well as to the new industries, stimulated by the war, in the Far West. By the 1970s, the trend became known as the "Sunbelt" phenomenon. [*Source:* Frank Levy, *Dollars and Dreams: The Changing American Income Distribution* (New York: Russell Sage Foundation, 1987), p. 106.]

Earlier waves of European immigrants had been absorbed by the expanding urban economy. During the 1950s, however, the flight of jobs and middle-class taxpayers to the suburbs made it difficult for African Americans and Hispanics to follow the same path. In the cities fewer jobs awaited them, while declining school systems made it harder for newcomers to acculturate. In the hardest hit urban areas, unemployment rose to over 40 percent.

By contrast, the suburbs remained beyond reach of most minorities. Since few black or Hispanic families could afford the cost of suburban living, they accounted for less than 5 percent of the population there. The few black suburbs that existed dated from before the war and had little in common with the newer white "bedroom communities." Black suburbanites were poorer, held lower-status jobs, lived in more ramshackle housing, and had less education than urban African Americans.

Minorities and suburbs

Those who could afford the suburbs discovered that most real estate agents refused to show them houses; bankers would not provide mortgages. And many communities adopted either restrictive covenants or zoning regulations that kept out "undesirable" home buyers. One African American, William Myers, finally managed in 1957 to buy a house from a white family in Levittown, Pennsylvania, but the developers did not sell directly to African Americans until 1960.

THE CULTURE OF SUBURBIA

Suburban home ownership was popularly associated with the broad middle classes: those workers who held white- or blue-collar jobs and made enough income to afford the housing. Unlike many urban neighborhoods, where immigrant parents or grandparents might be living on the same block or even in the same apartment, single-family dwellers often left their relatives and in-laws behind. As a result, ethnic lifestyles were less pronounced in the suburbs. The restrictive immigration policies of the 1920s had also eroded ethnicity by reducing the number of newly arrived foreign-born Americans.

Class distinctions were more pronounced between suburban communities than within them. The upper middle class clustered in older developments, often centered around country clubs. Working-class suburbs sprouted on the outskirts of large manufacturing centers, where blue-collar families eagerly escaped the city to own their own homes. Within these suburbs, where differences of class and ethnicity blurred, a more homogeneous suburban culture evolved. "We see eye to eye on most things," commented one Levittown resident, "about raising kids, doing things together with your husband . . . we have practically the same identical background."

American Civil Religion

If the move to the suburbs gradually stripped many ethnics of their native customs and languages, it seldom forced them to abandon their religious identities. Religion continued to be a distinctive and segregating factor during the 1950s. Catholics, Protestants, and Jews generally married within their own faiths, and in the suburbs they kept their social distance as well.

Daily Lives

PUBLIC SPACE/PRIVATE SPACE

The New Suburbia

When World War II ended, many Americans were happy to find housing of any kind. But prosperity in the 1950s brought a greater demand for houses that, like automobiles, reflected the status of those who owned them. No longer would William Levitt's standard 900-square-foot Cape Cod saltbox satisfy popular demand. Levitt's success inspired new designs, often created by builders rather than architects. Eager to please buyers rather than critics, they haphazardly mixed styles and colors.

Even so, suburban design did evolve from major architectural traditions. The most renowned of all suburban features, the picture window, traced its roots to architect Frank Lloyd Wright. Wright had come of age in the 1890s, at a time when "streetcar suburbs" were expanding around major urban areas. Wright's turn-of-the-century innovations combined open interior space, wide windows for natural lighting, and a horizontal, single-story layout. California architects translated Wright's ideas into the "ranch house," where rooms flowed into each other and indoor spaces opened to the outdoors to take advantage of the mild climate. Houses with fewer walls and defined spaces discouraged formality and even privacy.

Developers across the country seized upon the California "fantasy" style to conjure up dreams of informal living along with a touch of glamour. The use of picture windows allowed them to make small houses seem more spacious. Critics of suburban living suggested that the picture window was a means to ensure conformity. Why, after all, was the window most often placed looking onto the front yard, except to afford homeowners a means to keep an eye on neighbors who were watching them through their own picture windows? In truth, it made sense to have a picture window look onto the street in order to keep an eye on children. More important, the view provided about the only vantage point from which people could enjoy their front yards. Few suburbanites sat out front or actually used the lawn. But since front yards made an important statement about houses and their owners, families decorated and tended them with special care.

By 1955, economics forced developers to forsake the box shape of most suburban houses. Surveys showed that three-quarters of all would-be buyers wanted a single-story house. But with land prices rising and new zoning codes being enforced, builders could not fit enough floor space onto typical lots. To build a two-story house without seeming to, they hit upon the split-level or "raised ranch": something, as one critic wryly noted, that "looked like a ranch-style house that had fallen out of the air and landed on something else." The front door opened

The religious division   Communities that showed no obvious class distinctions were sometimes deeply divided along religious lines. Catholics attended parochial rather than public schools, formed their own clubs, and generally did not socialize with their Protestant neighbors. Protestant and Catholic members of the same country club usually did not play golf or tennis in the same foursomes. As for Jews, social historian Richard Polenberg has remarked that whereas a gulf divided many Catholics and Protestants, Jews and Gentiles "seem to have lived on the opposite sides of a religious Grand Canyon." Even superficial signs of friendliness masked underlying mistrust and the persistence of old stereotypes.

Daily Lives

In the wake of the baby boom and a demand for new homes, mass-produced houses soon filled suburban developments all across the United States. By varying styles only slightly, developers were able to construct houses quickly at prices many young couples could afford.

One magazine described the family room as "the newest room in the house, but also the oldest," for the concept originated in the middle-class Victorian front parlor. Like it, the 1950s living room acquired more elegant furnishings for use during holidays or special entertaining. That led to the conversion of what often had been a basement "rumpus" room for the kids into a family room. Here, families sought a cozier feel with pine paneling and furniture designed for comfort and durability, with the television as the focus of the room.

The growing families of the late 1950s needed more space to prepare and eat meals. Earlier kitchens had normally been small and limited largely to food preparation. Meals were eaten in a combined living–dining area. The new larger "live-in" kitchens were designed, one advertiser claimed, to make "mother a member of the family again." Everyone could gather while mom cooked. The same space would also hold appliances like dishwashers, dual ovens, and televisions, which became common kitchen features.

onto a landing halfway between the upper and lower floors, creating an illusion that it was only half the distance from one floor to the next. The basic construction, two simple boxes side by side, was cheap to build. By placing half the living space—either the kitchen, dining, and family rooms or the bedrooms—in what would otherwise be a basement, the split level created more habitable living space at little additional cost.

Most of all, homeowners in the 1950s wanted family rooms and "live-in kitchens."

Clearly, suburban houses were more than "Little boxes on the hillside/Little boxes all the same," as one folk-singing critic of the 1960s complained. To the people who flocked to suburbia, their homes represented a compromise between fantasy and practicality, fulfilling the American dream, "To own your own home."

Although such religious boundaries remained distinct, the consensus increased that religion was central to American life. Church membership rose to more than 50 percent for the first time in the twentieth century, and by 1957 the census bureau reported that 96 percent of the American people cited a specific affiliation when asked "What is your religion?" The religious upswing was supported in part by the prevailing cold war mood, since Communists were avowedly atheists. Cold war fervor led Congress in 1954 to add the phrase "under God" to the Pledge of Allegiance. With this phrase, commented one supporter, "we denounce the pagan doctrine of communism and declare 'under God' in favor of a free government and a free world."

Baptist Billy Graham led the revival of evangelistic denominations and sects. While his message emphasized the traditional fundamentalist themes of sin, redemption, and the Second Coming of Christ, his up-to-date methods took advantage of television, advertising, radio, and paperback books to reach the widest possible audience.

Television ministries

Such patriotic and anti-Communist themes were strong in the preaching of clergy who pioneered the use of television. Billy Graham, a Baptist revival preacher, warned Americans to repent, for God would not long abide the sin of materialism. Graham first attracted national attention at a tent meeting in Los Angeles in 1949. Following in the tradition of nineteenth-century revivalists like Charles Finney and Dwight Moody, he soon achieved an even wider impact by televising his meetings. Though no revivalist, the Roman Catholic Bishop Fulton J. Sheen became one of television's most popular celebrities. In his weekly program he extolled traditional values and attacked communism.

Even though religious differences remained profound, the growing consensus among Americans was that *any* religious belief was better than none. President Eisenhower joined the chorus of those extolling this view. "Our government makes no sense unless it is founded on a deeply religious faith," he proclaimed, "—and I don't care what it is." Children got the message too. Every Friday afternoon kids watching "The Howdy Doody Show" were exhorted by "Buffalo Bob" to worship "at the church or synagogue of your choice."

"Homemaking" Women in the Workaday World

The growth of a suburban culture revealed a contradiction in the lives of middle-class women. Never before were their traditional roles as housewives and mothers so central to American society. Yet never before did more women join the workforce outside the home.

Most housewives found that suburban homes and growing families required increasing time and energy. With relatives and grandparents less likely to live nearby, mothering became full-time work. Dependence on automobiles made many a suburban housewife the chauffeur for her family. In the 1920s grocers or milkmen had

To housewife and mother, many suburban women of the 1950s added the role of chauffeur. Husbands who once walked to work and children who walked to school now needed to be delivered and picked up. The average suburban woman spent one full working day each week driving and doing errands.

commonly delivered their goods from door to door; by the 1950s delivery services were being replaced by housewives doing "errands."

Working women

Yet between 1940 and 1960 the percentage of wives working outside the home doubled from 15 to 30 percent. While some women took jobs simply to help make ends meet, often more than financial necessity was involved. Middle-class married women went to work as often as lower-class wives, and women with college degrees were the most likely to get a job. Two-income families were able to spend far more on extras: gifts, education, recreation, and household appliances. In addition, women found status and self-fulfillment in their jobs, as well as a chance for increased social contacts.

More women were going to college, too, but that increased education did not translate into economic equality. The percentage of women holding professional jobs actually dropped between 1950 and 1960. And the gap between men's and women's wages was greater than in any other industrial nation. In the United States, the median wage for women was less than half that for men.

Media images of women

Despite women's wider roles in society, the modern media continued to portray women either as sex objects or as domesticated housewives and mothers. A typical article appearing in *Redbook* in 1957 made a heroine of Junior, a "little freckle-faced brunette" who had given up work. As the story closed, Junior nursed her baby at two in the morning, crooning "I'm glad, glad, glad I'm just a housewife." In 1950 Lynn White, the president of Mills College for women, advocated a curriculum that displaced traditional academic subjects with those that were "distinctly feminine," like crafts or home economics.

The media trivialized women in other ways. Where the films of the 1930s and 1940s often starred independent, confident women, the heroines of the 1950s appeared more vulnerable. Marilyn Monroe's voluptuous sensuality, combined with a little-girl innocence, clearly appealed to male tastes. Similarly, women's fashions portrayed a male vision of femininity. In 1947 Christian Dior introduced his "new look": narrow waistlines emphasizing shapely hips and a full bosom, rarely achieved without constricting foundation garments. The heels on shoes became ever higher and the toes pointier. As historian Lois Banner concluded, "Not since the Victorian era had women's fashions been so confining."

A Revolution in Sexuality?

The suburbs themselves encouraged other changes in sexual attitudes, especially among the middle classes who lived there. Throughout the twentieth century, a trend had been under way deemphasizing the tradition that sex within marriage was primarily for the procreation of children—a duty (especially for women) to be endured rather than enjoyed. During the 1920s reformer Ben Lindsey promoted the idea of "companionate marriage," stressing personal happiness and satisfaction as primary goals. That included the enjoyment of sex for both wife and husband. The suburban home of the 1950s encouraged such ideals, symbolizing as it did a place of relaxation and enjoyment. Unlike city apartments, where extended families often lived in crowded conditions, the suburban single-family houses provided greater privacy and more space for intimacy.

The Kinsey Report

The increased willingness to see sexual pleasure as an integral part of marriage received additional attention in 1948 with the publication of an apparently dry scientific study, *Sexual Behavior in the Human Male*. Its author, Professor Alfred Kinsey, hardly expected the storm of publicity received by that study or its companion, *Sexual Behavior in the Human Female* (1953). Kinsey began his research career as a zoologist with a zest for classifying data. During the 1940s he turned to collecting information on sexual behavior. Based on more than 10,000 interviews, Kinsey reached conclusions that were unorthodox and even startling for his day. Masturbation and premarital petting, he reported, were widespread. Women did not just endure sex as a wifely duty, they enjoyed it in much the same way men did. Extramarital sex was common for both husbands and wives. About 10 percent of the population was homosexual.

It is difficult in more sexually liberated times to appreciate the impact of Kinsey's work and the controversy surrounding it. Commentators called his first volume "the most talked about book of the twentieth century." Social scientists, with some justice, objected that Kinsey's sample was too limited. (Most of his subjects were midwestern, middle class, and well educated.) Later studies challenged some of his figures (for example, the percentage of homosexuals in the population). More strident critics of the day charged that Kinsey was a "menace to society" who would destroy the morals of the nation. Kinsey replied that he had published a "report on what people do which raises no question of what they should do." Polls indicated that most Americans felt comfortable about having such research published, perhaps partly because they found liberation in the discovery that behaviors once treated as sinful or perverse were widely practiced.

The Flickering Gray Screen

In the glow of postwar prosperity, most Americans found themselves with more leisure time and more income. In the suburbs, a yard to tend and a young family to

Even before the launch of *Sputnik* in 1957, Americans had begun devising fallout shelters for protection from the effects of a nuclear attack. This one was exhibited in 1955.

and foreign languages. At the same time, crash programs were undertaken to build basement fallout shelters to protect Americans in case of a nuclear attack. Democrats charged that the administration had allowed the United States to face an unacceptable "missile gap."

Thaws and Freezes

Throughout this series of crises, each superpower found it difficult to interpret the other's motives. The Russians exploited nationalist revolutions where they could—less successfully in Egypt, more so in Cuba. "We will bury you," Khrushchev admonished Americans, though it was unclear whether he meant through peaceful competition or military confrontation. More menacingly, in November 1958 he demanded that the Western powers withdraw all troops from West Berlin within six months. *Berlin crisis* Berlin would then become a "free city," and the Western powers could negotiate further access to it only with East Germany, a government the West had refused to recognize. When Eisenhower flatly rejected the ultimatum, Khrushchev backed away from his hard-line stance.

Rather than adopt a more belligerent course, Eisenhower determined to use the last 18 months of his presidency to improve Soviet–American relations. The shift in policy was made easier because Eisenhower knew from American intelligence (but could not admit publicly) that the "missile gap" was not real. While willing to spend more on missile development, he refused to heed the calls for a crash defense program at any cost. Instead, he took a more conciliatory approach by inviting Khrushchev to visit the United States in September 1959. Though the meetings produced no significant results, they eased tensions. And Khrushchev undertook a picturesque tour across America, swapping comments about manure with Iowa farmers, reacting puritanically to movie cancan dancers, and grousing when his visit to the new capitalist marvel, Disneyland, was canceled for security reasons.

The U-2 incident

Eisenhower's plans for a return visit to the Soviet Union were abruptly canceled in May, when a summit meeting in Paris collapsed. Only weeks earlier the Russians had shot down a high-altitude U-2 American spy plane over Soviet territory. At first Eisenhower claimed that the plane had strayed off course while doing weather research, but Khrushchev sprang his trap: the CIA pilot, Gary Powers, had been captured alive. The president then admitted that he had personally authorized the U-2 overflights for reasons of national security.

That episode ended Eisenhower's hopes that his personal diplomacy might create a true thaw in the cold war. Yet a less mature president might have led the United States into more severe conflict or even war. Eisenhower was not readily impressed by the promises of new weapon systems or worried talk about a "missile gap" between the United States and the Soviet Union. He left office with a warning that too much military spending would lead to "an unwarranted influence, whether sought or unsought" by the "military–industrial complex" at the expense of democratic institutions.

CIVIL RIGHTS AND THE NEW SOUTH

The struggle of African Americans for equality during the postwar era is filled with ironies. By the time barriers to legal segregation in the South began to fall, millions of black families were leaving for regions where discrimination was less easily challenged in court. The South they left behind was in the early stages of an economic boom. The cities where many migrated had entered a period of decline. Yet, as if to close a circle, the rise of large black voting blocs in major cities created political pressures that forced the nation to dismantle the worst legal and institutional barriers to racial equality. For black Americans, it might be said that these were the best and worst of times.

The Changing South and African Americans

After World War II the southern economy began to grow significantly faster than the national economy. The remarkable about-face began during the New Deal with federal programs like the Tennessee Valley Authority. World War II brought even more federal dollars to build and maintain military bases and defense plants. And the South attracted new business because it offered a "clean slate." In contrast to the more mature economies of the Northeast and Upper Midwest, the region had few unions, little regulation and bureaucracy, and low wages and taxes. Finally, there was the matter of climate, which later caused the region to be nicknamed the Sunbelt. Especially with improvements in air-conditioning, the South grew more attractive to skilled professionals, corporate managers, and affluent retirees.

Before World War II, 80 percent of African Americans lived in the South. Most raised cotton as sharecroppers and tenant farmers. But the war created a labor shortage at home as millions went off to fight or to work in armament factories. This shortage gave cotton growers an incentive to mechanize cotton picking. In 1950 only 5 percent of the crop was picked mechanically; by 1960 it was at least half. Farmers began to consolidate land into larger holdings. Tenant farmers, sharecroppers, and hired labor of both races, no longer in short supply, left the countryside for the city.

Mechanized cotton farming

The national level of wages also profoundly affected southern labor. When federal minimum wage laws forced lumber or textile mills to raise their pay scales, the mills no longer expanded. In addition, steel and other industries with strong national unions and manufacturers with plants around the country set wages by national standards. That brought southern wages close to the national average by the 1960s. As the southern economy grew, what had for many years been a distinct regional economy became more diversified and more integrated into the national economy.

As wages rose and unskilled work disappeared, job opportunities for black southerners declined. Outside of cotton farming, the lumber industry had provided the largest number of jobs for young black men. There, the number of black teenagers hired by lumber mills dropped 74 percent between 1950 and 1960. New high-wage jobs were reserved for white southerners, since outside industries arriving in the South made no effort to change local patterns of discrimination. So the ultimate irony arose. As per capita income rose and industrialization brought in new jobs, black laborers poured out of the region in search of work. They arrived in cities that showed scant tolerance for racial differences and little willingness or ability to hire unskilled black labor.

The NAACP and Civil Rights

In the postwar era the National Association for the Advancement of Colored People decided it would use the judicial system to attack Jim Crow laws. That stepped-up attack reflected the increased national political influence African Americans achieved as they migrated in great numbers out of the South. No longer could northern politicians readily ignore the demands black leaders made for greater equality. The Swedish scholar Gunnar Myrdal had amply documented the black case in his landmark work *The American Dilemma* (1944), sponsored by the Carnegie Corporation. Presidents Roosevelt and Truman had taken small but significant steps to address the worst forms of legal and economic discrimination. And across the South black churches and colleges became centers for organized resistance to segregation.

Thurgood Marshall emerged as the NAACP's leading attorney. Marshall had attended law school in the 1930s at Howard University in Washington. There, the law school's dean, Charles Houston, was in the midst of revamping the school and turning out sharp, dedicated lawyers. Marshall was not only sharp, he had the common touch. "Before he came along," one observer noted,

Thurgood Marshall

the principal black leaders—men like Du Bois and James Weldon Johnson and Charles Houston—didn't talk the language of the people. They were upper-class and upper-middle-class Negroes. Thurgood Marshall was *of* the people. . . . Out in Texas or Oklahoma or down the street here in Washington at the Baptist church, he would make these rousing speeches that would have 'em all jumping out of their seats. . . . "We ain't gettin' what we should," was what it came down to, and he made them see that.

During the late 1930s and early 1940s Marshall toured the South (in "a little old beat-up '29 Ford"), typing out legal briefs in the back seat, trying to get teachers to sue for equal pay, and defending blacks accused of murder in a Klan-infested county in Florida. He was friendly with whites, not shy, and black citizens who had never even considered the possibility that a member of their race might win a legal battle "would come for miles, some of them on muleback or horseback, to see 'the nigger lawyer' who stood up in white men's courtrooms."

For years NAACP lawyers had worked hard to organize local chapters, to support members of the community willing to risk their jobs, property, and lives in order to challenge segregation. But they waged a moderate, pragmatic campaign. They chose not to attack head-on the Supreme Court decision (*Plessy v. Ferguson*, 1896) that permitted "separate but equal" segregated facilities. They simply demonstrated that a black college or school might be separate, but it was hardly equal if it lacked a law school or even indoor plumbing.

The *Brown* Decision

In 1950 the NAACP changed tactics: it would now try to convince the Supreme Court to overturn the separate but equal doctrine itself. Oliver Brown was one of the people who provided a way. Brown was dissatisfied that his daughter Linda had to walk past an all-white school on her way to catch the bus to her segregated black school in Topeka, Kansas. A three-judge federal panel rejected Brown's suit because

Before the civil rights movement, facilities in the South were almost always separate—down to the drinking fountains—but seldom equal.

the schools in Topeka, while segregated, did meet the test of equality. But the NAACP had been making headway with other cases in other courts. After two years of arguments the Supreme Court in *Brown v. Board of Education of Topeka* (1954) overturned the lower court ruling.

Marshall and his colleagues succeeded in part because of a change in the Court itself. The year before, President Eisenhower had appointed Earl Warren, a liberal Republican from California, as chief justice. Warren, a forceful advocate, managed to persuade the last of his reluctant judicial colleagues that segregation as defined in *Plessy* rested on an untenable theory of racial supremacy. The Court thus ruled unanimously that separate facilities were inherently unequal. To keep black children segregated solely on the basis of race, it ruled, "generates a feeling of inferiority as to their status in the community that may affect their hearts and minds in a way unlikely ever to be undone."

Overturning Plessy

At the time of the *Brown* decision, 21 states and the District of Columbia operated segregated school systems. All of them had to decide, in some way, how to comply with the new ruling. The Court allowed a certain amount of leeway, handing down a second ruling in 1955 that required that desegregation be carried out "with all deliberate speed." Some border states reluctantly decided to comply, but in the Deep South, many called for diehard defiance. In 1956, a "Southern Manifesto" was issued by 19 U.S. senators and 81 representatives; it declared their intent to use "all lawful means" to reestablish legalized segregation.

A New Civil Rights Strategy

The *Brown* decision did not end segregation, but it combined with political and economic forces to usher in a new era of southern race relations. In December 1955 Rosa Parks, a 43-year-old black civil rights activist, was riding the bus home in Montgomery, Alabama. When the driver ordered her to give up her seat for a white man, as Alabama Jim Crow laws required, she refused. Police took her to jail and eventually fined her $14.

Rosa Parks

Determined to overturn the law, black leaders organized a boycott of Montgomery buses, whose ridership was predominantly black. The white community, in an effort to halt the unprecedented black challenge, resorted to various forms of legal and physical intimidation. No local agent would insure cars used to carpool black workers. A bomb exploded in the house of the Reverend Martin Luther King, Jr., the key boycott leader. And when that failed to provoke the violence whites could use to justify harsh reprisals, 90 black leaders were arrested for organizing an illegal boycott. Still they held out until November 23, 1956, when the Supreme Court ruled that bus segregation was illegal.

The triumph was especially sweet for Martin Luther King, Jr., whose leadership in Montgomery brought him national fame. Before becoming a minister at the Dexter Street Baptist Church, King had had little personal contact with the worst forms of white racism. He had grown up in the relatively affluent middle-class black community of Atlanta, Georgia, the son of one of the city's most prominent black ministers. He attended Morehouse College, an academically respected black school in Atlanta, and Crozer Theological Seminary in Philadelphia, before entering the doctoral program in theology at Boston University. As a graduate student, King embraced the pacifism and nonviolence of the Indian leader Mohandas Gandhi and the

Martin Luther King, Jr.

Angry white students, opposed to integration, menace black students during a recess at Little Rock's Central High. This was the first civil rights crisis covered by television; for weeks NBC correspondent John Chancellor took a chartered plane daily from Little Rock to Oklahoma City to deliver film footage for the nightly news program. Such national attention made people outside of the South more sensitive to civil rights issues.

activism of Christian reformers of the progressive era. King heeded the call to Dexter Street in 1954 with the idea of becoming a theologian after he served his active ministry and finished his dissertation.

As boycott leader it was King's responsibility to rally black support without triggering violence. Since local officials were all too eager for any excuse to use force, King's nonviolent approach was the ideal strategy. King offered his audience two visions. First, he reminded them of the many injustices they had been forced to endure. The boycott, he asserted, was a good way to seek redress. Then he counseled his followers to avoid the actions of their oppressors: "In our protest there will be no cross burnings. No white person will be taken from his home by a hooded Negro mob and brutally murdered." And he evoked the Christian and republican ideals that would become the themes of his civil rights crusade. "If we protest courageously, and yet with dignity and Christian love," he said, "when the future history books are written, somebody will have to say, 'There lived a race of people, of black people, of people who had the moral courage to stand up for their rights. And thereby they injected a new meaning into the history of civilization.'"

Indeed, the African Americans of Montgomery did set an example of moral courage that rewrote the pages of American race relations. Their firm stand caught the attention of the national news media. King and his colleagues were developing the tactics needed to launch a more aggressive phase of the civil rights movement.

Little Rock and the White Backlash

The civil rights spotlight moved the following year to Little Rock, Arkansas. White officials there had reluctantly adopted a plan to integrate the schools with a most deliberate lack of speed. Nine black students were scheduled to enroll in September 1957 at the all-white Central High School. Instead, the school board urged them to stay home. Governor Orval Faubus, generally a moderate on race relations, called out the Arkansas National Guard on the excuse of maintaining order. President Eisenhower tacitly supported Faubus in his defiance of court-ordered integration by remarking that "you cannot change people's hearts merely by laws."

Still, the Justice Department could not simply let Faubus defy the federal courts. It won an injunction against the governor, but when the nine blacks returned on September 23, a mob of 1000 abusive whites greeted them. So great was national attention to the crisis that President Eisenhower felt compelled to uphold the authority of the federal courts. He sent in federal troops and took control of the National Guard. For a year the Guard preserved order until Faubus, in a last-ditch maneuver, closed the schools. Only in 1959, under pressure of another federal court ruling, did Little Rock schools reopen and resume the plan for gradual integration.

In the face of such attitudes, Martin Luther King and other civil rights leaders recognized that the skirmishes of Montgomery and Little Rock were a beginning, not the end. Cultural attitudes and customs were not about to give way overnight.

CRACKS IN THE CONSENSUS

The fifties, then, were not a time of consensus on civil rights. In other ways, too, the era could hardly be painted as a decade of undisturbed calm. Intellectuals and social critics spoke out against the stifling features of a conformist corporate culture. Even a moderate like Eisenhower had warned of giving too much power to military, governmental, and industrial bureaucracies. At the fringes of American society, the "beatniks" rejected conformity, while the more mainstream rock 'n' roll movement broadcast its own brand of youthful rebellion. Such cultural ferment undercut the notion that the fifties were merely a decade of consensus.

Critics of Mass Culture

In Levittown, New Jersey, a woman who had invited her neighbors to a cocktail party eagerly awaited them dressed in newly fashionable Capri pants—a tight-fitting calf-length style. Alas, one early arriving couple glimpsed the woman through a window. What on earth was the hostess wearing? *Pajamas?* Who in their right mind would entertain in pajamas? The couple sneaked home, afraid they had made a mistake about the day of the party. They telephoned another neighbor, who anxiously called yet others on the guest list.

The neighbors finally mustered enough courage to attend the party. But when the hostess later learned of their misunderstanding, she put her Capri pants in the closet for good. Levittown was not ready for such a change in fashion.

Was America turning into a vast suburban wasteland, where the neighbors' worries over Capri pants would stifle all individuality? Many "highbrow" intellectuals worried openly about the homogenized lifestyle created by mass consumption, conformity, and mass media. Critics like Dwight Macdonald sarcastically attacked the culture of the suburban middle classes: *Reader's Digest* Condensed Books, uplifting film spectacles like *The Ten Commandments*, television dramas that pretended to be high art but in reality were little more than simplistic pontificating. "Midcult," Macdonald called it, which was his shorthand for middlebrow culture.

Other critics charged that the skyscrapers and factories of giant conglomerates housed an all too impersonal world. In large, increasingly automated workplaces, skilled laborers seemed little more than caretakers of machines. Large corporations required middle-level executives to submerge their personal goals in the processes and work routines of a large bureaucracy. David Riesman, a sociologist, condemned stifling conformity in *The Lonely Crowd* (1950). In nineteenth-century America, Riesman argued, Americans had been "inner directed." It was their own consciences that formed their values and drove them to seek success. In contrast, modern workers had developed a personality shaped not so much by inner convictions as by the opinions of their peers. The new "other-directed" society of suburbia preferred security to success. "Go along to get along" was its motto. In a bureaucratized economy, it was important to please others, to conform to the group, and to cooperate.

David Riesman's The Lonely Crowd

William Whyte carried Riesman's critique from the workplace to the suburb in *The Organization Man* (1956). Here he found rootless families, shifted from town to town by the demands of corporations. (IBM, went one standard joke, stood for "I've Been Moved.") The typical "organization man" was sociable but not terribly ambitious. He sought primarily to "keep up with the Joneses" and the number of consumer goods they owned. He lived in a suburban "split-level trap," as one critic put it, one among millions of "haggard" men, "tense and anxious" women, and "the gimme kids," who, like the cartoon character Dennis the Menace, looked up from the litter under the Christmas tree to ask, "Is that all?"

William Whyte's Organization Man

No doubt such portraits were overdrawn and overly alarmist. (Where, after all, did Riesman's nineteenth-century inner-directed Americans get their values, if not from the society around them?) But such critiques indicated the problems of adjustment faced by those working within large bureaucratic organizations and living in suburbs that were decentralized and self-contained.

The Rebellion of Young America

Young Americans were among suburbia's sharpest critics. Dance crazes, outlandish clothing, strange jargon, rebelliousness toward parents, and sexual precociousness— all these behaviors challenged middle-class respectability. More than a few parents and public figures felt challenged. They warned that America had spawned a generation of rebellious juvenile delinquents. Psychologist Frederic Wertheim told a group of doctors, "You cannot understand present-day juvenile delinquency if you do not take into account the pathogenic and pathoplastic [infectious] influence of comic books." Others laid the blame on films and the lyrics of popular music.

The center of the new teen culture was the high school. Whether in consolidated rural school districts, new suburban schools, or city systems, the large, comprehensive high schools of the 1950s were often miniature melting pots where middle-class students were exposed to, and often adopted, the style of the lower classes. Alarmed school administrators began to talk of the problems caused by "juvenile delinquents." They wore jeans and T-shirts, challenged authority, and defiantly smoked cigarettes, much like the motorcycle gang leader portrayed by Marlon Brando in the film *The Wild One* (1954).

Juvenile delinquency

In many ways the argument about juvenile delinquency was an argument about social class and, to a lesser degree, race. When adults complained that "delinquent" teenagers dressed poorly, lacked ambition, were irresponsible and sexually promiscuous, these were the same arguments traditionally used to denigrate other outsiders—immigrants, the poor, and African Americans. Nowhere were these racial and class undertones more evident than in the hue and cry greeting the arrival of rock and roll.

The rise of rock 'n' roll

Before 1954 popular music had been divided into three major categories: pop, country and western, and rhythm and blues. A handful of major record companies with almost exclusively white singers dominated the pop charts. On one fringe of the popular field was country and western, often split into cowboy musicians like Roy Rogers and Gene Autry and the hillbilly style associated with Nashville. The music industry generally treated rhythm and blues as "race music," whose performers and audience were largely black. Each of these musical traditions, it is worth noting, grew out of regional cultures. As the West and the South merged into the national culture, so were these musical subcultures gradually integrated into the national mainstream.

By the mid-1950s the distinctiveness of the three styles began to blur. Singers on the white pop charts recorded a few songs from country and from rhythm and blues. The popularity of crossovers such as "Sh-boom," "Tutti-Frutti," and "Earth Angel" indicated that a major shift in taste and market was under way. Lyrics still reflected the pop field's preoccupation with young love, marriage, and happiness, but the music reflected the rawer, earthier style of rhythm and blues. Country and western singer Bill Haley brought the new blend to the fore in 1954 with "Shake, Rattle, and Roll," the first rock song to reach the top ten on the pop charts.

And then—calamity! Millions of middle-class roofs nearly blew off with the appearance in 1955 of the rhythmic and raucous Elvis Presley. By background, Elvis was a country boy whose musical style combined elements of gospel, country, and blues. But it was his hip-swinging, pelvis-plunging performances that electrified teenage audiences. To more conservative adults, Presley's long hair, sideburns, and tight jeans seemed menacingly delinquent, an expression of hostile rebellion. What they often resented but rarely admitted was that Elvis looked lower class, sounded black, and really could sing.

The beat generation

Beyond the frenetic rhythms of rock 'n' roll, and even farther beyond the pale of suburban culture, a subculture flourished known as the beat generation. In run-down urban neighborhoods and college towns this motley collection of artists, intellectuals, musicians, and middle-class students dropped out of mainstream society. In dress and behavior the "beatniks" self-consciously rejected what they viewed as the excessive spiritual bankruptcy of America's middle-class culture. Cool urban "hipsters"—especially black jazz musicians like John Coltrane or Sonny Rollins—were their models. They read poetry, listened to jazz, explored Oriental philosophy, and experimented openly with drugs, mystical religions, and sex.

The "beats" viewed themselves as being driven to the margins of society, rejecting the culture of abundance, materialism, and conformity. "I saw the best minds of my generation destroyed by madness, starving hysterical naked," wrote Allen Ginsberg in his 1955 poem *Howl*. They had become "angelheaded hipsters . . . who in poverty and tatters and hollow-eyed and high sat up smoking in the supernatural

The King, Elvis Presley

darkness of cold-water flats floating across the tops of cities contemplating jazz." Jack Kerouac tapped the frenzied energy beneath the beatniks' cool facade in *On the Road* (1957), a novel based on his travels across the country with his friend Neal Cassady. Kerouac finished the novel in one frenetic three-week binge, feeding a 120-foot roll of paper through his typewriter and spilling out tales of pot, jazz, crazy sex, and all-night raps undertaken in a search for "IT"—the ultimate transcendental moment when mind and experience mesh.

The dreams of Kerouac and Ginsberg came from a world starkly different from the manicured lawns of suburbia. The world of the suburbs seemed content, middle-of-the-road, prosperous. The beats seemed restless, nonconformist, beyond the fringe. Yet the 1960s would demonstrate that the suburban era contained enough cracks in the consensus to launch an era of rebellion and reform. Those upheavals would test the limits of a liberal, even radical vision of American society. The fringes and the middle of the roaders were perhaps not so far apart as they seemed.

CHAPTER SUMMARY

The automobile and the culture of the highway were in many ways the ties that bound Americans to one another in the 1950s. Automobiles reflected the increasing abundance of the era, while the new interstate highway system symbolized a continuation of moderate New Deal–style involvement in the economy in the guise of Eisenhower's "modern Republicanism." Then, too, the new highways encouraged suburban growth as the most popular form of housing. The expanding economy and the rising numbers of Americans joining the suburban middle class led to the common view that society had developed a "consensus" about what it meant to be an American. This consensus blurred class distinctions and applauded the notion of "civil religion." It promoted an image of the ideal mother who found sufficient outlet for her talents through her housework and the care of a family, even though more women than ever worked outside the home.

Reflecting the politics of the era, President Eisenhower resisted the demands of conservative Republicans to dismantle New Deal programs. Instead, he championed his own brand of modern Republicanism. Initiating a number of modest social welfare programs, he rejected more far-reaching proposals of liberal Democrats to provide large-scale federal housing aid or a universal health-care system. The cold war dominated Eisenhower's foreign policy agenda. Under Secretary of State John Foster Dulles, the administration expressed a willingness to push to the "brink" of nuclear war in order to counteract Soviet influence. Regional conflicts in Vietnam, Quemoy and Matsu, Hungary, Guatemala, Iran, and the Middle East all demonstrated how the cold war struggle inflamed international tensions. During the Eisenhower years, moves toward conciliation (the Geneva Summit) mixed with renewed rivalry (the U-2 incident, the race into space, Castro's Cuban revolution).

Throughout the 1950s, cracks appeared in the national consensus. At a time when white Americans were moving to suburbs that were effectively segregated either by custom or by law, many African Americans were moving out of the rural South and into urban areas. Seeking to end legal segregation, the National Association for the Advancement of Colored People succeeded in challenging the

Supreme Court to overturn the prevailing doctrine of "separate but equal" in *Brown v. Board of Education*. Martin Luther King led a campaign to desegregate the city of Montgomery's bus system, while public school desegregation sparked conflict at Little Rock, Arkansas. Critics of the suburban consensus drew bleak portraits of the modern conglomerate's "organization man." On the fringes of society teenagers, intellectuals, and beatniks adopted ideas and behaviors that rejected the mainstream consensus. In the midst of postwar peace and prosperity, the United States began to build a new social and political agenda.

SIGNIFICANT EVENTS

1947	Levittown construction begins
1950	David Riesman's *The Lonely Crowd* published; Kefauver crime hearings
1952	Fertility rate in the United States reaches new high
1953	Mossadeq overthrown in Iran
1954	*Brown v. Board of Education;* St. Lawrence Seaway Act; CIA overthrows Arbenz in Guatemala; Geneva summit
1955	Montgomery bus boycott; Elvis Presley ignites rock and roll
1956	Interstate Highway Act; Eisenhower reelected; Suez crisis; "Southern Manifesto"
1957	*Sputnik* launched; Little Rock crisis; Eisenhower Doctrine
1958	Richard Nixon attacked in Latin America; marines sent into Lebanon; Berlin crisis; National Defense Education Act; NASA established
1959	Castro seizes power in Cuba; Khrushchev visits United States; Soviet probe hits moon
1960	Soviet Union captures CIA pilot; Paris summit canceled
1961	Eisenhower's farewell address warns of military–industrial complex

---

ADDITIONAL READING

No president's stock has risen more among historians than Dwight Eisenhower's. Contrast the dismissive view of Eisenhower in Eric Goldman, *The Crucial Decade and After, 1945–1960* (1960) with Stephen Ambrose, *Eisenhower: The President* (1984) or Fred Greenstein, *The Hidden Hand Presidency: Eisenhower as Leader* (1982). A similar revision has occurred in the treatment of his foreign policy, where Eisenhower receives credit that once went to Dulles. See, for example, Robert Divine, *Eisenhower and the Cold War* (1981) or Richard Melanson and David Mayers, eds., *Reevaluating Eisenhower: American Foreign Policy in the 1950s* (1987).

For an overview of the era, see John Diggins, *The Proud Decades: America in War and Peace, 1941–1960* (1988) or the even more readable, but less analytical, David Halberstam, *The Fifties* (1993). Among the many excellent studies of civil rights are Taylor Branch, *Parting the Waters: America in the King Years, 1954–63* (1988) and the reader for the PBS series, Juan Williams, *Eyes on the Prize: America's Civil Rights Years, 1954–1964* (1987). For a fuller list of readings, see the Bibliography.

30

Liberalism and Beyond

Six-year-old Ruby knew the lessons. She was to look straight ahead—not to one side or the other—and especially not at *them*. She was to keep walking. Above all, she was not to look back once she'd passed, because that would encourage them. Ruby's parents had instructed her carefully, but she still struggled to keep her eyes straight. The first day of school, federal marshals were there along with her parents. So were hundreds of nasty white people who came near enough to yell things like "You little nigger, we'll get you and kill you." Then she was within the building's quiet halls and alone with her teacher. She was the only person in class: none of the white students had come. As the days went by during that autumn of 1960, the marshals stopped walking with her, but the hecklers still waited. And once in a while Ruby couldn't help looking back, trying to see if she recognized the face of one woman in particular.

Ruby's parents were not social activists. They signed their daughter up for the white school because "we thought it was for all the colored to do, and we never thought Ruby would be alone." Her father's white employer fired him; letters and phone calls threatened the family's lives and home. Ruby seemed to take it all in stride, though her parents worried that she was not eating the way she used to. Often she left her school lunch untouched or refused anything other than packaged food such as potato chips. It was only after a time that the problem was traced to the hecklers. "They tells me I'm going to die, and that it'll be soon. And that one lady tells me every morning I'm getting poisoned soon, when she can fix it." Ruby was convinced that the woman owned the variety store nearby and would carry out her threat by poisoning the family's food.

Over the course of a year, white students gradually returned to class and life settled into a new routine. By the time Ruby was 10, she had developed a remarkably clear perception of herself. "Maybe because of all the trouble going to school in the beginning I learned more about my people. Maybe I would have anyway; because when you get older you see yourself and the white kids; and you find out the difference. You try to forget it, and say there is none; and if there is you won't say what it be. Then you say it's my own people, and so I can be proud of them instead of ashamed."

If the new ways were hard for Ruby, they were not easy for white southerners either—even those who saw the need for change. One woman, for years a dedicated teacher in Atlanta, vividly recalled a traumatic summer 10 years earlier when she

On August 28, 1963, more than 250,000 demonstrators joined the great civil rights march on Washington. The day belonged to the Reverend Martin Luther King, Jr., who movingly called on black and white Americans to join together in a color-blind society.

Ruby's drawings of a white girl (left) and herself

went north to New York City to take courses in education. There were black students living in the dormitory, an integrated situation she was not used to. One day as she stepped from her shower, so did a black student from the nearby stall. "When I saw her I didn't know what to do," the woman recalled. "I felt sick all over, and frightened. What I remember—I'll never forget it—is that horrible feeling of being caught in a terrible trap, and not knowing what to do about it. I thought of running out of the room and screaming, or screaming at the woman to get out, or running back into the shower. . . . My sense of propriety was with me, though—miraculously—and I didn't want to hurt the woman. It wasn't *her* that was upsetting me. I knew that, even in that moment of sickness and panic." So she ducked back into the shower until the other woman left.

Summer was almost over before she felt comfortable eating with black students at the same table. And when she returned home, she told no one about her experiences. "At that time people would have thought one of two things: I was crazy (for being so upset and ashamed) or a fool who in a summer had become a dangerous 'race mixer.'" She continued to love the South and to speak up for its traditions of dignity, neighborliness, and honor, but she saw the need for change. And so in 1961 she volunteered to teach one of the first integrated high school classes in Atlanta, even though she had her doubts. By the end of two years she concluded that she had never spent a more exciting time teaching. "I've never felt so useful, so constantly useful, not just to the children but to our whole society. American as well as Southern. Those children, all of them, have given me more than I've given them."

A LIBERAL AGENDA FOR REFORM

For Americans in all walks of life, the upheavals that swept America in the 1960s were wrenching. From the schoolrooms and lunch counters of the South to the college campuses of the North, from eastern slums to western migrant labor camps, American society was in ferment.

On the face of it, such agitation seemed to be a dramatic reversal of the placid fifties. Turbulence and change had overturned stability and consensus. Yet the events of the 1960s grew naturally out of the social conditions that preceded them.

The Social Structures of Change

The prosperity of the 1950s encouraged a confidence that problems like poverty and discrimination might finally be solved. At the same time, that prosperity did not reach all areas of the nation equally. While suburbs flourished, urban areas decayed. While more white Americans went to college, more African Americans found themselves out of work on southern farms or desperate for jobs in northern ghettos. As Mexican American migrant workers picked grapes in California or followed the harvest north from Texas, they saw their employers resist every attempt to unionize and improve their wages. Yet the general prosperity remained for all to see. And the success of the NAACP in wringing a policy of integration from the Supreme Court gave minorities new hopes that they too could win the rights due them.

The expansive years of the 1950s, in other words, proved to be a seedbed for reform movements of the 1960s. Time and again, the dissenters challenged the political system to deal with what the 1950s had done—and what had been left undone. As one friend of Martin Luther King predicted in 1958, "If the young people are aroused from their lethargy through this fight, it will affect broad circles throughout the country. . . ."

Inevitably, these forces for change brought hope and energy to the liberal tradition. Like the New Dealers and the progressives before them, liberals of the 1960s did not wish to overturn capitalism. They looked primarily to tame its excesses, taking a pragmatic approach to reforming American society. Like Franklin Roosevelt, they believed that the government should play an active role in managing the economy in order to soften the boom-and-bust swings of capitalism. Like progressives from the turn of the century, liberals looked to improve society by applying the intelligence of "experts." *The liberal tradition*

Liberals had confidence, at times bordering on arrogance, that poverty could be eliminated and the good society achieved. "The world seemed more plastic, more subject to human will," one liberal recalled. He and his fellow reformers believed that "the energy and commitment of multitudes could be linked to compel the enrichment of human life." That faith would prove naive, but during the early sixties such optimism was both infectious and energizing.

The Election of 1960

The first president to ride these currents of reform was John Fitzgerald Kennedy, at 43 the youngest man ever elected to the presidency. On the face of it, Kennedy's 1960 campaign promised to bring the breezes of change to Washington. The nation needed to find new challenges and "new frontiers," he proclaimed. Kennedy's rhetoric was noble, but the direction in which he would take the nation was far from clear.

The Catholic issue

Aside from political issues, there was a social one to be met. Jack Kennedy was a Roman Catholic out of Irish Boston, and no Catholic had ever been elected president. Conservative Protestants, many concentrated in the heavily Democratic South, were convinced that a Catholic president would never be "free to exercise his own judgment" if the pope ordered otherwise. Kennedy chose to confront the issue head on. In September he entered the lions' den, addressing an association of hostile Protestant ministers in Houston. The speech was the best of his campaign. "I believe in an America where the separation of church and state is absolute," he said, "—where no Catholic prelate would tell the President (should he be Catholic) how to act, and no Protestant minister would tell his parishioners how to vote." House Speaker Sam Rayburn, an old Texas pol, was astonished by Kennedy's bravura performance. "My God! . . . He's eating them blood raw."

Kennedy's opponent, Vice President Richard Nixon, ran on his record as an experienced leader and staunch anti-Communist, but his campaign faltered in October as unemployment rose. Nixon agreed to a series of debates with Kennedy—the first to be televised nationally. Image proved more telling than issues. According to one poll, radio listeners believed Nixon won the debate, but on television viewers saw a tired candidate with dark shadows on his face. A relaxed Kennedy convinced many in the audience that he could handle the job.

In the end religion, ethnicity, and race played decisive roles. One voter was asked if he voted for Kennedy because he was a Catholic. "No, because *I* am," he answered, and in key states Catholic support made a difference. "Hyphenated" Americans—Hispanic, Jewish, Irish, Italian, Polish, and German—voted Democratic in record numbers, while much of the black vote that had gone to Eisenhower in 1956 returned to the Democratic fold. Indeed, when Martin Luther King was imprisoned during a civil rights protest in Georgia, Kennedy attracted the support of black Americans by telephoning his sympathy to Dr. King's wife. Interest in the election ran so high that 64 percent of voters turned out, the largest number in 50 years. Out of 68.3 million ballots cast, Kennedy won by a margin of just 118,000.

The Hard-Nosed Idealists of Camelot

Many observers compared the Kennedy White House to Camelot, King Arthur's magical court. A popular musical of 1960 pictured Camelot as a land where skies were fair, men brave, women pretty, and the days full of challenge and excitement. With similar vigor, Kennedy brought into his administration bright, energetic liberal advisers. He and his stylish wife Jacqueline invited artists, musicians, and intellectuals to the White House. Impromptu touch football games on the White House lawn displayed a rough-and-tumble playfulness akin to Arthur's jousting tournaments of old.

In truth, Kennedy was not a liberal by temperament. Handsome and intelligent, he possessed an ironic, self-deprecating humor. Yet in Congress, he had had an undistinguished career, supported Senator Joe McCarthy, and earned a reputation as a playboy. Once Kennedy set his sights on the White House, however, he revealed an

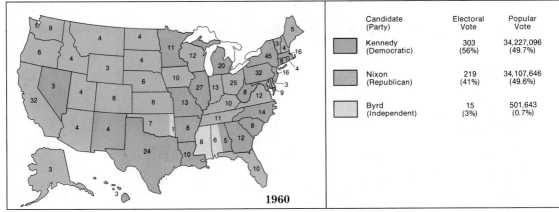

Candidate (Party)	Electoral Vote	Popular Vote
Kennedy (Democratic)	303 (56%)	34,227,096 (49.7%)
Nixon (Republican)	219 (41%)	34,107,646 (49.6%)
Byrd (Independent)	15 (3%)	501,643 (0.7%)

ELECTION OF 1960

astonishing capacity for political maneuver and organization. To woo the liberals, he surrounded himself with a distinguished group of intellectuals and academics.

Robert McNamara

Robert Strange McNamara typified the pragmatic, liberal bent of the new Kennedy team. Steely and brilliant, McNamara was one of the postwar breed of young executives known as the "whiz kids." As a Harvard Business School professor and later as president of Ford Motors, he specialized in using new quantitative tools to streamline business. As the new secretary of defense, McNamara intended to find more flexible and efficient ways of conducting the cold war.

Kennedy liked men like this—witty, bright, intellectual—because they seemed comfortable with power and were not afraid to use it. If Nikita Khrushchev spoke of waging guerrilla "wars of liberation," Americans could play that game, too. The president's leisure reading reflected a similar adventurous taste: the popular James Bond spy novels. Agent 007, with his license to kill, was sophisticated, a cool womanizer (as Kennedy himself continued to be), and ready to use the latest technology to deal with Communist villains. Ironically, Bond demonstrated that there could be plenty of glamour in being "hard-nosed" and pragmatic. That illicit pleasure was the underside, perhaps, of Camelot's high ideals.

NEW FRONTIERS

Kennedy had made the cold war a central theme of his campaign. The contest, he believed, had shifted from the traditional struggle over Europe to the developing nations in Asia, Africa, and Latin America. He wanted to arm the United States with a more flexible range of military and economic options.

Alliance for Progress and Peace Corps

The "Alliance for Progress," announced in the spring of 1961, indicated the course Kennedy would follow. He promised to provide $20 billion in foreign aid over 10 years—about four times the aid Latin America had been getting. In return,

The urbane and energetic John F. Kennedy was associated with both King Arthur (left, played by Richard Burton in the 1960 musical) and the spy James Bond (played by Sean Connery, right). Kennedy and his advisers prided themselves on their pragmatic, hard-nosed idealism. But while Bond used advanced technology and covert operations to save the world, in real life such approaches had their downside, as the growing civil war in Vietnam would demonstrate.

Latin American nations would agree to reform unfair tax policies and begin agricultural land reforms. If successful, the Alliance would discourage future Castro-style revolutions. With similar fanfare, the administration launched the Peace Corps, sending idealistic young men and women to Third World nations to provide technical, educational, and public health services. Under the Alliance, a majority of Peace Corps volunteers were assigned to Latin America.

To give economic programs some military muscle, the Pentagon created jungle warfare schools in North Carolina and the Canal Zone. These schools trained Latin American police and paramilitary groups to fight guerrilla wars. They also trained American "special forces" like the Green Berets in the arts of jungle warfare. If the Soviets aided wars of liberation, U.S. commandos would fight back.

Space program

Kennedy believed, too, that the Soviets had made space the final frontier of the cold war. Only a few months after the president's inauguration, a Russian cosmonaut orbited the world for the first time. In response, Kennedy challenged Congress to authorize a manned space mission to the moon that would land by the end of the decade. In February 1962 John Glenn circled the earth three times in a "fireball of a ride." Gradually, the American space program gained on the Russians. In July 1969, a lunar module from the *Apollo 11* spacecraft touched down on the moon. It was a showy triumph, fueled partly by cold war rivalry and partly by the liberal conviction that the government could attack and solve any problem set before it.

Cold War Frustrations

In more down-to-earth ways, high ideals did not translate easily into practical results. While Latin American governments eagerly accepted aid, they were much less able or willing to carry out reforms. Few welcomed the intrusive Yankee diplomats who came from north of the border to inspect their programs. Instability remained a key problem, for in the first five years of the Alliance, nine Latin American governments were overthrown by military coups. The Peace Corps, for its part, proved a tremendous public relations success and helped thousands of Third World farmers on a people-to-people basis. But individual Peace Corps workers could do little to change corrupt policies on a national level. Many returned home convinced the Third World needed revolution, not reform.

Nor did Kennedy succeed in countering revolutionary "wars of liberation." His prime target was Fidel Castro's Communist regime, only 90 miles south of Florida. After breaking diplomatic relations in 1960, the Eisenhower administration had secretly authorized the CIA to organize an invasion of Cuba. The CIA assured Kennedy that its 1400-member army of Cuban exiles could inspire their countrymen to overthrow Castro. Eager to establish his own cold war credentials, the president approved an attack. But the April invasion turned into a disaster. The poorly equipped rebel *Bay of Pigs* forces landed at the swampy Bay of Pigs, with no protective cover for miles. Within *invasion* two days Castro's army had rounded them up. Taking responsibility for the entire fiasco, Kennedy felt bitterly humiliated. That did not discourage further covert operations. Unrepentant for its fiasco, the CIA secretly hatched plans to embarrass or murder the Cuban leader.

Kennedy's advisers took a similar covert approach to the problem of South *Kennedy and* Vietnam. In former French Indochina a civil war with religious overtones was under *Vietnam* way. The autocratic government of Prime Minister Ngo Dinh Diem, a Catholic, remained in power, although it was growing more unpopular by the month. South Vietnamese Communists, known as the Vietcong, waged a guerrilla war against Diem with support from North Vietnam. Buddhist elements backed the rebellion. In May 1961, a month after the Bay of Pigs invasion, Kennedy secretly ordered 500 Green Berets and military advisers to Vietnam in hopes of helping Diem defeat the Vietcong. By 1963 the number of "military advisers" had risen to more than 16,000 men. Increasingly, they were being drawn into combat. Kennedy cited Eisenhower's domino theory to defend aid to Vietnam. "If South Vietnam went, it . . . would give the impression that the wave of the future in Southeast Asia was China and the Communists," he told the press.

By 1963 Diem's ruthless campaign against his Buddhist opposition had isolated the regime. Corruption and police state tactics created grave concern in Washington. Worse yet, he was not winning the war. As the Kennedy administration lost faith in Diem, it tacitly encouraged a military coup by other South Vietnamese military offi- *Diem falls* cers. To the surprise of American officials, the coup plotters captured Diem and shot him in November 1963. Despite Kennedy's policy of pragmatic idealism, the United States found itself mired in a Vietnamese civil war, which it had no clear strategy for winning.

Confronting Khrushchev

Vietnam and Cuba were just two areas in the Third World where the Kennedy administration sought to battle Communist forces. But the conflict between the United States and the Soviet Union soon overshadowed developments in Asia, Africa, and Latin America.

The discovery of Soviet offensive missile sites in Cuba, revealed by low-level American reconnaissance flights, led to the first nuclear showdown of the cold war. For several tense days in October 1962, President Kennedy met with his National Security Council to debate alternative responses.

June 1961 was the president's first chance to take the measure of Nikita Khrushchev, at a summit meeting held in Vienna. For two long days, Khrushchev was brash and belligerent. East and West Germany must be reunited, he demanded. In the divided capital of Berlin, located deep within East Germany (see map, page 998), citizens from across the nation were crossing from the eastern sector of the city into the free western zone as a way of escaping communist rule. This "problem" must be settled within six months, Khruschev insisted. Kennedy tried to stand up to Khrushchev's bullying, but he left Vienna worried that the Soviet leader perceived him as weak and inexperienced. By August events in Berlin confirmed his fears. Under cover of night, the Soviets threw up a heavily guarded wall sealing off any entry into West Berlin. Despite American protests, the wall stayed up.

The Berlin Wall

Tensions with the Soviet Union led the administration to rethink American nuclear strategy. Under the Dulles doctrine of massive retaliation, almost any incident threatened to trigger a launch of the full arsenal of nuclear missiles. Kennedy and McNamara sought to establish a "flexible response doctrine" that would limit the level of a first nuclear strike and therefore leave room for negotiation. In that case, however, conventional forces in Europe would have to be built up so that they could

A flexible nuclear response

better deter aggression. McNamara proposed equipping them with smaller tactical nuclear weapons.

But what if the Soviets were tempted to launch a first-strike attack to knock out American missiles? McNamara's flexible response policy required that enough American missiles survive in order to retaliate. If the Soviets knew the United States could survive a first strike, they would then be less likely to launch a surprise attack. So McNamara began a program to place missile sites underground and develop submarine-launched missiles. The new flexible response policies resulted in a 15 percent increase in the 1961 military budget, compared with only 2 percent increases during the last two years of Eisenhower's term. Under Kennedy, the military–industrial complex thrived.

The Missiles of October

The peril of nuclear confrontation became dramatically clear in the Cuban missile crisis of October 1962. President Kennedy had emphasized repeatedly that the United States would treat any attempt to place offensive weapons in Cuba as an unacceptable threat. Khrushchev had simultaneously promised that the Soviet Union had no such intention. Thus Kennedy was outraged when a CIA U-2 overflight on October 14 confirmed that offensive missile sites were being constructed. "He can't do that to me," the president snapped.

For a week, top security advisers met in secret strategy sessions. Hawkish advisers urged air strikes against the missile sites, but Kennedy worried that such an attack might lead to nuclear war. Indeed, evidence from Soviet archives indicates that, unknown to American officials, Soviet commanders in Cuba possessed the authority to launch short-range nuclear missiles if American forces invaded. Such an exchange almost certainly would have led to nuclear war. In the end Kennedy chose the more restrained option of imposing a naval blockade to intercept "all offensive military equipment under shipment to Cuba." On October 22, Americans were stunned when the president informed the nation about the crisis and his response. Tensions mounted as a Soviet submarine approached the line of American ships. On October 25 the navy stopped an oil tanker. Several Soviet ships reversed course.

A naval blockade

Meanwhile, Kennedy was making strenuous efforts to resolve the crisis through diplomatic channels. On October 26 he received a rambling message from Khrushchev agreeing to remove the missiles in return for an American promise not to invade Cuba. The next day came a more troubling message, insisting the United States must also dismantle its missile bases in Turkey, which bordered on the Soviet Union. Unwilling to strike that deal publicly, Kennedy decided to ignore the second letter and accept the offer in the first. When the Soviets agreed, the face-off ended on terms that saved either side from overt humiliation.

The nuclear showdown prompted Kennedy and his advisers to seek ways to control the nuclear arms race. "We all inhabit this small planet," he warned in June 1963. "We all breathe the same air. We all cherish our children's future. And we are all mortal." The administration negotiated a nuclear test ban with the Soviets, prohibiting all above-ground nuclear tests. Growing concern over radioactive fallout increased public support for the treaty. A telephone "hotline" was also installed, providing a direct communications link between the White House and the Kremlin for use in times of crisis. At the same time Kennedy's prestige soared for "standing up" to the Soviets.

Nuclear test ban treaty

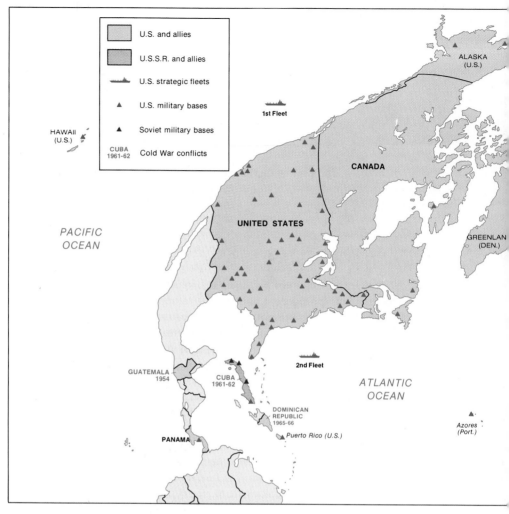

THE WORLD OF THE SUPERPOWERS
This map shows the extent of the cold war Soviet and American military buildup. The United States established a worldwide network of bases and alliances surrounding Soviet bloc nations, which extended from Japan and South Korea, South Vietnam, Pakistan, and Turkey in Asia to the nations of the NATO alliance in Europe. Soviet efforts to expand its influence in the Third World led to the creation of an outpost in Cuba. Around these strategic perimeters, "hotspots" and centers of crisis continued to simmer.

The (Somewhat) New Frontier at Home

Despite campaign promises for bold initiatives at home as well as abroad, the president's legislative achievements were modest. Once in the White House, he found himself hemmed in by a Democratic Congress dominated by conservatives. The modest Area Redevelopment Act of 1961 provided financial aid to depressed industrial and rural areas, and Congress raised the minimum wage to $1.25. But on key issues, including aid to education and medical health insurance, Kennedy made no headway.

He wavered, too, on how best to manage the economy. The president's liberal economic advisers favored increased government spending to reduce unemployment, even if that meant a budget deficit. Similarly, they argued that tax cuts could be used

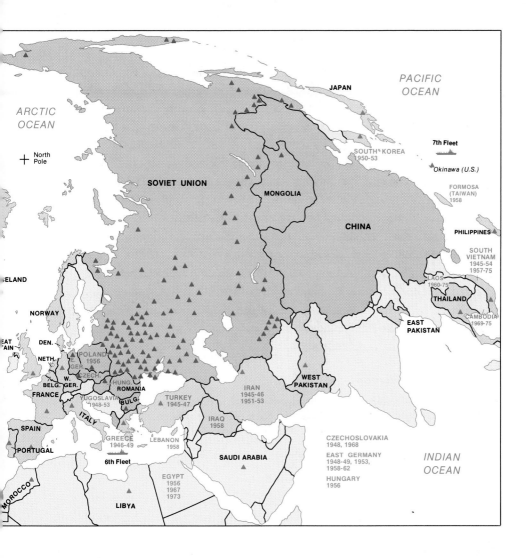

to increase consumer spending and so stimulate the economy. Kennedy toyed with both remedies, but conservatives continued to push for a balanced budget. So Kennedy moved cautiously, relieved at first to discover that the economy was growing quite nicely without a tax cut. Only in 1963 did he send a tax proposal to Congress.

Always the pragmatic politician, Kennedy hoped to work with, not against, the leaders of big business. He firmly believed that prosperity for large firms spelled growth for the whole nation. Thus the president asked Congress to ease antitrust restrictions and grant investment credits and tax breaks—all actions that perfectly suited corporate interests. But he did believe that the government should be able to limit wages and prices for large corporations and unions. If not, an inflationary spiral might result. Wage increases would be followed by price increases followed by even higher wage demands.

To prevent that, the Council of Economic Advisors proposed to stabilize prices by tying wage increases to improved productivity. In April 1962 the United Steel Workers, like most other major unions, agreed to a contract that followed those guidelines. The large steel corporations, however, broke their part of the informal bargain with substantial steel price raises. Such double-dealing enraged Kennedy. He called for investigations into price fixing, mounted antitrust proceedings, and shifted

Showdown with big steel

1069

I was sentenced to The State Penitentiary by The Circuit Court of Bay County, State of Florida. The present proceeding was commenced on a petition for a Writ of Habeus Corpus to The Supreme Court of The State of Florida to vacate The sentence, on the grounds that I was made to stand Trial without the aid of counsel, and, at all times of my incarseretion. The said Court refused To appoint counsel and therefore deprived me of Due process of law, and violate my rights in The Bill of Rights and the constitution of the United States.

Clarence Earl Gideon

5th day of Jan 1962 Petitioner

Notary Public

Gideon's Letter to the Supreme Court
John F. Davis, Clerk, Supreme Court of the United States

Clarence Earl Gideon (left) used this handwritten letter to bring his appeal to the attention of the Supreme Court. In the *Gideon* case the court ruled that even poor defendants have the right to legal counsel. Such incidents, while rare, restore faith in the idea of a government for the people.

Pentagon purchases to smaller steel companies that had not raised prices. The intense pressure caused the big companies to drop the price increases but soured relations between Kennedy and the business community.

The Reforms of the Warren Court

With the promise of new frontiers blocked by a conservative Congress, the Supreme Court broke the logjam. Chief Justice Earl Warren turned what was traditionally the least activist branch of government into a center of liberal reform. Until Warren's retirement in 1969, the Court continued to hand down a series of landmark decisions in broad areas of civil liberties and civil rights.

In 1960 the rights of citizens accused of a crime but not yet convicted were often unclear. Those too poor to afford lawyers often faced trial without representation. The police and the courts seldom informed those accused of a crime of their rights guaranteed under the Constitution. In a series of decisions, the Court ruled that the Fourteenth Amendment provided broad guarantees of due process under the law. *Gideon v. Wainwright* (1963), an appeal launched by a Florida prisoner, made it clear that all citizens were entitled to legal counsel in any case involving a possible jail sentence. In *Escobedo v. Illinois* (1964) and *Miranda v. Arizona* (1966) the Court declared that individuals detained for a crime must be informed of the charges against them, of their right to remain silent, and of their right to have an attorney present

Protecting due process

during questioning. Though these decisions applied to all citizens, they were primarily intended to benefit the poor, who were most likely to be in trouble with the law and least likely to understand their rights.

In *Engel v. Vitale* (1962), the Court issued a ruling that especially troubled conservative religious groups. The case involved a nonsectarian prayer written by the New York State Board of Regents that public school students were required to recite. Even if dissenting children could be excused, the Court ruled, they faced indirect pressure to recite the prayer. That violated the constitutional separation of church and state. The following year the Court extended the ban on school prayer to cover the reading of the Bible and the Lord's Prayer. *Banning school prayer*

Other decisions promoted a more liberal social climate. In *Griswold v. Connecticut* (1964) the Warren Court overturned a nineteenth-century law banning the sale of contraceptives or providing medical advice about their use. The Court demonstrated its distaste for censorship by greatly narrowing the legal definition of obscenity. A book had to be "utterly without redeeming social value" to permit censorship. The combination of decisions reforming criminal rights, prayer, free speech, and morality angered conservatives of almost all social and political backgrounds. These issues would again become a political battleground in the 1980s and 1990s.

The Court's most far-reaching decision was probably one of its least controversial, though politically most sensitive. As cities and suburbs grew, few states redrew their legislative districts to reflect the change. Rural (and generally conservative) elements continued to dominate state legislatures. In *Baker v. Carr* (1962) and a series of later cases the Court ruled that the states must apportion seats not by "land or trees or pastures," but as closely as possible by the principle of "one person, one vote." *One person, one vote*

THE CIVIL RIGHTS CRUSADE

In Greensboro, North Carolina, in 1960, four black students attending a local college read a pamphlet describing the 1955 bus boycott in Montgomery, Alabama. They decided it was time to make their own protest against segregation. Proceeding to the "whites only" lunch counter at a local store, they sat politely waiting for service. "The waitress looked at me as if I were from outer space," recalled one of the protesters. Rather than serve them, the manager closed the counter. Word of the action spread, and within two weeks, the courage of the Greensboro students had inspired 15 sit-ins across the South. By year's end, 50,000 people had demonstrated; 3000 had gone to jail.

Nothing did more to propel the liberalism of the 1960s—and in the end, to push beyond it—than the campaign for civil rights. By the late 1950s a generation of southern black Americans, many having moved from farms to cities, became increasingly unwilling to accept second-class citizenship. But how could they overturn the legal ramparts of segregation in the South as well as the racism evident in everyday life across the nation?

Riding to Freedom

The campaign for black civil rights gained momentum not through national movements but through a host of individual decisions by local groups and citizens. When New Orleans schools were desegregated in 1960, young Ruby's parents had not intended to make a social statement. But once involved, they refused to back down. The students at Greensboro had not been approached by the NAACP.

Newer civil rights organizations

Beginning in the 1960s, the push for desegregation moved from court actions launched by the NAACP and the Urban League to newer groups determined to take direct action. Since organizing the Montgomery boycott, Martin Luther King and his Southern Christian Leadership Conference (SCLC) had continued to advocate non-violent protest: "To resist without bitterness; to be cursed and not reply; to be beaten and not hit back." A second key organization, the Congress of Racial Equality (CORE), was more willing than the SCLC to force confrontations with the segregationist system. Another group, the Student Non-Violent Coordinating Committee (SNCC, pronounced "Snick") grew out of the Greensboro sit-in. SNCC represented the more militant, younger generation of black activists, who grew increasingly impatient with the slow pace of reform.

In May 1961 CORE director James Farmer led a group of black and white "freedom riders" on a bus trip into the heart of the South. They hoped their trip from Washington to New Orleans would focus national attention on the inequality of segregated facilities. Violent southern mobs gave them the kind of attention they feared.

CIVIL RIGHTS: PATTERNS OF PROTEST AND UNREST

The first phase of the civil rights movement was confined largely to the South, where the Freedom Ride of 1961 dramatized the issue of segregation. Beginning in the summer of 1964, urban riots brought the issue of race and politics home to the entire nation. Severe rioting followed the murder of Martin Luther King, Jr., in 1968, after which the worst violence subsided.

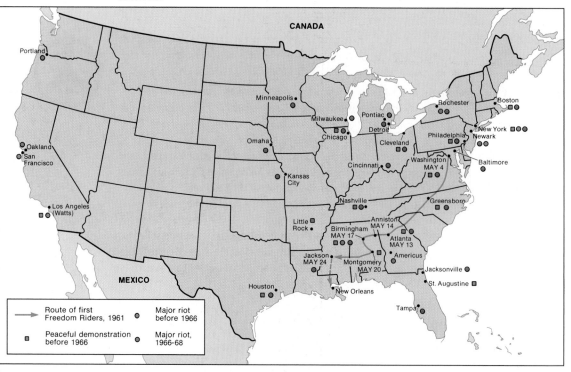

In South Carolina, thugs beat divinity student John Lewis as he tried to enter an all-white waiting room. Mobs in Anniston and Birmingham, Alabama, assaulted the freedom riders as police ignored the violence. One of the buses was burned.

President Kennedy had sought to avoid forceful federal intervention in the South. When the freedom riders persisted in their plans, he tried to convince Alabama officials to protect the demonstrators so that he would not have to send federal forces. His hopes were dashed. From a phone booth outside the bus terminal, John Doar, a Justice Department official in Montgomery, relayed the horror to Attorney General Robert Kennedy:

> Now the passengers are coming off. They're standing on a corner of the platform. Oh, there are fists, punching! A bunch of men led by a guy with a bleeding face are beating them. There are no cops. It's terrible! It's terrible! There's not a cop in sight. People are yelling, "There those niggers are! Get 'em, get 'em!" It's awful.

Appalled, Robert Kennedy ordered in 400 federal marshals, who barely managed to hold off the crowd. Martin Luther King, addressing a meeting in town, phoned the attorney general to say that their church had been surrounded by an angry mob of several thousand—jeering, throwing rocks, and carrying firebombs. As Kennedy later recalled, "I said that we were doing the best that we could and that he'd be as dead as Kelsey's nuts if it hadn't been for the marshals and the efforts that we made."

Both Kennedys understood that civil rights was the most divisive issue the administration faced. For liberals, civil rights measured Kennedy's credentials as a reformer. Kennedy needed black and liberal votes to win reelection. Yet an active federal role threatened to drive white southerners from the Democratic party. It was for that reason that Kennedy had hedged on his promise to introduce major civil rights legislation. Through executive orders, he assured black leaders, he could eliminate discrimination in the government civil service and in businesses filling government contracts. He appointed several African Americans to high administrative positions and five, including Thurgood Marshall, to the federal courts. The Justice Department beefed up its civil rights enforcement procedures. But the freedom riders, by their bold actions, forced the Kennedys to do more.

Civil Rights at High Tide

By the fall of 1961 Robert Kennedy had persuaded SNCC to shift tactics to voter registration, which he assumed would stir less violence. Voting booths, Kennedy noted, were not like schools, where people would protest, "We don't want our little blond daughter going to school with a Negro."

As SNCC and CORE workers arrived in southern towns in the spring of 1962, they discovered that voting rights was not a peaceful issue. Over two years in Mississippi they registered only 4000 out of 394,000 black adults. Angry racists attacked with legal harassment, jailings, beatings, bombings, and murders. Terrorized workers who called on the administration for protection found it woefully lacking. FBI agents often stood by taking notes while SNCC workers were assaulted. Undaunted, SNCC workers made it clear they intended to stay. They fanned out across the countryside to speak with farmers and sharecroppers who had never before dared to ask for a vote.

James Meredith

Confrontation increased when a federal court ordered the segregated University of Mississippi to admit James Meredith, a black applicant. When Governor Ross Barnett personally blocked Meredith's registration in September 1962, Kennedy faced the same crisis that had confronted Eisenhower at Little Rock in 1957. The president ordered several hundred federal marshals to escort Meredith into a university dormitory. Kennedy then announced on national television that the university had been integrated and asked students to follow the law of the land. Instead, a mob moved on campus, shooting out streetlights, commandeering a bulldozer, and throwing rocks and bottles. To save the marshals, Kennedy finally sent in federal troops, but not before 2 people were killed and 375 wounded.

"Letter from Birmingham Jail"

In Mississippi, President Kennedy had begun to lose control of the civil rights issue. The House of Representatives, influenced by television coverage of the violence, introduced a number of civil rights measures. And Martin Luther King led a group to Birmingham, Alabama, to force a showdown against segregation. From a prison cell there, he produced one of the most eloquent documents of the civil rights movement, his "Letter from Birmingham Jail." Addressed to local ministers who had counseled an end to confrontation, King defended the use of civil disobedience. The choice, he warned, was not between obeying the law and nonviolently breaking it to bring about change; it was between his way and streets "flowing with blood," as restive black citizens turned toward more militant ideologies.

Once freed, King led new demonstrations. Television cameras were on hand that May as Birmingham police chief "Bull" Connor, a man with a short fuse, unleashed attack dogs, club-wielding police, and fire hoses powerful enough to peel the bark off trees. When segregationist bombs went off in African American neighborhoods, black mobs retaliated with their own riot, burning a number of shops and businesses owned by whites. In the following 10 weeks, more than 750 riots erupted in 186 cities and towns, both North and South. King's warning of streets "flowing with blood" no longer seemed far-fetched.

In Birmingham, Alabama, firefighters used high-pressure hoses to disperse civil rights demonstrators. The force of the hoses was powerful enough to tear bark off trees. Pictures like this one aroused widespread sympathy for the civil rights movement.

Kennedy sensed that he could no longer compromise on civil rights. In phrases that, like King's, drew heavily on Christian and republican rhetoric, he asked the nation, "If [an American with dark skin] cannot enjoy the full and free life all of us want, then who among us would be content to have the color of his skin changed and stand in his place? Who among us would then be content with counsels of patience and delay?" The president followed his words with support for a strong civil rights bill to end segregation and protect black voters. When King announced a massive march on Washington for August 1963, Kennedy objected that it would undermine support for his bill. "I have never engaged in any direct action movement which did not seem ill-timed," King replied. Faced with the inevitable, Kennedy convinced the organizers to use the event to promote the administration's bill, much to the disgust of militant CORE and SNCC factions.

On August 28 some 250,000 people gathered at the Lincoln Memorial to march and sing in support of civil rights and racial harmony. Appropriately, the day belonged to King. In the powerful tones of a southern preacher, he reminded the crowd that the Declaration of Independence was a promise that applied to all people, black and white. "I have a dream," he told them, that one day "all of God's children, black men and white men, Jews and Gentiles, Protestants and Catholics, will be able to join hands and sing in the words of the old Negro spiritual, 'Free at last! Free at last! Thank God Almighty, we are free at last!'" Congress began deliberation of the civil rights bill, which was reported out of the Judiciary Committee on October 23.

The march on Washington

The Fire Next Time

While liberals applauded Kennedy's stand on civil rights and appreciative African Americans rejoined the Democratic party, substantial numbers of southern whites and northern ethnics deserted. The president scheduled a trip to Texas to recoup some southern support. On November 22, 1963, the people of Dallas lined the streets for his motorcade. Suddenly, a sniper's rifle fired several times. Kennedy slumped into his wife's arms, fatally wounded. His assassin, Lee Harvey Oswald, was caught several hours later. Oswald seemed a mysterious figure: emotionally unstable, he had spent several years in the Soviet Union. But his actions were never fully explained, because only two days after his arrest—in full view of television cameras—he was gunned down by a disgruntled nightclub operator named Jack Ruby. An investigative commission headed by Chief Justice Earl Warren concluded that Oswald had acted alone, a conclusion with which historians generally agree. But the commission acted so hastily, a host of critics arose, rejecting its conclusions in favor of theories placing Oswald as part of various conspiracies.

Tragedy in Dallas

In the face of the violence surrounding the civil rights campaign as well as the assassination of the president, many Americans came to doubt that programs of gradual reform could hold the nation together. A few black radicals believed that the Kennedy assassination was a payback to a system that had tolerated its own racial violence—the "chickens coming home to roost," as separatist Malcolm X put it. Many younger black leaders observed that civil rights received the greatest national coverage when white, not black, demonstrators were killed. They wondered, too, how Lyndon Johnson, a consummate southern politician, would approach the civil rights programs.

The new president, however, saw the need for action. Just as the Catholic issue had tested Kennedy's ability to lead, Johnson knew that without strong leadership on civil rights, "I'd be dead before I could ever begin." On November 23, his first day in office, he promised civil rights leaders that he would pass Kennedy's bill. Despite a *LBJ and the* southern filibuster in the Senate, the Civil Rights Act of 1964 became law the fol- *Civil Rights* lowing summer. The bill marked one of the great moments in the history of American *Act of 1964* reform. It barred discrimination in public accommodations such as lunch counters, bus stations, and hotels; it authorized the attorney general to bring suit to desegregate schools, museums, and other public facilities; it outlawed discrimination in employment by race, color, religion, sex, or national origin; and it gave additional protection to voting rights.

Still, the Civil Rights Act did not bar the techniques southern registrars routinely used to prevent black citizens from voting. A coalition of idealistic young black and white protesters had continued the Mississippi voting drive in what they called "Freedom Summer." In 1965 Martin Luther King led a series of demonstrations, climaxed by a 54-mile walk from Selma to Montgomery, Alabama. As pressure *Voting Rights* mounted, Johnson sent Congress a strong Voting Rights Act that was passed in *Act of 1965* August 1965. The act suspended literacy tests and authorized federal officials to supervise elections in many southern districts. With some justice Johnson called the act "one of the most monumental laws in the entire history of American freedom." Within a five-year period black registration in the South jumped from 35 to 65 percent.

Black Power

The civil rights laws, as comprehensive as they were, did not strike at the de facto segregation found outside the South. These were the forms of segregation not codified in law but practiced through unwritten custom. In large areas of America, African Americans were locked out of suburbs, kept out of decent schools, barred from exclusive clubs, and denied all but the most menial jobs. Nor did the Voting Rights Act deal with the sources of urban black poverty. The median income for urban black residents was approximately half that for white residents.

In such an atmosphere, militants sharply questioned the liberal goal of integration. Since the 1940s the Black Muslim religious sect, dedicated to complete separation from white society, had attracted as many as 100,000 members, mostly young men. During the early 1960s the sect drew even wider attention through the energetic *Malcolm X* efforts of Malcolm X. This charismatic leader had learned the language of the downtrodden from his own experience as a former hustler, gambler, and prison inmate. His militancy alarmed whites, though by 1965 Malcolm was in fact moving toward a more moderate position. He accepted integration but emphasized black community action. After he broke with the Black Muslims he was gunned down by rivals.

But by 1965–1966, even CORE and SNCC had begun to give up working for nonviolent change. If black Americans were to liberate themselves fully, militants argued, they could not merely accept rights "given" to them by whites—they had to claim them. Some members began carrying guns to defend themselves. In 1966 Stokely Carmichael of SNCC gave the militants a slogan—"Black Power"—and the defiant symbol of a gloved fist raised in the air. In its moderate form, the black power

Malcolm X

movement encouraged African Americans to recover their cultural roots, their African heritage, and a new sense of identity. African clothes and natural hairstyles became popular. On college campuses black students pressed universities to hire black faculty, create black studies programs, and provide segregated social and residential space.

For more militant factions like the Black Panther party of Oakland, California, violence became a revolutionary tool. Led by Huey P. Newton and Eldridge Cleaver, the Panthers called on the black community to arm. Since California law forbade carrying concealed weapons, Newton and his followers openly brandished shotguns and rifles as they patrolled the streets protecting blacks from police harassment. In February 1967 Newton found the showdown he had been looking for. "O.K., you big fat racist pig, draw your gun," he shouted while waving a shotgun. A gun battle with police left Newton wounded and in jail.

Black Panthers

Eldridge Cleaver, who assumed leadership of the party, attracted the attention of whites with his searing autobiography, *Soul on Ice.* But even at the height of the Black Panthers' power, the group never counted more than 2000 members nationwide. Most African Americans remained committed to the goals defined by the civil rights movement: nonviolence, not armed confrontation; integration, not segregation.

Violence in the Streets

No ideology shaped the reservoir of frustration and despair that existed in the ghettos. Often, a seemingly minor incident like an arrest or an argument on the streets would trigger widespread violence. A mob would gather and police cars and white-owned stores would be firebombed or looted. As police and the National Guard were ordered in, the violence escalated. Riots broke out in Harlem and Rochester, New York, in 1964, the Watts area of Los Angeles in 1965, Chicago in 1966, and Newark

A National Guardsman watches as flames consume large areas of the Watts section of Los Angeles during the 1965 riot. Often, a seemingly trivial event set off such scenes of violence, revealing the depth of explosive rage harbored within ghettos.

and Detroit in 1967. In the riot at Watts, more than $200 million in property lay in ruins and 34 people died, all of them black. It took nearly 5000 troops to end the bloodiest rioting in Detroit, where 40 died, 2000 were injured, and 5000 were left homeless.

To most whites the violence was unfathomable and inexcusable. Lyndon Johnson spoke for many when he argued that "neither old wrongs nor new fears can justify arson and murder." Martin Luther King, still pursuing the tactics of nonviolence, came to understand the anger behind it. Touring Watts only days after the riots, he was approached by a band of young blacks. "We won," they told him proudly. "How can you say you won," King countered, "when thirty-four Negroes are dead, your community is destroyed, and whites are using the riot as an excuse for inaction?" The youngsters were unmoved. "We won because we made them pay attention to us."

For Johnson, ghetto violence and black militance mocked his efforts to achieve racial progress. The Civil Rights and Voting Rights acts were essential parts of the "Great Society" he hoped to build. In that effort he had achieved a legislative record virtually unequaled by any president in the nation's history. What Kennedy had promised, Johnson delivered. But the growing white backlash and the anger exploding in the nation's cities exposed serious flaws in the theory and practice of liberal reform.

LYNDON JOHNSON AND THE GREAT SOCIETY

Like the state he hailed from, Lyndon Baines Johnson was in all things bigger than life. His gifts were greater, his flaws more glaring. Insecurity was his Achilles heel and the engine that drove him. If Kennedy had been good as president, Johnson would be "the greatest of them all, the whole bunch of them." If FDR won in a landslide in 1936, Johnson would produce an even larger margin in 1964. And to anyone who displeased him, he could be ruthlessly cruel. His scatological language and preoccupation with barnyard sex amused few and offended many. He counted himself among history's great figures. A visiting head of state once asked Johnson if he was born in a log cabin. "No, no," the president responded. "You have me confused with Abe Lincoln. I was born in a manger." Yet Johnson could not understand why so few people genuinely liked him; one courageous diplomat, when pressed, found the nerve to respond, "Because, Mr. President, you are not a very likable man."

Johnson was born in Stonewall, Texas, in the hill country outside Austin, where the dry climate and rough terrain only grudgingly yielded up a living. Schooled in manners by his overbearing mother and in politics by his father and his cronies, Johnson arrived in Washington in 1932 as an ardent New Dealer who loved the political game. When he became majority leader of the Senate in 1954, he cultivated an image as a moderate conservative who knew what strings to pull or levers to jog to get

The Johnson treatment

the job done. Johnson knew what made his colleagues run. On an important bill, he latched onto the undecided votes until they succumbed to the famous "Johnson treatment," a combination of arguments, threats, emotional or patriotic appeals, and enticing rewards. Florida Senator George Smathers likened Johnson to "a great overpowering thunderstorm that consumed you as it closed around you." Or as Ben Bradlee of the *Washington Post* recalled, "He never just shook hands with you. One

The irrepressible Lyndon Johnson had difficulty playing second fiddle to anyone, even when he was vice president. But his shrewd political instincts and folksy charm, which he knew how to deploy to good effect, often allowed him to outmaneuver his opponents.

hand was shaking your hand; the other was always someplace else, exploring you, examining you."

Despite his compulsion to control every person and situation, Johnson possessed certain bedrock strengths. No one was better at hammering out compromises among competing interest groups. To those who served him well he could be loyal and generous. As president, he cared sincerely about society's underdogs. His support for civil rights, aid to the poor, education, and the welfare of the elderly came from genuine conviction. He made the betterment of such people the goal of his administration.

The Origins of the Great Society

In the first months after the assassination, Johnson acted as the conservator of the Kennedy legacy. "Let us continue," he told a grief-stricken nation. Liberals who had dismissed Johnson as an unprincipled power broker grudgingly came to respect the energy he showed in steering reform through Congress. The Civil Rights Act and tax cut legislation were only two of the most conspicuous pieces of Kennedy business Johnson quickly finished.

Kennedy had come to recognize that prosperity alone would not ease the plight of America's poor. In 1962 Michael Harrington's book *The Other America* brought attention to the widespread persistence of poverty despite the nation's affluence. Harrington focused attention on the hills of Appalachia that stretched from western

Discovering poverty

Pennsylvania south to Alabama. In some counties a quarter of the population survived on a diet of flour and dried-milk paste supplied by federal surplus food programs. Under Kennedy Congress had passed a new food stamp program as well as laws designed to revive the economies of poor areas, replacing urban slums with newer housing and retraining the unemployed. Robert Kennedy also headed a presidential committee to fight juvenile delinquency in urban slums by involving the poor in "community action" programs. Direct participation, they hoped, would overcome "a sense of resignation and fatalism" that sociologist Oscar Lewis had found while studying the Puerto Rican community of New York City.

Economic Opportunity Act

It fell to Lyndon Johnson to fight Kennedy's "war on poverty." By August 1964 this master politician had driven through Congress the most sweeping social welfare bill since the New Deal. The Economic Opportunity Act addressed almost every major cause of poverty. It included training programs such as the Job Corps, granted loans to rural families and urban small businesses as well as aid to migrant workers, and launched a domestic version of the Peace Corps, known as VISTA (Volunteers in Service to America). The price tag for these programs was high. Johnson committed almost $1 billion to Sargent Shriver, a Kennedy brother-in-law, who directed the new Office of Economic Opportunity (OEO). When Michael Harrington complained that even $1 billion could barely scratch the surface, Shriver tartly replied, "Maybe you've spent a billion dollars before, but this is my first time around."

The speed Johnson demanded led inevitably to confusion, conflict, and waste. Officials at OEO often found themselves in conflict with other cabinet departments,

The Job Corps was one of many strategies Johnson's Great Society used to alleviate unemployment and poverty. The idea was to train the unskilled and retrain those whose skills were no longer needed

as well as state and local officials. For example, OEO workers organized voter registration drives in order to oust corrupt city officials. Others led rent strikes to force improvements in public housing. The director of city housing in Syracuse, New York, reacted typically: "We are experiencing a class struggle in the traditional Karl Marx style in Syracuse, and I do not like it." Such battles for power and bureaucratic turf undermined federal poverty programs.

The Election of 1964

In 1964, however, these controversies had not yet surfaced. Johnson's political stock remained high. To an audience at the University of Michigan in May, he announced his ambition to forge a "Great Society," in which poverty and racial injustice no longer existed. The chance to fulfill his dreams seemed open to him, for the Republicans nominated Senator Barry Goldwater of Arizona as their presidential candidate. Ruggedly handsome, Goldwater was a true son of the West who held a narrow view of what government should do, for he was at heart a libertarian. Government, he argued, should not dispense welfare, subsidize farmers, tax incomes on a progressive basis, or aid public education. At the same time, Goldwater was so anti-Communist that he championed a large defense establishment.

Goldwater's extreme views allowed Johnson to portray himself as a moderate. He chose Minnesota's liberal Senator Hubert Humphrey to give regional balance to the ticket. Only the candidacy of Governor George Wallace of Alabama marred Johnson's election prospects. In Democratic primaries, Wallace's segregationist appeal won nearly a third or more of the votes in Wisconsin, Indiana, and Maryland—hardly the Deep South. He was persuaded, however, to drop out of the race.

The election produced the landslide Johnson craved. Carrying every state except Arizona and four in the Deep South, he received 61 percent of the vote. Democrats gained better than two-to-one majorities in the Senate and House. All the same, the election was probably more a repudiation of Goldwater than a mandate for Johnson. The president realized that he had to move rapidly to exploit the momentum of his 1964 majority.

The Great Society

In January 1965 Johnson announced a legislative vision that would extend welfare programs on a scale beyond Franklin Roosevelt's New Deal. By the end of 1965, 50 bills had been passed, many of them major pieces of legislation, with more on the agenda for the following year.

As a former teacher, Johnson made education the cornerstone of his Great Society. Stronger schools would compensate the poor for their disadvantaged homes, he believed. Under the Elementary and Secondary School Act, students in low-income school districts were to receive educational equipment, money for books, and enrichment programs like "Project Headstart" for nursery-school-age children. As schools scrambled to create programs that would tap federal money, they sometimes spent more to pay middle-class educational professionals than to teach lower-income students.

Programs in education

President Johnson also pushed through the Medicare Act to provide the elderly with health insurance to cover hospital costs. Medicare targeted the elderly, because

Medicare and Medicaid

studies had shown that older people used hospitals three times more than other Americans and generally had incomes only half as large. Since Medicare made no provision for the poor who were not elderly, Congress also passed a program called Medicaid. Participating states would receive matching grants from the federal government to pay the medical expenses of those on welfare or too poor to afford medical care.

In many ways, Medicare and Medicaid worked. The poor and elderly received significantly more help when facing catastrophic illnesses. Over the next two decades, such aid helped to lower significantly the number of elderly poor. But as more patients used hospital services, Medicare budgets rose. In addition, nothing in the act restricted hospitals or doctors from raising their fees. The cost of the programs soared by more than 500 percent in the first 10 years.

HUD

Ten days after signing the Medicare bill, Johnson signed the Omnibus Housing Act, designed to subsidize rents for poor families unable to find adequate public housing. Four days later came the Voting Rights Act. Within two weeks Congress approved the creation of a new cabinet-level Department of Housing and Urban Development (HUD). To head it, Johnson named Robert Weaver, a former president of the NAACP. And in the tradition of the New Deal, which had patronized the arts under the WPA, Johnson created the National Foundation of the Arts and Humanities. Colleges and their students received support for scholarships and loans, research equipment, and libraries.

Immigration reform

The Great Society also reformed immigration policy. In 1924 the National Origins Act enshrined the racism of the era. It restricted immigration to 150,000 a year, almost all from northern Europe. The Immigration Act of 1965 abolished the national origins system. Now, 170,000 people a year would be admitted on an equitable basis. Racial provisions restricting Asian immigration were eliminated, although new limits were placed on immigration from the Western Hemisphere.

The environment

Nor did Johnson, in his efforts to outdo the New Deal, slight the environment. By the mid-1960s many Americans had become increasingly concerned about acrid smog from factories and automobiles; lakes and rivers polluted by detergents, pesticides, and industrial wastes; and the disappearance of wildlife. In 1964 Congress had

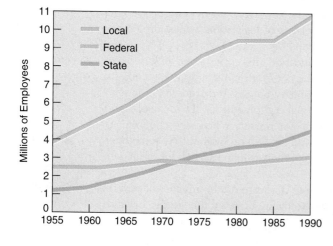

GROWTH OF GOVERNMENT, 1955–1990
Government has been a major growth industry since World War II. Most people think of "big government" as federal government. But even during the Great Society, far more people worked in state and local government. Despite the antigovernment rhetoric, federal employment grew substantially in the Reagan-Bush era.

already passed the National Wilderness Preservation System Act to set aside 9.1 million acres of wilderness as "forever wild." Lady Bird Johnson, the president's wife, campaigned to eliminate the garish billboards and junkyards along many of the nation's roads. Congress first established pollution standards for interstate waterways and a year later provided funds for sewage treatment and water purification. Legislation also tightened standards on air pollution. Environmental reform provoked opposition from groups like mining companies, cattle-grazers, and the timber industry, who wanted to continue using the public domain for their own purposes. But the public accepted the benefits of the new regulation. Among other accomplishments, by the mid-1990s smog had declined nationwide by about a third and the number of rivers and lakes suitable for swimming and fishing had doubled.

For all he had done, Johnson wanted to do more. In 1966 he pushed through bills to raise the minimum wage, improve auto safety, aid mass transit, and develop "model cities." But in time opposition mounted. "Doesn't matter what kind of majority you come in with," Johnson had predicted early on. "You've got just one year when they treat you right, and before they start worrying about themselves." Yet as late as 1968 Johnson pushed major legislation through Congress to ban discrimination in housing (Fair Housing Act), to build public housing, to protect consumers from unfair credit practices (Truth-in-Lending Act), and to protect scenic rivers and expand the national park system.

Historians have difficulty measuring the Great Society's impact. It produced more legislation and more reforms than the New Deal. It also carried a high price tag. Economic statistics suggested that general prosperity, accelerated by the tax cut bill, did more to fight poverty than all the OEO programs. And the inevitable scandals began to surface: Job Corps retrainees burglarizing homes in their off-hours, school equipment purchased that no one knew how to use. Conservatives and radicals alike objected that the liberal welfare state was intruding into too many areas of people's lives. Ethnic groups like Italian and Polish Americans objected to what they considered favoritism accorded black Americans and Hispanics under many programs.

Evaluating the Great Society

For all that, the Great Society established the high-water mark of interventionist government, a trend that began in the progressive era and flourished during the Great Depression and in World War II. While Americans continued to pay lip service to the notion that government should remain small and interfere little in citizens' lives, no strong movement emerged to eliminate Medicare or Medicaid. Few Americans disputed the right of the government to regulate industrial pollution or to control the excesses of large corporations or powerful labor unions. Even conservatives granted the government a role in managing the economy and providing citizens with a safety net of benefits in sickness and in old age. In this sense, the tradition of liberalism prevailed, whatever Johnson's failings.

THE COUNTERCULTURE

In 1964 some 800 students from Berkeley, Oberlin, and other colleges met in western Ohio to be trained for the voter registration campaign in the South. Middle-class students who had grown up in peaceful white suburbs found themselves being instructed for this "Mississippi Freedom Summer" by protest-hardened SNCC coordinators. The lessons were sobering. When beaten by police, the SNCC staff advised, assume the fetal position—hands protecting the neck, elbows covering the temples. That minimized injuries from nightsticks. A few days later, grimmer news arrived. A volunteer who had left for Mississippi two days earlier had already been arrested by local police. Now he and two others were reported "missing." Six weeks later, their mangled bodies were found, bulldozed into the earthworks of a freshly finished dam. That did not stop other sobered volunteers from heading to Mississippi.

By the mid-1960s dissatisfied members of the middle class—and especially the young—had launched a revolt against the conventions of society and politics as usual. The students who returned to campus from the voter registration campaign that summer of 1964 were the shock troops of a much larger movement. They included a curious mix of political activists and apolitical dropouts, labeled hippies.

Activists on the New Left

More than a few students had become disillusioned with the slow pace of reform. Since the "establishment"—whether it was liberal or conservative—blocked meaningful change, why not overthrow it? Tom Hayden, raised in a working-class family outside Detroit, went to college at the University of Michigan, then traveled to Berkeley, and soon joined civil rights workers in Mississippi. "At first, you thought, well, the southern system is some kind of historical vestige," he recalled. "Instead, we found out that the structure of power was very tied into the structure of power in the whole U.S. You'd find that Harvard was investing in Mississippi Power and Light, which was a company that economically dominated Mississippi."

SDS and Port Huron   Hayden, along with Al Haber, another student at the University of Michigan, was a driving force in forming the radical Students for a Democratic Society (SDS). SDS had little sympathy with an "old left" generation of radicals who grew up in the 1930s and still debated the merits of Marxism. Action was the route to change, Hayden argued: through sit-ins, protest marches, and direct confrontation. At a meeting in Port Huron, Michigan, in 1962 the group condemned the modern bureaucratic society exemplified by the "organization man" of the 1950s. The Port Huron Statement called for "participatory democracy," in which large organizations run by bureaucrats would be decentralized and turned into face-to-face communities where individual participation mattered. The Port Huron Statement did not exactly revolutionize America; only 60,000 copies of it were ever sold. It did, however, anticipate the dramatic increase in political and cultural conflict that was spreading across the nation.

COUNTERPOINT   Historians have debated the causes of the turbulent 1960s. Some scholars have favored a generational explanation. The United States has undergone periodic cycles of reform as each new generation has come of age—about once every 30 years. Thus the twentieth century began with progressive reformers pushing for change, only to give way to the quiet "normalcy" of the 1920s, which in turn was succeeded by the activist New Deal in the 1930s. Similarly, the "consensus" decade of the 1950s preceded liberalism's high tide in the 1960s. In that light, the Port Huron Statement can be read as a call for a new cycle of reform led by the nation's young baby boomers, who grew up during the 1950s. "There had to be a critical mass of students, and enough economic fat to cushion them," suggested one historian.

What triggered the upheavals of the 1960s?

favor of greater sensuality and freedom of expression. Nowhere was that more evident than in the costuming of the counterculture. Middle-class students began to let their hair grow. Levis and army–navy store military surplus replaced khakis and pleated skirts. The original impulse was less rebellion than a distinct youthful identity that blurred social class lines, just as rock and roll did.

"Hippies" added a more theatrical twist. They rejected commercial fashion, synthetic fabrics, and cosmetics in favor of a natural look. To express a return to nature, they adopted the Hispanic shawl and serape; the Indian fringed buckskin, beads, and moccasins; and the bright coloring of African, Oriental, and Caribbean cotton fabrics. This costuming became standard wear at folk and rock music festivals and "be-ins," as well as at political demonstrations. Much of the clothing and accessories was handcrafted and sold largely through street vendors, medieval-style craft fairs, and small shops. Often these same shops, located in college towns and artsy urban neighborhoods, did a lively business selling paraphernalia of the drug culture: water pipes, "bongs," rolling papers, roach clips, strobe lights, posters, and Indian print bedspreads.

Fashion had become a function of politics and rebellion. Traditional Americans saw beads, long hair, sandals, drugs, radical politics, and rock and roll as elements of a revolution. To them, hippies and radicals were equally threatening. To restore order, they tried to censor and even outlaw the trappings of the counterculture. Schools ex-pelled boys when their hair was too long and girls when their skirts were too short. It became indecent to desecrate the flag by sewing patches of red, white, and blue on torn blue jeans. Short-haired blue-collar workers harassed long-haired hippies and antiwar protestors. The personal fashions of the youth rebellion came to symbolize a "generation gap" between the young and their elders.

In time, however, that gap narrowed. Men especially broke with past tradition. Sideburns lengthened and mustaches and beards flourished as they had not since the nineteenth century. Men began to wear jewelry, furs, perfume, and shoulder-length hair. Subdued tweeds and narrow lapels gave way to bell-bottoms, broad floral ties, and wide-collared, sometimes psychedelic, shirts. By the early 1970s commercial success, not legal repression, had signaled an end to the revolution in fashion. As formerly hostile blue-collar workers and GIs began to sport long hair and hip clothes, fashion no longer made such clear distinctions. Even middle-aged men and women donned boots, let their hair grow a bit fuller, and slipped into modified bell-bottoms. Feminists rejected the more extreme styles as an example of the male-dominated fashion world that treated women as sex objects. Hippie garb, which was impractical in the office, was replaced by knee-length skirts or pants suits. Before long, three-piece suits, khakis, and short hair were back, although the democratic and eclectic spirit of the 1960s persisted. The new informality provided Americans of both sexes with a wider choice in fashions.

reflected the creativity of their music. Along with other English groups, like the Rolling Stones, they reconnected white American audiences with the rhythm-and-blues roots of rock and roll.

Dylan   Until 1965 Bob Dylan was the quintessential folk artist, writing about nuclear weapons, pollution, and racism. He appeared at concerts with longish frizzy hair, working-class clothes, an unamplified guitar, and a harmonica suspended on a wire support. But then Dylan shocked his fans by donning a black leather jacket and shifting to a "folk-rock" style featuring an electric guitar. His new songs seemed to suggest that the old America was almost beyond redemption. The Beatles, too, transformed themselves. After a pilgrimage to India to study transcendental meditation, they returned to produce *Sergeant Pepper's Lonely Hearts Club Band,* possibly the most influential album of the decade. It blended sound effects with music, alluded to trips taken with "Lucy in the Sky with Diamonds" (LSD), and concluded, "I'd love to turn you on." The new format was innovative, too. No longer were songs limited to the three-minute length of 45-rpm records and popular radio. Out in San Francisco, bands like the Grateful Dead pioneered "acid rock" with long pieces aimed to echo drug-induced states of mind.

The debt of white rock musicians to rhythm and blues led to increased integration in the music world. Before the 1960s black rhythm-and-blues bands had played primarily to black audiences, in segregated clubs, or over black radio stations. Black artists like Little Richard and Ray Charles wrote numerous hit songs made popular by white performers. The civil rights movement and a rising black social and political *Soul music* consciousness gave rise to "soul" music. One black disc jockey described soul as "the last to be hired, first to be fired, brown all year round, sit-in-the-back-of-the-bus feeling." Soul was the quality that expressed black pride and separatism: "You've got to live with us or you don't have it." Out of Detroit came the "Motown sound," which combined elements of gospel, blues, and big band jazz. Diana Ross and the Supremes, the Temptations, Stevie Wonder, and other groups under contract to Berry Gordy's Motown Record Company appealed to black and white audiences alike. Yet while soul music promoted black consciousness, it had little to offer by way of social commentary. It evoked the traditional blues themes of workday woes, unhappy marriages, and the troubles between men and women.

The West Coast Scene

For all of its themes of alienation, rebellion, and utopian quest, the counterculture also signaled the increasing importance of the West Coast in American popular culture. In the 1950s the shift of television production from the stages of New York to the film lots of Hollywood helped establish Los Angeles as a communications center. San Francisco became notorious as a center of the beat movement.

Then in 1958 the unthinkable happened. The Brooklyn Dodgers and the New York Giants baseball teams fled the Big Apple for Los Angeles and San Francisco. When Alaska and Hawaii became states in 1959, the national center of gravity shifted westward. Richard Nixon, a Californian, narrowly missed being elected president in 1960. By 1963 the "surfing sound" of West Coast rock groups like the Beach Boys and Jan and Dean had made southern California's preoccupation with surfing and cars into a national fad. And Mario Savio and the Free Speech Movement put Berkeley at the center of the nation's attention.

Before 1967 Americans were only vaguely aware of another West Coast phenomenon, the "hippies." But in January a loose coalition of drug freaks, Zen cultists, and political activists banded together to hold the first well-publicized "Be-In." The beat poet Allen Ginsberg was on hand to offer spiritual guidance. The

Grateful Dead and Jefferson Airplane, acid rock groups based in San Francisco, provided entertainment. A mysterious group called the Diggers somehow managed to supply free food and drink, while the notorious Hell's Angels motorcycle gang policed the occasion. Drugs of all kinds were plentiful. And a crowd attired in a bizarre mix of Native American, circus, Oriental, army surplus, and other costumes came to enjoy it all.

The West Coast had long been a magnet for Americans seeking opportunity, escape, and alternative lifestyles; now the San Francisco Bay area staked its claim as the spiritual center of the counterculture. The more politically conscious dropouts gravitated toward Berkeley; the apolitical "flower children" moved into Haight-Ashbury, a run-down San Francisco neighborhood of apartments, Victorian houses, and "head shops" selling drug paraphernalia, wall posters, Indian bedspreads, and other eccentric accessories. Similar dropout communities and communes sprang up across the country. Colleges became centers of hip culture, offering alternative courses, eliminating strict requirements, and tolerating the new sexual mores of their students.

In the summer of 1969 all the positive forces of the counterculture converged on Bethel, New York, in the Catskill Mountains resort area, to celebrate the promise of peace, love, and freedom. The Woodstock Music Festival attracted 400,000 people to the largest rock concert ever organized. For one long weekend the audience and performers joined to form an ephemeral community based on sex, drugs, and rock and roll. But even then, the counterculture was dying. Violence intruded on the laid-back urban communities hippies had formed. Organized crime and drug pushers muscled in on the lucrative trade in LSD, amphetamines, and marijuana. Bad drugs and addiction took their toll. Urban slum dwellers turned hostile to the strange middle-class dropouts who, in ways the poor could not fathom, found poverty ennobling. Free sex often became an excuse for rape, exploitation, and loveless gratification.

Much that had once seemed outrageous in the hippie world was readily absorbed into the marketplace. Rock groups became big business enterprises commanding huge fees. Slick concerts with expensive tickets replaced communal dances with psychedelic light shows. Yogurt, granola, and herbal teas appeared on supermarket shelves. Ironically, much of the world that hippies forged was co-opted by the society they had rejected.

By the late 1960s most dreams of human betterment seemed shattered—whether John Kennedy's New Frontier, Lyndon Johnson's Great Society, or the communal society of the hippie counterculture. Recession and inflation brought an end to the easy affluence that made liberal reform programs and alternative lifestyles seem so easily affordable. Poverty and unemployment menaced even middle-class youth who had found havens in communes, colleges, and graduate schools. Racial tensions divided black militants and the white liberals of the civil rights movement into sometimes hostile camps.

But the Vietnam War more than any other single factor destroyed the promise of Camelot and the Great Society. After 1965 the nation divided sharply as the American military role in Southeast Asia grew. Radicals on the left looked to rid America of a capitalist system that promoted race and class conflict at home and imperialism and military adventurism abroad. Conservatives who supported the war called for a return to more traditional values like law and order. Both the left and the right attacked the liberal center. Their combined opposition helped to undermine the consensus Lyndon Johnson had worked so hard to build.

CHAPTER SUMMARY

The first wave of dissent in the 1960s was liberal: it grew out of the pragmatic wish to tame the excesses of capitalism that had been seen earlier in the progressive era and in the New Deal. Like the progressives, John Kennedy depended on experts— "the best and the brightest"—to bring greater social justice at home, while he pursued the cold war more vigorously abroad. The "Alliance for Progress" with Latin America, the Peace Corps, and the pledge to reach the moon symbolized the idealism of Kennedy's foreign policy. The Bay of Pigs invasion and the Cuban missile crisis represented the dangers of the cold war in a nuclear age. Some of the most significant liberal reforms came from the Supreme Court under Chief Justice Earl Warren. In landmark decisions like *Gideon v. Wainwright, Escobedo v. Illinois,* and *Miranda v. Arizona* the Court expanded protection of civil rights and liberties. In other areas the Court eased censorship, banned school prayer, and increased voting rights.

The civil rights movement tested the liberalism of the era. At first, Kennedy only reluctantly supported efforts to end segregation. Leadership came from grass roots African American political and religious groups across the South. Through sit-ins, Freedom Rides, voter registration drives, and other forms of nonviolent protest, they pressed for change in the face of often violent resistance. The movement held a symbolic gathering in August 1963 in Washington. The stronger commitment to civil rights legislation did not die after Kennedy's assassination in November 1963. Lyndon Johnson pressed forward with the Civil Rights Act of 1964 and the Voting Rights Act of 1965. Determined to outshine even Franklin Roosevelt, Johnson then launched the "Great Society." His program included aid to education, health care to the poor and elderly, wilderness protection, job training, urban redevelopment, tax cuts, and more.

Johnson's efforts did not satisfy more radical and discontented elements of society. Out of the civil rights movement, a "New Left" emerged on college campuses, and a black power movement arose in cities torn by sporadic violence. Many young Americans rejected politics altogether. They gathered together in a counterculture dedicated to a freer, more sensual, and less materialistic lifestyle. In the end the counterculture began to collapse upon itself from the lack of a coherent philosophy, increasing violence, and invasive commercialism. As for the Great Society, Johnson's dreams for a just, liberal, and humane society became increasingly caught in the cold war conflict halfway across the globe, in Vietnam.

ADDITIONAL READING

Among historians, both John F. Kennedy and Lyndon Johnson have provoked controversy. Kennedy's stock has fallen sharply since the heady days of Camelot. That can be seen by contrasting the reverential treatments of Kennedy in Arthur Schlesinger,

Jr., *The Thousand Days* (1965) and Theodore Sorenson, *Kennedy* (1965) with David Burner and Thomas West, *The Torch Is Passed: The Kennedy Brothers and American Liberalism* (1992), Mark Stern, *Calculating Visions: Kennedy, Johnson and Civil Rights* (1992), and Thomas Paterson, ed., *Kennedy's Quest for Victory* (1989). Johnson receives a critical, but evenhanded, treatment in Doris Kearns, *Lyndon Johnson and the American Dream* (1976) and Robert Dallek, *Lyndon Johnson: Lone Star Rising* (1991) but is savaged in Robert Caro, *The Years of Lyndon Johnson: The Path to Power* (1982) and *Means of Ascent* (1990). On foreign policy under Kennedy and Johnson see Walter LaFeber, *America, Russia, and the Cold War* (8th ed., 1996).

For surveys of the upheavals of the 1960s see Allen Matusow, *The Unraveling of America* (1984) and Todd Gitlin, *The Sixties* (1987). The counterculture has no good surveys yet, but Terry H. Anderson, *The Movement and the Sixties* (1995) and Edward P. Morgan, *The 60s Experience* (1991) offer much insight into political activism. Of the many excellent works on civil rights, Taylor Branch, *Parting the Waters: America in the King Years, 1954–1963* (1988) is gripping, insightful reading, while Robert Weisbrot, *Freedom Bound: A History of America's Civil Rights Movement* (1990) provides an excellent survey. For a fuller list of readings, see the Bibliography.

SIGNIFICANT EVENTS

1958 — Kingston Trio popularizes folk music

1960 — Kennedy–Nixon debates; Greensboro sit-ins; Kennedy elected president

1961 — Alliance for Progress; Peace Corps begun; Alan Shepard, Jr., first American in space; Bay of Pigs invasion; Kennedy steps up U.S. role in Vietnam; Vienna summit; Berlin Wall built; Area Redevelopment Act; CORE freedom rides begin

1962 — Michael Harrington's *The Other America* published; Cuban missile crisis; James Meredith desegregates University of Mississippi; *Engel v. Vitale; Baker v. Carr;* SDS Port Huron Statement

1963 — Diem assassinated in Vietnam; nuclear test ban treaty; University of Alabama desegregation crisis; Kennedy introduces Civil Rights Bill; March on Washington; *Gideon v. Wainwright;* Kennedy assassinated

1964 — *Escobedo v. Illinois; Griswold v. Connecticut;* Civil Rights Act passed; SNCC Freedom Summer; Harlem and Rochester race riots; Johnson enacts Kennedy tax cuts; Economic Opportunity Act; VISTA established; Wilderness Preservation System Act; Johnson defeats Goldwater; Berkeley "Free Speech" Movement; Beatles introduce British rock

1965 — Johnson launches the Great Society; King's Selma protest; Voting Rights Act; Watts riots; Malcolm X assassinated; Medicare and Medicaid acts; Elementary and Secondary School Act; Omnibus Housing Act; Immigration Act; escalation in Vietnam

1966 — *Miranda v. Arizona;* Stokely Carmichael of SNCC coins "black power" slogan; Model Cities Act; minimum wages raised

1967 — Black Panthers battle Oakland, California, police; first "Be-In"

1968 — Fair Housing Act

1969 — Woodstock Music Festival

31

The Vietnam Era

Vietnam from afar: it looked almost like an emerald paradise. "I remember getting up on the flight deck and seeing one of the most beautiful visions I've ever seen in my life," recalled Thomas Bird, an army rifleman sent there in 1965: "A beautiful white beach with thick jungle background. The only thing missing was naked women running down the beach, waving and shouting 'Hello, hello, hello.'" Upon landing, Bird and his buddies were each issued a "Nine-Rule" card outlining proper behavior toward the Vietnamese. "Treat the women with respect, we are guests in this country and here to help these people."

But who were they helping and who were they fighting? When American troops sought to engage Vietcong forces, the VC generally disappeared into the jungle beyond the villages and rice fields. John Muir, a Marine rifleman, walked into a typical hamlet with a Korean lieutenant. To Muir the place looked ordinary, but the Korean had been in Vietnam a while. "We have a little old lady and a little old man and two very small children," he pointed out. "According to them, the rest of the family has been spirited away . . . either been drafted into one army or the other. So there's only four of them and they have a pot of rice that's big enough to feed fifty people. And rice, once it's cooked, will not keep. They gotta be feeding the VC." Muir, whose only experience with rice till then had been Minute Rice or Uncle Ben's, watched as the lieutenant set the house on fire. The roof "started cooking off ammunition because all through the thatch they had ammunition stored."

GIs soon learned to walk down jungle trails with a cautious shuffle, looking for a wire or a piece of vine that seemed too straight. "We took more casualties from booby traps than we did from actual combat," recalled David Ross, a medic. "It was very frustrating because how do you fight back against a booby trap? You're just walking along and all of a sudden your buddy doesn't have a leg. Or you don't have a leg." Yet somehow the villagers would walk the same paths and never get hurt. Who was the enemy and who the friend?

The same question was being asked half a globe away, on the campus of Kent *Kent State* State University in May 1970. By then the Vietnam War had dragged on for more than five years and had driven President Lyndon Johnson from office. And it had embroiled his successor, Richard Nixon, in controversy when he expanded the war into Cambodia. Kent State, just east of Akron, Ohio, was one of the many campuses that flourished in the 1950s and 1960s to accommodate the children of the baby boom.

In Vietnam, helicopters gave infantry unusual mobility — a critical element in a war with no real front line, since troops could be quickly carried from one battle to another. These soldiers await a pickup amid rice paddies south of Saigon.

Opposition to the war had become so intense in this normally apolitical community that 300 students had torn the Constitution from a history text and, in a formal ceremony, buried it. "President Nixon has murdered it," they charged. That evening demonstrators spilled into the nearby town, smashed shop windows, and returned to campus to burn down an old army ROTC building. The panicked mayor declared a state of emergency, and Governor James Rhodes ordered in 750 of the National Guard. Student dissidents were the "worst type of people we harbor in America," he announced. "We are going to eradicate the problem."

By background and education, the National Guard troops were little different from the students they had come to police. Almost all were white, between 18 and 30, and from Ohio. But guard veterans who fought in World War II or Korea disdained students who evaded or openly rejected their military obligation or who openly criticized their country. As his troops arrived at Kent, Guard Commander General Robert Canterbury remarked that "these students are going to have to find out what law and order is all about."

When demonstrators assembled for a rally on the college commons, the Guard ordered them to disperse, though the troops' legal right to break up a peaceful demonstration was debatable. The protesters stood their ground. Then the guardsmen advanced, wearing full battle gear and armed with M-1 rifles, whose high-velocity bullets had a horizontal range of almost two miles. Some students scattered; a few picked up rocks and threw them. The guardsmen suddenly fired into the crowd, many of whom were students passing back and forth from classes. Incredulous, a young woman knelt over Jeffrey Miller; he was dead. By the time calm was restored, three other students had been killed and nine more wounded, some caught innocently in the Guard's indiscriminate fire.

Jackson State   News of the killings swept the nation. At Jackson State, a black college in Mississippi, antiwar protesters seized a women's dormitory. On May 14 state police surrounding the building opened fire without provocation, killing two more students and wounding a dozen. In both incidents the demonstrators had been unarmed. The

Death at Kent State: who was the enemy, who was the friend?

events at Kent State and Jackson State turned sporadic protests against the American invasion of Cambodia into a nationwide student strike. Many students believed the ideals of the United States had been betrayed by those forces of law and order sworn to protect them.

Who was the friend and who the enemy? Time and again the war in Vietnam led Americans to ask that question. Not since the Civil War had the nation been so deeply divided. As the war dragged on, debate moved off college campuses and into the homes of middle Americans, where sons went off to fight and the war came home each night on the evening news. As no other war had, Vietnam seemed to stand the nation on its head. When American soldiers shot at Vietnamese "hostiles," who could not always be separated from "friendlies," or when National Guardsmen fired on their neighbors across a college green, who were the enemies and who were the friends?

THE ROAD TO VIETNAM

"The enemy must fight his battles far from his home base for a long time," one Vietnamese strategist wrote. "We must further weaken him by drawing him into protracted campaigns. Once his initial dash is broken, it will be easier to destroy him." The enemy in question was not American soldiers or the French but the Mongol invaders of A.D. 1284. For several thousand years Vietnam had struggled periodically to fight off foreign invasions. Buddhist culture penetrated eastward from India. More often Indochina faced invasion and rule by the Chinese from the north. After 1856 the French entered as a colonial power, bringing with them a strong Catholic tradition.

Ho Chi Minh was one Vietnamese who hoped to throw off French influence as well as the Chinese. In 1912, at the age of 22, Ho gave up life as a poor schoolteacher and hired out as a mess boy on a French ocean liner. By the end of World War I, he was in France when President Wilson came to Versailles calling for self-determination for small nations. Ho bought a formal pinstriped suit at a secondhand store and attended the peace conference to petition for Vietnam. When the delegates ignored his plea, he became a Communist, taking the recent Russian Revolution as his model. Visits to Moscow followed, after which he returned to the Indochina region to organize revolutionary activity.

Ho Chi Minh

Once Japan was defeated in 1945, Ho seized the opportunity to unite Vietnam under a nationalist government. But France moved to recover control of its old colony. Some of Ho's colleagues suggested approaching the Chinese Communists for help. But Ho was foremost a nationalist. He worried that Chinese aid might lead to permanent domination. "I prefer to smell French dung for five years rather than Chinese dung for the rest of my life," he concluded, and he accepted the French return. Soon after, negotiations for independence broke down. Ho and his forces began eight years of guerrilla war against the French, which led to victory at Dien Bien Phu in 1954 (page 1042). Ho's dream of an independent Vietnam seemed at hand. He agreed at the Geneva peace conference to withdraw his forces north of the 17th parallel in return for a promise to hold free elections in both the North and the South.

Nguyen Ai Quoc, who became Ho Chi Minh, once worked at London's posh Carlton Hotel in the pastry kitchen of the renowned French chef Escoffier. But he was soon swept up in socialist and nationalist politics, appearing at the Versailles Peace Conference (left) to plead for an independent Vietnam. By the time the United States was increasing its involvement in Vietnam, Ho had accumulated a lifetime of anticolonialist and revolutionary activity and become a revered leader of his people. He died in 1969, six years before his dream of a united Vietnam became a reality.

The United States, however, was determined to thwart Ho. Having supported the French in what they saw as a fight to contain communism, President Eisenhower helped install Ngo Dinh Diem and then supported Diem's decision not to hold elections. Frustrated South Vietnamese Communists—the Vietcong—began their guerrilla war once again. "I think the Americans greatly underestimate the determination of the Vietnamese people," Ho remarked in 1962, as President Kennedy was committing more American advisers to South Vietnam.

Ngo Dinh Diem

Lyndon Johnson's War

For Kennedy, Vietnam had been just one of many anticommunist skirmishes his activist advisers wanted to fight. As attention focused increasingly on Vietnam, Kennedy accepted President Eisenhower's "domino theory": if the pro-Western Catholic government fell to the Communists, all the other nations of Southeast Asia would collapse in a row. But even 16,000 American "advisers" had been unable to help the unpopular Diem, who was overthrown by the military in November 1963. When Kennedy was assassinated in the same month as Diem, the problem of Vietnam was left to Lyndon Johnson.

The domino theory

Johnson's political instincts told him to keep the Vietnam War at arm's length. He felt like a catfish, he remarked, who had "just grabbed a big juicy worm with a right sharp hook in the middle of it." Johnson's heart was in his Great Society programs. Yet fear of the political costs of defeat in Vietnam led him steadily toward deeper American involvement. He shared the assumptions of Kennedy holdovers like National Security Advisor McGeorge Bundy and Defense Secretary Robert McNamara that Vietnam was a key cold war test. And Republican presidential candidate Barry Goldwater raised the stakes by insisting on a "let's-win" policy of total military victory.

Always preferring the middle way, Johnson wanted a policy somewhere between total commitment and disengagement. Until August 1964 American advisers had focused on South Vietnam itself: guiding the South Vietnamese army in its struggle against the Vietcong. North Vietnam, for its part, had been infiltrating modest amounts of men and supplies along the Ho Chi Minh Trail, a primitive network of jungle routes threading through Laos and Cambodia into the highlands of South Vietnam. In the summer of 1964 North Vietnam began to modernize the trail so it could handle trucks in addition to the peasants who carried supplies on their backs or used modified bicycles. At the time American officials were unaware of the change, but they realized all too well that the Vietcong already controlled some 40 percent of South Vietnam. Johnson strategists decided to relieve the South by increasing pressure on North Vietnam itself.

American ships in the Gulf of Tonkin began to patrol the North Vietnamese coast and provide cover for secret South Vietnamese raids. On August 2, three North Vietnamese patrol boats exchanged fire with the American destroyer *Maddox*—neither side hurting the other—and then the Vietnamese boats fled. An angry Johnson chided several admirals. "You've got a whole fleet and all those airplanes, and you can't even sink three little ol' PT boats?" Two nights later, in inky blackness and a heavy thunderstorm, radar operators on the *C. Turner Joy* reported a torpedo attack. But a follow-up investigation could not establish whether enemy ships had even been near the scene. "The Gulf is a very funny place," explained one communications officer. "You get inversion layers there that will give you very solid radar contacts . . . that just aren't there. That may have happened to us." The president was not pleased. "For all I know our navy might have been shooting at whales out there," he remarked privately.

Tonkin Gulf incident

Whatever his doubts, the president called the incidents "open aggression on the high sea" and ordered retaliatory air raids on North Vietnam. He did not disclose that the navy and South Vietnamese forces had been conducting secret military operations at the time. Such deception would become standard practice. It allowed Johnson to ask Congress for authority to take "all necessary measures" to "repel any armed attack" on American forces and to "prevent future aggression." Congress overwhelmingly passed what became known as the Gulf of Tonkin resolution.

Senator Ernest Gruening of Alaska, one of the two lawmakers to object, sensed danger. The Tonkin Gulf resolution gave the president "a blank check" to declare war, a power the Constitution specifically reserved to Congress. Johnson insisted—no doubt sincerely at the time—that he had no such intention. But as pressure for an American victory increased, the president exploited the powers the resolution gave him.

Rolling Thunder

In January 1965 Johnson received a disturbing memorandum from McGeorge Bundy and Robert McNamara. "Both of us are now pretty well convinced that our present

CHINA

• Lao Cai

NORTH VIETNAM

• Thai Nguyen

Dien Bien Phu •

Red R.

Black R.

Hanoi •

Haiphong •

BURMA

GULF OF
TONKIN

Mekong R.

Luang •
Prabang

PLAIN
OF
JARS

Thanh Hoa •

LAOS

Vinh •

Hainan

Vientiane •

THAILAND

Yom R.

Ping R.

Po Sak R.

Mun R.

ANNAMESE

Sepone •

Con Thien
Quang Tri

Khe Sanh

Hue

SOUTH
CHINA
SEA

Da Nang

Kong R.

CORDILLERA

My Lai
Quang Ngai

Dak To

Kon Tum

Bangkok •

CAMBODIA

Tonle
Sap

Mekong R.

Pleiku

Qui Nhon

CENTRAL
HIGHLANDS

Tuy Hoa

SOUTH
VIETNAM

Pursat •

Nha Trang

Da Lat

Phnom Penh •

GULF
OF
THAILAND

Song Be

Chau Doc

PLAIN OF
REEDS

Saigon

Ben Tre

Can Tho

MEKONG
RIVER
DELTA

0   100   200 Miles

0   100   200 Kilometers

Ho Chi Minh
Trail

Major battles of
Tet offensive

policy can lead only to disastrous defeat," they said. The United States should either increase its attack—"escalate" was the term coined in 1965—or simply withdraw. In theory escalation would increase military pressure to the point at which further resistance cost more than the enemy was willing to bear. By taking gradual steps, the United States would demonstrate its resolve to win while leaving the door open to negotiations.

Escalation

But the theory that made so much sense in Washington did not work well in Vietnam. Each stage of American escalation only hardened the resolve of the Vietcong and North Vietnamese. When a Vietcong mortar attack in February killed seven Marines stationed at Pleiku airbase, Johnson ordered U.S. planes to begin bombing North Vietnam. Privately, McGeorge Bundy admitted that Pleiku was only an excuse to act. "Pleikus are like streetcars," he remarked; "there's one every ten minutes."

Restricted air strikes did not satisfy more hawkish leaders. Retired Air Force Chief of Staff Curtis LeMay complained, "We are swatting flies when we should be going after the whole manure pile." In March Johnson ordered Operation Rolling Thunder, a systematic bombing campaign aimed at bolstering confidence in South Vietnam and cutting the flow of supplies from the North. At the same time, he declared his willingness to negotiate an end to the war once North Vietnamese troops had left the South.

Air strikes

Rolling Thunder achieved none of its goals. American pilots could seldom spot the Ho Chi Minh Trail under its dense jungle canopy. Even when bombs hit, North Vietnamese crews kept the supplies moving by quickly filling the bomb craters or improvising pontoon bridges from woven bamboo stalks. Equally discouraging, South Vietnamese leaders spent their energy on political intrigue. One military government after another proved equally inept. And Ho Chi Minh refused to negotiate unless the bombing stopped and American troops went home.

Once the Americans established bases from which to launch the new air strikes, these, too, became targets for guerrilla attacks. When General William Westmoreland, the chief of American military operations in Vietnam, requested combat troops to defend the bases, Johnson sent in 3500 Marines, almost without considering the implication of his decision. Until then, only military "advisers" to the South Vietnamese had been sent. Once the crucial decision to commit combat troops had been taken, the urge to shore up and protect those already there became strong. Another 40,000 soldiers arrived in May and 50,000 more by July.

Johnson, as before, deliberately downplayed the escalation, because he feared a political backlash. McNamara ordered the decision carried out in a "low-keyed manner," both to prevent Soviet or Chinese intervention and "to avoid undue concern and excitement in the Congress and in domestic public opinion." By the end of 1965 almost 185,000 American troops had landed—and still the call for more continued. In

---

THE WAR IN VIETNAM
North Vietnam established the Ho Chi Minh Trail (red arrows) through central Laos in order to supply South Vietnam's Vietcong forces. In the earlier stages of the war supplies were transported by foot, but by 1964 the North Vietnamese were building roads and bridges that could handle heavy trucks.

1968, at the height of the war, 536,000 American troops were being supported with helicopters, jet aircraft, and other advanced military technologies. This was "escalation" with a vengeance.

SOCIAL CONSEQUENCES OF THE WAR

The impact of the war, naturally enough, fell hardest on the baby-boom generation of the 1950s. As these young people came of age, draft calls for the armed services were rising. At the same time, the civil rights movement and the growing counter-culture were encouraging students to question the goals of establishment America. Whether they fought in Vietnam or protested at home, supported the government or demonstrated against it, eventually these baby boomers—as well as Americans of all ages—were forced to take a stand on Vietnam.

The Soldiers' War

The social structure determining which Americans would be required to fight and which would remain civilian was the draft. The system in place generally favored the middle and upper classes, since college students and graduate students at first received deferments. Thus the Vietnam War increased male enrollment in colleges. As the war escalated the draft was changed, so that some students were called up through a lottery system. Still, those who knew the medical requirements might be able to produce a doctor's affidavit certifying a weak knee, flat feet, or bad eyes—all grounds for flunking the physical. About half of the potential draftees flunked—two to three times the rejection rate of those called up by the NATO allies. Of the 1200 men in Harvard's class of 1970, only 56 served in the military, and only 2 of them in Vietnam.

The poorest and least educated were also likely to escape service, because the Armed Forces Qualification Test and the physical often screened them out. Thus the sons of blue-collar America were most likely to accept Uncle Sam's letter of induction, as were the sons of Hispanic and black Americans, who, having fewer skills, were more often assigned to combat duty. The draft also made it a relatively young man's war. The average soldier serving in Vietnam was 19, compared with 26 years old for World War II.

Most American infantry came to Vietnam fairly well trained and with high morale. But the physical and psychological hardships inevitably took their toll. In a war of continual small skirmishes, booby traps, and search-and-destroy missions, it was hard to relax. An American force would fight its way into a Communist-controlled hamlet, clear and burn it, and move on—only to be ordered back days or weeks later because the enemy had moved in again. Since success could not be measured in territory gained, the measure became the "body count": the number of Vietcong killed. Unable to tell who was friendly and who was hostile, GIs regularly took out their frustrations on innocent civilians. Their deaths helped inflate the numbers used to prove that the Americans were winning.

Body counts

Other social factors affected the way soldiers fought. Only about one in nine sol-

The Vietcong often fought in small groups, using the dense vegetation to cover their movements. These suspects faced a difficult interrogation as U.S. soldiers tried to learn more about the location of Vietcong units.

diers was actually in combat; the rest supported them. Combat veterans particularly despised the rear-echelon soldiers who superintended supply depots or received combat pay for being lifeguards at beaches near Da Nang. Paradoxically, the miracles of modern technology also made the war hard to cope with. Helicopters could whisk GIs from the front lines of a steaming jungle back to Saigon, where they could catch overnight flights to Hawaii or the mainland. The sudden shift from the hell of war to civilian peace could be wrenching. John Kerry, later a senator from Massachusetts, recalled his homecoming: "There I was, a week out of the jungle, flying from San Francisco to New York. I fell asleep and woke up yelling, probably a nightmare. The other passengers moved away from me—a reaction I noticed more and more in the months ahead. . . . The feeling toward [Vietnam vets] was, 'Stay away—don't contaminate us with whatever you've brought back from Vietnam.'"

To support a technological war, American forces built the shell of a modern society in South Vietnam. By 1967 a million tons of supplies arrived in Vietnam each month—an average of a hundred pounds a day for every American in the country. South Vietnam's airports soon handled more flight traffic than New York, Rome, Tokyo, or any other city in the world. No matter where they were, ground forces could count on air strikes to strafe or bomb suspected enemy positions. Since the Vietcong routinely mixed with the civilian population, the chances for deadly error increased. Bombs of napalm (jellied gasoline) and white phosphorus rained liquid fire

Technology and its limits

from the skies, coating everything from village huts to the flesh of fleeing humans. Cluster bombs, designed to explode hundreds of pellets in midair, sprayed the enemy with high-velocity shrapnel. To clear jungle canopies and expose Vietcong camps and roads, American planes spread more than 100 million pounds of defoliants such as Agent Orange. ("Only You Can Prevent Forests" was the sardonic motto of one unit assigned to the task.) The forests destroyed totaled more than one-third of South Vietnam's timberlands—an area approximately the size of the state of Rhode Island. In many ways the ecological devestation was more severe than the military destruction.

By 1967 the war costs exceded more than $2 billion a month. The United States dropped more bombs on Vietnam than it had during all of World War II. After one air attack on a Communist-held provincial capital, American troops walked into the remains, now mostly ruined buildings and rubble. "We had to destroy the town in order to save it," an officer explained. As the human and material costs of the war increased, that statement stuck in the minds of many observers. What sense was there in a war that saved people by burning their homes?

The War at Home

As the war dragged on, such questions provoked anguished debate among Americans, especially on college campuses. Faculty members held "teach-ins" to explain the issues to concerned students. Scholars familiar with Southeast Asia questioned every major assumption the president used to justify escalation. The United States and South Vietnam had brought on the war, they charged, by violating the Geneva Accords of 1954. Moreover, the Vietcong were an indigenous rebel force with legitimate grievances against Saigon's corrupt government. The war was a civil war among the Vietnamese, not an effort by Soviet or Chinese Communists to conquer Southeast Asia, as Eisenhower, Kennedy, and Johnson had claimed.

Hawks and doves   By 1966 national leaders had similarly divided into opposing camps of "hawks" and "doves." The hawks argued that America must win in Vietnam to save Southeast Asia from communism, to preserve the nation's prestige, and to protect the lives of American soldiers fighting the war. A large majority of the American people supported those views. The doves were a prominent minority. They included New Left radicals as well as respected editorialist Walter Lippmann; Senator J. William Fulbright, head of the Foreign Relations Committee; and Dr. Benjamin Spock, the physician whose child care manuals had raised the generation of baby boomers.

African Americans as a group were far less likely than white Americans to support the war. Some resented the diversion of Geat Society resources from the cities to the war effort. Many black Americans' heightened sense of racial consciousness led them to identify with the Vietnamese people. Martin Luther King, SNCC, and CORE all opposed the war. Poet Nikki Giovanni set into vivid phrases the African American sense of alienation:

> We kill in Vietnam
> for them
> We kill for UN&NATO&SEATO&US
> And everywhere for all alphabet but BLACK.

Lyndon Johnson shocked reporters in October 1965 when he publicly exposed his surgical scar from a gallbladder operation. Political caricaturist David Levine caught the underlying irony of the Johnson presidency by drawing the scar in the shape of Vietnam.

Antiwar protests

By 1967 college students and faculty turned out in crowds of thousands to express their outrage: "Hey, hey, LBJ, how many kids have you killed today?" More than 300,000 people attended the demonstration organized in April 1967 in New York City. Sixty college protesters organized by SDS leaders from Cornell University burned their draft cards in defiance of federal law. In the fall more violent protests erupted as antiwar radicals stormed a draft induction center in Oakland, California. The next day 55,000 protesters, including some prominent writers and artists, ringed the Pentagon in Washington. Again, mass arrests followed.

Student protests forced policymakers and citizens to take a sobering look at the justice of the war. But the guerrilla tactics of more radical elements alienated many. It would be hard to exaggerate the shock university communities felt when radicals shut down Columbia University and clashed with police for a week in 1968. The following year black militant students—bandoliers draped across their shoulders, shotguns at their sides—seized the student union at Cornell. Even more shocking, a graduate student at the University of Wisconsin was killed in his lab when a bomb exploded there. The device had been planted by radicals protesting government-sponsored defense research.

On the other hand, key moderates both within and outside the government were convinced the United States could not win the war. Senator William Fulbright was among them. Having helped President Johnson push the Tonkin Gulf resolution through the Senate, Fulbright now held hearings sharply critical of American policy. The hawkish publisher of *Time* and *Life* magazines, Henry Luce, turned his editorials against the war in 1967. Even the strongest supporters of the war felt the pressure. Secretary of State Dean Rusk, a hard-liner throughout, was dismayed to hear his relatives back home in Cherokee County, Georgia: "Dean, if you can't tell us when this war is going to end, well then, maybe we just ought to chuck it."

McNamara loses faith

Defense Secretary Robert McNamara became the most dramatic defector. For years the statistically minded secretary had struggled to quantify the success of the war effort. General William Westmoreland duly provided body counts, number of bombs dropped, and pacification reports. For a time McNamara remained confident that there was indeed a "light at the end of the tunnel." But by 1967 the secretary had become skeptical. If Americans were killing 300,000 Vietnamese, enemy forces should be shrinking. Instead, intelligence estimates indicated that North Vietnamese infiltration had risen from 35,000 a year in 1965 to 150,000 by the end of 1967. McNamara came to have deep moral qualms. "The picture of the world's greatest superpower killing or seriously injuring 1,000 non-combatants a week, while trying to pound a tiny, backward nation into submission on an issue whose merits are hotly disputed, is not a pretty one," he advised.

Johnson, however, thought of himself as a moderate on the war. He weighed doves like McNamara against hawks like Senator John Stennis of Mississippi and General Westmoreland, who pressed to escalate further. Since Johnson did not want to be remembered as the first American president who lost a war, he sided more with the hawks. And so McNamara resigned.

Inflation

As the war dragged on, it had one severe economic consequence: inflation. By 1967 the cost of the war had soared to more than $50 billion a year. Medicare, education, housing, and other Great Society programs raised the domestic budget sharply, too. Through it all Johnson refused to raise taxes, for fear of losing support for his domestic programs. From 1950 to 1960 the average rate of inflation hovered at about 2 percent a year. From 1965 to 1970, as the war escalated, it jumped to around 4 percent. The economy was headed for trouble.

THE UNRAVELING

Almost all the forces dividing America seemed to converge in 1968. Until January of that year, most Americans had reason to believe General Westmoreland's estimate of the war. There was, he suggested, "light at the end of the tunnel." Johnson and his advisers, whatever their private doubts, in public painted an optimistic picture. With such optimism radiating from Washington, few Americans were prepared for the events on the night of January 30, 1968.

Tet Offensive

As the South Vietnamese began their celebration of Tet, the Vietnamese lunar new year, Vietcong guerrillas launched a series of concerted attacks. Assault targets included Saigon's major airport, the South Vietnamese presidential palace, and Hue, the ancient Vietnamese imperial capital. Perhaps most unnerving to Americans, 19 crack Vietcong commandos blasted a hole in the wall of the American embassy compound in Saigon and stormed in. They fought in the courtyard until all 19 lay dead. One reporter, stunned by the carnage, compared the courtyard to a butcher shop.

Tet must rank as one of the great American intelligence failures, on a par with Pearl Harbor or China's intervention in Korea. For nearly half a year the North Vietnamese had lured American troops to the countryside of South Vietnam. They engaged in pitched battles at remote outposts like Khe Sanh, Con Thien, Song Be, and Dak To. As American forces dispersed, the Vietcong infiltrated major population areas of Saigon and the delta region. A few audacious VC, disguised as South Vietnamese soldiers, even hitched rides on American jeeps and trucks. Though surprised by the Tet offensive, American and South Vietnamese troops quickly counterattacked, repulsing most of the assaults. Hue, the Communists' biggest conquest, took three weeks to retake. Appearing before the American press, General Westmoreland announced that the Vietcong had "very deceitfully" taken advantage of the Vietnamese holiday "to create maximum consternation" and that their "well-laid plans went afoul."

In a narrow military sense, Westmoreland was right. The enemy had been driven back, sustaining perhaps 40,000 deaths. Only 1100 American and 2300 South Vietnamese soldiers had been killed—a ratio of more than 10 to 1 (though 12,500 civilians died). But Americans at home received quite another message. Tet created a "credibility gap" between the administration's promises and the harsh reality. Westmoreland, Johnson, and other officials had repeatedly claimed that the Vietcong were on their last legs. Yet as Ho Chi Minh had coolly informed the French after World War II, "You can kill ten of my men for every one I kill of yours . . . even at those odds, you will lose and I will win." Highly respected CBS news anchor Walter Cronkite drew a gloomy lesson of Tet for his national audience: "To say that we are mired in stalemate seems the only realistic, yet unsatisfactory, conclusion."   *Stalemate*

Two months later, American forces remained edgy about Vietcong attacks. At the remote hamlet of My Lai, American troops under Lieutenant William Calley   *My Lai*

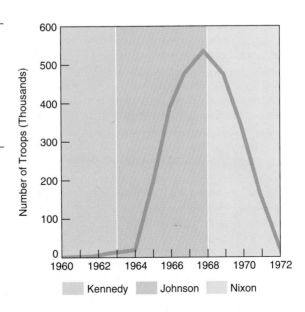

LEVELS OF U.S. TROOPS IN VIETNAM (AT YEAR END) This graph suggests one reason why protest against the war increased after 1964, peaked by 1968, and largely ended after 1972. (*Source:* U.S. Department of Defense.)

swept in, rounded up the villagers, and slaughtered more than 200 men, women, and children. The dead of My Lai would have been just more figures in the "body count," except that an army photographer had taken pictures and a helicopter pilot intervened. If returning veterans were to be believed, there had been hundreds of similar incidents, though perhaps few as bloody. On the communist side, vengeance was at times even more severe. Before Hue could be retaken, the Vietcong had shot, clubbed to death, or buried alive perhaps 3000 residents, many of them innocent civilians.

The Tet offensive sobered Lyndon Johnson as well as his new secretary of defense, Clark Clifford. Clifford was a Johnson loyalist and a stalwart believer in the war. But as he reviewed the American position in Vietnam, he could get no satisfactory answers from the Joint Chiefs of Staff, who had requested an additional 206,000 troops. "How long would it take to succeed in Vietnam?" Clifford recalled asking them.

> They didn't know. How many more troops would it take? They couldn't say. Were two hundred thousand the answer? They weren't sure. Might they need more? Yes, they might need more. Could the enemy build up [their own troop strength] in exchange? Probably. So what was the plan to win the war? Well, the only plan was that attrition would wear out the Communists, and they would have had enough. Was there any indication that we've reached that point? No, there wasn't.

Clifford decided to build a case for deescalation. To review policy, he formed a panel of "wise men," respected pillars of the cold war establishment, that included

"WHO? ? ?" taunts one poster behind Senator Eugene McCarthy after his strong showing against President Johnson in the New Hampshire Democratic primary. College students were among McCarthy's most fervent supporters.

Dean Acheson, Harry Truman's secretary of state; Henry Cabot Lodge, a Republican and former ambassador to South Vietnam; and several retired generals. Johnson's advisers had led him "down the garden path" on Vietnam, they concluded. The war could not be won, and he should seek a negotiated settlement.

Meanwhile, the antiwar forces had found a political champion in Senator Eugene McCarthy from Minnesota. McCarthy was something of a senatorial maverick who wrote poetry in his spare time. He announced that no matter what the odds, he would challenge Johnson in the 1968 Democratic primaries. Idealistic college students got haircuts and shaves in order to look "clean for Gene." Thus transformed, they canvassed New Hampshire voters. Johnson had not formally entered the 1968 presidential race, but his supporters sponsored a write-in campaign, confident of a decisive win in this opening primary. When the votes were counted, McCarthy had lost by only 300 out of 50,000 votes cast. For the president, so slim a victory was a stunning defeat. To the outrage of McCarthy supporters, Robert Kennedy, John Kennedy's younger brother, now announced his own antiwar candidacy.

"Clean for Gene"

"I've got to get me a peace proposal," the president told Clifford. The White House speechwriters finally put together an announcement that bombing raids against North Vietnam would be halted, at least partially, in hopes that peace talks could begin. They were still trying to write an ending when Johnson told them, "Don't worry; I may have a little ending of my own." On March 31 he supplied it, announcing: "I have concluded that I should not permit the presidency to become involved in the partisan divisions that are developing in this political year. . . . Accordingly I shall not seek, and I will not accept, the nomination of my party for another term as your president."

LBJ withdraws

COUNTERPOINT

Whose war?

In the spring of 1995 Robert McNamara published a memoir that stunned longtime defenders of the war and confirmed the beliefs of those who had opposed it. The war had been a great mistake, he concluded. The Johnson administration could—and should—have avoided sending hundreds of thousands of Americans into the conflict. Moreover, McNamara implied that if Kennedy had lived, he would not have escalated the war as Lyndon Johnson had. In other words, even though presidents from Truman through Kennedy had involved the United States in Southeast Asia, Vietnam was truly Lyndon Johnson's war. Some historians have argued that by the summer of 1963, Kennedy had become convinced that American forces had to be gradually withdrawn but that politically he dared not do so until the election of 1964. "If I tried to pull out now from Vietnam," one aide recalls him saying, "we would have another Joe McCarthy red scare on our hands."

Other historians have been more skeptical. They argue that even in 1965, no official of importance was suggesting that the United States should allow Vietnam to fall to the Communists. Senators Fulbright and Mike Mansfield and Undersecretary of State George Ball, who criticized Johnson by 1968, all backed the Tonkin Gulf resolution in 1965. Further, historians have evidence that President Kennedy would have escalated the war, though perhaps not as quickly. "We want the war to be won, the Communists to be contained, and the Americans to go home," Kennedy asserted only two months before his death; ". . . But we are not there to see a war lost." As one historian concluded, "The widespread and prevailing opinion in the administration, Congress, and the press and among the mass of Americans was that the United States simply could not walk away from Vietnam and sacrifice a pro-Western country to Communist aggression." In his view Vietnam was America's war: a product of the cold war mentality that had arisen over the previous two decades, not the act of a single, stubborn president.

Whether or not Johnson's tragedy was self-inflicted, the Vietnam War had pulled down one of the savviest, most effective politicians of the modern era. North Vietnam, for its part, responded to the speech by sending delegates to a peace conference in Paris, where negotiations quickly bogged down. And American attention soon focused on the chaotic situation at home, where all the turbulence, discontent, and violence of the 1960s seemed to be coming together.

The Shocks of 1968

The King and Kennedy assassinations

On April 4 Martin Luther King, Jr., traveled to Memphis to support striking sanitation workers. He was relaxing on the balcony of his motel when James Earl Ray, an escaped convict, fatally shot him. King's campaign of nonviolence was overshadowed by the frustration and anger that greeted news of his death. Riots broke out that evening in ghetto areas of the nation's capital; by the end of the week, disturbances rocked 125 more neighborhoods across the country. Almost before Americans could recover, a disgruntled Arab nationalist, Sirhan Sirhan, assassinated Robert Kennedy

Enthusiastic crowds followed Robert Kennedy on his Democratic primary campaign during the 1968 presidential election. The evening of his victory in California he was assassinated by a Palestinian refugee, Sirhan Sirhan, who later claimed he admired Kennedy.

on the evening of June 5. Running in opposition to the war, Kennedy had just won a crucial primary victory in California.

The deaths of King and Kennedy pained Americans deeply. In their own ways, both men exemplified the liberal tradition, which reached its high-water mark in the 1960s. King had retained his faith in a Christian theology of nonviolence. He sought change without resorting to the language of the fist and the gun. In the final years of his life, his campaign broadened to include the poor of all races. Robert Kennedy had begun his career as a pragmatic politician who, like his brother John, had not hesitated to use power ruthlessly. But Kennedy, like King, had come to reject the war his brother had supported, and he seemed genuinely to sympathize with the poor and minorities. At the same time, he was popular among traditional white ethnics and blue-collar workers. Would the liberal political tradition have flourished longer if these two charismatic figures had survived the turbulence of the sixties?

Chicago

Once violence had claimed the clearest liberal voices, it became obvious that the Democrats would choose Hubert Humphrey when their convention met at Chicago in August. Humphrey had begun his career as a progressive and a strong supporter of civil rights. But as Johnson's loyal vice president he was intimately associated with the war and the old-style liberal reforms that could never satisfy radicals. Humphrey's impending nomination meant, too, that no major candidate would speak for Americans disillusioned with the war or the status quo. The Republicans had chosen Richard Nixon, a traditional anti-Communist (now reborn as the "new," more moderate Nixon). As much as radicals disliked Johnson, they abhorred any Nixon, "new" or old.

Chicago, where the Democrats met, was the fiefdom of Mayor Richard Daley, long the symbol of machine politics and backroom deals. Daley was determined that the radicals who poured into Chicago would not disrupt "his" Democratic convention. The radicals were equally determined that they would. For a week the police skirmished with demonstrators: police clubs, riot gear, and tear gas versus the demonstrators' eggs, rocks, and balloons filled with paint and urine. When Daley refused to allow a peaceful march past the convention site, the radicals marched anyway. With the mayor's blessing, the police turned on the crowd in what a federal commission later labeled a police riot. In one pitched battle, many officers took off their badges and waded into the crowd, nightsticks swinging, chanting, "Kill, kill, kill." Reporters, medics, and other innocent bystanders were injured; at 3:00 a.m. police invaded candidate Eugene McCarthy's hotel headquarters and pulled some of his assistants from their beds.

With feelings running so high, President Johnson did not dare appear at his own party's convention. Theodore White, a veteran journalist covering the assemblage, scribbled his verdict in a notebook as police chased hippies down Michigan Avenue. "The Democrats are finished," he wrote.

Whose Silent Majority?

Radicals were not the only Americans alienated from the political system in 1968. Governor George Wallace of Alabama sensed the frustration among the "average man on the street, this man in the textile mill, this man in the steel mill, this barber, this beautician, the policeman on the beat." In running for president, Wallace sought the support of blue-collar workers and the lower middle classes.

Wallace had first come to national attention as he stood at the door barring integration of the University of Alabama. Briefly, he pursued the Democratic presidential nomination in 1964. For the race in 1968 he formed his own American Independent party with the hawkish General Curtis LeMay as his running mate. (LeMay spoke belligerently of bombing North Vietnam "back to the stone age.") Wallace's enemies were the "liberals, intellectuals, and long hairs [who] have run this country for too long." Wallace did not simply appeal to law and order, militarism, and white backlash; he was too sharp for that. With roots in southern Populism, he called for federal job-training programs, stronger unemployment benefits, national health insurance, a higher minimum wage, and a further extension of union rights. Polls in September revealed that many Robert Kennedy voters had shifted to Wallace. A quarter of all union members backed him.

In fact, Wallace had tapped true discontent among the working class. Many blue-collar workers despised hippies and peace marchers yet wanted the United States out of Vietnam. And they were suspicious, as Wallace was, of the upper-class "establishment" that held power. "We can't understand how all those rich kids—the kids with beards from the suburbs—how they got off when my son had to go over there and maybe get his head shot off," one blue-collar parent complained. Old-style radicals of the 1930s might have tried to tap such discontent, but the leaders of the New Left by and large had given up on traditional workers. They aimed their appeal at the newer minorities: students, Hispanics, African Americans, and the unorganized poor.

Richard Nixon also sought to attract traditionally Democratic voters, especially disaffected southern Democrats, away from Wallace into the Republican party. The Republicans, of course, had been reviled by the Populists of old as representatives of the money power, monopoly, and the old-line establishment. But Nixon himself had modest roots. His parents owned a general store in Whittier, California, where he had worked to help the family out. His high school grades were good enough to earn him a scholarship to Harvard, but fearing the cost of traveling east, he turned it down in favor of nearby Whittier College. At Duke Law School he was so pinched for funds, he lived in an abandoned toolshed. His dogged hard work earned him the somewhat dubious nickname of "iron pants." If ever there had been a candidate who could claim to be self-made, it was Nixon. And he well understood the disdain ordinary laborers felt for "kids with the beards from the suburbs"—hippies who wore flags sewn to the seat of their pants—who seemed always to be insisting, protesting, *demanding.*

Nixon's "silent majority" Nixon believed himself a representative of the "silent majority," as he later described it, not a vocal minority.

He thus set two fundamental requirements for his campaign: to distance himself from President Johnson on Vietnam and to turn Wallace's "average Americans" into a Republican "silent majority." The Vietnam issue was delicate, because Nixon had generally supported the president's efforts to end the war. He told his aide Richard Whalen, "I've come to the conclusion that there's no way to win the war. But we can't say that, of course. In fact, we have to seem to say the opposite." For most of his campaign he hinted that he had a secret plan to end the war but steadfastly refused to disclose it. He pledged only to find an honorable solution, at the same time promis-

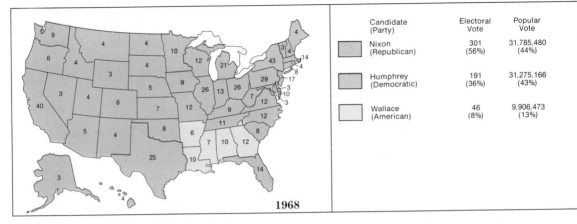

Candidate (Party)	Electoral Vote	Popular Vote
Nixon (Republican)	301 (56%)	31,785,480 (44%)
Humphrey (Democratic)	191 (36%)	31,275,166 (43%)
Wallace (American)	46 (8%)	9,906,473 (13%)

ELECTION OF 1968

ing to promote "law and order" while cracking down on "pot," pornography, protest, and permissiveness.

Hubert Humphrey had the more daunting task of surmounting the ruins of the Chicago convention. All through September antiwar protesters dogged his campaign with "Dump the Hump" posters. Finally the vice president distanced his position on Vietnam, however slightly, from that of his unpopular boss. The protests then faded, Humphrey picked up momentum, and traditional blue-collar Democrats began to return to the fold. By November his rallies were enthusiastic and well attended. But the late surge did not turn the tide. Nixon captured 43.4 percent of the popular vote to 42.7 percent for Humphrey and 13.5 percent for Wallace. More important, Nixon's "southern strategy" paid off; he and Wallace carried the entire southern tier of states except Texas. Some voters had punished the Democrats not just for the war but also for supporting civil rights. The majority of the American electorate seemed to have turned their backs on liberal reform.

The election of 1968

THE NIXON YEARS

In Richard Nixon, Americans had elected two men to the presidency. On the public side, he appeared as the traditional small-town, middle-class conservative who cherished individual initiative, Chamber-of-Commerce capitalism, Fourth-of-July patriotism, and Victorian mores. The private Nixon was a troubled man. His language among intimates was caustic and profane. He waxed bitter toward those he saw as enemies. Never a natural public speaker, he was physically rather awkward—a White House aide once found toothmarks on a "child-proof" aspirin cap the president had been unable to pry open. But Nixon seemed to search out challenges—"crises" to face and conquer.

The new president saw himself as a master of foreign policy. The Vietnam War stood in the way of his major goals. Hence, ending it became one of his first priori-

Henry
Kissinger

ties. He found a congenial ally in National Security Adviser Henry Kissinger. Kissinger, like Nixon, had a global vision of foreign affairs. Like Nixon, he had a tendency to pursue his ends secretly, skirting the traditional channels of government such as the Department of State.

Vietnamization—and Cambodia

To bring the Vietnam War to an end, Nixon and Kissinger wanted to negotiate a settlement that would bring American troops home, but they insisted on "peace with honor." That boiled down to preserving a pro-American South Vietnamese government. The strategy Nixon adopted was "Vietnamization," which involved a carrot and a stick. On its own initiative, the United States began gradually withdrawing troops as a way to advance the peace talks in Paris. The burden of fighting would shift to the South Vietnamese army, equipped now with massive amounts of American supplies. Critics likened this strategy to little more than "changing the color of the corpses." All the same, it helped reduce antiwar protests at home. Once the media shifted their focus from the war to the peace talks, the public had the impression that the war was winding down.

Using the stick, President Nixon hoped to drive the North Vietnamese into negotiating peace on American terms. Quite consciously, he traded on his reputation as a cold warrior who would stop at nothing. As he explained to his chief of staff, Robert Haldeman,

> I call it the Madman Theory, Bob. I want the North Vietnamese to believe that I've reached the point where I might do anything to stop the war. We'll just slip the word to them that, "for God's sake, you know Nixon is obsessed about Communists. We can't restrain him when he's angry—and he has his hand on the nuclear button"—and Ho Chi Minh himself will be in Paris in two days begging for peace.

To underline his point, Nixon in the spring of 1969 launched a series of bombing attacks against North Vietnamese supply depots inside neighboring Cambodia. Johnson had refused to widen the war in this manner, fearing domestic reaction. Nixon simply kept the raids secret.

The North Vietnamese refused to cave in to the bombing or the threats of the "Madman." Ho Chi Minh's death in 1969 changed nothing. His successors continued to reject any offer that did not end with complete American withdrawal and an abandonment of the South Vietnamese military government. Once again Nixon decided to turn up the heat. Over the opposition of his secretaries of defense and state, he or-

Invading
Cambodia

dered American troops into Cambodia to wipe out North Vietnamese bases there. This, to be sure, was Johnson's old policy of escalation—precisely the opposite of the withdrawal Nixon had promised. But the Joint Chiefs argued that such an attack would buy time to strengthen the South Vietnamese army.

Nixon recognized that a storm of protest would arise. (The administration was "going to get unshirted hell for doing this," he noted.) On April 30, 1970, he announced the "incursion" of American troops into Cambodia, proclaiming that he would not allow "the world's most powerful nation" to act "like a pitiful helpless giant." The wave of protests that followed included the Kent State tragedy as well as another march on Washington by 100,000 protesters. Even Congress was upset enough to repeal the Tonkin Gulf resolution, a symbolic rejection of Nixon's invasion. After two months American troops left Cambodia, having achieved little.

Fighting a No-Win War

For a time, Vietnamization seemed to be working. As more American troops went home, the South Vietnamese forces improved modestly. But for American GIs still in the country, morale became a serious problem. Obviously the United States was gradually pulling out its forces. After Tet, it was clear there would be no victory. So why were the "grunts" in the field still being asked to put their lives on the line? The anger surfaced increasingly in incidents known as "fragging," in which GIs threw fragmentation grenades at officers who pursued the war too aggressively.

Nor could the army isolate itself from the trends dividing American society. Just as young Americans "turned on" to marijuana and hallucinogens, so soldiers in Vietnam used drugs. The Pentagon estimated that by 1971 nearly a third of American troops there had experimented with either opium or heroin, easily obtained in Southeast Asia. Nor did black GIs leave black power issues at home. *Black power in Vietnam* Robert Rawls recalled that the brothers "used to make a shoestring that they braided up and tied around their wrist, and everywhere a whole lot of blacks used to go, they'd give a power sign." One white medic noticed that Muhammad Ali's re-

A helicopter machine gunner: cigarette dangling, a knife and "jungle juice" insect repellent stuck in his helmet. Increasingly, there were few illusions about this no-win war.

fusal to be drafted caused the blacks in his unit "to question why they were fighting the Honky's war against other Third World people. I saw very interesting relationships happening between your quick-talking, sharp-witted Northern blacks and your kind of easygoing, laid-back Southern blacks. . . . Many Southern blacks changed their entire point of view by the end of their tour and went home extremely angry."

The problem with morale only underlined the dilemma facing President Nixon. As the troops became restive, domestic opposition to the war grew. By repealing the Gulf of Tonkin resolution, Congress itself had put the president on notice that he would have to negotiate a settlement soon. Yet the North Vietnamese refused to yield, even after the American assaults in Cambodia.

The Move toward Détente

Despite Nixon's insistence on "peace with honor," Vietnam was not a war he had chosen to fight. Both Kissinger and Nixon recognized that the United States no longer had the strength to exercise unchallenged dominance across the globe. The Soviet Union, not Vietnam, remained their prime concern. Ever since Khrushchev had backed down at the Cuban missile crisis in 1962, the Soviets had steadily expanded their nuclear arsenal. Furthermore, the growing economies of Japan and Western Europe challenged American leadership in world trade. Continued instability in Southeast Asia, the Middle East, and other Third World areas threatened the strength of the non-Communist bloc. Thus Vietnam diverted valuable military and economic resources from more critical areas.

Nixon Doctrine   In what the White House labeled the new "Nixon Doctrine," the United States announced it would no longer expect to fight every battle, win every war, or draw every line to keep the global peace. Instead, Americans would shift some of the military burden for containment to such allies as Japan in the Pacific, the shah of Iran in the Middle East, Zaire in central Africa, and the apartheid government in South Africa. Over the next six years American foreign military sales jumped from $1.8 billion to $15.2 billion. At the same time, Nixon and Kissinger looked for new ways to contain Soviet power not simply by the traditional threat of arms but through negotiations to ease tensions. This policy was named, from the French, détente.

To pursue détente Kissinger and Nixon used "linkages," a system of making progress on one issue by connecting it with another. They recognized, for example, how much the cold war arms race burdened the Soviet economy. To ease that pressure, they would make concessions to the Soviets on nuclear arms. The Soviets in return would have to limit their arms buildup and, in a linked concession, pressure North Vietnam to negotiate an end to the war. To add pressure, Nixon and Kissinger developed a "China card." The United States would stop treating Mao Zedong as an archenemy and, instead, open diplomatic relations with the Chinese. Fearful of a more powerful China, the Soviets would be more conciliatory toward the United States.

It took a shrewd diplomatist to sense an opportunity to shift traditional cold war policy. Conservative Republicans in particular had denounced the idea of ever recognizing Mao's government, even after 20 years. They believed that the Soviets

Upon seeing China's Great Wall, an ebullient Richard Nixon pronounced it a "great wall," built by a great people. Perhaps precisely because he had been so staunch an anti-Communist, Nixon appreciated the enormous departure his trip marked in Sino-American relations.

responded only to force and that they were united with China in a monolithic communist conspiracy. Now Richard Nixon, the man who had built a career fighting communism, made overtures to the Communist powers. Kissinger slipped off to China on a secret mission (he was nursing a stomachache, his aides assured the press) and then reappeared having arranged a week-long trip to China for the president. During that visit in early 1972, Nixon pledged to normalize relations, a move the public enthusiastically welcomed, although some conservative Republicans were angered at the idea of betraying their old ally in Taiwan, Chiang Kai-shek. Only Nixon's impeccable anti-Communist credentials had allowed him to reverse the direction of America's China policy.

A new overture to the Soviet Union followed the China trip. Eager to acquire American grain and technology, Soviet Premier Leonid Brezhnev invited Nixon to visit Moscow in May 1972. Nixon saw in the Soviet market a chance to ease American trade deficits by selling grain surpluses. The two leaders struck a major wheat deal, but the most important benefit of the meeting was the signing of the first Strategic Arms Limitation Treaty (SALT I). In the agreement, both sides pledged not to develop a new system of antiballistic missiles, which would have accelerated the costly arms race. And they agreed to limit the number of intercontinental ballistic missiles each side would deploy.

SALT I

Both the China and Moscow visits strengthened Nixon's reputation as a global strategist. Americans were pleased at the prospect of lower cold war tensions. But it was not clear that the linkages achieved in Moscow and Beijing would help extricate the United States from Vietnam.

TIME AND TRAVEL

The Race to the Moon

In campaigning for the presidency in 1960 John F. Kennedy chided the Republicans for creating a "missile gap." While the American space program limped along, the Soviet Union had launched *Sputnik*. Only a few months after Kennedy's inauguration, Russian cosmonaut Yuri Gagarin orbited the world in a five-ton spacecraft. The first American space flight on May 6, 1961, succeeded only in carrying Commander Alan Shepard into a suborbital flight of 300 miles. Kennedy feared that if it lost the space race, the United States might lose the cold war as well.

Thus Kennedy ordered his science advisers "to shift our efforts in space from low to high gear." He announced on national television that the United States would do something truly dramatic: land a man on the moon and bring him back alive "before the decade is out." No matter how great the cost, Kennedy believed the investment was sound. "This is not merely a race," he remarked in an allusion to the Soviets' success. "Space is open to us now; and our eagerness to share its meaning is not governed by the efforts of others. We must go into space because whatever mankind must undertake, free men must fully share."

There were those like former President Eisenhower who thought anyone was "nuts" to spend billions for a space spectacular that promised little in the way of scientific discoveries. Nor was it clear that NASA could achieve such a feat in so short a time. To many members of Congress, however, the space program was a huge pork barrel, so they voted to fund Kennedy's "great new American enterprise." From then on the space program achieved a string of triumphs. In February 1962 Colonel John Glenn successfully circled the earth three times in "a fireball of a ride"; an unmanned satellite passed Venus later that year; and a Telstar communications satellite began relaying television broadcasts, launching an era of truly global mass communications.

One after another, the space spectaculars continued, much to the public's delight. In March 1965 American astronauts first maneuvered their capsule; in May Edward White took America's first space walk; the following year two vehicles met and docked for the first time. The Gemini program was followed by the Apollo missions, whose Saturn rockets powered their payloads into lunar orbit. From there, two astronauts planned to pilot a separate module to the moon's surface, while a third remained in the orbiting command module waiting for them and the return trip. By Christmas eve 1968 the *Apollo 8* mission was circling the moon. It seemed a "vast, lonely and forbidding sight," one astronaut remarked to hundreds of millions in a live telecast.

On July 20, 1969, the lunar module of *Apollo 11* at last touched down on the earth's closest neighbor. Commander Neil Armstrong, moving awkwardly in his bulky

Nixon's New Federalism

As a Republican, Nixon wanted to scale back many New Deal and Great Society programs. "After a third of a century of power flowing from the people and the states to Washington," he proclaimed, "it is time for a New Federalism in which power, funds, and responsibility will flow from Washington to the states and to the people."

Daily Lives

Landing on the moon may have been one small step for a man, but NASA spent $25 billion on the project, over $2 billion for each of the 12 astronauts who took lunar walks.

mand module, Armstrong brought along a quarter of the world's population, who monitored the moment live on television. "That's one small step for a man, one giant leap for mankind," he proclaimed.

For all its stunning success, the space program did not escape the political crosscurrents of the 1960s. Critics argued that those billions might better have been spent solving more earthly problems. And Richard Nixon turned *Apollo 11* into a public relations gold mine, even though Kennedy and Johnson had supported the space program against Republican attacks. "This is the greatest week in the history of the world since the Creation," Nixon told the astronauts after their capsule splashed down in the Pacific. Evangelist Billy Graham took exception to his friend's theological excess. What of Christ's birth, his death, and his resurrection, Graham wanted to know. "Tell Billy," Nixon wrote White House Chief of Staff H. R. Haldeman, "RN referred to a week not a day."

But *Apollo 11* marked the climax of a phase of exploration, not, like the Creation, a beginning. After *Apollo 17* and $25 billion in costs, Nixon predicted "this may be the last time in this century men will walk on the moon." Space travel since then has belonged largely to the space shuttles and to science fiction, where the crew of the starship *Enterprise* and their Kennedyesque captains, James T. Kirk and Jean Luc Picard, "boldly go where no man has gone before."

spacesuit, worked his way down a ladder to the white, chalky surface. He was not alone. Besides Edwin Aldrin, who followed him, and Michael Collins, orbiting in the com-

---

The New Federalism involved a system of revenue sharing in which Washington gave money in block grants to state and local governments. Rather than receiving funds earmarked for specific purposes, localities could decide which problems needed attention and how best to attack them. Congress passed a revenue-sharing act in 1972, which distributed $30 billion over the following five years. A similar approach influenced aid to individuals. Liberal programs from the New Deal to the

Revenue sharing

Great Society often provided specific services to individuals: job retraining programs, Head-Start programs for preschoolers, food supplement programs for nursing mothers. Republicans argued that such a "service strategy" too often assumed that federal bureaucrats best understood what the poor needed. Nixon favored an "income strategy" instead, which simply gave recipients money and allowed them to spend it as they saw fit. Such grants would encourage individual initiative, increase personal freedom, and reduce government bureaucracy.

The Family Assistance Plan

In this spirit Nixon encouraged a renegade liberal academic, Daniel Patrick Moynihan, to develop a program to replace the welfare system. His "Family Assistance Plan" stressed "workfare," not welfare; it targeted the working poor, not the undeserving poor. Poor families would be guaranteed a minimum annual income of $1600. An emphasis on family would encourage fathers to live at home. The plan also required recipients to register for employment to satisfy conservative critics who believed that too many welfare recipients were able-bodied workers addicted to handouts and too lazy to work. Though Moynihan's proposals died in Congress, they defined the general terms in which poverty and assistance to the poor would be debated into the 1990s.

Nixon reforms

Even if Nixon was determined to reverse the liberalism of the 1960s, critics were wrong to dismiss him as a knee-jerk conservative. His appeal to local authority and individual initiative in some ways echoed the New Left's rhetoric of "power to the people." In 1970 he signed a bill establishing an Occupational Safety and Health Agency (OSHA) to enforce health and safety standards in the workplace. And although the president was no crusader for the environment, he did support a Clean Air Act to reduce car exhaust emissions as well as a Clean Water Act to make polluters liable for their negligence and to deal with disastrous oil spills.

Stagflation

Ironically, economic distress, aggravated by the Vietnam War, forced Nixon to adopt liberal remedies. By 1970 the nation had entered its first recession in a decade. Traditionally a recession brought a decrease in demand for goods and a rise in unemployment as workers were laid off. Manufacturers then cut wages and prices in order to preserve profit margins and encourage demand for their goods. But in the recession of 1970, while unemployment rose as economists would have expected, wages and prices were also rising in an inflationary spiral. Americans were getting the worst of two worlds: a stagnant economy combined with rising prices—or "stagflation." Unfriendly Democrats labeled the phenomenon "Nixonomics," in which "all things that should go up—the stock market, corporate profits, real spendable income, productivity—go down, and all things that should go down—unemployment, prices, interest rates—go up."

To blame the recession on Nixon was hardly fair, since Lyndon Johnson had brought on inflation by refusing to raise taxes to pay for the war and Great Society social programs. In addition, wages continued their inflationary rise partly because powerful unions had negotiated automatic cost-of-living increases into their contracts. Similarly, in industries dominated by a few large corporations, like steel and oil, prices did not follow the market forces of a recession. So prices and wages continued to rise as demand and employment fell.

Mindful that his own "silent majority" were the people most pinched by the slower economy, Nixon decided that unemployment posed a greater threat than inflation. Announcing "I am now a Keynesian," he adopted a deficit budget designed to stimulate the growth of jobs. More surprising, in August 1971 he announced that to provide short-term relief, wages and prices would be frozen for 90 days. For a Republican to advocate federal wage and price controls was near heresy, almost as heretical as Nixon's overtures to China. Yet the president did not hesitate. For another year federal wage and price boards enforced the ground rules for any increases; most controls were lifted in January 1973. As in foreign policy, Nixon had reversed long-cherished economic policies to achieve practical results.

"SILENT" MAJORITIES AND VOCAL MINORITIES

During the 1968 campaign Richard Nixon had noticed a placard carried by a hopeful voter—"Bring Us Together." That became his campaign theme. Yet of necessity political coalitions cannot bring everyone together. Their goal is simply to assemble a majority on Election Day. Nixon recognized that in the three-way race of 1968, his 43 percent did not add up to a majority. But when Wallace's vote was added, the total came to an impressive 60 percent. If Nixon could add discontented southerners and blue-collar workers to the traditional GOP base, he could win in 1972.

These groups resented much that the civil rights movement had done to overcome racial inequalities. To add to that resentment, the civil rights movement inspired other minorities to demand greater equality for themselves. Just as the civil rights campaign gave way to black power militancy, so, too, other minority activists adopted increasingly disruptive tactics to press their causes. Their new visibility was crucial to Nixon's attempt to form his own countermajority.

Latino Activism

Part of the increased visibility of minorities resulted from a new wave of immigration from Mexico and Puerto Rico after World War II. That wave was augmented by Cubans after the 1959 revolution that brought Fidel Castro to power. Historical, cultural, ethnic, and geographic differences made it difficult to develop a common political agenda among Latinos. Still, some activists did seek greater unity.

After World War II a weak island economy and the lure of prosperity on the mainland brought more than a million Puerto Ricans into New York City. As citizens of the United States, they could move freely to the mainland and back home again. That dual consciousness discouraged many from establishing deep roots stateside. Equally important, the newcomers were startled to discover that, whatever their status at home, on the mainland they were subject to racial discrimination and most often segregated into urban slums. In 1964 approximately half of all recent immigrants lived below the poverty level, according to the Puerto Rican Forum. Their unemployment was three times greater than for whites and 50 percent higher than for blacks. Light-skinned migrants escaped those conditions by blending into the middle class as "Latin Americans." The Puerto Rican community thereby lost some of the leadership it needed to assert its political rights.

Cesar Chavez mobilized the largely Hispanic migrant workers into the United Farm Workers Union. His demands for recognition of the union by California growers led to a bitter strike (in Spanish, *huelga*) in 1966. In 1969 a call for boycotts against grapes and lettuce gained Chavez and the union national attention. In July 1970, after five years of conflict, the growers agreed to recognize the union.

Still, a shared island orientation preserved a strong group identity. By the 1960s, the urban barrios gained greater political consciousness as groups like "Aspira" adopted the strategies of civil rights activists and organizations like the Black and Puerto Rican Caucus created links with other minority groups. The Cubans who arrived in the United States after 1959—some 350,000 over the course of the decade— forged fewer ties with other Latinos. Most settled around Miami. An unusually large number came from Cuba's professional, business, and government class and were racially white and politically conservative.

Mexican Americans, on the other hand, constituted the largest segment of Latinos. Until the 1940s most were farmers and farm laborers in Texas, New Mexico, and California. But during the 1950s, the process of mechanization had affected them, just as it had southern blacks. By 1969 about 85 percent of Mexican Americans had settled in cities. With urbanization came a slow improvement of the range and quality of jobs they held. A body of skilled workers, middle-class professionals, and entrepreneurs emerged.

In 1960, frustrated by years of neglect by major parties, Latino political leaders from the region formed the Mexican American Political Association. MAPA declared its intent to be "proudly Mexican American, *openly* political, and *necessarily* bipartisan." By 1964 four Mexican Americans had been elected to Congress, but the growing activism across the nation altered traditional Hispanic approaches to politics.

Cesar Chavez   Younger Mexican Americans began to call themselves Chicanos. In 1965 Cesar

Chavez gained national attention by his efforts to organize migrant laborers into the United Farm Workers. He led them in *La Huelga*—The Strike—which they supported with a national boycott of California lettuce and grapes.

By the late 1960s Mexican Americans had clearly established an ethnic consciousness and a movement. Like blacks, Chicanos saw themselves as a people whose culture had been taken from them. Their heritage had been rejected, their labor exploited, and their opportunity for advancement denied. The new ethnic militancy led to the formation of *La Raza Unida* (The Race United). This third-party movement sought to gain power in communities in which Chicanos were a majority and to extract concessions from the Democrats and Republicans. The more militant "Brown Berets" adopted the paramilitary tactics and radical rhetoric of the Black Panthers.

The Choices of American Indians

Like African Americans and Latinos, Indians began to protest, yet the unique situation of Native Americans (as many had begun to call themselves) set them apart from other minorities. A largely hostile white culture had in past centuries sought either to exterminate or to assimilate American Indians. Ironically, the growing strength of the civil rights movement created another threat to Indian tribal identities. Liberals came to see the reservations not as oases of Indian culture but as rural ghettos. During the 1950s they joined conservatives eager to repeal the New Deal and western state politicians eyeing tribal resources to adopt a policy of "termination." The Bureau of Indian Affairs would reduce federal services, gradually sell off tribal lands, and push Indians into the "mainstream" of American life.

Termination

Although most full-blooded Indians objected to the policy, some mixed bloods and Indians already assimilated into white society supported the move. The resulting relocation of approximately 35,000 Indians accelerated a shift from rural areas to cities. The urban Indian population, which had been barely 30,000 in 1940, reached more than 300,000 by the 1970s.

The social activism of the 1960s inspired Indian leaders to shape a new political agenda. In 1968 urban activists in Minneapolis created AIM, the American Indian Movement. A year later similarly minded Indians living around San Francisco Bay formed Indians of All Tribes. Because the Bureau of Indian Affairs refused to address the problems of urban Indians, more militant members of the organization dramatized their dissatisfaction by seizing the abandoned federal prison on Alcatraz Island in San Francisco Bay.

American Indian Movement

The Alcatraz action inspired a national Pan-Indian rights movement. Richard Oakes, a Mohawk Indian from New York, declared that the Alcatraz protest was not "a movement to liberate the island, but to liberate ourselves." Then in 1973, AIM organizers Russell Means and Dennis Banks led a dramatic takeover of a trading post at Wounded Knee, on a Sioux reservation in South Dakota. Ever since white cavalry had gunned down over a hundred Sioux in 1890 (see page 690), Wounded Knee had symbolized for Indians the betrayal of white promises and the bankruptcy of reservation policy. Even more, Wounded Knee now demonstrated the problems that Indian activists faced. When federal officers surrounded the trading post, militants discovered that other Indians did not support their tactics and were forced to leave. A Pan-Indian movement was difficult to achieve when so many tribes were determined to go their own ways as distinct, self-regulating communities. Thus even activists who supported

Wounded Knee

In the 1890s Wounded Knee had been a symbol of conflict between the Sioux and whites. In 1973 these members of the American Indian Movement seized the hamlet of Wounded Knee, making it once again a symbol of conflict.

the Pan-Indian movement found themselves splintering. During the 1970s more than 100 different organizations were formed to unite various tribes pursuing political and legal agendas at the local, state, and federal levels.

Gay Rights

In 1972, Black Panther leader Huey Newton observed that homosexuals "might be the most oppressed people" in American society. Certainly Newton was qualified to recognize oppression when he saw it. But by then a growing number of homosexuals had embraced liberation movements that placed them among minorities demanding equal rights.

Even during the "conformist" 1950s, gay men founded the Mattachine Society (1951) to fight antihomosexual attacks and to press for a wider public acceptance of their lifestyle. Lesbians formed a similar organization, the Daughters of Bilitis, in 1955. Beginning in the mid-1960s, more radical gay and lesbian groups began organizing to raise individual consciousness and to establish a gay culture in which they felt free. One group called for "acceptance as full equals . . . basic rights and equality as citizens; our human dignity; . . . [our] right to love whom we wish."

The movement's defining moment came on Friday June 27, 1969, when New York City police raided the Stonewall Inn, a Greenwich Village bar. Such raids were common enough: gay bars were regularly harassed by the police in an attempt to control urban "vice." This time the patrons fought back, first with taunts and jeers, then with paving stones and parking meters. Increasingly, gay activists called on homosexuals to "come out of the closet" and publicly affirm their sexuality. In 1974 gays achieved a major symbolic victory when the American Psychiatric Association removed homosexuality from its list of mental disorders.

Social Policies and the Court

Many of the blue-collar and southern Democratic voters Nixon sought to attract resented the Supreme Court's use of school busing to achieve desegregation. Fifteen years after *Brown v. Board of Education* had ruled that racially separate school systems must be desegregated, many localities still had not complied. Busing to achieve racial balance aroused determined opposition from white neighborhoods. Parents resented having their children bused away from their neighborhood to more distant, formerly all-black schools. For their part, although black parents worried about the reception their children might receive in hostile white neighborhoods, by and large they supported busing as a means to better education.

School busing

Under President Nixon, federal policy on desegregation took a 180-degree turn. In 1969 when lawyers for Mississippi asked the Supreme Court to delay an integration plan, the Nixon Justice Department supported the state. The Court rejected that proposal, holding in *United States v. Jefferson County Board of Education* that all state systems, including Mississippi's, had an obligation "to terminate dual systems at once and to operate now and hereafter only unitary schools." Two years later, in *Swann v. Charlotte–Mecklenburg Board of Education* (1971), the Court further ruled that busing, balancing ratios, and redrawing school district lines were all acceptable ways to achieve integration.

To end the Court's liberal activism, Nixon looked to fill vacancies with more conservative justices. When Earl Warren resigned as chief justice in 1969, the president nominated Warren Burger, a jurist who accepted most of the Court's precedents but had no wish to break new ground. When another vacancy occurred in 1969, Nixon tried twice to appoint conservative southern judges. But since both nominees had reputations on the federal bench for opposing civil rights and labor unions, the Senate rejected them. In the end, Nixon chose Minnesotan Harry Blackmun, a moderate judge of unimpeachable integrity. In 1971 he made two additional appointments: Lewis Powell, a highly regarded Virginia lawyer, and William Rehnquist of Arizona, an extreme conservative.

Nixon and the Court

The successive appointments of Burger, Blackmun, Powell, and Rehnquist effectively transformed the Court. No longer would it lead the fight for minority rights, as it had under Chief Justice Earl Warren. But neither would it reverse the achievements of the Warren Court.

Us versus Them

In so many of his battles, as in the struggle to shape the Supreme Court, Nixon portrayed those who opposed him as foes of traditional American values. Just as Nixon had tended to equate liberal reformers with Communist "pinkos" during the 1950s, now his administration blurred the lines between honest dissent and radical criminals. In doing so, it reflected the president's tendency to see issues in terms of "us against them."

With Nixon's consent (and Lyndon Johnson's before him), J. Edgar Hoover and the FBI conducted a covert and often illegal war against dissent. The CIA and military intelligence agencies also allowed themselves to be used. Attorney General John Mitchell and his Justice Department aggressively prosecuted civil rights activists, antiwar groups like Vietnam Veterans Against the War, socially conscious members of the Catholic clergy, the Black Panthers, SDS activists, and leaders of the peace movement. In its war on the drug culture of hippies and radicals, the administration proposed a bill that would allow police to stage "no-knock" raids and use "preventive detention" to keep suspected criminals in jail without bail. It also lobbied for permission to use more phone taps and other means of electronic surveillance.

In the political arena, Nixon gave Vice President Spiro Agnew the task of political mudslinging that Nixon had once performed for Eisenhower. Aided by speechwriter William Safire, Agnew launched an alliterative assault on the administration's enemies. He referred to the press and television news commentators as "nattering nabobs of negativism" and "troubadours of trouble" who contributed to the "creeping permissiveness that afflicted America." Antiwar demonstrators were "an effete corps of impudent snobs." In the campaign between "us" and "them," the national press corps was clearly "them," a hostile establishment, giving the news a liberal slant.

Triumph

George McGovern

As the election of 1972 approached, Nixon's majority seemed to be falling into place, especially as the antiwar candidacy of Senator George McGovern of South Dakota became unstoppable. Under the new rules of the Democratic party, which McGovern had helped write, the delegate selection process was opened to all party members. Minorities, women, and young people all received proportional representation. No longer would party bosses handpick the delegates. McGovern's nomination gave Nixon the split between "us" and "them" he sought. The Democratic platform embraced all the activist causes that the silent majority resented. It called for immediate withdrawal from Vietnam, abolition of the draft, amnesty for war resisters, and a minimum guaranteed income for the poor. Those issues antagonized much of the traditional New Deal coalition of urban bosses, southerners, labor leaders, and white ethnic groups.

By November the only question to be settled was the size of Nixon's majority. An unsolved burglary at the Watergate complex in Washington, D.C., while vaguely linked to the White House, had not touched the president. He even captured some antiwar sentiment by announcing on election eve that peace in Vietnam was at hand. When the smoke cleared, only liberal Massachusetts and the heavily black District of Columbia gave McGovern a majority. Nixon received almost 61 percent of the popular vote. In the races for the Senate and governorships, however, the Democrats actually made gains, while losing only 13 House seats. As one pollster concluded, "Richard Nixon's 'new American majority' was the creation of George McGovern."

Even this overwhelming victory did not bring peace to Richard Nixon. He still felt that he had scores to settle with his political opponents. "We have not used the power in the first four years, as you know," he remarked to Haldeman during the campaign. "We haven't used the Bureau [FBI] and we haven't used the Justice

Department, but things are going to change now. And they are going to change and they're going to get it, right?" Haldeman could only agree.

THE END OF AN ERA

Nixon was particularly frustrated because peace in Vietnam still eluded him. The North Vietnamese refused any settlement that left the South Vietnamese government of General Nguyen Van Thieu in power. Nixon wanted to subdue his opponents through force but recognized that it would have been political suicide to send back American troops. Instead, he ordered Haiphong harbor mined and blockaded in May 1972, along with a sustained bombing campaign. Then on December 18 the president launched an even greater wave of attacks, as American planes dropped more bombs on the North in 12 days than they had during the entire campaign from 1969 to 1971.

Once again, Kissinger returned to Paris, hoping that the combination of threats and conciliation would bring a settlement. Ironically the Americans' ally, General Thieu, threw up the most stumbling blocks, for he was rightly convinced that his regime would not last once the United States departed. But in January 1973 a treaty was finally arranged, smoothed by Kissinger's promise of aid to the North Vietnamese to help in postwar reconstruction, as well as a secret pledge to Thieu to send troops again if they were needed. By March the last American units were home.

Paris peace treaty

"The enemy must fight his battles ... [in] protracted campaigns," wrote the Vietnamese strategist in 1284. For all concerned the American phase of the Vietnam War had been a bloody, wearying conflict. Between 1961 and 1973 the war claimed 57,000 American lives and left more than 300,000 wounded. The cost to Southeast Asia in lives and destruction is almost impossible to calculate. More than a million Vietnamese soldiers and perhaps half a million civilians died. Some 6.5 million South Vietnamese became refugees, along with 3 million Cambodians and Laotians. Nixon claimed the "peace with honor" he had insisted on, but experienced observers predicted that South Vietnam's days were numbered. By any real measure of military success the Vietcong peasant guerrillas and their lightly armed North Vietnamese allies had held off—and in that sense defeated—the world's greatest military power.

Truman may have started the United States down the road to Vietnam by promoting a doctrine of containment all across the globe. Certainly Eisenhower and Kennedy increased American involvement and Richard Nixon ended it. But fairly or not, Vietnam is remembered as Lyndon Johnson's war. He committed both the material and human resources of the United States to defeat communism in Southeast Asia. The decision to escalate eventually destroyed the political consensus that had unified Americans since the late 1940s. That consensus was built on two major assumptions. First, it assumed that the United States must bear the burden of containing communism around the world. Second, American leaders had believed that the prosperity generated by the American economy made it possible both to fight communism abroad and to solve major social problems at home.

Vietnam and the cold war

Liberal dreams died with Vietnam, too. The war in Southeast Asia shattered the optimism of the early sixties: the belief that the world could be remade with the help of enough brilliant intellectuals or enough federal programs. The war also eroded the prosperity upon which the optimism of the postwar era had rested. After 1973 the economy slid into a long recession that forced Americans to recognize they had entered an era of limits both at home and abroad. Lyndon Johnson, who sought to preserve both liberal dreams and the cold war consensus, died on January 22, 1973, one day before the American war in Vietnam ended.

CHAPTER SUMMARY

War in Vietnam involved the United States for almost three decades in an agonizing conflict. Presidents from Truman to Nixon claimed that communist expansionism threatened vital American interests in Southeast Asia. As the civil war deepened in 1964, Lyndon Johnson chose to escalate American involvement. To force the Vietcong to negotiate, Johnson ordered the bombing of supply routes and North Vietnam's cities. He then sent American troops first to defend the air bases, then to fight the Vietcong. Despite that pressure, Ho Chi Minh would agree only to a united Vietnam free of foreign influence.

As the war dragged on it divided the nation into hawks and doves. College campuses became the center of protest. But the Tet offensive in January 1968 shook even Middle America's faith in the war. After nearly losing the New Hampshire primary to peace candidate Eugene McCarthy, Lyndon Johnson announced a bombing pause and withdrew from the presidential campaign. Assassinations claimed the lives of Martin Luther King, Jr., and Johnson's rival Robert Kennedy. That left Hubert Humphrey to carry the Democratic banner, but he could not overcome the scars of the riotous Democratic convention.

Continued protests troubled Richard Nixon's efforts to force Hanoi to agree to "peace with honor." To help end the war, Nixon traveled to China and the Soviet Union. His policy of détente eased cold war tensions. At home, he attempted to forge a new Republican majority with an appeal to southern Democrats and blue-collar voters who resented the protests of Hispanics, American Indians, homosexuals, and other vocal minorities. A smashing victory over George McGovern in 1972 vindicated Nixon's strategy. When a new wave of bombing failed to break North Vietnam's resolve, Henry Kissinger negotiated terms that in 1973 brought the war to an end.

ADDITIONAL READING

A number of questions have framed the debate about American involvement in Vietnam. Over the past few years, historians have paid particular attention to Lyndon Johnson's responsibility for escalating the war. Larry Berman, *LBJ's War* (1990) raised the issue, which has more recently been taken up by George Herring, *LBJ and Vietnam* (1995), Lloyd Gardner, *Pay Any Price: Lyndon Johnson and the Wars for Vietnam* (1995), and LBJ biographer Robert Dallek, *Lone Star Rising* (1991), in "Lyndon Johnson and Vietnam," *Diplomatic History*, Spring, 1996.

Ralph Nader's dogged, ascetic style forced corporations like General Motors to examine more seriously issues of public safety in products they produced. Nader's organization, Public Citizen, expanded its efforts on behalf of consumers to a wide range of issues.

GM's embarrassed president, James Roche, publicly apologized, but by then Nader was a hero and *Unsafe at Any Speed* a bestseller. In 1966 Congress passed the National Traffic and Motor Vehicle Safety Act and the Highway Safety Act, which for the first time required safety standards for cars, tires, and roads. Nader used $425,000 from his successful lawsuit to launch his Washington-based Center for the Study of Responsive Law (1969) with a staff of five lawyers and a hundred college volunteers. "Nader's Raiders," as the group soon became known, investigated a wide range of consumer and political issues, lobbying against water pollution, influence-peddling in Congress, and abuses in old-age homes and in favor of consumer-oriented government agencies.

Highway Safety Act

Nader's Raiders were part of a diverse consumer movement comprised of people who ranged from modest reformers to radicals. The radicals viewed the system of markets in which consumers bought goods to be deeply flawed. Only a thorough overhaul of the system, carried out by an active, interventionist government, could empower citizen-consumers. Nader suggested both the radicals' tone and their agenda when he called on corporations "to stop stealing, stop deceiving, stop corrupting politicians with money, stop monopolizing, stop poisoning the earth, air and water, stop selling dangerous products, stop exposing workers to cruel hazards. . . ." To pressure corporate America, Nader created the Public Interest Research Group, whose branches across the country lobbied for consumer protection.

More moderate reformers concentrated on making the existing market economy more open and efficient. To be better consumers, people needed better information. Reformers identified specific abuses: unsafe toys, dangerous food additives, the health consequences of smoking, and defective products dubbed "lemons." They brought suit against unethical marketing strategies like "bait-and-switch advertising"

FOOD/DRINK/DRUGS

Fast-Food America

Before the 1960s, few Americans regularly ate food prepared outside the home. The rich with access to servants, restaurants, and clubs might regularly eat food prepared by a nonfamily member. So, too, might college students or the very poor who had to take their meals in prisons, soup kitchens, or other institutional settings. By the 1970s the consumption of prepared foods and meals had become common for most Americans. Fast-food chains, school and office cafeterias, vending machines, and other public facilities served up more than 40 percent of the meals Americans ate. Many home meals consisted of packaged foods like TV dinners or frozen entrées that required nothing but heating prior to consumption. Whether at home or away, the emphasis at mealtime was less on nutrition and more on speed, convenience, and economy.

As prepared foods became more popular, meals as social occasions for families became rarer. Common meals required the participants to foresake personal preferences and time schedules to share the same foods, served in the same order, at the same time. But in an age of fast-food chains and ethnic food takeouts, it became practical for individual family members to eat different foods at the same time or to break the "one-cook-to-one-family" pattern. In the process, eating became desocialized. The two most communal meals, breakfast and dinner, no longer brought families together. By the end of the 1970s some 75 percent of American families did not share breakfast, and the average family sat down to dinner fewer than three times a week. The meal seldom lasted more than 20 minutes. As formal meals lost their importance, snacking became common. Individual family members ingested food in some fashion as often as 20 times a day. More and more often, people combined the consumption of food with activities other than meals: popcorn and movies, beer and TV sports, coffee and commuting.

As important as where and how people ate were nutritional trends. In earlier societies meals had consisted largely of a core complex carbohydrate (rice, bread, potatoes, or noodles), served up with a fringe complement of meats, vegetables, and fruits, and seasoned perhaps with a sauce. The core carbohydrate provided most nutrition, calories, and satisfaction; the fringe abetted the eating of the core. In modern Western society, including the United States, that pattern reversed over time. By the 1970s the bulk of

and hidden credit costs that plagued the poor. Many consumer organizations concentrated on a single issue, such as auto safety, smoking, insurance costs, or health care.

Diversity of goals broadened the movement's appeal but also fragmented support. Consumerism often overlapped with other causes, such as environmentalism, civil rights, and the women's movement. Nader was never able to establish consumerism as a mass political movement, finding supporters largely among those in the more affluent upper middle class. Furthermore, a weak economy created fears that more regulation would drive up consumer prices and thus add to inflation. Still,

Daily Lives

Once limited largely to hamburgers, ice cream, and pancakes, fast-food chains now allow Americans to bolt down indifferently synthesized varieties of ethnic and regional foods as well.

Americans' calories came from protein foods like meat and eggs and even more from foods rich in sugars and fats.

As preoccupation with slimness grew, the direct consumption of sugar declined.

But since most Americans ate more prepared and precooked foods, the indirect consumption of sugar and sweeteners increased. Food manufacturers discovered that sugars and dense fats like palm and coconut oil improved flavor, texture, taste, and shelf life. Thus they included sweeteners or fats in places where most people did not expect them: table salt, coatings for fried foods, peanut butter, and "health" foods like granola. By the late 1970s the average American consumed some 130 pounds of sugar and sweeteners per year and about 40 percent of all calories in the form of animal and vegetable fats. That led to a steady increase in obesity and diet-related heart diseases and cancers.

So eating patterns suggest some basic contradictions of the 1970s. While traditionalists called for family values, most families discarded the most traditional ritual, "breaking bread together." And as the American diet, like the population, became more diverse, the basic sources of food energy became less varied. Further, while medical technologies added to life expectancy, most doctors ignored dietary patterns responsible for life-threatening diseases. In this way, the patterns of daily life may be more revealing than the great events of the era.

the consumer movement had placed its agenda in the mainstream of political debate, and powerful consumer groups continued to represent the public interest.

Environmentalism

The Santa Barbara oil spill was hardly the first warning that Americans were abusing the environment. As early as 1962 marine biologist Rachel Carson had warned in *Silent Spring* of the environmental damage done by the pesticide DDT. Though chemical companies tried to discredit her as a woman and a scientist, 40 state legislatures passed laws restricting DDT. Certainly, no one with a sense of irony could help but marvel that the oil-polluted Cuyahoga River running through Cleveland, Ohio, had burst into flames. Smog, nuclear fallout, dangerous pesticides, and polluted rivers were the not-so-hidden costs of a society wedded to technology and unbridled economic growth.

Conservation versus preservation

In some ways, the environmental movement echoed the concerns and approaches of both the traditional conservation movement associated with Teddy Roosevelt, Gifford Pinchot, and Harold Ickes and the preservationist philosophies of John Muir and the Sierra Club. Conservationists had always stressed the idea of proper *use* of both renewable and nonrenewable resources. Efficient use would ensure the nation's future prosperity. Engineers, lawyers, and economists shaped the conservation agenda. Preservationists shared the Romantics' vision of humankind's spiritual links to nature. They sought largely to save unique wilderness areas like Yellowstone, Yosemite, and the Grand Canyon from *any* development and commercial exploitation.

Barry Commoner and ecology

In addition the new environmental movement drew heavily on the field of ecology. Since the early twentieth century, this biological science had demonstrated how closely life processes throughout nature depend on one another. Barry Commoner in his book *The Closing Circle* (1971) argued that modern society courted disaster by trying to "improve on nature." American farmers, for example, had shifted from animal manures to artificial fertilizers to increase farm productivity. But the change also raised costs, left soil sterile, and poisoned nearby water sources. After laundry detergents artificially "whitened" clothes, they created foamy scum in lakes and rivers while nourishing deadly algae blooms. Industry profited in the short run, Commoner argued, but in the long run the environment was going bankrupt.

By the 1970s, environmentalists had organized to implement what biologist René Dubos had called a "new social ethic." They brought a lawsuit to block the plan of a consortium of oil companies to build an 800-mile pipeline across Alaska's fragile wilderness. In addition, they successfully lobbied in Congress to defeat a bill authorizing support for the supersonic transport plane, the SST, whose high-altitude flights threatened to deplete the earth's vital ozone layer. Similarly, environmental groups fought a proposed jet airport that threatened South Florida's water supply and the ecology of Everglades National Park.

EPA established

Even President Nixon, normally a friend of business and real estate interests, responded to the call for more stringent environmental regulation. His administration banned the use of DDT (though not its sale abroad) and supported the National Environmental Policy Act of 1969. The act required environmental impact statements for most public projects and made the government responsible for representing the public interest. Nixon also established the Environmental Protection Agency to enforce the law. Echoing Barry Commoner, he announced, "We must learn not how to master nature but how to master ourselves, our institutions, and our technology."

Earth Day

By the spring of 1970 a healthy environment had become a widely popular cause. Senator Gaylord Nelson of Wisconsin suggested a national "Earth Day" to celebrate this new consciousness. On April 22, 1970, for at least a few hours pedestrians reclaimed downtown city streets, millions of schoolchildren planted trees and picked up litter, college students demonstrated, and Congress adjourned. The enthusiasm reflected the movement's dual appeal: it combined the rationalism of science with a religious vision of life's organic unity. But at least one member of Congress recognized the movement's more radical implications: "The Establishment sees this as a great big anti-litter campaign. Wait until they find out what it really means . . . to clean up our earth."

Earth Day did not signal a consensus on an environmental ethic. President Nixon, for one, was unwilling to restrict economic development. In his own Earth Day speech he supported the oil industry's Alaskan pipeline project, which threatened huge caribou herds and the Arctic's fragile ecology. Despite a long series of court challenges construction began in 1973. "We are not going to allow the environmental issue . . . to destroy the system," he announced in 1972.

Nixon's political instincts were shrewd. Conflict between social classes underlay the environmental debate. To those he courted for his silent majority, the issue came down to jobs versus the environment. "Out of work? Hungry? Eat an environmentalist," declared one bumper sticker. During the 1960s many middle Americans came to resent the veterans of the counterculture, civil rights, and antiwar movements who now found an outlet in environmental activism. But so long as pollution threatened, the environmental movement would not go away. Whether conservative hunters in Ducks Unlimited or mainstream nature lovers in the Wilderness Society or radical groups like Greenpeace, numerous groups continued the fight to protect the environment.

Because historians have often been sympathetic to the goals of environmentalists, they have tended to interpret the movement somewhat uncritically. Mainstream accounts often point out flattering continuities with the progressive movement, such as a reliance on the authority of science. Biology, for example, caused progressives to discard once popular theories of human exceptionalism and to see nature not as a simple warehouse of useful resources but as a series of interlinking systems. In similar ways, environmentalists have relied on ecological studies to provide a more sophisticated understanding of how those systems were interacting.

COUNTERPOINT

Interpreting the environmental movement

More recently some historians have become more critical of environmentalism. One confessed, "Where once I saw a movement founded in science, now I see a utopian political program." He compared modern environmentalism to the temperance crusade at the turn of the century. Although temperance advocates were divided over how to attack alcohol abuse, the more extreme factions successfully promoted prohibition and the Eighteenth Amendment. It was a utopian experiment that, in the end, was doomed to fail. Similarly, some environmental reformers have called for "global schemes of economic and political control," according to this point of view. Environmentalist Paul Ehrlich's popular book *The Population Bomb* (1968), for example, warned of the dire consequences of overpopulation. Ehrlich suggested that voluntary efforts at family planning were likely to fail and that the state might have to step in to control birthrates, especially in developing nations.

The parallel between the environmentalists and the temperance reformers is instructive. Progressivism, we have seen, displayed a mix of reform and control. Its middle- and upper-middle-class advocates worried about what the unruly masses might do without the guidance of "experts." A similar tension can be seen in the environmental movement, whose professional, white-collar advocates during the 1960s and 1970s paid scant attention to the environmental problems specific to poor urban residents. Only in the 1980s did a number of new organizations focus greater attention on the effects of hazardous industrial sites on lower-class neighborhoods or the danger of pesticides to migrant workers.

Feminism

Organized struggle for women's rights and equality in the United States began before the Civil War. Sustained political efforts had won women the vote in 1920. But the women's movement of the 1960s and 1970s began to push for equality in broader, deeper ways.

Writer Betty Friedan was one of the earliest to voice dissatisfaction with the cultural attitudes that flourished after World War II. Even though more women were entering the job market, the media routinely glorified housewives and homemakers, while discouraging those who aspired to independent careers. In *The Feminine Mystique* (1963) Friedan identified the "problem that has no name," a dispiriting boredom or emptiness in the midst of affluent lives. "Our culture does not permit women to accept or gratify their basic need to grow and fulfill their potentialities as human beings."

The Feminine Mystique gave new life to the women's rights movement. The Commission on the Status of Women appointed by President Kennedy proposed the 1963 Equal Pay Act and helped add gender to the forms of discrimination outlawed by the 1964 Civil Rights Act. Women had also assumed an important role in both the civil rights and antiwar movements. They accounted for half the students who went south for the "Freedom Summers" in 1964 and 1965. Living with violence, assuming heavy responsibilities, they discovered new freedom and self-confidence.

Movement women also realized that they were themselves victims of systematic discrimination. Male reformers often limited them to behind-the-scenes services such as cooking, laundry, and fulfilling sexual needs. Casey Hayden, a veteran of SDS and SNCC, confronted the male leadership. The "assumptions of male superiority are as widespread . . . and every bit as crippling to the woman as the assumptions of white superiority are to the Negro," she wrote. By 1966 activist women were less willing to see their grievances eclipsed by other political constituencies. Friedan joined a group of 24 women and 2 men who formed the National Organization for Women (NOW). The new feminists sought to force the Johnson administration to take bolder action to eliminate discrimination in such areas as jobs and pay. When feminists argued that "sexism" was not qualitatively different from racism, Johnson accepted the argument and in 1967 included women as well as African Americans, Hispanics, and other minorities as groups covered by federal affirmative action programs.

Broader social trends established a receptive climate for the feminist appeal. After 1957 the birthrate began a rapid decline; improved methods of contraception, such as the birth control pill, permitted more sexual freedom and smaller family size. By 1970 more than 40 percent of all women, an unprecedented number, were employed outside the home. Education also spurred the shift from home to the job market and increased consciousness of women's issues. Higher educational levels allowed women to enter an economy oriented increasingly to white-collar service industries rather than blue-collar manufacturing.

The Feminine Mystique [margin note]

National Organization for Women [margin note]

Ms. magazine, edited by feminist Gloria Steinem, gave the women's movement a means to reach a broader audience. The cover of the first issue, published in 1972, uses the image of a many-armed Hindu goddess to satirize the multiple roles of the modern housewife.

As much as women sought liberation from old restrictions, their new circumstances raised problems. Men did not readily share traditional family responsibilities with working women; obligations of a job were added to domestic routines. Because women often took part-time jobs or jobs treated as "female" work, they earned far less than men. And though greater sexual freedom implied more gender equality, the media continued to promote the image of women as sex objects.

By 1970 feminists had captured the media's attention. Fifty thousand women participated in NOW's Strike for Equality Parade down New York's Fifth Avenue. Television cameras zeroed in on signs with such slogans as "Don't Cook Dinner— Starve a Rat Today." Some newscasters reported that marchers had burned their bras to protest sexual stereotyping. "Bra burners" became the media's condescending phrase used to deny credibility to militant feminists like Kate Millett, whose *Sexual Politics* (1970) condemned a male-dominated "patriarchal" society.

Strike for equality

Equal Rights and Abortion

With its influence growing, the feminist movement sought to translate women's grievances into a political agenda. NOW members could agree in 1967 to a "Bill of Rights" that called for maternity leave for working mothers, federally supported day-care facilities, child care tax deductions, and equal education and job training. But they divided on two other issues: the passage of an Equal Rights Amendment to the Constitution and a repeal of all state antiabortion laws.

At first, support seemed strong for an Equal Rights Amendment that would forbid all discrimination on the basis of gender. By the 1970s public opinion polls showed that even a majority of American men were sympathetic to the idea. In 1972 both the House and the Senate passed the Equal Rights Amendment (ERA) virtually without opposition. Within a year 28 of the necessary 38 states had approved the ERA. It seemed only a matter of time before 10 more state legislatures would complete its ratification.

Many in the women's movement also applauded the Supreme Court's decision, in *Roe v. Wade* (1973), to strike down 46 state laws restricting a woman's access to abortion. In his opinion for the majority, Justice Harry Blackmun observed that a woman in the nineteenth century had "enjoyed a substantially broader right to terminate a pregnancy than she does in most states today." As legal abortion in the first three months of pregnancy became more readily available, the rate of maternal deaths from illegal operations, especially among minorities, declined.

Women divided   But the early success of the Equal Rights Amendment and the feminist triumph in *Roe v. Wade* masked underlying divisions among women's groups. *Roe v. Wade* triggered a sharp backlash from many Catholics, Protestant fundamentalists, and socially conservative women. Their opposition inspired a crusade for a "right to life" amendment to the Constitution. A similar conservative reaction breathed new life into the "STOP ERA" crusade of Phyllis Schlafly, an Illinois political organizer. Although Schlafly was a professional working woman herself, she believed that women should embrace their traditional role as homemakers subordinate to their husbands. "Every change [that the ERA] requires will deprive women of a right, benefit, or exemption that they now enjoy," she argued.

In the middle ground stood women (and a considerable number of men) who wanted to use the political system, rather than a constitutional amendment, to correct the most glaring inequalities between the sexes. Within a year after Congress passed the ERA, the National Women's Political Caucus conceded that the momentum to ratify was waning. Although Congress in 1979 extended the deadline for state legislatures to act for another three years, it became clear that the amendment would fail. Determined feminists vowed to continue the fight, but they, too, had discovered the limits of the era.

The Activist Legacy

To say that the organized environmental, consumer, and feminist movements lost ground after the early 1970s is not to say that they failed. Rather, each crusade fell short in its effort to forge a consensus. There would be no new ecological consciousness, no consumer-directed economy, and no absolute gender equality. Indeed, none of the movements could ever agree just what those ideas would mean in practice.

Even so, the United States was left after the early 1970s with an abiding concern for ecology, consumer rights, and the blatant and subtle forms of sexism. Advocates of reform had learned to use the media, to lobby politicians, to fight in the courts, and to organize. Older organizations like the National Audubon Society and League of Women Voters had been revitalized. New organizations like NOW and Friends of the Earth had become part of the political infrastructure. Within government the Environmental Protection Agency, the Federal Trade Commission, and other agencies had been given a mandate to enforce the court decisions and laws that reformers had won. In that way the advocates of reform breathed renewed life into the activist tradition of progressivism and the New Deal.

POLITICAL LIMITS: WATERGATE

To Richard Nixon, his 1972 reelection offered sweet revenge. In 49 of the 50 states he had defeated George McGovern, the candidate of liberal environmentalists, consumer advocates, feminists, and the youthful counterculture. Yet while Nixon sought to stem the liberal tide, he continued to concentrate federal power away from Congress and the Supreme Court and more in an "imperial presidency." That trend had been under way since the early twentieth century, but the cold war with its sense of ongoing crisis had accelerated the shift.

The President's Enemies

Encouraged by his victory, Nixon determined to use the power of his office even more broadly. The president and his advisers wanted to destroy the radical counterculture that they saw as a menace to American society. Members of his staff began compiling an "enemies list"—including everyone from CBS correspondent Daniel Schorr to actress and antiwar activist Jane Fonda. Some on the list were targeted for audits by the Internal Revenue Service or similar harassment.

    Then in June 1971 the *New York Times* published a secret, often highly critical military study of the Vietnam War, soon dubbed the Pentagon Papers. Nixon was so irate, he authorized his aide John Ehrlichman to organize a team known as "the plumbers" to find and plug security leaks. The government prosecuted Daniel Ellsberg, the disillusioned official who had leaked the Pentagon Papers. The plumbers also went outside the law: they illegally burglarized the office of Ellsberg's psychiatrist in hopes of finding personally damaging material. *The "plumbers"*

    When Congress passed a number of programs Nixon opposed, he simply refused to spend the appropriated money. Some members of Congress claimed that the practice, called impoundment, violated the president's constitutional duty to execute the laws of the land. By 1973 Nixon had used impoundment to cut some $15 billion out of more than 100 federal programs. The courts eventually ruled that impoundment was illegal. But the president continued his campaign to consolidate power and reshape the more liberal social policies of Congress to his own liking. *Impoundment*

    Convinced of the need for firm action in a crisis, suspicious of his "enemies," delighting in personal trappings of power—such traits made it easier for Richard Nixon to break or bend the rules in the service of what he believed was a good cause. In the end, his refusal to acknowledge the limits of power brought him down.

Break-In

Nixon's fall began with what seemed a minor event. In June 1972 burglars had entered the Democratic National Committee headquarters, located in Washington's plush Watergate apartment complex. The *Washington Post* assigned this routine story to a couple of cub reporters, Bob Woodward and Carl Bernstein. But the five burglars proved an unusual lot. They wore business suits, carried walkie-talkies as well as bugging devices and tear-gas guns, and had more than $2000 in crisp new hundred-dollar bills. One of the burglars had worked for the CIA. Another was carrying an address book whose phone numbers included that of a Howard Hunt at the "W. House." *Woodward and Bernstein*

Woodward and Bernstein sensed that this was no simple break-in. When Woodward called the mysterious "W. House" number, he discovered that Hunt was indeed a White House consultant. Nixon's press secretary dismissed the break-in as "a third rate burglary attempt" and warned that "certain elements may try to stretch this beyond what it is." In August, Nixon himself announced that White House counsel John Dean's own thorough investigation had concluded that "no one on the White House staff . . . was involved in this very bizarre incident. What really hurts in matters of this sort is not the fact that they occur," the president continued. "What really hurts is if you try to cover up."

Matters were not so easily settled, however. Woodward and Bernstein traced some of the burglars' money back to the Nixon reelection campaign, which had a secret "slush fund" to pay for projects to harass the Democrats. The dirty tricks included forged letters, false news leaks, and spying on Democratic campaign workers.

To the Oval Office

In January 1973 the five burglars plus former White House aides E. Howard Hunt, Jr., and G. Gordon Liddy went on trial before Judge John Sirica. Sirica, a no-nonsense judge tagged with the nickname "Maximum John," was not satisfied with the defen-

Under the leadership of North Carolina Senator Sam Ervin (left), the Senate Committee investigating the Watergate scandal attracted a large television audience. John Dean (right), the former White House legal counsel, provided the most damning testimony linking President Nixon to the cover-up. But only when the existence of secretly recorded White House tapes became known was there a chance to corroborate his account.

dants' guilty plea. He wanted to know whether anyone else had directed the burglars and why "these hundred dollar bills were floating around like coupons."

Facing a stiff jail sentence, one of the Watergate burglars cracked. He admitted that other government officials had been involved, that the defendants had been bribed to plead guilty, and that they had perjured themselves. The White House then announced on April 17 that all previous administration statements on the Watergate scandal had become "inoperative." Soon after, the president accepted the resignations of his two closest aides, H. R. Haldeman and John Ehrlichman. He also fired John Dean, his White House counsel, after Dean agreed to cooperate with prosecutors.

Over the summer of 1973 a string of administration officials testified at televised Senate hearings. Each witness took the trail of the burglary and its cover-up higher into White House circles. Attorney General John Mitchell, it became clear, had attended meetings in 1972 where Gordon Liddy outlined preliminary plans for a campaign of dirty tricks. Liddy and others had also worked as the plumbers under the direction of Ehrlichman in the White House. *Senate hearings*

Then White House counsel John Dean gave his testimony. Young, with a Boy Scout's face, Dean declared in a quiet monotone that the president had personally been involved in the cover-up as recently as April. The testimony stunned the nation. Still, it remained Dean's word against the president's—until Senate committee staff discovered, almost by chance, that since 1970 Nixon had been secretly recording all conversations and phone calls in the Oval Office. The reliability of Dean's testimony was no longer central, for the tapes could tell all.

Obtaining that evidence proved no easy task. In an effort to restore confidence in the White House, the president agreed to appoint a special prosecutor, Harvard law professor Archibald Cox, to investigate the new Watergate disclosures. When Cox subpoenaed the tapes, the president refused to turn them over, citing executive privilege and matters of national security.

As that battle raged and the astonished public wondered if matters could possibly get worse, they did. Evidence unrelated to Watergate revealed that Vice President Spiro Agnew had systematically solicited bribes, not just as governor of Maryland but while serving in Washington. To avoid jail, he agreed to resign the vice presidency in October and to plead no contest to a single charge of federal income tax evasion. Under provisions of the Twenty-Fifth Amendment, Nixon appointed Representative Gerald R. Ford of Michigan to replace Agnew. *Agnew resigns*

Meanwhile, when Special Prosecutor Cox demanded the tapes, the president offered to submit written summaries instead. Cox no longer had any reason to trust the president and rejected the offer. On Saturday night, October 20, Nixon fired Cox. Reaction to this "Saturday Night Massacre" was overwhelming. The president's own attorney general resigned in protest, 150,000 telegrams poured into Washington, and by the following Tuesday, 84 House members had sponsored 16 different bills of impeachment. The beleaguered president agreed to hand over the tapes. And he appointed Texas lawyer Leon Jaworski as a new special prosecutor. By April 1974, Jaworski's investigations led him to request additional tapes. Again the president refused, although he grudgingly supplied some 1200 pages of typed transcripts of the tapes. *"Saturday Night Massacre"*

Even the transcripts damaged the president's case. Littered with cynicism and profanity, they revealed Nixon talking with his counsel John Dean about how to "take care of the jackasses who are in jail." When Dean estimated it might take a million dollars to shut them up, Nixon replied, "We could get that. . . . You could get a million dollars. And you could get it in cash. I know where it could be gotten." When the matter of perjury came up, Nixon suggested a way out: "You can say, 'I don't remember.' You can say, 'I can't recall.'"

Even those devastating revelations did not produce the "smoking gun" demanded by the president's defenders. When Special Prosecutor Jaworski petitioned the Supreme Court to order the release of additional tapes, the Court in *United States v. Nixon* ruled unanimously in Jaworski's favor.

Resignation

The end came quickly. The House Judiciary Committee adopted three articles of impeachment, charging that Nixon had illegally obstructed justice, had abused his constitutional authority in improperly using federal agencies to harass citizens, and had hindered the committee's effort to investigate the cover-up.

The "smoking gun"

The tapes produced the smoking gun. Conversations with Haldeman on June 23, 1972, only a few days after the break-in, showed that Nixon knew the burglars were tied to the White House staff, knew that his attorney general had been involved, and knew that Mitchell had acted to limit an FBI investigation. Not willing to be the first president convicted in a Senate impeachment trial, Nixon resigned on August 8, 1974. The following day Gerald Ford became president. "The Constitution works," Ford told a relieved nation. "Our long national nightmare is over."

Had the system worked? In one sense, yes. The wheels of justice had turned, even if slowly. For the first time a president had been forced to leave office. Four cabinet officers, including Attorney General John Mitchell, the highest law officer in the nation, were convicted of crimes. Twenty-five Nixon aides eventually served prison terms ranging from 25 days to more than 4 years.

Fair Campaign Practices Act

Yet what would have happened if Woodward and Bernstein had been less resourceful? With the exception of the *Washington Post* and one or two other newspapers, the media had accepted the administration's cover-up. Later abuses within the executive branch, such as the "Irangate" scandals under Ronald Reagan, have demonstrated that the imperial powers of the presidency are still largely unchecked. The Fair Campaign Practices Act was adopted in 1974 in an attempt to enforce greater financial accountability on campaigns. Yet special interest groups have circumvented the law by funneling money through political action committees. The system works, as the Founding Fathers understood, only when citizens and public servants respect the limits of government power.

A FORD, NOT A LINCOLN

Gerald Ford inherited a presidential office almost crippled by the Watergate scandals. As the first unelected president, he had no popular mandate. He was little known outside Washington and his home district around Grand Rapids, Michigan.

Ford's success as the House minority leader came from personal popularity, political reliability, and party loyalty, qualities that suited a member of Congress better than an unelected president.

Ford respected the limits of government. His easy manner came as a relief after the mercurial styles of Johnson and Nixon. By all instincts a conservative, he was determined to continue Nixon's foreign policy of cautious détente and a domestic program of social and fiscal conservatism.

Kissinger and Foreign Policy

As Nixon's star fell, that of his Secretary of State and National Security Adviser Henry Kissinger rapidly rose. Kissinger cultivated reporters, who relished his witty quips, intellectual breadth, and willingness to leak stories to the press. Kissinger viewed himself as a realist, a man for whom order and stability were more important than principle. In that way he offended idealists on the political left and right. Quoting the German writer Goethe, Kissinger acknowledged, "If I had to choose between justice and disorder, on the one hand, and injustice and order on the other, I would always choose the latter."

Kissinger had struggled to prevent Vietnam and Watergate from eroding the president's power to conduct foreign policy. He believed Congress was too sensitive to public opinion and special-interest groups to pursue consistent long-term policies. But after Vietnam congressional leaders were eager to curtail presidential powers. The War Powers Act of 1973 required the president to consult Congress whenever *War Powers* possible before committing troops, to send an explanation for his actions within 2 *Act* days, and to withdraw any troops after 60 days unless Congress voted to retain them. Such limits often led Kissinger to take a covert approach, as he did in an attempt to quell political ferment in Chile.

In 1970 Chile ranked as one of South America's few viable democracies. When a coalition of Socialists, Communists, and radicals elected Salvador Allende Gossens as president, the Central Intelligence Agency determined that his victory created a danger to the United States. Kissinger pressed the CIA to bribe the Chilean Congress *Coup in Chile* and to promote a military coup against Allende. When those attempts failed, Kissinger resorted to economic warfare between the United States and the Allende government. By 1973 a conservative Chilean coalition with CIA backing had driven the Socialists from power, attacked the presidential palace, and killed Allende. The United States immediately recognized the new government, which over the next decade deteriorated into a brutally repressive dictatorship. Kissinger argued that the United States had the right to destroy this democracy because Communists themselves threatened an even longer-term dictatorship.

The Limits of American Influence

Kissinger understood that the United States no longer had the economic strength to dominate the affairs of the non-Communist bloc of nations even in areas like Central America and the Middle East, where it had once prevailed. Soaring inflation was a major source of weakness. In addition key American industries were crippled by inefficient production, products of poor quality, and high wages. They faced mounting

After having won a Nobel Peace Prize in 1973 for his role in ending the Vietnam War, Henry Kissinger (left) entered the Ford administration as something of a hero. But his efforts to improve relations with the Soviet Union by strengthening détente aroused the ire of the Republican right wing, while liberals accused Kissinger of being too secretive and friendly to dictators. Here, he briefs President Ford on a train, on the way to a 1974 summit meeting in Vladivostok in the Soviet Union.

competition from more efficient manufacturers in Europe and in nations along the Pacific rim (Japan, South Korea, Taiwan, Hong Kong, Singapore, and the Philippines). Reacting to these changes, American-based multinational corporations moved high-wage jobs overseas to take advantage of lower costs and cheap labor. The bellwether industry of the American economy, automobile manufacturing, steadily lost sales to Japan and Germany. Speaking on behalf of its blue-collar workers, the AFL–CIO complained that the loss of high-wage manufacturing jobs would create "a nation of hamburger stands, a country stripped of industrial capacity . . . a nation of citizens busily buying and selling cheeseburgers and root beer floats."

War in the Middle East soon made inflation at home even worse. On October 6, 1973, Syria and Egypt launched a devastating surprise attack against Israel, on the Jewish holy day of Yom Kippur. The Soviet Union airlifted supplies to the Arabs; the United States countered on October 15 by resupplying its Israeli allies while pressing the two sides to accept a cease-fire. The seven Arab members of the Organization of Petroleum Exporting Countries (OPEC) backed Egypt and Syria by imposing a boycott of oil sales to countries seen as friendly to Israel. The boycott from October 1973 until March 1974 staggered the economies of Western Europe and Japan, which imported 80 to 90 percent of their oil from the Middle East. As the price of oil soared, recession spread.

Yom Kippur War and the energy crisis

The United States depended on foreign oil far more than most Americans had appreciated. With just 7 percent of the world's population, the United States consumed about 30 percent of its energy. The nation's postwar prosperity came in large part from the use of cheap energy. In November 1973 President Nixon warned the nation, "We are heading toward the most acute shortage of energy since World War II." As the price of petroleum-based plastics soared, everything from records to raincoats cost more. In some places motorists hoping to buy a few gallons of gas waited for hours in lines miles long.

Shuttle Diplomacy

Kissinger believed that stability in the Middle East would ease pressures on the western economies. He wanted the Arab states to view the United States as neutral in their conflict with Israel. That would make them less likely to resort to oil blackmail. And as American prestige rose, Kissinger could reduce Soviet influence in the region. From January to April 1974 Kissinger intermittently engaged in "shuttle diplomacy" between Sadat's government in Cairo and the Israeli government of Golda Meir in Jerusalem. Flying back and forth, Kissinger persuaded Israel to withdraw its troops from the west bank of the Suez Canal. He also arranged a disengagement between Israel and Syria in the Golan Heights.

Still, Kissinger's whirlwind efforts could not stem the erosion of American power everywhere. While the secretary of state struggled to restore order to the Middle East, the American client government in South Vietnam was near defeat by North Vietnam. President Ford asked Congress for $1 billion in aid to Vietnam, Cambodia, and Laos. This time, Congress refused to spend money on a lost cause. As North Vietnamese forces marched into Saigon in April 1973, desperate South Vietnamese civilian and military leaders rushed to escape Communist retribution.

South Vietnam falls

Détente

Vietnam, Chile, and the Yom Kippur War indicated that the spirit of détente had not ended Soviet–American rivalry over the Third World. Seeking to ease tensions, Ford met with Soviet leader Leonid Brezhnev in November 1974. Since economic stagnation also dogged the Soviet Union, Brezhnev came to Vladivostok eager for more American trade; Ford and Kissinger wanted a limit on nuclear weapons that preserved the current American advantage. Though many issues could not be resolved, the two sides agreed in principle to a framework for a second SALT treaty.

Helsinki summit

A similar hope to extend détente brought Ford and Brezhnev together with European leaders at Helsinki, Finland, in August 1975. There they agreed to recognize the political boundaries that had divided Eastern and Western Europe since 1945. For the first time the United States sent an ambassador to East Germany. In return Brezhnev eased restrictions on the right of Soviet Jews to emigrate.

The erosion of American power, symbolized by Kissinger's overtures to the Soviet Union, dismayed Republican conservatives. The 1976 presidential hopeful Ronald Reagan criticized Ford and Kissinger for selling out American interests and weakening the nation's power. In an effort to subdue the critics, Ford in 1976 stripped Kissinger of his post as national security adviser.

The Limits of a Post-Watergate President

At home, Gerald Ford found himself facing a Congress determined to restrain an "imperial presidency." Since Ford himself had served in Congress for many years, he enjoyed a brief honeymoon with the legislative branch. But after only a month in office the new president granted Richard Nixon a pardon for any crimes committed during the Watergate affair. In trying to put Watergate in the past, Ford only managed to reopen the wounds. Pardon meant no prosecution, leaving charges against Nixon unanswered and crimes unpunished. The move was especially controversial because at the same time President Ford refused to provide any similar full pardon to draft resisters from the Vietnam War for any wrongdoing. Instead, the president offered them conditional amnesty after review by a government panel.

CIA and FBI abuses

If Ford was willing to forgive and forget presidential sins, Congress was not, especially after reports surfaced of misconduct by the nation's intelligence agencies. Senate investigations as well as a presidential commission appointed by Ford revealed that the CIA had routinely violated its charter by spying on American citizens at home. It had opened private mail, infiltrated domestic protest organizations—even conducted experiments on unwitting subjects using the hallucinogenic drug LSD. Abroad, the CIA had been involved in the assassination or attempted murder of foreign leaders in Cuba, Chile, South Vietnam, the Dominican Republic, and the Congo. The FBI had also used illegal means to infiltrate and disrupt domestic dissidents, including an attempt by J. Edgar Hoover to drive Martin Luther King to suicide. In an effort to bring the executive branch under control, the Senate created an oversight committee to monitor the intelligence agencies.

Fighting Inflation

By the time Ford gave Congress his first State of the Union message in January 1975, he faced the twin scourges of inflation and recession. Inflation had climbed to almost

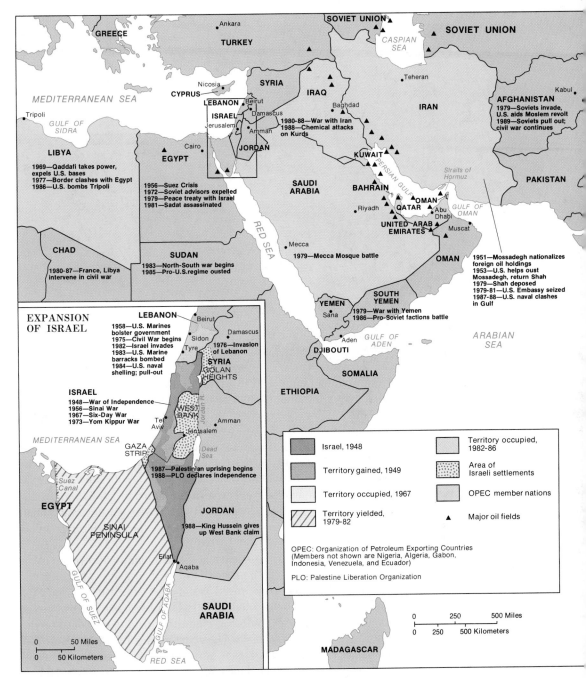

OIL AND CONFLICT IN THE MIDDLE EAST, 1948–1988

After World War II, the Middle East became a vital geopolitical region beset by big-power rivalry and complicated by local tribal, ethnic, and religious divisions and political instability. Much of the world's known oil reserves lie along the Persian Gulf. Proximity to the former Soviet Union and vital trade routes like the Suez Canal have defined the region's geographic importance. Revolutions in Iran and Afghanistan, intermittent warfare between Arabs and Jews, the unresolved questions of Israel's borders and a Palestinian homeland, the disintegration of Lebanon, and a long, bloody war between Iran and Iraq were among the conflicts that unsettled the region.

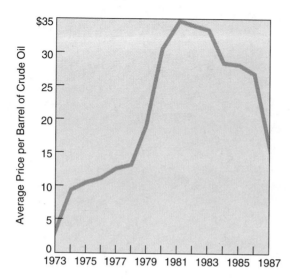

OPEC OIL PRICES, 1973–1987
Prices fell even further than the
chart shows after 1980 because
the dollar was worth much less
than in 1973. By the late 1980s
gasoline was actually cheaper than
in the 1950s.

14 percent, and unemployment exceeded 7 percent. At the heart of the economic crisis lay the problem of rising energy costs. By 1976 oil consumption had returned to
1973 levels, even though domestic oil production had fallen by more than 1 million
barrels. Before the Arab oil boycott, OPEC crude oil had been selling at around $2
to $3 a barrel. In a matter of months the price had tripled; by 1976 it was averaging
$12 a barrel. (And the worst was yet to come: prices would peak in 1981 at nearly $35
a barrel.)

Energy policy   Congress responded in 1975 by passing the Energy Policy and Conservation Act.
It authorized the Federal Energy Administration to order utilities to burn abundant
coal rather than expensive oil. In addition, the act created a strategic petroleum reserve as a hedge against future boycotts and ordered the auto industry to improve the
energy efficiency of the engines it produced. And as a final—but environmentally
dangerous—stopgap measure, the government encouraged the rapid development of
nuclear power plants.

The energy-driven recession struck hardest at the older industrial centers of the
Northeast and Upper Midwest, which imported most of their energy. Housing and
plants built in the days of cheap energy proved wasteful and inefficient. Nixon's and
Ford's fiscal conservatism hurt, too. Cutbacks in federal spending fell hardest on
major cities with shrinking tax bases, outmoded industries, and heavy social service
costs. The crisis for "rust belt" cities came to a head in October 1975 when New York
City announced that it faced bankruptcy. New York's plight reflected the wrenching
adjustments faced in an era of economic limits. A shrinking economic base could not
support high wages and expensive public services.

The Election of 1976

In the 1976 presidential campaign the greatest debates occurred within rather than
between the major parties. Ford's challenge came from former California governor,
movie actor, and television pitchman Ronald Reagan. Once a supporter of Franklin

In the 1976 election African American votes provided Jimmy Carter with the crucial margin for victory. Here Carter, a born-again Christian, worships with black leaders including (to his right) Coretta Scott King, widow of Martin Luther King, Jr.

Roosevelt, Reagan discovered true conservatism after his marriage to actress Nancy Davis. The polished Reagan won crowds with an uncompromising but amiable conservatism. "Under Messrs. Nixon and Ford this nation has become Number Two in military power," he would tell enthusiastic audiences. Ford barely eked out the nomination at the convention.

Jimmy Carter

Before 1976 few Democrats had ever heard of presidential hopeful James Earl (Jimmy) Carter. That allowed Carter, a peanut farmer and former governor of Georgia, to run as a Washington outsider. Carter managed to address controversial issues like abortion without offending large groups on either side. (He was "personally opposed to abortion" as a Christian but against a constitutional amendment overturning *Roe v. Wade*.) As a southerner and a "born-again" Christian he appealed to voters who had recently left the Democratic party.

Since both candidates rejected Great Society activism, party loyalty determined the outcome. Most voters (80 percent of Democrats and 90 percent of Republicans) backed their party's candidate, giving Carter 50.1 percent of the vote, a popular edge of almost 1.7 million. Carter's overwhelming margin among African Americans (90 percent) carried the South and offset Ford's margin among whites, especially in the western states, which all went Republican. Resounding Democratic majorities in Congress indicated more accurately than the presidential race how much the weak economy had hurt Ford's campaign.

JIMMY CARTER: RESTORING THE FAITH

Jimmy Carter looked to invest the White House with a new simplicity and directness. Rather than the usual Inauguration Day ride down Pennsylvania Avenue in the presidential limousine, the new president and his wife Rosalynn walked. Carter shunned the formal morning coat and tails for a business suit. But Congress, too, was determined to see that the executive branch would no longer be so imperial. Because the president and many of his staff were relative newcomers to Washington, Carter found it difficult to reach many of his goals.

The Search for Direction

Although the president possessed an ability to absorb tremendous amounts of information, too often he focused on details. His larger goals remained obscure. Carter's key appointments reflected this confusion. In foreign policy, a rivalry arose between National Security Adviser Zbigniew Brzezinski and Secretary of State Cyrus Vance. Brzezinski harbored the staunch cold warrior's preoccupation with containing the Communist menace. Vance believed negotiations with the Communist bloc were both possible and potentially profitable. Stronger economic ties would reduce the risk of superpower conflict. At different times, Carter gravitated in both directions.

The president found that it was no easy task to make government more efficient, responsive to the people, and ethical. His first push for efficiency—calling for the elimination of 19 expensive pork barrel water projects—angered many in Congress, including the leaders of his own party. They promptly threatened to bury his legislative program. Even the weather seemed to conspire against the Carter administration. The year 1977 brought one of the most severe winters in modern history, as heavy snows and fierce cold forced many schools and factories to close. Supplies of heating fuels dwindled, and prices shot up. Like Ford, Carter preferred voluntary restraint to mandatory rules for conserving energy and controlling fuel costs. The nation should adopt energy conservation measures as the "moral equivalent of war," he announced in April 1977.

Carter correctly sensed that conservation was the cheapest and most practical way to reduce dependence on foreign oil. But homilies about "helping our neighbors" did not sell the president's program. Most controversial were new taxes to discourage wasteful consumption. The American way, as domestic oil producers were quick to argue, was to produce more, not live with less. Americans were too wedded to gas-guzzling cars, air conditioners, inefficient electrical appliances, and warm houses to accept limits as long as fuel was available. Although Congress did agree to establish a cabinet-level Department of Energy, it rejected most of Carter's energy taxes and proposals to encourage solar energy alternatives.

Department of Energy

By 1978 what Carter had called the "moral equivalent of war" was sounding more like its acronym: MEOW. Renewed administration efforts resulted in a weak National Energy Act, which provided tax credits for installation of energy-saving equipment, encouraged utility conversion to coal, and allowed prices to rise for newly discovered natural gas. As a result, the nation was ill prepared for the dislocation in international oil markets that followed the 1978 revolution against the shah of Iran. Renewed shortages allowed OPEC to raise prices steeply again. Carter could only complain that such hikes were unfair while asking Americans to lower thermostats to 65 degrees, take only essential car trips, and "drive 55."

Three Mile Island

The nuclear power industry had long touted its reactors as the best alternative to buying foreign oil. But on March 28, 1979, a valve stuck in the cooling system of the Three Mile Island nuclear power plant near Harrisburg, Pennsylvania. A cloud of radioactive gas floated into the atmosphere, and for a time, officials worried that they

Oil shortages in the 1970s increased American dependence on nuclear power as an alternative energy source. The danger became evident in 1979 when an accident closed a nuclear power plant at Three Mile Island near Harrisburg, Pennsylvania. The large towers pictured on this *Time* Magazine cover are part of the cooling system in which the accident occurred. Huge construction costs, the unsolved problem of nuclear waste disposal, and safety issues soon soured many Americans on nuclear energy.

faced a "meltdown" of the reactor core. About a hundred thousand nearby residents fled their homes. The debate that followed revealed that public utilities had often constructed nuclear power plants before installing adequate safeguards or solving the problem of where to dispose of the nuclear radioactive wastes generated by the plant. Large construction cost overruns and concerns about safety inspired a growing antinuclear backlash. By the time of the accident at Three Mile Island, many energy experts believed that nuclear plants could be no more than a temporary response to the nation's long-term needs.

Three Mile Island gave President Carter another opportunity to press for his energy program, most of which Congress rejected. By May motorists once again faced long lines at the gas pumps. Not until spring 1980 did Congress pass a bill taxing some windfall profits of oil companies, regulating nuclear power more stringently, and establishing a solar-energy program. Carter had promoted sacrifice as a way to "seize control of our common destiny"; Congress preferred halfhearted measures that left America's energy future in OPEC's hands.

A Sick Economy

Rapid OPEC price hikes dislocated an economy built on cheap energy. Inflation shot from just below 6 percent in 1976 to almost 14 percent by 1979. Federal policies added to these inflationary pressures. Government subsidies to farmers continued to keep prices artificially high, as did laws protecting key industries like steel from foreign competition. As prices rose, wages could not keep pace. Workers took home more dollars, but inflation guaranteed that those dollars, in real terms, were worth less.

Within factories, the news was no better. If workers' real income was declining, so, too, was their productivity. It was difficult to produce efficiently when so many industrial plants had become outdated and union rules blocked innovation. Furthermore, wage contracts with built-in cost-of-living adjustments (COLAs) lowered the competitive standing of American industry in world markets. Plants in Japan and other Pacific Rim nations were newer, labor costs were lower, and the products turned out were often better.

The plight of the automobile industry reflected this economic malaise. Americans had turned in increasing numbers to higher-quality and more fuel-efficient Japanese cars. By 1978 Chrysler Corporation, the nation's tenth largest business enterprise, stood on the brink of bankruptcy unless the government provided a billion-dollar tax credit. The threat of massive unemployment persuaded Congress to guarantee a $1.5 billion loan. New financing and concessions from union workers brought Chrysler off the critical list. Still, disgruntled liberals and conservatives laughed when folk singer Tom Paxton announced,

The Chrysler bailout

> I'm changing my name to Chrysler.
> I'll be waiting in that great receiving line.
> So when they hand a billion grand out,
> I'll be standing with my hand out;
> Mister I'll get by.

"Hard choices," not stopgap loans, were needed to place the economy back on a competitive footing, the *Wall Street Journal* argued. That might mean higher taxes and cuts in popular programs like social security or subsidies to farmers. But Carter called only for voluntary restraints on prices and wages, while seeking to restore the strength of the dollar in international trade. Meanwhile, high interest rates struck hardest at American consumers addicted to installment and credit-card buying. Before Carter's economic remedies could work, OPEC began another round of oil price hikes that increased energy costs almost 60 percent. Interest rates shot up to almost 20 percent. Such high rates discouraged American consumers who bought on credit. With the Federal Reserve determined to keep interest rates high in order to dampen inflation, recession seemed to doom Carter's political future.

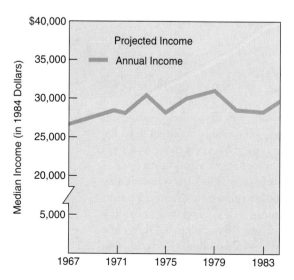

INCOME PROJECTIONS OF TWO-INCOME FAMILIES, 1967–1984
Had the economy maintained its earlier growth, family earnings (Projected Income line) would have continued to rise. In the age of limits, family income leveled off instead. It stayed relatively even, rather than falling, only because more wives entered the workforce. Wages for individual workers fell, when calculated in real dollars. [*Source:* Frank Levy, *Dollars and Dreams: The Changing American Income Distribution* (New York: Russell Sage Foundation, 1987), p. 204.]

Leadership, Not Hegemony

Presidents battered on the domestic front often find that a strong foreign policy can restore power and prestige. Carter approached foreign policy with a set of ambitious, yet reasonable, goals. Like Nixon and Kissinger, he accepted the fact that in a post-colonial world, American influence could not be heavy-handed. The United States should exert "leadership without hegemony," Carter announced. Unlike Nixon and Kissinger, Carter believed that a knee-jerk fear of Soviet power and disorder had led Americans to support too many right-wing dictators simply because they professed to be anti-Communist. Carter reasserted the nation's moral purpose by giving a higher priority to preserving human rights.

Human rights

Though this policy was often jeered at by foreign policy "realists," it did make a difference. At least one Argentinian Nobel Peace Prize winner, Adolfo Pérez Esquivel, claimed he owed his life to it. So did hundreds of others in countries like the Philippines, South Korea, Argentina, and Chile, where dissidents were routinely tortured and murdered. The Carter administration exerted economic pressure to promote more humane policies.

Debate over American influence in the Third World soon focused on the Panama Canal, long a symbol of American intervention in Latin America. Most Americans were under the impression that the United States owned the canal—or if it didn't, it at least deserved to. Senator S. I. Hayakawa of California spoke for defenders of the American imperial tradition when he argued, "It's ours. We stole it fair and square." In reality the United States held sovereignty over a 10-mile-wide strip called the Canal Zone and administered the canal under a perpetual lease. Since the 1960s Panamanians had resented, and sometimes rioted against, the American presence. Secretary of State Vance believed conciliation would reduce anti-American sentiment in the region. He convinced Carter in 1977 to sign treaties that would return the canal to Panama by 1999. The United States did reserve the right to defend and use the waterway.

From 1979 on, however, it was not Vance but Zbigniew Brzezinski who dominated the administration's foreign policy. Brzezinski was determined to reimpose a cold war framework, even in Latin America. Unrest troubled all the region's struggling nations, especially Nicaragua. Its dictator, Anastasio Somoza, had proved so venal and predatory that even the normally conservative propertied classes disliked him. Only the United States, at Brzezinski's urging, proved willing to support Somoza. With support from Nicaragua's business leaders, the Sandinistas toppled him. They then rejected American aid in favor of a nonaligned status and friendliness toward Communist Cuba.

Brzezinski and Central America

Revolution soon spread to neighboring El Salvador. The Carter administration also found it hard to make a case for the Salvadoran government, which had systematically murdered its own people as well as four American Catholic churchwomen. But hard-liners grew more alarmed when the Sandinistas began supplying the Salvadoran rebels. Worried about the spread of communism in Latin America, Carter agreed to assist El Salvador while encouraging the overthrow of the leftist government in Nicaragua.

The Wavering Spirit of Détente

The United States was not the only superpower with a flagging economy and problems in the Third World. The Soviet Union struggled with an aging leadership and an economy that produced guns but little butter. Even though the Russians led the world in oil production, income from rising oil prices was drained off by inefficient industries. Support for impoverished allies in Eastern Europe, Cuba, and Vietnam and attempts to extend Soviet influence in the Middle East and Africa proved costly.

Economic weakness made the Soviets receptive to greater cooperation with the United States. In that spirit President Carter and Soviet premier Leonid Brezhnev in 1977 issued a joint statement on a Middle East peace. But domestic opposition to any Soviet role as a peacemaker in the Middle East was immediate and powerful. Carter quickly rendered his understanding with Brezhnev inoperative. The Soviets then renewed arms shipments to Israel's archenemy, Syria. And in that troubled environment, *Reviving the China card* Zbigniew Brzezinski flew off to Beijing to revive "the China card"—Kissinger's old hope of playing the two communist superpowers against each other. The United States extended formal recognition to China in 1979, and trade doubled within a year.

For the Russians the China card was a blow to détente. A potential Japanese–Chinese–American alliance threatened their Asian border. In an attempt to save détente Brezhnev met Carter at Vienna in 1979. Following through on the summit with *SALT II* President Ford, their talks produced an arms control treaty–SALT II—to limit nuclear launchers and missiles with multiple warheads (MIRVs). But neither the Americans nor the Soviets would agree to scrap key weapons systems. Conservative critics saw the SALT agreements as another example of the bankruptcy of détente. Nuclear "parity" (an equal balance of weapons on the American and Soviet sides) was to them yet another insulting symbol of declining American power. They successfully blocked ratification of the treaty in the Senate.

With détente under attack Carter turned to Brzezinski and his hard-line approach to the Soviet Union. Confrontation and a military buildup replaced the Vance policy of negotiation and accommodation. The president expanded the defense budget, built American bases in the Persian Gulf region, and sent aid to anti-Communist dictators whatever their record on human rights. The Soviet Union responded with similar hostility.

The Middle East: Hope and Hostages

Before World War I, the unstable Balkans had proved to be the spark setting off a larger conflict. For the superpowers in the 1970s and 1980s, the Middle East promised a similar threat. Oil and the Soviets' nearby southern border gave the area its geopolitical importance. Religious, tribal, national, and ethnic rivalries created chronic instability, dramatized by the wars between Israel and its Arab neighbors in 1948, 1956, 1967, and 1973. The United States had to balance its strong ties to oil-rich Saudi Arabia with its commitment to the survival of Israel.

Preservation of the peace was one key to American policy. As a result, Americans were greatly encouraged when President Anwar Sadat of Egypt made an unprecedented trip to Israel to meet with Prime Minister Menachem Begin. To encourage *Camp David Accords* the peace process, Carter invited Begin and Sadat to Camp David in September 1978. For 13 days the talks waxed hot and cold, often breaking into argument and heated debate. When the marathon session ended, Carter had succeeded in helping the two long-standing rivals reach agreement. The 30-year state of war between Israel and Egypt finally ended. Israel accommodated Egypt by agreeing to withdraw from the Sinai Peninsula, which it had occupied since 1967. Carter compensated

It was at Camp David, in private talks sponsored by President Jimmy Carter, that Egyptian President Anwar el-Sadat (left) and Israeli Prime Minister Menachem Begin (right) hammered out a "Framework for Peace in the Middle East" as a first step toward ending decades of war and mistrust. For their efforts Begin and Sadat shared the Nobel Peace Prize of 1978, but the prize justifiably might have gone to Carter.

Israel by offering $3 billion in military aid. Begin and Sadat shared a Nobel Peace Prize that might just as fairly have gone to Carter for his critical role in pushing the two leaders to compromise.

The shah of Iran, with his American-equipped military forces, was another key to American hopes for stability in the Middle East. A strong Iran, after all, blocked Soviet access to the Persian Gulf and its oil. But in the autumn of 1978, the shah's regime was challenged by Iranian Islamic fundamentalists. They objected to the Western influences flooding their country, especially the tens of thousands of American advisers. Brzezinski urged Carter to support the shah with troops if necessary; Vance recommended meetings with the revolutionary leaders, distance from the shah, and military restraint.

The Iranian revolution

Carter waffled between the two approaches. He encouraged the shah to use force but refused any American participation. When the shah's regime collapsed in February 1979, fundamentalists established an Islamic republic led by a religious leader, the Ayatollah Ruhollah Khomeini. The new government was particularly outraged when Carter admitted the ailing shah to the United States for medical treatment. In November student revolutionaries stormed the American embassy in Teheran, occupying it and taking 53 Americans hostage. In the face of this insult the United States seemed helpless to act. Would Muslim Shiite fundamentalists spread their revolution to neighboring Arab states? Worse yet, would the Soviets prey upon a weakened Iran?

The Soviet Union invades Afghanistan

In fact, the Soviets were equally worried that religious zeal might spread to their own restless minorities, especially to Muslims within their borders. In December 1979 Leonid Brezhnev ordered Soviet troops into neighboring Afghanistan to subdue anti-Communist Muslim guerrillas. President Carter condemned the invasion, but the actions he took to protest it were largely symbolic, especially the decision to withdraw the American team from the 1980 Olympic games in Moscow. And he announced a Carter Doctrine: the United States would intervene unilaterally if the Soviet Union threatened American interests in the Persian Gulf.

A President Held Hostage

The spectacle of "America held hostage" shown on nightly newscasts dimmed Carter's hopes for another term. It did not help that Iran's turmoil led to another round of OPEC price hikes and new inflationary pressures.

Once again Carter faced a test of his leadership. Even more than the 53 Americans in Teheran, Jimmy Carter had been taken hostage by events there. His ratings in national polls sank to record lows (77 percent negative). Carter responded by reviving the cold war rhetoric of the 1950s and accelerating the development of nuclear weapons. But where the CIA in 1953 had successfully overthrown an Iranian government, an airborne rescue mission launched in 1980 ended in disaster. Eight marines died when two helicopters and a plane collided in Iran's central desert. Cyrus Vance, a lonely voice of moderation, finally resigned.

Crisis of confidence

By 1980 the United States was mired in what Carter himself described as "a crisis of confidence." Visions of Vietnam, Central America, and the Middle East produced a nightmare of waning American power. Economic dislocations at home revived fears of a depression. None of these problems had begun with Jimmy Carter. The inflationary cycle and declining American productivity had their roots in the Vietnam era. And ironically, America's declining influence abroad reflected long-term success in bringing economic growth to Europe and the Pacific rim.

In that sense, Carter's failure was largely symbolic. But the uneasiness of the late 1970s reflected a widespread disillusionment with liberal social programs and even with pragmatic "engineers" like Carter. Had the government become a drag on the American dream? Tom Wolfe's "Me Generation" seemed to be rejecting Carter's appeals to sacrifice. It turned instead to promoters of self-help therapy, fundamentalist defenders of the faith, and staunch conservatives who promised both spiritual and material renewal for the 1980s.

CHAPTER SUMMARY

As the radical groups of the 1960s fragmented, three movements continued to seek reform. Consumer advocates like Ralph Nader wanted a national effort to eliminate dangerous products and devious business practices. Environmentalists pressed for action to fight pollution and clean up the earth. Feminists came to focus their efforts to achieve equality for women on an Equal Rights Amendment. Although all three groups fell short of their broader goals, they each achieved major successes.

President Richard Nixon also faced the realities of an era of limits. He battled Congress on many fronts, using impoundment to cut programs he opposed. Privately his staff made war against groups and individuals Nixon saw as "enemies." Their efforts led to a break-in at the Watergate complex. Despite efforts to cover up White House involvement, reporters Bob Woodward and Carl Bernstein, the Senate Committee chaired by Sam Ervin, and Special Prosecutors Archibald Cox and Leon Jaworski eventually produced the "smoking gun" that led to a threat of impeachment and forced Nixon to resign.

President Gerald Ford and Henry Kissinger pursued a foreign policy that acknowledged the decline of American power. Kissinger especially sought stability in the Middle East, where war between Israel and its Arab neighbors led to an oil boycott and an energy crisis. Attempts to ease tensions through détente with the Soviet Union only provoked the opposition of conservative Republicans. Ford, whose popularity suffered for his pardon of Richard Nixon, fought an unsuccessful battle against inflation. Defeating Ford in 1976, Jimmy Carter sought to bring honesty and simplicity to the White House and a human rights agenda to foreign policy. Entrenched interests blocked him from cutting wasteful programs. Inflation and a new energy crisis crippled the economy. In foreign policy Carter negotiated the eventual return of the Panama Canal to Panama and brought Israel's Menachim Begin and Egypt's Anwar Sadat together at Camp David to hammer out peace accords. When Iranian revolutionaries held American diplomats hostage, Carter became trapped by the crisis. A Soviet invasion of Afghanistan added to the region's instability. By 1980 crisis in the Middle East and a sick economy mired the nation in what Carter himself described as a "crisis of confidence."

ADDITIONAL READING

Of late, historians have become engaged in the debate over environmental reform. The story began with Barry Commoner, *The Closing Circle* (1971), which introduced many Americans to the core ideas of ecology. Donald Worster, *Nature's Economy* (3d ed., 1994) offers a rich history of the ideas informing environmentalism, while Samuel Hays, *Beauty, Health, and Permanence* (1987) surveys the postwar era. Charles Rubin, *The Green Crusade* (1994) challenges the methods and assumptions of some of the movement's central figures, including Rachel Carson and Commoner. Robert Gottlieb provides another critical perspective in *Forcing the Spring: The Transformation of the American Environmental Movement* (1996).

On consumerism see Robert Mayer, *The Consumer Movement* (1989), and on feminism see Sara Evans, *Personal Politics: The Roots of Women's Liberation in the Civil Rights Movement and New Left* (1980) or Jane Maysbridge, *Why We Lost ERA* (1986). Among the books on Watergate are J. Anthony Lukas, *Nightmare* (2d ed., 1988), Stanley Kutler, *The Wars of Watergate* (1990), and Stephen Ambrose, *Nixon: The Triumph of a Politician* (1989). Kissinger's own memoirs, *The White House Years* (1979) and *Years of Upheaval* (1982), contrast with the more critical study by Walter Isaacson, *Kissinger* (1992). For foreign policy during the Carter years, see Gaddis Smith, *Morality, Reason, and Power* (1986). Peter Carroll offers a survey of the 1970s in *It Seemed Like Nothing Happened* (1982). For a fuller list of readings, see the Bibliography.

SIGNIFICANT EVENTS

1962 — Rachel Carson's *Silent Spring* published

1965 — Ralph Nader's *Unsafe at Any Speed* published

1966 — National Traffic and Motor Vehicle Safety Act; NOW established

1969 — *Apollo 11* moon mission; Santa Barbara oil spill; National Environmental Policy Act

1970 — First Earth Day; Environmental Protection Agency created; NOW organizes Strike for Equality

1971 — Barry Commoner's *The Closing Circle* published; Pentagon Papers published

1972 — Congress passes Equal Rights Amendment; Woodward and Bernstein investigate Watergate burglary

1973 — Watergate burglars convicted; *Roe v. Wade;* Haldeman and Ehrlichman resign; Ervin Committee hearings; Archibald Cox appointed special prosecutor; Spiro Agnew resigns; Saturday Night Massacre; War Powers Act; OPEC oil boycott triggers U.S. recession

1974 — *United States v. Nixon;* House adopts articles of impeachment; Nixon resigns; Ford becomes president; Fair Campaign Practices Act; Kissinger Arab–Israeli "shuttle" diplomacy; Ford–Brezhnev meeting at Vladivostok; Ford pardons Nixon; Church Committee exposes CIA and FBI abuses

1975 — Thieu government falls in South Vietnam; Helsinki Summit; Energy Policy and Conservation Act; New York City faces bankruptcy

1976 — Carter defeats Ford

1977 — Department of Energy established; Panama Canal treaties

1978 — Revolution in Iran; Chrysler bailout; Camp David meetings on the Middle East

1979 — Three Mile Island crisis; energy crisis; United States recognizes Peoples' Republic of China; SALT II agreement; Iran hostage crisis; Soviet Union invades Afghanistan

1980 — Inflation and recession hurt economy; Carter adopts sanctions against the Soviet Union; U.S. hostage mission fails

1982 — Ratification of ERA fails

NICHOLAS G BROOKS · TANNER M BROWN Jr · ROBERT
· GARDNER DORSEY · FRANK M DUNSMORE Jr · HARRY E FARMER · ROGER W F
· RAUL GARCIA Jr · STEVEN L GREEN · WILLIE J HAYES · ROGER W KVERNES
· KENNETH H McLENDON · BARNEY M SMITH · DALLAS R SNODGRASS · EDDIE LEE SPI
· DENNIS E DEBNER · ROBERT C WRIGHT · GARY L DAVIS · RICHARD T DERO
WILBERT WALTON · ROBERT J FATICA · CYE GARY · RONALD A JENNIGES · CLAUDE A KNIGH
· CHARLES R OLSON · GENE J OLSON · KENNETH E PERRY · MATTHEW P ROCH
· LAWRENCE R WARE · HERMAN H BAN · THOMAS L BLANKS · PAUL B BLUNT Jr
· JOHNNY LEE HAWKINS · DAVID S JONES · REGINALD W LINDSEY · RICHARD M MAHON
· PETER PULASKI Jr · FRANCIS J SNEE Jr · BERNARD A SOWDER · JAMES S VANO
· JAMES R WHITMORE · JIMMY A WHITSON · RICHARD C WILLIAMS · WALDO A WILLIAMS
· JAMES F BRENNAN Jr · HUBERT E BRINSON · ROBERT W BURNES · GARY W ERICSON
· PATRICK HOP SUNG HU · MAX D KERSEY · LARRY N LAMB · DONALD E LEW
· JOEL M MAGRASS · TOM A METCAL · ARLES T MOORE · EUGENIO ORTIZ

The Contested Ground
of Collective Memory

Perhaps the nation's most cherished commemorative space lies along the mall in Washington,
D.C. On the south side of its grassy boulevards
the Smithsonian Institution holds room after
room of artifacts from the nation's past. Across the
way is the National Gallery of Art. And the mall's
western end is dominated by memorials to
Washington and Lincoln. If anywhere, the collective memories of the republic are on display here.

As the mall makes clear, a culture defines itself by the history it elevates in public places. Such
markers are hardly limited to Washington. Town
squares boast statues; post office murals portray
the deeds of forebears; even sports arenas hang
honored jerseys from the rafters. As scholars of
commemoration point out, all societies find visible
ways to affirm their collective values.

For the historian, the Washington mall presents one singular puzzle. Today the most frequently visited and publically acclaimed site also
happens to be the least epic. Unlike Washington's
555-foot obelisk, this memorial does not soar.
Unlike Lincoln's Greek temple, there are no

columns evoking classical grandeur. In fact, at
any reasonable distance the memorial cannot
even be seen. It is simply a V of highly polished
black granite incised into the ground—a V whose
wide arms, each 247 feet long, converge 10 feet
below the surface of the boulevard. This is the
Vietnam Veterans Memorial. Amid considerable
controversy, the memorial was built in the wake
of what was not only the nation's longest war but
a divisive one that the United States lost.

Why, in a mall that takes special care to burnish the nation's proudest memories, has this
memorial moved so many Americans?

That question intrigues historians, who have
been drawn in recent years to the study of collective memories. Their interest is not the traditional concern over whether this or that recollection is accurate. At issue instead is the *process* of
memory-making: "how people together searched
for common memories to meet present needs,
how they first recognized such a memory and
then agreed, disagreed, or negotiated over its
meaning. . . ." At first, the definition seems un-

Maya Lin

necessarily complex. But the process of forging a collective memory *is* complex and can take years or even decades.

For example, most people today take for granted commemorative statues honoring two sworn enemies, Ulysses S. Grant and Robert E. Lee. Yet the tradition that allows us to venerate *both* generals is possible only because of a collective memory that emphasizes the heroism of all Americans who fought. That memory began to take form in the 1880s, when northern and southern veterans started to hold joint reunions.

But for African Americans of that era, Confederate leaders like Lee symbolized slavery, making this emerging collective memory difficult to endorse. Frederick Douglass, a former slave and prominent Republican, warned that monuments honoring Lee would only "reawaken the confederacy." He argued that emancipation, not martial valor, deserved the most emphasis. To that end, he supported efforts of African Americans to erect the Freedman's Memorial Monument in Washington. The nation may "shut its eyes to the past . . ." he warned, "but the colored people of this country are bound to keep the past in lively memory till justice shall be done them." Even today the collective memories of the Civil War remain contested ground.

The same can be said for the war in Vietnam. By the 1980s the vast majority of Americans, whether they had opposed or defended American involvement in Vietnam, agreed that the war had been a mistake. How then would a nation used to celebrating success find a way to remember failure?

Vietnam veteran Jan Scruggs took an approach that was consciously apolitical. Rather than celebrate the war, Scruggs proposed a monument honoring the veterans themselves. From 1959 to 1975 over three million American men and women had served in Vietnam, of whom 75,000 returned home permanently disabled. Yet many felt their sacrifices had been lost amid the debate over the war. To promote reconciliation Congress in 1980 set aside a two-acre site on the mall, almost equidistant from the Washington and Lincoln memorials.

In the competition to select a design for the memorial over 1400 entries were submitted, all judged anonymously. The panel's unanimous choice came as a surprise: the entry of Maya Ying Lin, a Chinese American student at Yale University's School of Arts and Architecture. The idea for the design had occurred to her when she visited the projected site. "I thought about what death is . . . ," Lin recalled, "a sharp pain that lessens with time, but can never heal over. A scar. Take a knife and cut open the earth, and with time the grass would heal it."

Despite his personal dislike of the statue (because the slave was kneeling rather than proudly standing) Frederick Douglass helped dedicate the Freedmen's Memorial Monument to Abraham Lincoln in 1876. Douglass believed emancipation was central to remembering the Civil War.

To view the monument a visitor descends a gentle incline. Because there are no steps, the handicapped have easy access. The memorial's polished black granite sets a somber tone, yet the open sky and reflection of the sun dispel any sense that this is a tomb or mausoleum. A person beginning the descent at first sees only a few names carved into the granite, but as the wall deepens, so does the procession of names. Altogether, 70 panels enumerate over 54,000 Americans who died in Vietnam. As Lin insisted, "you cannot ever forget that war is not just a victory or loss. It's really about individual lives."

The design immediately roused controversy. Some critics resented Lin's relative youth, her ethnicity, and the fact that she was a woman.

Others objected to the memorial's abstract and decidedly unheroic character. Lin had rejected a traditional approach in favor of a more feminine and nonwestern sensibility. "I didn't set out to conquer the earth, or to overpower it the way Western man usually does," she acknowledged. Ross Perot, a major financial supporter and later a presidential candidate, called the memorial a slap in the face to veterans. Others less politely described it as a public urinal. To them the black granite seemed a mark of shame and the descent below ground level an admission of wrongdoing.

So loud were these objections that in 1982 the secretary of the interior refused a construction permit until the memorial's sponsors agreed to add to the site a realistic sculpture by Frederick Hart (below). Hart, one of Lin's most outspoken critics, created three soldiers with an American flag, installed in 1984. This provoked a female Vietnam veteran, Diane Carlson Evans, to lead a campaign for one additional monument, to honor the women of Vietnam. This third sculptural piece (also realistic) portrays three nurses, one holding a wounded soldier.

Who captured the contested terrain of Vietnam commemoration? For the historian, the evidence lies in the crowds who flock to Maya Lin's memorial. Often, visitors seek out the name of someone they knew and make a rubbing of it to take with them. So many have left flowers, flags, personal objects, along with messages and poems, that the Park Service has created a museum for them. The messages vary wildly, from the hopeful and resolute to the sorrowful and disgusted:

Thank you for having the courage to fight . . .
You never would listen to anyone and you finally screwed up . . .
I am sorry Frankie, I know we left you, I hope you did not suffer too much . . .

Given such diverse reactions, Lin's choice of polished black marble was inspired. "The point," she said, "is to see yourself reflected in the names." The reflective marble and the wall's abstract design allow people to find their own meaning in the memorial.

As for the historian who passes by—even a century from now—the site will always bear witness to Vietnam's contested ground. As on a real battlefield, the opposing sides stand arrayed: heroic, realistic figures on one side, challenged and ultimately outflanked by the wide embrace of that silent granite V. In aesthetic terms, traditional realism wars with abstract modernity. But that contrast only reflects a deeper cultural divide over the way we choose to remember war. Maya Lin's commemoration would have been unthinkable in 1946, when a triumphant United States was emerging as one of the world's superpowers. In an age of limits, when even superpowers falter, the gleam of black marble reflects faces less certain that martial valor can guarantee a nation's immortality.

BIBLIOGRAPHY. A useful introduction to the concept of collective memory is *Memory and American History* (1990), edited by David Thelen. Suzanne Vromen summarizes the controversy over Maya Lin's memorial in "The Vietnam Veterans Memorial, Washington, D.C.: Commemorating Ambivalence," *Focaal*, 25 (1995), 95–102. For more detail see Jan C. Scruggs and Joel T. Swerdlow, *To Heal a Nation* (1985), Brent Ashabranner, *Always to Remember: The Story of the Vietnam Veterans Memorial* (1988), and James Mayo's more interpretive *War Memorials as Political Landscapes* (1988). For Maya Ying Lin, see Peter Tauber, "Monument Maker," *New York Times Sunday Magazine*, February 24, 1991: 49–55 and a fine documentary film, "Maya Lin: A Strong, Clear Vision" (1995).

33

A Nation Still Divisible

n the early 1970s San Diego city officials looked out at a downtown that was growing seedier each year as stores and shoppers fled to the suburban malls that ringed the city. Nor was San Diego an exception. Across the nation many once-thriving downtown retail centers became virtual ghost towns at the close of the business day. But San Diego found a way to bounce back. The city launched a $3 billion redevelopment plan calling for a convention center, a marina, hotels, and apartment complexes.

At the core of the redevelopment plan was Horton Plaza, a mall with the look of an Italian hill town. Stores with stucco facades fronted twisting pedestrian thoroughfares where Renaissance arches lured customers to upscale stores like Banana Republic, to jewelers, and to sporting goods shops. Jugglers and clowns wandered the streets, while guitarists serenaded passersby. Horton Plaza soon ranked just behind the zoo and Sea World as San Diego's prime tourist attraction. By 1986 it drew more than 12 million shoppers and tourists.

For all its extravagance, Horton Plaza was hardly an innovation. The first enclosed mall, Southdale Center, had been completed nearly 20 years earlier in Edina, Minnesota, near Minneapolis. Edina had good reason for enclosure: with chilling winters and 100 days a year of rain, shopping conditions were hardly ideal for outdoor strollers. The mall's planners had approached Victor Gruen, an architect seeking ways to reclaim urban downtowns from what he saw as the tyranny of the automobile. Gruen contrasted the pedestrian-dominated streets and fountain-filled squares of European villages with the acres of sterile parking lots surrounding suburban shopping centers. As he noted in his manifesto, *The Tired Heart of Our Cities*, automobiles added pollution and congestion to the urban environment. Southdale provided an alternative: a climate-controlled marketplace where shoppers could browse or get a bite to eat at a café without dodging cars or inhaling exhaust fumes.

At first retailers feared that customers who couldn't drive by their stores or park in front wouldn't stop and shop. Success dispelled those fears. By 1985, when Horton Plaza opened, Southdale had expanded to a three-level, 144-store complex, spreading over 1.1 million square feet. Nationwide, there were more shopping centers (25,000) than either school districts or hospitals. Some 2800 were enclosed, like Southdale.

With their soaring atriums, lavish food courts, and splashing fountains malls became the cathedrals of American material culture. Shopping on Sunday rivaled churchgoing as the weekly family ritual. Where American youth culture centered on the high school in the 1950s and on college campuses in the 1960s, in the 1970s and

Bringing a touch of Disney World–style magic to urban redevelopment, San Diego succeeded in luring shoppers back to its downtown retail center with Horton Plaza, a replica of an Italian hill town.

1980s it gravitated toward mall fast-food stores and video amusement arcades. For single men and women, malls became a place to find a date. Older people in search of moderate exercise discovered that the controlled climate was ideal for "mall walking." Malls even had their counterculture—"mall rats" who hung out and survived by shoplifting.

Malls as symbols of an age

The new cathedrals of consumption served as an appropriate symbol of a society that in the 1980s turned from protests and crusades to more private paths of spiritual fulfillment. Confronted by an age of limits, some turned to evangelical religion, with its emphasis on the conversion of "born-again" individuals. Others extolled the virtues of the traditional family and lauded private charity and volunteerism as an alternative to the activist social policies of a modern welfare state. Along less orthodox paths, the "human potential movement" focused on techniques like yoga, transcendental meditation, and "bioenergetics" to bring inner fulfillment.

So it was not surprising, perhaps, that in 1980 Ronald Reagan chose to evoke Puritan John Winthrop's seventeenth-century vision of an American "city on a hill"—that city Winthrop hoped would inspire the rest of the world. For conservatives, the image carried strong religious overtones. The Puritans, after all, sought to create a Christian commonwealth that was both well ordered and moral. Reagan's vision updated the Puritans', embracing nineteenth-century ideals of "manifest destiny" as well. (America should "stand tall," he insisted, as the world's number one military power.) And Reagan affirmed the laissez-faire ideals of the late nineteenth century, encouraging citizens to promote the public good through the pursuit of private wealth. "Government is not the solution to our problem," he asserted. "Government is the problem."

Critics contended that Reagan could no more succeed with his revolution than John Winthrop had been able to impose his Puritan utopia on a disorderly world. History, they argued, had shown that private enterprise was unable to prevent or regulate the environmental damage caused by acid rain, oil spills, or toxic waste dumps. Furthermore, a severely limited federal government would prove unable to cope with declining schools, urban violence, or the AIDS epidemic. To liberals the Reagan agenda amounted to a flight from public responsibility into a fantasy world no more authentic than the Italian hill town nestled in downtown San Diego. John Winthrop's austere vision risked being transformed into a city on a hill with climate control, where the proprietors of Muzak-filled walkways banished all problems beyond the gates of the parking lots.

Throughout the 1980s and 1990s Americans gravitated between the born-again vision of the conservative revolution and more secular, centrist politics. The election in 1992 of activist Bill Clinton seemed to halt the revolution, but Republican conservatives led by Representative Newt Gingrich captured the House and Senate in 1994. As the successors of Ronald Reagan zealously promoted their campaign for a born-again America, the nation returned in 1996 to the moderate path Bill Clinton had chosen.

THE CONSERVATIVE REBELLION

In 1964 conservative candidate Barry Goldwater had proclaimed on billboards across America: "In Your Heart You Know He's Right." Beneath one of the billboards an unknown Democratic wag unfurled his own banner: "Yes—Extreme Right." In 1964 most citizens voted with the wag, perceiving Goldwater's platform as too conservative, too extreme, too dangerous for the times.

By 1980 rising prices, energy shortages, and similar economic uncertainties fed a growing resistance to a liberal agenda. Hard-pressed workers resented increased competition from minorities, especially those supported by affirmative action quotas and government programs. Citizens resisted the demands for higher taxes to support social welfare spending. The traditional family, too, seemed under siege as divorce rates and births to single mothers soared. Increasingly the political agenda was determined by those who wanted to restore a strong family, traditional religious values, patriotism, and limited government.

Born Again

At one center of the conservative rebellion was the call for a revival of religion. That call came most insistently from white Protestant evangelicals. Fundamentalist Protestants had since the 1920s increasingly separated themselves from the older, more liberal denominations. In the decades after World War II their membership grew dramatically—anywhere from 400 to 700 percent, compared with less than 90 percent for mainline denominations. By the 1980s they had become a significant third force in Christian America, after Roman Catholics and traditional Protestants.

During the late 1970s and the 1980s conservatives increasingly spoke out against abortion and in favor of the right to life for unborn children. Adopting the tactics of protest and civil disobedience once common to radicals in the 1960s, they clash here with pro-choice demonstrators outside Faneuil Hall in Boston.

The Reverend Jerry Falwell's Moral Majority attempted to apply religious convictions in the political arena. Falwell actively supported Ronald Reagan's military buildup and political candidates who shared the Moral Majority's social agenda, including opposition to abortion.

The election of Jimmy Carter, himself a born-again Christian, reflected their new-found visibility.

Like fundamentalists of the 1920s, the evangelicals of the 1980s resisted the trend toward more secular values, especially in education. They pressed states and the federal government to adopt a "school prayer" amendment allowing officially sanctioned prayer in classrooms. They urged the teaching of "Creationism" as an acceptable alternative to Darwinian evolution. Frustrated with public schools, they created private Christian academies to insulate their children from the influence of "secular humanism." They condemned modernist notions of a materially determined world in which all truths were relative and in which circumstances rather than absolute moral precepts determined ethical behavior.

Evangelicals

Although evangelicals denounced the modern media as secular agencies, they eagerly used broadcast technology to sell their message. Cable and satellite broadcasting allowed "televangelists" to reach national audiences. The Reverend Pat Robertson, the son of a Virginia politician, introduced his "700 Club" over the Christian Broadcast Network from Virginia Beach, Virginia. His success inspired a "700 Club" regular, Jim Bakker, to launch a spin-off program called the "Praise the Lord Club"—PTL for short. Within a few years PTL had the largest audience of any daily show in the world. The content was Pentecostal in background: gospel singing, fervent sermons, faith healing, and speaking in tongues. The format, however, imitated that of sophisticated network "talk shows," including Bakker's Christian monologue, testimonials from celebrity guests, and musical entertainment.

It was the Reverend Jerry Falwell who first made the step from religious to political activism. In 1979 he formed the Moral Majority, Inc., an organization to attract campaign contributions and examine candidates around the country on issues important to Christians. America, Falwell proclaimed, possessed "more God-fearing citizens per capita than any other nation on earth." Using computerized mailing lists to identify donors and target audiences, the Moral Majority sent out more than a billion pieces of mail during the 1980 election.

The Catholic Conscience

American Catholics faced their own decisions about the lines between religion and politics. In the 1960s a social activist movement had arisen out of the church council known as Vatican II (1962–1965). Convened by Pope John XXIII and continued by his successor, Pope Paul VI, the council sought to revitalize the church and to reappraise its role in the modern world. The reforms of Vatican II reduced the amount of Latin in the mass, invited greater participation by ordinary church members, and encouraged closer ties to other Christians and to Jews.

Disturbed by these currents, Catholic conservatives found support for their views when the magnetic John Paul II assumed the papacy in 1979. Pope John Paul reined in the modern trends inspired by Vatican II. He ruled against a wider role for women in the church hierarchy and stiffened church policy against birth control. That put him at odds with a majority of American Catholics. The American church also faced a crisis as fewer young men and women chose celibate lives as priests and nuns.

Pope John Paul II

Though conservative Catholics and Protestant evangelicals were sometimes wary of one another, they shared certain views. Both groups lobbied for the government to provide federal aid to parochial schools and fundamentalist academies. But it was the issue of abortion that attracted the greatest mutual support. Pope John Paul reaffirmed the church's teaching that all life begins at conception and that abortion amounts to murder of the unborn. Evangelicals, long suspicious of the power of secular technology and science, attacked abortion as another instance in which science had upset the natural moral order of life.

COUNTERPOINT

It is not an easy task to pinpoint the underlying elements that unite the conservative rebellion. Some analysts, focusing on the movement's political leadership, have viewed matters cynically. Ronald Reagan, George Bush, and their ilk are simply members of the established and wealthy business elite who have tapped the resentments of ordinary people in order to attain power and provide others of their class with tax and regulatory relief. In this view, "hot button" issues like school prayer, abortion, and gun control can be used "as a means to ignite people who do not normally support Republicans," in the words of one conservative political adviser. Such an analysis emphasizes the differences within the conservative movement. On the one side, libertarians and free-enterprising businessmen would keep the government out of regulating public morals as well as out of regulating the economy. On the other side cultural conservatives urge the government to take an active role in restoring morality.

Defining the new conservatism

Other historians concede the existence of this split but stress the cultural roots that unite both sides: the rejection of a liberalism that brought activism to government and a secular perspective to society at large. Conservatives of all stripes, one can argue, hold up the values of a purer past, one free, in their view, from government interference and invigorated by a clear moral order. In 1955, when William F. Buckley, Jr., began his conservative magazine, *National Review,* he proclaimed it his job to "stand athwart History and shout Stop!" In the eyes of some historians, it is this fixation on a past—an idealized one, at that—which unites the new right. "People became conservatives," suggested one analyst, "when they experienced 'the horrible feeling' that a society they took for granted might suddenly cease to exist."

The Media as Battleground

Both evangelists and political conservatives viewed the mass media as an establishment that was liberal in its politics and permissive in its tolerance of sex and violence. Because film and television had come to occupy such a prominent place in American life, they became a battleground where conservatives and liberals clashed.

Topical sitcoms

By the late 1960s the film industry had left behind the strict standards of its Production Code, established in 1930 to police Hollywood's morals. Soft-core pornography with simulated sex and partial nudity had been exceeded in the 1970s by hard-core films. Even the traditionally inoffensive television programming became more topical. In 1971 producer Norman Lear introduced *All in the Family*, whose main character, Archie Bunker, was a rough-hewn blue-collar father. Archie treated his addlepated wife like a doormat, struggled to understand his modestly rebellious daughter, and shouted endless insults at his Polish American son-in-law. Americans were supposed to laugh at Archie's outrageous references to "Hebes," "Spics," and "Commie crapola," but many in the audience were not laughing. Some minority leaders charged that by making Archie lovable, the show legitimized the very prejudices it seemed to attack.

M*A*S*H, a popular television series launched in 1972, was more clearly liberal in its sympathies. Although set in a medical unit during the Korean War, its real inspiration was Vietnam and the growing disillusionment with the war. *M*A*S*H* twitted bureaucracy, authority, pretense, bigotry, and snobbery. As newer liberal sensitivities emerged during the decade, the show adapted as well. "Hawkeye" Pierce and his fellow army doctors began as hard-drinking, womanizing foes of war and army life. Ten years later they still hated the army and war, but Hawkeye had become more vulnerable and respectful to women, while "Hotlips" Hoolihan was transformed from an overly patriotic military martinet into Margaret Hoolihan, a career woman struggling for respect. For conservatives, antiauthoritarian shows like *M*A*S*H* demonstrated how deeply liberal values pervaded American life. That same bias, they believed, affected newspaper and television reporters. For their part, feminists and minority groups complained that television portrayed them as stereotypes, when it bothered to portray them at all.

Perhaps inevitably, the wars for the soul of prime time spilled into the political arena. Norman Lear, Archie Bunker's creator, went on to form People for the American Way, a lobbying group that campaigned for more diversity in American life and attempted to counteract pressure groups like the Moral Majority. Conservatives, looking to make a stronger political impact, in 1980 embraced an amiable former movie actor who had long preached their gospel.

The Election of 1980

Jimmy Carter might be born again, but Ronald Reagan spoke the language of true conservatism. "I think there is a hunger in this land for a spiritual revival, a return to a belief in moral absolutes," he told his followers. Such a commitment to fundamentalist articles of faith was more important than the fact that Reagan actually had no church affiliation and seldom attended services.

The defection of many southern evangelical Protestants to the Republicans was just one of Jimmy Carter's problems. His rapid military buildup and cutbacks in social programs offended liberals, while rampant inflation and a weak economy alienated blue-collar voters. Preoccupied with the Iran hostage crisis, the president refrained from vigorous campaigning. When undecided voters saw Reagan as a

The Reagan landslide

candidate with the power to lead, the race turned into a landslide. Equally impressive, the Republicans won their first majority in the Senate since 1954. Reagan had splintered the New Deal Democratic coalition. Although his support was greatest

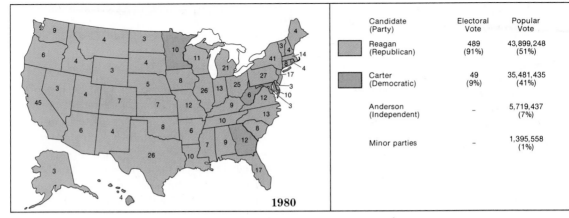

Candidate (Party)	Electoral Vote	Popular Vote
Reagan (Republican)	489 (91%)	43,899,248 (51%)
Carter (Democratic)	49 (9%)	35,481,435 (41%)
Anderson (Independent)	–	5,719,437 (7%)
Minor parties	–	1,395,558 (1%)

ELECTION OF 1980

among those who were over 45, white, and earning more than $50,000 a year, he made striking gains among union workers, southern white Protestants, Catholics, and Jews. For the next decade and beyond, conservatives would dominate the terms of debate in public policy.

PRIME TIME WITH RONALD REAGAN

Ronald Reagan brought the bright lights of Hollywood to Washington. His managers staged one of the most extravagant inaugurations in the nation's history. Nancy Reagan became the most fashion-conscious first lady since Jackie Kennedy, while the new administration made the conspicuous display of wealth once again a sign of success and power.

The Great Communicator

Ronald Reagan came to Washington with a simple message. "It is time to reawaken the industrial giant, to get government back within its means, and to lighten our punitive tax burden," he announced on inauguration day. A strong national defense and a determined effort to revive the cold war crusade would reestablish the United States as the number one power in the world. Commentators began referring to the president as "the great communicator" because of his mastery of television and radio.

The Reagan style

Reagan's skill as an actor obscured contradictions between his rhetoric and reality. With his jaunty wave and jutting jaw, he projected physical vitality and the charismatic good looks of John Kennedy. Yet at age 69, he was the oldest president to take office, and none since Calvin Coolidge slept as soundly or as much. Reagan had begun his political life as a New Deal Democrat, but over the next two decades he moved increasingly to the right. By the 1950s he had become an ardent anti-Communist, earning a reputation among conservatives as an engaging after-dinner

Ronald Reagan's image as a plainspoken westerner helped build his reputation as "the great communicator."

speaker and corporate spokesperson for General Electric. In 1966 he began two terms as governor of California with a promise to pare down government programs and balance budgets. In fact, spending jumped sharply during his term in office. Similarly, he continued to champion family values, although he was divorced and estranged from some of his children.

Similar inconsistencies marked Reagan's leadership as president. Outsiders applauded his "hands-off" style: less management, not more, was what the nation needed after a succession of activist presidents from Kennedy to Carter. Reagan set the tone and direction, letting his advisers take care of the details. On the other hand, many within the administration, like Secretary of the Treasury Donald Regan, were shocked to find the new president remarkably ignorant of and uninterested in important matters of policy. "The Presidential mind was not cluttered with facts," Regan lamented.

Nancy Reagan (aided by an astrologer) often dictated the president's schedule, helped select his advisers, and sometimes even determined the major issues the president addressed. Yet the public believed that the president was firmly in charge and, until the Iran arms scandal in 1986, consistently approved his conduct. His capacity for deflecting responsibility for mistakes earned him a reputation as the "Teflon president," since no criticism seemed to stick.

Reagan's fortune

In addition, Reagan was blessed by remarkable fortune: a number of events beyond his control broke in his favor. The deaths of three aging Soviet leaders, beginning with Leonid Brezhnev in 1982, compounded that country's economic weakness and reduced Russian influence abroad. Members of the OPEC oil cartel quarreled among themselves, exceeded production quotas, and thus forced oil prices lower. That removed a major inflationary pressure on the American economy. The day Reagan took office, the Iranians released the American hostages, relieving the president of his first major foreign policy crisis. And when a would-be assassin shot the president in the chest on March 30, 1981, the wound was not life-threatening. His courage in the face of death impressed even his critics.

The Reagan Agenda

Reagan set out with two major goals: to reestablish the prestige of a presidency battered by Watergate and to weaken big government. His budget would become an instrument to reduce bureaucracy and to undermine activist federal agencies in the areas of civil rights, environmental and consumer protection, poverty programs, urban renewal, transportation, the arts, and education. In essence, Reagan wanted to return government to the size and responsibility it possessed in the 1950s, before the reforms of Kennedy and Johnson.

Supply-side economics

At the heart of the Reagan revolution was a commitment to supply-side economics, a program that in many ways resembled the trickle-down economic theories of the Harding–Coolidge era. Supply-side theorists argued that high taxes and government regulation stifled enterprising businesses and economic expansion. The key to revival lay in a large tax cut—a politically popular though economically controversial proposal. Such a cut threatened to reduce revenues and increase an already large deficit. Not so, argued supply-side economist Arthur Laffer. The economy would be so stimulated that tax revenues would actually rise, even though the tax rate was cut.

The president's second target for action was inflation, the "silent thief" that had burdened the economy during the Ford–Carter years. Reagan resisted certain traditional cures for inflation: tight money, high interest rates, and wage and price controls. He preferred two approaches unpopular with Democrats: higher unemployment and weakened unions to reduce labor costs.

Lower public spending, a favorite Republican remedy, might have seemed one likely method of reducing inflation. But the third element of Reagan's agenda was a sharp rise in military outlays: a total of $1.5 trillion to be spent over five years. The American military would gain the strength to act unilaterally anywhere in the world to beat back communist threats. This was a remarkably expansive goal: Presidents Nixon, Ford, and Carter had all looked to scale back American commitments, either through détente or by shifting burdens to allies in Western Europe. Reagan recognized no such limits. And rather than emphasize either nuclear defense or conventional weapons, Defense Secretary Caspar Weinberger lobbied Congress for both.

Military buildup

The Reagan Revolution in Practice

The administration soon found an opportunity to "hang tough" against unions when air traffic controllers went on strike, claiming that understaffing and long working hours threatened air safety. But because the controllers were civil service employees, the strike was technically illegal. Without addressing the merits of the controllers' complaints, Reagan simply fired them for violating their contract. The defeat of the air controllers signaled a broader attack on unions. When a recession enveloped the nation, major corporations wrung substantial concessions on wages and work rules. Organized labor witnessed a steady decline in membership and political power.

The president's war against government regulation took special aim at environmental rules. Conservatives, especially in the West, dismissed the environmental lobby as "nature lovers." Preservation of wild lands restricted mining, cattle grazing, farming, and real estate development—all powerful western industries. Reagan appointed westerner James Watt, an outspoken champion of this "sagebrush rebellion," to head the Interior Department. Watt, in turn, devoted himself to opening federal lands for private development, including lumbering and offshore oil drilling. A series of rash statements forced Watt to resign in 1983, but the administration continued to oppose most efforts to regulate or protect the environment. The president even refused to accept the conclusion of scientists that the smoke from coal-fired power plants in the Ohio valley was sending destructive acid rain over the lakes and forests of eastern Canada and the United States.

Environmental controversies

Most important, by the summer of 1981 Reagan had pushed his supply-side legislation through Congress. The Economic Recovery Tax Act (ERTA) provided a 25 percent across-the-board reduction for all taxpayers. The president hailed it, along with recently passed budget cuts, as an antidote to "big government's" addiction to spending and a stimulus to the economy. Opponents pointed out that an "equal" cut of 25 percent for all taxpayers left far more dollars in the hands of the wealthy.

Tax cuts

The Supply-Side Scorecard

The impact of Reagan's supply-side economics was mixed. By 1982 a recession had pushed unemployment above 10 percent. The Federal Reserve Board's tight money policies and high interest rates deepened the recession. But 1983 saw the beginning of an economic expansion that was to last through Reagan's presidency, thanks in part to increased federal spending and lowered interest rates. Then, too, falling energy costs and improved industrial productivity also contributed to renewed prosperity. While many workers earned less per hour, the flow of women into the labor market kept family incomes from falling too much.

Even so, the Reagan tax cut was one of a series of policy changes that brought about a substantial transfer of wealth from poor and lower-middle-class workers to the upper middle classes and the rich. For the wealthiest Americans, the 1980s were the best of times. The top 1 percent commanded a greater share of the nation's wealth (37 percent) than at any other time since 1929. Their earnings averaged about $560,000 per year as opposed to $20,000 or less for the bottom 40 percent. What counterculture hippies were to the 1960s, high-salaried "yuppies" (young, upwardly mobile professionals) were to the 1980s.

The transfer of wealth

On the surface, the buoyant job market seemed to signal a more general prosperity as well. By the end of Reagan's term, more than 14.5 million jobs had been created for Americans. Yet these jobs were spread unevenly by region, class, and gender. More than 2 million were in finance, insurance, real estate, and law, all services used by the wealthy, not the poor. In highly paid "Wall Street" jobs—those involving financial services—more than 70 percent went to white males, only 2 percent to African Americans. New employment for women was concentrated in the areas of health, education, social services, and government, where approximately 3 million jobs opened, most dependent on government support. New jobs for the poor (more than 3 million) were largely restricted to minimum wage, part-time, dead-end jobs in hotels, fast-food restaurants, and retail stores.

Because Reaganomics preached the virtues of free markets and free trade, the administration did little to discourage high-wage blue-collar jobs from flowing to cheap labor markets in Mexico and Asia. Furthermore, Reagan aimed the sharpest edge of his budget ax at programs for the poor: food stamps, Aid to Families with Dependent Children, Medicaid, school lunches, and housing assistance. The programs trimmed back least were middle-class entitlements like social security and Medicare. Those programs affected Americans over 65, who, as social activist Michael Harrington observed, as a general class "are not now, and for a long time have not been, poor."

As more income flowed toward the wealthy and as jobs were lost to overseas competitors, the percentage of Americans below the poverty level rose from 11.7 percent in 1980 to 15 percent by 1982. There the level remained through the Bush administration. Reagan's successful war on inflation, which dropped to less than 2 percent by 1986, contributed to a rise in unemployment. Even during the recovery, the figure dropped below 6 percent of the workforce only in the months before the 1988 election. (By contrast, the highest rate under Jimmy Carter was 5.9 percent.) Thus the Reagan boom was an uneven one, despite continued economic expansion.

litical skin. But the Iran–Contra congressional hearings, held during the summer of 1987, left the role of President Reagan unexplained. Admiral John Poindexter, his national security adviser, testified that he had kept Reagan in ignorance "so that I could insulate him from the decision and provide some future deniability for the president if it ever leaked out. . . . On this whole issue, you know, the buck stops here, with me." In that way, Iran–Contra revealed a presidency out of control. An unelected segment within the government had taken upon itself the power to pursue its own policies beyond legal channels.

As one analyst noted, Reagan's ideological approach to foreign policy tended to give his aides an "absolute certainty of their own rightness." Since they were operating with "pure hearts," they found it all too easy to justify working with "dirty hands." In doing so, however, they subverted the constitutional system of checks and balances.

From Cold War to *Glasnost*

Since few in Congress wanted to impeach a genial president, the hearings came to a sputtering end. Reagan's popularity returned, in part because of substantial improvement in Soviet–American relations. By the 1980s the Soviet Union was far weaker than American experts, including the CIA, had ever recognized. The Soviet economy

Soviet Premier Mikhail Gorbachev (right) used his summits with Ronald Reagan to reduce Soviet–American tensions, although the spirit of *glasnost* did not ease the skirmishes between his wife, Raisa, and Nancy Reagan, who waged a quiet war over fashion and ideology. Gorbachev came to rival Reagan as a "great communicator," with many Americans applauding his efforts to reform Soviet society and to slow the arms race.

stagnated; the Communist party was mired in corruption. The war in Afghanistan had become a Russian Vietnam. By accelerating the arms race, Reagan placed additional pressure on the Russians.

Mikhail Gorbachev

In 1985 a fresh spirit entered the Kremlin. Unlike the aged leaders who preceded him, Mikhail Gorbachev was young and saw the need for reform within the Soviet Union. Gorbachev's fundamental restructuring, or *perestroika,* set about improving relations with the United States. He reduced military commitments and adopted a policy of openness (*glasnost*) about problems in the Soviet Union. In October, the two leaders held their second summit in Reykjavík, Iceland. Gorbachev dangled the possibility of abolishing all nuclear weapons. Reagan seemed receptive to the idea, apparently unaware that if both sides eliminated all nuclear weapons, Soviet conventional forces would far outnumber NATO troops in Europe. In the end, the president refused to sacrifice his Star Wars system for so radical a proposal.

Despite the immediate impasse, negotiations continued after the summit. In December 1987 Reagan traveled to Moscow, where he signed the Intermediate Nuclear Force treaty, which eliminated an entire class of nuclear missiles with ranges of 600 to 3400 miles. Both sides agreed to allow on-site inspections of missile bases and the facilities where missiles would be destroyed.

The Election of 1988

Thus as the election of 1988 approached, the president could claim credit for improved relations with the Soviet Union. Loyalty to Ronald Reagan made Vice President George Bush the Republican heir apparent. Bush appealed most to party professionals, white Protestants, and the affluent middle class that had benefited from Reaganomics.

The Democratic challenger, Governor Michael Dukakis of Massachusetts, tried to call attention to weaknesses in the American economy. An alarming number of savings and loan institutions had failed, and Dukakis recognized that poor and even many middle-class Americans had lost ground during the 1980s. But Bush put the lackluster Dukakis on the defensive. With the economy reasonably robust, Bush won by a comfortable margin, taking 54 percent of the popular vote. The Reagan agenda remained on track.

AN END TO THE COLD WAR

President George Herbert Walker Bush was born to both privilege and politics. The son of a Connecticut senator, he attended an exclusive boarding school and then the ivy-league Yale University. That background made him part of the East Coast establishment often scorned by more populist Republicans. Yet once the oil business lured Bush to Texas, he moved to the right, becoming a Goldwater Republican when he ran for the Senate in 1964. Although he once supported Planned Parenthood and a woman's right to abortion, Bush eventually adopted the conservative right-to-life position. In truth, foreign policy interested him far more than domestic politics. But in

Justice Clarence Thomas survived a bitter Senate battle during his Supreme Court confirmation hearings. Here, he is sworn in by Chief Justice William Rehnquist as Thomas's wife and President George Bush and Barbara Bush look on. Thomas's conservative views on abortion and affirmative action were later confirmed by the votes he cast as a justice.

federal circuit court had gone so far as to claim (in *Hopwood v. State of Texas et. al.*) that race could not be a factor in college admissions.

Court decisions on abortion and religion in public schools demonstrated a similar desire to set limits on the established precedents. *Planned Parenthood v. Casey* (1992) upheld a woman's constitutional right to an abortion, but it also allowed states to place new restrictions on the procedure. Other Court decisions let stand laws restricting abortions and even abortion counseling by clinics or hospitals receiving federal funds. And while the Court affirmed that religious teachings or prayer could have no official status in public schools, it allowed students to engage in voluntary prayer as well as to form religious clubs meeting after school.

Disillusionment and Anger

Ronald Reagan had given a sunny face to conservatism. He had assured voters that if taxes were cut, the economy would revive and deficits would fall. He promised that if "big government" could be scaled back, there would be a new "morning in America." Yet after a decade of conservative leadership, with its hands-off approach, the deficit had ballooned and state and local governments were larger than ever. A growing number of Americans felt that the institutions of government had come seriously off track. Indeed, such cynicism was fueled by the attacks on big government by Reagan and Bush.

Daily Lives

PUBLIC AND PRIVATE SPACE

Life in the Underclass

During the 1880s Jacob Riis "discovered" a class of people he described as invisible. They were "individuals who have lost connection with home life, or never had any, or whose homes had ceased to be sufficiently separated, decent, and desirable to afford what are regarded as ordinary wholesome influences of home and family." A century later investigators for the Chicago *Tribune* discovered in American cities "a lost society dwelling in enclaves of despair and chaos that infect and threaten the communities at large." This ghetto world, of dilapidated housing, poverty, and despair, was home to as many as 5 million Americans. Yet while many of its spaces and avenues were public, it, too, was invisible, except when its private behavior became so violent or criminal that the news forced the broad middle class to pay attention.

Like Riis the *Tribune* reporters portrayed this urban blight through the story of individual lives. Dorothy Sands was one. In 1957 Dorothy, her mother, Ora Streeter, and the rest of her family lived in a one-room shack in rural Mississippi. Conditions there had improved little since the days of Reconstruction. The shack had neither electricity nor indoor plumbing. Ora finally decided to escape the South, her job, and her abusive husband. She took six small children to Chicago, where her mother lived. For her daughter Dorothy, "It was something like going to a new world."

Life in Chicago imposed disappointments and cruelties of its own. For several years Streeter struggled to make a decent life for her family. Arthritis finally prevented her from working and forced her to sign up for public assistance. Dorothy, the oldest child, assumed responsibility for the household. With what little time she had for herself, she reached the ninth grade. But at age 15 her dream of a nursing career ended when she discovered she was pregnant. In 1965, after her mother died, Dorothy began a relationship with Carra Little, a man who promised he could not get her pregnant. Within a year, Dorothy had her second child. She asked the doctors to sterilize her, but they refused. And the children kept arriving—four more of them. "When you are young, you don't really think about the future," Dorothy recalled. "You say, 'If I have another baby, then I have another child.'"

After Little died suddenly of a heart attack in 1976, the household disintegrated. Dorothy's oldest daughter, Barbara, like her mother and grandmother before her, became pregnant at age 15. By 1985 Dorothy was suffering from chronic depression and considered suicide. She was a 37-year-old grandmother living in a three-room apartment with five of her six children, her daughter LaWanda's new boyfriend, two grandchildren ages 7 and 2, and two teenage runaways. In 20 years, the family had never been off welfare and no one in

A series of longer-term crises contributed to this sense of disillusionment. One
S&L crisis of the most threatening centered on the nation's savings and loan institutions. By the end of the decade these thrifts were failing at the highest rate since the Great Depression. To help increase bank profits, the Reagan administration and Congress had agreed to cut back federal regulations. That allowed savings and loan institutions to invest their funds more speculatively. Few depositors noticed or cared, since their

In the cramped and decaying spaces of this inner-city apartment, a hot plate doubles as a clothes dryer.

every time they turned on the water, plaster fell into the tub. The building manager reneged on his promise to make repairs. So the children just stood over the sink and washed their clothes by hand. An electrical wire attached to a bare bulb doubled as a clothesline. Only Dorothy had a room of her own. The girls slept on canvas cots in one room, while the boys took turns between cots and a mattress on the living room floor. Meals were irregular affairs, since money was scarce and no one liked to cook. For two weeks each month the family splurged on eggs for breakfast and Spam for dinner. More often they got by on hot dogs, rice, and beans.

Of the neighborhood's 61,500 people, more than half received some form of welfare. People lucky enough to find work quickly moved away. The social agencies that existed to help people in trouble had largely stopped trying. One government official described "a caste of people almost totally dependent on the state, with little hope of breaking free." By the late 1980s murders, drive-by shootings, and guns in school had become commonplace. For the rest of the American people, more fortunate in their circumstances, a question persisted: how could the problems of the largely invisible underclass be solved before the violence and desperation of their private world overwhelmed the city streets? As rioting swept Los Angeles in the spring of 1992 Americans had to wonder if that question had gone too long unanswered.

the household had held a regular job. Only one of her children attended school other than briefly.

With public assistance money Dorothy could afford only rooms in a dilapidated three-story building on Chicago's West Side. Each evening people pried open the building's front door to do "crack" or drink 100 percent grain alcohol. Sometime in 1985 the family stopped bathing because

money was insured by the Federal Savings and Loan Insurance Corporation. The government, however, had to pay depositors if these banks failed. Reagan's advisers as well as members of Congress ignored the warnings that fraud and mismanagement were increasing sharply. Only during the Bush administration did it become clear that the cost of rebuilding the savings banks and paying off huge debts might run into hundreds of billions of dollars.

As the AIDS epidemic spread in the 1980s, quilts like these expressed sorrow for lost friends and loved ones. The quilts also served to raise public awareness of the need for a more effective policy to aid the afflicted and fight the disease.

The late 1980s also brought a public health crisis. Americans were spending a higher percentage of their resources on medical care than citizens in other nations, yet they were no healthier. New technologies that improved care also burdened the system with heavy expenses. Doctors complained of excessive paperwork. As medical costs soared, more than 30 million Americans had no health insurance. The crisis was worsened by a fatal disorder that physicians began diagnosing in the early 1980s: acquired immune deficiency syndrome, or AIDS. With no cure available, the disease threatened to take on epidemic proportions not only in the United States but across the globe. Yet because the illness at first struck hardest at the male homosexual community and intravenous drug users, many groups in American society were hesitant to address the problem.

Riots in Los Angeles   The widespread disillusion had an angry edge as well. In 1991 Los Angeles police were videotaped while arresting a black motorist for speeding and drunken driving. The tape showed a man, Rodney King, lying prone and being struck more than 50 times by officers wielding nightsticks. When a suburban white jury acquitted the officers the following year, the black community of central Los Angeles exploded. Stores were looted, some 600 buildings were set ablaze, and more than 50 people were killed. Clearly, the anger in central Los Angeles over racism was also fueled by the stresses of high unemployment, urban poverty, and economic decline.

Bank failures, skyrocketing health costs, anger over poverty and discrimination—none of these problems by themselves had the power to derail the conservative rebellion. Still, the various crises demonstrated how pivotal government had become in providing social services and limiting the abuses of powerful private interests in a highly industrialized society. Neither the Reagan nor the Bush administration had developed a clear way to address such problems without the intervention of government—the sort of intervention envisioned by a more activist Republican, Teddy Roosevelt, at the turn of the century.

The Election of 1992

In the end, George Bush's inability to rein in soaring government deficits proved most damaging to his reelection prospects. "Read my lips! No new taxes," he had pledged to campaign audiences in 1988. But the president and Congress were at loggerheads over how to reach the holy grail of so many conservatives: a balanced budget. In 1985 Congress had passed the Gramm–Rudman Act, establishing a set of steadily increasing limits on federal spending. These limits were meant to force Congress and the president to make hard choices needed to reach a balanced budget. If they did not, automatic across-the-board cuts would go into effect. By 1990 the law's automatic procedures were threatening programs like Medicare, which Republicans and Democrats alike supported. Facing such unpopular cuts, Bush agreed to a package of new taxes along with budget cuts. Conservatives felt betrayed, and in the end, the deficit grew larger all the same.

As the election of 1992 approached, unemployment stood at more than 8 percent, penetrating to areas of the economy not affected by most recessions. Statistics showed that wages for middle-class families had not increased since the early 1970s and had actually declined during Bush's presidency. Many Reagan Democrats seemed ready to return to the party of Franklin Roosevelt, who had mobilized an activist government in a time of economic depression. Other disillusioned voters were drawn to the maverick candidacy of Texas computer billionaire H. Ross Perot. The blunt-talking, jug-eared Perot (he, too, made fun of his ears) demanded a government run like a business but free of big-business lobbyists. He declared his willingness to administer the bitter medicine needed to lower the deficit.

White-collar unemployment

Meanwhile, the Democrats gave their nomination to Governor Bill Clinton of Arkansas. Clinton had personal hurdles to surmount: he was dogged by reports of marital infidelity, by his lame admission that he had tried marijuana while a student (but had not inhaled), and by his youthful opposition to the war in Vietnam. Still, he gained ground by hammering away at Bush for failing to revive the economy. "It's the economy, stupid!" read the sign tacked up at his election headquarters to remind Clinton workers of the campaign's central theme. Clinton painted himself as a new kind of Democrat: moderate, willing to work with business, and not a creature of liberal interest groups.

"It's the economy . . ."

The Bush campaign miscalculated by allowing the most conservative members of the party to dominate the Republican convention. Middle-of-the-road voters turned to Perot and Clinton. Clinton himself proved a resourceful campaigner, even willing to play his saxophone on MTV. On Election Day, he captured 43 percent of the popular vote (to Bush's 38 and Perot's 19) in the largest turnout—55 percent—in 20 years. The election of four women to the Senate, including the first African American woman, Carol Moseley Braun, indicated that gender had become an electoral factor.

ELECTION OF 1992

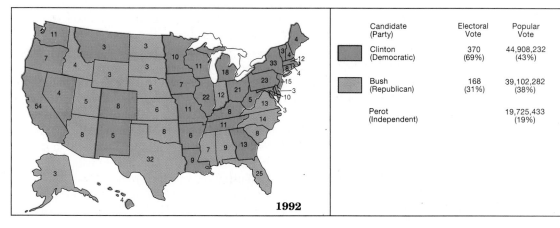

Candidate (Party)	Electoral Vote	Popular Vote
Clinton (Democratic)	370 (69%)	44,908,232 (43%)
Bush (Republican)	168 (31%)	39,102,282 (38%)
Perot (Independent)		19,725,433 (19%)

1992

THE CLINTON PRESIDENCY

Did Clinton's victory in 1992 signal a reversal of fortune for the conservatives? Sixty-two percent had voted against the Republicans, but only 43 percent voted for the man who now looked to lead the nation.

An activist presidency

Still, William Jefferson Clinton intended to be an activist president. He shared with his wife, Hillary Rodham Clinton, a love for politics and government as well as a determination to address problems Reagan and Bush had left unattended. An activist executive could accomplish much, he insisted, "even a president without a majority mandate coming in, if the president has a disciplined, aggressive agenda. . . ." Certainly Clinton's agenda was ambitious. Beyond seeking to revive the economy and rein in the deficit, he called for systematic reform of the welfare and health care systems, as well as measures to lessen the increasing violence in American life.

Whitewater

The president seemed less able to provide the "disciplined, aggressive" approach needed to push his agenda through Congress. His administration's first months were squandered by controversies over cabinet appointments and an attempt—which Clinton quickly backed away from—to strike down the policy of excluding homosexuals from the military. Allegations about the president's past continued to appear, including rumors of womanizing and a sexual harassment suit. The most troubling controversy, known as the Whitewater affair, stemmed from charges that the Clintons may have received special treatment in a failed Arkansas real estate venture a decade earlier. A Senate committee and a special prosecutor investigated those charges throughout 1997.

The New World Disorder

Determined to focus on domestic issues, Clinton hoped to pay less attention to foreign affairs. Yet the "new world order," hailed by both Mikhail Gorbachev and George Bush, seemed more than ever to be disrupted by regional conflicts. Clinton's policies seemed indecisive at first, though by 1996 he had scored enough limited triumphs to aid his reelection.

Civil wars in Somalia and Rwanda

In sub-Saharan Africa, corruption and one-party rule had severely weakened most economies, tribal violence had mounted, and AIDS had become epidemic. Brutal civil wars broke out in both Somalia and Rwanda. Clinton did support President Bush's decision in December 1992 to send troops to aid famine-relief efforts in Somalia. But attempts to install a stable government proved difficult. Similarly, the United States as well as European nations remained reluctant to intervene in Rwanda, where over a million people were massacred in 1994.

In Yugoslavia, Serbs fought Croats and Muslims who had broken off to form the independent state of Bosnia-Herzegovina. Western Europeans and Americans were dismayed by the systematic slaughter and rape of Muslims that Serbs justified in the name of "ethnic cleansing." By the end of 1995 the international War Crimes Tribunal had charged nearly 50 Serbs with crimes against humanity, including Radovan Karadzic, the Bosnian Serbs' leader. But with Europeans divided over how to combat Serbian aggression, the administration remained reluctant to involve U.S. troops in an open-ended peacekeeping mission. Finally, in November 1995 the United States hosted peace talks in Dayton, Ohio. The resulting Dayton Accord called for Bosnia to remain a single nation, but governed as two separate republics. To help guarantee the peace, Clinton sent 20,000 American ground troops to Bosnia as part of an international peacekeeping mission.

Instability in Haiti pushed the president to take a bolder approach in a region closer to home. In 1991 Haitian military leaders had forced their country's elected president, Jean-Bertrand Aristide, to leave the country. The harsh rule that followed prompted over 35,000 refuges to flee toward the United States, often in homemade boats and rafts. When a U.N.-sponsored economic embargo failed to oust the military regime, the Security Council in 1994 approved an invasion of Haiti by a multinational force. Although Clinton was attacked for taking a leading role in the invasion, American troops proved crucial in convincing the military to leave. The following year a smaller U.N. force continued to maintain order as new elections were held. *Intervention in Haiti*

Steps forward in Haiti and Bosnia could not quiet fears of a new Middle East crisis. Since 1987, protests and rioting by Palestinians in the Israeli-occupied territories of Gaza and the West Bank at first gave way to hopeful signs of peace. Palestinian leader Yasir Arafat and Israeli Prime Minister Itzak Rabin had overcome the resistance of hard-liners. At a ceremony hosted by President Clinton in 1993, Israel and the PLO signed a peace agreement permitting self-rule for Palestinians in the Gaza Strip and in Jericho on the West Bank. In 1995 Arafat became head of the West Bank Palestinian National Authority. Still, a full settlement remained elusive. In November 1995, an angry Orthodox Jew assassinated Prime Minister Rabin. Arab extremists responded with suicide bombings in urban areas of Israel.

Throughout the negotiations, Clinton found he had limited leverage to broker a lasting peace. Whether in the Middle East, Eastern Europe, Africa, or the Caribbean, such regional crises demonstrated that a new global "world order" would be difficult to maintain.

Recovery—but Reform?

As president, Bill Clinton intended to focus on domestic policy. He made that clear in his first appearance before a joint session of Congress in February 1993. In a graceful performance, Clinton improvised nearly half of his speech when his teleprompter broke down, a feat that would have eluded either Ronald Reagan or George Bush. The new president proposed a program of economic recovery that combined deficit reduction with a package of investments to stimulate the economy and repair the nation's decaying infrastructure.

But the president's facility for public speaking by no means ensured his command of Congress. Republicans blocked the stimulus portion of Clinton's program. In August 1993 a compromise budget bill passed by only a single vote in the Senate. Still, it was a remarkable achievement. During the Reagan–Bush years deficits had risen sharply, despite conservative rhetoric about balancing the budget. Economic projections indicated that by 1996 the federal deficit would fall by nearly half as a percentage of the gross domestic product, reflecting Clinton's deficit-reduction package.

The victory in the fight over the budget bill provided Clinton with some momentum in other battles. In the fall he hammered together a bipartisan coalition to pass NAFTA, the North American Free Trade Agreement. With the promise of *NAFTA* greater trade and more jobs, the pact linked the United States more closely with Canada and Mexico. The president even helped supporters of gun control overcome the powerful opposition of the National Rifle Association to pass the Brady Bill, requiring a five-day waiting period on gun purchases. And with inner-city violence and drive-by shootings making headlines, the president pushed through a compromise crime bill in September 1994.

Health care
reform

Clinton's most ambitious plans were for the reform of health care—and in that area he stumbled. A task force led by Hillary Rodham Clinton developed a plan to provide health coverage for all Americans, including the 37 million who in 1994 remained uninsured. The plan rejected a more sweeping "single payer" system, in which the government would act as the central agency reimbursing medical expenses. At the same time, it proposed more far-reaching changes than a Republican proposal merely to reform insurance laws in order to make private medical coverage more readily available. But a host of interest groups attacked the proposal, especially small businesses who worried that they would bear the brunt of the system's financing. Despite last-minute lobbying, even a compromise bill lacked the votes needed to win approval.

If the Clintons' plan had passed, the president and the Democratic majority in Congress might have staked their claim to a government that was actively responding to some of the long-term problems facing American society. But the failure of health

President Clinton's most ambitious attempt at reform was to overhaul the nation's health care system to provide all Americans with basic health care (along with a card to guarantee it). But medical interest groups defeated the proposal, arguing it would create yet another huge and inefficient bureaucracy. In 1996 Congress passed a more modest medical reform bill that made it easier for workers to retain health insurance if they lost or changed jobs.

care reform heightened the perception of an ill-organized administration and a well-entrenched Congress content with the status quo. Republicans, sensing the level of public frustration, stepped up their opposition to other Democratic legislation, which only increased the sense of stalemate.

Revolution Reborn

The 1994 midterm elections confirmed the public's anger over political gridlock. For the first time since the Eisenhower years, Republicans captured majorities in both the House and the Senate. The combative new Speaker of the House, Newt Gingrich of Georgia, proclaimed himself a "genuine revolutionary" and vowed to complete what Ronald Reagan had begun. Gingrich used the first hundred days of the new Congress to bring to a vote ten popular proposals from his campaign document "The Contract with America." The Contract proposed a balanced budget amendment, tax cuts, and term limits for all members of Congress. To promote family values, its anticrime package included a broader death penalty and welfare restrictions aimed at reducing teen pregnancy. With the exception of term limits, nine of the ten proposals were passed by the House.

The whirlwind performance was impressive. "When you look back five years from now," enthused Republican Governor Tommy Thompson of Wisconsin, "you're going to say they came, they saw, they conquered." But the Senate was less eager to enact the House proposals. And as Republicans assembled a more comprehensive budget, it became clear that the public was increasingly worried about the Gingrich revolution. Fiscally, the Republicans set out to balance the federal budget by the year 2002 while still cutting taxes by $245 billion. To do that, they proposed scaling back Medicare expenditures by $270 billion and allowing Medicare premiums to double. Republicans also sought to roll back environmental legislation that had been passed over the previous quarter century. Their proposals reduced protection for endangered species, relaxed pollution controls set up by the Clean Water Act, and gave mining, ranching, and logging interests greater freedom to develop public lands. Even moderate Republicans in Congress complained to the Speaker that their party "had taken a beating this year over missteps in environmental policy."

When President Clinton threatened to veto the Republican budget, freshmen Republicans (among Gingrich's most committed troops) pushed the Speaker toward confrontation. Twice Republicans forced the federal government to shut down rather than compromise with the president. The result was a disaster for the self-proclaimed revolutionaries, since most of the public viewed their stance as intransigent. Republicans were forced to back down. At the same time, right-wing extremist

The revolution stumbles

"I am a genuine revolutionary," House Speaker Newt Gingrich proclaimed, and the newly elected Republican freshmen in Congress led the charge to complete the Reagan revolution. By clothing Newt's followers as stiff-armed, flag-waving militarists, illustrator Anita Kunz recalls Mussolini's overzealous Brown Shirts. Enough of the public agreed, forcing the Republicans to backpedal.

groups were linked to the bombing of a federal building in Oklahoma City, which killed 169 men, women, and children. The incident made Americans aware of the many right-wing militia groups operating on the fringes of American society. Though they ranged from religious cults to survivalists, anti-Semites, skinheads, and rabid nativists, what did seem to unite them was a profound mistrust of the federal government.

Clinton moves to the center
At the same time, President Clinton began moving steadily toward the center of the political spectrum. In his earlier efforts at reducing public debt, he had been willing to settle for a $200 billion annual budget deficit into the indefinite future. (It had run as high as $290 billion under George Bush.) By the time Clinton confronted the Republican Congress in 1995, he was proposing his own route toward a balanced budget by 2002. Similarly, in August 1996 the president signed into law a sweeping reform of welfare. The law owed as much to Republican ideas as it did to his. For the first time in 60 years, the social welfare policies of the liberal democratic state were being substantially reversed. The bill ended guarantees of federal aid to poor children, turning over such programs to the states. Food stamp spending was cut, and the law placed a five-year limit on payments to any family, requiring most adults receiving payments to work within two years.

Welfare reform

Thus as the election of 1996 approached, the Republican revolution had been chastened. "By popular demand," one reporter joked, Newt Gingrich had become "a political hermit." At the same time, Clinton had adroitly adopted many issues that Republicans had once called their own. Following a lackluster primary campaign, the Republicans nominated former Senator Bob Dole, an aging political technician, to run for president. Dole and his running mate, Jack Kemp, sought to stir voters with promises of a 15 percent tax cut. But the economy was robust, and voters, wary of Republican revolutionaries and the deficits of the Reagan–Bush years, remained skeptical that Dole could balance the budget and still deliver his tax cut. In November Bill Clinton became the first Democrat since Franklin Roosevelt to win a second term in the White House.

ELECTION OF 1996

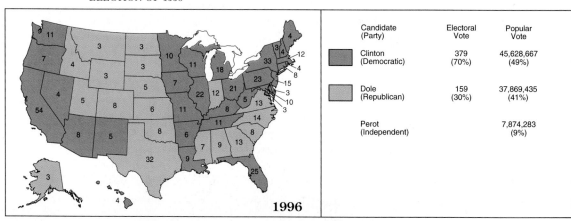

Candidate (Party)	Electoral Vote	Popular Vote
Clinton (Democratic)	379 (70%)	45,628,667 (49%)
Dole (Republican)	159 (30%)	37,869,435 (41%)
Perot (Independent)		7,874,283 (9%)

1996

A NATION OF NATIONS IN THE TWENTY-FIRST CENTURY

When George Washington took the oath of office in 1789, he understood all too well the odds against the survival of the United States. History had demonstrated that few republics ever endured for long. Certainly none had endured with a population of 4 million people spread across a million square miles of territory. As the United States approaches the twenty-first century, its population has risen to more than 250 million, with territory exceeding 3.6 million square miles. Such size and diversity would have astonished Washington. Given the present state of the world, in which so many nations and empires have fallen prey to ethnic, religious, and nationalist rivalries, the survival of the American republic should perhaps astonish us as well.

How well it has dealt with the conflicts among its diverse citizenry has depended on the ability of different groups to participate equally and openly in the political system. The republic's most dramatic failure came with the Civil War. That breakdown occurred, it might be argued, because enslaved African Americans were forbidden any participation in the system. Indeed, they were treated as the property of other Americans who could and did exercise political power. Many pivotal moments in American history have turned on the attempts of new groups to be heard and to exercise effective political power—whether western Populists or eastern immigrants, militant suffragettes or concerned evangelicals, civil rights workers or overtaxed middle-class voters.

In a nation where more than half the population changed addresses between 1985 and 1995 and where immigration during the decade reached new highs, diversity and mobility remain hallmarks of American society. Inevitably, the debate over equal participation will continue.

The New Immigration

During the 1980s, more than 7 million immigrants entered the country legally—more than in any decade in American history except 1901–1910. Adding another 300,000 to 500,000 illegal immigrants each year, the total was even greater than the 8.8 million arriving in the first decade of the century. The percentage of the population that was foreign-born jumped from a low of 4.8 in 1970 to 8.7 in 1994.

Latin American immigrants accounted for as much as 40 percent of the yearly influx, as they had since the 1960s. But now, in addition to Mexicans, Cubans, and Puerto Ricans, the Latino population included communities of Dominicans and Central Americans. Most moved to the Sunbelt states of Florida, Texas, and California, as well as to Illinois and New York. Like immigrants at the turn of the century, established Latino families provided housing for newer immigrants, who were often single. The newcomers hoped to save money from their weekly paychecks to send to relatives in Mexico or Central America. However, in an economy increasingly divided between skilled jobs in the service sectors and low-paying unskilled jobs, Latinos lagged behind Anglos and blacks in education. Often, the lack of adequate English-language skills discouraged success, especially among older Latino immigrants. On the other hand, one study of immigrants to Southern California showed that younger Latino immigrants generally learned English (about 70 percent) and had a lower poverty rate than older immigrants.

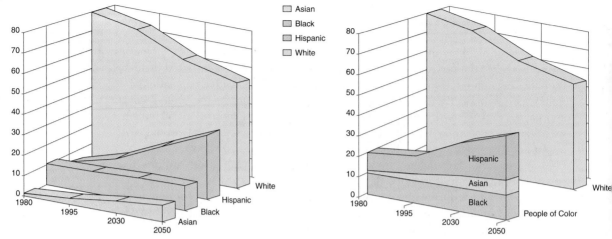

PROJECTED POPULATION SHIFTS: 1980–2050

Census figures project an increasing ethnic and racial diversity for the United States. White population is expected to drop from 80 percent in 1980 to about 53 percent in 2050, with the nation's Hispanic population rising most sharply. Which graph presents the data most effectively?

The political climate of the 1990s led many Hispanic Americans to worry about their own future. The welfare reform bill passed in 1996 prohibited legal immigrants who had not become citizens from receiving most federal welfare benefits. Furthermore, pressures to restrict immigration were rising, especially in California. In response, applications by legal immigrants to become U.S. citizens rose sharply: from about 446,000 in 1995 to 1.2 million in 1996. "I'm afraid they're trying to take everything away from us," one legal immigrant explained. "I pay my taxes all the time. I've been very straight with the government here. So why are they coming after us?" In October 1996 Latinos from all over the country gathered in Washington for the Latino and Immigrants' Rights March, to protest welfare and immigration legislation.

Asian Americans   After the Immigration Act of 1965 eliminated the national origins quota system, immigration from Asia increased heavily. By 1990 about 7.3 million Asian Americans lived in the United States. Like earlier immigrants from Europe, those from the Pacific rim came in waves. Some, like the Vietnamese "boat people" of the late 1970s, were driven from their homes by economic or political turmoil. Others were drawn to reunite families or realize greater opportunities in the Western Hemisphere. "My brother-in-law left his wife in Taiwan and came here as a student to get a Ph.D. in engineering," explained Subi Lin Felipe. "After he received his degree, he got a job in San Jose. Then he brought in a sister and his wife, who brought over one of her brothers and me. And my brother's wife then came."

Professional Asian Indians emigrated in search of better jobs. Doctors and nurses constituted a large percentage of the early Korean immigrants. But letters home soon attracted a more diverse population, which concentrated in small businesses. By the mid-1980s Indians owned more than 50 percent of the nonchain motels in the United States, and Koreans often replaced Jews and Italians as owners of small inner-city delicatessens and produce stores.

The presence of other Asian Americans and an international atmosphere drew many Asians to New York City, but climate made Hawaii and California particularly popular destinations. In 1977 alone some 40,000 Filipinos migrated to Honolulu, many eager to escape from the corrupt regime of dictator Ferdinand Marcos. Of more than 800,000 Korean Americans, about a quarter lived around Los Angeles in 1990. So, too, the 1.4 million Japanese Americans settled primarily in California and Hawaii. By contrast, the federal government attempted to disperse nearly half a million Vietnamese (as well as Cambodians and Laotians) who fled after the American withdrawal from Southeast Asia.

Even successful new immigrants encountered subtle forms of discrimination. "Many Asian Americans hoping to climb the corporate ladder face an arduous ascent," reported the *Wall Street Journal*. "Ironically, the same companies that pursue them for technical jobs often shun them when filling managerial and executive positions." Hard work has overcome some, though by no means all, of these prejudices. Many immigrant families have brought business and educational experience to America, as well as a powerful work ethic. Japanese American wages are 10 percent above white wages and 50 percent higher than African American and Hispanic wages.

Such success led the media to stereotype Asians as a "model minority," yet the experience of Asian immigrants remains widely diverse, encompassing high-income Filipino-American doctors and low-income agricultural laborers, Japanese Americans

The willingness of immigrants to work hard for low wages contributed to the prosperity of the 1990s. The irony of this picture should not be lost in a nation where patriotic rhetoric is routinely used to support restrictions on immigrants, such as California's Proposition 187, passed in 1996.

who are poor and elderly as well as those who are younger, upwardly mobile technicians. Ethnic tensions, made worse by job losses and an American trade deficit with Asian countries, gave rise to scattered acts of violence. During the 1992 Los Angeles riots, Korean shops were often the targets of looters and arsonists.

Equality Still Denied

Fear of immigration had economic as well as ethnic and racial sources. During the 1990s economic inequality continued to worsen. Those workers with advanced technical skills and financial resources saw their wages and personal assets grow at an astonishing rate. A sustained boom in the stock market accounted for many of their gains. Where once they might have put money aside in a savings account, bonds, or other secure investments, in the 1990s they put it into mutual funds investing in stocks. As the market rose, so did the fortunes of upper-income Americans.

Downsizing

Much of the rise in stock prices reflected higher corporate profits. During the 1980s American businesses vastly improved their competitive position in world markets, in part through improved production efficiencies. Sometimes that meant shifting jobs to lower-cost labor markets in Asia or Latin America. But it also meant downsizing, the strategy of doing more business with fewer workers. Almost every week the news reported that a major company had eliminated tens of thousands of jobs. Thus, even as the economy expanded and the number of jobs grew, middle- and lower-class Americans felt considerable economic insecurity.

Opportunity lost

The prognosis was not rosy for a nation which believes in economic opportunity for all. "There is little doubt," one economist concluded: "Permanent inequality is going up." American wage earners from the middle 50th to the bottom 10th percentile all lost ground in the 1990s. More disturbing was the decline in economic mobility. In 1980 high school graduates with six years on the job stood a 17 percent chance of moving from the bottom to the second fifth of income earners. By 1990 they had only a 10 percent chance.

Prospects for African Americans

Such trends only confirmed the anxieties of the African American community. Over the 1970s and 1980s a significant minority of them had successfully achieved the American dream. Almost three times more black Americans held public office than in the 1960s. They made substantial strides in the professions, management, sports, and entertainment. The earnings of black households rose faster than those of whites in the 1970s and 1980s, although they remained 20 percent lower.

But the surge of African Americans into middle-class occupations tended to disguise the persistence of poverty tied to race. In the 1970s and 1980s, more young families were counted among the nation's poor. Those families were increasingly headed by single women. More than 40 percent of all black families (versus 12 percent of whites) were headed by women, and the number was growing. To make matters worse, the largest numbers of black families were concentrated in urban areas hard hit by the recessionary economy. Black unemployment, particularly severe among teenagers and young adults, was twice the national average. More shocking still, the infant mortality rate for African Americans was double the white average and worse than that for some Third World nations. African Americans made up nearly one-third of all AIDS cases. Homicide was the leading cause of death for black males between 15 and 34, of whom about 20 percent had prison records. These were the cruelest realities of poverty.

One event starkly dramatized the ongoing currents of racial tension in America: the murder trial of O.J. Simpson. Born into a ghetto family, Simpson had become first a football legend, then a movie star and television personality. He seemed to defy all notions that race prejudice restricted African Americans. But in June 1994 police charged Simpson with the brutal murders of his white wife, Nicole, and a friend. During televised proceedings eagerly billed as the "trial of the century," Simpson's attorneys transformed what seemed to be a strong prosecution case into a debate over whether Simpson had been the victim of systematic police racism. The defense revealed that the lead police officer in the case had lied on the stand about his own prejudices and his use of racial slurs like *nigger.* After a trial lasting almost a year, a jury took just four hours to acquit. Regardless of Simpson's guilt or innocence, the trial demonstrated the lines of race dividing American society. The vast majority of whites believed Simpson guilty; most African Americans thought he was innocent. Clearly white and black Americans disagreed because they held differing opinions of whether the American system of justice permitted a fair trial for all its citizens.

The O.J. case

To what degree should the political system move to ease such tensions? In the United States, where diversity—and therefore conflict—remains central to its history, the debate will continue over how strongly government should intervene to manage the conflicts of a modern state. For better or worse, the long-term trend has been clear. As economic power became more concentrated in the late nineteenth century and as cycles of boom and bust periodically wracked the nation, government increased its powers to curb the excesses of the market and to provide both economic protection and social guarantees for its citizens. The election of Bill Clinton brought to power a leader who seemed determined, like both the Roosevelts, Wilson, Kennedy, and Lyndon Johnson, to use government more actively. Yet the conservative movement of the past 16 years demonstrates that many Americans remain deeply suspicious not only of the power of big business but also of big government. In a world where national, ethnic, and racial discord continues to threaten the stability of a global economy, a democratic republic remains the best practical hope for resolving conflict. It remains to be seen whether Americans can rise to the task of making diversity the strength, not the weakness, of a nation of nations.

CHAPTER SUMMARY

In the wake of social upheaval and a wrenching war abroad, the nation's political agenda was increasingly determined by a conservative movement seeking to restore traditional religious and family values, patriotism, and limited government. At the core of the revival was an evangelical Christian movement sharply critical of the secular-oriented modern media, with their more explicit portrayals of sex and violence. In the political arena, Ronald Reagan led this conservative tide with legislation that reduced government regulation, lowered taxes, and sharply increased military spending. Although the economy recovered from recession, the national debt rose sharply, as did the gap between rich and poor. Reagan gave some legislative support to the conservatives' social agenda, but he and his successor George Bush advanced it most by appointing five conservative justices to the Supreme Court. The Court's decisions set increasing limits in the areas of civil rights, affirmative action, abortion, and the separation of church and state.

In foreign policy, the Reagan administration's most serious setback arose from a secret attempt to free hostages in the Middle East by sending arms to Iran—and using the profits from those sales to aid right-wing guerrillas in Latin America. The resulting Iran–Contra scandal revealed a broad pattern of illegality and constitutional abuses but did not lead to the president's impeachment. Both Reagan and Bush welcomed reforms set in motion by Mikhail Gorbachev, reforms that led in 1991 to the breakup of the Soviet Union and a reduction in the nuclear arms race. But regional conflicts continued to present problems. Under the auspices of the United Nations, President Bush formed an allied coalition that routed Iraq in Operation Desert Storm. Both Bush and President Bill Clinton worked to end civil wars in Africa (Somalia and Rwanda) and Bosnia. For Bush, however, a continuing recession, high deficits, and high unemployment undermined his bid for reelection. When Bill Clinton failed to pass an ambitious program of medical reform in 1994, opposition from Republicans led to a gridlock in Congress and to an overwhelming victory for conservatives. But Speaker Newt Gingrich's revolution proved too ambitious as well, leading to Clinton's reelection in 1996. Despite these swings, the conservative rebellion had led the president to promise a balanced budget by the year 2002 and to abandon the traditional liberal approach to welfare. It remained to be seen whether those compromises could bridge the differences within a nation in which immigration had created a more diverse population than ever before and economic insecurities had aggravated tensions over race and ethnicity.

ADDITIONAL READING

The Reagan presidency inspired numerous memoirs and exposés, among which are Haynes Johnson, *Sleep Walking through History: America in the Reagan Years* (1991), Jane Mayer and Doyle McManus, *Landslide: The Unmaking of the President, 1984–88* (1988), and Garry Wills, *Reagan's America* (1987). Especially good on recent religious issues is Garry Wills, *In God We Trust* (1991). A powerful, if controversial, study of recent racial patterns is Nicholas Lemann, *The Promised Land* (1991). David Reimers, *Still the Golden Door* (1985) and Ronald Takaki, *Strangers from a Different Shore* (1989) are excellent on immigration. Little of value has yet been written on the Bush years, but Thomas Friedman, *From Beirut to Jerusalem* (1990) describes the political currents in the Middle East that helped launch Desert Storm, and Dilip Hiro, *Desert Shield to Desert Storm: The Second Gulf War* (1992) offers a military and political history from a non-American perspective.

To trace the Republican revolution and its unfulfilled promise, start with David Stockman, *The Triumph of Politics: The Inside Story of the Reagan Revolution* (1986). Then look at Dan Balz and Ronald Brownstein, *Storming the Gates: Protest Politics and the Republican Revival* (1996), followed by Elizabeth Drew, *Showdown: The Struggle between the Gingrich Congress and the Clinton White House* (1996) and David Maraniss and Michael Weisskopf, *"Tell Newt to Shut Up"* (1996). All these are neatly summarized in Garry Wills, "What Happened to the Revolution," *New York Review of Books,* vol. XLIII, No. 10, June 6, 1996, 11–16. For a fuller list of readings, see the Bibliography.

SIGNIFICANT EVENTS

1978 — *Bakke v. Regents of the University of California*

1979 — Moral Majority established; Sandinistas overthrow Somoza in Nicaragua

1980 — Reagan defeats Carter

1980s — Asians pass Hispanics in numbers of legal immigrants

1981 — Military buildup; Reagan breaks air controllers' strike; recession sets in; Economic Recovery Tax Act; United States begins aiding Nicaraguan Contras

1982 — Attack on U.S. Marine barracks in Lebanon

1983 — Reagan proposes the Strategic Defense Initiative; invasion of Grenada

1984 — Boland Amendment passed; Reagan defeats Mondale

1985 — Gramm–Rudman Act sets in motion a plan to balance budget; increase in hostages taken by terrorists; United States begins secret arms-for-hostages negotiations with Iran

1986 — Oliver North begins diverting Iran arms sales profits to Contras; Reykjavík summit; Iran–Contra scandal breaks

1988 — Congress passes drug and welfare reform bills; Bush elected president

1989 — Eastern European nations break with Soviet Union; China crushes revolt in Tiananmen Square; Berlin Wall taken down

1990 — Iraq invades Kuwait; Clean Air Act; Bush agrees to higher taxes in budget agreement with Congress

1991 — Operation Desert Storm launched; Strategic Arms Reduction Treaty (START) concluded; Clarence Thomas hearings; 11 former republics of the Soviet Union become the Commonwealth of Independent States

1992 — Los Angeles riots; *Planned Parenthood v. Casey* sets new restrictions on abortion; Clinton defeats Bush and Perot

1993 — Clinton succeeds in passing budget legislation reducing annual deficits; NAFTA trade agreement approved

1994 — U.S. leads U.N.-sponsored invasion of Haiti; Clinton health care reform defeated; congressional election gives Republicans control of both the House and the Senate

1995 — Federal building in Oklahoma City bombed; O.J. Simpson acquitted in murder trial; Dayton Accords signed, ending civil war in Bosnia; Republicans shut down federal government in confrontation with Clinton

1996 — Welfare reform legislation signed; Clinton defeats Dole

APPENDIX

THE DECLARATION OF INDEPENDENCE

In Congress, July 4, 1776,

THE UNANIMOUS DECLARATION OF THE
THIRTEEN UNITED STATES OF AMERICA

When, in the course of human events, it becomes necessary for one people to dissolve the political bands which have connected them with another, and to assume, among the powers of the earth, the separate and equal station to which the laws of nature and of nature's God entitle them, a decent respect to the opinions of mankind requires that they should declare the causes which impel them to the separation.

We hold these truths to be self-evident, that all men are created equal; that they are endowed by their Creator with certain unalienable rights; that among these, are life, liberty, and the pursuit of happiness. That, to secure these rights, governments are instituted among men, deriving their just powers from the consent of the governed; that, whenever any form of government becomes destructive of these ends, it is the right of the people to alter or to abolish it, and to institute a new government, laying its foundation on such principles, and organizing its powers in such form, as to them shall seem most likely to effect their safety and happiness. Prudence, indeed, will dictate that governments long established, should not be changed for light and transient causes; and, accordingly, all experience hath shown, that mankind are more disposed to suffer, while evils are sufferable, than to right themselves by abolishing the forms to which they are accustomed. But, when a long train of abuses and usurpations, pursuing invariably the same object, evinces a design to reduce them under absolute despotism, it is their right, it is their duty, to throw off such government and to provide new guards for their future security. Such has been the patient sufferance of these colonies, and such is now the necessity which constrains them to alter their for-

mer systems of government. The history of the present King of Great Britain is a history of repeated injuries and usurpations, all having, in direct object, the establishment of an absolute tyranny over these States. To prove this, let facts be submitted to a candid world:

He has refused his assent to laws the most wholesome and necessary for the public good.

He has forbidden his governors to pass laws of immediate and pressing importance, unless suspended in their operation till his assent should be obtained; and, when so suspended, he has utterly neglected to attend to them.

He has refused to pass other laws for the accommodation of large districts of people, unless those people would relinquish the right of representation in the legislature; a right inestimable to them, and formidable to tyrants only.

He has called together legislative bodies at places unusual, uncomfortable, and distant from the depository of their public records, for the sole purpose of fatiguing them into compliance with his measures.

He has dissolved representative houses repeatedly for opposing, with manly firmness, his invasions on the rights of the people.

He has refused, for a long time after such dissolutions, to cause others to be elected; whereby the legislative powers, incapable of annihilation, have returned to the people at large for their exercise; the state remaining, in the meantime, exposed to all the danger of invasion from without, and convulsions within.

He has endeavored to prevent the population of these States; for that purpose, obstructing the laws for naturalization of foreigners, refusing to pass others to encourage their migration hither, and raising the conditions of new appropriations of lands.

He had obstructed the administration of justice, by refusing his assent to laws for establishing judiciary powers.

He has made judges dependent on his will

alone, for the tenure of their offices, and the amount and payment of their salaries.

He has erected a multitude of new offices, and sent hither swarms of officers to harass our people, and eat out their substance.

He has kept among us, in time of peace, standing armies, without the consent of our legislatures.

He has affected to render the military independent of, and superior to, the civil power.

He has combined, with others, to subject us to a jurisdiction foreign to our Constitution, and unacknowledged by our laws; giving his assent to their acts of pretended legislation:

For quartering large bodies of armed troops among us:

For protecting them by a mock trial, from punishment, for any murders which they should commit on the inhabitants of these States:

For cutting off our trade with all parts of the world:

For imposing taxes on us without our consent:

For depriving us, in many cases, of the benefit of trial by jury:

For transporting us beyond seas to be tried for pretended offences:

For abolishing the free system of English laws in a neighboring province, establishing therein an arbitrary government, and enlarging its boundaries, so as to render it at once an example and fit instrument for introducing the same absolute rule into these colonies:

For taking away our charters, abolishing our most valuable laws, and altering, fundamentally, the powers of our governments:

For suspending our own legislatures, and declaring themselves invested with power to legislate for us in all cases whatsoever.

He has abdicated government here, by declaring us out of his protection, and waging war against us.

He has plundered our seas, ravaged our coasts, burnt our towns, and destroyed the lives of our people.

He is, at this time, transporting large armies of foreign mercenaries to complete the works of death, desolation, and tyranny, already begun, with circumstances of cruelty and perfidy scarcely paralleled in the most barbarous ages, and totally unworthy the head of a civilized nation.

He has constrained our fellow citizens, taken captive on the high seas, to bear arms against their country, to become the executioners of their friends, and brethren, or to fall themselves by their hands.

He has excited domestic insurrections amongst us, and has endeavored to bring on the inhabitants of our frontiers, the merciless Indian savages, whose known rule of warfare is an undistinguished destruction of all ages, sexes, and conditions.

In every stage of these oppressions, we have petitioned for redress, in the most humble terms; our repeated petitions have been answered only by repeated injury. A prince, whose character is thus marked by every act which may define a tyrant, is unfit to be the ruler of a free people.

Nor have we been wanting in attention to our British brethren. We have warned them, from time to time, of attempts made by their legislature to extend an unwarrantable jurisdiction over us. We have reminded them of the circumstances of our emigration and settlement here. We have appealed to their native justice and magnanimity, and we have conjured them, by the ties of our common kindred, to disavow these usurpations, which would inevitably interrupt our connections and correspondence. They, too, have been deaf to the voice of justice and consanguinity. We must, therefore, acquiesce in the necessity which denounces our separation, and hold them as we hold the rest of mankind, enemies in war, in peace, friends.

We, therefore, the representatives of the United States of America, in general Congress assembled, appealing to the Supreme Judge of the world for the rectitude of our intentions, do, in the name, and by the authority of the good people of these colonies, solemnly publish and declare, that these united colonies are, and of right ought to be, free and independent states: that they are absolved from all allegiance to the British Crown, and that all political connection between them and the state of Great Britain is, and ought to be, totally dissolved; and that, as free and independent states, they have full power to levy war, conclude peace, contract alliances, establish commerce, and to do all other acts and things which independent states may of right do. And, for the support of this declaration, with a firm reliance on the protection of Divine Providence, we mutually pledge to each other our lives, our fortunes, and our sacred honor.

The foregoing Declaration was, by order of Congress, engrossed, and signed by the following members:

JOHN HANCOCK

New Hampshire
Josiah Bartlett
William Whipple
Matthew Thornton

Massachusetts Bay
Samuel Adams
John Adams
Robert Treat Paine
Elbridge Gerry

Rhode Island
Stephen Hopkins
William Ellery

Connecticut
Roger Sherman
Samuel Huntington
William Williams
Oliver Wolcott

New York
William Floyd
Philip Livingston
Francis Lewis
Lewis Morris

New Jersey
Richard Stockton
John Witherspoon
Francis Hopkinson
John Hart
Abraham Clark

Pennsylvania
Robert Morris
Benjamin Rush
Benjamin Franklin
John Morton
George Clymer
James Smith
George Taylor
James Wilson
George Ross

Delaware
Caesar Rodney
George Read
Thomas M'Kean

Maryland
Samuel Chase
William Paca
Thomas Stone
Charles Carroll,
    of Carrollton

Virginia
George Wythe
Richard Henry Lee
Thomas Jefferson
Benjamin Harrison
Thomas Nelson, Jr.
Francis Lightfoot Lee
Carter Braxton

North Carolina
William Hooper
Joseph Hewes
John Penn

South Carolina
Edward Rutledge
Thomas Heyward, Jr.
Thomas Lynch, Jr.
Arthur Middleton

Georgia
Button Gwinnett
Lyman Hall
George Walton

Resolved, That copies of the Declaration be sent to the several assemblies, conventions, and committees, or councils of safety, and to the several commanding officers of the continental troops; that it be proclaimed in each of the United States, at the head of the army.

THE CONSTITUTION OF THE UNITED STATES OF AMERICA[1]

We the People of the United States, in Order to form a more perfect Union, establish Justice, insure domestic Tranquility, provide for the common defence, promote the general Welfare, and secure the Blessings of Liberty to ourselves and our Posterity, do ordain and establish this CONSTITUTION for the United States of America.

ARTICLE I

Section 1. All legislative Powers herein granted shall be vested in a Congress of the United States, which shall consist of a Senate and House of Representatives.

Section 2. The House of Representatives shall be composed of Members chosen every second Year by the People of the several States, and the Electors in each State shall have the Qualifications requisite for Electors of the most numerous Branch of the State Legislature.

No Person shall be a Representative who shall not have attained to the Age of twenty-five Years, and been seven Years a Citizen of the United States, and who shall not, when elected, be an Inhabitant of that State in which he shall be chosen.

[Representatives and direct Taxes[2] shall be apportioned among the several States which may be included within this Union, according to their respective Numbers, which shall be determined by adding to the whole Number of free Persons, including those bound to Service for a Term of Years, and excluding Indians not taxed, three fifths of all other Persons.][3] The actual Enumeration shall be made within three Years after the first Meeting of the Congress of the United States, and within every subsequent Term of ten Years, in such Manner as they shall by Law direct. The Number of Representatives shall not exceed one for every thirty Thousand, but each State shall have at Least one Representative; and until such enumeration shall be made, the State of New Hampshire shall be entitled to chuse three, Massachusetts eight, Rhode-Island and Providence Plantations one, Connecticut five, New York six, New Jersey four, Pennsylvania eight, Delaware one, Maryland six, Virginia ten, North Carolina five, South Carolina five, and Georgia three.

When vacancies happen in the Representation from any State, the Executive Authority thereof shall issue Writs of Election to fill such Vacancies.

The House of Representatives shall chuse their Speaker and other Officers; and shall have the sole Power of Impeachment.

Section 3. The Senate of the United States shall be composed of two Senators from each State, chosen by the Legislature thereof, for six Years; and each Senator shall have one Vote.

Immediately after they shall be assembled in Consequence of the first Election, they shall be divided as equally as may be into three Classes. The Seats of the Senators of the first Class shall be vacated at the Expiration of the second Year, of the second Class at the Expiration of the fourth Year, and of the third Class at the Expiration of the sixth Year, so that one-third may be chosen every second Year; and if Vacancies happen by Resignation, or otherwise, during the Recess of the Legislature of any State, the Executive thereof may make temporary Appointments until the next Meeting of the Legislature, which shall then fill such Vacancies.

No Person shall be a Senator who shall not have attained to the Age of thirty Years, and been nine Years a Citizen of the United States, and who shall not, when elected, be an Inhabitant of that State for which he shall be chosen.

The Vice President of the United States shall be President of the Senate, but shall have no vote, unless they be equally divided.

The Senate shall chuse their other Officers, and also a President pro tempore, in the absence of the Vice President, or when he shall exercise the Office of President of the United States.

[1]This version follows the original Constitution in capitalization and spelling. It is adapted from the text published by the United States Department of the Interior, Office of Education.

[2]Altered by the Sixteenth Amendment.

[3]Negated by the Fourteenth Amendment.

The Senate shall have the sole Power to try all Impeachments. When sitting for that purpose they shall be on Oath or Affirmation. When the President of the United States is tried, the Chief Justice shall preside: And no person shall be convicted without the Concurrence of two thirds of the Members present.

Judgment in Cases of Impeachment shall not extend further than to removal from Office, and disqualification to hold and enjoy any Office of honor, Trust, or Profit under the United States: but the Party convicted shall nevertheless be liable and subject to Indictment, Trial, Judgment, and Punishment, according to Law.

Section 4. The Times, Places and Manner of holding Elections for Senators and Representatives, shall be prescribed in each State by the Legislature thereof; but the Congress may at any time by Law make or alter such Regulations, except as to the Places of Chusing Senators.

The Congress shall assemble at least once in every Year, and such Meeting shall be on the first Monday in December, unless they shall by Law appoint a different Day.

Section 5. Each House shall be the Judge of the Elections, Returns and Qualifications of its own Members, and a Majority of each shall constitute a Quorum to do Business; but a smaller number may adjourn from day to day, and may be authorized to compel the Attendance of absent Members, in such Manner, and under such Penalties, as each House may provide.

Each House may determine the Rules of its Proceedings, punish its Members for disorderly Behaviour, and, with the Concurrence of two thirds, expel a Member.

Each House shall keep a Journal of its Proceedings, and from time to time publish the same, excepting such Parts as may in their Judgment require Secrecy; and the Yeas and Nays of the Members of either House on any question shall, at the Desire of one fifth of those Present, be entered on the Journal.

Neither House, during the Session of Congress, shall, without the Consent of the other, adjourn for more than three days, nor to any other Place than that in which the two Houses shall be sitting.

Section 6. The Senators and Representatives shall receive a Compensation for their Services, to be ascertained by Law, and paid out of the Treasury of the United States. They shall in all Cases, except Treason, Felony, and Breach of the Peace, be privileged from Arrest during their Attendance at the Session of their respective Houses, and in going to and returning from the same; and for any Speech or Debate in either House, they shall not be questioned in any other Place.

No Senator or Representative shall, during the Time for which he was elected, be appointed to any civil Office under the Authority of the United States, which shall have been created, or the Emoluments whereof shall have been increased, during such time; and no Person holding any Office under the United States shall be a Member of either House during his continuance in Office.

Section 7. All Bills for raising Revenue shall originate in the House of Representatives; but the Senate may propose or concur with Amendments as on other bills.

Every Bill which shall have passed the House of Representatives and the Senate, shall, before it become a Law, be presented to the President of the United States; If he approve he shall sign it, but if not he shall return it, with his Objections, to that House in which it shall have originated, who shall enter the Objections at large on their Journal, and proceed to reconsider it. If after such Reconsideration two thirds of that House shall agree to pass the bill, it shall be sent, together with the objections, to the other House, by which it shall likewise be reconsidered, and if approved by two thirds of that House, it shall become a Law. But in all such Cases the Votes of both Houses shall be determined by Yeas and Nays, and the Names of the Persons voting for and against the Bill shall be entered on the Journal of each House respectively. If any Bill shall not be returned by the President within ten Days (Sundays excepted) after it shall have been presented to him, the Same shall be a Law, in like Manner as if he had signed it, unless the Congress by their Adjournment prevent its Return, in which Case it shall not be a Law.

Every Order, Resolution, or Vote to which the Concurrence of the Senate and House of

Representatives may be necessary (except on a question of Adjournment) shall be presented to the President of the United States; and before the Same shall take Effect, shall be approved by him, or being disapproved by him, shall be repassed by two thirds of the Senate and House of Representatives, according to the Rules and Limitations prescribed in the Case of a Bill.

Section 8. The Congress shall have Power To lay and collect Taxes, Duties, Imposts and Excises, to pay the Debts and provide for the common Defence and general Welfare of the United States; but all Duties, Imposts and Excises shall be uniform throughout the United States;

To borrow money on the credit of the United States;

To regulate Commerce with foreign Nations, and among the several States, and with the Indian Tribes;

To establish an uniform rule of Naturalization, and uniform Laws on the subject of Bankruptcies throughout the United States;

To coin Money, regulate the Value thereof, and of foreign Coin, and fix the Standard of Weights and Measures;

To provide for the Punishment of counterfeiting the Securities and current Coin of the United States;

To establish Post Offices and post Roads;

To promote the Progress of Science and useful Arts, by securing for limited Times to Authors and Inventors the exclusive Right to their respective Writings and Discoveries;

To constitute Tribunals inferior to the Supreme Court;

To define and punish Piracies and Felonies committed on the high Seas, and Offenses against the Law of Nations;

To declare War, grant Letters of Marque and Reprisal, and make Rules concerning Captures on Land and Water;

To raise and support Armies, but no Appropriation of Money to that Use shall be for a longer Term than two Years;

To provide and maintain a Navy;

To make Rules for the Government and Regulation of the land and naval forces;

To provide for calling forth the Militia to execute the Laws of the Union, suppress Insurrections and repel Invasions;

To provide for organizing, arming, and disciplining the Militia, and for government such Part of them as may be employed in the Service of the United States, reserving to the States respectively, the Appointment of the Officers, and the Authority of training the Militia according to the discipline prescribed by Congress;

To exercise exclusive Legislation in all Cases whatsoever, over such District (not exceeding ten Miles square) as may, by Cession of particular States, and the acceptance of Congress, become the Seat of the Government of the United States, and to exercise like Authority over all Places purchased by the Consent of the Legislature of the State in which the Same shall be, for the Erection of Forts, Magazines, Arsenals, Dock-yards, and other needful Buildings;—And

To make all Laws which shall be necessary and proper for carrying into Execution the foregoing Powers, and all other Powers vested by this Constitution in the Government of the United States, or in any Department or Officer thereof.

Section 9. The Migration or Importation of such Persons as any of the States now existing shall think proper to admit, shall not be prohibited by the Congress prior to the Year one thousand eight hundred and eight, but a tax or duty may be imposed on such Importation, not exceeding ten dollars for each Person.

The privilege of the Writ of Habeas Corpus shall not be suspended, unless when in Cases of Rebellion or Invasion the public Safety may require it.

No bill of Attainder or ex post facto Law shall be passed.

No capitation, or other direct, Tax shall be laid unless in Proportion to the Census or Enumeration herein before directed to be taken.

No Tax or Duty shall be laid on Articles exported from any State.

No Preference shall be given by any Regulation of Commerce or Revenue to the Ports of one State over those of another: nor shall Vessels bound to, or from, one State, be obliged to enter, clear, or pay Duties in another.

No Money shall be drawn from the Treasury, but in Consequence of Appropriations made by Law; and a regular Statement and Account of the Receipts and Expenditures of all public Money shall be published from time to time.

No Title of Nobility shall be granted by the United States: And no Person holding any Office of Profit or Trust under them, shall, without the Consent of the Congress, accept of any present, Emolument, Office, or Title, of any kind whatever, from any King, Prince, or foreign State.

Section 10. No State shall enter into any Treaty, Alliance, or Confederation; grant Letters of Marque and Reprisal; coin Money; emit Bills of Credit; make any Thing but gold and silver Coin a Tender in Payment of Debts; pass any Bill of Attainder, ex post facto Law, or Law impairing the Obligation of Contracts, or grant any Title of Nobility.

No State shall, without the Consent of the Congress, lay any Imposts or Duties on Imports or Exports, except what may be absolutely necessary for executing its inspection Laws; and the net Produce of all Duties and Imposts, laid by any State on Imports or Exports, shall be for the use of the Treasury of the United States; and all such Laws shall be subject to the Revision and Control of the Congress.

No state shall, without the Consent of Congress, lay any duty of Tonnage, keep Troops, or Ships of War in time of Peace, enter into any Agreement or Compact with another State, or with a foreign Power, or engage in War, unless actually invaded, or in such imminent Danger as will not admit of delay.

ARTICLE II

Section 1. The executive Power shall be vested in a President of the United States of America. He shall hold his Office during the Term of four years, and, together with the Vice President, chosen for the same Term, be elected, as follows:

Each State shall appoint, in such Manner as the Legislature thereof may direct, a Number of Electors, equal to the whole Number of Senators and Representatives to which the State may be entitled in the Congress: but no Senator or Representative, or Person holding an Office of Trust or Profit under the United States, shall be appointed an Elector.

[The Electors shall meet in their respective States, and vote by Ballot for two persons, of whom one at least shall not be an Inhabitant of the same State with themselves. And they shall make a List of all the Persons voted for, and of the Number of Votes for each; which List they shall sign and certify, and transmit sealed to the Seat of the Government of the United States, directed to the President of the Senate. The President of the Senate shall, in the Presence of the Senate and House of Representatives, open all the Certificates, and the Votes shall then be counted. The Person having the greatest Number of Votes shall be the President, if such Number be a Majority of the whole Number of Electors appointed; and if there be more than one who have such Majority, and have an equal Number of Votes, then the House of Representatives shall immediately chuse by Ballot one of them for President; and if no Person have a Majority, then from the five highest on the List the said House shall in like Manner chuse the President. But in chusing the President, the Votes shall be taken by States, the Representation from each State having one Vote; a quorum for this Purpose shall consist of a Member or Members from two-thirds of the States, and a Majority of all the States shall be necessary to a Choice. In every Case, after the Choice of the President, the Person having the greatest Number of Votes of the Electors shall be the Vice President. But if there should remain two or more who have equal votes, the Senate shall chuse from them by Ballot the Vice President.][4]

The Congress may determine the Time of chusing the Electors, and the Day on which they shall give their Votes; which Day shall be the same throughout the United States.

No person except a natural-born Citizen, or a Citizen of the United States, at the time of the Adoption of this Constitution, shall be eligible to the Office of President; neither shall any Person be eligible to that Office who shall not have attained to the Age of thirty-five years, and been fourteen Years a Resident within the United States.

In Case of the Removal of the President from Office, or of his Death, Resignation, or Inability to discharge the Powers and Duties of the said Office, the same shall devolve on the Vice President, and the Congress may by Law provide for the Case of Removal, Death, Resignation, or Inability, both of the President and Vice President,

---

[4]Revised by the Twelfth Amendment.

declaring what Officer shall then act as President, and such Officer shall act accordingly, until the disability be removed, or a President shall be elected.

The President shall, at stated Times, receive for his Services a Compensation, which shall neither be increased nor diminished during the Period for which he shall have been elected, and he shall not receive within that Period any other Emolument from the United States, or any of them.

Before he enter on the execution of his Office, he shall take the following Oath or Affirmation:—"I do solemnly swear (or affirm) that I will faithfully execute the Office of President of the United States, and will, to the best of my Ability, preserve, protect, and defend the Constitution of the United States."

Section 2. The President shall be Commander in Chief of the Army and Navy of the United States, and of the Militia of the several States, when called into the actual Service of the United States; he may require the Opinion, in writing, of the principal Officer in each of the executive Departments, upon any subject relating to the Duties of their respective Offices, and he shall have Power to Grant Reprieves and Pardons for Offenses against the United States, except in Cases of Impeachment.

He shall have Power, by and with the Advice and Consent of the Senate, to make Treaties, provided two-thirds of the Senators present concur; and he shall nominate, and by and with the Advice and Consent of the Senate, shall appoint Ambassadors, other public Ministers and Consuls, Judges of the supreme Court, and all other Officers of the United States, whose Appointments are not herein otherwise provided for, and which shall be established by Law: but the Congress may by Law vest the Appointment of such inferior Officers, as they think proper, in the President alone, in the Courts of Law, or in the Heads of Departments.

The President shall have Power to fill up all Vacancies that may happen during the Recess of the Senate, by granting Commissions which shall expire at the End of their next Session.

Section 3. He shall from time to time give to the Congress Information of the State of the Union, and recommend to their Consideration such Measures as he shall judge necessary and expedient; he may, on extraordinary occasions, convene both Houses, or either of them, and in Case of Disagreement between them, with respect to the Time of Adjournment, he may adjourn them to such Time as he shall think proper; he shall receive Ambassadors and other public Ministers; he shall take care that the Laws be faithfully executed, and shall Commission all the Officers of the United States.

Section 4. The President, Vice President and all civil Officers of the United States, shall be removed from Office on Impeachment for, and Conviction of, Treason, Bribery, or other high Crimes and Misdemeanors.

ARTICLE III

Section 1. The judicial Power of the United States, shall be vested in one supreme Court, and in such inferior Courts as the Congress may from time to time ordain and establish. The Judges, both of the supreme and inferior Courts, shall hold their Offices during good Behaviour, and shall, at stated Times, receive for their Services, a Compensation, which shall not be diminished during their Continuance in Office.

Section 2. The judicial Power shall extend to all Cases, in Law and Equity, arising under this Constitution, the Laws of the United States, and Treaties made, or which shall be made, under their Authority;—to all Cases affecting ambassadors, other public ministers and consuls;—to all cases of admiralty and maritime Jurisdiction;—to Controversies to which the United States shall be a Party;—to Controversies between two or more States;—between a State and Citizens of another State;[5]—between Citizens of different States—between Citizens of the same State claiming Lands under Grants of different States, and between a State, or the Citizens thereof, and foreign States, Citizens, or Subjects.

In all Cases affecting Ambassadors, other public Ministers and Consuls, and those in which a State shall be Party, the supreme Court shall have original Jurisdiction. In all the other Cases

[5]Qualified by the Eleventh Amendment.

before mentioned, the supreme Court shall have appellate Jurisdiction, both as to Law and Fact, with such Exceptions, and under such Regulations as the Congress shall make.

The trial of all Crimes, except in Cases of Impeachment, shall be by Jury; and such Trial shall be held in the State where the said Crimes shall have been committed; but when not committed within any State, the Trial shall be at such Place or Places as the Congress may by Law have directed.

Section 3. Treason against the United States, shall consist only in levying War against them, or in adhering to their Enemies, giving them Aid and Comfort. No Person shall be convicted of Treason unless on the Testimony of two Witnesses to the same overt Act, or on Confession in open Court.

The Congress shall have power to declare the Punishment of Treason, but no Attainder of Treason shall work Corruption of Blood, or Forfeiture except during the Life of the Person attainted.

ARTICLE IV

Section 1. Full Faith and Credit shall be given in each State to the public Acts, Records, and judicial Proceedings of every other State. And the Congress may by general Laws prescribe the Manner in which such Acts, Records and Proceedings shall be proved, and the Effect thereof.

Section 2. The Citizens of each State shall be entitled to all Privileges and Immunities of Citizens in the several States.

A Person charged in any State with Treason, Felony, or other Crime, who shall flee from Justice, and be found in another State, shall on demand of the executive Authority of the State from which he fled, be delivered up, to be removed to the State having Jurisdiction of the crime.

No Person held to Service or Labour in one State, under the Laws thereof, escaping into another, shall, in Consequence of any Law or Regulation therein, be discharged from such Service or Labour, but shall be delivered up on Claim of the Party to whom such Service or Labour may be due.

Section 3. New States may be admitted by the Congress into this Union; but no new State shall be formed or erected within the Jurisdiction of any other State; nor any State be formed by the Junction of two or more States, or parts of States, without the Consent of the Legislatures of the States concerned as well as of the Congress.

The Congress shall have Power to dispose of and make all needful Rules and Regulations respecting the Territory or other Property belonging to the United States; and nothing in this Constitution shall be so construed as to Prejudice any Claims of the United States, or of any particular State.

Section 4. The United States shall guarantee to every State in this Union a Republican Form of Government, and shall protect each of them against Invasion; and on Application of the Legislature, or of the Executive (when the Legislature cannot be convened) against domestic Violence.

ARTICLE V

The Congress, whenever two-thirds of both Houses shall deem it necessary, shall propose Amendments to this Constitution, or, on the Application of the Legislatures of two-thirds of the several States, shall call a Convention for proposing Amendments, which, in either Case, shall be valid to all Intents and Purposes, as part of this Constitution, when ratified by the Legislatures of three-fourths of the several States, or by Conventions in three-fourths thereof, as the one or the other Mode of Ratification may be proposed by the Congress; Provided that no Amendment which may be made prior to the Year One thousand eight hundred and eight shall in any Manner affect the first and fourth Clauses in the Ninth Section of the first Article; and that no State, without its Consent, shall be deprived of its equal Suffrage in the Senate.

ARTICLE VI

All Debts contracted and Engagements entered into, before the Adoption of this Constitution, shall be as valid against the United States under this Constitution, as under the Confederation.

This Constitution, and the Laws of the United States which shall be made in Pursuance thereof; and all Treaties made, or which shall be

Section 2. The Congress shall assemble at least once in every year, and such meeting shall begin at noon on the 3d day of January, unless they shall by law appoint a different day.

Section 3. If, at the time fixed for the beginning of the term of the President, the President elect shall have died, the Vice-President elect shall become President. If a President shall not have been chosen before the time fixed for the beginning of his term or if the President elect shall have failed to qualify, then the Vice-President elect shall act as President until a President shall have qualified; and the Congress may by law provide for the case wherein neither a President elect nor a Vice-President elect shall have qualified, declaring who shall then act as President, or the manner in which one who is to act shall be selected, and such person shall act accordingly until a President or Vice-President shall have qualified.

Section 4. The Congress may by law provide for the case of the death of any of the persons from whom the House of Representatives may choose a President whenever the right of choice shall have devolved upon them, and for the case of the death of any of the persons from whom the Senate may choose a Vice-President whenever the right of choice shall have devolved upon them.

Section 5. Sections 1 and 2 shall take effect on the 15th day of October following the ratification of this article.

Section 6. This article shall be inoperative unless it shall have been ratified as an amendment to the Constitution by the legislatures of three-fourths of the several States within seven years from the date of its submission.

[AMENDMENT XXI][18]

Section 1. The eighteenth article of amendment to the Constitution of the United States is hereby repealed.

Section 2. The transportation or importation into any State, Territory, or possession of the United States for delivery or use therein of intoxicating

[18]Adopted in 1933.

liquors, in violation of the laws thereof, is hereby prohibited.

Section 3. This article shall be inoperative unless it shall have been ratified as an amendment to the Constitution by conventions in the several States, as provided in the Constitution, within seven years from the date of the submission hereof to the States by the Congress.

[AMENDMENT XXII][19]

No person shall be elected to the office of the President more than twice, and no person who has held the office of President, or acted as President, for more than two years of a term to which some other person was elected President shall be elected to the office of the President more than once.

But this Article shall not apply to any person holding the office of President when this Article was proposed by the Congress, and shall not prevent any person who may be holding the office of President, or acting as President, during the term within which this Article becomes operative from holding the office of President or acting as President during the remainder of such term.

This article shall be inoperative unless it shall have been ratified as an amendment to the Constitution by the legislatures of three-fourths of the several states within seven years from the date of its submission to the states by the Congress.

[AMENDMENT XXIII][20]

Section 1. The District constituting the seat of Government of the United States shall appoint in such manner as the Congress may direct:

A number of electors of President and Vice-President equal to the whole number of Senators and Representatives in Congress to which the District would be entitled if it were a State, but in no event more than the least populous State; they shall be in addition to those appointed by the States, but they shall be considered, for the purpose of the election of President and Vice-

[19]Adopted in 1961.

[20]Adopted in 1961.

President, to be electors appointed by a State; and they shall meet in the District and perform such duties as provided by the twelfth article of amendment.

Section 2. The Congress shall have power to enforce this article by appropriate legislation.

[AMENDMENT XXIV][21]

Section 1. The right of citizens of the United States to vote in any primary or other election for President or Vice-President, for electors for President or Vice-President, or for Senator or Representative in Congress, shall not be denied or abridged by the United States or any state by reason of failure to pay any poll tax or other tax.

Section 2. The Congress shall have the power to enforce this article by appropriate legislation.

[AMENDMENT XXV][22]

Section 1. In case of the removal of the President from office or of his death or resignation, the Vice-President shall become President.

Section 2. Whenever there is a vacancy in the office of the Vice President, the President shall nominate a Vice President who shall take office upon confirmation by a majority vote of both Houses of Congress.

Section 3. Whenever the President transmits to the President Pro Tempore of the Senate and the Speaker of the House of Representatives his written declaration that he is unable to discharge the powers and duties of his office, and until he transmits to them a written declaration to the contrary, such powers and duties shall be discharged by the Vice-President as Acting President.

Section 4. Whenever the Vice-President and a majority of either the principal officers of the executive departments or of such other body as Congress may by law provide, transmit to the President Pro Tempore of the Senate and the Speaker of the House of Representatives their

written declaration that the President is unable to discharge the powers and duties of his office, the Vice President shall immediately assume the powers and duties of the office as Acting President.

Thereafter, when the President transmits to the President Pro Tempore of the Senate and the Speaker of the House of Representatives his written declaration that no inability exists, he shall resume the powers and duties of his office unless the Vice President and a majority of either the principal officers of the executive departments or of such other body as Congress may by law provide, transmit within four days to the President Pro Tempore of the Senate and the Speaker of the House of Representatives their written declaration that the President is unable to discharge the powers and duties of his office. Thereupon Congress shall decide the issue, assembling within forty-eight hours for that purpose if not in session. If the Congress, within twenty-one days after receipt of the latter written declaration, or, if Congress is not in session, within twenty-one days after Congress is required to assemble, determines by two-thirds vote of both Houses that the President is unable to discharge the powers and duties of his office, the Vice President shall continue to discharge the same as Acting President; otherwise, the President shall resume the powers and duties of his office.

[AMENDMENT XXVI][23]

Section 1. The right of citizens of the United States, who are eighteen years of age or older, to vote shall not be denied or abridged by the United States or by any State on account of age.

Section 2. The Congress shall have power to enforce this article by appropriate legislation.

[AMENDMENT XXVII][24]

No law, varying the compensation for the services of the Senators and Representatives, shall take effect, until an election of Representatives shall have intervened.

[21]Adopted in 1964.
[22]Adopted in 1967.

[23]Adopted in 1971.
[24]Adopted in 1992.

PRESIDENTIAL ADMINISTRATIONS

The Washington Administration (1789–1797)

Vice President	John Adams	1789–1797
Secretary of State	Thomas Jefferson	1789–1793
	Edmund Randolph	1794–1795
	Timothy Pickering	1795–1797
Secretary of Treasury	Alexander Hamilton	1789–1795
	Oliver Wolcott	1795–1797
Secretary of War	Henry Knox	1789–1794
	Timothy Pickering	1795–1796
	James McHenry	1796–1797
Attorney General	Edmund Randolph	1789–1793
	William Bradford	1794–1795
	Charles Lee	1795–1797
Postmaster General	Samuel Osgood	1789–1791
	Timothy Pickering	1791–1794
	Joseph Habersham	1795–1797

The John Adams Administration (1797–1801)

Vice President	Thomas Jefferson	1797–1801
Secretary of State	Timothy Pickering	1797–1800
	John Marshall	1800–1801
Secretary of Treasury	Oliver Wolcott	1797–1800
	Samuel Dexter	1800–1801
Secretary of War	James McHenry	1797–1800
	Samuel Dexter	1800–1801
Attorney General	Charles Lee	1797–1801
Postmaster General	Joseph Habersham	1797–1801
Secretary of Navy	Benjamin Stoddert	1798–1801

The Jefferson Administration (1801–1809)

Vice President	Aaron Burr	1801–1805
	George Clinton	1805–1809
Secretary of State	James Madison	1801–1809
Secretary of Treasury	Samuel Dexter	1801
	Albert Gallatin	1801–1809
Secretary of War	Henry Dearborn	1801–1809
Attorney General	Levi Lincoln	1801–1805
	Robert Smith	1805
	John Breckinridge	1805–1806
	Caesar Rodney	1807–1809

Postmaster General	Joseph Habersham	1801
	Gideon Granger	1801–1809
Secretary of Navy	Robert Smith	1801–1809

The Madison Administration (1809–1817)

Vice President	George Clinton	1809–1813
	Elbridge Gerry	1813–1817
Secretary of State	Robert Smith	1809–1811
	James Monroe	1811–1817
Secretary of Treasury	Albert Gallatin	1809–1813
	George Campbell	1814
	Alexander Dallas	1814–1816
	William Crawford	1816–1817
Secretary of War	William Eustis	1809–1812
	John Armstrong	1813–1814
	James Monroe	1814–1815
	William Crawford	1815–1817
Attorney General	Caesar Rodney	1809–1811
	William Pinkney	1811–1814
	Richard Rush	1814–1817
Postmaster General	Gideon Granger	1809–1814
	Return Meigs	1814–1817
Secretary of Navy	Paul Hamilton	1809–1813
	William Jones	1813–1814
	Benjamin Crowninshield	1814–1817

The Monroe Administration (1817–1825)

Vice President	Daniel Tompkins	1817–1825
Secretary of State	John Quincy Adams	1817–1825
Secretary of Treasury	William Crawford	1817–1825
Secretary of War	George Graham	1817
	John C. Calhoun	1817–1825
Attorney General	Richard Rush	1817
	William Wirt	1817–1825
Postmaster General	Return Meigs	1817–1823
	John McLean	1823–1825
Secretary of Navy	Benjamin Crowninshield	1817–1818
	Smith Thompson	1818–1823
	Samuel Southard	1823–1825

The John Quincy Adams Administration (1825–1829)

Vice President	John C. Calhoun	1825–1829
Secretary of State	Henry Clay	1825–1829
Secretary of Treasury	Richard Rush	1825–1829
Secretary of War	James Barbour	1825–1828
	Peter Porter	1828–1829
Attorney General	William Wirt	1825–1829
Postmaster General	John McLean	1825–1829
Secretary of Navy	Samuel Southard	1825–1829

The Jackson Administration (1829–1837)

Vice President	John C. Calhoun	1829–1833
	Martin Van Buren	1833–1837
Secretary of State	Martin Van Buren	1829–1831
	Edward Livingston	1831–1833
	Louis McLane	1833–1834
	John Forsyth	1834–1837
Secretary of Treasury	Samuel Ingham	1829–1831
	Louis McLane	1831–1833
	William Duane	1833
	Roger B. Taney	1833–1834
	Levi Woodbury	1834–1837
Secretary of War	John H. Eaton	1829–1831
	Lewis Cass	1831–1837
	Benjamin Butler	1837
Attorney General	John M. Berrien	1829–1831
	Roger B. Taney	1831–1833
	Benjamin Butler	1833–1837
Postmaster General	William Barry	1829–1835
	Amos Kendall	1835–1837
Secretary of Navy	John Branch	1829–1831
	Levi Woodbury	1831–1834
	Mahlon Dickerson	1834–1837

The Van Buren Administration (1837–1841)

Vice President	Richard M. Johnson	1837–1841
Secretary of State	John Forsyth	1837–1841
Secretary of Treasury	Levi Woodbury	1837–1841
Secretary of War	Joel Poinsett	1837–1841
Attorney General	Benjamin Butler	1837–1838
	Felix Grundy	1838–1840
	Henry D. Gilpin	1840–1841
Postmaster General	Amos Kendall	1837–1840
	John M. Niles	1840–1841
Secretary of Navy	Mahlon Dickerson	1837–1838
	James Paulding	1838–1841

The William Harrison Administration (1841)

Vice President	John Tyler	1841
Secretary of State	Daniel Webster	1841
Secretary of Treasury	Thomas Ewing	1841
Secretary of War	John Bell	1841
Attorney General	John J. Crittenden	1841
Postmaster General	Francis Granger	1841
Secretary of Navy	George Badger	1841

The Tyler Administration (1841–1845)

Vice President	None	
Secretary of State	Daniel Webster	1841–1843
	Hugh S. Legaré	1843
	Abel P. Upshur	1843–1844
	John C. Calhoun	1844–1845
Secretary of Treasury	Thomas Ewing	1841
	Walter Forward	1841–1843
	John C. Spencer	1843–1844
	George Bibb	1844–1845
Secretary of War	John Bell	1841
	John C. Spencer	1841–1843
	James M. Porter	1843–1844
	William Wilkins	1844–1845
Attorney General	John J. Crittenden	1841
	Hugh S. Legaré	1841–1843
	John Nelson	1843–1845
Postmaster General	Francis Granger	1841
	Charles Wickliffe	1841
Secretary of Navy	George Badger	1841
	Abel P. Upshur	1841
	David Henshaw	1843–1844
	Thomas Gilmer	1844
	John Y. Mason	1844–1845

The Polk Administration (1845–1849)

Vice President	George M. Dallas	1845–1849
Secretary of State	James Buchanan	1845–1849
Secretary of Treasury	Robert J. Walker	1845–1849

Secretary of War	William L. Marcy	1845–1849
Attorney General	John Y. Mason	1845–1846
	Nathan Clifford	1846–1848
	Isaac Toucey	1848–1849
Postmaster General	Cave Johnson	1845–1849
Secretary of Navy	George Bancroft	1845–1846
	John Y. Mason	1846–1849

The Taylor Administration (1849–1850)

Vice President	Millard Fillmore	1849–1850
Secretary of State	John M. Clayton	1849–1850
Secretary of Treasury	William Meredith	1849–1850
Secretary of War	George Crawford	1849–1850
Attorney General	Reverdy Johnson	1849–1850
Postmaster General	Jacob Collamer	1849–1850
Secretary of Navy	William Preston	1849–1850
Secretary of Interior	Thomas Ewing	1849–1850

The Fillmore Administration (1850–1853)

Vice President	None	
Secretary of State	Daniel Webster	1850–1852
	Edward Everett	1852–1853
Secretary of Treasury	Thomas Corwin	1850–1853
Secretary of War	Charles Conrad	1850–1853
Attorney General	John J. Crittenden	1850–1853
Postmaster General	Nathan Hall	1850–1852
	Sam D. Hubbard	1852–1853
Secretary of Navy	William A. Graham	1850–1852
	John P. Kennedy	1852–1853
Secretary of Interior	Thomas McKennan	1850
	Alexander Stuart	1850–1853

The Pierce Administration (1853–1857)

Vice President	William R. King	1853–1857
Secretary of State	William L. Marcy	1853–1857
Secretary of Treasury	James Guthrie	1853–1857

Secretary of War	Jefferson Davis	1853–1857
Attorney General	Caleb Cushing	1853–1857
Postmaster General	James Campbell	1853–1857
Secretary of Navy	James C. Dobbin	1853–1857
Secretary of Interior	Robert McClelland	1853–1857

The Buchanan Administration (1857–1861)

Vice President	John C. Breckinridge	1857–1861
Secretary of State	Lewis Cass	1857–1860
	Jeremiah S. Black	1860–1861
Secretary of Treasury	Howell Cobb	1857–1860
	Philip Thomas	1860–1861
	John A. Dix	1861
Secretary of War	John B. Floyd	1857–1861
	Joseph Holt	1861
Attorney General	Jeremiah S. Black	1857–1860
	Edwin M. Stanton	1860–1861
Postmaster General	Aaron V. Brown	1857–1859
	Joseph Holt	1859–1861
	Horatio King	1861
Secretary of Navy	Isaac Toucey	1857–1861
Secretary of Interior	Jacob Thompson	1857–1861

The Lincoln Administration (1861–1865)

Vice President	Hannibal Hamlin	1861–1865
	Andrew Johnson	1865
Secretary of State	William H. Seward	1861–1865
Secretary of Treasury	Samuel P. Chase	1861–1864
	William P. Fessenden	1864–1865
	Hugh McCulloch	1865
Secretary of War	Simon Cameron	1861–1862
	Edwin M. Stanton	1862–1865
Attorney General	Edward Bates	1861–1864
	James Speed	1864–1865
Postmaster General	Horatio King	1861
	Montgomery Blair	1861–1864
	William Dennison	1864–1865
Secretary of Navy	Gideon Welles	1861–1865
Secretary of Interior	Caleb B. Smith	1861–1863
	John P. Usher	1863–1865

The Andrew Johnson Administration (1865–1869)

Vice President	None	
Secretary of State	William H. Seward	1865–1869
Secretary of Treasury	Hugh McCulloch	1865–1869
Secretary of War	Edwin M. Stanton	1865–1867
	Ulysses S. Grant	1867–1868
	Lorenzo Thomas	1868
	John M. Schofield	1868–1869
Attorney General	James Speed	1865–1866
	Henry Stanbery	1866–1868
	William M. Evarts	1868–1869
Postmaster General	William Dennison	1865–1866
	Alexander Randall	1866–1869
Secretary of Navy	Gideon Welles	1865–1869
Secretary of Interior	John P. Usher	1865
	James Harlan	1865–1866
	Orville H. Browning	1866–1869

The Grant Administration (1869–1877)

Vice President	Schuyler Colfax	1869–1873
	Henry Wilson	1873–1877
Secretary of State	Elihu B. Washburne	1869
	Hamilton Fish	1869–1877
Secretary of Treasury	George S. Boutwell	1869–1873
	William Richardson	1873–1874
	Benjamin Bristow	1874–1876
	Lot M. Morrill	1876–1877
Secretary of War	John A. Rawlins	1869
	William T. Sherman	1869
	William W. Belknap	1869–1876
	Alphonso Taft	1876
	James D. Cameron	1876–1877
Attorney General	Ebenezer Hoar	1869–1870
	Amos T. Ackerman	1870–1871
	G. H. Williams	1871–1875
	Edwards Pierrepont	1875–1876
	Alphonso Taft	1876–1877
Postmaster General	John A. J. Creswell	1869–1874
	James W. Marshall	1874
	Marshall Jewell	1874–1876
	James N. Tyner	1876–1877

Secretary of Navy	Adolph E. Borie	1869
	George M. Robeson	1869–1877
Secretary of Interior	Jacob D. Cox	1869–1870
	Columbus Delano	1870–1875
	Zachariah Chandler	1875–1877

The Hayes Administration (1877–1881)

Vice President	William A. Wheeler	1877–1881
Secretary of State	William M. Evarts	1877–1881
Secretary of Treasury	John Sherman	1877–1881
Secretary of War	George W. McCrary	1877–1879
	Alex Ramsey	1879–1881
Attorney General	Charles Devens	1877–1881
Postmaster General	David M. Key	1877–1880
	Horace Maynard	1880–1881
Secretary of Navy	Richard W. Thompson	1877–1880
	Nathan Goff, Jr.	1881
Secretary of Interior	Carl Schurz	1877–1881

The Garfield Administration (1881)

Vice President	Chester A. Arthur	1881
Secretary of State	James G. Blaine	1881
Secretary of Treasury	William Windom	1881
Secretary of War	Robert T. Lincoln	1881
Attorney General	Wayne MacVeagh	1881
Postmaster General	Thomas L. James	1881
Secretary of Navy	William H. Hunt	1881
Secretary of Interior	Samuel J. Kirkwood	1881

The Arthur Administration (1881–1885)

Vice President	None	
Secretary of State	F. T. Frelinghuysen	1881–1885

Secretary of Treasury	Charles J. Folger	1881–1884
	Walter Q. Gresham	1884
	Hugh McCulloch	1884–1885
Secretary of War	Robert T. Lincoln	1881–1885
Attorney General	Benjamin H. Brewster	1881–1885
Postmaster General	Timothy O. Howe	1881–1883
	Walter Q. Gresham	1883–1884
	Frank Hatton	1884–1885
Secretary of Navy	William H. Hunt	1881–1882
	William E. Chandler	1882–1885
Secretary of Interior	Samuel J. Kirkwood	1881–1882
	Henry M. Teller	1882–1885

The Cleveland Administration (1885–1889)

Vice President	Thomas A. Hendricks	1885–1889
Secretary of State	Thomas F. Bayard	1885–1889
Secretary of Treasury	Daniel Manning	1885–1887
	Charles S. Fairchild	1887–1889
Secretary of War	William C. Endicott	1885–1889
Attorney General	Augustus H. Garland	1885–1889
Postmaster General	William F. Vilas	1885–1888
	Don M. Dickinson	1888–1889
Secretary of Navy	William C. Whitney	1885–1889
Secretary of Interior	Lucius Q. C. Lamar	1885–1888
	William F. Vilas	1888–1889
Secretary of Agriculture	Norman J. Colman	1889

The Benjamin Harrison Administration (1889–1893)

Vice President	Levi P. Morton	1889–1893
Secretary of State	James G. Blaine	1889–1892
	John W. Foster	1892–1893
Secretary of Treasury	William Windom	1889–1891
	Charles Foster	1891–1893
Secretary of War	Redfield Proctor	1889–1891
	Stephen B. Elkins	1891–1893
Attorney General	William H. H. Miller	1889–1893

Postmaster General	John Wanamaker	1889–1893
Secretary of Navy	Benjamin F. Tracy	1889–1893
Secretary of Interior	John W. Noble	1889–1893
Secretary of Agriculture	Jeremiah M. Rusk	1889–1893

The Cleveland Administration (1893–1897)

Vice President	Adlai E. Stevenson	1893–1897
Secretary of State	Walter Q. Gresham	1893–1895
	Richard Olney	1895–1897
Secretary of Treasury	John G. Carlisle	1893–1897
Secretary of War	Daniel S. Lamont	1893–1897
Attorney General	Richard Olney	1893–1895
	James Harmon	1895–1897
Postmaster General	Wilson S. Bissell	1893–1895
	William L. Wilson	1895–1897
Secretary of Navy	Hilary A. Herbert	1893–1897
Secretary of Interior	Hoke Smith	1893–1896
	David R. Francis	1896–1897
Secretary of Agriculture	Julius S. Morton	1893–1897

The McKinley Administration (1897–1901)

Vice President	Garret A. Hobart	1897–1901
	Theodore Roosevelt	1901
Secretary of State	John Sherman	1897–1898
	William R. Day	1898
	John Hay	1898–1901
Secretary of Treasury	Lyman J. Gage	1897–1901
Secretary of War	Russell A. Alger	1897–1899
	Elihu Root	1899–1901
Attorney General	Joseph McKenna	1897–1898
	John W. Griggs	1898–1901
	Philander C. Knox	1901
Postmaster General	James A. Gary	1897–1898
	Charles E. Smith	1898–1901
Secretary of Navy	John D. Long	1897–1901
Secretary of Interior	Cornelius N. Bliss	1897–1899
	Ethan A. Hitchcock	1899–1901
Secretary of Agriculture	James Wilson	1897–1901

The Theodore Roosevelt Administration (1901–1909)

Vice President	Charles Fairbanks	1905–1909
Secretary of State	John Hay	1901–1905
	Elihu Root	1905–1909
	Robert Bacon	1909
Secretary of Treasury	Lyman J. Gage	1901–1902
	Leslie M. Shaw	1902–1907
	George B. Cortelyou	1907–1909
Secretary of War	Elihu Root	1901–1904
	William H. Taft	1904–1908
	Luke E. Wright	1908–1909
Attorney General	Philander C. Knox	1901–1904
	William H. Moody	1904–1906
	Charles J. Bonaparte	1906–1909
Postmaster General	Charles E. Smith	1901–1902
	Henry C. Payne	1902–1904
	Robert J. Wynne	1904–1905
	George B. Cortelyou	1905–1907
	George von L. Meyer	1907–1909
Secretary of Navy	John D. Long	1901–1902
	William H. Moody	1902–1904
	Paul Morton	1904–1905
	Charles J. Bonaparte	1905–1906
	Victor H. Metcalf	1906–1908
	Truman H. Newberry	1908–1909
Secretary of Interior	Ethan A. Hitchcock	1901–1907
	James R. Garfield	1907–1909
Secretary of Agriculture	James Wilson	1901–1909
Secretary of Labor and Commerce	George B. Cortelyou	1903–1904
	Victor H. Metcalf	1904–1906
	Oscar S. Straus	1906–1909
	Charles Nagel	1909

The Taft Administration (1909–1913)

Vice President	James S. Sherman	1909–1913
Secretary of State	Philander C. Knox	1909–1913
Secretary of Treasury	Franklin MacVeagh	1909–1913
Secretary of War	Jacob M. Dickinson	1909–1911
	Henry L. Stimson	1911–1913
Attorney General	George W. Wickersham	1909–1913
Postmaster General	Frank H. Hitchcock	1909–1913
Secretary of Navy	George von L. Meyer	1909–1913
Secretary of Interior	Richard A. Ballinger	1909–1911
	Walter L. Fisher	1911–1913
Secretary of Agriculture	James Wilson	1909–1913
Secretary of Labor and Commerce	Charles Nagel	1909–1913

The Wilson Administration (1913–1921)

Vice President	Thomas R. Marshall	1913–1921
Secretary of State	William J. Bryan	1913–1915
	Robert Lansing	1915–1920
	Bainbridge Colby	1920–1921
Secretary of Treasury	William G. McAdoo	1913–1918
	Carter Glass	1918–1920
	David F. Houston	1920–1921
Secretary of War	Lindley M. Garrison	1913–1916
	Newton D. Baker	1916–1921
Attorney General	James C. McReynolds	1913–1914
	Thomas W. Gregory	1914–1919
	A. Mitchell Palmer	1919–1921
Postmaster General	Albert S. Burleson	1913–1921
Secretary of Navy	Josephus Daniels	1913–1921
Secretary of Interior	Franklin K. Lane	1913–1920
	John B. Payne	1920–1921
Secretary of Agriculture	David F. Houston	1913–1920
	Edwin T. Meredith	1920–1921
Secretary of Commerce	William C. Redfield	1913–1919
	Joshua W. Alexander	1919–1921
Secretary of Labor	William B. Wilson	1913–1921

The Harding Administration (1921–1923)

Vice President	Calvin Coolidge	1921–1923
Secretary of State	Charles E. Hughes	1921–1923

Secretary of Treasury	Andrew Mellon	1921–1923
Secretary of War	John W. Weeks	1921–1923
Attorney General	Harry M. Daugherty	1921–1923
Postmaster General	Will H. Hays	1921–1922
	Hubert Work	1922–1923
	Harry S. New	1923
Secretary of Navy	Edwin Denby	1921–1923
Secretary of Interior	Albert B. Fall	1921–1923
	Hubert Work	1923
Secretary of Agriculture	Henry C. Wallace	1921–1923
Secretary of Commerce	Herbert C. Hoover	1921–1923
Secretary of Labor	James J. Davis	1921–1923

The Coolidge Administration (1923–1929)

Vice President	Charles G. Dawes	1925–1929
Secretary of State	Charles E. Hughes	1923–1925
	Frank B. Kellogg	1925–1929
Secretary of Treasury	Andrew Mellon	1923–1929
Secretary of War	John W. Weeks	1923–1925
	Dwight F. Davis	1925–1929
Attorney General	Henry M. Daugherty	1923–1924
	Harlan F. Stone	1924–1925
	John G. Sargent	1925–1929
Postmaster General	Harry S. New	1923–1929
Secretary of Navy	Edwin Derby	1923–1924
	Curtis D. Wilbur	1924–1929
Secretary of Interior	Hubert Work	1923–1928
	Roy O. West	1928–1929
Secretary of Agriculture	Henry C. Wallace	1923–1924
	Howard M. Gore	1924–1925
	William M. Jardine	1925–1929
Secretary of Commerce	Herbert C. Hoover	1923–1928
	William F. Whiting	1928–1929
Secretary of Labor	James J. Davis	1923–1929

The Hoover Administration (1929–1933)

Vice President	Charles Curtis	1929–1933
Secretary of State	Henry L. Stimson	1929–1933
Secretary of Treasury	Andrew Mellon	1929–1932
	Ogden L. Mills	1932–1933
Secretary of War	James W. Good	1929
	Patrick J. Hurley	1929–1933
Attorney General	William D. Mitchell	1929–1933
Postmaster General	Walter F. Brown	1929–1933
Secretary of Navy	Charles F. Adams	1929–1933
Secretary of Interior	Ray L. Wilbur	1929–1933
Secretary of Agriculture	Arthur M. Hyde	1929–1933
Secretary of Commerce	Robert P. Lamont	1929–1932
	Roy D. Chapin	1932–1933
Secretary of Labor	James J. Davis	1929–1930
	William N. Doak	1930–1933

The Franklin D. Roosevelt Administration (1933–1945)

Vice President	John Nance Garner	1933–1941
	Henry A. Wallace	1941–1945
	Harry S Truman	1945
Secretary of State	Cordell Hull	1933–1944
	Edward R. Stettinius, Jr.	1944–1945
Secretary of Treasury	William H. Woodin	1933–1934
	Henry Morgenthau, Jr.	1934–1945
Secretary of War	George H. Dern	1933–1936
	Henry A. Woodring	1936–1940
	Henry L. Stimson	1940–1945
Attorney General	Homer S. Cummings	1933–1939
	Frank Murphy	1939–1940
	Robert H. Jackson	1940–1941
	Francis Biddle	1941–1945
Postmaster General	James A. Farley	1933–1940
	Frank C. Walker	1940–1945
Secretary of Navy	Claude A. Swanson	1933–1940
	Charles Edison	1940
	Frank Knox	1940–1944
	James V. Forrestal	1944–1945
Secretary of Interior	Harold L. Ickes	1933–1945
Secretary of Agriculture	Henry A. Wallace	1933–1940
	Claude R. Wickard	1940–1945

Secretary of Commerce	Daniel C. Roper	1933–1939
	Harry L. Hopkins	1939–1940
	Jesse Jones	1940–1945
	Henry A. Wallace	1945
Secretary of Labor	Frances Perkins	1933–1945

The Truman Administration (1945–1953)

Vice President	Alben W. Barkley	1949–1953
Secretary of State	Edward R. Stettinius, Jr.	1945
	James F. Byrnes	1945–1947
	George C. Marshall	1947–1949
	Dean G. Acheson	1949–1953
Secretary of Treasury	Fred M. Vinson	1945–1946
	John W. Snyder	1946–1953
Secretary of War	Robert P. Patterson	1945–1947
	Kenneth C. Royall	1947
Attorney General	Tom C. Clark	1945–1949
	J. Howard McGrath	1949–1952
	James P. McGranery	1952–1953
Postmaster General	Frank C. Walker	1945
	Robert E. Hannegan	1945–1947
	Jesse M. Donaldson	1947–1953
Secretary of Navy	James V. Forrestal	1945–1947
Secretary of Interior	Harold L. Ickes	1945–1946
	Julius A. Krug	1946–1949
	Oscar L. Chapman	1949–1953
Secretary of Agriculture	Clinton P. Anderson	1945–1948
	Charles F. Brannan	1948–1953
Secretary of Commerce	Henry A. Wallace	1945–1946
	W. Averell Harriman	1946–1948
	Charles W. Sawyer	1948–1953
Secretary of Labor	Lewis B. Schwellenbach	1945–1948
	Maurice J. Tobin	1948–1953
Secretary of Defense	James V. Forrestal	1947–1949
	Louis A. Johnson	1949–1950
	George C. Marshall	1950–1951
	Robert A. Lovett	1951–1953

The Eisenhower Administration (1953–1961)

Vice President	Richard M. Nixon	1953–1961
Secretary of State	John Foster Dulles	1953–1959
	Christian A. Herter	1959–1961
Secretary of Treasury	George M. Humphrey	1953–1957
	Robert B. Anderson	1957–1961
Attorney General	Herbert Brownell, Jr.	1953–1958
	William P. Rogers	1958–1961
Postmaster General	Arthur E. Summerfield	1953–1961
Secretary of Interior	Douglas McKay	1953–1956
	Fred A. Seaton	1956–1961
Secretary of Agriculture	Ezra T. Benson	1953–1961
Secretary of Commerce	Sinclair Weeks	1953–1958
	Lewis L. Strauss	1958–1959
	Frederick H. Mueller	1959–1961
Secretary of Labor	Martin P. Durkin	1953
	James P. Mitchell	1953–1961
Secretary of Defense	Charles E. Wilson	1953–1957
	Neil H. McElroy	1957–1959
	Thomas S. Gates, Jr.	1959–1961
Secretary of Health, Education, and Welfare	Oveta Culp Hobby	1953–1955
	Marion B. Folsom	1955–1958
	Arthur S. Flemming	1958–1961

The Kennedy Administration (1961–1963)

Vice President	Lyndon B. Johnson	1961–1963
Secretary of State	Dean Rusk	1961–1963
Secretary of Treasury	C. Douglas Dillon	1961–1963
Attorney General	Robert F. Kennedy	1961–1963
Postmaster General	J. Edward Day	1961–1963
	John A. Gronouski	1963
Secretary of Interior	Stewart L. Udall	1961–1963
Secretary of Agriculture	Orville L. Freeman	1961–1963
Secretary of Commerce	Luther H. Hodges	1961–1963

Secretary of Labor	Arthur J. Goldberg	1961–1962
	W. Willard Wirtz	1962–1963
Secretary of Defense	Robert S. McNamara	1961–1963
Secretary of Health, Education, and Welfare	Abraham A. Ribicoff	1961–1962
	Anthony J. Celebrezze	1962–1963

The Lyndon Johnson Administration (1963–1969)

Vice President	Hubert H. Humphrey	1965–1969
Secretary of State	Dean Rusk	1963–1969
Secretary of Treasury	C. Douglas Dillon	1963–1965
	Henry H. Fowler	1965–1969
Attorney General	Robert F. Kennedy	1963–1964
	Nicholas Katzenbach	1965–1966
	Ramsey Clark	1967–1969
Postmaster General	John A. Gronouski	1963–1965
	Lawrence F. O'Brien	1965–1968
	Marvin Watson	1968–1969
Secretary of Interior	Stewart L. Udall	1963–1969
Secretary of Agriculture	Orville L. Freeman	1963–1969
Secretary of Commerce	Luther H. Hodges	1963–1964
	John T. Connor	1964–1967
	Alexander B. Trowbridge	1967–1968
	Cyrus R. Smith	1968–1969
Secretary of Labor	W. Willard Wirtz	1963–1969
Secretary of Defense	Robert F. McNamara	1963–1968
	Clark Clifford	1968–1969
Secretary of Health, Education, and Welfare	Anthony J. Celebrezze	1963–1965
	John W. Gardner	1965–1968
	Wilbur J. Cohen	1968–1969
Secretary of Housing and Urban Development	Robert C. Weaver	1966–1969
	Robert C. Wood	1969
Secretary of Transportation	Alan S. Boyd	1967–1969

The Nixon Administration (1969–1974)

Vice President	Spiro T. Agnew	1969–1973
	Gerald R. Ford	1973–1974
Secretary of State	William P. Rogers	1969–1973
	Henry A. Kissinger	1973–1974
Secretary of Treasury	David M. Kennedy	1969–1970
	John B. Connally	1971–1972
	George P. Shultz	1972–1974
	William E. Simon	1974
Attorney General	John N. Mitchell	1969–1972
	Richard G. Kleindienst	1972–1973
	Elliot L. Richardson	1973
	William B. Saxbe	1973–1974
Postmaster General	Winton M. Blount	1969–1971
Secretary of Interior	Walter J. Hickel	1969–1970
	Rogers Morton	1971–1974
Secretary of Agriculture	Clifford M. Hardin	1969–1971
	Earl L. Butz	1971–1974
Secretary of Commerce	Maurice H. Stans	1969–1972
	Peter G. Peterson	1972–1973
	Frederick B. Dent	1973–1974
Secretary of Labor	George P. Shultz	1969–1970
	James D. Hodgson	1970–1973
	Peter J. Brennan	1973–1974
Secretary of Defense	Melvin R. Laird	1969–1973
	Elliot L. Richardson	1973
	James R. Schlesinger	1973–1974
Secretary of Health, Education, and Welfare	Robert H. Finch	1969–1970
	Elliot L. Richardson	1970–1973
	Caspar W. Weinberger	1973–1974
Secretary of Housing and Urban Development	George Romney	1969–1973
	James T. Lynn	1973–1974
Secretary of Transportation	John A. Volpe	1969–1973
	Claude S. Brinegar	1973–1974

The Ford Administration (1974–1977)

Vice President	Nelson A. Rockefeller	1974–1977
Secretary of State	Henry A. Kissinger	1974–1977

Secretary of Treasury	William E. Simon	1974–1977
Attorney General	William Saxbe	1974–1975
	Edward Levi	1975–1977
Secretary of Interior	Rogers Morton	1974–1975
	Stanley K. Hathaway	1975
	Thomas Kleppe	1975–1977
Secretary of Agriculture	Earl L. Butz	1974–1976
	John A. Knebel	1976–1977
Secretary of Commerce	Frederick B. Dent	1975–1976
	Rogers Morton	1975–1976
	Elliot L. Richardson	1976–1977
Secretary of Labor	Peter J. Brennan	1974–1975
	John T. Dunlop	1975–1976
	W. J. Usery	1976–1977
Secretary of Defense	James R. Schlesinger	1974–1975
	Donald Rumsfeld	1975–1977
Secretary of Health, Education, and Welfare	Caspar Weinberger	1974–1975
	Forrest D. Mathews	1975–1977
Secretary of Housing and Urban Development	James T. Lynn	1974–1975
	Carla A. Hills	1975–1977
Secretary of Transportation	Claude Brinegar	1974–1975
	William T. Coleman	1975–1977

The Carter Administration (1977–1981)

Vice President	Walter F. Mondale	1977–1981
Secretary of State	Cyrus R. Vance	1977–1980
	Edmund Muskie	1980–1981
Secretary of Treasury	W. Michael Blumenthal	1977–1979
	G. William Miller	1979–1981
Attorney General	Griffin Bell	1977–1979
	Benjamin R. Civiletti	1979–1981
Secretary of Interior	Cecil D. Andrus	1977–1981
Secretary of Agriculture	Robert Bergland	1977–1981
Secretary of Commerce	Juanita M. Kreps	1977–1979
	Philip M. Klutznick	1979–1981
Secretary of Labor	F. Ray Marshall	1977–1981

Secretary of Defense	Harold Brown	1977–1981
Secretary of Health, Education, and Welfare	Joseph A. Califano	1977–1979
	Patricia R. Harris	1979
Secretary of Health and Human Services	Patricia R. Harris	1979–1981
Secretary of Education	Shirley M. Hufstedler	1979–1981
Secretary of Housing and Urban Development	Patricia R. Harris	1977–1979
	Moon Landrieu	1979–1981
Secretary of Transportation	Brock Adams	1977–1979
	Neil E. Goldschmidt	1979–1981
Secretary of Energy	James R. Schlesinger	1977–1979
	Charles W. Duncan	1979–1981

The Reagan Administration (1981–1989)

Vice President	George Bush	1981–1989
Secretary of State	Alexander M. Haig	1981–1982
	George P. Shultz	1982–1989
Secretary of Treasury	Donald Regan	1981–1985
	James A. Baker, III	1985–1988
	Nicholas Brady	1988–1989
Attorney General	William F. Smith	1981–1985
	Edwin A. Meese III	1985–1988
	Richard Thornburgh	1988–1989
Secretary of Interior	James Watt	1981–1983
	William P. Clark, Jr.	1983–1985
	Donald P. Hodel	1985–1989
Secretary of Agriculture	John Block	1981–1986
	Richard E. Lyng	1986–1989
Secretary of Commerce	Malcolm Baldrige	1981–1987
	C. William Verity, Jr.	1987–1989
Secretary of Labor	Raymond Donovan	1981–1985
	William E. Brock	1985–1987
	Ann D. McLaughlin	1987–1989
Secretary of Defense	Caspar Weinberger	1981–1987
	Frank Carlucci	1987–1989

Secretary of Health and Human Services	Richard Schweiker	1981–1983
	Margaret Heckler	1983–1985
	Otis R. Bowen	1985–1989
Secretary of Education	Terrel H. Bell	1981–1985
	William J. Bennett	1985–1988
	Lauro F. Cavazos	1988–1989
Secretary of Housing and Urban Development	Samuel Pierce	1981–1989
Secretary of Transportation	Drew Lewis	1981–1983
	Elizabeth Dole	1983–1987
	James H. Burnley	1987–1989
Secretary of Energy	James Edwards	1981–1982
	Donald P. Hodel	1982–1985
	John S. Herrington	1985–1989

The Bush Administration (1989–1993)

Vice President	J. Danforth Quayle	1989–1993
Secretary of State	James A. Baker III	1989–1992
Secretary of Treasury	Nicholas Brady	1989–1993
Attorney General	Richard Thornburgh	1989–1991
	William P. Barr	1991–1993
Secretary of Interior	Manuel Lujan	1989–1993
Secretary of Agriculture	Clayton K. Yeutter	1989–1991
	Edward Madigan	1991–1993
Secretary of Commerce	Robert Mosbacher	1989–1992
	Barbara Franklin	1992–1993
Secretary of Labor	Elizabeth Hanford Dole	1989–1991
	Lynn Martin	1991–1993
Secretary of Defense	Richard Cheney	1989–1993
Secretary of Health and Human Services	Louis W. Sullivan	1989–1993
Secretary of Education	Lauro F. Cavazos	1989–1991
	Lamar Alexander	1991–1993
Secretary of Housing and Urban Development	Jack F. Kemp	1989–1993

Secretary of Transportation	Samuel K. Skinner	1989–1992
	Andrew H. Card, Jr.	1992–1993
Secretary of Energy	James D. Watkins	1989–1993
Secretary of Veterans Affairs	Edward J. Derwinski	1989–1993

The Clinton Administration (1993–   )

Vice President	Albert Gore	1993–
Secretary of State	Warren Christopher	1993–1997
Secretary of Treasury	Lloyd Bentsen	1993–1995
	Robert E. Rubin	1995–
Attorney General	Janet Reno	1993–
Secretary of Interior	Bruce Babbitt	1993–
Secretary of Agriculture	Michael Espy	1993–1995
	Dan Glickman	1995–
Secretary of Commerce	Ronald Brown	1993–1996
Secretary of Labor	Robert B. Reich	1993–1997
Secretary of Defense	Les Aspin	1993–1994
	William J. Perry	1994–1997
Secretary of Health and Human Services	Donna Shalala	1993–
Secretary of Housing and Urban Development	Henry G. Cisneros	1993–1997
Secretary of Education	Richard W. Riley	1993–
Secretary of Transportation	Federico Peña	1993–1997
Secretary of Energy	Hazel R. O'Leary	1993–1997
Secretary of Veterans Affairs	Edward J. Derwinski	1993–

JUSTICES OF THE SUPREME COURT

	Term of Service	Years of Service	Life Span		Term of Service	Years of Service	Life Span
John Jay	1789–1795	5	1745–1829	John M. Harlan	1877–1911	34	1833–1911
John Rutledge	1789–1791	1	1739–1800	William B. Woods	1880–1887	7	1824–1887
William Cushing	1789–1810	20	1732–1810	Stanley Matthews	1881–1889	7	1824–1889
James Wilson	1789–1798	8	1742–1798	Horace Gray	1882–1902	20	1828–1902
John Blair	1789–1796	6	1732–1800	Samuel Blatchford	1882–1893	11	1820–1893
Robert H. Harrison	1789–1790	—	1745–1790	Lucius Q. C. Lamar	1888–1893	5	1825–1893
James Iredell	1790–1799	9	1751–1799	*Melville W. Fuller*	1888–1910	21	1833–1910
Thomas Johnson	1791–1793	1	1732–1819	David J. Brewer	1890–1910	20	1837–1910
William Paterson	1793–1806	13	1745–1806	Henry B. Brown	1890–1906	16	1836–1913
John Rutledge°	1795	—	1739–1800	George Shiras, Jr.	1892–1903	10	1832–1924
Samuel Chase	1796–1811	15	1741–1811	Howell E. Jackson	1893–1895	2	1832–1895
Oliver Ellsworth	1796–1800	4	1745–1807	Edward D. White	1894–1910	16	1845–1921
Bushrod Washington	1798–1829	31	1762–1829	Rufus W. Peckham	1895–1909	14	1838–1909
Alfred Moore	1799–1804	4	1755–1810	Joseph McKenna	1898–1925	26	1843–1926
John Marshall	1801–1835	34	1755–1835	Oliver W. Holmes	1902–1932	30	1841–1935
William Johnson	1804–1834	30	1771–1834	William R. Day	1903–1922	19	1849–1923
H. Brockholst				William H. Moody	1906–1910	3	1853–1917
Livingston	1806–1823	16	1757–1823	Horace H. Lurton	1909–1914	4	1844–1914
Thomas Todd	1807–1826	18	1765–1826	Charles E. Hughes	1910–1916	5	1862–1948
Joseph Story	1811–1845	33	1779–1845	*Edward D. White*	1910–1921	11	1845–1921
Gabriel Duval	1811–1835	24	1752–1844	Willis Van Devanter	1911–1937	26	1859–1941
Smith Thompson	1823–1843	20	1768–1843	Joseph R. Lamar	1911–1916	5	1857–1916
Robert Trimble	1826–1828	2	1777–1828	Mahlon Pitney	1912–1922	10	1858–1924
John McLean	1829–1861	32	1785–1861	James C. McReynolds	1914–1941	26	1862–1946
Henry Baldwin	1830–1844	14	1780–1844	Louis D. Brandeis	1916–1939	22	1856–1941
James M. Wayne	1835–1867	32	1790–1867	John H. Clarke	1916–1922	6	1857–1945
Roger B. Taney	1836–1864	28	1777–1864	William H. Taft	1921–1930	8	1857–1930
Philip P. Barbour	1836–1841	4	1783–1841	George Sutherland	1922–1938	15	1862–1942
John Catron	1837–1865	28	1786–1865	Pierce Butler	1922–1939	16	1866–1939
John McKinley	1837–1852	15	1780–1852	Edward T. Sanford	1923–1930	7	1865–1930
Peter V. Daniel	1841–1860	19	1784–1860	Harlan F. Stone	1925–1941	16	1872–1946
Samuel Nelson	1845–1872	27	1792–1873	*Charles E. Hughes*	1930–1941	11	1862–1948
Levi Woodbury	1845–1851	5	1789–1851	Owen J. Roberts	1930–1945	15	1875–1955
Robert C. Grier	1846–1870	23	1794–1870	Benjamin N. Cardozo	1932–1938	6	1870–1938
Benjamin R. Curtis	1851–1857	6	1809–1874	Hugo L. Black	1937–1971	34	1886–1971
John A. Campbell	1853–1861	8	1811–1889	Stanley F. Reed	1938–1957	19	1884–1980
Nathan Clifford	1858–1881	23	1803–1881	Felix Frankfurter	1939–1962	23	1882–1965
Noah H. Swayne	1862–1881	18	1804–1884	William O. Douglas	1939–1975	36	1898–1980
Samuel F. Miller	1862–1890	28	1816–1890	Frank Murphy	1940–1949	9	1890–1949
David Davis	1862–1877	14	1815–1886	*Harlan F. Stone*	1941–1946	5	1872–1946
Stephen J. Field	1863–1897	34	1816–1899	James F. Brynes	1941–1942	1	1879–1972
Salmon P. Chase	1864–1873	8	1808–1873	Robert H. Jackson	1941–1954	13	1892–1954
William Strong	1870–1880	10	1808–1895	Wiley B. Rutledge	1943–1949	6	1894–1949
Joseph P. Bradley	1870–1892	22	1813–1892	Harold H. Burton	1945 – 1958	13	1888–1964
Ward Hunt	1873 – 1882	9	1810–1886	*Fred M. Vinson*	1946–1953	7	1890–1953
Morrison R. Waite	1874 – 1888	14	1816–1888	Tom C. Clark	1949–1967	18	1899–1977

	Term of Service	Years of Service	Life Span		Term of Service	Years of Service	Life Span
Sherman Minton	1949–1956	7	1890–1965	Lewis F. Powell, Jr.	1972–1987	15	1907–
Earl Warren	1953–1969	16	1891–1974	William H. Rehnquist	1972–1986	14	1924–
John Marshall Harlan	1955–1971	16	1899–1971	John P. Stevens III	1975–	—	1920–
William J. Brennan, Jr.	1956–1990	33	1906–	Sandra Day O'Connor	1981–	—	1930–
Charles E. Whittaker	1957–1962	5	1901–1973	*William H. Rehnquist*	1986–	—	1924–
Potter Stewart	1958–1981	23	1915–	Antonin Scalia	1986–	—	1936–
Bryon R. White	1962–1993	31	1917–	Anthony M. Kennedy	1988–	—	1936–
Arthur J. Goldberg	1962–1965	3	1908–1990	David H. Souter	1990–	—	1939–
Abe Fortas	1965–1969	4	1910–1982	Clarence Thomas	1991–	—	1948–
Thurgood Marshall	1967–1991	24	1908–1992	Ruth Bader Ginsberg	1993–	—	1933–
Warren C. Burger	1969–1986	17	1907–	Stephen Breyer	1994–	—	1938–
Harry A. Blackmun	1970–1994	24	1908–				

*Appointed and served one term, but not confirmed by the Senate.

Note: Chief justices are in italics.

A SOCIAL PROFILE OF THE AMERICAN REPUBLIC

POPULATION

Year	Population	Percent Increase	Population Per Square Mile	Percent Urban/ Rural	Percent Male/ Female	Percent White/ Nonwhite	Persons Per Household	Median Age
1790	3,929,214		4.5	5.1/94.9	NA/NA	80.7/19.3	5.79	NA
1800	5,308,483	35.1	6.1	6.1/93.9	NA/NA	81.1/18.9	NA	NA
1810	7,239,881	36.4	4.3	7.3/92.7	NA/NA	81.0/19.0	NA	NA
1820	9,638,453	33.1	5.5	7.2/92.8	50.8/49.2	81.6/18.4	NA	16.7
1830	12,866,020	33.5	7.4	8.8/91.2	50.8/18.1	81.9/18.1	NA	17.2
1840	17,069,453	32.7	9.8	10.8/89.2	50.9/49.1	83.2/16.8	NA	17.8
1850	23,191,876	35.9	7.9	15.3/84.7	51.0/49.0	84.3/15.7	5.55	18.9
1860	31,443,321	35.6	10.6	19.8/80.2	51.2/48.8	85.6/14.4	5.28	19.4
1870	39,818,449	26.6	13.4	25.7/74.3	50.6/49.4	86.2/13.8	5.09	20.2
1880	50,155,783	26.0	16.9	28.2/71.8	50.9/49.1	86.5/13.5	5.04	20.9
1890	62,947,714	25.5	21.2	35.1/64.9	51.2/48.8	87.5/12.5	4.93	22.0
1900	75,994,575	20.7	25.6	39.6/60.4	51.1/48.9	87.9/12.1	4.76	22.9
1910	91,972,266	21.0	31.0	45.6/54.4	51.5/48.5	88.9/11.1	4.54	24.1
1920	105,710,620	14.9	35.6	51.2/48.8	51.0/49.0	89.7/10.3	4.34	25.3
1930	122,775,046	16.1	41.2	56.1/43.9	50.6/49.4	89.8/10.2	4.11	26.4
1940	131,669,275	7.2	44.2	56.5/43.5	50.2/49.8	89.8/10.2	3.67	29.0
1950	150,697,361	14.5	50.7	64.0/36.0	49.7/50.3	89.5/10.5	3.37	30.2
1960	179,323,175	18.5	50.6	69.9/30.1	49.3/11.4	88.6/11.4	3.33	29.5
1970	203,302,031	13.4	57.4	73.5/26.5	48.7/51.3	87.6/12.4	3.14	28.0
1980	226,545,805	11.4	64.0	73.7/26.3	48.6/51.4	86.0/14.0	2.76	30.0
1990	248,709,873	9.8	70.3	NA	48.7/51.3	80.3/19.7	2.63	32.9
2000°	276,382,000	7.1	75.8	NA	48.9/51.5	82.6/17.4	NA	NA

NA = Not available.
°Projections.

VITAL STATISTICS (rates per thousand)

Year	Births	Year	Births	Deaths°	Marriages°	Divorces°
1800	55.0	1900	32.3	17.2	NA	NA
1810	54.3	1910	30.1	14.7	NA	NA
1820	55.2	1920	27.7	13.0	12.0	1.6
1830	51.4	1930	21.3	11.3	9.2	1.6
1840	51.8	1940	19.4	10.8	12.1	2.0
1850	43.3	1950	24.1	9.6	11.1	2.6
1860	44.3	1960	23.7	9.5	8.5	2.2
1870	38.3	1970	18.4	9.5	10.6	3.5
1880	39.8	1980	15.9	8.8	10.6	5.2
1890	31.5	1990	16.7	8.6	9.8	4.6

NA = Not available.
°Data not available before 1900.

LIFE EXPECTANCY (in years)

Year	Total Population	White Females	Nonwhite Females	White Males	Nonwhite Males
1900	47.3	48.7	33.5	46.6	32.5
1910	50.1	52.0	37.5	48.6	33.8
1920	54.1	55.6	45.2	54.4	45.5
1930	59.7	63.5	49.2	59.7	47.3
1940	62.9	66.6	54.9	62.1	51.5
1950	68.2	72.2	62.9	66.5	59.1
1960	69.7	74.1	66.3	67.4	61.1
1970	70.9	75.6	69.4	68.0	61.3
1980	73.7	78.1	73.6	70.7	65.3
1990	75.4	79.3	76.3	72.6	68.4

THE CHANGING AGE STRUCTURE

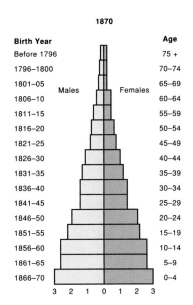

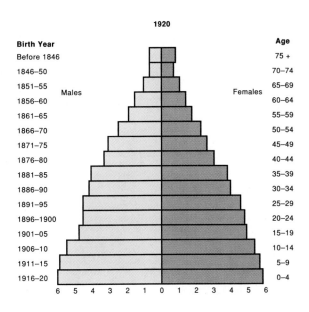

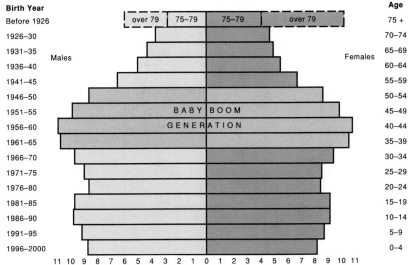

Before the twentieth century, the age distribution of Americans could be charted roughly as a pyramid, as seen in the figures for 1870 and 1920. High birthrates create a broad base at the bottom, while mortality rates winnow the population to a small tip of elderly. But as the year 2000 approaches, the pyramid has been transformed more nearly into a cylinder. Over the past two centuries fertility rates have undergone a steady decline, pulling in the base of the pyramid, while higher living standards have allowed Americans to live longer, broadening the top. Only the temporary bulge of the baby boom distorts the shape.

REGIONAL ORIGIN OF IMMIGRANTS (percent)

Years	Total Number of Immigrants	Total Europe	Europe North and West	Europe East and Central	Europe South and Other	Western Hemisphere	Asia
1821–1830	143,389	69.2	67.1	—	2.1	8.4	—
1831–1840	599,125	82.8	81.8	—	1.0	5.5	—
1841–1850	1,713,251	93.8	92.9	0.1	0.3	3.6	—
1851–1860	2,598,214	94.4	93.6	0.1	0.8	2.9	1.6
1861–1870	2,314,824	89.2	87.8	0.5	0.9	7.2	2.8
1871–1880	2,812,191	80.8	73.6	4.5	2.7	14.4	4.4
1881–1890	5,246,13	90.3	72.0	11.9	6.3	8.1	1.3
1891–1900	3,687,546	96.5	44.5	32.8	19.1	1.1	1.9
1901–1910	8,795,386	92.5	21.7	44.5	6.3	4.1	2.8
1911–1920	5,735,811	76.3	17.4	33.4	25.5	19.9	3.4
1921–1930	4,107,209	60.3	31.7	14.4	14.3	36.9	2.4
1931–1940	528,431	65.9	38.8	11.0	16.1	30.3	2.8
1941–1950	1,035,039	60.1	47.5	4.6	7.9	34.3	3.1
1951–1960	2,515,479	52.8	17.7	24.3	10.8	39.6	6.0
1961–1970	3,321,677	33.8	11.7	9.4	12.9	51.7	12.9
1971–1980	4,493,300	17.8	4.3	5.6	8.4	44.3	35.2
1981–1990	7,338,000	10.4	5.9	4.8	1.1	49.3	37.3

Dash indicates less than 0.1 percent.

RECENT TRENDS IN IMMIGRATION (in thousands)

	1961–1970	1971–1980	1981–1990	1991	Percent 1961–1970	Percent 1971–1980	Percent 1981–1990
All countries	3,321.7	4,493.3	7,338.0	1,827.2	100.0	100.0	100.0
Europe	1,123.5	800.4	761.5	146.7	33.8	17.8	10.4
Austria	20.6	9.5	18.9	3.5	0.6	0.2	0.3
Hungary	5.4	6.6	5.9	0.9	0.2	0.1	0.1
Belgium	9.2	5.3	6.6	0.7	0.3	0.1	0.1
Czechoslovakia	3.3	6.0	5.4	0.6	0.1	0.1	0.1
Denmark	9.2	4.4	2.8	0.6	0.3	0.1	0.1
France	45.2	25.1	92.1	4.0	1.4	0.6	1.3
Germany	190.8	74.4	159.0	10.9	5.7	1.7	2.2
Greece	86.0	92.4	31.9	2.9	2.6	2.1	0.4
Ireland	33.0	11.5	67.2	4.6	1.0	0.3	0.9
Italy	214.1	129.4	12.3	30.3	6.4	2.9	0.2
Netherlands	30.6	10.5	4.2	1.3	0.9	0.2	0.1
Norway	15.5	3.9	83.2	0.6	0.5	0.1	1.1
Poland	53.5	37.2	40.3	17.1	1.6	0.8	0.5
Portugal	76.1	101.7	20.5	4.6	2.3	2.3	0.3
Spain	44.7	39.1	11.1	2.7	1.3	0.9	0.2
Sweden	17.1	6.5	8.0	1.2	0.5	0.1	0.1
Switzerland	18.5	8.2	57.6	1.0	0.6	0.2	0.8
USSR	2.5	39.0	18.7	31.6	0.1	0.9	0.3
United Kingdom	213.8	137.4	159.2	16.8	6.4	3.1	2.2
Yugoslavia	20.4	30.5	37.3	2.8	0.6	0.7	0.5
Other Europe	9.1	18.9	7.7	1.2	0.2	0.2	0.0

RECENT TRENDS IN IMMIGRATION (in thousands)

	1961–1970	1971–1980	1981–1990	1991	Percent 1961–1970	1971–1980	1981–1990
Asia	427.6	1,588.2	2,738.1	342.2	12.9	35.2	37.3
China	34.8	124.3	298.9	24.0	1.0	2.8	4.1
Hong Kong	75.0	113.5	98.2	15.9	2.3	2.5	1.3
India	27.2	164.1	250.7	42.7	0.8	3.7	3.4
Iran	10.3	45.1	116.0	9.9	0.3	1.0	1.6
Israel	29.6	37.7	44.2	5.1	0.9	0.8	0.6
Japan	40.0	49.8	47.0	5.6	1.2	1.1	0.6
Korea	34.5	267.6	333.8	25.4	1.0	6.0	4.5
Philippines	98.4	355.0	548.7	68.8	3.0	7.9	7.5
Turkey	10.1	13.4	23.4	3.5	0.3	0.3	0.3
Vietnam	4.3	172.8	281.0	14.8	1.1	3.8	3.8
Other Asia	36.5	176.1	631.4	126.4	1.1	3.8	8.6
America	1,716.4	1,982.5	3,615.6	1,297.6	51.7	44.3	49.3
Argentina	49.7	29.9	27.3	4.2	1.5	0.7	0.4
Canada	413.3	169.9	158.0	19.9	12.4	3.8	2.2
Colombia	72.0	77.3	122.9	19.3	2.2	1.7	1.7
Cuba	208.5	264.9	144.6	9.5	6.3	5.9	2.0
Dominican Rep.	93.3	148.1	252.0	42.4	2.8	3.3	3.4
Ecuador	36.8	50.1	56.2	10.0	1.1	1.1	0.8
El Salvador	15.0	34.4	213.5	46.9	0.5	0.8	2.9
Haiti	34.5	56.3	138.4	47.0	1.0	1.3	1.9
Jamaica	74.9	137.6	208.1	23.0	2.3	3.1	2.8
Mexico	453.9	640.3	1,655.7	947.9	13.7	14.3	22.6
Other America	264.4	373.8	639.3	128.4	7.9	8.3	8.7
Africa	29.0	80.8	176.8	33.5	0.9	1.8	2.4
Oceania	25.1	41.2	45.2	7.1	0.8	0.9	0.6

Figures may not add to total due to rounding.

AMERICAN WORKERS AND FARMERS

Year	Total Number of Workers (thousands)	Percent of Workers Male/Female	Percent of Female Workers Married	Percent of Workers in Female Population	Percent of Workers in Labor Unions	Farm Population (thousands)	Farm Population as Percent of Total Population
1870	12,506	85/15	NA	NA	NA	NA	NA
1880	17,392	85/15	NA	NA	NA	21,973	43.8
1890	23,318	83/17	13.9	18.9	NA	24,771	42.3
1900	29,073	82/18	15.4	20.6	3	29,875	41.9
1910	38,167	79/21	24.7	25.4	6	32,077	34.9
1920	41,614	79/21	23.0	23.7	12	31,974	30.1
1930	48,830	78/22	28.9	24.8	7	30,529	24.9
1940	53,011	76/24	36.4	27.4	27	30,547	23.2
1950	59,643	72/28	52.1	31.4	25	23,048	15.3
1960	69,877	68/32	59.9	37.7	26	15,635	8.7
1970	82,049	63/37	63.4	43.4	25	9,712	4.8
1980	108,544	58/42	59.7	51.5	23	6,051	2.7
1990	117,914	55/45	58.4	44.3	16	4,591	1.8

THE ECONOMY AND FEDERAL SPENDING

Year	Gross National Product (GNP) (in billions)°	Foreign Trade (in millions)			Federal Budget (in billions)	Federal Surplus/Deficit (in billions)	Federal Debt (in billions)
		Exports	Imports	Balance of Trade			
1790	NA	$ 20	$ 23	$ −3	$ 0.004	$ +0.00015	$ 0.076
1800	NA	71	91	−20	0.011	+0.0006	0.083
1810	NA	67	85	−18	0.008	+0.0012	0.053
1820	NA	70	74	−4	0.018	−0.0004	0.091
1830	NA	74	71	+3	0.015	+0.100	0.049
1840	NA	132	107	+25	0.024	−0.005	0.004
1850	NA	152	178	−26	0.040	+0.004	0.064
1860	NA	400	362	−38	0.063	−0.01	0.065
1870	$ 7.4	451	462	−11	0.310	+0.10	2.4
1880	11.2	853	761	+92	0.268	+0.07	2.1
1890	13.1	910	823	+87	0.318	+0.09	1.2
1900	18.7	1,499	930	+569	0.521	+0.05	1.2
1910	35.3	1,919	1,646	+273	0.694	−0.02	1.1
1920	91.5	8,664	5,784	+2,880	6.357	+0.3	24.3
1930	90.7	4,013	3,500	+513	3.320	+0.7	16.3
1940	100.0	4,030	7,433	−3,403	9.6	−2.7	43.0
1950	286.5	10,816	9,125	+1,691	43.1	−2.2	257.4
1960	506.5	19,600	15,046	+4,556	92.2	+0.3	286.3
1970	992.7	42,700	40,189	+2,511	195.6	−2.8	371.0
1980	2,631.7	220,783	244,871	+24,088	590.9	−73.8	907.7
1990	5,546.1	394,030	495,042	−101,012	1,251.8	−220.5	3,233.3
1994	6,738.4	512,627	663,256	−150,629	1,460.6	−203.4	4,692.8

°For 1990 and after, gross domestic product (GDP) is given.

AMERICAN WARS

	U.S. Military Personnel (thousands)	Personnel as % of Population	U.S. Deaths	U.S. Wounds	Direct Cost 1990 Dollars (millions)
American Revolution Apr. 1775–Sept. 1783	184–250	9–12	4,004	6,004	$100–140
War of 1812 June 1812–Feb. 1815	286	3	1,950	4,000	87
Mexican War May 1846–Feb. 1848	116	0.5	13,271	4,102	82
Civil War: Union	3,393	14	360,222	275,175	2,302
Civil War: Confederacy Apr. 1861–Apr. 1865	1,034	11	258,000	NA	1,032
Spanish-American War Apr. 1898–Aug. 1898	307	0.4	2,446	1,662	270
World War I Apr. 1917–Nov. 1918	4,714	5	116,516	204,002	32,740
World War II Dec. 1941–Aug. 1945	16,354	12	405,399	670,846	360,000
Korean War June 1950–June 1953	5,764	4	54,246	103,284	50,000
Vietnam War Aug. 1964–June 1973	8,400	4	47,704	219,573	140,644
Persian Gulf War Jan. 1991–Feb. 1991	467	0.1	293	467	NA

BIBLIOGRAPHY

CHAPTER 17: RECONSTRUCTING THE UNION

General Histories
James McPherson, *Ordeal by Fire: The Civil War and Reconstruction* (1982); Kenneth M. Stampp, *The Era of Reconstruction, 1865–1877* (1965).

National Politics
Herman Belz, *Emancipation and Equal Rights: Politics and Constitutionalism in the Civil War Era* (1978); Michael Les Benedict, *A Compromise of Principle: Congressional Republicans and Reconstruction* (1974); W. R. Brock, *An American Crisis: Congress and Reconstruction, 1865–1867* (1963); John and LaWanda Cox, *Politics, Principles, and Prejudice, 1865–1866* (1963); James M. McPherson, *The Struggle for Equality: Abolitionists and the Negro in the Civil War and Reconstruction* (1964); Hans L. Trefousse, *The Radical Republicans: Lincoln's Vanguard for Racial Justice* (1969).

Reconstruction and the Constitution
William Gillette, *The Right to Vote: Politics and the Passage of the Fifteenth Amendment* (1965); Harold M. Hyman, *A More Perfect Union: The Impact of the Civil War and Reconstruction on the Constitution* (1973); Joseph James, *The Framing of the Fourteenth Amendment* (1956); William E. Nelson, *The Fourteenth Amendment: From Political Principle to Judicial Doctrine* (1988).

The Black Experience in Reconstruction
James D. Anderson, *The Education of Blacks in the South, 1860–1935* (1988); Herbert G. Gutman, *The Black Family in Slavery and Freedom, 1750–1925* (1976); Janet Sharp Hermann, *The Pursuit of a Dream* (1981); Howard Rabinowitz, ed., *Southern Black Leaders in Reconstruction* (1982); Vernon L. Wharton, *The Negro in Mississippi, 1865–1890* (1947); Joel Williamson, *After Slavery: The Negro in South Carolina during Reconstruction* (1966).

Reconstruction in the South
Richard N. Current, *Those Terrible Carpetbaggers: A Reinterpretation* (1988); William C. Harris, *Day of the Carpetbagger: Republican Reconstruction in Mississippi* (1979); Michael Perman, *Reunion without Compromise:*

The South and Reconstruction, 1865–1868 (1973); George C. Rable, *But There Was No Peace: The Role of Violence in the Politics of Reconstruction* (1984); James Sefton, *The United States Army and Reconstruction, 1865–1877* (1967); Ted Tunnell, *Crucible of Reconstruction: War, Radicalism, and Race in Louisiana, 1862–1877* (1974); Allen Trelease, *White Terror: The Ku Klux Klan Conspiracy and Southern Reconstruction* (1967); Sarah Woolfolk Wiggins, *The Scalawag in Alabama Politics, 1865–1881* (1977).

Social and Economic Reconstruction
George R. Bentley, *A History of the Freedmen's Bureau* (1955); Eric Foner, *Nothing But Freedom: Emancipation and Its Legacy* (1983); Steven Hahn, *The Roots of Southern Populism: Yeoman Farmers and the Transformation of the Georgia Upcountry, 1850–1890* (1983); Jacqueline Jones, *Soldiers of Light and Love: Northern Teachers and Georgia Blacks, 1865–1873* (1980); Donald Nieman, *To Set the Law in Motion: The Freedmen's Bureau and the Legal Rights of Blacks, 1865–1868* (1979); Claude F. Oubre, *Forty Acres and a Mule: The Freedmen's Bureau and Black Landownership* (1978); Lawrence N. Powell, *New Masters: Northern Planters during the Civil War and Reconstruction* (1984); Roger L. Ransom and Richard Sutch, *One Kind of Freedom: The Economic Consequences of Emancipation* (1977); Mark W. Summers, *Railroads, Reconstruction, and the Gospel of Prosperity* (1984).

The End of Reconstruction
Paul Buck, *The Road to Reunion, 1865–1900* (1937); Keith Ian Polakoff, *The Politics of Inertia: The Election of 1876 and the End of Reconstruction* (1973); C. Vann Woodward, *Reunion and Reaction: The Compromise of 1877 and the End of Reconstruction* (1951).

Biographies
Fawn M. Brodie, *Thaddeus Stevens: Scourge of the South* (1959); David Donald, *Charles Sumner and the Rights of Man* (1970); William S. McFeely, *Yankee Stepfather: General O. Howard and the Freedmen* (1968) and *Grant: A Biography* (1981); Brooks D. Simpson, *Let Us Have Peace: Ulysses S. Grant and the Politics of War and Reconstruction, 1861–1868* (1991); Hans L. Trefousse, *Andrew Johnson: A Biography* (1989).

CHAPTER 18: A NEW INDUSTRIAL ORDER

General Studies
Daniel Boorstin, *The Americans: The Democratic Experience* (1973); John A. Garraty, *The New Commonwealth* (1968); Ray Ginger, *The Age of Excess* (1963); Samuel P. Hays, *The Response to Industrialism, 1885–1914* (1957); Edward C. Kirkland, *Industry Comes of Age: Business, Labor, and Public Policy, 1860–1897* (1967); Martin V. Melosi, *Coping with Abundance: Energy and Environment in Industrial America* (1985); Robert Wiebe, *The Search for Order, 1877–1920* (1968).

The Economy
Frederick Lewis Allen, *The Great Pierpont Morgan* (1949); W. Elliot Brownlee, *Dynamics of Ascent: A History of the American Economy*, rev. ed. (1979); Stuart Bruchey, *Growth of the Modern American Economy* (1975); Milton Friedman and Anna Schwartz, *Monetary History of the United States, 1867–1960* (1963); Robert L. Heilbroner, *The Economic Transformation of America* (1977); Robert Higgs, *The Transformation of the American Economy, 1865–1914* (1971); Susan Previant Lee and Peter Passell, *A New Economic View of American History* (1979); Harold G. Vatter, *The Drive to Industrial Maturity: The United States Economy, 1860–1914* (1975).

The Railroads
Alfred D. Chandler, Jr., *The Railroads: The Nation's First Big Business* (1965); Robert Fogel, *Railroads and American Economic Growth* (1964); Julius Grodinsky, *Jay Gould* (1957); Gabriel Kolko, *Railroads and Regulation, 1877–1916* (1965); Albro Martin, *James J. Hill and the Opening of the Northwest* (1976) and *Railroads Triumphant: The Growth, Rejection, and Rebirth of a Vital American Force* (1992); John F. Stover, *American Railroads* (1970).

The Rise of Big Business
Alfred Chandler, Jr., *Strategy and Structure: Chapters in the History of American Industrial Enterprise* (1962), *The Visible Hand: The Managerial Revolution in American Business* (1977) and *Scale and Scope: The Dynamics of Industrial Capitalism* (1990); Thomas Cochrane, *Business in American Life* (1972); Naomi Lamoreaux, *The Great Merger Movement in American Business, 1895–1904* (1985); Harold C. Livesay, *Andrew Carnegie and the Rise of Big Business* (1975); Alan Nevins, *Study in Power: John D. Rockefeller*, 2 vols. (1953); Glenn Porter, *The Rise of Big Business* (1973); Martin J. Sklar, *The Corporate Reconstruction of American Capitalism, 1890–1916: The Market, Law and Politics* (1988); Richard Tedlow, *The Rise of the American Business Corporation* (1991); Alan Trachtenberg, *The Incorporation of America* (1982); Joseph Wall, *Andrew Carnegie* (1970); Olivier Zunz, *Making America Corporate, 1870–1920* (1990).

Invention and Industry
Robert Bruce, *Alexander Graham Bell and the Conquest of Solitude* (1973); Robert Conot, *A Streak of Luck* (1979); Ruth Schwartz Cowan, *A Social History of American Technology* (1996); Siegfried Giedion, *Mechanization Takes Command* (1948); David Hounshell, *From the American System to Mass Production, 1800–1932* (1984);

John F. Kasson, *Civilizing the Machine* (1976); Carolyn Marvin, *When Old Technologies Were New: Thinking about Electric Communication in the Late Nineteenth Century* (1988); David Nye, *Electrifying America: Social Meanings of a New Technology, 1890–1940* (1990); Harold Passer, *The Electrical Manufacturers, 1875–1900* (1953); Leonard S. Reich, *The Making of Industrial Research: Science and Business at GE and Bell, 1876–1926* (1985); Nathan Rosenberg, *Technology and American Economic Growth* (1972); Peter Temin, *Iron and Steel in Nineteenth Century America* (1964); Frederick A. White, *American Industrial Research Laboratories* (1961).

Capitalism and Its Critics
Robert Bannister, *Social Darwinism: Science and Myth in Anglo-American Social Thought* (1979); Robert H. Bremner, *American Philanthropy* (1988); Carl N. Degler, *In Search of Human Nature: The Decline and Revival of Darwinism in America* (1991); Sidney Fine, *Laissez Faire and the General Welfare State: A Study of Conflict in American Thought, 1865–1900* (1956); Louis Galambos, *The Public Image of Big Business in America, 1880–1940: A Quantitative Study of Social Change* (1975); Richard Hofstadter, *Social Darwinism in American Thought*, rev. ed. (1955); Edward C. Kirkland, *Dream and Thought in the Business Community, 1860–1900* (1956); Ellen Condliffe Lagemann, *The Politics of Knowledge: The Carnegie Corporation, Philanthropy, and Public Policy* (1989); T. Jackson Lears, *No Place of Grace: Antimodernism and the Transformation of American Culture, 1880–1920* (1981); George E. Pozzetta, ed., *Americanization, Social Control, and Philanthropy* (1991); John Thomas, *Alternative America: Henry George, Edward Bellamy, Henry Demarest Lloyd, and the Adversary Tradition* (1983).

The Culture of Work
American Social History Project, *Who Built America? Working People and the Nation's Economy, Politics, Culture, Society*, Volume Two: *From the Gilded Age to the Present* (1992); Cindy Sondik Aron, *Ladies and Gentlemen of the Civil Service: Middle-Class Workers in Victorian America* (1987); James R. Barrett, *Work and Community in the Jungle: Chicago's Packinghouse Workers, 1894–1922* (1990); John Bodnar, *Immigration and Industrialization: Ethnicity in an American Mill Town* (1977); John T. Cumbler, *Working Class Community in Industrial America: Work, Leisure, and Struggle in Two Industrial Cities, 1880–1930* (1979); David Emmons, *The Butte Irish: Class and Ethnicity in an American Mining Town, 1875–1925* (1989); Michael Frisch and Daniel Walkowitz, eds., *Working-Class America: Essays on Labor, Community, and American Society* (1983); James R. Green, *World of the Worker: Labor in Twentieth Century America* (1980); Herbert Gutman, *Work, Culture and Society in Industrializing America: Essays in American Working-Class History* (1976); Tamara Hareven, *Family, Time, and Industrial Time: The Relationship between the Family and Work in a New England Industrial Community* (1982); William H. Harris, *The Harder We Run: Black Workers since the Civil War* (1982); Jacqueline Jones, *Labor of Love, Labor of Sorrow: Black Women, Work and the Family, from Slavery to the Present* (1985); Susan Kennedy, *If All We Did Was to Weep at Home: A History*

and Free Speech (1987); Walton Rawls, Wake Up America! World War I and the American Poster (1987); Ronald Schaffer, America in the Great War: The Rise of the War Welfare State (1991); Jordan Schwarz, The Speculator: Bernard M. Baruch in Washington, 1917–1965 (1981); Dale N. Shook, William G. McAdoo and the Development of National Economic Policy, 1913–1918 (1987); Barbara Steinson, American Women's Activism in World War I (1982); John A. Thompson, Reformers and War: Progressive Publicists and the First World War (1987); Joe William Trotter, Jr., ed., The Great Migration in Historical Perspective (1991); Stephen Vaughn, Holding Fast the Inner Lines: Democracy, Nationalism, and the Committee on Public Information (1979); James Weinstein, The Decline of Socialism in America, 1912–1923 (1967); Neil A. Wynn, From Progressivism to Prosperity: World War I and American Society (1986).

Versailles
Thomas Bailey, Woodrow Wilson and the Great Betrayal (1945) and Woodrow Wilson and the Lost Peace (1944); Robert Ferrell, Woodrow Wilson and World War I (1985); Inga Floto, Colonel House at Paris (1980); John Gaddis, Russia, the Soviet Union, and the United States (1978); Lloyd Gardner, Safe for Democracy: The Anglo-American Response to Revolution, 1913–1923 (1984); Thomas J. Knock, To End All Wars: Woodrow Wilson and the Quest for a New World Order (1992); Arno Mayer, Politics and Diplomacy of Peacemaking: Containment and Counterrevolution at Versailles (1965); Charles Mee, Jr., The End of Order, Versailles, 1919 (1980); Ralph Stone, The Irreconcilables: The Fight against the League of Nations (1970); William C. Widenor, Henry Cabot Lodge and the Search for an American Foreign Policy (1980).

Aftermath
David Brody, Labor in Crisis: The Steel Strike of 1919 (1965); Stanley Coben, A. Mitchell Palmer: Politician (1963); Stanley Cooperman, World War I and the American Mind (1970); Roberta Feuerlicht, Justice Crucified (1977); Dana Frank, Purchasing Power: Consumer Organizing, Gender, and the Seattle Labor Movement, 1919–1929 (1994); Robert Murray, The Red Scare (1955); Burl Noggle, Into the Twenties (1977); Stuart Rochester, American Liberal Disillusionment in the Wake of World War I (1977); Francis Russell, A City in Terror (1975); William Tuttle, Jr., Race Riot: Chicago in the Red Summer of 1919 (1970); Stephen Ward, ed., The War Generation: Veterans of the First World War (1975).

CHAPTER 24: THE NEW ERA

General Studies
Frederick Lewis Allen, Only Yesterday: An Informal History of the 1920s (1931); John Braeman et al., eds., Change and Continuity in Twentieth Century America: The 1920s (1968); Ann Douglas, Terrible Honesty: Mongrel Manhattan in the 1920s (1995); Lynn Dumenil, Modern Temper: American Culture and Society in the 1920s (1995); Ellis Hawley, The Great War and the Search for a Modern Order (1979); John Hicks, The Republican Ascendancy, 1921–1933 (1960); Isabel Leighton, ed., The Aspirin Age (1949); William Leuchtenburg, The Perils of Prosperity,

1914–1932 (1958); Donald McCoy, Coming of Age (1973); Geoffrey Perrett, America in the Twenties (1982); Arthur Schlesinger, Jr., The Crisis of the Old Order (1957); David Shannon, Between the Wars: America, 1919–1940 (1979).

Economics, Business, and Labor
Irving Bernstein, The Lean Years: A History of the American Worker, 1920–1933 (1960); David Brody, Steelworkers in America (1960) and Workers in Industrial America (1980); Lizabeth Cohen, Making a New Deal: Industrial Workers in Chicago, 1919–1939 (1990); Alfred D. Chandler, Jr., Strategy and Structure: Chapters in the History of American Industrial Enterprise (1962); Ed Cray, Chrome Colossus: General Motors and Its Times (1980); Gilbert Fite, George Peek and the Fight for Farm Parity (1954); James Flink, The Car Culture (1975); Louis Galambos, Competition and Cooperation (1966); James Gilbert, Designing the Industrial State (1972); Allan Nevins and Frank Hill, Ford, 3 vols. (1954–1963); Jim Potter, The American Economy between the Wars (1974); John Rae, American Automobile (1965) and The Road and the Car in American Life (1971); George Soule, Prosperity Decade (1947); Keith Sward, The Legend of Henry Ford (1948); Leslie Woodcock Tentler, Wage Earning Women: Industrial Work and Family Life in the United States, 1900–1930 (1979); Bernard Weisberger, The Dress Maker (1979); Robert Zieger, Republicans and Labor, 1919–1929 (1969) and American Workers, American Unions, 1920–1980 (1986).

Mass Society and Mass Culture
Erick Barnouw, A Tower of Babel: A History of American Broadcasting in the United States to 1933 (1966); Daniel Boorstin, The Americans: The Democratic Experience (1973); Paul Carter, Another Part of the Twenties (1977); Robert Creamer, Babe (1974); Kenneth Davis, The Hero: Charles A. Lindbergh (1954); Stuart Ewen, Captains of Consciousness: Advertising and the Social Roots of the Consumer Culture (1976); Richard Wrightman Fox and T. J. Jackson Lears, eds., The Culture of Consumption: Critical Essays in American History, 1880–1980 (1983); Jackson Lears, Fables of Abundance: A Cultural History of Advertising in America (1994); Robert Lynd and Helen Lynd, Middletown: A Study in Modern Culture (1929); Roland Marchand, Advertising the American Dream: Making Way for Modernity, 1920–1940 (1985); Lary May, Screening Out the Past (1980); Leonard Mosley, Lindbergh: A Biography (1976); Otis Pease, The Responsibilities of American Advertising (1959); Daniel Pope, The Making of Modern Advertising (1983); Randy Roberts, Jack Dempsey, The Manassa Mauler (1979); Philip Rosen, The Modern Stentors: Radio Broadcasting and the Federal Government, 1920–1933 (1980); Robert Sklar, Movie-Made America: A Cultural History of American Movies (1975); Kevin Starr, Material Dreams: Southern California through the 1920s (1990); Susan Strasser, Satisfaction Guaranteed: The Making of the American Mass Market (1990).

High Culture
Carlos Baker, Hemingway (1956); Malcolm Cowley, Exile's Return (1934); Robert Crunden, From Self to Society: Transition in Modern Thought, 1919–1941 (1972); Frederick Hoffman, The Twenties (1949); Arthur Mizner,

The Far Side of Paradise (1951); Roderick Nash, *The Nervous Generation: American Thought, 1917–1930* (1969); Mark Shorer, *Sinclair Lewis* (1961); Marvin Singleton, *H. L. Mencken and the "American Mercury" Adventure* (1962).

Women, Youth, and Minorities
Lois Banner, *American Beauty* (1983); Susan D. Becker, *The Origins of the Equal Rights Amendment* (1981); Kathlenn M. Blee, *Women of the Klan: Racism and Gender in the 1920s* (1991); Dorothy M. Brown, *Setting a Course: American Women in the 1920s* (1987); William Chafe, *The American Women: Her Changing Social, Economic, and Political Roles, 1920–1970* (1972); Nancy Cott, *The Grounding of Modern Feminism* (1987); David Cronon, *Black Moses: The Story of Marcus Garvey* (1955); Melvin Patrick Ely, *The Adventures of Amos 'n' Andy: A Social History of an American Phenomenon* (1991); Paula Fass, *The Damned and Beautiful: American Youth in the 1920s* (1977); Linda Gordon, *Woman's Body, Woman's Right: A Social History of Birth Control in America* (1976); Peter Gottlieb, *Making Their Own Way: Southern Blacks' Migration to Pittsburgh, 1916–1930* (1987); Florette Henri, *Black Migration: Movement North, 1900–1920* (1975); Nathan Huggins, *Harlem Renaissance* (1971); Jacqueline Jones, *Labor of Love, Labor of Sorrow: Black Women, Work, and Family, from Slavery to the Present* (1985); J. Stanley Lemons, *The Woman Citizen: Social Feminism in the 1920s* (1973); David Levering Lewis, *When Harlem Was in Vogue* (1981); Glenna Matthews, *"Just a Housewife!" The Rise and Fall of Domesticity in America* (1987); Cary D. Mintz, *Black Culture and the Harlem Renaissance* (1988); Wilson Moses, *The Golden Age of Black Nationalism, 1850–1925* (1988); Kathy H. Ogren, *The Jazz Revolution: Twenties America and the Meaning of Jazz* (1989); Arnold Rampersad, *The Life of Langston Hughes*, 2 vols. (1986–1988); Ricardo Romo, *East Los Angeles: History of a Barrio* (1983); George J. Sanchez, *Becoming Mexican American: Ethnicity, Culture and Identity in Chicano Los Angeles, 1900–1945* (1993); Lois Scharf, *To Work and to Wed* (1980); Virginia Scharff, *Taking the Wheel: Women and the Coming of the Motor Age* (1991); Alan Spear, *Black Chicago* (1967); Judith Stein, *The World of Marcus Garvey: Race and Class in Modern Society* (1986); Joe William Trotter, Jr., *Black Milwaukee: The Making of an Industrial Proletariat* (1985); Theodore Vincent, *Black Power and the Garvey Movement* (1971); Winifred Wandersee, *Women's Work and Family Values, 1920–1940* (1981).

Political Fundamentalism
Paul Avrich, *Sacco-Vanzetti: The Anarchist Background* (1991); David Burner, *The Politics of Provincialism* (1968); David Chalmers, *Hooded Americanism: The History of the Ku Klux Klan* (1965); Norman Clark, *Deliver Us from Evil* (1976); Robert Divine, *American Immigration Policy* (1957); Norman Furniss, *The Fundamentalist Controversy, 1918–1933* (1954); Ray Ginger, *Six Days or Forever? Tennessee v. John Scopes* (1958); Joseph Gusfeld, *Symbolic Crusade* (1963); John Higham, *Strangers in the Land: Patterns of American Nativism, 1860–1925* (1955); Kenneth Jackson, *The Ku Klux Klan in the City, 1915–1930* (1967); Don Kirschner, *City and Country: Rural Responses to Urbanization in the 1920s* (1970); Shawn

Lay, ed., *The Invisible Empire in the West: Toward a New Historical Appraisal of the Ku Klux Klan of the 1920s* (1992); Nancy MacLean, *Behind the Mask of Chivalry: The Making of the Second Ku Klux Klan* (1994); George Maraden, *Fundamentalism and American Culture* (1980); Leonard J. Moore, *Citizen Klansmen: The Ku Klux Klan in Indiana, 1921–1928* (1991); Andrew Sinclair, *Prohibition: The Era of Excess* (1962); William Wilson, *Coming of Age: Urban America, 1915–1945* (1974).

Politics, Public Policy, and the Election of 1928
Kristi Andersen, *The Creation of a Democratic Majority* (1979); Paula Edler, *Governor Alfred E. Smith: The Politician as Reformer* (1983); James Giglio, *H. M. Daugherty and the Politics of Expediency* (1978); Oscar Handlin, *Al Smith and His America* (1958); Ellis Hawley, *Herbert Hoover as Secretary of Commerce: Studies in New Era Thought and Practice* (1974); Robert Himmelberg, *The Origins of the National Recovery Administration: Business, Government, and the Trade Association Issue, 1921–1933* (1976); J. Joseph Huthmacher, *Massachusetts People and Politics, 1919–1933* (1959); Alan Lichtman, *Prejudice and the Old Politics* (1979); Richard Lowitt, *George Norris*, 2 vols. (1971); Donald McCoy, *Calvin Coolidge* (1967); Robert Murray, *The Harding Era* (1969) and *The Politics of Normalcy* (1973); Burl Noggle, *Teapot Dome* (1962); Elisabeth Perry, *Belle Moskowitz: Feminine Politics and the Exercise of Power in the Age of Alfred E. Smith* (1987); George Tindall, *The Emergence of the New South* (1967); Eugene Trani and David Wilson, *The Presidency of Warren G. Harding* (1977).

CHAPTER 25: CRASH AND DEPRESSION

General Studies
Frederick Lewis Allen, *Since Yesterday* (1939); John A. Garraty, *The Great Depression* (1987); Robert McElvaine, *The Great Depression: America, 1929–1941* (1984); Broadus Mitchell, *Depression Decade* (1947); Arthur Schlesinger, Jr., *The Crisis of the Old Order* (1957); T. H. Watkins, *The Great Depression: America in the 1930s* (1991).

The Great Crash and the Origins of the Great Depression
Michael A. Bernstein, *The Great Depression: Delayed Recovery and Economic Change in America, 1929–1939* (1987); Lester Chandler, *America's Greatest Depression, 1929–1941* (1970); Milton Friedman and Ana Schwartz, *The Great Contraction, 1929–1933* (1965); John Kenneth Galbraith, *The Great Crash*, rev. ed. (1988); Susan Kennedy, *The Banking Crisis of 1933* (1973); Charles Kindleberger, *The World in Depression* (1973); Robert Sobel, *The Great Bull Market: Wall Street in the 1920s* (1968); Peter Temin, *Did Monetary Forces Cause the Great Depression?* (1976); Gordon Thomas and Max Morgan-Witts, *The Day the Bubble Burst: The Social History of the Wall Street Crash of 1929* (1979).

Depression Life
Edward Anderson, *Hungry Men* (1935); Robert Angel, *The Family Encounters the Depression* (1936); Ann Banks, *First Person America* (1980); Caroline Bird, *The Invisible Scar* (1966); The Federal Writers' Project, *These Are Our*

Lives (1939); John Garraty, *Unemployment in History: Economic Thought and Public Policy* (1978); Mirra Komarovsky, *The Unemployed Man and His Family* (1940); Robert Lynd and Helen Lynd, *Middletown in Transition* (1937); Robert McElvaine, ed. *Down & Out in the Great Depression* (1983); Harvey Levenstein, *Paradox of Plenty: A Social History of Eating in Modern America* (1993); H. Wayne Morgan, *Drugs in America: A Social History, 1800–1980* (1981); David Musto, *The American Disease, Origins of Narcotics Control*, rev. ed. (1988); Lois Scharf, *To Work and to Wed: Female Employment, Feminism, and the Great Depression* (1980); Tom Terrill and Jerrold Hirsch, eds., *Such as Us: Southern Voices of the Thirties* (1978); Studs Terkel, *Hard Times: An Oral History of the Great Depression* (1970); Winifred Wandersee, *Women's Work and Family Values, 1920–1940* (1981); Susan Ware, *Holding Their Own: American Women in the 1930s* (1982); Jeane Westin, *Making Do: How Women Survived the '30s* (1976).'

Ethnicity and Race
Rodolfo Acuna, *Occupied America*, rev. ed. (1981); Ralph Bunche, *The Political Status of the Negro in the Age of FDR* (1973); Dan Carter, *Scottsboro: A Tragedy of the American South* (1969); Sarah Deutsch, *No Separate Refuge: Culture, Class, and Gender on an Anglo-Hispanic Frontier in the American Southwest, 1880–1940* (1987); Abraham Hoffman, *Unwanted Mexican-Americans in the Great Depression* (1974); Richard Polenberg, *One Nation Divisible: Class, Race, and Ethnicity in the United States since 1938* (1980); Bernard Sternsher, ed., *The Negro in Depression and War* (1969); Robert Weisbrot, *Father Divine and the Struggle for Racial Equality* (1983); Nancy Weiss, *The National Urban League* (1974); Raymond Wolters, *Negroes and the Great Depression* (1970).

Depression Culture
Daniel Aaron, *Writers on the Left* (1961); James Agee, *Let Us Now Praise Famous Men* (1941); Andrew Bergman, *We're in the Money: Depression America and Its Films* (1971); Eileen Eagan, *Class, Culture and the Classroom* (1981); Neal Gabler, *An Empire of Their Own: How the Jews Invented Hollywood* (1988); Lawrence Levine, *The Unpredictable Past: Explorations in American Cultural History* (1993); Jeffrey Meikle, *Twentieth Century Limited: Industrial Design in America, 1925–1939* (1979); Richard Pells, *Radical Visions and American Dreams: Culture and Social Thought in the Depression Years* (1973); Thomas Schatz, *The Genius of the System: Hollywood Filmmaking in the Studio Era* (1988); John Steinbeck, *The Grapes of Wrath* (1939); William Stott, *Documentary Expressionism and Thirties America* (1973); Warren Susman, *Culture as History: The Transformation of American Society in the Twentieth Century* (1984); Twelve Southerners, *I'll Take My Stand: The South and the Agrarian Tradition* (1937).

Radicalism and Protest
Irving Bernstein, *The Lean Years: A History of the American Worker, 1920–1933* (1960); Robert Cohen, *When the Old Left Was Young: Student Radicals and America's First Mass Student Movement, 1929–1941* (1993); Roger Daniels, *The Bonus March* (1971); John Hevener, *Which Side You On? The Harlan County Coal Miners, 1931–1939* (1978); Harvey Klehr, *The Heyday of American Communism: The Depression Decade* (1984); Donald Lisio, *The President and Protest: Hoover, Conspiracy, and the Bonus Riot* (1974); Mark Naison, *Communists in Harlem during the Depression* (1983); Theodore Saloutos and John Hicks, *Twentieth Century Populism: Agrarian Protest in the Middle West, 1900–1939* (1951); John Shover, *Cornbelt Rebellion: The Farmers' Holiday Association* (1965).

The Hoover Years
David Burner, *Herbert Hoover: A Public Life* (1979); Roger Daniels, *The Bonus March* (1971); Martin Fausold, *The Presidency of Herbert C. Hoover* (1985); Martin Fausold and George Mazuzun, eds., *The Hoover Presidency* (1974); George Nash, *The Life of Herbert Hoover* (1983); James Olson, *Herbert Hoover and the Reconstruction Finance Corporation* (1977); Albert Romasco, *The Poverty of Abundance: Hoover, the Nation, the Depression* (1965); Elliot A. Rosen, *Hoover, Roosevelt, and the Brains Trust: From Depression to New Deal* (1977); Jordan Schwarz, *The Interregnum of Despair* (1970); Joan Hoff Wilson, *Herbert Hoover: Forgotten Progressive* (1975).

CHAPTER 26: THE NEW DEAL

General Studies
John Braeman et al., *The New Deal*, 2 vols. (1975); Paul Conkin, *The New Deal* (1967); Steve Fraser and Gary Gerstle, eds., *The Rise and Fall of the New Deal Order, 1930–1980* (1989); Otis Graham, Jr., *Encore for Reform: The Old Progressives and the New Deal* (1967); Barry Karl, *The Uneasy State* (1983); William Leuchtenburg, *Franklin D. Roosevelt and the New Deal, 1932–1940* (1963); Robert McElvaine, *The Great Depression: America, 1929–1941* (1984); Gerald Nash, *The Great Depression and World War II* (1979); Harvard Sitkoff, ed., *Fifty Years Later: The New Deal Evaluated* (1985).

Franklin and Eleanor
James Burns, *Roosevelt: The Lion and the Fox* (1956); Rochelle Chadakoff, ed., *Eleanor Roosevelt's My Day: Her Acclaimed Columns, 1936–1945* (1989); Blanche Wiesen Cook, *Eleanor Roosevelt*, Volume One, *1884–1933* (1992); Kenneth Davis, *FDR*, 4 vols. (1972–1993); Frank Freidel, *Franklin D. Roosevelt*, 4 vols. (1952–1973) and *Franklin D. Roosevelt: A Rendezvous with Destiny* (1990); Joseph Lash, *Eleanor and Franklin* (1971); Ted Morgan, *FDR: A Biography* (1985); Eleanor Roosevelt, *This Is My Story* (1937) and *This I Remember* (1949); Lois Scharf, *Eleanor Roosevelt: First Lady of American Liberalism* (1987); Arthur Schlesinger, Jr., *The Age of Roosevelt*, 3 vols. (1957–1960); Rexford Tugwell, *The Democratic Roosevelt: A Biography of Franklin D. Roosevelt* (1957); Geoffrey Ward, *Before the Trumpet: Young Franklin Roosevelt* (1985) and *A First Class Temperament: The Emergence of Franklin Roosevelt* (1989).

The New Deal and New Dealers
Anthony J. Badger, *The New Deal: The Depression Years, 1933–1940* (1989); Barton J. Bernstein, "The New Deal: The Conservative Achievements of New Deal Reform," in Barton J. Bernstein, ed., *Towards a New Past: Dissenting*

Essays in American History (1968); Michael Beschloss, *Kennedy and Roosevelt: The Uneasy Alliance* (1980); John Blum, *From the Morgenthau Diaries*, 3 vols. (1959–1965); Harold Ickes, *The Secret Diaries of Harold L. Ickes*, 3 vols. (1953–1954); Peter Irons, *The New Deal Lawyers* (1982); Joseph Lash, *Dealers and Dreamers: A New Look at the New Deal* (1988); Katie Lockheim, ed., *The Making of the New Deal: The Insiders Speak* (1983); Richard Lowitt, *George W. Norris: The Triumph of a Progressive, 1933–1944* (1978); George Martin, *Madame Secretary: Frances Perkins* (1976); George McJimsey, *Harry Hopkins: Ally of the Poor and Defender of Democracy* (1987); Raymond Moley, *After Seven Years* (1939); Frances Perkins, *The Roosevelt I Knew* (1946); Samuel Rosenman, *Working for Roosevelt* (1952); Jordan Schwarz, *Liberal: Adolf A. Berle and the Vision of an American Era* (1987) and *The New Dealers: Power Politics in the Age of Roosevelt* (1993); Robert Sherwood, *Roosevelt and Hopkins: An Intimate History* (1948); Bernard Sternsher, *Rexford Tugwell and the New Deal* (1964); Susan Ware, *Beyond Suffrage: Women and the New Deal* (1981) and *Partner and I: Molly Dewson, Feminism, and New Deal Politics* (1987); T. H. Watkins, *The Righteous Pilgrim: The Life and Times of Harold L. Ickes* (1990).

Recovery and Reform
Bernard Belush, *The Failure of the NRA* (1975); Donald R. Brand, *Corporatism and the Rule of Law: A Study of the National Recovery Administration* (1988); Walter L. Creese, *TVA's Public Planning: The Vision, the Reality* (1990); Colin Gordon, *New Deals: Business, Labor, and Politics in America, 1920–1935* (1994); Ellis Hawley, *The New Deal and the Problems of Monopoly* (1966); Barry Karl, *Executive Reorganization and Reform in the New Deal* (1963); Susan E. Kennedy, *The Banking Crisis of 1933* (1973); Mark Leff, *The Limits of Symbolic Reform: The New Deal and Taxation, 1933–1939* (1984); Thomas McCraw, *TVA and the Public Power Fight* (1970); James Olson, *Saving Capitalism: The RFC and the New Deal, 1933–1940* (1988); Michael Parrish, *Securities Regulation and the New Deal* (1970); Richard Polenberg, *Reorganizing Roosevelt's Government* (1966); Albert Romasco, *The Politics of Recovery: Roosevelt's New Deal* (1983).

Agriculture and Conservation
Sidney Baldwin, *Poverty and Politics: The Rise and Decline of the Farm Security Administration* (1967); David Conrad, *The Forgotten Farmers: The Story of Sharecroppers in the New Deal* (1965); James Gregory, *American Exodus: The Dust Bowl Migration and Okie Culture in California* (1989); Richard Kirkendall, *Social Scientists and Farm Politics in the Age of Roosevelt* (1966); Richard Lowitt, *The New Deal and the West* (1984); Percy H. Merrill, *Roosevelt's Forest Army: A History of the Civilian Conservation Corps, 1933–1942* (1981); Paul Mertz, *The New Deal and Southern Rural Poverty* (1978); Van Perkins, *Crisis in Agriculture* (1969); Donald Worster, *Dust Bowl: The Southern Plains in the 1930s* (1979) and *Rivers of Empire: Water, Aridity, and the Growth of the American West* (1986).

Relief and the Rise of the Semi-Welfare State
Searle Charles, *Minister of Relief* (1963) [about Harry Hopkins]; Paul Conkin, *FDR and the Origins of the Welfare State* (1967); Phoebe Cutler, *The Public Landscape of the New Deal* (1986); Linda Gordon, *Pitied but Not Entitled: Single Mothers and the History of Welfare* (1994); Richard Lowitt and Maurine Beasley, eds., *One Third of a Nation: Lorena Hickok Reports on the Great Depression* (1981); Roy Lubove, *The Struggle for Social Security* (1968); Jerre Mangione, *The Dream and the Deal: The Federal Writers' Project, 1935–1943* (1972); Jane deHart Matthews, *The Federal Theater, 1935–1939* (1967); Richard McKinzie, *The New Deal for Artists* (1973); Barbara Melosh, *Engendering Culture: Manhood and Womanhood in New Deal Public Art and Theater* (1991); Francis O'Connor, ed., *Art for the Millions: Essays from the 1930s by Artists and Administrators of the WPA Federal Art Project* (1973); Karen Benker Orhn, *Dorothea Lange and the Documentary Tradition* (1980); Marlene Park and Gerald Markowitz, *Democratic Vistas: Post Offices and Public Art in the New Deal* (1984); John Salmond, *The Civilian Conservation Corps* (1967); Bonnie Schwartz, *The Civil Works Administration, 1933–1934* (1984).

Dissent and Protest
Alan Brinkley, *Voices of Protest: Huey Long, Father Coughlin, and the Great Depression* (1982); Donald Grubbs, *Cry from Cotton: The Southern Tenant Farmers Union and the New Deal* (1971); Abraham Holzman, *The Townsend Movement* (1963); Glen Geansonne, *Gerald L. K. Smith: Minister of Hate* (1988); Robin D. G. Kelly, *Hammer and Hoe: Alabama Communists during the Great Depression* (1990); R. Alan Lawson, *The Failure of Independent Liberalism, 1930–1941* (1971); Greg Mitchell, *The Campaign of the Century: Upton Sinclair's Epic Race for Governor of California and the Birth of Media Politics* (1992); Mark Naison, *Communists in Harlem during the Depression* (1983); Leo Ribuffo, *The Old Christian Right: The Protestant Far Right from the Great Depression to the Cold War* (1983); Vicki Ruiz, *Cannery Women/Cannery Lives: Mexican Women, Unionization, and the California Food Processing Industry, 1930–1950* (1987); Charles Tull, *Father Coughlin and the New Deal* (1965); T. Harry Wiliams, *Huey Long* (1969); Frank Warren, *Liberals and Communism: The "Red Decade" Revisited* (1966) and *An Alternative Vision: The Socialist Party in the 1930s* (1976); George Wolfskill, *Revolt of the Conservatives: A History of the American Liberty League, 1934–1940* (1962).

Labor
Jerold Auerback, *Labor and Liberty: The La Follette Committee and the New Deal* (1966); John Barnard, *Walter Reuther and the Rise of the Auto Workers* (1983); Irving Bernstein, *Turbulent Years: A History of the American Worker, 1933–1941* (1969); Lizabeth Cohen, *Making a New Deal: Industrial Workers in Chicago, 1919–1939* (1990); Melvyn Dubofsky and Warren Van Tine, *John L. Lewis: A Biography* (1977); Sidney Fine, *Sit-Down: The General Motors Strike of 1936–1937* (1969); Steven Fraser, *Labor Will Rule: Sidney Hillman and the Rise of American Labor* (1991); Peter Friedlander, *The Emergence of a UAW Local* (1975); Nelson Lichenstein, *"The Most Dangerous Man in Detroit": Walter Reuther and the Fate of American Labor* (1995); August Meier and Elliott Rudwick, *Black Detroit and the Rise of the UAW* (1979); David Milton,

The Politics of U.S. Labor: From the Great Depression to the New Deal (1980); Ronald Schatz, *The Electrical Workers* (1983); Robert H. Zieger, *John L. Lewis* (1988).

New Deal Politics
John Allswang, *The New Deal in American Politics* (1978); Frank Freidel, *FDR and the South* (1965); J. Joseph Huthmacher, *Senator Robert Wagner and the Rise of Urban Liberalism* (1968); Gregg Mitchell, *The Campaign of the Century: Upton Sinclair's Race for Governor and the Birth of Media Politics* (1992); James Patterson, *Congressional Conservatism and the New Deal* (1967) and *The New Deal and the States* (1969); William Leuchtenburg, "The Origins of Franklin D. Roosevelt's 'Court Packing' Plan," in Philip Kurland, ed., *The Supreme Court Review* (1966).

Minorities
Laurence Kelly, *The Assault on Assimilation: John Collier and the Origins of Indian Policy Reform, 1920–1954* (1983); Harry A. Kersey, Jr., *The Florida Seminoles and the New Deal, 1933–1942* (1989); John Kirby, *Black Americans in the Roosevelt Era: Liberalism and Race* (1980); Carey McWilliams, *North from Mexico* (1949); Donald Parman, *The Navajoes and the New Deal* (1976); Kenneth Philp, *John Collier's Crusade for Indian Reform, 1920–1934* (1977); Francis Prucha, *The Indians in American Society: From the Revolutionary War to the Present* (1985); Mark Reisler, *By the Sweat of Their Brow: Mexican Immigrant Labor in the United States, 1900–1940* (1976); Harvard Sitkoff, *A New Deal for Blacks* (1978); Raymond Walters, *Negroes and the Great Depression: The Problem of Economic Recovery* (1970); Graham D. Taylor, *The New Deal and American Indian Tribalism: The Administration of the Indian Reorganization Act, 1934–1945* (1980); Nancy Weiss, *Farewell to the Party of Lincoln: Black Politics in the Age of FDR* (1983); Robert Zangrando, *The NAACP Crusade against Lynching* (1980).

CHAPTER 27: AMERICA'S RISE TO GLOBALISM

The Roosevelt Era and the Coming of World War II

Dorothy Borg, *The United States and the Far Eastern Crisis of 1933–1938* (1964); James MacGregor Burns, *Roosevelt: The Lion and the Fox* (1956); Wayne S. Cole, *Roosevelt and the Isolationists, 1932–1945* (1983); Robert Dallek, *Franklin D. Roosevelt and American Foreign Policy, 1932–1945* (1979); Charles DeBenedetti, *The Peace Reform Movement in American History* (1980); John Findling, *Close Neighbors, Distant Friends: United States–Central American Relations* (1987); Lloyd Gardner, *Economic Aspects of New Deal Diplomacy* (1964) and *The Great Powers Partition Europe, from Munich to Yalta* (1993); Irwin Gellman, *Good Neighbor Diplomacy* (1979); Patrick Headen, *Roosevelt Confronts Hitler: America's Entry into World War II* (1987); Edwin Herzstein, *Roosevelt and Hitler: Prelude to War* (1989); Akira Iriye and Warren Cohen, eds., *American, Chinese, and Japanese Perspectives on Asia, 1931–1949* (1990); Warren Kimball, *The Most Unsordid Act: Lend Lease, 1939–1941* (1969);

Walter LaFeber, *Inevitable Revolutions: The United States in Central America* (1993); Douglas Little, *Malevolent Neutrality: The United States, Great Britain, and the Origins of the Spanish Civil War* (1985); Arthur Morse, *While Six Million Died* (1968); Arnold Offner, *The Origins of the Second World War* (1975); Gordon Prange, *At Dawn We Slept* (1981); Michael Slackman, *Target: Pearl Harbor* (1990); John Toland, *Infamy* (1982); Jonathan Utley, *Going to War with Japan, 1937–1941* (1985); Roberta Wohlstetter, *Pearl Harbor: Warning and Decision* (1962); Bryce Wood, *The Making of the Good Neighbor Policy* (1961); David Wyman, *The Abandonment of the Jews* (1984).

War and Strategy
John Dower, *War without Mercy: Race and Power in the Pacific War* (1986); David Eisenhower, *Eisenhower at War, 1943–1945* (1986); Richard B. Frank, *Guadalcanal* (1990); B. H. Liddell Hart, *History of the Second World War* (1970); Max Hastings, *OVERLORD: D-Day and the Battle of Normandy* (1984); Akira Iriye, *Power and Culture: The Japanese-American War, 1941–1945* (1981); D. Clayton James with Anne Sharp Wells, *A Time for Giants: Politics of the American High Command during World War II* (1987); John Keegan, *The Second World War* (1989); Eric Larabee, *Commander in Chief: Franklin Delano Roosevelt, His Lieutenants, and Their War* (1987); William Manchester, *American Caesar* (1979); Karal Ann Marling and John Wetenhall, *Iwo Jima* (1991); Ken McCormick and Hamilton Perry, *Images of War: The Artists' Vision of World War II* (1990); Nathan Miller, *War at Sea: A Naval History of World War II* (1995); Samuel Eliot Morison, *The Two Ocean War* (1963); Bernard C. Nalty, *Strength for the Fight: A History of Black Americans in the Military* (1986); Geoffrey Perret, *There's a War to Be Won: The United States Army and World War II* (1991) and *Winged Victory: The American Air Force in World War II* (1993); Forrest Pogue, *George C. Marshall*, 3 vols. (1963–1975); Paul P. Rogers, *The Good Years: MacArthur and Sutherland* (1990); Ronald Schaffer, *Wings of Judgment: American Bombing in World War II* (1985); Michael Sherry, *The Rise of American Air Power* (1987); Bradley Smith, *The Shadow Warriors: O.S.S. and the Origins of the C.I.A.* (1983); Ronald Spector, *The Eagle against the Sun: The American War with Japan* (1985); James Stokesbury, *A Short History of World War II* (1980).

The Home Front at War
Michael Adams, *The Best War Ever: Americans and World War II* (1994); Karen T. Anderson, *Wartime Women: Sex Roles, Family Relations, and the Status of American Women during World War II* (1981); Matthew Baigall and Julia Williams, eds., *Artists against War and Fascism* (1986); M. Joyce Baker, *Images of Women on Film: The War Years, 1941–1945* (1981); David Brinkley, *Washington Goes to War* (1988); John Costello, *Virtue under Fire: How World War II Changed Our Social and Sexual Attitudes* (1985); George Q. Flynn, *The Draft, 1940–1973* (1993); Paul Fussell, *Wartime* (1989); Sherna Berger Gluck, *Rosie the Riveter Revisited: Women, the War, and Social Change* (1987); Doris Kearns Goodwin, *No Ordinary Time, Franklin and Eleanor Roosevelt: The Homefront in World War II* (1994); Susan Hartmann, *The Home Front and Beyond: American Women in the 1940s* (1982); Maurice Isserman, *Which Side Were You On? The*

American Communist Party during the Second World War (1982); Clayton Koppes and Gregory Black, *Hollywood Goes to War* (1987); Ruth Milkman, *Gender at Work: The Dynamics of Job Segregation by Sex during World War II* (1987); Gerald Nash, *The American West Transformed: The Impact of the Second World War* (1985); Richard Polenberg, *War and Society: The United States, 1941–1945* (1972); David Robertson, *Sly and Able: A Political Biography of James F. Byrnes* (1994); George H. Roeder, Jr., *The Censored War: American Visual Experience during World War II* (1993); Studs Turkel, *The Good War: An Oral History of World War II* (1984); William Tuttle, *Daddy's Gone to War: The Second World War in the Lives of America's Children* (1993); Harold Vatter, *The American Economy in World War II* (1985).

Minorities and the War
Robert Abzug, *Inside the Vicious Heart: Americans and the Liberation of the Nazi Concentration Camps* (1985); Allan Bérubé, *Coming Out under Fire: Gay Men and Women in World War Two* (1990); Richard Breitman and Alan Kraut, *American Refugee Policy and European Jewry, 1933–1945* (1987); A. Russell Buchanan, *Black Americans in World War II* (1977); Dominic Capeci, Jr., *Race Relations in Wartime Detroit* (1984) and *The Harlem Race Riot of 1943* (1977); Richard Dalfiume, *Desegregation of the U.S. Armed Forces* (1969); Clete Daniel, *Chicano Workers and the Politics of Fairness: The Fair Employment Practices Commission and the Southwest 1941–1945* (1990); Roger Daniels, *Concentration Camps U.S.A.* (1981) and *Prisoners without Trials: The Japanese-Americans in World War II* (1993); Leonard Dinnerstein, *America and the Survivors of the Holocaust* (1982); Masayo Umezawa Duus, *Unlikely Liberators: The Men of the 100th and 442nd* (1987); Lee Finkel, *Forum for Protest: The Black Press during World War II* (1975); Peter Irons, *Justice at War: The Story of the Japanese American Internment Cases* (1983); Deborah Lipstadt, *Beyond Belief: The American Press and the Coming of the Holocaust, 1933–1945* (1986); Mauricio Mazon, *The Zoot Suit Riots* (1984); Phillip McGuire, ed., *Taps for a Jim Crow Army: Letters from Black Soldiers in World War II* (1982); Sandra Taylor, *Jewel of the West: Japanese-American Internment at Topaz* (1993); Patrick Washburn, *A Question of Sedition: The Federal Government and the Investigation of the Black Press during World War II* (1986); Neil Wynn, *The Afro-American and the Second World War* (1976); Norman Zucker and Naomi Flink Zucker, *The Guarded Gate: The Reality of American Refugee Policy* (1987).

Atoms and Diplomacy
Gar Alperovitz, *The Decision to Use the Bomb* (1995); Edward M. Bennett, *Franklin D. Roosevelt and the Search for Victory: American-Soviet Relations, 1935–1945* (1990); Henry Blumenthal, *Illusion and Reality in Franco-American Diplomacy, 1914–1945* (1982); McGeorge Bundy, *Danger and Survival: Choices about the Atom Bomb in the First Fifty Years* (1988); James MacGregor Burns, *Roosevelt: The Soldier of Freedom* (1970); Winston Churchill, *The Second World War*, 6 vols. (1948–1953); Herbert Feis, *Roosevelt, Churchill, Stalin: The War They Waged and the Peace They Sought* (1957), *Between War and Peace: The Potsdam Conference* (1960), and *The Atomic Bomb and the End of World War II* (1966); John

L. Gaddis, *The United States and the Origins of the Cold War* (1972); Fraser J. Harbutt, *The Iron Curtain: Churchill, America, and the Origins of the Cold War* (1986); George Herring, *Aid to Russia, 1941–1946* (1977); John Hersey, *Hiroshima* (1946); Richard Hewlett and Oscar Anderson, *The New World* (1962); "Hiroshima in History and Memory: A Symposium," *Diplomatic History*, vol. 19, No. 2, Spring, 1995, 197–365; Godfrey Hodgson, *The Colonel: The Life and Wars of Henry Stimson* (1990); Warren Kimball, ed., *Churchill and Roosevelt: The Complete Correspondence, 1939–1945* (1984); Gabriel Kolko, *The Politics of War* (1968); William Roger Louis, *Imperialism at Bay: The United States and the Decolonization of the British Empire, 1941–1945* (1978); Mark H. Lytle, *The Origins of the Iranian-American Alliance, 1941–1953* (1987); David Painter, *Oil and the American Century: The Political Economy of U.S. Foreign Oil Policy, 1941–1954* (1986); Richard Rhodes, *The Making of the Atomic Bomb* (1986); Keith Sainsbury, *Roosevelt, Stalin, Churchill, and Chiang Kai-shek, 1943: The Moscow, Cairo, and Tehran Conferences* (1985); Gaddis Smith, *American Diplomacy during the Second World War, 1941–1945* (1985); Michael B. Stoff, *Oil, War, and American Security: The Search for a National Policy on Foreign Oil, 1941–1947* (1980), and as ed., *The Manhattan Project: A Documentary Introduction* (1991); Randall B. Woods, *A Changing of the Guard: Anglo-American Relations, 1941–1946* (1990).

CHAPTER 28: COLD WAR AMERICA

The Postwar Era
Paul Boyer, *By the Bomb's Early Light* (1986); H. W. Brands, *The Devil We Knew: America and the Cold War* (1993); Robert Ferrell, *Harry S Truman: A Life* (1994); Eric Goldman, *The Crucial Decade and After* (1960); Landon Jones, *Great Expectations: America and the Babyboom Generation* (1980); George Lipsitz, *Class and Culture in Postwar America* (1981); James O'Connor, ed., *American History/American Television* (1983); William O'Neill, *American High* (1986); Richard Pells, *The Liberal Mind in a Conservative Age* (1985); Dana Polan, *Power and Paranoia: History, Narrative, and the American Cinema, 1940–1950* (1986); Leila Rupp and Verta Taylor, *Survival in the Doldrums: The American Women's Rights Movement, 1945 to the 1960s* (1987); Mark Silk, *Spiritual Politics: Religion and America since World War II* (1988); Jules Tygiel, *Baseball's Great Experiment: Jackie Robinson and His Legacy* (1983); Martin Walker, *The Cold War: A History* (1994).

The Cold War in the West
Dean Acheson, *Present at the Creation* (1969); Stephen Ambrose, *The Rise to Globalism* (1983); Douglas Brinkley, ed., *Dean Acheson and the Making of American Foreign Policy* (1993); Richard Wightman Fox, *Reinhold Niebuhr: A Biography* (1985); Richard Freeland, *The Truman Doctrine and the Origins of McCarthyism* (1970); John L. Gaddis, *Strategies of Containment* (1982) and *The Long Peace: Inquiries into the History of the Cold War* (1987); Lloyd Gardner, *Architects of Illusion* (1970); David Green, *The Containment of Latin America* (1971); Gregg Herken, *The Winning Weapon* (1980); Michael Hogan, *The Marshall Plan: America, Britain, and the Reconstruction*

Presidency: A Re-evaluation (1993); Gerald Ford, *A Time to Heal* (1979); Raymond Garthoff, *Détente and Confrontation: American–Soviet Relations from Nixon to Reagan* (1985); Millicent Gates and Bruce Geelhoed, *The Dragon and the Snake: An American Account of the Turmoil in China, 1976–1977* (1986); Michael Hogan, *The Panama Canal in American Politics* (1986); Henry Jackson, *From the Congo to Soweto: U.S. Foreign Policy toward Africa since 1960* (1982); Burton Kaufman, *The Presidency of James Earl Carter, Jr.* (1993); Walter LaFeber, *The Panama Canal*, rev. ed. (1989); J. Anthony Lukas, *Nightmare: The Underside of the Nixon Years* (1988); Richard Pipes, *U.S.–Soviet Relations in the Era of Détente* (1981); William Quandt, *Camp David* (1986); A. James Reichley, *Conservatives in an Age of Change: The Nixon and Ford Administrations* (1981); Robert Schulzinger, *Henry Kissinger: Doctor of Diplomacy* (1989); Gary Sick, *All Fall Down* (1985); John Sirica, *To Set the Record Straight* (1979); Seth Tillman, *The U.S. in the Middle East* (1982); Cyrus Vance, *Hard Choices* (1983); Theodore White, *Breach of Faith* (1975); Bob Woodward and Carl Bernstein, *All the President's Men* (1974) and *The Final Days* (1976).

CHAPTER 33: A NATION STILL DIVISIBLE

Contemporary American Society

Bruce Bawer, *A Place at the Table: The Gay Individual and American Society* (1994); Robert Bellah et al., *Habits of the Heart: Individualism and Commitment in American Life* (1985) and *The Good Society* (1991); Dallas Blanchard, *The Anti-Abortion Movement* (1994); Stephen Carter, *The Culture of Disbelief: How American Law and Politics Trivialize Religious Devotion* (1993); William Dietrich, *In the Shadow of the Rising Sun: The Political Roots of American Economic Decline* (1991); Thomas Byrne Edsall, *The New Politics of Inequality* (1984); Barbara Ehrenreich, *Fear of Falling: The Inner Life of the Middle Class* (1989) and *The Worst Years of Our Lives* (1990); Susan Faludi, *Backlash: The Undeclared War against American Women* (1991); Elizabeth Fee and Daniel Fox, eds., *AIDS: The Burdens of History* (1992); Henry Louis Gates, Jr., *Loose Canons: Notes on the Culture Wars* (1993); Michael Goldfield, *The Decline of Organized Labor in the United States* (1987); Otis Graham, Jr., *Losing Time: The Industrial Policy Debate* (1992); Michael Harrington, *The New American Poverty* (1984); Richard Herrnstein and Charles Murray, *The Bell Curve: Intelligence and Class Structure in American Life* (1994); Robert Hughes, *Culture of Complaint: The Fraying of America* (1993); Paul Krugman, *Peddling Prosperity: Economic Sense and Nonsense in the Age of Diminished Expectations* (1994); Frank Levy, *Dollars and Dreams: The Changing American Income Distribution* (1987); Steve Levy, *Insanely Great: The Life and Times of Macintosh, the Computer That Changed Everything* (1994); Jane Maysbridge, *Why We Lost the ERA* (1986); Joseph Nocera, *A Piece of the Action: How the Middle Class Joined the Money Class* (1994); Juliet Schor, *The Overworked American: The Unexpected Decline of Leisure* (1991); Studs Terkel, *The Great Divide* (1988); Thomas Toch, *In the Name of Excellence: The Struggle to Reform the Nation's Schools* (1991); James Trabor and Eugene Gallagher, *Why Waco? Cults in the Battle for Religious Freedom* (1995).

Politics from Reagan to Clinton

Charles Allen, *The Comeback Kid: The Life and Career of Bill Clinton* (1992); Earl Black and Merle Black, *The Vital South: How Presidents Are Elected* (1992); Sidney Blumenthal, *The Rise of the Counter-Establishment from Conservative Ideology to Political Power* (1988), and with Thomas Byrne Edsall, eds., *The Reagan Legacy* (1988); Paul Boyer, ed., *Reagan as President: Contemporary Views of the Man, His Politics, and His Policies* (1990); William Brennan, *America's Right Turn from Nixon to Bush* (1994); Barbara Bush, *Barbara Bush: A Memoir* (1994); Michael Deaver, *Behind the Scenes* (1987); Theodore Draper, *A Very Thin Line: The Iran–Contra Affairs* (1991); Elizabeth Drew, *On the Edge: The Clinton Presidency* (1994); Ken Gross, *Ross Perot: The Man Behind the Myth* (1992); David Hoeveler, Jr., *Watch on the Right: Conservative Intellectuals in the Reagan Era* (1991); Peter Irons, *Brennan vs. Rehnquist: The Battle for the Constitution* (1994); Jonathan Kwitny, *The Crimes of Patriots: A True Tale of Dope, Dirty Money, and the CIA* (1987); Jonathan Lash, *A Season of Spoils: The Story of the Reagan Administration's Attack on the Environment* (1984); Theodore Lowi, *The End of the Republican Era* (1995); Mary Matlin and James Carville, *All's Fair: Love, War, and Running for President* (1994); *The New Yorker,* "Special Politics Issue," October 21 & 28, 1996; Kevin Phillips, *The Politics of Rich and Poor: Wealth and the American Electorate in the Reagan Aftermath* (1990) and *Boiling Point: Republicans: Democrats and the Decline of Middle Class Prosperity* (1993); John Podhoretz, *Hell of a Ride: Backstage at the White House Follies, 1989–1993* (1993); Dan Quayle, *Standing Firm: A Vice-Presidential Memoir* (1994); Donald Regan, *For the Record* (1988); Tom Rosenstiel, *Strange Bedfellows: How Television and the Presidential Candidates Changed American Politics, 1992* (1993); Randy Shilts, *And the Band Played On: Politics, People and the AIDS Epidemic* (1987); David Stockman, *The Triumph of Politics: The Inside Story of the Reagan Revolution* (1986); Stephen Vaugh, *Ronald Reagan in Hollywood: Movies and Politics* (1994); Gary Wills, *Reagan's America* (1987); Daniel Wirls, *The Politics of Defense in the Reagan Era* (1992); Bob Woodward, *The Agenda: Inside the Clinton White House* (1994).

Foreign Policy into the 1990s

Michael Beschloss and Strobe Talbot, *At the Highest Levels: The Inside Story of the End of the Cold War* (1993); Raymond Bonner, *Weakness and Deceit: U.S. Policy and El Salvador* (1984); William Broad, *Teller's War: The Top Secret Story behind the Star Wars Deception* (1992); Bradford Burns, *At War with Nicaragua* (1987); Leslie Cockburn, *Out of Control* (1987); Christopher Coker, *The United States and South Africa, 1968–1985* (1986); Thomas Friedman, *From Beirut to Jerusalem* (1989); John Lewis Gaddis, *The United States and the End of the Cold War* (1992); Roy Gutman, *Banana Diplomacy* (1988); Alexander Haig, Jr., *Caveat: Realism, Reagan, and Foreign Policy* (1984); Delip Hiro, *Desert Shield to Desert Storm* (1992); Bruce Jentleson, *Pipeline Politics: The Complex Political Economy of East–West Trade* (1986); Robert Kaplan, *Balkan Ghosts* (1993); Walter LaFeber, *Inevitable Revolutions* (1993); John Mueller, *Policy and Opinion in the Gulf War* (1994); Robert Pastor, *Condemned to Repetition: The United States and*

Nicaragua (1987); Jonathan Schell, *The Fate of the Earth* (1982); David Schoenbaum, *The United States and the State of Israel* (1993); Strobe Talbott, *Deadly Gambits: The Reagan Administration and the Stalemate in Nuclear Arms Control* (1984); Sanford Ungar, *Africa* (1985); William Vogele, *Stepping Back: Nuclear Arms Control and the End of the Cold War* (1994). Thomas Walker, ed., *Reagan versus the Sandinistas* (1987); Bob Woodward, *Veil: The Secret Wars of the CIA* (1987).

Minorities and American Culture
Ken Auletta, *The Underclass* (1982); Richard Bernstein, *Multiculturalism and the Battle for America's Future* (1994); Ellis Cose, *The Rage of the Privileged Class: Why Are Middle Class Blacks Angry?* (1994); Roger Daniels et al., eds., *Japanese-Americans: From Relocation to Redress* (1986); Reynolds Farley and Walter Allen, *The Color Line and the Quality of Life in America* (1987); Lawrence Fuchs, *The American Kaleidoscope: Race, Ethnicity, and the Civic Culture* (1990); Douglas Glasgow, *The Black Underclass* (1980); Andrew Hacker, *Two Nations: Black and White, Separate, Hostile, Unequal* (1992); Denis Heyck, ed., *Barrios and Borderlands: Cultures of Latinos and Latinas in the United States* (1993); Bill Ong Hing, *Making and Remaking Asian America through Immigration Policy, 1850–1990* (1993); David Hollinger, *Postethnic America: Beyond Multiculturalism* (1995); Christopher Jencks, *The Homeless* (1994); Jonathan Kozol, *Savage Inequalities: Children in America's Schools* (1991); Oscar Martinez, *Border People: Life and Society in the U.S.–Mexico Border Lands* (1994); Joan Moore and Harry Pachon, *Hispanics in the United States* (1985); Adolph Reed, *The Jesse Jackson Phenomenon: The Crisis of Purpose in Afro-American Politics* (1986); Sam Roberts, *Who Are We? A Portrait of America Based on the Latest U.S. Census* (1994); Arthur Schlesinger, Jr., *The Disuniting of America* (1991); Peter Skerry, *Mexican-Americans: The Ambivalent Minority* (1993); Robert C. Smith, *Racism in the Post–Civil Rights Era: Now You See It, Now You Don't* (1995); The Staff of the Chicago Tribune, *The American Millstone: An Examination of the Nation's Permanent Underclass* (1986); Shih-Shan Henry Tsai, *The Chinese Experience in America* (1986); William Wei, *The Asian American Movement* (1993).

PHOTO CREDITS

INDEX